ETHICS AND LAW FOR SCHOOL PSYCHOLOGISTS

ETHICS AND LAW FOR SCHOOL PSYCHOLOGISTS

Seventh Edition

Susan Jacob
Dawn M. Decker
Elizabeth Timmerman Lugg

WILEY

Published by John Wiley & Sons, Inc., Hoboken, New Jersey.
Published simultaneously in Canada.

For general information on our other products and services, please contact our Customer Care Department within the U.S. at 800-956-7739, outside the U.S. at 317-572-3986, or fax 317-572-4002.

Wiley publishes in a variety of print and electronic formats and by print-on-demand. Some material included with standard print versions of this book may not be included in e-books or in print-on-demand. If this book refers to media such as a CD or DVD that is not included in the version you purchased, you may download this material at http://booksupport.wiley.com. For more information about Wiley products, visit www.wiley.com.

Library of Congress Cataloging-in-Publication Data

Names: Jacob, Susan, 1949- author. | Decker, Dawn M. author. | Lugg,
    Elizabeth T. (Elizabeth Timmerman) author.
Title: Ethics and law for school psychologists / Susan Jacob, Dawn M. Decker,
    Elizabeth Timmerman Lugg.
Description: Seventh edition. | Hoboken, New Jersey : John Wiley & Sons,
    Inc., 2016. | Includes index.
Identifiers: LCCN 2016018222 | ISBN 9781119157069 (hardback) |
    ISBN 9781119157168 (epub)
Subjects: LCSH: School psychologists—Legal status, laws, etc.—United
    States. | School psychologists—Professional ethics—United States. |
    BISAC: PSYCHOLOGY / Education & Training.
Classification: LCC KF4192.5.P8 J33 2016 | DDC 174/.9371713—dc23
LC record available at https://lccn.loc.gov/2016018222

Cover Design: Wiley
Cover Image: © annasir/Shutterstock

Printed in the United States of America

SEVENTH EDITION

HB Printing V10007443_010819

This book is dedicated to the memory of Tim and Nancy Hartshorne's children, Michael David Salem Hartshorne (1984–1992) and Katherine Swift Hartshorne (1991–1992)

And to the memory of Susan Jacob's son, Andrew Alan Neal (1982–2009)

The brevity of their lives reminds us just how precious are all children.

Contents

Preface

There are a number of excellent texts, journal articles, and book chapters on ethics in psychology, legal issues in school psychology, and special education law. However, in the late 1980s, the authors of the first edition of this book recognized a need for a single sourcebook on ethics and law specifically written to meet the unique needs of the psychologist in the school setting. Consequently, *Ethics and Law for School Psychologists* was written to provide up-to-date information on ethical principles and standards and law pertinent to the delivery of school psychological services. Our goals for this seventh edition of the book remain unchanged. We hope that the book will continue to be useful as a basic textbook or supplementary text for school psychology students in training and as a resource for practitioners. In addition, we hope it will also be a valuable resource for scholars interested in ethical and legal issues in the field of school psychology.

As stated in the preface to the first edition, one goal in writing the book was to bring together various ethical and legal guidelines pertinent to the delivery of school psychological services. We also introduce an ethical-legal decision-making model. We concur with the suggestion that the educated practitioner is the best safeguard against ethical-legal problems (Koocher & Keith-Spiegel, 2008). School psychologists with a broad knowledge base of ethics and law are likely to anticipate and prevent problems. Use of a decision-making model allows the practitioner to make informed, well-reasoned choices in resolving problems when they do occur (Eberlein, 1987; M. A. Fisher, 2013; Tymchuk, 1986).

WHAT'S IN THE BOOK

Chapter 1 provides an introduction to ethical codes; an ethical-legal decision-making model; and the four broad ethical principles of respect for the dignity and rights of all persons, professional competence and responsibility, honesty and integrity in professional relationships, and responsibility to schools, families, communities, the profession, and society. We also describe ethics committees and sanctions for unethical conduct. Chapter 2 provides an introduction to the legal underpinnings of school-based practice and to public school law that protects the rights of students and their parents. We also address certification and licensure of school psychologists—

mechanisms that help to ensure that psychologists meet specified qualifications before they are granted a legal sanction to practice. The chapter closes with a brief discussion of tort liability of schools and practitioners. In Chapter 3, we discuss privacy, informed consent, confidentiality, privileged communication, and record keeping—ethical-legal concerns that cut across all of the school psychologist's many roles.

The remaining chapters focus on ethical-legal issues associated with specific roles. Chapters 4 and 5 address the delivery of services to students with disabilities. Psycho-educational assessment within the context of a school psychologist–client relationship is discussed in Chapter 6. Chapter 7 addresses academic and behavioral interventions within a multitiered system of service delivery and therapeutic interventions such as counseling. Chapters 8 and 9 focus on indirect services. We discuss ethical-legal issues associated with consultative services to teachers and parents in Chapter 8 and systems-level consultation in Chapter 9. A number of special consultation topics are covered in Chapter 9, including the ethical-legal concerns associated with large-scale assessment programs (high-stakes testing, screening to identify students at risk for harm to self or others); instructional policies and practices (grade retention, instructional grouping, programs for English language learners and gifted and talented students); school discipline; and discrimination, harassment, and bullying. In Chapter 10, ethical-legal issues associated with research are discussed, and Chapter 11 provides a brief overview of issues associated with school-based supervision of school psychologists in training. And, finally, in the epilogue, we discuss advocacy.

WHAT'S NOT IN THE BOOK

We have chosen to focus on ethical-legal issues of interest to current and future school-based practitioners. Consistent with this focus, we did not include a discussion of issues associated with private practice. Interested readers are encouraged to consult C. B. Fisher (2012); Knapp, Gottlieb, Handelsman, and VandeCreek (2012); and Knapp and VandeCreek (2012). We also did not address the legal rights of psychologists as employees in the public schools. However, we did address situations in which the freedoms of ordinary citizens must be balanced with the school psychologist's professional roles and responsibilities.

SEVENTH EDITION REVISIONS

A rapid increase in the use of digital technology for "generation, storage, and communication of information" in the schools has occurred in recent years (L. D. Armistead, 2014b, p. 459). The seventh edition of *Ethics and Law for School Psychologists* gives new attention to ethical-legal considerations associated with the use of digital-age technologies by school districts, school psychologists, and schoolchildren. For example, in Chapter 1, we address potential ethical-legal problems associated with the use of online social media by school psychologists. Chapter 3 addresses digital storage of student school psychological records and the use of electronic communication by practitioners. Computer-assisted testing and scoring are discussed in Chapter 6.

In addition, new vignettes challenge readers to apply their knowledge of ethics and law to contemporary issues raised by the increased use of digital technologies.

The seventh edition includes a summary of, and citations to, the Every Student Succeeds Act (ESSA, Pub. L. No. 114-95), signed into law on December 10, 2015. The ESSA is the most recent set of amendments to the Elementary and Secondary Education Act of 1965. The ESSA citations in this book are to the text of the Senate Bill, S. 1177.

Throughout the seventh edition, we incorporated citations to recent publications and legal decisions. However, we also continued to cite older works that provided the foundation for more recent scholarship in the area of ethics and law for school psychologists. As Koocher and Keith-Spiegel (2008) observed, ignoring important older publications on a topic is disrespectful of the efforts of early scholars. Furthermore, researchers and writers "who pass over earlier work may conclude that they discovered something fresh and innovative when in fact the same findings were published many years ago" (p. 524)

To assist the reader, a list of acronyms that are frequently used in this volume now appears in Appendix E. An updated instructor's manual and Microsoft PowerPoint slides are available for trainers who adopt the textbook. These supplements are available by contacting your John Wiley & Sons sales representative (visit http://www.wiley.com).

A number of the changes made in the seventh edition were suggested by readers. We welcome your suggestions for improving future editions of *Ethics and Law for School Psychologists*. Please contact Susan Jacob, Professor Emeritus, Central Michigan University. E-mail: jacob1s@cmich.edu.

DISCLAIMERS

The portions of this book that address legal issues were written to provide the reader with a framework for understanding federal and state law pertinent to the delivery of school psychological services and a foundation for future learning in the area of legal issues. We hope that the material on legal issues will alert practitioners to professional practices that law deems appropriate or inappropriate (Sales, Miller, & Hall, 2005); prompt them to seek consultation with knowledgeable supervisors when legal questions arise; and encourage thoughtful decisions that are respectful of student rights and decisions that, under public scrutiny, will foster trust in school psychologists. This book is not a legal text, and nothing in the book should be construed as legal advice. The court cases and judicial opinions summarized here were selected to provide a historical background for understanding legal issues in the field of school psychology, to illustrate terms and principles, to provide insight into contemporary interpretations of law pertinent to practice, or to serve as a cautionary tale regarding missteps to avoid in the delivery of services. Unlike a legal text, we do not provide a comprehensive set of citations to authoritative judicial decisions when legal issues are discussed in the book.

In addition, our interpretations of ethical codes and standards should not be viewed as reflecting the official opinion of any specific professional association.

CAST OF CHARACTERS

Throughout the text, we have included a number of case incidents to illustrate specific principles. Some of the incidents are from case law, some were suggested by practitioners in the field, and others are fictitious. To make it easier for the reader to follow who's who in the vignettes, we have used the same six school psychologists throughout the book:

MARIA DELGADO serves as a member of a school psychological services team in a medium-size city. She is particularly interested in school-based consultative services.

CARRIE JOHNSON provides school psychological services in a rural area. She faces the special challenges of coping with professional isolation and works in a community where resources are limited.

DAVID KIM is currently a doctoral intern in a suburban school district.

JAMES LEWIS, a school psychologist in a large metropolitan district, is a strong advocate of school efforts to prevent mental health problems.

PEARL MEADOWS is a school psychologist in a small university town. She works with a diverse student population, including students from farm families who live on the district's outskirts, Native American students from the neighboring Indian reservation, and children from many different cultures whose parents are part of the university community. Pearl also provides on-site supervision to school psychology interns.

WANDA ROSE provides services at the preschool and elementary level in a small town. Children, babies, parents, and teachers love her. She has been a school psychology practitioner for many years. Wanda needs an occasional push from her colleagues to keep current with changing practices, however.

SUSAN JACOB
Ann Arbor, Michigan

DAWN M. DECKER
Central Michigan University
Mt. Pleasant, Michigan

ELIZABETH T. LUGG
Illinois State University
Normal, Illinois

Acknowledgments

The first edition of *Ethics and Law for School Psychologists* would not have come to fruition without the support and scholarship of Dr. Timothy S. Hartshorne as co-author. Dr. Hartshorne was also instrumental in ensuring that subsequent editions addressed emerging ethical and legal issues in a comprehensive and informed manner, particularly issues relevant to the consultative and therapeutic intervention roles of school psychology practitioners. In the years since the first edition of the book was published in 1991, Dr. Hartshorne has become an internationally respected speaker, writer, and researcher dedicated to understanding, and sharing his understanding of, the development of children with CHARGE syndrome, a relatively rare genetic syndrome. He also became an outstanding chair of the Psychology Department at Central Michigan University (CMU, 1995–2002), a professor recognized for his teaching excellence (1996 CMU Excellence in Teaching Award), and a wise and valued friend to Susan Jacob. Dr. Hartshorne decided not to participate in this revision of the book, in part because of the demands associated with his research commitment to children with CHARGE and his role as teacher and mentor to CMU school psychology trainees. For those of you who know Tim, please rest assured that he is doing well and continues to enjoy his faculty position in the school psychology training program at CMU.

In addition to acknowledging Tim's contributions to this book, we would like to thank the following colleagues for reading drafts of portions of the text and providing excellent suggestions and invaluable guidance:

Dr. Leigh D. Armistead, Winthrop University
Dr. John M. Garruto, School Psychologist, Kingsford Park Elementary School, Oswego, NY
Dr. Samuel Y. Kim, Western Kentucky University
Dr. Daniel D. Drevon, Central Michigan University
Dr. William Pfohl, Western Kentucky University

We also appreciate the research assistance provided by Michael James Hetzler and CMU school psychology program graduate students Julie Grech and Cody Bartow.

We are grateful for the excellent support provided by our Wiley editor, Marquita Flemming, and for the thoughtful and careful work done by Wiley production editor Maria Sunny Zacharias.

Finally, a special thank you also is due to family members for their encouragement and patience during the completion of the book.

Chapter 1 ———————————————————————————

ETHICS IN SCHOOL PSYCHOLOGY: AN INTRODUCTION

Who are *school psychologists*? As Fagan (2014) observed, the term *school psychologist* has been defined in many different ways. For the purposes of this book, we adopted the definition developed by the National Association of School Psychologists (NASP): *School psychologists* are professionals who

> provide effective services to help children and youth succeed academically, socially, behaviorally, and emotionally. School psychologists provide direct educational and mental health services for children and youth, as well as work with parents, educators, and other professionals to create supportive learning and social environments for all children. (NASP, 2010b)

Because the decisions made by school psychologists have an impact on human lives, and thereby on society, the practice of school psychology rests on the public's trust. To build and maintain society's trust in school psychology, it is essential that every school psychologist is sensitive to the ethical and legal components of his or her work, knowledgeable regarding broad ethical principles and rules of professional conduct, and committed to a proactive stance in ethical thinking and conduct.

QUALITY CONTROL IN SCHOOL PSYCHOLOGY

Four sources of "quality control" protect the rights and welfare of students and other recipients of school psychological services. Professional codes of ethics for the delivery of psychological services are discussed in this chapter. Chapter 2 provides an introduction to law that protects the rights of students and their parents in the school setting. Educational law provides a second source of quality control. Chapter 2 also addresses the credentialing of school psychologists, a third mechanism of quality assurance. Credentialing helps to ensure that psychologists meet specified qualifications before they are granted a legal sanction to practice (Fagan & Wise, 2007). Training-program accreditation is an additional mechanism of quality control. Program accreditation helps to ensure the adequate preparation of school psychologists during their graduate coursework and field experiences.

This chapter focuses on the what and why of professional ethics, ethics training and competencies, and the codes of ethics of the NASP and the American Psychological Association (APA). Four broad ethical principles are introduced along with an ethical-legal decision-making model. We also describe ethics committees and sanctions for unethical conduct.

WHAT AND WHY OF PROFESSIONAL ETHICS

The term *ethics* generally refers to a system of principles of conduct that guide the behavior of an individual. *Ethics* derives from the Greek word *ethos*, meaning character or custom, and the phrase *ta ethika*, which Plato and Aristotle used to describe their studies of Greek values and ideals (Solomon, 1984). Accordingly,

> ethics is first of all a concern for individual character, including what we call "being a good person," but it is also a concern for the overall character of an entire society, which is still appropriately called its "ethos." Ethics is participation in, and an understanding of, an ethos, the effort to understand the social rules which govern and limit our behavior. (p. 5)

A system of ethics develops in the context of a particular society or culture and is connected closely to social customs. Ethics is composed of a range of acceptable (or unacceptable) social and personal behaviors, from rules of etiquette to more basic rules of society.

The terms *ethics* and *morality* are often used interchangeably. However, according to philosophers, the term *morality* refers to a subset of ethical rules of special importance. Solomon (1984) suggested that moral principles are "the most basic and inviolable rules of a society." Moral rules are thought to differ from other aspects of ethics in that they are more important, fundamental, universal, rational, and objective (pp. 6–7). W. D. Ross (1930), a twentieth-century Scottish philosopher, identified a number of moral duties of the ethical person: *nonmaleficence, fidelity, beneficence, justice,* and *autonomy.* These moral principles have provided a foundation for the ethical codes of psychologists and other professionals (Bersoff & Koeppl, 1993).

Our focus here is on *applied* or *practical professional ethics*, the application of broad ethical principles and specific rules to the problems that arise in professional practice (Beauchamp & Childress, 2013). Applied ethics in school psychology is, thus, a combination of ethical principles and rules, ranging from more basic rules to rules of professional etiquette, that guide the conduct of the practitioner in his or her professional interactions with others. Furthermore, although school psychologists are employed in a variety of settings, in this text we emphasize the special challenges of school-based practice.

Professionalism and Ethics

Professionalization has been described as:

> the process by which an occupation, usually on the basis of a claim to special competence and a concern for the quality of its work and benefits to society, obtains the exclusive right to perform a particular kind of work, to control training criteria and access to the profession, and to determine and evaluate the way the work is to be performed. (Chalk, Frankel, & Chafer, 1980, p. 3)

Professional associations or societies function to promote the profession by publicizing the services offered, safeguarding the rights of professionals, attaining benefits for its members, facilitating the exchange of and development of knowledge, and promoting standards to enhance the quality of professional work by its members (Chalk et al., 1980). Codes of ethics appear to develop out of the self-interests of the profession and a genuine commitment to protect the interests of persons served. Most professional associations have recognized the need to balance self-interests against concern for the welfare of the consumer. Ethical codes are one mechanism to help ensure that members of a profession will deal justly with the public (Bersoff & Koeppl, 1993).

However, the development of a code of ethics also serves to foster the profession's self-interests. A code of ethics is an indicator of the profession's willingness to accept responsibility for defining appropriate conduct and a commitment to self-regulation of members by the profession (Chalk et al., 1980). The adoption of a code of ethics often has been viewed as the hallmark of a profession's maturity. Ethical codes thus may serve to enhance the prestige of a profession and reduce the perceived need for external regulation and control.

The field of psychology has a long-standing commitment to activities that support and encourage appropriate professional conduct. As will be seen in this chapter, both the NASP and the APA have developed and adopted codes of ethics. These codes are drafted by committees within professional organizations and reflect the beliefs of association members about what constitutes appropriate professional conduct. They serve to protect the public by sensitizing professionals to the ethical aspects of service delivery, educating practitioners about the parameters of appropriate conduct, and helping professionals to monitor their own behavior. Furthermore, because the codes of ethics of psychologists can now be accessed using the Internet, they also increasingly serve to educate the public and recipients of services about the parameters of expected professional conduct by school psychologists. Finally, professional codes of ethics also provide guidelines for adjudicating complaints (Behnke & Jones, 2012).

By encouraging appropriate professional conduct, the NASP and the APA help to ensure that each person served will receive the highest quality of professional service. As a result, the public's trust in psychologists and psychology is enhanced and maintained.

Ethical Codes Versus Ethical Conduct

Codes of ethics serve to protect the public. However, ethical conduct is not synonymous with simple conformity to a set of rules outlined in professional codes and standards (J. N. Hughes, 1986). As Kitchener (2000) and others (Bersoff, 1994; Welfel, 2012) have noted, codes of ethics are imperfect guides to behavior for several reasons. First, ethical codes in psychology are composed of broad, abstract principles along with a number of more specific statements about appropriate professional conduct. They are at times vague and ambiguous (Bersoff, 1994).

Second, competing ethical principles often apply in a particular situation (Bersoff & Koeppl, 1993; Haas & Malouf, 2005), and specific ethical guidelines may conflict with federal or state law (Koocher & Keith-Spiegel, 2008). In some situations, a primary or overriding consideration can be identified in choosing a course of action. In other situations, however, no one principle involved clearly outweighs the other(s) (Haas & Malouf, 2005). For example, the decision to allow a minor child the freedom to choose or refuse to participate in psychological services often involves a consideration of law, ethical principles (respect for autonomy and self-determination versus the welfare of the child), and the likely practical consequences of affording choices (enhanced treatment outcomes versus refusal of treatment).

A third reason ethical codes are imperfect is because they tend to be reactive. They frequently fail to address new and emerging ethical issues (Bersoff & Koeppl, 1993; Welfel, 2012). Committees within professional associations often are formed to study the ways existing codes relate to emerging issues, and codes may be revised in response to new ethical concerns. Concern about the ethics of behavior modification techniques was a focus of the 1970s; in the 1980s, psychologists scrutinized the ethics of computerized psychodiagnostic assessment. In the 1990s, changes in codes of ethics reflected concerns about sexual harassment and fair treatment of individuals, regardless of their sexual orientation. In recent years, codes have emphasized the need for practitioner competence in the delivery of services to individuals from diverse experiential, linguistic, and cultural backgrounds. Codes also have been scrutinized to ensure relevance to the use of digital technologies.

Ethical codes thus provide guidance for the professional in his or her decision making. Ethical conduct, however, involves careful choices based on knowledge of broad ethical principles and code statements, ethical reasoning, and personal values. In many situations, more than one course of action is acceptable. In some situations, no course of action is completely satisfactory. In all situations, the responsibility for ethical conduct rests with the individual practitioner (L. D. Armistead, Williams, & Jacob, 2011; Eberlein, 1987).

ETHICS TRAINING AND COMPETENCIES

Prior to the late 1970s, many applied psychology graduate programs (clinical psychology, school psychology) required little formal coursework in professional ethics (Welfel, 2012). Ethics was often taught in the context of supervised practica and internship experiences, a practice Handelsman (1986) labeled "ethics training by 'osmosis'" (p. 371). A shortcoming of this approach is that student learning is limited by supervisor awareness and knowledge of ethical-legal issues and the types of situations encountered in the course of supervision (Handelsman, 1986). Consensus now exists that ethics, legal aspects of practice, and a problem-solving model need to be explicitly taught during graduate training (Dailor & Jacob, 2010; Haas, Malouf, & Mayerson, 1986; Tymchuk, 1985). Both the NASP and the APA graduate program training standards require coursework in professional ethics. Furthermore, in *School Psychology: A Blueprint for Training and Practice* (Ysseldyke et al., 2006), prepared by a task force composed of leaders in the field, knowledge of the ethical and legal aspects of professional practice was identified as a foundational competency for school psychologists, one that permeates all aspects of the provision of services.

In the 1980s, psychology trainers began to ask "What should be the goals of ethics education in psychology?" (Haas et al., 1986; Kitchener, 1986); and "What are the desired cognitive, affective, and behavioral 'ethics competencies' for school psychologists?" More recently, trainers have raised these questions: "How do school psychology students and practitioners gain competence, and ultimately expertise, in ethical decision making?" (Dailor & Jacob, 2010); "How do they gain a sense of themselves as ethical professionals?" (Handelsman, Gottlieb & Knapp, 2005, p. 59); and "How should ethics be taught?" A number of goals for ethics training have been suggested in the literature. An emerging picture of desired competencies includes these:

- Competent practitioners are sensitive to "the ethical components of their work" and are aware that their actions "have real ethical consequences that can potentially harm as well as help others" (Kitchener, 1986, p. 307; also Welfel & Kitchener, 1992).

- Competent psychologists have a sound working knowledge of the content of codes of ethics, professional standards, and law pertinent to the delivery of services (Fine & Ulrich, 1988; Welfel & Lipsitz, 1984).

- Competent practitioners are committed to a proactive rather than a reactive stance in ethical thinking and conduct (Tymchuk, 1986). They use their broad knowledge of codes of ethics and law along with ethical reasoning skills to anticipate and prevent problems from arising.

- Skilled practitioners are able to analyze the ethical dimensions of a situation and demonstrate a well-developed "ability to reason about ethical issues" (Kitchener, 1986, p. 307). They have mastered and make use of a problem-solving model (L. D. Armistead et al., 2011; de las Fuentes & Willmuth, 2005; Tymchuk, 1981, 1986).

- Competent practitioners recognize that a system of ethical rules and ideals develops in the context of a specific culture, and they are sensitive to the ways their own values and standards for behavior may be similar to or different from those of individuals from other cultural groups. They "strive to understand the manner in which culture influences their own view of others and other's view of them" (Ortiz, Flanagan, & Dynda, 2008, p. 1721).

- Competent psychologists are aware of their own feelings and beliefs. They recognize that personal feelings, beliefs, and values influence professional decision making (Handelsman et al., 2005; Kitchener, 2000).

- Competent practitioners do their best to engage in *positive ethics*; that is, they strive for excellence rather than meeting minimal obligations outlined in codes of ethics and law (Knapp & VandeCreek, 2012).

- Competent practitioners appreciate the complexity of ethical decisions and are tolerant of ambiguity and uncertainty. They acknowledge and accept that there may be more than one appropriate course of action (de las Fuentes & Willmuth, 2005; Kitchener, 2000).

- Competent practitioners have the personal strength to act on decisions made and accept responsibility for their actions (de las Fuentes & Willmuth, 2005; Kitchener, 1986).

Two paradigms describe how students and school psychology practitioners develop ethical competence: the acculturation model (Handelsman et al., 2005) and a stage model (Dreyfus, 1997). Handelsman et al. (2005) described ethics training of psychology graduate students as a dynamic, multiphase acculturation process.[1] They suggested that psychology, as a discipline and profession, has its own culture that encompasses aspirational ethical principles, ethical rules, professional standards, and values. Students develop their own "professional ethical identity" based on a process that optimally results in an adaptive integration of personal moral values and the ethics culture of the profession. Trainees who do not yet have a well-developed personal sense of morality, and those who do not understand and accept critical aspects of the ethics culture of psychology, may have difficulty making good ethical choices as psychologists.

The stage model describes a process whereby practitioners progress through five levels (Dreyfus, 1997). *Novice* practitioners are rules-bound and slow to make decisions. With some experience in applying rules of practice, *advanced beginners* become more capable of identifying multiple aspects of a complex situation and taking context into account, but they are still focusing on technical mastery of their skills. *Competent* practitioners are better able to identify key elements of a situation, see relationships among elements, recognize subtle differences between similar situations, balance skills and empathy, and consider the long-term effects of their decisions. However, because they are more skilled in considering relevant elements, competent practitioners are at times overwhelmed by the complexity of real-world problems. Practitioners who are *proficient* recognize situational patterns and subtle differences more quickly, and they are able to prioritize elements in decision making more effortlessly. Proficient practitioners may not be conscious of the knowledge and thinking processes that provide the foundation for choices. Finally, because of many experiences with diverse situations, *experts* are able to rely on past decisions to inform future decisions, base decisions on subtle qualitative distinctions, and often have an intuitive grasp of what needs to be done without extensive analyses. Based on their review of research on the acquisition of expertise, Ericsson and Williams (2007) suggested that expertise is acquired by early supervised practice coupled with deliberate practice over an extended period of time, usually 10 years.

How should ethics be taught? Growing professional support exists for a planned, multilevel approach to training in ethics and law (Conoley & Sullivan, 2002; Dailor & Jacob, 2011; Welfel, 2012). Tryon (2000) and others (Dailor & Jacob, 2011) recommended that formal coursework in ethics and law be required at the beginning of graduate training to prepare students to participate in discussions of ethical and legal issues throughout their program. Because many aspects of school-based practice are regulated by law as well as ethics, we recommend integrated rather than separate instruction in ethics and law; furthermore, key concepts, such as privacy, informed consent, and confidentiality, have roots in both ethics and law. A foundational course can introduce students to broad ethical principles, codes of ethics, the major provisions of school law pertinent to practice, and an ethical-legal decision-making model. In addition, Handelsman et al. (2005) recommended that early coursework include activities to heighten self-awareness of personal values and beliefs. For example, they suggested

---

[1]Portions of this section also appeared in Dailor and Jacob (2010).

asking students to write an ethics autobiography in which they reflect on their own values, as well as those of their families and cultures of origin, and consider what it means to be an ethical professional (p. 63; also Bashe, Anderson, Handelsman, & Klevansky, 2007). (For a discussion of methods in teaching ethical and legal issues in school psychology, see Welfel, 2012, and Williams, Sinko, & Epifanio, 2010).

A foundational course in ethics and law can provide opportunities for students to apply what they are learning about the ethical-legal aspects of practice by role-playing difficult situations and analyzing case incidents (Dailor & Jacob, 2010). However, while such coursework provides a critically important foundation for subsequent training, it is not sufficient to achieve desired practitioner competencies in ethics and law. If students have only one course in ethics and law, they may not be prepared to apply this knowledge across various domains of practice. In order for students to progress beyond the stage of advanced beginner, discussion of ethical-legal issues associated with diverse situations and professional roles must be a component of coursework in assessment, academic remediation, behavioral interventions, counseling, and consultation. For this reason, Tryon (2000) recommended that all graduate program course instructors discuss ethical issues related to their specialty areas.

Supervised field experiences provide a vitally important opportunity for students to apply their knowledge to multiple real-world situations (Harvey & Struzziero, 2008). With appropriate supervisory support, internship is "a prime time to develop ethical frameworks that will be useful throughout a professional career" (Conoley & Sullivan, 2002, p. 135). Field- and university-based supervisors consequently have a special obligation to model sound ethical-legal decision making and to monitor, assist, and support supervisees and early-career practitioners as they first encounter real-world challenges (Conoley & Sullivan, 2002; Handelsman et al., 2005; Harvey & Struzziero, 2008).

Although growing professional support exists for a planned, multilevel approach to graduate preparation in ethics, Dailor and Jacob (2011) surveyed a nationally representative sample of public school psychology practitioners and found that only 24% of the 208 respondents reported receiving multilevel university ethics training that included coursework in ethics, discussion of ethical issues in multiple courses, and supervised discussion of ethical issues in practica and internships.

Few empirical investigations of the effectiveness of formal ethics training have appeared in the literature (Tryon, 2001; Welfel, 2012). Baldick (1980) found that clinical and counseling interns who received formal ethics training were better able to identify ethical issues than interns without prior coursework in ethics. Tryon (2001) surveyed school psychology doctoral students from APA-accredited programs and found that students who had taken an ethics course and those who had completed more years of graduate study felt better prepared to deal with the ethical issues presented in the survey than those who had not taken an ethics course and who had completed fewer years of graduate education. Student ratings of their preparedness to deal with ethical issues were positively associated with the number of hours of supervised practicum experience completed. More recently, Dailor and Jacob (2011) found an association between the types of university training school psychology practitioners had received and their preparedness to handle ethical issues on the job, with those who had received multilevel university preparation in ethics reporting higher levels of preparedness to handle ethical issues. Preparedness was not associated with degree level (doctoral or nondoctoral) or years of experience on the job (five or fewer years versus more than five years).

Several studies, however, have reported a gap between knowledge of the appropriate course of action and willingness to carry out that action (Bernard & Jara, 1986; Smith, McGuire, Abbott, & Blau, 1991; Tryon, 2000). Even when practitioners can identify what ought to be done, many would choose to do less than they believe they should (Bernard & Jara, 1986). Thus, at this time, additional research is needed to identify the types of ethics training that are most effective in developing the skills and necessary confidence for psychologists to take appropriate actions in ethically difficult situations (Tymchuk, 1985; Welfel, 2012).

CODES OF ETHICS

D. T. Brown (1979) suggested that school psychology emerged as an identifiable profession in the 1950s. Two professional associations, the APA and the NASP, have shaped the development of the profession. Each professional association has formulated its own code of ethics. Within the APA, Division 16 is the Division of School Psychology.[2]

APA and NASP Codes of Ethics

In joining the APA or the NASP, members agree to abide by that association's ethical principles. Additionally, psychologists who are members of the National School Psychologist Certification System are obligated to abide by the NASP's code of ethics. We believe school psychology practitioners should be thoroughly familiar with the NASP's (2010b) "Principles for Professional Ethics" and the APA's (2010) "Ethical Principles of Psychologists and Code of Conduct," whether they are members of a professional association or not. A psychologist with a broad knowledge base of ethical principles will likely be better prepared to make sound choices when ethically challenging situations arise. Furthermore, regardless of association membership or level of training, trainees and practitioners may be expected to know and abide by both the APA and NASP ethics codes in their work setting (Flanagan, Miller, & Jacob, 2005).

The NASP's "Principles for Professional Ethics"

The NASP's "Principles for Professional Ethics" (NASP-PPE) was first adopted in 1974 and revised in 1984, 1992, 1997, 2000, and 2010 (also see L. D. Armistead et al., 2011, for a brief history of the early development of the code). The 2010 code is reprinted in Appendix A. The NASP's code of ethics focuses on the special challenges of school-based practice. *School-based practice* is defined as "the provision of school psychological services under the authority of a state, regional, or local educational agency" whether the school psychologist "is an employee of the schools or contracted by the schools on a per case or consultative basis" (NASP-PPE Definition of Terms).

---

[2]For information about the history of APA's Division 16 and NASP, see Fagan and Wise (2007).

The team of NASP members responsible for drafting the 2010 revision of the "Principles for Professional Ethics" shared a commitment to ensuring that the code, like its precursors, would address the unique circumstances associated with providing school-based psychological services and would emphasize protecting the rights and interests of schoolchildren and youth (NASP-PPE Introduction). More specifically, they attempted to incorporate the following special considerations of school-based practice:

- School psychologists must "balance the authority of parents to make decisions about their children with the needs and rights of those children, and the purposes and authority of schools." Within this framework, school psychologists "consider the interests and rights of children and youth to be their highest priority in decision making, and act as advocates for all students" (NASP-PPE Introduction).
- The mission of schools is to maintain order, ensure student safety, and educate children (*Burnside v. Byars*, 1966). As school employees, "school psychologists have a legal as well as an ethical obligation to take steps to protect all students from reasonably foreseeable risk of harm" (NASP-PPE Introduction).
- As school employees, school psychology practitioners are *state actors*; that is, their actions are seen to be an extension of the state's authority to educate children. This creates a special obligation for school psychologists to know and respect the rights of schoolchildren under federal and state law (NASP-PPE Introduction).
- Like other mental health practitioners, school psychologists often provide assessment and intervention services within the framework of an established psychologist–client relationship. However, at other times, as members of a school's instructional support team, school psychologists may provide consultative services to student assistance teams, classrooms, schools, or other recipients of service that do not fall within the scope of an established psychologist–client relationship (NASP-PPE Definition of Terms). This distinction is particularly important for school practitioners because, in law and ethics, the rules for informed consent are linked to whether services are provided within the context of a school psychologist–client relationship.
- Recent years have witnessed growing interest in better protection of sensitive student information. Partly as a result of changes that have occurred in health care settings, many parents now have a greater expectation of control of physical and mental health information about their children, even when information is to be shared internally in the school setting (Gelfman & Schwab, 2005b; Schwab & Gelfman, 2005a, 2005b; Schwab et al., 2005). In addition, since 1999, many states have broadened the scope of their laws governing privilege to include confidential communications that occur within a school psychologist–client relationship.
- "School-based practitioners work in a context that emphasizes multidisciplinary problem solving and intervention" (NASP-PPE Introduction).

The NASP's 2010 code of ethics is organized around four broad ethical themes: Respecting the Dignity and Rights of All Persons; Professional Competence and

Responsibility; Honesty and Integrity in Professional Relationships; and Responsibility to Schools, Families, Communities, the Profession, and Society. These themes were derived from the literature on ethical principles (e.g., Bersoff & Koeppl, 1993; Prilleltensky, 1997; W. D. Ross, 1930) and other ethical codes, especially that of the Canadian Psychological Association (CPA, 2000). The four broad themes subsume 17 ethical principles, and each principle is then further articulated by specific standards. The "broad themes, corollary principles, and ethical standards are to be considered in ethical decision making" (NASP-PPE Introduction). However, the broad themes statements are aspirational; NASP will seek to enforce only the 17 ethical principles and associated standards of conduct. The NASP's broad ethical themes, corollary principles, and associated standards of conduct will be discussed in more detail in this and subsequent chapters.

APA's "Ethical Principles of Psychologists and Code of Conduct"

The "Ethical Standards of Psychologists" was first adopted by the APA in 1953. Eight revisions of the APA's code of ethics were published between 1959 and 1992. The current version, "Ethical Principles of Psychologists and Code of Conduct" (APA-EP), was adopted in 2002 and amended in 2010. (See Appendix B.) The APA's "Ethical Principles" differs from the NASP's "Principles for Professional Ethics" in that it was developed for psychologists with training in diverse specialty areas (clinical, industrial-organizational, school psychology) and who work in a number of different settings (private practice, industry, hospitals and clinics, public schools, university teaching, research).

The "Ethical Principles of Psychologists and Code of Conduct" consists of these sections: Introduction and Applicability, Preamble, General Principles, and Ethical Standards. The General Principles section includes five broadly worded aspirational goals to be considered by psychologists in ethical decision making, and the Ethical Standards section sets forth enforceable rules for conduct. General Principle A, Beneficence and Nonmaleficence, means that psychologists engage in professional actions that are likely to benefit others, or at least do no harm (Behnke & Jones, 2012).

Principle B is Fidelity and Responsibility. Consistent with this principle, psychologists build and maintain trust by being aware of and honoring their professional responsibilities to clients and the community. Principle C, Integrity, obligates psychologists to be open and honest in their professional interactions and faithful to the truth and to guard against unclear or unwise commitments. In accordance with Principle D, Justice, psychologists seek to ensure that all persons have access to and can benefit from what psychology has to offer. They strive for fairness and nondiscrimination in the provision of services. Principle E, Respect for People's Rights and Dignity, encourages psychologists to respect the worth of all people and their rights to privacy, confidentiality, autonomy, and self-determination (Flanagan et al., 2005).

The APA's Ethical Standards (enforceable rules for conduct) are organized into six general sections: Resolving Ethical Issues, Competence, Human Relations, Privacy and Confidentiality, Advertising and Other Public Statements, and Record Keeping and Fees. These are followed by four sections: Education and Training, Research and Publication, Assessment, and Therapy (APA, 2010). (For additional information on the APA's 2010 ethics code, see Behnke & Jones, 2012; C. B. Fisher, 2012; Knapp & VandeCreek, 2012.)

Professional Versus Private Behavior

Professional codes of ethics apply "only to psychologists' activities that are part of their scientific, educational, or professional roles as psychologists.... These activities shall be distinguished from the purely private conduct of psychologists, which is not within the purview of the Ethics Code" (APA, 2010, Introduction and Applicability). Similarly, the NASP's code states: "School psychologists, in their private lives, are free to pursue their personal interests, except to the degree that those interests compromise professional effectiveness" (NASP-PPE III.4.1). Ethics code thus obligate school psychologists to avoid actions that would diminish their professional credibility and effectiveness. In addition, it is important for school-employed practitioners to understand that school boards, parents, other community members, and the courts may hold elementary and secondary school (K–12) educators to a higher standard of moral character and conduct than others because K–12 educators serve as role models for schoolchildren (*Ambach v. Norwick*, 1979).

As Pipes, Holstein, and Aguirre (2005, p. 332) observed, the boundaries between professional and personal behaviors are often "fuzzy." School psychologists are encouraged to aspire to high standards of ethical conduct in their personal, as well as professional, lives and to think critically about the boundaries between the two (Pipes et al., 2005). For example, if a psychologist engages in socially undesirable behavior in a public setting (e.g., a school psychologist is verbally abusive of the referee at a high school football game), the behavior may negatively impact his or her credibility, diminish trust in school psychologists, and confuse students and others who hear about or witness the event.

School psychology practitioners and trainees must also be mindful of the fuzzy boundaries between their private and professional lives in cyberspace (L. D. Armistead, 2014b; Pham, 2014). Ethically, inappropriate posts on social networking sites can result in loss of trust in the school psychologist and impair his or her effectiveness. Legally, inappropriate social networking posts can threaten the job standing of school-employed practitioners or justify dismissal of a graduate student from his or her training program. The courts have upheld the right of school districts to discipline or dismiss employees for sharing information on their personal social networking sites—even on their own time and using their own electronic devices—if the material posted threatens to undermine the authority of school administrators; disrupts coworker relationships in the school, especially those based on trust and confidentiality; impairs the employee's performance of his or her duties; or could disrupt the learning atmosphere of the school (e.g., *Richerson v. Beckon*, 2008; *Spanierman v. Hughes*, 2008). Furthermore, because K–12 educators are expected to serve as role models for children, the courts have upheld the right of training programs to dismiss students whose social networking posts show poor professional judgment and conduct unbecoming to a public school educator (*Snyder v. Millersville University*, 2008). (The right of school psychologists to make statements about matters of public concern is addressed in the epilogue.)

Professional Models for Service Delivery

Professional models for the delivery of school psychological services differ from ethical codes in both scope and intent. The NASP's *Model of Comprehensive and Integrated Services by School Psychologists* (2010a) represents a consensus among practitioners and trainers about the roles and duties of school psychologists, desirable conditions for the effective delivery of services, the components of a comprehensive school psychological services delivery system, and standards for best practices. This document can be used to inform practitioners, students, trainers, administrators, policy makers, and consumers about the nature and scope of appropriate and desirable services. The NASP and the APA seek to ensure that members abide by their respective ethical codes and investigate and adjudicate code violations. In contrast, the NASP's *Model of Comprehensive and Integrated Services by School Psychologists* identifies standards for excellence in the delivery of comprehensive school psychological services, and it is recognized that not all school psychologists or all school psychological service units will be able to meet every identified standard. (See R. J. Armistead & Smallwood, 2014.)

FOUR BROAD ETHICAL PRINCIPLES

The four broad themes that appear in the NASP's 2010 "Principles for Professional Ethics" provide an organizational framework for the introduction to ethical issues in school psychology in this section of the chapter. As noted previously, these themes also can be found in the literature on ethical principles (e.g., Bersoff & Koeppl, 1993; Prilleltensky, 1997; W. D. Ross, 1930) and other ethical codes, especially that of the CPA (2000). In this book we emphasize principles-based ethics. We encourage readers to think about the spirit and intent of broad ethical themes outlined in this section and to enhance their understanding of ethics by becoming familiar with other philosophical systems (see Knapp & VandeCreek, 2012).

Respect for the Dignity of Persons

Psychologists "accept as fundamental the principle of respect for the dignity of persons" (CPA, 2000, p. 9); also see APA-EP Principle E). "School psychologists are committed to the application of their professional expertise for the purpose of promoting improvement in the quality of life for students, families, and school communities. This objective is pursued in ways that protect the dignity and rights of those involved. School psychologists consider the interests and rights of children and youth to be their highest priority in decision making" (NASP-PPE Introduction). The general principle of respect for the dignity of all persons encompasses respect for the rights of individuals to *self-determination and autonomy*, *privacy and confidentiality*, and *fairness and justice* (NASP-PPE I; also CPA, 2000).

Self-Determination and Autonomy

"In their words and actions, school psychologists demonstrate respect for the autonomy of persons and their right to self-determination" (NASP-PPE I). They "respect the right of persons to participate in decisions affecting their own welfare" (NASP-PPE I.1). School psychologists apply the ethical principle of respect for self-determination and autonomy to their professional practices by seeking informed consent to establish a school psychologist–client relationship and by ensuring that the individuals with whom they work have "a voice and a choice" in decisions that affect them.

Except for urgent situations, school psychologists generally seek the informed consent of an adult (the parent or guardian of a child) to establish a school psychologist–client relationship (NASP-PPE I.1.2). They respect the right of the individual providing consent to choose or decline the services offered (NASP-PPE I.1.5). School psychologists also honor, to the maximum extent appropriate, the right of children to assent to or decline school psychological services. (See Chapters 3 and 7.)

However, when working with children, sometimes it is necessary to balance the rights of self-determination and autonomy against concerns for the welfare of the child. The NASP's code of ethics states: "Ordinarily, school psychologists seek the student's assent to services; however, it is ethically permissible to bypass student assent to services if the service is considered to be of direct benefit to the student and/or is required by law" (NASP-PPE I.1.4; also see CPA, 2000). If a child's assent is not solicited, school psychologists nevertheless ensure that the child is informed about the nature of the services being provided and is afforded opportunities to participate in decisions that affect him or her (NASP-PPE I.1.4, II.3.11).

As noted, school psychologists often provide services within the framework of an established school psychologist–client relationship. However, as members of a school's instructional support team, practitioners also provide consultative services to student assistance teams, classrooms, or schools that do not fall within the scope of an established school psychologist–client relationship (NASP-PPE Definition of Terms). Thus, while school practitioners encourage parental participation in school decisions affecting their children (NASP-PPE I.1.1, II.3.10), not all of their consultative services require informed parent consent, particularly if the resulting interventions are under the authority of the teacher and within the scope of typical classroom interventions (NASP-PPE I.1.1). (Also see Chapter 7.)

During their careers, school psychologists will encounter dilemmas regarding how to balance the rights of parents to make informed decisions about their children with the rights and needs of those children. For example: Under what circumstances should minors have the right to seek school psychological services on their own, without parent permission? When should a minor be afforded the opportunity to make a choice whether to participate in or refuse the psychological services being offered?

Privacy and Confidentiality

Psychologists "respect the right of persons to choose for themselves whether to disclose their private thoughts, feelings, beliefs, and behaviors" (NASP-PPE I.2; also APA-EP Principle E), and every effort is made to avoid undue invasion of privacy (APA-EP Principle E; NASP-PPE I.2.2). School psychologists "do not seek or store private information about clients that is not needed in the provision of services" (NASP-PPE I.2.2; APA-EP 4.04).

Practitioners also use appropriate safeguards to protect the confidentiality of client disclosures. Except for urgent situations, they inform clients of the boundaries of confidentiality at the outset of establishing a school psychologist–client relationship. They seek a shared understanding with clients regarding the types of information that will and will not be shared with third parties and recognize that it may be necessary to discuss how confidential information will be managed at multiple points in an ongoing professional relationship (NASP-PPE I.2.3). In light of these obligations, how should Carrie (Case 1.1) handle Joanne's disclosures?

Case 1.1

Samantha's first- and second-grade teachers observed that she experienced difficulties with concentration and memory. She frequently failed to remember letter sounds and math facts she had previously mastered. Now in third grade, Samantha continues to perform well below grade level even after multiple individualized interventions were attempted in the classroom. Samantha's mother, Joanne, agrees with the third-grade teacher that Samantha should be evaluated to determine whether she is eligible for special education services.

Carrie Johnson, the school psychologist, meets with Joanne to ensure she is informed about the nature and scope of the psychoeducational evaluation and to gather information about Samantha's developmental history. Joanne is employed as a classroom teacher aide at the same small, rural school her daughter attends. In the meeting with Carrie, Joanne discloses that she was involved "with the wrong boyfriend" during her first semester away at college. She "partied a lot, used all kinds of drugs, and got pregnant." Because she was "too messed up" to realize she was pregnant, she continued to use drugs during the early months of her pregnancy but then moved back home with her parents and "got straightened out." Joanne went on to tell the psychologist: "Please don't tell anyone about this. I've never even told any of my doctors because my mom said it would be difficult for me to get a good job if drug abuse showed up in my medical records. And if my drug use history gets out at this school—you know how this community is and how people talk—it could hurt Samantha and I might even lose my job."

Carrie will assure Joanne that her disclosure of drug use during pregnancy will be held in strict confidence and not shared with anyone else, and not included in Samantha's school psychology records (NASP-PPE I.2.2; APA-EP 4.04). Carrie recognizes that she has a special ethical obligation to safeguard the confidentiality of sensitive and private medical information (NASP-PPE I.2.7). Furthermore, the information that Joanne disclosed about her pregnancy is not needed for the purpose of determining Samantha's eligibility for special education services or for planning appropriate educational interventions for her (NASP-PPE I.2.2, I.2.5), and could have negative repercussions for Joanne and Samantha if made available to others.

In situations in which confidentiality is promised or implied, school psychologists do not reveal information to third parties "without the agreement of a minor child's parent or legal guardian (or an adult student), except in those situations in which failure to release information would result in danger to the student or others, or where otherwise required by law." Furthermore, when practitioners share information with third parties, they "discuss and/or release confidential information only for professional purposes and only with persons who have a legitimate need to know" (NASP-PPE I.2.5).

The ethical and legal issues of privacy, confidentiality, and privilege will create challenges for practitioners. For example, what information do teachers and other instructional staff need to know about a child's physical health, mental health, and family background to provide effective individualized instruction? Do parents have a right to know what their child tells a school psychologist? What if a young teenager discloses that he or she is planning to hurt someone or has committed a crime? These issues will be explored further in the chapters ahead.

Fairness and Justice

Respect for the dignity of all persons also encompasses the ethical obligation to ensure fairness, nondiscrimination, and justice. School psychologists "use their expertise to cultivate school climates that are safe and welcoming to all persons regardless of actual or perceived characteristics, including race, ethnicity, color, religion, ancestry, national origin, immigration status, socioeconomic status, primary language, gender, sexual orientation, gender identity, gender expression, disability, or any other distinguishing characteristics" (NASP-PPE I.3; also APA-EP Principle E). They do not engage in or condone actions or policies that discriminate against persons, including students and their families, other recipients of service, supervisees, and colleagues based on these or any other actual or perceived characteristics (I.3.1). Furthermore, school psychologists "work to correct school practices that are unjustly discriminatory" (NASP-PPE I.3.3).

The school psychologist's obligation to students from diverse cultural, linguistic, and experiential backgrounds goes beyond striving to be impartial and unprejudiced in the delivery of services. Practitioners have an ethical responsibility to actively "pursue awareness and knowledge of how diversity factors may influence child development, behavior, and school learning" (NASP-PPE I.3.2) and to pursue the skills needed to promote the mental health and education of diverse students (NASP-PPE II.1.2). Ignoring or minimizing the importance of characteristics such as ethnicity, disabilities, sexual orientation, or socioeconomic background may result in approaches that are ineffective and a disservice to children, parents, teachers, and other recipients of services (see NASP-PPE I.3.2; also Jacob, Drevon, Abbuhl, & Taton, 2010; Lopez, 2014; Miranda, 2014; Rogers & Lopez, 2002).

Consistent with the broad ethical principle of justice, school psychologists also "strive to ensure that all children have equal opportunity to participate in and benefit from school programs and that all students and families have access to and can benefit from school psychological services" (NASP-PPE I.3.4, IV; also APA-EP Principle D; Shriberg et al., 2008). (See Harrison & Thomas, 2014.)

Responsible Caring (Professional Competence and Responsibility)

A shared theme in ethical codes of the helping professions is that of beneficence. *Beneficence*, or responsible caring, means that psychologists engage in actions that are likely to benefit others, or at least do no harm (CPA, 2000; Welfel, 2012; also APA-EP Principle A; NASP-PPE II). "To do this, school psychologists must practice within the boundaries of their competence, use scientific knowledge from psychology and education to help clients and others make informed choices, and accept responsibility for their work" (NASP-PPE II).

Competence

The NASP code of ethics requires that school psychologists "engage only in practices for which they are qualified and competent" (NASP-PPE II.1; also APA-EP 2.01). As noted previously, the term *competent* generally suggests that the practitioner is able to integrate professional knowledge and skills with an understanding of the client and situation and make appropriate decisions, based on a consideration of both the immediate and long-term effects (Dreyfus, 1997; Nagy, 2012). Practitioners must consider their competence to provide various types of services and to use techniques that are new to them. Like David in Case 1.2, they also must consider whether they are competent to provide services in light of client characteristics such as age; disability; ethnic, racial, and language background; and sexual orientation and gender identity. Psychologists who step beyond their competence place the student at risk for misdiagnosis, misclassification, miseducation, and possible psychological harm.

Case 1.2

A Kia Motors assembly plant opened near the school district where David Kim is completing his school psychology internship. A number of Korean Kia employees and their families were relocated to the United States and now live in David's school district. Some of the adults and children are quite fluent in English; others speak little English. The special education director asked David to conduct a school psychological evaluation of an 8-year-old girl, Seo-yeon, because she appeared to be struggling academically more than other Korean students at her school. Although Seo-yeon has acquired some conversational English proficiency, her parents speak little English. Consistent with codes of ethics, David, a second-generation Korean American, needed to carefully consider whether he was competent to conduct a valid bilingual assessment of Seo-yeon using Korean and English.

David consulted his university internship supervisor and his on-site supervisor about the special education director's request. They discussed David's self-assessment of his Korean language competence and his lack of prior supervised experience conducting a bilingual assessment. As a result, David met with the special education director and offered to review Seo-yeon's school records from Korea and conduct a screening of Seo-yeon to determine whether a full evaluation was needed. He respectfully explained why he was not qualified to conduct a comprehensive bilingual assessment of Seo-yeon if a disability is suspected. He also offered to attend school-parent meetings with Seo-yeon's parents, noting that he would be able to help establish culturally sensitive "*jeong*" (rapport) with family members. In addition,

David recommended that a trained interpreter attend the meetings with the parents because he was not proficient enough in Korean to explain the specialized terms used in meetings with parents of students who are struggling academically.

The students who attend our nation's schools have become increasingly diverse in terms of race, ethnicity, language, national origin, and family composition (Miranda, 2014). In addition, gay, lesbian, and transgender youth now "come out" at earlier ages than in previous generations, often during their middle or high school years (Jacob et al., 2010). Consequently, all practitioners must assess and periodically reassess their competence to provide services to a diverse clientele and seek the knowledge necessary to provide culturally sensitive services in the schools where they work. Where understanding of age, gender, race, ethnicity, national origin, religion, sexual orientation, gender identity or expression, disability, language, or socioeconomic status is essential for providing effective services, school psychologists are expected to have or to obtain the training, experience, consultation, or supervision necessary to provide effective services. If a school practitioner is not competent to provide services to a particular client, then he or she is obligated to refer the client to a professional who is qualified to provide the needed services (APA-EP 2.01; also NASP-PPE I.3.2).

School psychologists are ethically obligated to "remain current regarding developments in research, training, and professional practices that benefit children, families, and schools. They also should demonstrate an understanding that professional skill development beyond that of the novice practitioner requires well-planned continuing professional development and professional supervision" (NASP-PPE II.1.4; also APA-EP 2.03). Our codes of ethics encourage practitioners to engage in the lifelong learning that is necessary to achieve and maintain expertise in the field of school psychology (Welfel, 2012). (See L. D. Armistead, 2014a.)

Responsibility

In all areas of service delivery, school psychologists strive to maximize benefit and avoid doing harm. Consistent with this principle of responsible caring, school psychologists use the science of psychology to assist students, teachers, parents, and others in making informed choices (APA-EP Preamble; NASP-PPE II). In addition, practitioners monitor the impact of their professional decisions and the consequences of those decisions, work to correct ineffective recommendations, and strive to offset any harmful consequences of decisions made (APA-EP Principle B; NASP-PPE II.2, II.2.2).

Under the broad principle of professional competence and responsibility, the NASP's code of ethics has specific standards for responsible assessment and intervention practices (II.3), school-based record keeping (II.4), and use of professional materials (II.5).

Honesty and Integrity in Professional Relationships

A psychologist–client relationship is a *fiduciary* relationship, that is, one based on trust. To build and maintain trust, school psychologists must demonstrate integrity in professional relationships. The broad principle of integrity encompasses the moral obligations of fidelity, nonmaleficence, and beneficence. *Fidelity* refers to a continuing faithfulness to the truth and to one's professional duties (Bersoff & Koeppl, 1993). Practitioners are obligated to be open and honest in their interactions with others and to adhere to their professional promises (CPA, 2000; APA-EP Principle B; NASP-PPE III).

Consistent with the broad principle of honesty in professional relationships, school psychologists provide a forthright explanation of the nature and scope of their services, roles, and priorities (NASP-PPE III.2). They "explain all professional services to clients in a clear, understandable manner" (NASP-PPE III.2.1). Case 1.3 illustrates the importance of openly defining the parameters of the services to be offered in the school setting. Madeleine has become Maria's consultee in this school psychologist–consultee relationship. In this situation, Maria is bound by the obligation and expectation that what is shared and learned in their professional interaction is confidential; she may not share information about her consultee with the principal without Madeleine's explicit consent to do so. However, as is discussed in Chapter 8, not all psychologist–teacher consultative relationships are confidential.

In defining their job roles to the school community, school psychologists also identify the services they provide and those that are outside the scope of their job roles (NASP-PPE III.2.2; APA-EP Principle E). It is the job role of the principal, not the school psychologist, to gather information on teacher effectiveness (also NASP-PPE III.2.4). If Maria violates the confidentiality of the consultative relationship and shares information about Madeleine's teaching with the school administration, her actions would most likely undermine teacher trust in school psychologists and diminish her ability to work with other teachers in need of consultative services. The ethical issues associated with the consultation role are also discussed in Chapters 8 and 9.

Furthermore, consistent with the general principle of integrity in professional relationships, psychologists must be honest and straightforward about the boundaries of their competencies (NASP-PPE III.1.1, III.2.1). "Competency levels, education, training, experience, and certification and licensing credentials are accurately represented to clients, recipients of services, and others" (NASP-PPE III.1.1; also APA-EP

Case 1.3

Madeleine Fine, a new first-grade teacher, asks Maria Delgado, the school psychologist, for some ideas on handling Kevin, a child who has demonstrated some challenging behaviors in the classroom. After Maria observes in the classroom, it is evident to her that Madeleine needs some help working with Kevin and developing effective classroom management strategies. Maria offers to meet with Madeleine once a week over a six-week period to work on classroom management skills, and Madeleine agrees. Shortly after their third consultation session, the principal asks Maria for her assessment of Madeleine's teaching competence. The principal indicates that she plans to terminate Madeleine during her probationary period if there are problems with her teaching effectiveness. Maria is not sure how to respond to the principal's request.

Principle C). School psychology interns and practicum students identify themselves as such when seeking to establish a school psychologist–client relationship. Practitioners inform clients if they are offering a service that is new to them so that clients can make informed choices about whether to accept the service.

School psychologists also respect and understand the areas of competence of other professionals in their work settings and communities, and they work in full cooperation with others "in relationships based on mutual respect" to meet the needs of students (NASP-PPE III.3; also APA-EP Principle B). As noted previously, school-based practitioners work in a context that emphasizes multidisciplinary problem solving and intervention. Consistent with their professional duties, they "encourage and support the use of all resources to serve the interests of students" (NASP-PPE III.3.1).

In addition, the principle of integrity in professional relationships also requires school psychologists to avoid multiple relationships and conflicts of interest that may interfere with professional effectiveness (NASP-PPE III.4; APA-EP 3.05a). "School psychologists attempt to resolve such situations in a manner that provides greatest benefit to the client" (NASP-PPE III.4.2). Multiple relationships occur when a psychologist is in a professional role with a client and at the same time is in another role with that person or in a relationship with an individual related to or closely associated with the client. The APA's ethics code states that a psychologist should refrain from entering into a multiple relationship "if it can reasonably be expected to impair the psychologist's objectivity, competence, or effectiveness" in providing services (APA-EP 3.05a; also NASP-PPE III.4.2). For example, it would not be appropriate to provide services to a friend's child. However, the APA's code recognizes that multiple relationships are not always unethical. School psychologists must think carefully about whether the existence of multiple roles (e.g., professional, social, business) in relation to a client or his or her family will impair professional objectivity or effectiveness (Flanagan et al., 2005).

Practitioners also avoid conflicts of interest. "When personal beliefs, conflicts of interests, or multiple relationships threaten to diminish professional effectiveness or would be viewed by the public as inappropriate, school psychologists ask their supervisor for reassignment of responsibilities, or they direct the client to alternative services" (NASP-PPE III.4.2).

Furthermore, school psychologists "do not exploit clients, supervisees, or graduate students through professional relationships or condone these actions by their colleagues. They do not participate in or condone sexual harassment." They "do not engage in sexual relationships with individuals over whom they have evaluation authority" and "do not engage in sexual relationships with their current or former pupil-clients; the parents, siblings, or other close family members of current pupil-clients; or current consultees" (NASP-PPE III.4.3; also APA-EP 3.02, 3.08).

Consistent with the general principle of honesty and integrity, psychologists also do not take credit for work that is not their own (APA-EP Principle C; NASP-PPE IV.5.8, IV.5.9). "When publishing or presenting research or other work, school psychologists do not plagiarize the works or ideas of others" (NASP-PPE IV.5.8). Furthermore, they take credit "only for work they have actually performed or to which they have contributed" (APA-EP 8.12; also NASP-PPE IV.5.9).

Responsibility to Schools, Families, Communities, the Profession, and Society

"Psychology functions as a discipline within the context of human society. Psychologists, both in their work and as private citizens, have responsibilities to the societies in which they live and work, such as the neighbourhood or city, and to the welfare of all human beings in those societies" (CPA, 2000, p. 27; also APA-EP Principle B; Prilleltensky, 1991; Shriberg & Moy, 2014). Consistent with these ideas, the NASP's fourth broad aspirational principle states:

> School psychologists promote healthy school, family, and community environments. They assume a proactive role in identifying social injustices that affect children and schools and strive to reform systems-level patterns of injustice. They maintain the public trust in school psychologists by respecting law and encouraging ethical conduct. School psychologists advance professional excellence by mentoring less experienced practitioners and contributing to the school psychology knowledge base. (NASP-PPE IV)

Under the fourth broad principle of responsibility to schools, families, communities, the profession, and society, the NASP's code of ethics has specific standards for promoting healthy school, family, and community environments (IV.1); respecting law and the relationship of law and ethics (IV.2); maintaining public trust by self-monitoring and peer monitoring (IV.3); contributing to the profession by mentoring, teaching, and supervision (IV.4); and contributing to the school psychology knowledge base (IV.5).

James's conduct (Case 1.4) is consistent with our ethical responsibility to speak up for the needs and rights of students even when it is difficult to do so (NASP-PPE Introduction) and to use our professional expertise "to promote school, family, and community environments that are safe and healthy for children" (NASP-PPE IV.1). School psychologists are ethically obligated to help ensure that all youth can attend school, learn, and develop their personal identities in an environment free from discrimination, harassment, violence, and abuse (NASP-PPE IV.1.2). Through advocacy and education of staff and students, James will work to foster a school climate that

---

Case 1.4

After several incidents of harassment of gay teens and students who do not conform to gender-role expectations, James Lewis, school psychologist, became increasingly convinced that the schools in his district were not a safe or supportive place for lesbian, gay, biattractional, or transgender (LGBT) youth. He began to read about the developmental needs and challenges of LGBT youth and those questioning (Q) their sexual orientation or gender identity, and he spent time talking with LGBTQ teens about their experiences at school. He then formed alliances with school and community leaders who shared his concerns. Although he may face opposition, James will advocate for districtwide changes to reduce harassment and improve the school climate for LGBTQ youth.

promotes not only understanding and acceptance of individual differences but also a respect for and valuing of those differences.

In keeping with our responsibilities to the communities in which we live and work, school psychologists know and respect federal and state law and school policies (NASP-PPE IV.2; see "Relationship between Ethics and Law" later in this chapter). Also consistent with the broad principle of responsibility to schools, families, communities, the profession, and society, school psychologists monitor their own conduct to ensure that it conforms to high ethical standards, and they monitor the conduct of their professional colleagues. Self- and peer monitoring for ethical compliance safeguards the welfare of others and fosters trust in psychology (Johnson, Barnett, Elman, Forrest, & Kaslow, 2012). If concerns about unethical conduct by another psychologist cannot be resolved informally through a collegial problem-solving process, practitioners take further action appropriate to the situation, such as notifying the practitioner's work-site supervisor of their concerns or filing a complaint with a professional ethics committee (NASP-PPE IV.3.3; also APA-EP 1.04). (See the section titled "Unethical Conduct" later in this chapter.)

School psychologists also contribute to the profession by mentoring, teaching, and supervision: "As part of their obligation to students, schools, society, and their profession, school psychologists mentor less experienced practitioners and graduate students to assure high quality services, and they serve as role models for sound ethical and professional practices and decision making" (NASP-PPE IV.4).

Finally, psychologists accept the obligation to contribute to the knowledge base of psychology and education in order to further improve services to children, families, and others and, in a more general sense, promote human welfare (CPA, 2000; APA-EP Principle B; NASP-PPE IV.5). For this reason, they are encouraged to participate in, assist in, or conduct and disseminate research (NASP-PPE IV.5). When school psychologists engage in research activities, they "respect the rights, and protect the well-being, of research participants" (NASP-PPE IV.5.2). (See Chapter 10.)

Summary

In this section, four broad ethical principles were introduced. The first was respect for the dignity of persons. Consistent with this principle, we value client autonomy and safeguard the client's right to self-determination, respect client privacy and the confidentiality of disclosures, aspire to fairness in interactions with the client and others, and promote justice in the environments where we work and live. The second broad principle was responsible caring. We engage in actions that are likely to benefit others. To do so, we work within the boundaries of our professional competence and accept responsibility for our actions. The third principle was integrity in professional relationships. We are candid and honest about the nature and scope of the services we offer and work in cooperation with other professionals to meet the needs of children in the schools. The fourth principle was responsibility to schools, families, communities, the profession, and society. We recognize that our profession exists within the context of society and work to ensure that the science of psychology is used to promote human welfare.

ETHICAL AND LEGAL DECISION MAKING

In this portion of the chapter, we address these questions: What makes a situation ethically challenging? What if ethical obligations conflict with law? When the needs and rights of multiple parties conflict, is our primary responsibility to the student, parent, teacher, or school system? How do we evaluate whether a course of action is ethical? And how can we make good choices when ethical-legal dilemmas arise?

What Makes a Situation Ethically Challenging?

Jacob-Timm (1999) surveyed school psychology practitioners and asked them to describe ethically challenging situations that they had encountered in their work. She found that ethical-legal dilemmas can be created by situations involving competing ethical principles, conflicts between ethics and law, the conflicting interests of multiple parties, dilemmas inherent in the dual roles of employee and student advocate, poor educational practices resulting in potential harm to students, and because it is difficult to decide how broad ethics code statements apply to a particular situation. In a more recent survey of school psychology practitioners, Dailor and Jacob (2011) found that almost three-fourths of the 208 respondents indicated they had encountered at least one of eight types of ethical dilemmas during the previous year. Whereas some ethical dilemmas are quickly and easily resolved, others are troubling and time-consuming (Sinclair, 1998). These findings support the view that, in addition to knowledge of the content of ethical codes, skill in using a systematic decision-making procedure is needed.

Relationship Between Ethics and Law

As noted previously, *professional ethics* is a combination of broad ethical principles and rules that guide the conduct of a practitioner in his or her professional interactions with others. *Law* is a body of rules of conduct prescribed by the state that has binding legal force. Both the APA and NASP codes of ethics require practitioners to know and respect the law (APA-EP Introduction and Applicability; NASP-PPE Introduction, IV.2.2; also see Behnke & Jones, 2012).

Professional codes of ethics are generally viewed as requiring decisions that are "more correct or more stringent" than required by law (Ballantine, 1979, p. 636). The APA's ethics code states that if the code "establishes a higher standard of conduct than is required by law, psychologists must meet that higher ethical standard" (APA-EP Introduction and Applicability; also NASP-PPE Introduction).

In the delivery of school psychological services, practitioners may face decisions involving possible conflicts between codes of ethics and law. In such circumstances, practitioners are encouraged to ask themselves: "Do I understand my legal obligations correctly? What actions does the law specifically require or prohibit (*must* do, *can't* do)? What actions does the law permit (*can* do)? Even if an action is legal, is it ethical? Do I understand my ethical obligations correctly?" (Knapp, Gottlieb, Berman, & Handelsman, 2007; Stefkovich, 2006).

If the ethical responsibilities of psychologists conflict with law, regulations, or other governing legal authority, psychologists clarify the nature of the conflict, make known their commitment to their code of ethics, and take steps to resolve the conflict in a responsible manner. The APA code states: "Under no circumstances may this standard be used to justify or defend violating human rights" (APA-EP 1.02, also 1.03; also see NASP-PPE Introduction, IV.2.3). The NASP's code of ethics states: "When conflicts between ethics and law occur, school psychologists take steps to resolve the conflict through positive, respected, and legal channels. If not able to resolve the conflict in this manner, they may abide by the law, as long as the resulting actions do not violate basic human rights" (NASP-PPE IV.2.3).

Ethical Challenge of Multiple Clients

School psychologists frequently face the challenge of considering the needs and rights of multiple clients and other recipients of services, including children, parents, teachers, and systems (Dailor & Jacob, 2011; NASP-PPE Introduction; also see M. A. Fisher, 2013). The *Canadian Code of Ethics for Psychologists* states: "Although psychologists have a responsibility to respect the dignity of all persons with whom they come in contact in their role as psychologists, the nature of their contract with society demands that their greatest responsibility be to those persons in the most vulnerable position" (CPA, 2000, Principle I, p. 9). Consistent with the idea that ethical priority should be given to the most vulnerable persons, the NASP's code of ethics states: "School psychologists consider the interests and rights of children and youth to be their highest priority in decision making, and act as advocates for all students" (NASP-PPE Introduction; also see APA-EP Principle E).

How Do We Evaluate Whether a Course of Action Is Ethical or Unethical?

Ethics involves "making decisions of a moral nature about people and their inter-actions in society" (Kitchener, 1986, p. 306). Individuals may make choices of a moral nature primarily on an intuitive level or a critical-evaluative level (Hare, 1981; Kitchener, 1986). Choices made on the intuitive level are based on "people's immediate feeling responses to situations," along with personal beliefs about what they should or should not do (Kitchener, 1986, p. 309).

Psychologists, however, have special obligations when making ethical choices in the context of a professional relationship (Behnke & Jones, 2012; Haas & Malouf, 2005). In the provision of psychological services, decision making on a critical-evaluative level is consistent with sound professional practice. The critical-evaluative level of ethical decision making involves following a systematic procedure. This procedure may involve the exploration of feelings and beliefs, but also includes consideration of general ethical principles and codes of ethics and possibly consultation with colleagues. Psychologists need to be aware of their own feelings and values and how they may influence their decisions (N. D. Hansen & Goldberg, 1999; Newman, 1993). However, reliance on feelings and intuition alone in professional decision making may result in poor decisions or confusion (Kitchener, 1986).

How do we evaluate whether a course of action is ethical or unethical? Haas and Malouf (2005, p. 3) suggested that an act or a decision is likely to be viewed as ethical if it has these three characteristics: (1) The decision is *principled*, based on generally accepted ethical principles; (2) the action is a *reasoned* outcome of a consideration of the principles; and (3) the decision is *universalizable*, that is, the psychologist would recommend the same course of action to others in a similar situation. The consequences of the course of action chosen must also be considered—namely, will the action chosen result in more good than harm? Evaluation of whether a course of action is ethical thus involves consideration of characteristics of the decision itself (based on accepted principles and universality), the process of decision making (reasoned), and the consequences of the decision.

Knapp and VandeCreek (2012) have called for a greater emphasis on *positive ethics* in choosing a course of action. A positive approach to ethics encourages psychologists to focus on moral excellence rather than meeting minimal obligations outlined in codes of ethics. Psychologists are encouraged to become familiar with philosophical systems of ethics, to internalize schemas for moral excellence, and to integrate schemas of moral excellence into their professional decision making.

Eight-Step Problem-Solving Model

Three broad types of ethical-legal challenges arise in professional practice: ethical dilemmas, ethical transgressions, and legal quandaries. Ethical dilemmas occur when "there are good but contradictory ethical reasons to take conflicting and incompatible courses of action" (Knauss, 2001, p. 231; also Beauchamp & Childress, 2013), and may foster moral distress among psychologists (Austin, Rankel, Kagan, Bergum, & Lemermeyer, 2005). Ethical transgressions or violations are those acts that go against professional expectations for ethical conduct and violate enforceable ethics codes. Ethical transgressions can result in harm to students or others and create a problematic situation for colleagues who must decide whether and how to confront the misconduct (Dailor & Jacob, 2011). Finally, disregard for federal or state law can result in infringement of the legal rights of students and families; parent–school disputes, especially with regard to special education law; and legal action against the school or school psychologist.

Sinclair (1998) observed that "some ethical decision making is virtually automatic and the individual may not be aware of having made an ethical decision. In other situations, ethical decision making is not automatic but leads rapidly to an easy resolution," particularly if a clear-cut standard exists. However, "some ethical issues ... require a time-consuming process of deliberation" (p. 171). Eberlein (1987) and others (Behnke & Jones, 2012; Knapp & VandeCreek, 2012; Tymchuk, 1986) suggested that mastery of an explicit decision-making model or procedure may help the practitioner make informed, well-reasoned choices when dilemmas arise in professional practice. Tymchuk (1986) has also noted that in difficult situations, the course of action chosen may be challenged. Use of a systematic problem-solving strategy will allow the practitioner to describe *how* a decision was made. This may afford some protection when difficult decisions come under the scrutiny of others. Furthermore, practitioners may find a systematic decision-making model helpful in anticipating and preventing problems from occurring (Sinclair, 1998).

We recommend that practitioners use an eight-step problem-solving model adapted from Koocher and Keith-Spiegel (2008, pp. 21–25). Note that, when using this decision-making model, it is not necessary to follow the steps in sequence. For example, a practitioner might consult with a colleague (step 3) to identify the ethical-legal issues pertinent to a situation (step 2):

1. Describe the parameters of the situation.
2. Define the potential ethical-legal issues involved.
3. Consult ethical and legal guidelines and district policies that might apply to the resolution of each issue (N. D. Hansen & Goldberg, 1999). Consider the broad ethical principles as well as specific mandates involved (N. D. Hansen & Goldberg, 1999; Kitchener, 1986).
4. Evaluate the rights, responsibilities, and welfare of all affected parties (e.g., student, teachers, classmates, other school staff, parents, siblings). N. D. Hansen and Goldberg (1999) encouraged consideration of the cultural characteristics of affected parties that may be salient to the decision (also Cottone, 2012).
5. Generate a list of alternative decisions possible for each issue.
6. Enumerate the consequences of making each decision. Evaluate the short-term, ongoing, and long-term consequences of each possible decision, considering the possible psychological, social, and economic costs to affected parties (Tymchuk, 1986). Eberlein (1987, p. 353) advised consideration of how each possible course of action would "affect the dignity of and the responsible caring for all of the people involved." Consultation with colleagues may be helpful.
7. Consider any evidence that the various consequences or benefits resulting from each decision will actually occur (i.e., a risk-benefit analysis).
8. Make the decision. Consistent with codes of ethics (APA, NASP), the school psychologist accepts responsibility for the decision made and monitors the consequences of the course of action chosen.

When faced with a difficult dilemma, the use of a decision-making model is now widely considered be a "best practice" and one that is recommended in the NASP's code of ethics (NASP-PPE Introduction). Additional research is needed to assess the impact of various decision models on the quality of ethical choices made by psychologists (Cottone, 2012). However, as Cottone (2012) noted, "the profession has advanced to the degree that a psychologist who makes a crucial ethical decision without the use of a model would appear naive, uneducated, or potentially incompetent" (p. 117).

Dailor and Jacob (2011) asked school psychology survey participants to identify the types of problem-solving strategies they used when handling difficult situations in the previous year. Less than one-quarter of respondents reported using a systematic decision-making model. Respondents who had received multilevel university training (coursework in ethics, discussion of ethical issues in multiple courses, and supervised discussion of ethical issues in practica and internships) were more likely to report use of a systematic decision-making model than those who had not received multilevel ethics preparation. However, two-thirds of survey participants did report consulting with colleagues when faced with a challenging situation. Gottlieb (2006) identified best practices in providing consultation to colleagues who are facing a difficult ethical situation.

UNETHICAL CONDUCT

As noted previously, one of the functions of professional associations is to develop and promote standards to enhance the quality of work by its members (Chalk et al., 1980). By encouraging appropriate professional conduct, associations such as the APA and the NASP strive to ensure that each person served will receive the highest quality of service. By so doing, the associations build and maintain public trust in psychology and psychologists. Failure to do so is likely to result in increased external regulation of the profession.

Appropriate professional conduct is defined through the development and frequent revision of codes of ethics and professional standards.

> The presence of a set of ethical principles or rules of conduct is only part, albeit an important one, of the machinery needed to effect self-regulation. The impact of a profession's ethical principles or rules on its members' behavior may be negligible ... without appropriate support activities to encourage proper professional conduct, or the means to detect and investigate possible violations, and to impose sanctions on violators. (Chalk et al., 1980, p. 2)

The APA and the NASP support a range of activities designed to educate and sensitize practitioners to the parameters of appropriate professional conduct. Both include ethics coursework as a required component in their standards for graduate training, and each organization disseminates information on professional conduct through publications and the support of symposia. In addition, continued professional training in the area of ethics is required for renewal of the Nationally Certified School Psychologist (NCSP) credential, and many states require continuing education credits in ethics for renewal of licensure.

The APA and the NASP also each support a standing ethics committee. Ethics committees are made up of volunteer members of the professional association. Ethics committees respond to informal inquiries about ethical issues, investigate complaints about possible ethics code violations by association members, and attempt to educate and/or impose sanctions on violators.

Ethics Committees and Sanctions

The APA (2007a) developed an extensive set of rules and procedures for investigation and adjudication of ethical complaints against APA members. According to the "Rules and Procedures," the primary objectives of the APA's ethics committee are to "maintain ethical conduct by psychologists at the highest professional level, to educate psychologists concerning ethical standards, [and] to endeavor to protect the public against harmful conduct by psychologists" (Part I, #1). The ethics committee investigates complaints alleging violation of the ethics code by APA members. It also investigates notices of action or charges pending against APA members from entities such as state licensing boards to determine whether the member also violated the APA's code of ethics. Possible sanctions for ethics violations include issuance of an educative letter, reprimand or censure, expulsion, and stipulated resignation (APA, 2007a; also see Behnke & Jones, 2012).

The purposes of the NASP's Ethical and Professional Practices Committee (EPPC) are: "(1) to promote and maintain ethical conduct by school psychologists, (2) to educate school psychologists regarding NASP ethical standards, and (3) to protect the general well-being of consumers of school psychological services" (National Association of School Psychologists Ethical and Professional Practices Committee, 2014b, p. 1). The EPPC responds to questions regarding appropriate professional practices and is committed to resolving concerns informally, if possible. The committee investigates alleged ethical misconduct of NASP members or any psychologist who holds an NCSP credential (p. 1). If, after investigation, the committee determines that a violation of the NASP's "Principles for Professional Ethics" has occurred, the committee may require the respondent to engage in remedial activities, such as education or training, and to provide restitution or apology. The committee also may recommend probation, suspension, or termination of NASP membership and/or revocation of the NCSP.

The legality of ethical complaint adjudication was tested in court in the case of *Marshall v. American Psychological Association* (1987). The plaintiff in this case claimed that the APA had no legal right to expel him or to publicize his expulsion from the association following an investigation of ethical misconduct. The court upheld the authority of the APA to expel the plaintiff, noting that he agreed to be bound by the APA's ethical principles when he joined the association, that the principles were repeatedly published, and that he had detailed hearing rights to respond to any and all charges.

Complaints to Ethics Committees

The APA's ethics committee periodically publishes an analysis of its actions in the *American Psychologist*. In 2014, the APA ethics committee received 68 complaints against members and 52 notices of action pending against a member from entities such as state licensing boards. Complaints were filed against fewer than 1 member per 1,000; notices were received regarding fewer than 1 member per 1,000. Ten new cases were opened in 2014. Based on categorization of the underlying behaviors (rather than the basis for processing the case), problem areas were sexual misconduct; nonsexual dual relationships; inappropriate professional practices (e.g., providing services outside of areas of competence); and false, fraudulent, or misleading public statements (APA, 2015).

Between July 2014 and May 2015, the NASP's EPPC responded to numerous requests for assistance and addressed five cases of possible ethics code violations at various stages of investigation and resolution. The possible ethics code violations involved theft from colleagues, dual relationships, falsification of records, and inappropriate sharing of university exam questions. Because many requests for assistance are handled at the regional level, no precise count of the inquiries to EPPC members is available. Documented inquiries to the EPPC included multiple questions regarding the use of digital communication and record keeping, district noncompliance with special education law, and the provision of school psychological services without parent consent or notice (screening of students, counseling). In addition, questions were received regarding provision of services to a student in a virtual high school program, university versus internship site responsibility for unsatisfactory intern performance, access to student records by parent advocates, confidentiality in a counseling relationship, an individual practicing without appropriate credentials, and the use of outdated tests (National Association of School Psychologists Ethical and Professional Practices Committee, 2014a, 2015).

Reasons for Unethical Conduct

In their survey of school psychology practitioners, Dailor and Jacob (2011) found that most of the respondents in their sample had witnessed at least one of nine types of ethical transgression by a school psychologist within the past year. According to Koocher and Keith-Spiegel (2008), no one profile describes psychologists who become ethics violators. Ethics violations may occur because the psychologist is unaware of the parameters of appropriate conduct or not competent to provide the services being offered. Transgressions may occur because the psychologist is poorly trained, is inexperienced, or fails to maintain up-to-date knowledge. Violations also may occur when a psychologist who usually works within the parameters of appropriate practice fails to think through a situation carefully. Some psychologists suffer from emotional problems or situational stressors that impair professional judgment and performance. Some practitioners lack sensitivity to the needs and rights of others; others may engage in unethical conduct because they are irresponsible or vengeful. Finally, a few psychologists (fortunately only a few) are self-serving and knowingly put their needs before those of their clients. (Also see Mahoney & Morris, 2012.)

Peer Monitoring

Both the APA and the NASP require members to monitor the ethical conduct of their professional colleagues (APA-EP Principle B; NASP-PPE IV, IV.3). Both associations also support attempts to resolve concerns informally before filing a complaint. The NASP's code of ethics states: "When a school psychologist suspects that another school psychologist or another professional has engaged in unethical practices, he or she attempts to resolve the suspected problem through a collegial problem solving process, if feasible" (NASP-PPE IV.3.2; also see APA-EP 1.04). If, however, an apparent ethical violation cannot be resolved informally, school psychologists take further action appropriate to the situation, such as discussing the situation with a supervisor in the employment setting or other institutional authorities, referral to a professional ethics committee, or referral to a state certification or licensing board (APA-EP 1.05; NASP-PPE IV.3.3). If a decision is made to file an ethics complaint, the appropriate professional organization is contacted for assistance and its procedures for resolving concerns about ethical practices are followed (see APA, 2007a; NASP, 2014b).

Although most psychologists are aware of their obligation to report unethical practices if the situation cannot be resolved informally, many are reluctant to do so (Pope, Tabachnick, & Keith-Spiegel, 1987). In her study of students' beliefs about their preparation to deal with ethical issues, Tryon (2001) found that fewer than half of the advanced students in school psychology doctoral programs (fifth year and beyond) believed they were prepared to deal with ethical violations by colleagues. Similarly, Dailor and Jacob (2011) found that about 25% of public school psychology practitioners had witnessed multiple instances of unethical conduct by a colleague within the past year but only 38% of the respondents perceived themselves to be "very well prepared" to address unethical conduct by colleagues. Survey participants who reported receiving multilevel training in ethics (coursework in ethics, discussion of ethical issues in multiple courses, and supervised discussion of ethical issues during field experiences) were more likely to report that they felt prepared to address unethical conduct by others than those who did not receive multilevel ethics training.

CONCLUDING COMMENTS

Students and practitioners often complain that codes of ethics are bothersome to read, confusing and boring lists of "shoulds" and "should nots." Wonderly (1989) suggested, however, that codes of ethics in psychology are not so overwhelming if we remember their primary purpose: namely, to protect the public. Professionals do not have *rights* under a code of ethics, only *obligations*. We will be exploring those obligations in more detail in the chapters ahead.

STUDY AND DISCUSSION

Questions for Chapter 1

1. What are the sources of quality control in the provision of school psychological services?
2. What does the term *ethics* mean?
3. What does the term *applied professional ethics* mean?
4. Why do professional groups, such as school psychologists, develop a code of ethics?
5. Summarize the desired ethics competencies of school psychology practitioners.
6. Why are codes of ethics imperfect guides to behavior?
7. Summarize the broad ethical principles discussed in Chapter 1.
8. How do you evaluate whether a course of action is ethical?
9. What are some of the reasons for unethical conduct?
10. What are your responsibilities with regard to peer monitoring?

Discussion

Tanya Howard, a newly hired school psychologist, was upset by a meeting she had with the parents of a child with a disability and the director of special education. The parents were concerned because their son was being called "retard," "monkey brains," and other names at school, and he no longer wanted to get on the school bus in the morning. The special educator director's only response was that "kids will be kids" and "a school can't be expected to stop kids from teasing kids." The boy's parents, from India, silently accepted these statements. Because of the special education director's overbearing manner, Tanya could not find an opportunity to speak up and express her concern about the bullying or to explore ways to address the problem. That evening, at home and using her own computer, Tanya vented her anger and frustration on Facebook. She did not use any real names, but in a post to her Facebook friends she described "the special education director" as "a bully and an arrogant creep" who "doesn't really give a crap about kids." She also wrote: "Parents from other countries need to learn to speak up for their children's rights like American parents do." Using the NASP's code of ethics as a guide (Appendix A), what are the ethical issues associated with Tanya's Facebook post? Should practitioners who use social media expect their posts to be private and confidential?

Related Activities

Do you think Tanya could face disciplinary sanction by her employer for her Facebook post? If you would like to read about the outcome of a similar situation, go to your university's online law data base (e.g., LexisNexis or WestlawNext) or "Google Scholar" and enter "Richerson" and "Beckon" where it allows you to search for a court case by the names of the parties.

Does your school psychology training program have policies to ensure that social media are used by students and faculty in ethically and professionally appropriate ways? If yes, review them with your classmates. If not, read Pham (2014) for ideas on this issue.

Review the pictures and posts on your own social networks. Have you posted material that shows poor judgment or conduct unbecoming a K–12 educator?

Vignettes

Eberlein (1987) and others have suggested that mastery of an explicit decision-making model or procedure may help the practitioner make well-reasoned ethical choices when difficult situations arise in professional practice. In this chapter, we introduced an eight-step problem-solving model adapted from Koocher and Keith-Spiegel (2008). The incidents that follow are included to provide an opportunity to practice the problem-solving model. At first, use of a decision-making model may seem quite cumbersome. However, it is important for practitioners to remember that ethical decision making "applies to almost everything psychologists do." Over time, if such a problem-solving model is practiced regularly, it is likely to become almost automatic (Tryon, 2000, p. 278).

In the situations described, assume the role of the school psychologist and then follow a decision-making model to determine the course of action most appropriate. Compare your decisions with those of colleagues or fellow students.

1. A few months after Carrie Johnson was hired as the school psychologist in a rural school district, the district superintendent of schools asked to meet with her. During this meeting, he said, "You'll be working closely with the principal at Pine Lake. Rumor has it he drinks a lot on the job. He's been caught twice and fined for driving while intoxicated. I think he's nuts, and we've got to get rid of him. Keep notes on what he says and does. I want a report later." How should Carrie handle this situation? (Vignette source unknown.)

2. As part of her effort to build a strong working relationship with school staff and community members, Maria Delgado joined the Parent-Teacher Association (PTA) and regularly attends its meetings. During a public meeting of the PTA, a parent openly complained about the treatment her daughter was receiving in a world history class at a school where Maria is the school psychologist. The parent contended that the history teacher lacked mental stability and consequently was causing her child much anguish. How should Maria handle this situation? (Adapted from Bailey, 1980.)

3. Michelle Phillips was born with Sanfilippo syndrome, a genetic disorder that results in progressive neurological deterioration and limited life expectancy. No effective treatment for the disorder exists. Wanda Rose, a school psychologist, has worked with the Phillips family since Michelle was diagnosed six years ago, and she has formed a warm working relationship with them. Michelle is now in the third and final phase of the disorder. She shows little awareness of her surroundings, is unable to communicate, and is unable to sit or walk without support. She has difficulty swallowing and chokes frequently.

   Mr. and Mrs. Phillips have made an appointment with Wanda. They believe Michelle is experiencing much pain and suffering. Although they want all comfort care to continue for their daughter, they do not want medical interventions that would prolong her life. They have brought along do not resuscitate (DNR) orders (do not institute basic choking rescue) from Michelle's physician, and they would like Wanda's help in ensuring that the orders will be honored at school. How should Wanda respond to this situation? (See Schwab & Gelfman, 2005b.)

4. You and a fellow student (a friend) are placed at the same school for your first practicum experience. You are aware that she is a problem drinker, but thus far, she has been able to conceal her problem from the program faculty. You discover that your fellow student drinks before coming to practicum, and you have observed some erratic behavior and poor judgment at the practicum site. What should you do? What will you do? Why? (Adapted from Bernard & Jara, 1986.)

Activities

To learn more about the APA and the NASP, visit their Web sites: http://www.apa.org and http://www.nasponline.org

For vignettes illustrating the use of a problem-solving model and additional practice vignettes, see L. D. Armistead et al. (2011) and Klose and Lasser (2014).

Many different acronyms are used in school psychology and special education. Appendix E is a list of acronyms frequently used in this volume. For a more complete list of acronyms commonly used in the schools, visit the Center for Parent Information and Resources: http://www.parentcenterhub.org/repository/acronyms/

Chapter 2 ————————————————————

LAW AND SCHOOL PSYCHOLOGY: AN INTRODUCTION

As noted in Chapter 1, codes of ethics are one source of quality control in the provision of school psychological services. This chapter explores two other mechanisms of quality assurance: public school law and the credentialing of school psychologists. We also further explore the legal implications of school-based practice. The term *school-based practice* means that the school psychologist is an employee of the schools, whether full time, part time, or on a per-case or consultative basis. In contrast, the term *private practice* refers to situations in which a school psychologist enters into an agreement with a client rather than an educational agency to provide services, and the fee for services is the responsibility of the client or his or her representative (National Association of School Psychologists [NASP], 2010b, Definition of Terms).

In this chapter, the reader will learn that in the United States, state governments, rather than the federal government, have assumed the duty to educate children and the power to do so. This authority to educate children and ensure student safety is further delegated by state governments to school boards. When principals, teachers, and school psychologists employed by a school board make decisions in their official roles, such acts are seen as an extension of the authority of state government; in legal parlance, school-based practitioners are considered to be *state actors* (Russo, 2012; Wells, 2004).

In our discussions with school psychologists, we have found that the subtle but important differences between school-based practice and private practice (or employment in other nonschool settings) often are misunderstood. Under the U.S. Constitution and federal and state statutory law, students and their parents have many legal rights in our public schools. School-based practitioners, as state actors, must know and respect those legal rights. Furthermore, as employees of a school board, school-based practitioners have a legal obligation to protect all students from reasonably foreseeable risk of harm. This duty extends to all students, not just clients (Russo, 2012).

THE U.S. CONSTITUTION

The three basic sources of public school law are the U.S. Constitution, statutes and regulations, and case law. The U.S. Constitution is the supreme law of the land. All statutes enacted by the U.S. Congress, state and local governments, and even boards of education are subject to the provisions of the Constitution (Russo, 2012). The original Constitution outlined the duties and powers of the federal government. Concern that the Constitution provided the foundation for a federal government that was too powerful led to the passage in 1791 of 10 amendments to the Constitution, the Bill of Rights. The Bill of Rights was created to provide a more distinct balance of power between the federal government and the states and to safeguard the rights of individual citizens. The remaining amendments, 11th through 26th, were adopted between 1795 and 1971.

No fundamental right to an education is guaranteed to citizens in the Constitution; however, the right to a public school education is seen to fall within the penumbra of the Constitution (see *San Antonio Independent School District v. Rodriguez*, 1973). As will be seen, the Constitution has been the foundation for many decisions affecting public school education, including the right to equal educational opportunity, student rights in the school setting, and church-state-school relationships. Portions of the Constitution most pertinent to education law are shown in Exhibit 2.1. The 10th, 14th, First, and Fourth Amendments are discussed next.

The 10th Amendment

The Constitution does not specifically refer to education as a duty of the federal government. Under the 10th Amendment, "The powers not delegated to the United States by the Constitution, nor prohibited by it to the states, are reserved to the states respectively, or to the people." Thus, under the 10th Amendment, state governments have assumed the duty to educate, the power to tax citizens of the state to finance education, and the power to compel school attendance.

Both federal and state governments have an interest in an "educated citizenry," as educated citizens are more capable of self-government and of making a positive contribution to community life (Hubsch, 1989). Most states delegate much of the authority for the management of public schools to local school boards. Public schools consequently are considered to be an arm of the government (Russo, 2012). Thus, when school boards, principals, teachers, and school psychologists make decisions in their official roles, their actions are seen as actions by the state. A public education is considered to be an *entitlement* given by the state to its citizens under state constitutional or statutory law. On the basis of state law, all children within a state have a legitimate claim of entitlement to a public education. This right to a public education given by state law is considered to be a *property right*.

The 14th Amendment

As noted, the Bill of Rights was passed to ensure a clearer balance of power between the federal government and the states and to safeguard the rights of individual citizens. The 14th Amendment was created to prevent state governments from trespassing on the rights of individual citizens: "No state shall make or enforce any law which shall abridge the privileges or immunities of citizens of the United States ... without due process of law." The Bill of Rights has been incorporated by the 14th Amendment to apply to states as well as the federal government, including public schools.

Exhibit 2.1 The U.S. Constitution: Selected Amendments

Amendment 1

Freedom of Religion, Speech, and the Press; Rights of Assembly and Petition

Congress shall make no law respecting an establishment of religion, or prohibiting the free exercise thereof; or abridging the freedom of speech, or of the press; or the right of the people peaceably to assemble, and to petition the government for a redress of grievances.

Amendment 4

Search and Arrest Warrants

The right of the people to be secure in their persons, houses, papers, and effects, against unreasonable searches and seizures, shall not be violated, and no warrants shall issue, but upon probable cause, supported by oath or affirmation, and particularly describing the place to be searched, and the persons or things to be seized.

Amendment 9

Powers Retained by the People

The enumeration in the Constitution, of certain rights, shall not be construed to deny or disparage others retained by the people.

Amendment 10

Powers Retained by the States and the People

The powers not delegated to the United States by the Constitution, nor prohibited by it to the states, are reserved to the states respectively, or to the people.

Amendment 14

Civil Rights

No state shall make or enforce any law which shall abridge the privileges or immunities of citizens of the United States; nor shall any state deprive any person of life, liberty, or property, without due process of law; nor deny to any person within its jurisdiction the equal protection of the laws.

Because education is a duty left to the states, the courts have long held the position that "judicial interposition in the operation of the public school system requires care and restraint" (*Epperson v. State of Arkansas*, 1968). As the Supreme Court stated in *Epperson*,[1] "By and large, public education in our Nation is committed to the control of state and local authorities. Courts do not and cannot intervene in the resolution of conflicts which arise in the daily operation of school systems and which do not directly and sharply implicate basic constitutional values" (p. 104).

The 1950s, 1960s, and 1970s were decades of increasing federal court involvement in school-related issues, however, because of school actions that violated the constitutional rights of students and their parents. Two aspects of the 14th Amendment have been extremely important in decisions regarding schools: the *equal protection clause* and the requirement for *procedural due process*.

Equal Protection Clause

The equal protection clause provides that no state shall "deny any person within its jurisdiction the equal protection of the laws." Beginning in the years of the Warren Court (1953–1969), this clause has been interpreted to mean that a state may not make a free public education available to some children but not to others in the state and that the state must provide equal educational opportunity to all citizens within its jurisdiction.

In the 1954 landmark Supreme Court ruling *Brown v. Board of Education*, the Court made it clear that each state must provide equal educational opportunity to all children in its jurisdiction regardless of race. The Court ruled that the assignment of African American children to separate public schools is a denial of equal protection under the 14th Amendment of the Constitution. In two important subsequent cases, *Pennsylvania Association for Retarded Children v. Commonwealth of Pennsylvania* (1971, 1972) and *Mills v. Board of Education of District of Columbia* (1972), the courts ruled that exclusion of children with handicaps[2] from public school education is a denial of equal protection.

In the years since *Brown*, the courts have sent an unwavering message to the states that they have a duty to provide equal educational opportunities to all children regardless of race, color, national origin, native language, sex, and disability under the 14th Amendment. The 14th Amendment equal protection clause also protects the school access rights of pregnant and married students.

Due Process

The 14th Amendment also provides that no state shall "deprive any person of life, liberty, or property, without due process of law." Courts have identified two aspects of due process: substantive and procedural. *Substantive due process* applies to the content of a law. A state may not pass a law that deprives citizens of life, liberty, or property if the law

---

[1] This case concerned an Arkansas state law that prohibited the teaching of the Darwinian theory of evolution in the schools. The Supreme Court held the law to be an unconstitutional violation of First Amendment safeguards of freedom of speech and inquiry and belief.

[2] The term *handicaps*, rather than *disability*, is used when historically accurate.

is not related to a legitimate governmental purpose; arbitrary and capricious laws that impact on citizens' rights will be ruled unconstitutional. In the public schools, substantive due process has been interpreted to mean that school rules restricting student rights must be reasonably related to the purpose of schooling. (See the discussion of *Tinker v. Des Moines Independent Community School District* [1969] later in this chapter.)

Procedural due process means that a state may not take away life, a liberty interest, or a property right without some sort of procedural fairness to safeguard citizens from unfair or wrongful infringement of rights by the government (Reschly & Bersoff, 1999). The requirement for procedural due process applies only to the infringement or deprivation of a liberty or property interest protected by the 14th Amendment; citizens are guaranteed procedural due process only if a substantive liberty or property interest is affected. The specific liberty and property interests protected under the umbrella of the 14th Amendment have been identified in court interpretations of the scope of substantive rights. In *Goss v. Lopez* (1975), the Supreme Court held that education is a property right protected by the 14th Amendment.

Procedural due process "is a flexible concept whose precise contours change relative to the nature and gravity of the interest infringed" (Bersoff & Prasse, 1978, p. 402). Notice (being told what action the state proposes to take and the reason for that action) and the opportunity to be heard are basic components of due process when state action may deprive a citizen of a liberty or property interest.

Under the due process clause of the 14th Amendment, schools may not suspend or expel children from school (and therefore deprive them of their property interest) without some sort of fair, impartial due process procedures. The due process procedures required for school suspension or expulsion generally do not have to be complex or elaborate but must include notice and the opportunity to be heard (*Goss v. Lopez*, 1975). (The suspension or expulsion of students with disabilities for more than 10 days requires more formal procedures because of the protections afforded students with disabilities under statutory law. See Chapter 9.)

The due process clause of the 14th Amendment also protects individuals from arbitrary or unwarranted stigmatization by the state that may interfere with the ability to acquire property (*Wisconsin v. Constantineau*, 1971). More specifically, the courts have ruled that a school may not label a child as "mentally retarded" or "emotionally disturbed" without due process, that is, without some sort of fair decision-making procedure that includes parent notice of the proposed classification and the right to an impartial hearing to protest the classification (see Chapter 4).

As noted previously, the 14th Amendment also protects the basic personal freedoms of citizens outlined in the Bill of Rights from arbitrary infringement by the state. The First and Fourth Amendments are important sources of fundamental rights.

The First and Fourth Amendments

In 1969, the Supreme Court decided an important case concerning student rights in the public schools, *Tinker v. Des Moines Independent Community School District*. This case involved three students who were suspended from school for violating a school policy prohibiting students from wearing black armbands in protest of the war in Vietnam. In *Tinker*, the Court recognized the need to balance the school's interest in maintaining discipline in order to foster learning and the fundamental personal freedoms guaranteed citizens in the Bill of Rights. In the Court's view, the school's policy of banning armbands was an unreasonable violation of the students' constitutional right to freedom of expression because there was no evidence that the silent wearing of armbands interfered with or disrupted the functioning of the school.

Thus, although children in the school setting are not afforded the full range of personal freedoms guaranteed citizens by the Bill of Rights, they do maintain certain fundamental rights in the school setting. In *Tinker*, the Court stated that "students in school as well as out of school are 'persons' under our Constitution … possessed of fundamental rights which the State must respect" (p. 511). Students do not "shed their constitutional rights to freedom of speech or expression at the schoolyard gate" (p. 507).

Freedom of Speech and Assembly

The First Amendment prohibits the government from interfering with the rights of free speech and assembly and freedom of religious choice. In *Tinker* and subsequent cases, the courts generally have acknowledged the right of students to free speech and assembly, as long as the exercise of those rights does not significantly interfere with or disrupt the functioning of the school. Freedom of speech and assembly can be restricted when their exercise "materially and substantially" interferes with schooling. The right to free speech does not protect the use of "obscene" language, gestures, or materials (*Bethel School District No. 403 v. Fraser*, 1986); speech promoting drug use (*Morse v. Frederick*, 2007); or speech that includes true threats (*D. J. M. v. Hannibal Public School District #60*, 2011).

As noted in Chapter 1, school psychologists are ethically obligated to speak up for the best interests of schoolchildren. However, tension exists between the school psychologist's obligation to advocate for the bests interests of students and the limitations to his or her free speech as a public school employee. The First Amendment protections of the speech of school-employed psychologists are addressed in the epilogue of the book.

Privacy Rights

No "right to privacy" is mentioned expressly in the Constitution. A number of different privacy rights have been carved out of the First Amendment concept of "liberty," Fourth Amendment prohibition against unreasonable search and seizure, Fifth Amendment protections against self-incrimination, and Ninth Amendment reservation of rights to the people (Hummel, Talbutt, & Alexander, 1985).

The courts generally have held that students have a Fourth Amendment right to be free from unreasonable search and seizure in the schools. The courts have ruled that students have a legitimate expectation of *privacy rights with regard to their person and possessions*, but they have allowed a more lenient standard of "reasonable suspicion" as opposed to "probable cause" for conducting searches in school. (Privacy is discussed further in Chapter 3.)

The right to *informational privacy* has been acknowledged in several Supreme Court opinions (e.g., *Whalen v. Roe*, 1977). A lower court described this right as protecting "the individual from government inquiry into matters in which it does not have a legitimate and proper interest" (*Eastwood v. Depart. of Corrections of State of Okl.*, 1988, p. 631). However, because the Supreme Court has not provided guidance on the meaning of *informational privacy*, the lower courts have defined it with various broad or narrow interpretations (Waldman, 2015). The lower courts also have adopted differing tests with regard to whether an individual's informational privacy interests have been violated by a government actor. Most, however, use a balancing test that weighs the government's interest in the invasion of informational privacy against the individual's privacy interests. Furthermore, "case law is also murky as to whether the informational privacy right applies to government *acquisition* of personal information or whether it solely covers the further *disclosure* of such information" (p. 708).

At least three federal circuits have ruled that minors have informational privacy rights, but the implication of these rulings for public school students and their parents is not clear (Waldman, 2015). Do such rulings provide greater informational privacy rights to students and their families than afforded by federal public education laws (e.g., Family Educational Rights and Privacy Act of 1974)? In an older court case, a federal district court ruled that parents of schoolchildren have a right to be free from the invasion of family privacy by the school (*Merriken v. Cressman*, 1973). In light of contemporary concerns about the collection of extensive quantities of personally identifiable student information by schools and its disclosure to third parties (Reidenberg et al., 2013; also Chapter 3 in this volume), future court decisions may provide new guidance on the appropriate balance between the school's need for information about students and their families and the right of students and parents to be free from inquiry into matters in which the school does not have "a legitimate and proper" interest.

Freedom of Religion

The First Amendment also ensures the basic right to free exercise of religious choice, and, under the 14th Amendment, both Congress and the states are prohibited from passing laws "respecting an establishment of religion." The First Amendment is the source of two types of church-school-state cases: those involving the use of public funds for parochial schools and those involving school policies or classroom procedures objected to on religious grounds. (For a discussion of cases involving school-sponsored prayer or other religious activities, see Russo, 2012.)

In general, court interpretations of the First Amendment suggest that the state is not allowed to provide funds directly to parochial schools. However, under the "child benefit theory," the state may provide educational services (e.g., remedial instruction and school psychological services) for students attending parochial schools as long as those services directly aid the student, they are not used for the purpose of religious instruction, and there is no impermissible entanglement of church and state (*Agostini v. Felton*, 1997; *Wolman v. Walter*, 1977).

In 2002, the Supreme Court decided *Zelman v. Simmons-Harris*, a case concerning whether the First Amendment prohibition against Congress establishing a religion prevents a state from providing tuition monies to parents and allowing them to use that aid to enroll their children in a private school of their own choosing, without regard to whether the school is religiously affiliated. In a narrow 5–4 ruling, the Court held that such school voucher plans are constitutionally permissible, so long as the money that flows to the parochial schools results from the true choice of schools by parents.

STATUTES AND REGULATIONS

A second source of law in the U.S. legal system is statutory law. The U.S. government is composed of three parallel systems of government at the federal, state, and local levels, a form of government known as *federalism* (H. R. Turnbull & Turnbull, 2000). At the federal level, the Constitution is the basic law of the land. Congress is empowered to enact federal laws as long as they do not violate the U.S. Constitution. Similarly, each state has its own constitution and legislative body for enacting laws at the state level. State laws may not violate either the state's constitution or the federal constitution.

Many countries have a nationalized school system operated by the central government (Hubsch, 1989). Under the 10th Amendment of the Constitution, Congress is forbidden from creating a nationalized school system. However, the U.S. Congress has the power to shape educational policy and practices by offering monies to states contingent on compliance with federal mandates. This is called *categorical aid*. Congress has passed two types of legislation that have had a dramatic impact on the public schools, *antidiscrimination legislation* and *federal education legislation*. Key federal statutes affecting the schools are highlighted in the paragraphs that follow.

Federal Education Legislation

Some federal education legislation is grant legislation; that is, funds are provided to states on the condition that schools comply with certain educational policies and practices. The Elementary and Secondary Education Act of 1965 and the Individuals with Disabilities Education Improvement Act of 2004 are important examples of this type of legislation. Other federal education legislation stipulates that no federal funds will be made available to schools unless they adhere to specific educational policies and practices outlined in the law; the Family Educational Rights and Privacy Act of 1974 (FERPA) is an example of this type of legislation.

Elementary and Secondary Education Act of 1965

As noted previously, education generally has been regarded as a responsibility of state and local governments. The Elementary and Secondary Education Act of 1965 (ESEA; Pub. L. No. 89-750) was one of the first major federal programs to aid education. With the passage of ESEA, Congress accepted the proposition that although "education is primarily a state function ... the Federal Government has a secondary obligation to see that there is a basic floor under those essential services for all adults and children in the United States" (Taft, 1965, p. 1450). A major thrust of early amendments of the law was to target funds more specifically for economically disadvantaged schoolchildren.

The ESEA initially was a permissive law that gave the schools much latitude in how funds would be spent. With subsequent re-authorizations, however, the law became more prescriptive. The 2001 re-authorization of ESEA, the No Child Left Behind

Act (NCLB, Pub. L. No. 107-110), gave states little discretion regarding selection of educational goals, how funds could be spent, and the ways in which school and student performance were to be measured (i.e., accountability requirements). The most recent re-authorization of ESEA is the Every Student Succeeds Act (ESSA, Pub. L. No. 114-95), signed into law by President Barack Hussein Obama on December 10, 2015.[3] Its purpose is "to provide all children significant opportunity to receive a fair, equitable, and high-quality education, and to close educational achievement gaps" (Sec. 1001). Like its precursors, ESSA "advances equity by upholding critical protections for America's disadvantaged and high-needs students" (U.S. Department of Education, 2016). Unlike NCLB, however, ESSA returns much flexibility to the states to determine educational goals and how student and school performance will be documented. ESSA authorizes funds for low-performing schools (defined as schools performing in the bottom 5%), for high schools where less than two-thirds of students graduate, and to improve educational outcomes for subgroups of children who chronically struggle to succeed at school (Sec. 1111 [c][4][C–D]). Funds are also targeted for literacy education, early childhood education, and for children who are English language learners, Native American, migratory, homeless, neglected, delinquent, or at risk of dropping out. In addition, some ESSA funds are provided as block grants to states. The block grants consolidate programs that were previously funded separately (Klein, 2016). Of special importance to school psychology, these funds may be used for "initiatives to expand access to or coordinate school counseling and mental health programs" (Sec. 4104 [b][3][B][ii][II]), and the term *school-based mental health services provider* is defined to include state-certified or state-licensed school psychologists (Sec. 4102 [6]).

Individuals with Disabilities Education Improvement Act

Prior to 1990, the Education for the Handicapped Act (EHA) referred to a series of federal statutes concerning the education of children with handicapping conditions (e.g., Pub. L. No. 94-142). In 1990, President George H. W. Bush signed into law the Education of the Handicapped Act Amendments of 1990 (Pub. L. No. 101-476), which changed the name of EHA to the Individuals with Disabilities Education Act (IDEA). In 1997, President Bill Clinton signed into law the Individuals with Disabilities Education Act Amendments of 1997 (Pub. L. No. 105-117). This Act reauthorized IDEA and introduced a number of changes to improve the law. Most recently, President George W. Bush signed into law the Individuals with Disabilities Education Improvement Act of 2004 (IDEIA, Pub. L. No. 108-445).

IDEIA—Part B allocates funds to states that provide a free and appropriate education to all children with disabilities as defined by the law. To receive funds, each state must have developed a plan that offers every child with a disability an opportunity to receive special education and related services in conformance with an individualized education program (IEP). Children must be assessed on the basis of nondiscriminatory testing and evaluation procedures and provided with an IEP in the least

---

[3] ESSA citations are to (Senate Bill) S.1177, available at https://www.gpo.gov/fdsys/pkg/BILLS-114s1177enr/pdf/BILLS-114s1177enr.pdf

restrictive environment appropriate for each child. The "least restrictive environment" is the educational setting selected from a continuum of alternative placements (ranging from a residential facility to the general education classroom) that is closest to the general education classroom but also meets the special education needs of the child with a disability. Individualized education planning decisions are made by a multidisciplinary team that includes the student's parents, and a number of safeguards are required in the law to ensure parent participation in decision making. IDEIA—Part C provides funds to states that offer early intervention programs for infants and toddlers with known or suspected disabilities in conformance with an individualized family service plan (see Chapter 4).

Family Educational Rights and Privacy Act of 1974

The Family Educational Rights and Privacy Act of 1974 (FERPA) was an amendment to the Elementary and Secondary Education Act of 1965 (Pub. L. No. 93-380). Under FERPA, no federal funds will be made available to schools unless they adhere to the student record-keeping procedures outlined in the law. FERPA record-keeping guidelines are designed to safeguard confidentiality of records and parent access to school records concerning their children. In accordance with FERPA, parents have access to all school education records of their children, the right to challenge the accuracy of those records, and the right to a hearing regarding their accuracy. Aside from parents, student records are to be available only to those in the school setting with a legitimate educational interest in the student, and, although there are some exceptions, parent consent generally must be obtained before records are released to agencies outside of the school. (See Chapter 3.)

Protection of Pupil Rights Act

The Protection of Pupil Rights Act (PPRA) was a 1978 amendment to the Elementary and Secondary Education Act of 1965. PPRA was amended in 1994 and 2001 (Pub. L. No. 107-110 § 1061). The Act requires school districts that receive federal funds to notify parents when the school intends to administer a survey, analysis, or evaluation that reveals one or more of eight types of personal information, including political affiliations or beliefs; potentially embarrassing psychological problems; illegal, antisocial, and self-incriminating behavior; sexual behaviors and attitudes; and religious beliefs or practices. It also requires school districts that receive federal funds to ensure that parents have the opportunity to review the content of the survey or other instrument prior to distribution. School districts also must allow parents to have their child opt out of survey participation. Parent consent is required if the survey or other evaluation is funded by the U.S. Department of Education (DOE). (See Chapter 3.)

Federal Antidiscrimination Legislation

Congress also has passed antidiscrimination or civil rights legislation that has had an impact on public school policies and practices. These statutes prohibit state and school authorities from discriminating against individuals on the basis of race, color, or national origin;[4] sex;[5] or disability[6] in any program or activity receiving any federal funding. A state department of education (SDE) may choose not to pursue monies available under federal grant statutes (e.g., funds for infants and toddlers with disabilities). School districts must comply with antidiscrimination legislation if they receive *any* federal funds for any purpose, however.

Federal antidiscrimination laws also protect students from harassment based on race, color, national origin, sex, or disability. The term *harassment* means oral, written, graphic, or physical conduct relating to an individual's race, color, national origin, sex, or disability that is sufficiently severe, pervasive, or persistent so as to interfere with or limit the ability of an individual to participate in or benefit from the district's programs or activities (see U.S. Department of Education & Bias Crimes Task Force of the National Association of Attorneys General, 1999). *Sexual harassment* means unwanted and unwelcome sexual advances that are sufficiently severe, pervasive, or persistent so as to interfere with or limit the ability of an individual to participate in or benefit from the district's programs or activities. The federal laws cited make schools responsible for taking reasonable steps to remedy harassment.

The U.S. DOE Office for Civil Rights (OCR) provides guidance regarding the interpretation and implementation of antidiscrimination law in the schools and conducts investigations of schools after receiving a discrimination complaint. If evidence of discrimination is found, the OCR may order a school district to engage in remedial actions to correct the discrimination. If voluntary compliance cannot be achieved through informal actions, the OCR may take steps to suspend federal funding to the school.

Federal statutory law does not explicitly prohibit discrimination in the public schools based on religion or sexual orientation, gender identity, or gender expression. However, in a 2010 *Dear Colleague Letter* to school districts, the OCR specifically extended its protections to include discrimination and harassment based on a student's religion. In addition, the OCR made known that, as part of national efforts to reduce bullying in schools and to ensure equal educational opportunity for all students, it now explicitly interprets Title IX as prohibiting harassment and bullying based on sexual orientation or nonconformity to gender role stereotypes. Furthermore, if harassment based on sexual orientation or nonconformity to gender-role stereotypes results in a hostile learning environment for a student, schools "have an obligation to take immediate and effective action to eliminate the hostile environment" (Ali, 2010, p. 8). (See Chapter 9.)

Rehabilitation Act of 1973

Section 504 of the Rehabilitation Act of 1973 (Pub. L. No. 93-112) specifically prohibits discrimination against any otherwise qualified individual solely on the basis of a handicapping condition in any program or activity receiving federal financial assistance. Section 504 is discussed in Chapter 5.

---

[4]Title VI of the Civil Rights Act of 1964.
[5]Title IX of the Education Amendments of 1972.
[6]Title II of the Americans with Disabilities Act of 1990.

Americans With Disabilities Act of 1990

The Americans with Disabilities Act of 1990 (ADA) (Pub. L. No. 101-336) is considered to be the most significant federal law ensuring the civil rights of all individuals with disabilities. It was amended by the Americans with Disabilities Act Amendments of 2008 (ADAA, Pub. L. No. 110-325). The ADAA guarantees equal opportunity in employment, public accommodation, transportation, state and local government services, and telecommunications to individuals with disabilities. Title II, Subtitle A, is the portion of the law most pertinent to public schools (see Chapter 5).

Civil Rights Act of 1871

School personnel also should be familiar with Section 1983 of the Civil Rights Act of 1871. This statute was passed following the Civil War as a reaction to the mistreatment of African Americans, and it originally was known as the Ku Klux Klan Act. Under Section 1983, any person whose constitutional rights (or rights under federal law) have been violated by a government (school) official may sue for damages in federal court, and the official may be held liable for damages (see the section "Lawsuits Against Schools and School Psychologists" later in this chapter).

Rules and Regulations

When federal legislation is enacted, an executive agency is charged with the responsibility for developing rules and regulations implementing the law. For example, rules and regulations implementing IDEIA and FERPA are issued by the U.S. DOE. For all intents and purposes, *rules and regulations have the same impact as actual legislation.* School psychologists need to be familiar with both the statute itself and the regulations implementing the law.

Federal statutes are compiled and published in the *United States Code* (U.S.C.). Rules and regulations implementing a law first appear in a daily publication called the *Federal Register* (Fed. Reg.) and subsequently are published in the *Code of Federal Regulations* (CFR). The *Code of Federal Regulations* has 50 titles, and each volume is updated once each calendar year. These government publications can be found at https://www.gpo.gov/fdsys/browse/collectionCfr.action?collectionCode=CFR and in state and university libraries. In addition, the Electronic Code of Federal Regulations (e-CFR) can be accessed on the Internet at www.ecfr.gov. The e-CFR is updated daily, but it is not considered to be the "official" legal edition of federal regulations. The U.S. DOE Web site also has links to statutes and regulations pertinent to education (http://www.ed.gov). Citations for important federal statutes are provided in Appendix D at the back of this book.

State Education Laws

As Hubsch (1989) noted, the majority of public school *statutory* law is enacted at the state level. School psychologists must become familiar with the laws pertinent to the delivery of school psychological services in the state where they are employed, in addition to federal statutes and regulations. Copies of state laws affecting education typically can be purchased from a state's department of education, downloaded from its Web site, or found in a college library law collection.

CASE LAW

A third source of law is case law. Case law, or common law, is law that emerges from court decisions (Russo, 2012). The common law system can be traced back to medieval England. At that time, it was widely accepted that there were "laws of nature" to guide solutions to problems if those laws could be discovered. Legal scholars studied past court decisions for the purpose of discovering those "natural laws." The rules and principles that judges customarily followed in making decisions were identified and, at times, articulated in case decisions, and judges tended to base new decisions on those earlier legal precedents. Common law is thus discovered law rather than enacted law (Russo, 2012, p. 1). Many aspects of public school law today are based on common law rather than enacted law, as Russo pointed out. For example, the courts generally have upheld a teacher's right to use corporal punishment to discipline students where no state laws or school board policies prohibit its use. Acceptance of the use of corporal punishment in the schools by courts has a long history in case law (see Chapter 9).

In the United States, the federal court system has three tiers or layers; most state court systems also have three tiers or layers. As H. R. Turnbull and Turnbull (2000, p. 6) observed, "Why a case may be tried in one court, appealed or reviewed by another, and finally disposed of by yet another is a matter of great complexity." A brief discussion of the state and federal court systems follows.

State court systems vary in organization and complexity. Cases filed in the lowest court may be appealed to an intermediate-level court, if a state has one. Decisions then may be appealed to the supreme court of the state, the "court of last resort" (Russo, 2012). The U.S. Supreme Court may review cases from a state court if a question of federal law is involved.

Within the federal system, at the lowest level are the trial courts, called district courts. Nearly 100 federal district courts exist. At the intermediate level are 11 numbered federal circuits or geographical areas and the District of Columbia. Each court at this level is called a circuit court of appeals. These courts hear appeals from the district courts. They decide issues of law, not fact. The highest court in the federal system is the U.S. Supreme Court. A person who loses a case in a federal court of appeals or the highest state court may submit a written petition requesting the Supreme Court to review the case. The Supreme Court agrees to review a case by granting a *writ of certiorari* (an order calling up a case from a lower court for review). However, the Supreme Court selects only those cases it considers most important to review, and consequently, only a small percentage of the requests for review are granted.

The federal court system decides both civil and criminal cases. Criminal cases involve crimes prosecuted by the government, not private citizens (e.g., murder, theft, and assault). Civil cases are lawsuits brought by private parties. Federal courts rule only on cases that involve federal constitutional or statutory law or cases that involve parties from two different states. The U.S. Supreme Court has the final authority in interpreting the U.S. Constitution and federal statutes. State courts also decide both civil and criminal cases. State courts rule on cases involving state constitutional and statutory law but also may rule on cases involving the federal Constitution and statutory laws.

The role of the courts is to resolve disputes involving citizens, organizations, and the government. Courts also decide the guilt or innocence of those accused of crimes. In education, most disputes are decided in civil court. Courts decide conflicts by applying law to a given set of facts and interpreting the meaning of the law in that context. It is the function of courts to say what the Constitution or statute means in a given case, set forth the findings of fact that the interpretation is based on, and enter an order commanding the parties in the case to take certain action (or, if the case is on appeal, the judge may enter an order for another court to take action). If there is no *codified* law (no constitutional or statutory provision) found controlling in a case, the court is likely to rely on common law (legal precedents) in rendering a decision (Hubsch, 1989; H. R. Turnbull & Turnbull, 2000).

In reading about court rulings, remember that decisions of the U.S. Supreme Court are binding throughout the country. The decisions of the lower federal courts are binding only within their jurisdictions, and the decisions of state courts are binding only within the state (Russo, 2012).

SUMMARY

We have explored the three basic sources of public school law within the American legal system, namely, the Constitution, statutes and regulations, and case law. It is evident from the material presented that the federal courts and legislature have had a powerful impact on public schools, particularly since *Brown* in 1954. But, as Hubsch (1989) pointed out, the role that the federal government can play in fostering quality public education in our nation's schools is limited. Court decisions spanning more than 60 years have sent a clear message that our schools must provide equal educational opportunities for all children. Equal educational opportunity for all children is not the same as a quality education for all, however, as Hubsch noted. By providing grants and resources, the federal government can encourage quality educational programs, but the bulk of the responsibility for ensuring a quality education for all children must be carried at the state and local levels. Individual teachers, principals, and school psychologists must accept and share in this responsibility.

LEGAL TRAINING FOR SCHOOL PSYCHOLOGISTS

Leaders in the field of school psychology called for increased training in the legal aspects of practice in the mid-1970s, the years coinciding with the passage of federal special education legislation, Section 504 of The Rehabilitation Act of 1973, and FERPA (Kaplan, Crisci, & Farling, 1974). As noted previously, the NASP publication *School Psychology: A Blueprint for Training and Practice* (Ysseldyke et al., 2006) now identifies *legal*, ethical, and social responsibility as a foundational domain relevant to all areas of service delivery.

A search of the literature did not yield any contemporary studies describing the legal training school psychologists receive during their graduate school preparation or graduate perceptions of the adequacy of the legal training they received. As discussed in Chapter 1, Dailor and Jacob (2010), M. A. Fisher (2013), and others have recommended integrated rather than separate instruction in law and ethics because many aspects of the practice of psychology are regulated by law as well as professional codes of ethics, and key concepts, such as privacy, informed consent, and confidentiality, have roots in both ethics and law. Furthermore, for school psychologists to be able to fulfil their ethical obligations, practitioners must know law pertinent to interpretation of codes of ethics and their domain of practice (Behnke & Jones, 2012). In their discussion of the relationship between ethics and law, Behnke and Jones (2012) reported that "the word *law* or some variant" (p. 71) occurs more than 20 times in the APA's code of ethics; similarly, *law* or *legal* occurs more than 50 times in the NASP's ethics code.

As Phillips (1983) observed, school-based practitioners must be knowledgeable of federal and state education law and familiar with state law that regulates psychology. We believe that school psychology trainees should acquire knowledge of the major provisions of federal education law early in their coursework so that they have a foundational framework for understanding and applying state education regulations during field experiences and at their employment site (Dailor & Jacob, 2010). In addition, graduate coursework should introduce students to provisions of state law that regulate mental health providers if those provisions are pertinent to school-based practice (e.g., privilege and nondisclosure laws).

The scope and depth of legal training required for school psychologists should be appropriate to the range and type of legal decisions they make in their job setting. Unlike psychologists in private practice, school-employed practitioners work under the supervision of school administrators. The individual practitioner bears responsibility for ensuring that his or her independent decisions are in compliance with district policies and law, but many of his or her decisions are subject to administrative oversight. In addition, school-employed practitioners work in a context that emphasizes multidisciplinary assessment and intervention planning. For example, the legal determination of special education eligibility, classification, and appropriate education in the least restrictive environment is determined by a group of professionals and the child's parents. This emphasis on shared decision making in schools serves as a safeguard against legally incorrect determinations that might be made by a professional acting alone.

In Chapter 1, we discussed the goals of ethics training for school psychologists and provided a list of desired ethical-legal competencies. Several additional competencies specific to law are identified here. Competent school practitioners are alert to situations that involve legal issues and seek consultation with knowledgeable supervisors (or, when appropriate, with experts on mental health law) when legal questions arise. They strive to make informed decisions that are respectful of student and parent legal rights and the legal rights of others, and they ensure that parents, students, and other clients understand their legal rights in the school setting. They recognize that law impacting public schools is complex and that misunderstandings of contemporary school law are not uncommon (Zirkel, 2012). When anticipated or real school administrative policies, practices, or decisions appear contrary to what the law deems appropriate, school practitioners raise questions through appropriate administrative channels after first "checking the facts" by consulting authoritative sources. Finally, school psychologists recognize that their actions may come under public scrutiny in a due process hearing, U.S. DOE OCR complaint investigation, or in court. They engage in actions that safeguard the legal rights of students and others; make decisions that are in compliance with law and with sound professional practices and that foster trust in school psychologists; and they document the decisions made and the basis for those decisions.

CREDENTIALING OF SCHOOL PSYCHOLOGISTS

As part of the obligation to protect the health and welfare of their citizens, state governments enact laws to regulate the provision of psychological services. State credentialing of professionals, such as school psychologists, protects the consumer by requiring individuals to hold specified qualifications before they are granted a legal sanction to practice in the state.

Credentialing for School-Based Practice

In most states, the SDE credentials school psychologists for practice in the school setting. The credential issued by the SDE may be called a "certificate," "endorsement," or "license" (Rossen, 2014). An SDE credential generally permits school-based practice only; that is, the practitioner may work for the schools either as a regular school employee or on a contractual basis, but the credential typically does not authorize a school psychologist to engage in private practice. An SDE credential is the state credential most commonly held by school psychology practitioners (Curtis, Castillo, & Gelley, 2012).

The credentialing of school psychologists for school-based practice is a state matter. The highest degree required for an SDE credential is the specialist degree (about 60 credit hours); no state currently requires a doctorate (Rossen, 2014). Although commonalities in credentialing standards exist across states, equivalence of requirements between states is the exception rather than the rule. Furthermore, different states may use different titles or designations (e.g., "school psychologist," "school diagnostician"), and some states have more than one level of SDE credential, depending on the level of graduate preparation and years of experience.

Fagan and Wise (2007) identified two models of SDE credentialing: *transcript review* and *program approval*. *Transcript review* requires submission of transcripts and other supporting materials to a state credentialing agency. The agency then determines whether the applicant successfully has completed the prescribed set of courses and field experiences outlined in the SDE's credentialing standards. The *program approval* process means that applicants who have the recommendation from an approved state training program will be credentialed by the SDE. The procedure used for SDE credentialing may be different for applicants from in-state training programs and those from out-of-state programs. (See Rossen, 2014.)

Because credentialing is controlled at the state level, students and practitioners need to contact the state in which they wish to practice for up-to-date information about SDE requirements for credentialing. The NASP maintains a National School Psychology Certification and Licensure Online Resource List that provides a summary of the requirements for licensure and certification in various states (see http://www .nasponline.org/certification/state_info_list.aspx).

Credentialing for Private Practice

Licensure acts typically regulate the private practice of psychology. Licenses for the private practice of psychology usually are issued by a state psychology board or a board that regulates mental health providers (Rossen, 2014). Some states, but not many, license school psychologists for unsupervised private practice at the subdoctoral level; some states license school psychologists for private practice at the subdoctoral level but only if they are supervised by a fully licensed doctoral psychologist. See Rossen (2014) and DeMers and Schaffer (2012) for additional discussion. Information on licensing boards is available at http://www.nasponline.org/certification/state_info_list.aspx and http://www.asppb.org

Nonpractice Credentials

In addition to state credentials to practice, nonpractice credentials recognize the quality of professional preparation. The National School Psychology Certification System allows school psychologists who complete training consistent with NASP standards, who achieve a passing score on the National School Psychology Examination, and who meet continuing education requirements to be identified as a Nationally Certified School Psychologist (NCSP). About 12,700 individuals hold the NCSP credential (Rossen & Williams, 2013). It is important to recognize that the NCSP title alone does not authorize a school psychologist to render services; practitioners must hold a valid certificate or license in the state where they wish to practice. However, 31 states use the NCSP as part of their standards for certification (Rossen & Williams, 2013). For more information, see Rossen (2014) or visit the NASP's Web site at http://www .nasponline.org

LAWSUITS AGAINST SCHOOLS AND SCHOOL PSYCHOLOGISTS

In the last portion of this chapter, we discuss lawsuits against schools and school psychologists.

Lawsuits against Schools Under State Laws

Civil liability, simply stated, "means that one can be sued for acting wrongly toward another or for failing to act when there was a recognized duty to do so" (Hopkins & Anderson, 1985, p. 21). Civil liability rests within the basic framework of the law of tort.

A tort is a civil (not criminal) wrong that does not involve a contract. It is a complex area of law. In general, the court considers four questions in tort cases: (1) Did injury occur? *Injury* means a wrong or damage done to the student's person, rights, reputation, or property. (2) Did the school owe a duty in law to the student? (3) Was there a breach of duty? That is, did the school fail to do what it should have done? A tort can arise when either an improper act or a failure to act causes injury to the student. (4) Is there a proximate cause relationship between the injury and the breach of duty? (Evans, 1997).

The most common tort committed by school personnel is negligence (Evans, 1997). Negligence suits often are precipitated by a physical injury to a student (e.g., injury resulting from student-on-student violence). When a student suffers harm and his or her parents seek vindication in court, the parents are most likely to file a negligence lawsuit in state court (Schill, 1993). Such lawsuits generally allege that the school had a duty (under state common or statutory law) to protect students from foreseeable harm, had knowledge of a specific danger, negligently failed to take reasonable precautions to protect the student, and thus caused the injury by allowing the incident to occur (Schill, 1993; Wood & Chestnutt, 1995).

As noted previously, public schools are an arm of state government. Historically, under common law, a school district could not be held liable for torts committed by the district, officials, or other employees (Russo, 2012). In some states, the immunity of school districts was based on the old English doctrine of *sovereign immunity*: "The king (state) can do no wrong; you can't sue the king." In other states, immunity of school districts was based on the fact that state law provides no funds for the payment of damages; funds for education could not be diverted to pay legal claims (Russo, 2012).

Currently, the doctrine of immunity of school districts has been modified by legislation or case law in most states. However, the exceptions to the doctrine of immunity vary from state to state, making it extremely difficult to make generalizations about the kinds of tort actions that will be successful against school districts in various states. Immunity usually exists to the extent that the school's or school board's liability insurance does not cover the particular injury suffered (Schill, 1993, p. 1). This means that, in many states, state legislation or case law permits lawsuits against school districts but allows recovery only up to the limits of the school's liability insurance (see Russo, 2012).

School-based practitioners must remember that they are state actors and district employees. As a result of a long history of negligence lawsuits against schools, school-based practitioners, like other school employees, have a legal duty to take steps to protect students from *reasonably foreseeable risk of harm*. This obligation extends to all students, not just student clients. Furthermore, school employment contracts often contain a provision whereby any act or failure to act that jeopardizes student health, safety, or welfare can result in the suspension or termination of employment. However, schools are not guarantors of student safety. Schools are not likely to be held liable when spontaneous, unforeseeable acts by students result in injury (Wood & Chestnutt, 1995; see, e.g., *Kok v. Tacoma School District No. 10,* 2013).

Whether a state will allow recovery of damages in lawsuits against school districts is a complicated matter. Whether individual school employees can be sued is also a complicated matter, determined by state legislation and case law. State courts typically have held teachers and other individual school employees immune from liability during performance of duties within the scope of their employment.[7] They may, however, be disciplined by their district for inappropriate actions.

School-based practitioners thus have a widely recognized duty to protect students from reasonably foreseeable risk of harm. Psychologists in nonschool settings also may have a professional obligation under the laws of the state where they practice to take steps to protect their clients from self-harm and to forewarn individuals whom their client has threatened to harm. However, where they exist, state laws governing mental health practitioners often use language that requires the psychologist to take preventive actions only in situations suggesting "clear and imminent" danger to the client or a targeted victim. Thus, a difference may exist between school-based practitioners and those in nonschool settings with regard to the threshold for breaking confidentiality of the psychologist—client relationship to protect a student or others from harm (i.e., reasonably foreseeable risk of harm versus imminent danger). (Also see Chapter 3.)

As noted, many of the negligence suits filed against school districts by parents are precipitated by a physical injury to a student (Evans, 1997). In the 1970s and 1980s, however, a number of so-called *instructional malpractice* suits were decided. These suits were filed by students or their parents when a student graduated from high school but was unable to read or write well enough to secure employment or when the student did not achieve academically what his or her parents expected. The plaintiffs in these cases claimed that poor instruction (instructional malpractice) was the cause of the injury (student failure to learn). Such claims generally failed for several reasons. First, the courts prefer not to intervene in the administration of the public schools except in unusual circumstances involving clear violations of constitutional rights or federal law. Second, the courts have held that the award of monetary damages for instructional malpractice suits would be overly burdensome to the public education system in terms of both time and money (*Peter W. v. San Francisco Unified School District*, 1976). In addition, as noted in *Donohue v. Copiague Union Free School District* (1979), it would be difficult, if not impossible, to prove a causal link between a school's instructional practices and student academic failure.

Lawsuits Under Federal Law (Section 504, ADAA, IDEIA, and Section 1983)

Federal antidiscrimination laws, such as Section 504, ADAA, and Title IX of the Education Amendments of 1972, allow parents to sue a school district for violation of their child's rights under those laws. In successful suits, parents have been able to secure a court order commanding the school to take steps to comply with the law, and at times they have been awarded monetary damages (see Chapters 5 and 9).

IDEIA also allows parents of special education students to file a lawsuit when they believe their child's rights under the law have been violated. Except for unusual circumstances, parents are required to exhaust administrative remedies (e.g., due process hearings) available to them before they pursue a court action under IDEIA. If parents prevail in a court action under IDEIA, they may recover their attorney fees and/or be reimbursed for private school tuition or compensatory education for their child

---

[7]School employees are not immune from liability for intentional torts or criminal acts.

(see Chapter 4). Parents typically have not been able to recover monetary damages under IDEIA.

In addition to claims filed under Section 504, ADAA, and IDEIA, an increasing number of lawsuits are filed against schools and school personnel under Section 1983 of the Civil Rights Act of 1871. In accordance with Section 1983, any person whose constitutional rights (or rights under federal law) have been violated by a government official may sue for damages in federal court, and the official may be held liable for the actual damages. Section 1983 lawsuits often are referred to as "constitutional torts," and, similar to common torts, the court decides whether there was a duty to a student, whether the duty was breached (i.e., the student was deprived of his or her rights under constitutional or federal statutory law by a public official), whether the student suffered injury, and whether the breach of duty was the proximate cause of the student's injury. A student whose civil rights were violated under Section 1983 may sue the school board, principal, teacher, and/or the school psychologist responsible in federal court, thereby bypassing any state law granting school personnel immunity from liability during performance of their job duties.

A number of student lawsuits concerning school disciplinary actions (e.g., illegal search and seizure, unreasonable corporal punishment) have been filed under Section 1983. School officials may have qualified immunity from Section 1983 lawsuits. The standard for qualified immunity applicable to government (school) officials is as follows: "Government officials performing discretionary functions are shielded from liability for civil damages unless their conduct violated clearly established statutory or constitutional rights of which a reasonable person would have known" (*Harlow v. Fitzgerald*, 1982, p. 817). Hummel et al. (1985, p. 78) suggested that school personnel generally will not be held liable in Section 1983 lawsuits as long as they are "acting clearly within the scope of their authority for the betterment of those they serve" (e.g., *Landstrom v. Illinois Department of Children and Family Services*, 1990).

Professional Malpractice

Professional malpractice suits are civil lawsuits (torts) filed against individual practitioners under state statutory and common law. Professional malpractice occurs when, in the context of a psychologist–client relationship, a client suffers harm and it is determined that the harm was caused by departure from acceptable professional standards of care (Bennett et al., 2006). The likelihood of a psychologist being sued for malpractice is small. Bennett et al. (2006) estimated that, each year, approximately 1% of psychologists are subject to either a malpractice suit or a licensing board complaint. As noted, whether an individual school-based practitioner is immune from liability under state law during performance of his or her job duties varies from state to state. Psychologists in private practice, however, can be held liable for malpractice in all states.

When a professional–client relationship exists and the psychologist is acting in a professional capacity, he or she is expected to provide "due care," or a level of care that is "standard" in the profession. To succeed in a malpractice claim, the plaintiff must prove four facts: (1) a professional relationship was formed between the psychologist and plaintiff so that the psychologist owed a legal duty of care to the plaintiff; (2) the duty of care was breached; that is, a standard of care exists and the practitioner breached that standard; (3) the client suffered harm or injury; and (4) the practitioner's breach of duty to practice within the standard of care was the proximate cause of the client's injury; that is, the injury was a reasonably foreseeable consequence of the breach (Bennett et al., 2006).

How does the court determine the standard of care? In most cases, the courts look to the profession itself to identify the customary standard of care used by others in the same field. Expert testimony may be used to establish the customary standard of care. In addition, codes of ethics may be presented as evidence of the parameters of accepted practice. Sometimes the client's condition is a key factor in determining the expected standard of care (e.g., acceptable and reasonable actions in handling a suicidal adolescent). If the psychologist is not qualified to work with a particular type of problem situation, he or she is obligated to refer the client to someone with appropriate training (Bennett et al., 2006).

According to Woody (1988), the key words related to defining the appropriate standard of care are *ordinary*, *reasonable*, and *prudent*. *Ordinary* pertains to what is accepted or customary practice. *Reasonable* relates to the appropriate and adequate use of professional knowledge and judgment. *Prudent* means the exercise of caution, not in the sense of being traditional or conservative but rather maintaining adequate safeguards.

Risk Management

School psychologists should be familiar with the term *risk management*. Unlike ethical decision-making models that have the primary goal of safeguarding the welfare of the client, a *risk management analysis* is conducted to minimize exposure of the school or the practitioner to legal liability (Behnke & Jones, 2012). It is understandable that school districts and school psychologists wish to avoid lawsuits and other legal actions against them. Lawsuits and due process hearings are stressful, time consuming, and expensive. However, it is important "to avoid placing the protection of [the school] or the professional from legal action above the welfare of the client" (Welfel, 2012, p. 284). Experts in ethics and law agree that the best way to avoid lawsuits is "to do the right thing" (Knapp, Bennett, & VandeCreek, 2012; Welfel, 2012). For school districts, this means knowing and respecting the legal rights of students and parents. For individual practitioners, this means knowing and making decisions consistent with our codes of ethics and aspirational ethical principles as well as working to safeguard the legal rights of schoolchildren and other clients (Knapp, Bennett, et al., 2012; Welfel, 2012). Readers interested in risk management strategies are referred to Bennett et al. (2006); Knapp, Bennett, et al. (2012); and Sales, Miller, and Hall (2005).

Professional Liability Insurance

To protect themselves and perhaps ease their fear of litigation, some school psychologists purchase professional liability insurance. Prior to purchasing a policy, school psychologists should investigate what type of coverage, if any, is provided by their employers and whether any professional liability insurance is provided by their membership in a professional union, such as the National Education Association or American Federation of Teachers. Both the NASP (http://www.nasponline.org)

and the American Psychological Association (http://www.apa.org) have information about professional liability insurance on their Web sites. Internship students are well advised to consider purchasing liability insurance (often available at a student rate) because they may not be covered by their school district's policies.

In choosing an insurance policy, several points should be kept in mind. First, be sure to study the policy carefully to know what is and is not covered. Some professional liability policies cover school psychologists only when their services are performed during school-based practice. In other words, they do not cover private practice. Such policies are generally much less expensive than those that cover private work. Second, policies may be either based on claims made or occurrence based. Under the former, the practitioner is covered only if insured when the alleged malpractice took place *and* when the claim was filed. Under the latter, called an occurrence-based policy, the practitioner is covered as long as he or she was insured when the alleged malpractice took place, regardless of when the claim was filed. Third, many policies reserve the right to select legal counsel and to settle the case. This may be discouraging to practitioners who want their day in court. The psychologist may still hire his or her own attorney to work with the one supplied by the insurance carrier, but that is an additional expense. (See Knapp, Bennett, et al., 2012, for additional information.)

CONCLUDING COMMENTS

This chapter provided a brief overview of public school law pertinent to school psychology. School psychologists are ethically and professionally obligated to be familiar with law and to keep abreast of changes in law affecting practices. We concur with Reschly and Bersoff's (1999) view that understanding of law is important "as means to protect precious rights, as well as a method to resolve disagreements over rights and responsibilities. The better understanding of legal influences is one way to enhance opportunities for implementing the best professional practices" (p. 1077).

STUDY AND DISCUSSION

Questions for Chapter 2

1. What are the three sources of public school law in the U.S. legal system?
2. Why was the Bill of Rights passed? What is the significance of the 10th Amendment with regard to public education? Do citizens have a right to a public education under the U.S. Constitution?
3. Identify the two aspects of the 14th Amendment that have been extremely important in court decisions regarding public schools.
4. What was the significance of the Supreme Court decision in *Tinker v. Des Moines Independent Community School District* (1969)?
5. If public education is a duty of the states, how does the U.S. Congress have the power to shape educational policy and practices? Cite two examples of federal education legislation and two examples of federal antidiscrimination legislation.

6. What is case law, and why is it important?
7. What is civil liability?
8. What is professional malpractice? What aspects of the situation do courts evaluate to determine whether malpractice occurred? How is appropriate standard of care generally determined?

Activities

1. The majority of public school statutory law is enacted at the state level. School psychologists must become familiar with the laws pertinent to the delivery of school psychological services in the state where they are employed. Obtain a copy of the rules governing special education and school psychological services in the state where you live. Copies of state laws affecting education typically can be purchased from a state's department of education, downloaded from its Web site, or located in a college library law collection.

2. During the course of their careers, many school psychologists will be asked to provide testimony in legal proceedings, such as a special education due process hearing. Read about school psychologists' involvement in special education due process hearings (Elias, 1999) and the legal and ethical issues associated with being an expert witness in the courtroom (Bennett et al., 2006).

Chapter 3 —————————————————————

PRIVACY, INFORMED CONSENT, CONFIDENTIALITY, AND RECORD KEEPING

This chapter explores four important ethical-legal concepts in the delivery of psychological services in the schools: *privacy, informed consent, confidentiality*, and *privileged communication*. School record keeping also is discussed. Privacy, informed consent, confidentiality, and record keeping are discussed together in this chapter because they are ethical-legal concerns that cut across all of the school psychologist's many roles. The chapter closes with a discussion of parent access to test protocols and digital record keeping and communication.

PRIVACY

The term *privacy* meshes together complicated concepts from case law, statutory law, and professional ethics. We first briefly explore privacy as a legal concept and then discuss respect for privacy as an ethical mandate.

Privacy and Law

The privacy rights of students and their parents have been addressed in case and statutory law. However, there are many areas in which the legal boundaries of student privacy are not clearly delineated. Furthermore, some tension between the school's perceived need for personal information about students and the right of students and parents to be free from unnecessary intrusions on their privacy is likely inevitable, even as additional privacy guidelines become available.

Case Law

As noted in Chapter 2, the Constitution does not mention "right to privacy" explicitly. However, a number of privacy rights have been carved out of the First, Fourth, Fifth, and Ninth Amendments.

Court decisions regarding the rights of students have recognized the need to balance the interest of the state (school) in fulfilling its duty to educate children, maintain order, and ensure student safety against the personal freedoms and rights generally afforded citizens. Thus, in the school setting, students do not have the full range of privacy rights afforded adult citizens. Two cases that addressed the issue of student privacy rights are *Merriken v. Cressman* (1973) and *New Jersey v. T.L.O.* (1985); *Sterling v. Borough of Minersville* (2000) also may have implications for the privacy rights of students.

In *New Jersey v. T.L.O.* (1985), the Supreme Court held that students have the Fourth Amendment right to be free from unreasonable search and seizure in schools. The case concerned whether school officials had the right to search a student's purse. The Court engaged in a two-part inquiry to determine the legality of the search, namely, "Was the search justified at its inception?" and "Was the search, as actually conducted, reasonably related in scope to the circumstances which justified the search in the first place?" While holding that students have a legitimate expectation of privacy rights with regard to their person and possessions in school, the Court in *T.L.O.* upheld the standard of *reasonable suspicion* as opposed to *probable cause* for conducting individual searches, thus giving more latitude in the case of students than provided adults by the Fourth Amendment. School officials must, however, have reasonable grounds to suspect that a search will produce evidence that the student violated school rules or committed a crime; the search must be justified at its inception by more than a rumor or hunch. Consistent with *T.L.O.*, some courts have held that search of the contents of a student's cell phone by school officials must be based on reasonable suspicion that the search will yield evidence that the student violated school rules or committed a crime (e.g., *Gallimore v. Henrico County School District*, 2014).

The Court in *T.L.O.* also noted that a search must not be "excessively intrusive in light of the age and gender of the pupil and the nature of the infraction" (*T.L.O.*, 1985, p. 342). The more personal the search (the closer the search comes to the body), the more serious the reasons the school must have for conducting the search. Thus, a search of a student's body for a weapon would likely be viewed as more legally permissible than an intrusive search for missing money. In our opinion, strip searches should be avoided if at all possible because they may result in emotional distress, anger, and alienation and legal challenges. (Also see *Safford Unified School District No. 1 v. Redding*, 2009, and Pinard, 2003.)

Student lockers and desks are the property of the school, and school officials generally have been afforded the legal right to search them as part of an effort to foster a safe educational environment. Districts are encouraged, however, to forewarn students that lockers and desks might be searched at any time, thereby dispelling any expectation of privacy. In addition, some school districts have policies stating that, as a condition of a student receiving permission to park on campus, the student must grant school officials the right to search his or her car at any time (Russo, 2012).

Merriken v. Cressman (1973) is a case that concerned the right to privacy of personal information. In this case, decided in federal district court, a school planned to administer a questionnaire to students as part of a program designed to identify student drug abusers, provide their names to the school administration, and then subject those students to intervention. The questionnaire inquired about the nature of the parent–child relationship and parenting practices and was to be administered without parent consent. After a parent challenged the use of the questionnaire as an unconstitutional invasion of privacy, the court ruled that parents of schoolchildren have a right to be free from invasion of family privacy by the school. However, this right to privacy was recognized for the parents only; the court did not address the issue of a student's independent right to privacy in the schools. (This case is discussed further in Chapter 10.)

A case decided in federal appeals court may have implications for informational privacy rights with regard to sexual orientation. In *Sterling v. Borough of Minersville* (2000), police officers told a young man, a senior in high school, of their intent to inform his family that he was gay. The teenager subsequently committed suicide. In his suicide note, the boy expressed fear that disclosure of his sexual orientation would damage the lives of his family. His mother subsequently filed a Section 1983 lawsuit against the police (state actors), alleging that their actions violated her son's constitutional right to privacy and caused harm. In his opinion, the federal judge wrote:

> We thus carefully guard one's right to privacy against unwarranted government intrusion. It is difficult to imagine a more private matter than one's sexuality and a less likely probability that the government would have a legitimate interest in disclosure of sexual identity. (*Sterling v. Borough of Minersville*, 2000, p. 196)

In *Sterling,* the Third Circuit interpreted the right to informational privacy to include "the right to be free from forced disclosure of sexual orientation" (Weinstein, 2005, p. 815). However, when an individual's right to privacy regarding sexual orientation is violated, there are many barriers to a successful Section 1983 lawsuit. In the *Sterling* case, the police officers were not held liable for any wrongdoing in the initial trial, but this verdict was set aside. To end the ordeal, the boy's mother settled for $100,000 in damages while a second trial was pending (Weinstein, 2005). To date, although there have been many reports of students suffering harm as a result of being "outed" by school administrators, most of these incidents appear to have been resolved out of court, and none led to a successful Section 1983 lawsuit against the school officials involved. Nevertheless, legal experts advise school employees to refrain from disclosing the sexual orientation or gender identity of students to others without their permission. In a model letter to school administrators on constitutional privacy rights of students, Esseks (2012) stated:

> Without full and voluntary consent by the student, it is against the law to disclose a student's sexual orientation or gender identity, or compel a student to disclose his or her sexual orientation or gender identity, even to a student's parents or other school administrators. (p. 1)

Statutory Law

The Individuals with Disabilities Education Improvement Act (IDEIA), the Protection of Pupil Rights Act (PPRA), and the Family Educational Rights and Privacy Act of 1974 (FERPA) provide some statutory protection for the privacy rights of students and their parents. IDEIA requires informed consent for an initial evaluation to determine whether a student is eligible for special education and protects the privacy of student special education records (see Chapters 4 and 6). The requirements of FERPA are discussed in "Record Keeping in the Schools" later in this chapter.

The PPRA, enacted in 1978, provides protection from school actions that intrude on student or family privacy. It was amended in 1994 (Pub. L. No. 103-227) and 2001 (Pub. L. No. 107-110 § 1061). The Act has two major provisions regarding the collection of sensitive information from students. First, in accordance with PPRA, no student may be required to submit without prior consent to a survey, analysis, or evaluation funded by the U.S. Department of Education (DOE) that reveals one or more of eight types of information: (1) political affiliations or beliefs of the student or the student's parent; (2) mental and psychological problems potentially embarrassing to the student or his or her family; (3) sex behavior and attitudes; (4) illegal, antisocial, self-incriminating, and demeaning behavior; (5) critical appraisals of other individuals with whom respondents have close family relationships; (6) legally recognized privileged and analogous relationships; (7) religious practices, affiliations, or beliefs of the student or student's parent; or (8) income, other than required by law to determine eligibility for participation in a program or for receiving financial assistance under a program. *Prior consent* is defined as the prior consent of the student if the student is an adult or emancipated minor, or prior written consent of the parent or guardian if the student is an unemancipated minor (20 U.S.C. § 1232h). These privacy protections of PPRA apply only to schools that receive and use federal funds in connection with the use or administration of surveys, analyses, or evaluations concerning one or more areas listed in the statute (*Altman v. Bedford Central School District,* 1999).

A second provision of the PPRA requires local school districts that receive *any* federal funds to develop policies, in consultation with parents, to notify parents when the school intends to administer a survey that reveals one or more of the eight types of information listed in the preceding paragraph. The parent of a student must be given the opportunity to inspect the survey, upon request, prior to its distribution. Parents must be given the opportunity to have their student opt out of the information-gathering activity.

If an adult or emancipated student, or the parent of a minor child, feels that he or she has been affected by a violation of PPRA, he or she may file a complaint with the Family Policy Compliance Office, U.S. DOE.

Privacy as an Ethical Issue

Privacy is also an ethical issue. Siegel (1979) defined privacy as "the freedom of individuals to choose for themselves the time and the circumstances under which and the extent to which their beliefs, behaviors, and opinions are to be shared or withheld from others" (p. 251). School psychologists have a special professional obligation to safeguard the privacy of clients.

Consistent with the general principle of respect for the dignity of all persons and the valuing of autonomy, psychologists respect the right of the client to self-determine whether to disclose private information (NASP-PPE I.2; also APA-EP Principle E). Furthermore, every effort is made to minimize intrusions on privacy (APA-EP Principle E, 4.04; NASP-PPE I.2.2). School psychologists do not seek or store private information about students, parents, teachers, or others that is not needed in the provision of services (NASP-PPE I.2.2; also APA-EP 4.04).

INFORMED CONSENT TO ESTABLISH A SCHOOL PSYCHOLOGIST–CLIENT RELATIONSHIP

Ethical codes and law are consistent in respecting the individual's right to self-determine whether to share private thoughts, behaviors, and beliefs with others. In ethics and law, the requirement for informed consent grew out of deep-rooted notions of the importance of individual privacy. As Bersoff (1983) noted, "It is now universally agreed, though not always honored in practice, *that human beings must give their informed consent prior to any significant intrusion of their person or privacy*" (p. 150, emphasis added).

As mentioned in Chapters 1 and 2, school psychologists often, but not always, provide services within the framework of an established school psychologist–client relationship (NASP-PPE Definition of Terms). When a school psychologist—whether employed by the schools or in private practice—establishes a psychologist–client professional relationship, he or she assumes special ethical and legal obligations to the parties who enter the relationship (Haas & Malouf, 2005), such as the obligation to ensure informed consent for services (NASP-PPE I.1.2; APA-EP Principle E, 3.10–3.11). This ethical obligation to obtain consent to establish a school psychologist–client relationship for the purpose of individualized psychological assessment and intervention is consistent with IDEIA. Codes of ethics and law thus show agreement that, with the exception of urgent situations, informed consent should be obtained to establish a school psychologist–client relationship.

However, as one of the members of a school's instructional staff and/or mental health team, a practitioner also provides consultative services to student assistance teams, classrooms, or schools that do not fall within the scope of an established school psychologist–client relationship (NASP-PPE Definition of Terms). Not all school-based consultative services require informed parent consent, particularly if the resulting interventions are under the authority of the teacher, within the scope of typical classroom interventions, and not intrusive of student or family privacy beyond what might be expected in the course of ordinary school activities (NASP-PPE I.1.1; also Corrao & Melton, 1988). (See Chapter 7.)

Meaning of *Informed Consent*

Case law and statutory regulations concur that the three key elements of informed consent are that it must be *knowing*, *competent*, and *voluntary* (Dekraai, Sales, & Hall, 1998). *Knowing* means that the individual giving consent must have a clear understanding of what he or she is consenting to. The person seeking consent must make a good-faith effort to disclose enough information to the person from whom consent is sought so that the individual can make an *informed choice* regarding whether to enter a school psychologist–client relationship (Barnett, Wise, Johnson-Greene, & Bucky, 2007; Dekraai et al., 1998).

In seeking consent to establish a professional relationship with a client (or clients) for the provision of psychological services, the practitioner is obligated to provide information about the nature and scope of services offered, assessment-intervention goals and procedures, the expected duration of services, any foreseeable risks or discomforts (including any risks of psychological or physical harm), the cost of the services (if any), the benefits that reasonably can be expected, the possible consequences and risks of not receiving services, and information about alternative treatments or services that may be beneficial. The extent to which confidentiality of information will be maintained also should be discussed as part of the informed consent procedures. This information must be provided in language (or by other mode of communication) understandable to the person giving consent (Weithorn, 1983; also NASP-PPE I.1.3).

The individual giving consent also must be *legally competent* to give consent. As Bersoff and Hofer (1990) observed, the law presumes that every adult is competent to consent, unless judged incompetent following a full hearing conducted by an impartial fact finder. However, in the legal system, children generally are presumed to be incompetent and not capable of making legally binding decisions (Bersoff, 1983). Consequently, in the school setting, informed consent to establish a school psychologist–client relationship typically is sought from the parent or guardian of a minor child, or from the student if an adult. Parent consent may be bypassed in emergency situations (see NASP-PPE I.1.2).

The National Association of School Psychologists' (NASP's) code of ethics notes that the term *parent* may be defined in law (e.g., special education law) or district policy, "and can include the birth or adoptive parent, an individual acting in the place of a natural or adoptive parent (a grandparent or other relative, stepparent, or domestic partner), and/or an individual who is legally responsible for the child's welfare" (NASP-PPE Definition of Terms). Practitioners should consult their school administrator or attorney if there are questions regarding who can make educational decisions for a child.

The third element of informed consent is that it must be *voluntary*. Consent must be "obtained in the absence of coercion, duress, misrepresentation, or undue inducement. In short, the person giving consent must do so freely" (Bersoff & Hofer, 1990, p. 951). Practitioners should ensure that the individual from whom consent is sought has sufficient time to decide whether to agree to the services offered. It is also important to ensure that the individual providing consent understands that he or she is free to decline the services offered.

When establishing a school psychologist–client relationship, practitioners are ethically obligated to appropriately document oral or written consent (NASP-PPE I.1.3). It is important for school psychologists to recognize that consent is an ongoing process, particularly if there is a significant change in the previously agreed-on assessment or intervention goals or procedures. Furthermore, clients must be allowed to withdraw consent at any time without negative repercussions (NASP-PPE Definition of Terms; also Barnett, Wise, et al., 2007; IDEIA). Specific ethical and legal requirements for informed consent vary across different situations within the school setting. Informed consent for release of student education records is discussed in this chapter. Consent for psychoeducational assessment is addressed in Chapter 6; consent for school-based interventions is covered in Chapter 7; and participation in research is discussed in Chapter 10.

Consent of Minors for Psychological Services

In this portion of the chapter, we explore children's competence to consent to psychological services from legal, ethical, and cognitive-developmental perspectives.

Consent of Minors as a Legal Issue

As noted earlier, legally, in the school setting, informed consent to establish a school psychologist–client relationship typically rests with the parent of a minor child. Legislators and the courts generally have presumed that minors are not developmentally competent to make sound judgments on their own regarding their need for psychological services. The courts have viewed parents as typically acting in their children's best interests and have reasoned that allowing minors a right to refuse services or treatment independent of parental wishes might be disruptive to the parent–child relationship and interfere with effective treatment programs (*Parham v. J.R.*, 1979).

Parham (1979) was an important case regarding the competence of minors to participate in decisions affecting their own welfare. In *Parham*, the Supreme Court upheld a Georgia statute allowing parents to commit a minor child to a mental institution for treatment (with the approval of a physician) in the absence of a formal or quasi-formal hearing to safeguard the child from arbitrary commitment. Although the Court recognized that children have an interest in being free from misdiagnosis and unnecessary confinement, the Court viewed minors as incompetent to make decisions concerning their own need for treatment.

It should be noted, however, that minors are granted access to medical care without parental consent in emergency situations, and most states allow minors access to treatment independent of parent notice or consent for certain health-related conditions (e.g., sexually transmitted disease, alcohol abuse, drug abuse) (English, Bass, Boyle, & Eshragh, 2010). More than 20 states also permit minors to consent to outpatient mental health treatment on their own at an age earlier than 18 years (Bartow, Jacob, Malta, Schmittel, & Zielinski, 2014).

Consent of Minors as an Ethical Issue

Although minors are not generally seen as legally competent to consent to or refuse psychological services in the schools, practitioners are ethically obligated to respect the dignity, autonomy, and self-determination of their clients. As discussed in the paragraphs that follow, we find the notion of developmentally appropriate rights to self-determination and autonomy suggested in the *Canadian Code of Ethics for Psychologists* (Canadian Psychological Association [CPA], 2000) more satisfactory than an absolute stance that children should always (or never) be afforded the choice to accept or refuse psychological services. The term *assent*, rather than *consent*, typically is used to refer to a minor's affirmative agreement to participate in psychological services. (Also see NASP-PPE Definition of Terms.)

Minors and Capacity to Consent: A Research Perspective

What standards are used to determine whether a client is competent to provide consent to psychological treatment? In law and professional practice, four tests or standards of competency to consent have been applied in psychological treatment situations involving adult clients: (1) there is a simple expression of a preference relative to alternative treatment choices; (2) the choice is seen as one a reasonable person might make; (3) a logical or rational decision-making process was followed; and (4) the person giving consent demonstrates understanding (factual or abstract) of the situation, choice made, and probable consequences (adapted from Weithorn, 1983, pp. 244–245). Evidence of a preference is probably the most lenient standard, and evidence of understanding is the most stringent (Weithorn, 1983).

Findings from cognitive-developmental research suggest that many children have a greater capacity to make competent choices about psychological treatment than is recognized in law. Research suggests that a child's capacity to participate effectively in treatment decisions depends on a number of factors, including cognitive and personal-social development and functioning, motivation to participate, prior experiences with decision making, and the complexity of the situation and choices under consideration (Melton, Koocher, & Saks, 1983).

Preschoolers have limited language and reasoning abilities. However, they may be able to express preferences when choices are presented in concrete, here-and-now terms (Ferguson, 1978). Although children in middle childhood (ages 6 to 11) have not attained adult reasoning capabilities, research suggests they typically are able to make sensible treatment choices (Weithorn, 1983), and parents and professionals have judged the participation of children this age in treatment decisions to be effective (Taylor, Adelman, & Kaser-Boyd, 1985).

The years between ages 11 and 14 are seen as transitional ones with much individual variation in cognitive development and the ability to make truly voluntary choices. Students in this age range, like younger children, may defer to authority in decisions, or they may make choices based on anti-authority feelings. Minors age 14 and older typically have reasoning capabilities similar to adults, and many are capable of participating in treatment decisions as effectively as adults (Grisso & Vierling, 1978; Steinberg, Cauffman, Woolard, Graham, & Banich, 2009; also Abramovitch, Freedman, Henry, & Van Brunschot, 1995). Cooper (1984) proposed the use of a written therapist–child agreement as a strategy for involving minors ages 9 and older in treatment decisions.

Research findings suggest not only that minors have greater capacity to make treatment decisions than generally recognized in law, but that a child's participation in intervention decisions may lead to enhanced motivation for treatment, an increased sense of personal responsibility for self-care, greater treatment compliance, and reduced rates of early treatment termination (Holmes & Urie, 1975; Kaser-Boyd, Adelman, & Taylor, 1985; Weithorn, 1983). For these reasons, Weithorn (1983) suggested that practitioners permit and encourage student involvement in decision making within the parameters of the law and the child's capacity to participate. However, psychologists must guard against overwhelming children with choices they do not wish to make for themselves. Furthermore, when children are given a choice of whether to accept school psychological services, it is important to recognize that they may have little knowledge of or may have misconceptions about the services offered. The practitioner should ensure that the student understands what participation means before soliciting assent so that the child can make an informed choice. For example, a psychologist might ask a student to attend a counseling group session before making a choice about participation (see NASP-PPE I.1.4; also APA-EP 3.10d).

In sum, the decision to allow a minor child the opportunity to choose or refuse psychological services and participate in treatment decisions involves a consideration of law, ethical issues (self-determination versus welfare of the client), the child's competence to make choices, and the likely consequences of affording choices (enhanced treatment outcomes versus choice to refuse treatment). As suggested in the *Canadian Code of Ethics for Psychologists* (CPA, 2000), it may be ethical to proceed without the child's explicit assent if the service is considered to be of direct benefit to the child. We concur with Corrao and Melton (1988) that it is disrespectful to solicit assent from the child if refusal will not be honored (NASP-PPE I.1.4).

It also is important to distinguish between the right to consent to (or refuse) services and *the right to be informed about the services offered* (Fleming & Fleming, 1987). Practitioners have an ethical obligation to inform student-clients of the scope and nature of psychological services whether they are given a choice about participating or not (NASP-PPE I.1.4).

Informed Consent Versus Notice

Informed consent differs from notice. *Notice* means that the school supplies information about impending actions. *Consent* requires "affirmative permission before actions can be taken" (Bersoff & Hofer, 1990, p. 950). Wanda's letter to parents (Case 3.1) is an example of notice; it does not meet the requirements for informed consent to establish a school psychologist–client relationship. If parents do not receive the letter, they have no opportunity to deny consent (J. H. Correll in Canter, 1989).

In seeking informed consent from the parents, Wanda is obligated to describe the nature, scope, and goals of the counseling sessions; their expected duration; any foreseeable risks or discomforts for the student (e.g., loss of student and family privacy); any cost to parent or student (e.g., loss of classroom instructional time), any benefits that can reasonably be expected (e.g., the possibility of enhanced adjustment to parent separation); alternative services available; and the likely consequences of not receiving services. After consideration of the ethical issues involved and the possible consequences of her decision, Wanda also must decide whether to offer each child the opportunity to make an informed choice about participating (or not participating) in the counseling groups.

Case 3.1

Wanda Rose is concerned about the children in her elementary school experiencing adjustment difficulties related to parent separation and divorce. She decides to form counseling groups for children experiencing parent separation or divorce. She asks teachers to identify students who might benefit from the group counseling and then sends letters home with the children, notifying parents that their child will be seen for group counseling sessions. She asks parents to contact her if further information about the counseling is desired.

CONFIDENTIALITY

Siegel (1979) described confidentiality as "an explicit promise or contract to reveal nothing about an individual except under conditions agreed to by the source or subject" (p. 251). Although confidentiality is primarily a matter of professional ethics, in some states psychologists can be held civilly liable under state law for impermissible breach of client confidentiality (see "Nondisclosure Laws and Privileged Communication" later in this chapter). The NASP's code of ethics states:

> School psychologists respect the confidentiality of information obtained during their professional work. Information is not revealed to third parties without the agreement of a minor child's parent or legal guardian (or an adult student), except in those situations in which failure to release information would result in danger to the student or others, or where otherwise required by law. Whenever feasible, student assent is obtained prior to disclosure of his or her confidences to third parties, including disclosures to the student's parents. (NASP-PPE I.2.4; also APA-EP 4.05)

The interpretation of the principle of confidentiality as it relates to the delivery of psychological services in the school setting is a complicated matter. However, three guidelines can be found in our codes of ethics and the literature on confidentiality in school-based practice. First, with the exception of urgent situations, school psychologists define the parameters of confidentiality at the outset of establishing a school psychologist–client professional relationship (Davis & Sandoval, 1982; also APA-EP Principle E, 4.02; NASP-PPE I.2.3).

Second, if information learned within a school psychologist–client relationship is shared with third parties, such information is disclosed only on a *need-to-know* basis. "School psychologists discuss and/or release confidential information only for professional purposes and only with persons who have a legitimate need to know" (NASP-PPE I.2.5). Furthermore, only information "essential to the understanding and resolution" of a student's difficulties is disclosed (Davis & Sandoval, 1982, p. 548; also APA-EP Principle E, 4.04, 4.05; NASP-PPE I.2; Schwab & Gelfman, 2005a).

Third, school physical and mental health professionals, including school psychologists, must recognize that medical or other sensitive personal information "belongs to the student and family, not the school." Therefore, it is generally the parent's (or student's) "right to control who has access to that information, especially when disclosure might cause harm" (Schwab & Gelfman, 2005a, pp. 266–267; also see NASP-PPE I.2).

In the paragraphs that follow, we discuss confidentiality and its limits when school-based services are provided within the context of these types of school psychologist–client relationships: direct services to the student, collaboration with the parent and/or teacher, and consultative services to a teacher-consultee.

Confidentiality and Direct Services to the Student

For our purposes here, the provision of direct services to the student means that the practitioner works with the student directly (e.g., individual counseling) as part of a process of ongoing, planned interactions between a school psychologist and a student. When establishing a school psychologist–client relationship, the initial interview "should include a direct and candid discussion of the limits that may exist with respect to any confidences communicated in the relationship" (Koocher & Keith-Spiegel, 2008, p. 194; also M. A. Fisher, 2013; APA-EP 4.02; NASP-PPE I.2.).[1] Because a student who is a minor has no legal right to confidentiality independent of the parents, it is critically important to discuss confidentiality and its limits with parents when seeking consent to provide direct services to a minor. The practitioner must explain to parents why a promise of confidentiality to the student can be essential to an effective helping relationship, particularly if the student is entering adolescence or is older, and must seek parent understanding and agreement that the psychologist will not share with the parent specific confidences disclosed by the child without the child's assent to do so. Parents need to be reassured, however, that the practitioner will let them know what they can do to help their child and that the practitioner will inform them immediately if there is a serious situation, such as one suggesting that their child is in danger.

Much has been written about the importance of confidentiality for building and maintaining the trust essential to a helping relationship (M. A. Fisher, 2013; Siegel, 1979). However, a promise of confidentiality can help or hinder the psychologist's effectiveness when the client is a minor child (Taylor & Adelman, 1989). As Pitcher and Poland (1992) observed, for a troubled student, candor about the limits of confidentiality may be more important in fostering trust in adult helpers than a promise of absolute confidentiality that is later broken. Consequently, school psychologists must weigh a number of factors in deciding the boundaries of a promise of confidentiality (e.g., age and maturity of the student, self-referral or referral by others, reason for referral). Whatever the parameters, the circumstances under which the psychologist might share student confidences with others must be made clear.

In the provision of direct services to the student, there are three situations in which the school psychologist may be obligated to share confidential student disclosures with others. First, it is usually appropriate to disclose student confidences to others when the student requests it. Second, as noted previously, confidential information may be disclosed when there is a situation involving danger to the student or others. Situations involving danger are discussed in the next subsection, "Duty to Protect." Third, it may be necessary for the psychologist to disclose confidential information when there is a legal obligation to testify in a court of law. This is discussed in the next main section, "Nondisclosure Laws and Privileged Communication."

Taylor and Adelman (1989) provided suggestions regarding how to create an atmosphere of safety and trust in which the student knows and understands the exceptions to the promise of confidentiality yet is motivated to disclose personal thoughts, feelings, and important information. Findings from a study by Muehleman, Pickens, and Robinson (1985) suggested that discussion of the limits of confidentiality with clients does not limit self-disclosure if self-disclosure is encouraged verbally.

---

[1] It is generally not necessary to discuss confidentiality with preschool-age student/clients. Preschool children lack cognitive awareness that their own thoughts and feelings differ from those of the people around them, and consequently, discussions of confidentiality have little meaning for this age group.

As Poland (1989) noted, the ideal situation is for mental health professionals to discuss the limits of confidentiality at the outset of establishing a psychologist–client relationship. However, at times students are referred for assessment of whether they are a threat to self or others or self-refer because they are in immediate need of assistance. In such situations, Poland suggested gathering the most complete information possible about the student's thoughts and plans first and then dealing with the issue of the limits of confidentiality (also APA-EP 4.02; NASP-PPE I.2.1). If students offer to disclose personal matters "on the condition that the counselor promises not to tell anyone," the practitioner should not enter into such an agreement, as the student is likely to feel betrayed if the promise cannot be kept.

If it becomes apparent in working with a student that confidentiality must be broken, only information essential to the resolution of the student's difficulties should be disclosed to others and only to persons who need to know (Davis & Sandoval, 1982, p. 548; also APA-EP 4.05; NASP-PPE I.2.5). The decision to divulge information also should be discussed with the student. The NASP's code of ethics states, "*Whenever feasible*, student assent is obtained prior to disclosure of his or her confidences to third parties, including the student's parents" (I.2.4, emphasis added). Taylor and Adelman (1989) suggested three steps: (1) explaining to the student the reason for disclosure, (2) exploring with the student the likely repercussions in and outside the student–psychologist relationship, and (3) discussing with the student how to proceed in a manner that will minimize negative consequences and maximize potential benefits. In their work with troubled youth, Pitcher and Poland (1992) found that if handled with sensitivity, most students come to understand that a decision to disclose confidential information to others is based on the need to help the student or protect others.

Duty to Protect

School psychologists have an ethical obligation to safeguard the confidentiality of information learned in a psychologist–client relationship. However, as discussed in Chapter 2, school-based practitioners also have a legal obligation to protect all students from reasonably foreseeable risk of harm. For this reason, the NASP's code of ethics allows disclosure of confidences "in those situations in which failure to release information would result in danger to the student or others, or where otherwise required by law" (NASP-PPE I.2.4; also APA-EP 4.05).

In contrast, depending on state statutory and common law, psychologists in non-school settings may or may not have a legal duty to breach confidentiality to protect a client or others from danger (see Benjamin, Kent, & Sirikantraporn, 2009). Historically, most state duty-to-protect mandates governing the practice of psychology were a result of the *Tarasoff* case, summarized in Case 3.2. The *Tarasoff I* court decision triggered a lengthy debate between American Psychological Association (APA) psychologists who asserted that confidentiality is absolute and can be broken under no circumstances and those who insisted that limits to confidentiality be built into APA's ethical code. The 1981 revision of the APA's code of ethics included the statement that psychologists reveal confidential information to others "only with the consent of the

---

Case 3.2

Prosenjit Poddar, a foreign student from India attending the University of California–Berkeley, was in psychotherapy with a psychologist at the university's health center. The psychologist recognized that Poddar was quite dangerous, based in part on his pathological attachment to Tatiana Tarasoff, his ex-girlfriend, toward whom he made some threats. After consultation with his supervisor, the psychologist notified the campus police that Poddar was dangerous and should be committed. The police visited Poddar, who denied he had any intentions of harming Tarasoff. Poddar subsequently refused to return for therapy and two months later killed Tarasoff. Tarasoff's parents brought suit against the regents, the student health center staff members involved, and the campus police. Ultimately, the California Supreme Court ruled twice on the case.

The 1974 ruling (*Tarasoff I*) held that the therapists had a duty to warn Tarasoff. The court held that "public policy favoring protection of the confidential character of patient-psychotherapist relationships must yield in instances in which disclosure is essential to avert danger to others; the protective privilege ends where the public peril begins" (*Tarasoff v. Regents of California*, 1974, p. 566). The second ruling, in 1976 (*Tarasoff II*), held that a therapist has a "duty to exercise reasonable care to protect the foreseeable victim" from harm (*Tarasoff v. Regents of California*, 1976, p. 345).

---

person or the person's legal representative, *except in those unusual circumstances where not to do so would result in clear danger to the person or others*" (emphasis added). The current code states: "Psychologists disclose confidential information without the consent of the individual only as mandated by law, or where permitted by law for a valid purpose, such as to ... protect the client/patient, psychologist, or others from harm" (APA-EP 4.05; also NASP-PPE I.2.4). Psychologists refer to this obligation to breach confidentiality to ensure the safety of the client or others as the *duty to warn* (*Tarasoff I*) or, more generally, a *duty to protect* (*Tarasoff II*). Following the *Tarasoff* decisions, some, but not all, states enacted laws requiring psychologists to make reasonable efforts to warn potential victims of violent clients, and in some states, appropriate law enforcement agencies must be notified as well.

In summary, although direct service to the student is in some ways analogous to the psychologist–client relationship in nonschool settings, it is important to recognize that a school-based practitioner has special duty-to-protect obligations. Furthermore, most students are minors. Consequently, in school-based practice, student confidences must be shared with others when necessary to safeguard students from *reasonably foreseeable risk of harm* to self or others, a less stringent standard for disclosure of confidential information than *clear* or *imminent danger*, terms often used in state laws regulating mental health providers. (Also see Chapter 7.)

Collaboration and Confidentiality

As noted earlier, school psychologists may provide direct services to the student. However, they typically work in collaboration with teachers, parents, and others to assist the student, a situation that complicates the translation of the principle of confidentiality into appropriate action. In collaboration, the individuals involved carry joint responsibility for assisting the student (J. C. Hansen, Himes, & Meier, 1990). Thus, if the psychologist is working in collaboration with the teacher and/or parent in assisting the student, information will most likely be shared by those involved in the collaborative effort.

At the outset of establishing a professional relationship with a client, the school psychologist needs a clear prior agreement about confidentiality and its limits among those involved in the collaborative effort. The student is informed of those who will receive information regarding the services and the type of information they will receive (NASP-PPE I.2.3, II.4.1). In interactions with the parent, practitioners discuss confidentiality and its limits and parent and student rights regarding "creation, modification, storage, and disposal of psychological and educational records that result from the provision of services" (NASP-PPE II.4.1). Teachers and other staff involved in the collaborative effort also need a clear understanding of the parameters of confidentiality. Furthermore, "School psychologists recognize that it may be necessary to discuss confidentiality at multiple points in a professional relationship to ensure client understanding and agreement regarding how sensitive disclosures will be handled" (NASP-PPE I.2.3).

If information received in a confidential situation subsequently is disclosed to assist the teacher or parent in meeting the needs of a student, it is recommended that *only generalizations*, not specific confidences, are shared (Davis & Sandoval, 1982; also APA-EP 4.04; NASP-PPE I.2.5). Zingaro (1983) suggested that the psychologist share insights about students with others in terms of what they can do to help the child.

In sum, the need-to-know ethical principle dictates that information obtained in a professional relationship and subsequently shared with others is discussed only for professional purposes and only with persons clearly concerned with the situation (APA-EP 4.04). Disclosure of information is "limited to the minimum that is necessary to achieve the purpose [of the disclosure]" (APA-EP 4.04; NASP-PPE I.2.5).

In Case 3.3, Carrie may wish to discuss the parent conference with Amy's teacher in a private setting, but she must take care not to disclose specific information conveyed during her conferences with Mrs. Farwell. For example, Amy's teacher, in working with Mrs. Farwell, may need to know about her difficulty in accepting Amy's disabilities. She does not need to know about Mrs. Farwell's specific disclosures (e.g., the details of her search for a miracle cure).

As Davis and Sandoval (1982) observed, sometimes social pressures to gossip exist, particularly in the teacher's lounge or lunchroom, in order to be accepted as part of the school staff. Resisting the temptation to join in when teachers and other staff share their frustrations about students, parents, and school life may be particularly difficult for Carrie because of her professional isolation in a rural area. However, to safeguard confidential disclosures and maintain teacher trust in her as a professional, Carrie must

=== **Case 3.3** ===

Carrie Johnson is exhausted. She just completed another parent conference with Mrs. Farwell. Mrs. Farwell's daughter, Amy, age 5, was diagnosed as having a rare genetic disorder characterized by mild to moderate intellectual disability. After the diagnosis was made more than a year ago, Mr. Farwell soon focused his attention on how to best help his daughter, but Mrs. Farwell has not yet been able to accept her daughter's diagnosis. Even after the original diagnosis was confirmed by a second genetics expert, Mrs. Farwell spent thousands of dollars shopping for a different diagnosis and seeking "miracle cures" on the Internet. She has refused Carrie's referrals for family counseling and involvement with a support group for parents of children with disabilities. Although she finally acquiesced to special education services for her daughter, she continues to insist that Amy will "grow out of it" and doesn't seem to hear Carrie's careful explanations of Amy's abilities, limitations, and needs. Today, Carrie learned that Mr. and Mrs. Farwell have separated and that Amy's older siblings are showing many adjustment problems at home and in school. She enters the teacher's lounge for a cup of coffee and is greeted by Amy's teacher, who asks, "How's it going with the Farwells?" What, if anything, should Carrie disclose?

avoid discussing her knowledge of students, parents, or school staff in casual conversations with others.

Confidentiality and Teacher Consultation

When a school psychologist provides consultation to a teacher, the parameters of confidentiality must be discussed at the outset of the delivery of consultative services. At a minimum, teachers should clearly understand what and how information will be used, by whom, and for what purposes (APA-EP 4.02; NASP-PPE I.2.3; also Erchul & Young, 2014; Sandoval, 2014). Whatever the parameters of the promise of confidentiality, violation of those parameters is likely to result in a loss of trust in the school psychologist and to impair his or her ability to work with the consultee and other staff. School psychologists also must ensure a shared understanding with school administrators regarding the parameters of confidentiality of school psychologist–teacher consultative relationships.

The confidentiality agreement is likely to vary depending on the nature of the consultative services being provided. When a consultative relationship is established between an individual school psychologist and a teacher, the parameters of confidentiality will likely be similar to those of a traditional psychologist–client relationship (Sandoval, 2014). However, the school psychologist may be a member of a team providing instructional and behavioral consultation to teachers with information shared freely among team members (Erchul & Young, 2014). In such situations, the school psychologist must clarify that the school psychologist–teacher consultative relationship is not confidential (also see Chapter 8).

NONDISCLOSURE LAWS AND PRIVILEGED COMMUNICATION

In psychology, "privileged communication" generally refers to the legal right of a client to prevent disclosure to third parties of information shared in a confidential professional relationship. Two types of laws protect the confidentiality of client disclosures to a mental health provider in the context of an established mental health provider–client relationship: *nondisclosure laws* and *evidentiary privilege laws.*[2]

Nondisclosure Laws

In the course of a school psychological assessment or intervention, a child or his or her parents may divulge sensitive information, including information that, if disclosed to third parties, would create risks of harm to the child or family members (see Exhibit 3.1). *Nondisclosure laws*[3] are not found in all states but may be established in state codes that regulate the delivery of health and mental health services, including

---

Exhibit 3.1 Risks of Disclosing Confidential Communications

The following are examples of confidential communications to a school psychologist that create risk to the client's rights or reputation if disclosed to third parties.

Legal Risk

As a result of conversations with a child referred for academic assessment, the school psychologist becomes aware that the child's father is an illegal immigrant who fears deportation.

Risk to Right to Attend School and Academic Standing

A high school student referred for depression confides that he plagiarized several term papers because of parental pressure to get As and to be accepted at a prestigious college.

Social Risk (Risk to Reputation, Loss of Social Standing)

In a meeting with parents regarding their teen who may be suicidal, the parents confide that they are divorcing because one parent is leaving the marriage for a same-sex partner, resulting in turmoil at home.

---

[2]Portions of this section were adapted from Jacob and Powers (2009).

[3]In this edition of the book, the term *nondisclosure laws* replaces *professional privilege laws* to better distinguish the two types of law protecting confidential disclosures and to align our terminology with that recommended by experts (e.g., M. A. Fisher, 2013). It is important to note, that state laws sometimes use the terms *confidential* and *privileged* interchangeably.

occupation codes, mental health codes, and/or health and safety codes. Where found, such laws prohibit mental health providers from disclosing confidential client information except under certain circumstances. These laws mean that a mental health provider could be held civilly liable under state law for an impermissible breach of client confidentiality. Impermissible breach of client confidentiality also could result in discipline by the state's licensure or certification board.

In addition to safeguarding the confidentiality of client information, nondisclosure laws also enumerate situations in which it is legally permissible for a mental health provider to disclose confidential information without the client's consent. State laws vary, but the confidentiality of client communications to a mental health provider is typically not protected when: (a) the disclosure leads the professional to believe that the client poses a risk of imminent danger to others, (b) the professional is obligated by mandated reporting laws to report suspected abuse of a child or elderly person or individual with a disability, or (c) the client has filed a legal action or complaint against the mental health provider. School psychologists are advised to learn about the scope and language of nondisclosure laws in the state where they practice and to consult someone knowledgeable of mental health law if they are unsure of the implications of such laws for school-based practice.

McDuff v. Tamborlane (1999) provides an example of a civil suit filed against a school psychologist for a violation of state nondisclosure law (see Case 3.4). The reader is advised that this case only serves as a cautionary tale. It is an unpublished case (i.e., it is not a legal precedent for future similar cases except as allowed within the court's jurisdiction). No record of further legal proceedings could be located, so the outcome is unknown.

Case 3.4

In *McDuff v. Tamborlane* (1999), a school psychologist employed by a public school district was providing psychological counseling to a high school student. In order to assist the school psychologist in providing appropriate treatment for her daughter, the girl's mother informed the school psychologist that her daughter had been involved in a larceny. The mother assumed that this disclosure was confidential. The school psychologist subsequently shared the information about the student's crime with the vice principal, who notified the police, and the student was arrested. The student's family filed a malpractice suit against the school psychologist alleging she had violated the confidential nature of the communication by the mother to the psychologist as well as the state's privileged communication statutes. In the opinion of a superior court of Connecticut, the communication of a client's past criminal activity is privileged, whether the information is disclosed by the client or by a member of his or her family. The judge also noted that there was no imminent risk of injury to the student, others, or property that would justify the breach of confidentially.

Note: This is an unpublished case.

Evidentiary Privilege

The duty for witnesses to testify in judicial proceedings in order to ensure justice at times conflicts with the need to safeguard the trust and privacy essential to special relationships (e.g., attorney–client, husband–wife, psychotherapist–patient). Evidentiary (or testimonial) privilege laws govern the admissibility of evidence in a trial or legal procedure. *Evidentiary privilege* is a legal term that refers to the right of a person in a special relationship to prevent the disclosure in court of information given in confidence in the special relationship. Where evidentiary privilege is extended to school psychologists, it generally means that a client can prevent the psychologist from disclosing information shared in a psychologist–client relationship in a legal proceeding. The client may voluntarily waive privilege (i.e., give consent for the psychologist to disclose privileged communications), and then the psychologist must provide relevant testimony. The waiver belongs to the *client*, and the psychologist has no independent right to invoke privilege against the client's wishes (Knapp & VandeCreek, 1985).

Rules of evidence are used to determine what evidence is admissible in a trial or other legal proceeding. Federal courts follow the Federal Rules of Evidence, while state courts may follow their own rules (Legal Information Institute [LII], n.d.[a]). At the federal level, except as required by the Constitution or the U.S. Congress, privilege, including whether communications between a psychologist and client are protected from disclosure, is determined by case law (Article V. Privileges, Rule 501. General Rule; LII, n.d.[a]). Prior to the late 1990s, federal case law recognized "psychotherapist–patient privilege," with the term *psychotherapist* meaning a psychiatrist or licensed doctoral-level psychologist. In 1996, however, in *Jaffee v. Redmond*, the Supreme Court ruled that communications between a psychotherapist who was a master's-level social worker and her client were privileged and protected from disclosure in federal court cases. Subsequent decisions in the lower federal courts extended privilege to the clients of a broad range of nondoctoral mental health providers.

State courts follow their own rules of evidence. At the state level, rules governing evidentiary privilege are established by common law or found in one section or several different sections of state codes. In 1892, a nongovernmental body, the National Conference on Commissioners on Uniform State Laws, was formed to promote uniformity in state laws (LII, n.d.[b]). This group, comprised of attorneys from each state, drafted and continues to draft "uniform laws" on various subjects that are sometimes, but not always, adopted in whole or in part by states. As a result of the *Jaffee v. Redmond* decision and parallel developments in state law, the Uniform Rules of Evidence were revised in 1999 to broaden the scope of mental health provider privilege (Aronson, 2001). The components of the 1999 Uniform Rules of Evidence addressing mental health provider privilege are described in the paragraphs that follow. It is important to remember, however, that states rarely use the verbatim language of a uniform law (LII, n.d.[b]).

The Uniform Rules of Evidence now recognize privileged communication status for "mental health providers," identified as "a person authorized, in any State … , or reasonably believed by the patient to be authorized, to engage in the diagnosis or treatment of a mental or emotional condition, including addiction to alcohol or drugs"

(Beam & Whinery, 2001, Rule 503[a][5], p. 474). The general rule of evidentiary privilege is that a client has a privilege to refuse to disclose, and to prevent a mental health provider from disclosing, confidential communications made for the purpose of diagnosis or treatment of the client's physical, mental, or emotional condition (Beam & Whinery, 2001, Rule 503[b]). Privilege includes the confidential communications of family members who are participating in the diagnosis and treatment of the client (Beam & Whinery, 2001, Rule 503[a][1], p. 474). Note that under the Uniform Rules, the mental health provider does not have to be licensed or certified; the only requirement is that the client reasonably believes that the person is an authorized mental health provider.

Thus, under the Uniform Rules, *privileged communication status* for school psychologists generally means that a psychologist cannot disclose confidential information about the client in a legal proceeding without client consent (or the consent of a minor's parents) to do so. There are, however, exceptions to privilege. To fall within the Uniform Rules scope of privileged communication, *the communication must occur in the context of a practitioner–client relationship, and privilege applies only if the client has a reasonable expectation that his or her communications are privileged* (Beam & Whinery, 2001, Rule 503[a][5]). Case 3.5, *People v. Vincent Moreno* (2005), and Case 3.6, *J.N. v. Bellingham School District No. 501* (1994), exemplify this exception to privilege. The Uniform Rules also identify other exceptions to privilege (e.g., legal proceeding to hospitalize a client for mental illness). While state laws may include the exceptions to privilege outlined in the Uniform Rules, other exceptions may exist as well (Glosoff, Herlihy, & Spence, 2000).

In sum, *evidentiary privilege* gives the client the right to decide whether a school psychologist will disclose client information in a legal proceeding. Evidentiary privilege for school psychologist–client communications are protected in federal courts and may or may not be protected in state courts, depending on state law. If a client waives privilege or a judge rules that client communications to a school psychologist do not have privileged communication status, the psychologist is then required to testify in court, and refusal to testify may result in the psychologist being held in contempt of court.

Case 3.5

In *People v. Vincent Moreno* (2005), a student, Vincent, confessed to a school psychologist that he shot and killed a man during an attempt to rob the victim of his necklace. However, the school psychologist had forewarned Vincent of the limits of confidentiality. More specifically, she had cautioned him that if he were to tell her something "really serious," she would be obligated to take it to a higher level ("Psychologist–Patient Privilege," 2002). The defense attorneys for Vincent argued that his confession to the school psychologist was privileged communication. The court held that a psychologist–patient privilege did not exist in this case because, among other things, a client–psychologist relationship did not exist at the time of the confession, and the school psychologist had forewarned Vincent that her professional obligations prevented her from keeping such an admission confidential.

Case 3.6

In *J. N. v. Bellingham School District No. 501* (1994), a student, "A.B.," sexually assaulted another student, "J.N." The victim's parents subsequently filed suit against the school district, alleging that the school had prior knowledge that A.B. posed a threat to other students and, in light of this knowledge, was negligent in supervision of A.B. When the attorney for the victim's parents asked to see A.B.'s school psychological records to establish that A.B. was a foreseeable risk to others, the school refused to release them on the basis that the records were privileged communication between the school psychologist and A.B.'s parents, although the records were released with parent consent to members of the school's multidisciplinary special education assessment team. The court held that psychologist–patient privilege "does not apply where it is manifest that the communication was not intended to be confidential" (1994, p. 26). When information is recorded and shared for the purpose of making a recommendation to a teacher or school multidisciplinary team, the information is not privileged.

In addition, some states have *nondisclosure laws* protecting the confidentiality of communications to a school psychologist. If school psychologists disclose client information to others in violation of those laws, they may put themselves at risk for a malpractice suit (e.g., *McDuff v. Tamborlane*, 1999; Case 3.4) or sanction by their state credentialing board, including possible loss of certification or licensure.

Jacob and Powers (2009) analyzed trends in state privilege laws (evidentiary and nondisclosure) and found that most states (75%) have broadened the scope of their laws governing patient–psychotherapist privilege with language that would likely include nondoctoral as well as doctoral school psychologists. In accordance with the NASP's code of ethics (I.2.2), school psychologists "recognize that client-school psychologist communications are privileged in most jurisdictions, and do not disclose information that would put the student or family at legal, social, or other risk if shared with third parties, except as permitted by the mental health provider–client privilege laws in their state." Practitioners thus have an ethical and legal obligation to be informed of the scope, language, and exemptions of privilege law in the state in which they work and to consult an attorney for advice when difficult situations arise.

Subpoenas and Court Orders

In the course of their professional careers, school psychologists may receive a subpoena or court order regarding a client's records. A *subpoena,* typically issued by the clerk of a court, is a command to produce certain documents or to appear at a certain time and place to give testimony. Attorneys use subpoenas to gather information relevant to a case. A subpoena differs from a *court order*, a legal document issued by a judge that compels the psychologist to appear in court or produce documents. Failure to comply with a court order can result in being held in contempt of court (see M. A. Fisher, 2013). Although subpoenas and court orders may appear legally threatening and may seem to demand an immediate response, school-employed practitioners are cautioned to remember that student education records belong to the school,[4] not the individual practitioner, and decisions regarding their release in response to a subpoena or court order is the responsibility of the school district's administration, not the individual practitioner. A school-employed practitioner who receives a subpoena or court order for student education records or is asked to testify in a legal proceeding regarding a student should forward such requests to the appropriate school administrative official.

FERPA identifies situations in which the school district may release student education records without the consent of the parent (or an eligible student) in response to a lawfully issued subpoena or court order. However, unless the disclosure is to comply with certain types of subpoenas or court orders, school districts generally "must make a reasonable effort to notify the parent or eligible student of the order or subpoena in advance of compliance, so that the parent or eligible student may seek protection action" (34 CFR § 99.31[a][9][ii]). The practitioner's private notes are not "student education records" under FERPA and may be protected by state privilege laws.

M. A. Fisher (2013) and the APA's Committee on Legal Issues (1996) provided information for private practitioners regarding how to respond to a subpoena or court order.

RECORD KEEPING IN THE SCHOOLS

In 1925, the National Education Association recommended that schools maintain health, guidance, and psychological records on each student so that information would be available about the "whole child" along with the academic record (Schimmel & Fischer, 1977). Although these records were made available to governmental agents, employers, and other nonschool personnel, they were to be closed to parents and students. In 1969, the Russell Sage Foundation (1970) convened a conference on the ethical and legal aspects of school record keeping, and many abuses of school records began to be identified:

- Public elementary and secondary school officials released student records to law enforcement agencies, creditors, prospective employers, and others without obtaining permission from parents or students.
- Parents and students typically had little knowledge of the contents of student records or how those records were used. Parent and student access to records usually was limited to attendance and achievement records.
- The secrecy with which the records were maintained made it difficult for parents or students to ascertain the accuracy of information contained in them. Because procedures for challenging the veracity of the information did not exist, an unverified allegation of misconduct could become part of a student's permanent record and be passed on—without the student's or parents' knowledge—to potential employers, law enforcement agencies, and other educational institutions.

---

[4]Psychological reports prepared by a school-employed practitioner are "works for hire" and belong to the school (U.S. Copyright Office, 2012).

- Few provisions existed for protecting school records from examination by unauthorized persons.
- Formal procedures for regulating access to records by nonschool personnel did not exist in most schools.

Family Educational Rights and Privacy Act

In 1974, FERPA was passed as an amendment to the Elementary and Secondary Education Act of 1965 (20 U.S.C. § 1232g; 34 CFR Part 99). This legislation specifically addresses the privacy of student records and access to those records. This summary of FERPA focuses on the law as it applies to elementary and secondary schools. The regulations cited here were downloaded from the *Electronic Code of Federal Regulations* on April 7, 2015, and were current as of that date.

Although FERPA was passed more than 40 years ago, interpretation of the law and its regulations continues to generate considerable confusion among teachers, school officials, and school psychologists. Furthermore, the original law was written prior to the introduction of digital management and storage of student education records. Today, some school systems maintain and manage student education records on a district server. Other districts may lease space from commercial services and store records on remote computers "in the cloud" (L. D. Armistead, 2014b). Cloud storage offers advantages, such as unlimited storage capacity and a reduced need for on-site computer hardware and its maintenance. However, electronic storage and management of student education records, whether on a district server or in the cloud, raises questions about the security of students' personally identifiable information (PII) and parent access to the records of their own child. The U.S. DOE allows third-party cloud storage of student education records as long as resulting practices are compliant with FERPA regulations (see U.S. DOE, 2008; 2011a). Some of the potential risks and benefits of digital storage of PII will be identified in the remaining portions of the chapter.

In the text that follows, FERPA is discussed under these five subheadings: (1) Education Records Defined, (2) Right to Inspect and Review Records, (3) Right to Confidentiality of Records, (4) Right to Request Amendment of Records, and (5) Complaints. IDEIA also has requirements for safeguarding the confidentiality of the education records of children with disabilities and ensuring parent access to those records. The summary here focuses on FERPA with reference to IDEIA requirements where they are more extensive. In addition to knowledge of federal law, school psychology practitioners need to be familiar with their state's laws regarding student records.

Education Records Defined

Under FERPA, *education records* are defined as any records maintained by the schools (or contractors, consultants, or other parties to whom a school has outsourced school services or functions) that are directly related to the student. A *record* means any information recorded in any way (34 CFR §§ 99.3, 99.35). At the elementary and secondary levels, the term *education record* typically includes student education records maintained by the school nurse, school psychologist, and special education student records (U.S. Department of Health and Human Services [U.S. HHS] & U.S. DOE, 2008).

However, there are a number of different types of records maintained by schools that are explicitly excluded from the definition of *education records* under FERPA. For example, FERPA excludes records maintained by a school-based law enforcement unit for the purpose of law enforcement and records of employees who are not also students. In the case of an eligible student (one who is 18 or attending a postsecondary institution), the term *education record* does not apply to records made or maintained by a physician, psychiatrist, psychologist, or paraprofessional in connection with treatment of the student and disclosed only to those providing the treatment, unless that treatment is in the form of remedial education or is a part of the instructional program. The term *education record* also excludes grades on papers corrected by classmates before they are collected and recorded by a teacher (see *Owasso Independent School District v Falvo*, 2002).

The Act also excludes *directory information* from its definition of *education record*. Directory information is "information contained in an education record of a student that would not generally be considered harmful or an invasion of privacy if disclosed" (34 CFR § 99.3). This category includes information such as name, address, telephone number, electronic mail address, activities and sports participation, and degrees and awards received. As long as the school informs parents or eligible students about the types of directory information they maintain, and gives them an opportunity to object to the release of this information, the school may freely release such information (34 CFR § 99.3).

The definition of *education record* under FERPA also does not include *sole possession records*, which are described as follows: "Records that are kept in the sole possession of the maker, are used only as a personal memory aid, and are not accessible or revealed to any other person except a temporary substitute for the maker of the record" (34 CFR § 99.3). In its comments regarding "sole possession records," "personal notes," or "private notes," made in 2000, the U.S. DOE stated:

> The main purpose of this exception to the definition of "educational records" is to allow school officials to keep personal notes private. For example, a teacher or a counselor who observes a student and takes a note to remind himself or herself of the student's behavior has created a sole possession record, so long as he or she does not share the note with anyone else. (U.S. DOE, July 6, 2000, p. 41856)

Under FERPA, it is permissible for school psychologists to keep personal notes about their contacts with students, parents, or other recipients of service (Martin, 1979). Private notes are to jog the memory and include *information that is to be kept absolutely confidential*. Parents do not have a right under FERPA to access private notes. If a practitioner believes that it is necessary to keep notes regarding confidential client disclosures, such information should be recorded in the school psychologist's private notes and not shared with anyone, be kept separately from student education records and in a secure file not accessible to anyone but the psychologist, and be destroyed as soon as the information is no longer needed.

Pearl (Case 3.7) may want to make private notes regarding her promise to help Mrs. Rupert locate an appropriate counselor and to remind herself to follow up with Mrs. Rupert in several weeks. Mrs. Rupert's disclosure should not be shared with anyone (also see NASP-PPE I.2.2).

Case 3.7

Dillon Rupert, a fourth grader, has always tested the patience of his teachers with his classroom antics. This year, however, his attention-seeking behavior appears to be spiraling out of control. Before planning a behavioral intervention with Dillon's teacher, Pearl Meadows meets with Mrs. Rupert, a divorced single mother who has sole custody of her three young boys. In her meeting with Pearl, Mrs. Rupert discloses that she is feeling overwhelmed by the pressures of her job and parenting, and confides that on occasion she has had four or five alcoholic drinks after the children are in bed at night. She is worried about Dillon's behavior at school and home and her own drinking habits. Mrs. Rupert asks Pearl to help her locate a counselor for herself and other sources of support.

In contrast, because parents must have access to the data that forms the basis of educational decisions regarding their child, information that the psychologist discloses or makes available to others in the school setting should be placed in the student's education record (Martin, 1979; also see *Parents Against Abuse in Schools v. Williamsport Area School District*, 1991). As noted previously, information included in the student's school psychological file or other education record as defined by FERPA cannot be considered privileged because it is accessible to parties outside of an established school psychologist–client professional relationship (see Case 3.6, *J.N. v. Bellingham School District No. 501*, 1994). Also, as discussed under "Parental Access to Test Protocols" (later in this chapter), test data and a student's answers recorded on test protocols are not considered to fall within the category of private notes.

School psychologists who keep private notes need to be aware that a psychologist's personal notes can be subpoenaed. In a court of law, the problem reverts to one of privilege. Let us suppose that, several months after their meeting, Mrs. Rupert's former husband attempts to have Pearl's private notes subpoenaed as part of a child custody suit. If Pearl has shared information from her private notes with anyone, she can no longer claim that the notes are privileged, and it would be difficult to prevent their disclosure in a legal proceeding.

Right to Inspect and Review Records

FERPA was developed to ensure appropriate access to school education records by parents or eligible students. *Parent* is defined as a parent of a student and includes "a natural parent, a guardian, or an individual acting as a parent in the absence of a parent or guardian" (34 CFR § 99.3). Parental separation, divorce, and custody do not affect the right to inspect records, unless a court order or legally binding document specifically revokes parental right to access records (34 CFR § 99.4). In the absence of an official legal notification to the contrary, school personnel may assume that a noncustodial parent has access to the records of his or her child (see *Fay v. South Colonie Central School District*, 1986).

In secondary schools, an *eligible student* is a student who is 18 years of age or older. When a student reaches the age of 18, the rights of the parent transfer to the student (34 CFR § 99.5). Parents maintain the right to inspect and review the files of a high school student age 18 or older, however, as long as the student is a dependent as defined by federal tax law (34 CFR § 99.31[a][8]). At age 18, a student may have psychological treatment records that are under his or her own control and not accessible to parents, but only if his or her treatment is not part of the school's instructional program for the student (34 CFR § 99.3[b][4]).

Under FERPA, schools must provide annual notice to parents and eligible students of their right to inspect, review, and request amendments of the student's education records (34 CFR § 99.7). Schools receiving funds under the Every Student Succeeds Act of 2015 (ESSA, Pub. L. No. 114-95) are required to notify parents if PII will be shared with individuals other than school officials in charge of educating students, such as when student information is outsourced to a third party provider for data management or analysis (Sec. 8037 of the Elementary and Secondary Education Act of 1965 as amended by Sec. 8545 of ESSA). In addition, IDEIA requires that parents of children with disabilities be provided, on request, a list of the types and locations of education records collected, maintained, or used by the education agency (34 CFR § 300.616).

When parents or eligible students make a request to inspect records, FERPA requires the school to comply with the request for access to records "within a reasonable period of time, but in no case more than 45 days after it has received the request" (34 CFR § 99.10[b]). The school must respond to "reasonable requests for explanations and interpretations of the records" (34 CFR § 99.10[c]). Also, if "circumstances effectively prevent the parent or eligible student from exercising the right to inspect and review the student's education records," the school must "provide the parent or eligible student a copy of the records requested" or make "other arrangements" for them to review and inspect the records (34 CFR § 99.3[d]). The school may charge a fee for copies unless the fee effectively prevents parents or eligible students from exercising their right to inspect records (34 CFR § 99.11). The school may not destroy any records if there is an outstanding request to review them (34 CFR § 99.10[e]).

Digital storage and management of education records potentially can improve parent access to the student education records of their own child, particularly for a parent who resides at a location distant from the school. With today's technology, it is possible to create a parent "log in" portal so that parents can access their child's digitally stored school records from any location. Such programs also can provide parent access to their child's special education records. In addition, digital storage is likely to facilitate the quick transfer of a student's education records when he or she enrolls at a new school. Furthermore, because third-party service providers typically have redundant backup systems for the information they store, cloud storage may decrease the likelihood of the loss of student education records in the event of a disaster such as hurricane Katrina (Devereaux & Gottlieb, 2012).

Right to Confidentiality of Records

FERPA was designed in part to protect the informational privacy rights of students and their parents. The school may not disclose PII from student education records without the informed consent of the parent or eligible student, except for disclosures specifically authorized by FERPA. *Disclosure* means permitting access to, or the release, transfer, or other communication of personally identifiable information by any means, including oral, written, or electronic (34 CFR § 99.3[c]). Information in an education record is considered to be *personally identifiable* if it includes or is linkable to direct personal identifiers, such as student name or Social Security number, or indirect identifiers, such as mother's maiden name, that alone or in combination would allow identification of the individual student (see 34 CFR 99.3).

When student education records are disclosed to specific persons or agencies at the request of the parent or an eligible student, the school must obtain the signed and written consent of the parent or eligible student. Electronic signatures are permitted. The written consent must specify the records to be disclosed, state the purpose of the disclosure, and identify the party to whom the disclosure may be made (34 CFR § 99.30).

Certain disclosures of education records are authorized by FERPA and do not require the permission of the parent or eligible student. Schools may disclose information from education records without consent to school officials, including teachers, who have been determined to have *legitimate educational interests* in the information. *Legitimate educational interest* means the school official "needs to review an education record in order to fulfill his or her professional responsibility" (U.S. DOE, 2011b, p. 75654). It is important to recognize that, although FERPA permits disclosure of information from student school psychological education records to teachers without the consent of the parent or eligible student, school psychologists are ethically obligated to release student information to others in the school setting only on a need-to-know basis (NASP-PPE I.2.5, II.4.5).

FERPA allows schools to outsource record-keeping functions to an external agency without parent consent if certain contractual conditions are met. The regulations also permit schools to disclose information from education records without parent consent (or the consent of an eligible student) to certain parties under specific circumstances, such as:

- Appropriate officials in cases of health and safety emergencies (34 CFR § 99.36)
- Specified officials for audit and evaluation purposes (34 CFR § 99.35)
- Organizations conducting studies for or on behalf of educational agencies or institutions to develop, validate, or administer predictive tests; or improve instruction (34 CFR § 99.31[a][6] (see Chapters 6, 7, and Chapter 10)
- Parties conducting research using de-identified student information (34 CFR § 99.31[b])
- Other schools to which a student is transferring or intending to enroll (34 CFR § 99.31[a][2])
- State and local authorities within a juvenile justice system in accordance with state law (34 CFR § 99.31[a][5], § 99.38)
- Subpoena or court order (34 CFR § 99.31[a][9]) (see "Subpoenas and Court Orders" earlier in this chapter)

Although FERPA regulations generally permit these types of disclosures without parent consent (or the consent of an eligible student), the reader should consult the cited regulations for detailed guidance. Furthermore, as noted, ESSA requires parent notice when PII is shared or outsourced to parties other than school officials in charge of educating students.

FERPA regulations also require schools to maintain a list of the names of educational and other authorities who may access education records without parent consent and maintain a record of each request for access to, and each disclosure of, personally identifiable information from the education records of each student (see 34 CFR § 99.32; also §§ 99.34–99.39). In addition, IDEIA requires each educational agency to identify one official responsible for ensuring the confidentiality of PII for students with disabilities (34 CFR § 300.623). With digital storage of student education records, a school official or the third-party cloud provider can easily generate records of the persons who accessed each individual student education record and the date and time the records were accessed (Devereaux & Gottlieb, 2012).

Right to Request Amendment of Records

A parent or eligible student has three bases for requesting an amendment to records: that the information (1) is inaccurate, (2) is misleading, or (3) violates the privacy or other rights of the student. The school then may agree and so amend the record, or disagree and so advise the parent or eligible student and inform the parent or student of their right to a hearing on the matter (34 CFR §§ 99.20–99.21).

The hearing is to be conducted by an individual who has no direct interest in the outcome, but it may be an official of the school. The parent or eligible student may present any evidence he or she chooses and be represented by any individual he or she chooses. The school then makes a decision about whether to amend the record and must present written findings related to its decision. If the school agrees with the parent or student, the record is then amended. If it disagrees, the parent or student may then place in the file a statement commenting on the record (34 CFR §§ 99.21–99.22).

Complaints

Persons may file complaints about violations of FERPA with the Family Policy Compliance Office, U.S. DOE. Complaints are investigated by the Family Policy Compliance Office, and the DOE may terminate federal funds to schools that do not comply with FERPA within a specified time period (34 CFR § 99.63). Prior to 2002, some federal courts allowed parents to pursue Section 1983 lawsuits against school districts because of alleged FERPA violations. In 2002, however, the Supreme Court ruled that FERPA does not confer a personal right to enforcement under Section 1983 (*Gonzaga University v. John Doe*, 2002).

Summary

Schools must have a written policy consistent with FERPA regarding parent access to education records and confidentiality of records and provide annual notice to parents and eligible students of their right to inspect records.

Parental Access to Test Protocols

Two questions often arise with regard to school psychological records: (1) Do parents have the right to inspect and review their child's school psychological test protocols? And (2) is it ever ethically and legally permissible to make copies of test protocols for review by parents or by a mental health professional qualified to interpret psychological tests?

Right to Inspect and Review Protocols

The U.S. DOE Office of Special Education Programs and Office for Civil Rights (OCR) have responded to numerous inquiries from school personnel, parents, and attorneys regarding parent access to school psychological test protocols. Their responses to letters of inquiry and reports subsequent to complaints are published in the *Individuals with Disabilities Education Law Report* (IDELR). Reschly and Bersoff (1999) reviewed 115 interpretations of the issue of parent access to test protocols that appeared in the IDELR and concluded that it is "unequivocal" that a student's psychological test protocol on which the child's answers were recorded is part of the student's education record under FERPA and IDEA. In the Analysis of Comments and Changes section of the 1999 IDEA regulations (U.S. DOE, 1999) and in more recent responses to letters of inquiry (Guard, 2007; Rooker, 2008), the U.S. DOE again reiterated its long-standing policy that the form on which an individual student's answers are recorded is an education record as defined by FERPA. Thus, parents have a legal right to inspect and review their child's responses recorded on a school psychological test protocol. Protocols cannot be considered private notes. (Also see *John K. and Mary K. v. Board of Education for School District #65, Cook County*, 1987; *Newport-Mesa Unified School District v. State of California Department of Education*, 2005).

Is it permissible for schools to simply destroy school psychological test protocols so as to avoid allowing parents to review their child's answers written on those protocols? Schools are cautioned against destroying protocols from individually administered psychological or educational tests if such actions could deny parents their legal right to access to information used in educational decision making about their child (Reschly & Bersoff, 1999; Rosenfeld, 2010; also see Rooker, 2005, 2008). IDEIA requires that the information obtained from evaluation sources is documented (34 CFR § 300.306 [c][ii]). In McKinney Independent School District Texas State Educational Agency (2010), a special education hearing officer required a school district to pay for an independent educational evaluation of a child because the district did not have the test protocols from its own evaluation of the child. In *Woods v. Northport Public Schools* (2012), the school's failure to provide a child's test protocols to a licensed psychologist as requested by the parents was determined to an IDEIA violation.

Although school-based psychologists must balance the obligation to protect test security (NASP-PPE II.5.1) against the parent's (or eligible student's) legal right to inspect answers on a test protocol, the parent's right to inspect education records is of paramount importance. The NASP's ethics code states: "School psychologists respect the right of parents to inspect, but not necessarily to copy, their child's answers to school psychological test questions, even if those answers are recorded on a test protocol" (II.4.4). However, practitioners may be able to avoid parent requests to inspect test protocols by establishing a good collaborative relationship early in the evaluation process, by explaining the conflict between their professional obligation to maintain test security and the parents' right to review their child's answers on test protocols, and by communicating assessment findings in a manner that satisfies the parents' need for information about their child. Providing handouts for parents that describe what a test measures with fictitious sample items may be helpful (e.g., Sattler, 2008, pp. 268–269).

If, nevertheless, parents do request to see their child's test protocols, parents should be encouraged to review protocols under the supervision of the school psychologist or other appropriately trained person (see *Newport-Mesa Unified School District v. State of California Department of Education*, 2005; Case 3.8). This review might include a discussion of sample questions and answers. Parents have a right to review the test questions "where the test booklet includes both the test questions and the student's written answers.... No exception under FERPA would permit the district to redact [to obscure or remove] the test questions from the test booklet" (Rooker, 2008, p. 1). However, school psychologists have no obligation under FERPA to disclose "nonidentifying information" to parents. Thus, it is appropriate to deny parent requests to inspect test materials (e.g., manuals and stimulus materials) that are not part of the child's individual performance record (Hehir, 1993).

Many states have adopted freedom of information laws to ensure that citizens have access to information regarding the activities of government and to safeguard against abuse of power by officials. Parents and others occasionally request access to test questions and answers under such laws. Tests used in academic settings typically are exempt from disclosure under freedom of information acts unless a court determines that public interest in disclosure outweighs public interest in nondisclosure. Practitioners need to consult their state laws on this matter, however.

Parent Request for Copies of Test Protocols

As Canter (2001a) observed, "One of the more controversial issues regarding release of school psychologists' records concerns the actual copying of test protocols for parents, other professionals or attorneys" (p. 30). Under FERPA, a school is not legally required to provide copies of a child's test protocols to parents except under the following unusual circumstances:

> If circumstances effectively prevent the parent or eligible student from exercising the right to inspect and review the student's education records, the educational agency or institution, or SEA [state educational agency] or its component, shall—
>
> (1) Provide the parent of eligible student with a copy of the records requested; or
>
> (2) Make other arrangements for the parent or eligible student to inspect and review the requested records. (34 CFR § 99.10)

Thus, a school must provide parents a copy of a student's education records, including a child's answers on school psychological test protocols, if the parent is unable to come into the school because of unusual circumstances, such as extended travel or serious illness, or must make other arrangements for the parent to review the requested records. Making a copy of a test protocol, rather than simply allowing parents to review it, raises additional ethical and legal concerns. Test publishers warn users that any reproduction of a test protocol without permission is a violation of copyright.

However, in 1999, Reschly and Bersoff suggested that providing a single copy of a used protocol probably would fall under the fair use provisions of copyright law (also Rosenfeld, 2010). The judge in a 2005 court ruling agreed (see Case 3.8). In *Newport-Mesa Unified School District v. State of California Department of Education,*

Case 3.8

In *Newport-Mesa Unified School District v. State of California Department of Education* (2005), a federal district court addressed the issue of parents' rights to copies of their child's test protocols under IDEIA and California state law. In this case, Mr. Anthony, a parent of a child with special education needs, requested copies of his child's test protocols to review before a scheduled individualized education program meeting. Section 56504 of California's Education Code allows parents of special education students to have copies of their child's test protocols. The district declined to provide Mr. Anthony with copies of the test protocols, however, citing its potential liability for copyright violations. Mr. Anthony subsequently filed a complaint with the California Department of Education (CDOE), and the CDOE subsequently ordered the school district to revise its policies regarding student records to comply with Section 56504. The school district brought the matter to a U.S. district court, contending that federal copyright law prevents it from providing copies of copyrighted test protocols to parents. The court invited Harcourt Assessment and Riverside Publishing, copyright holders of assessment instruments such as the Wechsler Intelligence Scale for Children IV (Wechsler, 2003), to intervene and assert a copyright interest. After a review of relevant case decisions and federal copyright law and weighing the competing interests involved, the court found that giving a copy of a copyrighted test protocol to the parents of special education students falls within the "fair use doctrine" of federal copyright law (17 U.S.C. § 107). Schools need to provide a copy of only those portions of the protocol that show the child's answers. Furthermore, "To minimize the risk of improper use, the District may choose to use appropriate safeguards, such as requiring a review by parents of the original test protocols before obtaining a copy, a written request for a copy, a nondisclosure of confidentiality agreement, or other reasonable measures" (p. 1179). It is important to note, however, that the court did not issue an opinion on whether the test publishing companies have a trade secret interest in the test protocols.

a federal district court found that giving a copy of the child's test protocol to the parent of a special education student falls within the "fair use doctrine" of federal copyright law. However, schools may implement safeguards, such as requiring a nondisclosure of test content agreement with parents.

In summary, one court has ruled that providing a copy of a child's answers on his or her test protocol to parents is not a violation of federal copyright law. At this time, however, there is no definitive answer regarding whether making copies of a used test protocol for parents might be viewed as a violation of the test publishers' trade secret (intellectual property) rights. Because there are many unanswered questions, it is important for school districts to have policies on parent access to test protocols that are consistent with evolving federal and state law and that are communicated to parents and school staff.

It also is important for school-based practitioners to recognize that it is *ethically permissible* (and good practice) to provide a copy of a student's test protocol to another professional who is qualified to interpret it (e.g., a psychologist in private practice), as long as consent to release the record has been obtained from the parents. Providing a protocol to another psychologist may allow parents to obtain a second opinion on their child's educational needs without additional testing. This parallels our right to have a second medical opinion without having to retake medical tests that were already done. Furthermore, because our primary concern is the welfare of the student, we must recognize that it is not appropriate to subject a child to retesting if parent concerns about the school's psychological evaluation might be resolved with an external review of existing data. Furthermore, a second assessment can result in less valid findings because the instruments used in the first evaluation should have been the best and most appropriate for the student, and retesting with the same instrument can result in a practice effect. Finally, the cost of retesting a student is likely to be significantly higher than simply having another psychologist review existing data. A second full and independent evaluation can be done if a review of existing records (including protocols) does not result in clear answers about the child's needs.

Privacy of Sensitive Health Information in Schools: New and Complex Challenges

The Health Insurance Portability and Accountability Act (HIPAA, Pub. L. No. 104-191) is a 1996 federal law created to protect the privacy and security of patient physical and mental health information and to ensure the efficient electronic exchange of patient information and health care claims. Psychologists who work in health care settings and private practice typically are required to comply with HIPAA. The HIPAA *Privacy Rule* requires procedures to effectively control access to and disclosure of "protected health information" (PHI) which is health information that can be linked to a specific individual. The *Security Rule* addresses standards for creation and maintenance of electronic private health records within a health care agency. The HIPAA *Administrative Simplification Rules for Transactions and Code Sets and Identifiers* assures secure and uniform electronic transmission of patient information, such as when Medicaid or other health insurance claims are made.

The U.S. HHS together with the U. S. DOE issued joint guidance on the intersection of FERPA and HIPAA:

> When a school provides health care to students in the normal course of business, such as through its health clinic, it is also a "health care provider" as defined by HIPAA. If the school also conducts any covered transactions electronically in connection with that health care, it is then a covered entity under HIPAA. As a covered entity, the school must comply with the HIPAA Administrative Simplification Rules for Transactions and Code Sets and Identifiers with respect to its transactions. However, many schools, even those that are HIPAA covered entities, are not required to comply with the HIPAA Privacy Rules because the only health records maintained by the school are "education records" or "treatment records" of eligible students under FERPA, both of which are excluded from coverage under the HIPAA Privacy Rule.... In addition, the exception for records covered by FERPA applies to ... the HIPAA Security Rule. (2008, p. 3)

The 2008 document prepared by the U.S. HSS and the U.S. DOE provides detailed discussion of the relationship between FERPA and HIPAA including implications of HIPAA for Medicaid billing, school-based health clinics, and contracted health services. Medicaid (along with the Patient Protection and Affordable Health Care Act of 2010, Pub. L. 111-148) allows states to reimburse schools for specific health and mental health services, and some states include school psychologists as qualified health care providers. Schools that electronically bill Medicaid for health care services provided by a school-employed school psychologist must, in compliance with FERPA, obtain parental consent in order to disclose information for Medicaid billing purposes, and comply with the HIPAA standards for electronically submitting health care claims (U.S. HHS & U.S. DOE, 2008, p. 4). The HIPAA-compliant billing functions are the responsibility of the school district, not the individual school-employed practitioner. Although a school district bills for health insurance reimbursement for services provided by an employee, a student's PII is protected by FERPA, not by HIPAA Security Rules and Privacy Rules, including student education records that are maintained electronically.

Most school psychologists are employed by a public school district (Curtis, Castillo, & Gelley, 2012) and generally they are required to comply with FERPA but not with HIPAA.[5] As noted previously, FERPA does not make a distinction between student health records and other types of student education records at the K–12 level. Because education records created or maintained by K–12 schools may include sensitive health information about a student, some states have experienced pressure for state legislation and district policies to better protect the privacy of physical and mental health information maintained by elementary and secondary schools. Furthermore, most parents have received information regarding their privacy rights under HIPAA during visits to health care providers, and now many have *a greater expectation of ownership and control of physical and mental health information about their children in the school setting.* For these reasons, district policies may be more

---

[5]If a private school is not subject to FERPA, the student education records are not exempt from HIPAA.

protective of the privacy of education records maintained by school physical and mental health professionals than of other school education records (see Schwab & Gelfman, 2005a; Schwab et al., 2005).

Also, in many states, penalties exist for unauthorized disclosure of certain types of student health status information by school personnel. Such laws often are located in the state's public health code. For example, in Michigan, with the exception of unusual circumstances, the unauthorized disclosure of information about a person with a serious communicable disease by school personnel is a felony punishable by a prison term of up to three years and a $5,000 fine or both (Public Act 488, § 5131[10]). However, these same state laws typically allow school personnel to contact public health departments for assistance without penalty (see Chapter 7).

Sensitive physical or mental health information might be received by a school psychologist in a report written by a physician or mental health provider that was released by the parents to the school; the information might be communicated orally by the parent or student (e.g., Case 1.1, in which the mother disclosed drug abuse during pregnancy); or a practitioner might uncover sensitive information as a result of the assessment process (e.g., Dr. Kim's mental health diagnosis of a somatic symptom disorder, Case 6.2). Although FERPA has specific requirements for the written consent of the parent (or eligible student) prior to disclosure of PII to external (nonschool) professionals and agencies, FERPA regulations provide little guidance regarding what, if any, sensitive student physical or mental health information to share with others who have "legitimate educational interests" in the student *within* the school setting (Schwab & Gelfman, 2005a).

Consistent with the need-to-know principle that appears in our codes of ethics (NASP-PPE I.2.5), Schwab and Gelfman (2005a) advised school-based physical and mental health professionals to disclose sensitive student health information to others within the school setting only "when necessary in order to benefit the student" and only as allowed by state law (p. 267). Information disclosure should focus on communicating the student's functional health, academic, and behavioral difficulties and how to respond. Furthermore, in keeping with recommended standards for the management of sensitive student health information in K–12 schools (see Exhibit 3.2), it is appropriate to have a certified or licensed school-based physical or mental health professional review, *in collaboration with the parent or eligible student*, any sensitive medical or mental health information received, to determine what information within those records should be disclosed, and to whom, in order to assist the student.

In summary, consistent with ethical obligations to respect family privacy and the need-to-know principle, school nurses, school psychologists, and other school health professionals should be allowed to serve as gatekeepers who, in partnership with parents or eligible students, control disclosure of sensitive information about students to others within the school setting. Exhibit 3.2 identifies guidelines for managing sensitive physical and mental health information. Digital storage of student physical and mental health records would allow schools to limit access to those records by allowing only parents and appropriate school professionals to access them electronically.

Exhibit 3.2   Protecting Confidential Student Health Information

School psychologists have both ethical and legal obligations to safeguard the confidentiality of sensitive student physical and mental health information. Eight guidelines follow.

1. "School psychologists recognize that it may be necessary to discuss confidentiality at multiple points in a professional relationship to ensure client understanding and agreement regarding how sensitive disclosures will be handled" (NASP-PPE I.2.3).

2. School-based practitioners advocate for school record-keeping policies that distinguish student physical and mental health information from other types of school education records and that give school psychologists the authority to control access to school psychological records (National Task Force on Confidential Student Health Information [National Task Force], 2000; Schwab et al., 2005).

3. Consistent with ethical obligations, school psychologists release student information internally only for professional purposes and only with persons who have a legitimate need to know (NASP-PPE I.2.5). When preparing school psychological evaluation reports for a multidisciplinary evaluation team, student assistance team, teachers, or other school staff, school psychologists focus on providing information that will be useful in determining the student's school-related needs, such as the information required for determining eligibility for special education, planning individualized instruction, and identifying recommended school services and accommodations (also see Schwab et al., 2005).

4. School psychologists advocate for district policies that *generally* require "written, informed consent from the parent and, when appropriate, the student, to release medical and psychiatric diagnoses to other school personnel" (National Task Force, 2000, Guideline V; also Schwab et al., 2005). School policies are consistent with state law regarding the disclosure of student health status information by school personnel (e.g., student is infected with a communicable disease).

5. School psychologists advocate for district policies and clear procedures for protecting confidentiality during the creation, storage, transfer, and destruction of electronic and paper student health and mental health records (see Schwab et al., 2005; National Task Force, 2000).

6. School psychologists advocate for the establishment of standard district-wide procedures "for requesting needed health information from outside sources and for releasing confidential health information, with parental consent, to outside agencies and individuals" (National

Task Force, 2000, Guideline VII). They recommend the district use HIPAA-compliant authorization forms when requesting health information from outside persons and agencies. Such forms should identify the names of the certified or licensed school staff (e.g., school nurse, school psychologist) who are being given permission to receive and use the health information. The forms also should identify the specific type of information requested, why the information has been requested, and how it will be used. As Schwab et al. (2005) noted, requesting a child's complete medical or mental health records is rarely appropriate.

7. School psychologists advocate for school districts to provide "regular, periodic training for all new staff, contracted service providers, substitute teachers, and school volunteers concerning the district's policies and procedures for protecting confidentiality" (National Task Force, 2000, Guideline VIII; also Schwab et al., 2005).

8. School psychology practitioners begin meetings to discuss the needs of an individual student with a brief review of the boundaries of the confidentiality of information to be shared during the meeting and ensure that such meetings are private and cannot be overheard by others.

Storage and Disposal of Psychological Records

Psychologists ethically are obligated to maintain records to document their professional work with sufficient detail to be useful in decision making by another professional (NASP-PPE II.4.2; also APA, 2007b; APA-EP 6.01). Furthermore, because school psychological records may be used in special education due process hearings or other legal proceedings, practitioners have a responsibility to maintain records "with sufficient detail to withstand scrutiny if challenged in a due process or other legal procedure" (NASP-PPE II.4.2; also APA, 2007b). However, practitioners respect privacy and do not seek or store sensitive information that is not needed in the provision of services (NASP-PPE I.2.2; also APA-EP Principle E, 4.04), and they include "only documented and relevant information from reliable sources" in their records (NASP-PPE II.4.3). School psychologists also are obligated to "discuss with parents and adult students their rights regarding creation, modification, storage, and disposal of psychological and educational records that result from the provision of services" (NASP-PPE II.4.1).

School psychologists have an ethical obligation to "safeguard the privacy of school psychological records and to ensure parent access to the records of their own children" (NASP-PPE II.4). Under federal special education law (IDEIA), schools must establish policies regarding the storage, retrieval, and disposal of education records, and parents of students with disabilities must be provided a summary of the school's record-keeping policies (34 CFR § 300.612[a][3]). The federal government provides little guidance, however, regarding how school education records should be stored to ensure compliance with FERPA and IDEIA. Thus, policies for the retention and destruction of student education records are largely a state matter. Some states have detailed policies for school record keeping; others only specify minimal requirements regarding the retention of records of attendance, grades, and graduation (Gelfman & Schwab, 2005b).

Physical copies of student test protocols often require a sizable amount of storage space. Is it legally and ethically permissible to scan student answers/responses that are recorded on test protocols and store them digitally? To the best of our knowledge, there is no authoritative guidance on this issue. Because of the legal uncertainties, seeking permission from the test publisher to scan and store student test protocols may be the best course of action. Ethically, school psychologists are obligated to protect test security and the privacy of the examinee's answers. Consequently, scanned protocols should be password-protected, under the control of the school psychologist, and not accessible to persons not qualified to administer and interpret psychological tests.

School-based practitioners occasionally receive reports from professionals or agencies outside the school setting that include sensitive information about a student or a student's family (e.g., information regarding marital problems or parent incarceration, sensitive private health information) that is not needed in the school setting. This may pose a dilemma for the practitioner who believes the report should not become part of the student's education record, yet it also includes information about the student that is helpful in addressing educational needs. A strategy for handling this dilemma is to return the report to the sender with a request that the sender delete any information that is not needed in the school setting (see Schwab et al., 2005, Standard 3).

How long should school psychological records be maintained? We are not aware of any federal guidance with regard to how long school psychological records should be maintained, except that the school may not destroy any records if an outstanding request to review them exists. Also, under IDEIA, schools must notify parents when student education records are no longer needed for providing special educational services, and, upon parent request, obsolete records must be destroyed (34 CFR § 300.624). A concern about cloud storage of student education records by a third-party service provider is ensuring that records are in fact destroyed at the request of the school (Devereaux & Gottlieb, 2012).

In the absence of laws controlling how long psychological records must be retained, the APA (2007b) suggests psychologists retain full records on adult clients until seven years after the last date of service and retain the records of minor clients for three years after the minor has reached the age of majority (the age at which an individual legally ceases to be a minor) in the state where the psychologist practices. The APA points out that decisions must be made on a case-by-case basis, however, after consideration of the risks associated with storage of outdated information and the possible benefits of having a record of the early manifestation of a disorder. Bernstein and Hartsell (1998) advised retaining records beyond the state statute of limitations for filing a lawsuit against the psychologist. The statute of limitations for filing a due process complaint under IDEIA is two years unless different explicit time limitations are identified in state law (34 CFR § 300.507[a][2]).

The NASP's code of ethics encourages school psychologists to work in collaboration with school administrators and other staff "to establish district policies regarding the storage and disposal of school psychological records that are consistent with law and sound professional practice" (NASP-PPE II.4.9; also Doll, Strein, Jacob, & Prasse, 2011; Exhibit 3.2). As Canter suggested (2001b), it may be desirable to specify different time lines for storage of different types of psychological records in the district's policies. She recommended that reports and summaries of psychological services be maintained "at least five years beyond the student's graduation or last day of enrollment, or until the date required by state law" (p. 19). If permitted under state law, test protocols and other raw data might be maintained for a shorter period. However, in our opinion, it is advisable to retain a student's test protocols until there is a pattern of relatively stable findings across multiple reevaluations, at which time protocols and other raw data from early evaluations might be destroyed. (See NASP-PPE II.4.9 for a list of recommended practices and policies regarding storage and disposal of school psychological records.)

Digital Record Keeping and Communication

The first portion of this section focuses on the ethical-legal issues associated with the use of digital technologies to manage *student education records* as defined by FERPA. The second portion of this section briefly addresses digital storage and communication of student information by individual practitioners.

District Cloud Storage of Student Education Records

The NASP's ethics code states: "School psychologists, in collaboration with administrators and other school staff, work to establish district policies regarding storage and disposal of school psychological records that are consistent with law and sound professional practice" (II.4.9). Maria (Case 3.9) has an obligation to advocate for district policies that "safeguard the security of school psychological records while facilitating appropriate parent access to those records" (II.4.9). After reading several authoritative sources, Maria learns that the district's proposed outsourcing of student education records is legally permissible under FERPA if certain conditions are met. Furthermore,

---

Case 3.9

The school district where Maria Delgado works has formed a committee to explore cloud management of student education records by a third-party service provider, and Maria has been invited to serve on the committee. The district plans to begin with cloud storage of student attendance records and grades and will provide a portal for parent access to those records. In the second phase of cloud management of education records, student special education records will be maintained in the cloud, including the school psychologist's assessment results that are part of a multidisciplinary team evaluation of a child with a suspected disability. Maria sets out to learn about the ethical-legal issues associated with cloud storage of student education records and recommended best practices.

when third-party contractors act as "school officials with legitimate educational interests," FERPA permits disclosure of records to them without parent consent (34 CFR
§ 99.31). However, ESSA requires schools to notify parents if student information is
outsourced to individuals other than school officials in charge of educating students.

After some additional research, Maria discovers that, in recent years, potential
problems associated with the release of PII by schools to third parties captured the
attention of the lawmakers and the media. However, most of the concern was triggered
by the use of third-party service providers to conduct *data analytic functions* for school
districts or state departments of education. *Data analytic services* are designed to
aggregate and analyze student data; report on performance trends; pinpoint areas for
district-wide performance improvement; and identify schools, teachers, and students
"in need of assistance" (Reidenberg et al., 2013, p. 17). Public concern focused on the
security of PII released for data analytic functions, the right of parents to access the
outsourced PII of their child, whether third parties would use PII in unauthorized
ways (e.g., to target students and their families for marketing purposes or for identity
theft), whether schools were collecting and releasing PII that was not needed for data
analytic functions, whether data were destroyed when no longer needed, and school
district "transparency" with parents regarding the release of PII to third parties.

Although her district is considering the use of a third-party service provider for a
different purpose, namely to manage student education records, Maria recognizes that
many of the expert recommendations for best practices in cloud-based data analytic
services are pertinent to her efforts to ensure legally and ethically acceptable district
student record-keeping policies. For example, district-wide policies regarding cloud
storage are needed and those policies and practices should be transparent to parents
(Reidenberg et al., 2013; U.S. DOE, 2011a). It is important for the district to select a
reputable and established third-party provider of cloud services, one that has a history
of success in handling sensitive private information (Devereaux & Gottlieb, 2012).
The district must also ensure that contracts between school districts and third-party
vendors are consistent with FERPA and IDEIA requirements, have adequate privacy
protection provisions, ensure parent access to the student education records of their
own child, and address the issue of destruction of outdated records (Reidenberg
et al., 2013). Although, generally, public schools are required to comply with FERPA
and not HIPAA, Maria will recommend that the district select a third-party vendor
that is in compliance with HIPAA "best practice" standards for data security and
privacy-protection training of its employees.

Maria will also recommend that, consistent with ESSA, the district policy includes
parent notification regarding cloud storage of student education records on the district's Web site and in their parent handbook. In addition, she will ensure that her colleagues are knowledgeable of the benefits and risks of cloud storage of PII and are able
to discuss them with parents at the outset of establishing a school psychologist–client
relationship. Furthermore, she will remind her colleagues to not include information
in school psychology multidisciplinary team reports that is not needed for eligibility
determination or other provision of school services and to seek parent permission prior
to including sensitive student or family information. Finally, she will encourage her district to assume a proactive stance by developing a planned response to any breach of
confidential student information.

Digital Storage and Communication by Individual Practitioners

School psychologists often serve multiple schools within a district or regional cooperative, making it necessary and efficient for them to use a personal cloud or portable device for managing case records and report writing. As an increasing number of districts likely have policies for digital management of student information, practitioners should consult their district policies regarding acceptable practices and keep abreast of literature on best practices in the use of new digital technologies. The NASP's code of ethics states: "To the extent that school psychological records are under their control, school psychologists protect electronic files from unauthorized release or modification (e.g., by using passwords and encryption), and they take reasonable steps to ensure that school psychological records are not lost due to equipment failure" (NASP-PPE II.4.7; also see APA-EP 6.01; Schwab et al., 2005, Standard 7). Practitioners also take steps to ensure that no one can recover confidential information from old or failed computers (or other hardware) after their disposal (NASP-PPE II.4.9). In addition, practitioners are ethically obligated to notify clients of the electronic storage and transmission of personally identifiable school psychological records and any known risks to privacy (NASP-PPE II.4.1; APA-EP 4.02c).

Practitioners are advised to password-protect documents that include PII or other confidential information when using laptops, a personal cloud storage system, and devices such as USB flash drives, memory cards, CDs, and DVDs (L. D. Armistead, 2014b). File encryption provides additional security. FERPA is silent on methods to safeguard digitally stored PII; HIPAA security rules require encryption or a reasonable equivalent alternative for protected patient health information (45 CFR § 164.312[a][2][iv] and [e][2][ii]). As a result, psychologists generally consider the use of both passwords and file encryption to be "best practice" for the protection of sensitive confidential information (Devereaux & Gottlieb, 2012).

As L. D. Armistead (2014b) observed, "It is difficult to imagine practicing school psychology today without e-mail, file-attachments, and text services" (p. 464). These modes of communication with colleagues, parents, and others are quick and inexpensive. However, it is important for practitioners to consult and respect their district policies regarding use of electronic communication. If a practitioner wishes to communicate with parents or other clients using e-mail, it is appropriate to seek their permission to do so at the outset of offering services. E-mails are not confidential. For that reason, if e-mail is used to send PII about a student or his or her family within the district or in communication with parents, the information should not be included in the text of the e-mail itself but attached as a password-protected file.

Do e-mails that contain PII about a student fall within the meaning of *student education records* as defined by FERPA? The court's opinion in *S.A. v. Tulare County Office of Education* (2009) suggested that only e-mails that are filed and maintained in a child's student education record, either as a paper copy or in a digital format, meet the FERPA definition of *student education record*. The *S.A. v. Tulare County Office of Education* decision was based on *Owasso Independent School District v. Falvo* (2002), a U.S. Supreme Court ruling that held that peer-grading of classwork does not violate FERPA because the grades on students' classwork are not *student education records* until the teacher has entered them into the gradebook. School district administrators are likely pleased with the reluctance of the courts to rule that e-mails that contain PII are *student education records*. If all e-mail and other digital communications that contain PII were considered to be *education records* under FERPA, then parents would have the right to request and review all digital communications by school staff that include PII about their child. Such requests would likely place a time-consuming, challenging, and costly burden on schools.

As part of district-wide notice regarding its record-keeping policies, parents should be informed that e-mails are not generally considered *student education records* under FERPA unless the e-mail is subsequently filed in their child's education records. If parents send an e-mail with information that typically would be included in a student's school records, it seems advisable to file and maintain the e-mail as if it were a letter or fax from the parents, particularly if the communication involves the exercise of parental rights under IDEIA or another law.

CONCLUDING COMMENTS

In light of the ethical-legal issues of privacy, confidentiality, and school record keeping, Eades's (1986) recommendation continues to be helpful: School psychologists need to ensure that the statements they make orally or in writing are necessary, permitted, and required as a part of their employment and their professional responsibility to their clients.

STUDY AND DISCUSSION

Questions for Chapter 3

1. What is *privacy*?
2. Do schoolchildren have a legal right to privacy in the public schools?
3. The chapter states, "Codes of ethics and law thus show agreement that ... informed consent should be obtained to establish a school psychologist–client relationship." What does *informed consent* mean?
4. Under what circumstances is it ethically permissible to provide psychological services to a child without his or her explicit assent for services?
5. What does *confidentiality* mean? Identify three situations in which the school psychologist is obligated to share student disclosures with others.
6. What is the *need-to-know* principle?
7. What is *privileged communication*? Who has the right to waive privilege in a legal proceeding?
8. Briefly discuss school responsibilities under FERPA with regard to: (a) ensuring parent access to student's records, (b) safeguarding the privacy of student's records, and (c) affording parents opportunities to ensure the accuracy of records.

Discussion

In this chapter, we recommended that school psychology practitioners encourage a child's participation in treatment decisions to the maximum extent appropriate to the child and the situation. This statement reflects our belief that children are individuals who should be given choices when feasible. This valuing of autonomy, choice, and independence has its foundation in Anglo-European culture and American psychology. In contrast, in many other cultures, children are seen as an extension of the parent; they are expected to obey authority, and they are not offered choices to make on their own (Lynch & Hanson, 2011). Discuss how contrasting beliefs about allowing a child to participate in decisions might affect psychologist–parent communication and collaboration when working with families from culturally diverse backgrounds (see Lynch & Hanson, 2011).

Vignettes

1. Reread Case 3.9. Maria seeks to inform her school psychology colleagues about the ethical-legal issues associated with third-party cloud storage of student special education records. What potential benefits of cloud storage in meeting FERPA obligations were identified in this chapter? What are the potential risks? Can you think of additional risks and benefits?

2. David Kim, a school psychology doctoral intern, is interested in using personal cloud storage for the school psychology reports he is preparing in his role as intern. As noted in the chapter, David's first step is to consult his on-site supervisor to ask about their school district policies regarding personal cloud storage of personally identifiable student information. His second step is to consult with his university supervisor. If he is given permission to store reports in a personal cloud, what steps should David take to safeguard the confidentiality of the reports he is preparing?

3. Pearl Meadows, a school psychologist, began an assessment of Melanie as part of the initial evaluation to determine whether she is eligible for special education under IDEIA. Before Pearl completed her evaluation, Melanie's mother, Francine, who is in the army, was deployed overseas. Melanie is now living with her grandmother while Francine is completing her tour of duty.

   Francine has requested via e-mail that Pearl send her a copy of the school psychological assessment report on Melanie as an e-mail attachment. She has also requested that IQ and other test protocols showing Melanie's answers be scanned and sent to her as e-mail attachments so that she can review all of the evaluation findings and documentation before the team meeting to discuss her daughter's eligibility for special education. Because Francine has a right to participate in the special education team meeting to determine Melanie's eligibility under IDEIA, she has asked to do so via video-conferencing (e.g., Skype). How should Pearl respond? Based on the information provided in this chapter, what are the ethical and legal issues associated with this situation?

4. As a result of Carrie Johnson's assessment and other information gathered by the school's multidisciplinary team, the school has recommended, in the team meeting with his parents, that John Malamo be classified as cognitively impaired. John's father, furious with Carrie and the school, has made an appointment with Carrie to review the results of the school psychological evaluation in more detail. When he appears for his appointment, Mr. Malamo demands copies of all information in John's psychological file, including the Wechsler Intelligence Scale for Children V (Wechsler, 2014) test protocol, so that he can seek an independent opinion about John's needs from a psychologist in private practice. How should Carrie handle this situation?

Chapter 4 —————————————————————————————————

ETHICAL-LEGAL ISSUES IN THE EDUCATION OF STUDENTS WITH DISABILITIES UNDER IDEIA

Education law is one thing; educational action is quite another. Between the two events, the passing of a law and the behavior of the school, must occur a chain of intermediate events: the interpretation of the law in terms of practice; the study of the feasibility of the interpretation; the successive adjustments, reorganizations, retrainings, and redesign of administrative procedures; the self-monitoring and reporting—the reality testing. (Page, 1980, p. 423)

This chapter provides a summary of law pertinent to providing services to children with disabilities. It focuses on the Individuals with Disabilities Education Improvement Act of 2004 (IDEIA). Special education services for children with disabilities ages 3 through 21 are discussed first in some detail (IDEIA—Part B). This is followed by a summary of the federal legislation that provides funds for early intervention services for infants and toddlers with disabilities (IDEIA—Part C).

EDUCATION OF CHILDREN WITH DISABILITIES: A HISTORICAL PERSPECTIVE

It is important for school psychology practitioners to have some knowledge of the history of IDEIA to appreciate fully the meaning of current law. In the text that follows, we have summarized case law and early legislation that foreshadowed the most important special education law, the Education for All Handicapped Children Act of 1975 (Pub. L. No. 94-142), later replaced by the Individuals with Disabilities Education Act of 1990 (IDEA).

Right-to-Education Case Law

As discussed in Chapter 2, no fundamental right to an education is mentioned in the U.S. Constitution. Public education is an entitlement granted to citizens of a state under state law. However, on the basis of state laws, all children within a state have a legitimate claim to an education at public expense. In legal terms, education is a property right protected by the 14th Amendment of the Constitution, which provides that no state shall "deny to any person within its jurisdiction the equal protection of the laws."

For many years, children with disabilities, particularly those with severe or multiple impairments, were routinely excluded from a public education. School districts typically had policies that required a child to meet certain admissions standards (e.g., toilet trained, ambulatory, mental age of at least 5 years) before they were allowed to enter school. One of the responsibilities of many school psychologists prior to 1975 was to evaluate children to certify that they were not eligible to attend public school and, therefore, were excused from school attendance. Children who were behavior problems in the classroom or simply too difficult to teach were often expelled from school.

Few options existed for the parents of children who did not qualify to attend public school. Institutionalization was the recommended treatment for children with disabilities prior to the 1960s. Affluent families often placed their children in private schools. Others kept their children at home.

In the 1960s, following successful court challenges to racial discrimination in the public schools (e.g., *Brown v. Board of Education*, 1954), parents of children with disabilities began to file lawsuits against public school districts, alleging that the equal protection clause of the 14th Amendment prohibits states from denying school access to children because of their disabilities. Two landmark court cases, *Pennsylvania Association for Retarded Children (P.A.R.C.) v. Commonwealth of Pennsylvania* (1971, 1972) and *Mills v. Board of Education of District of Columbia* (1972), marked a turning point in the education of children with disabilities and gave impetus to the development of federal legislation ensuring a free and appropriate education for all children with disabilities.

Pennsylvania Association for Retarded Children (P.A.R.C.) v. Commonwealth of Pennsylvania

In *P.A.R.C.* (1972), parents of children with mental retardation[1] brought suit against the state of Pennsylvania in federal court because their children were denied access to public education. In a consent decree (where parties involved in a lawsuit consent to a court-approved agreement), parents won access to public school programs for children with mental retardation, and the court ordered comprehensive changes in policy and practices regarding the education of children with mental retardation within the state. The consent decree in *P.A.R.C.* marked the beginning of a redefinition of education in this country, broadened beyond the "three Rs" to include training of children with disabilities toward self-sufficiency (Martin, 1979). The consent decree in *P.A.R.C.* (1971) stated:

> Expert testimony in this action indicates that all mentally retarded persons are capable of benefiting from a program of education and training; that the greatest number of retarded persons, given such education and training, are capable of achieving self-sufficiency, and

---

[1]In 2010, with the passage of Rosa's Law (Pub. L. No. 111-256), the term *mental retardation* was replaced with *an intellectual disability* in federal health and education law. As of April 2015, the term *mental retardation* had not been changed to *intellectual disability* in the federal regulations implementing IDEIA. In this chapter, we use the term *mental retardation* when historically accurate and *intellectual disability* when discussing contemporary law.

the remaining few, with such education and training, are capable of achieving some degree of self-care; that the earlier such education and training begins, the more thoroughly and the more efficiently a mentally retarded person can benefit at any point in his life and development from a program of education and training. (p. 1259)

The *P.A.R.C.* case is particularly important because it foreshadowed and shaped subsequent federal laws regarding schools' responsibilities in educating children with disabilities. The state of Pennsylvania was required to locate and identify all school-age persons excluded from the public schools, to place all children in a "free program of education and training appropriate to the child's capacity" (1971, p. 1258), to provide home-bound instruction if appropriate, and to allow tuition grants for children who needed alternative school placements. The *P.A.R.C.* consent decree also required parent notice before children were assigned to special education classes and an opportunity for an impartial hearing if parents were unsatisfied with the placement recommendation for their child.

Mills

Mills (1972) was a lawsuit filed on behalf of seven children with behavioral, emotional, and learning impairments in the District of Columbia.[2] The court order in *Mills* reiterated many of the requirements of *P.A.R.C.,* and a number of additional school responsibilities in educating children with disabilities were identified. The decision required the schools to "provide each handicapped child of school age a free and suitable publicly supported education regardless of the degree of the child's mental, physical or emotional disability or impairment" (p. 878). The decision also required the schools to prepare a proposal outlining a suitable educational program for each child with a disability, and set limits on the use of disciplinary suspensions and expulsions of children with disabilities.

Following the successful resolution of *P.A.R.C.* and *Mills,* right-to-education cases were soon filed in 27 jurisdictions (Martin, 1979). These cases signaled to Congress that a need existed for federal laws to ensure educational opportunities for all children with disabilities.

Early Legislation

Congress's attempts to address the needs of students with disabilities took two routes: the passage of antidiscrimination legislation and the amendment of federal education laws (Martin, 1979). One of the first bills that attempted to ensure equal educational opportunity for children with "handicaps"[3] in the public schools was an amendment to Title VI of the Civil Rights Act of 1964. The bill later became Section 504 of the Rehabilitation Act of 1973, civil rights legislation that prohibits discrimination against students with handicaps in school systems receiving federal financial assistance. School

---

[2]The suit was initially resolved by a consent decree in 1972. However, the District of Columbia Board of Education failed to comply with the consent decree, and the suit ultimately resulted in a contempt of court judgment against the school board.

[3]*Handicap*, rather than *disability*, is used when historically accurate.

responsibilities under Section 504 to students with physical or mental impairments are discussed in Chapter 5.

In addition to antidiscrimination legislation, Congress attempted to meet the needs of students with disabilities by amending federal education laws. In 1966, Congress amended the Elementary and Secondary Education Act of 1965 (Pub. L. No. 89-750) to provide grants to states to assist them in developing and improving programs to educate children with disabilities. In 1970, Congress repealed the 1966 law but established a similar grant program to encourage states to develop special education resources and personnel (Pub. L. No. 91-230; H. R. Turnbull & Turnbull, 2000). Four years later, Congress passed the Education Amendments of 1974 (Pub. L. No. 93-380), which increased aid to states for special education and served to put the schools on notice that federal financial assistance for special education would be contingent on the development of state plans with "a goal of ... full educational opportunities to all handicapped children." Congress intended that this interim legislation would encourage states to begin a period of comprehensive planning and program development to meet the needs of students with disabilities. The Education Amendments of 1974 are primarily of historical interest now, except for Section 513, the Family Educational Rights and Privacy Act (Martin, 1979).

INDIVIDUALS WITH DISABILITIES EDUCATION IMPROVEMENT ACT

The most important federal statute concerning the education of children with disabilities is the Education for All Handicapped Children Act of 1975 (Pub. L. No. 94-142). This legislation was introduced as a Senate bill in 1972. A Senate subcommittee on the handicapped held extensive hearings on the proposed legislation. The witnesses (numbering more than 100) included teachers, parents, education associations, parent organizations, and legislators (Martin, 1979). Their testimony made it increasingly evident that more clear-cut federal incentives were needed to assure educational opportunities for children with disabilities. As of 1975, it was estimated that there were more than eight million children with handicaps in the United States. More than half were not receiving an appropriate education, and one million were excluded from public education entirely (Pub. L. No. 94-142, § 601[b]).

The purpose of the Education of All Handicapped Children Act of 1975 was to assure that all handicapped children have available to them:

> a free appropriate education which emphasizes special education and related services designed to meet their unique needs; to assure that the rights of handicapped children and their parents or guardians are protected; to assist States and localities to provide for the education of all handicapped children; and to assess and assure the effectiveness of efforts to educate handicapped children. (Pub. L. No. 94-142, § 601[c])

The Education for the Handicapped Act Amendments of 1990 (Pub. L. No. 101-476) changed the name of the Education for All Handicapped Children Act to the Individuals with Disabilities Education Act (IDEA). Throughout the law, the term *handicap* was replaced by *disability*. Seven years later, the Individuals with Disabilities Education Act Amendments of 1997 was signed into law (Pub. L. No. 105-17). The 1997 amendments focused on improving educational outcomes for students with disabilities.

The Individuals with Disabilities Education Improvement Act was passed in 2004 (Pub. L. No. 108-446). Although, technically, the correct abbreviation for Pub. L. No. 108-446 is *IDEIA*, readers should know that the 2004 law continues to be referred to as *IDEA* at government Web sites and in the literature. This set of amendments to the IDEA was based on congressional findings that education of children with disabilities can be made more effective by having high achievement expectations; ensuring access to the general education curriculum; making special education a service rather than a place; and providing funds for evidence-based early reading programs, positive behavioral interventions, and early intervening services. The authors of the 2004 amendments also recognized that the increasing diversity of the nation's population requires greater responsiveness to the needs of culturally and linguistically diverse schoolchildren (Pub. L. No. 108-446, § 682[c]).

IDEIA provides funds to state and local educational agencies that provide a free and appropriate education to children with disabilities in conformance with the requirements of the law. The law has four parts: Part A, General Provisions; Part B, Assistance for Education of All Children with Disabilities; Part C, Infants and Toddlers with Disabilities; and Part D, National Activities to Improve Education of Children with Disabilities. IDEIA—Part B refers to special education legislation that provides funds for services to children with disabilities ages 3 through 21. IDEIA—Part C provides funds for early intervention services for infants and toddlers and is discussed later in this chapter.

It is important to recognize that IDEIA is not a fully funded federal statute; it funds only a modest portion of the extra expenses schools incur in providing special education to students with disabilities. The 2004 amendments allowed each state to receive 40% of the average per-pupil expenditure in public elementary and secondary schools multiplied by the number of children ages 3 to 21 with disabilities in the state who receive special education and related services (Pub. L. No. 108-446, § 611[a]). However, there is no guarantee that Congress will make these funds available. For example, the final funding for federal year 2014 fell far short of the 40% per-pupil funding allowed under IDEIA and was at about 16% of the estimated excess cost of educating students with disabilities (New America Foundation, 2015).

Under IDEIA, states may set aside up to 10% of their monies for a "high-cost" fund. This account can be used to reimburse districts when the cost of providing special education and related services to a high-need child with a disability is greater than three times the average pupil expenditure (34 CFR § 300.704). School districts also are allowed to allocate up to 15% of their federal funds to develop and implement coordinated early intervening services (34 CFR § 300.226).

Rules and regulations implementing IDEIA are developed by the U.S. Department of Education (DOE) and are revised following changes in the law. The Part B and Part C regulations are codified at Title 34 of the Code of Federal Regulations (34 CFR Parts 300 and 303, respectively). The Part B final regulations implementing IDEIA were published in 2006. Final regulations for Part C were published in 2011.

The Electronic Code of Federal Regulations (e-CFR), updated as of April 30, 2015, was used to prepare this chapter. To ensure accuracy, we used the verbatim wording of the regulations where feasible. However, for readability, we omitted cross-references to other sections of the regulations and subsection designators and, for brevity and clarity, at times modified the original wording. Interested readers are encouraged to consult the e-CFR for the exact language of the regulations and http://idea.ed.gov for up-to-date information about IDEIA. Readers also are encouraged to become familiar with special education law in the state where they practice.

The major provisions of IDEIA—Part B are discussed under these chapter headings: "State Plans and Single-Agency Responsibility," "The Zero Reject Principle," "Children Eligible for Services," "Early Intervening Services," "Evaluation Procedures," "Individualized Education Program," "Least Restrictive Environment," "The Meaning of *Appropriate Education*," "The Scope of Required Related Services," "Procedural Safeguards," and "Right to Private Action."

State Plans and Single-Agency Responsibility

Each state must develop a plan to provide special education and related services to students with disabilities. The state's lead education agency (i.e., Department of Education, Department of Instruction) is responsible for carrying out the state's IDEIA—Part B plan.

State Plans

To receive funds, IDEIA requires each state educational agency (SEA) to have on file with the U.S. DOE a plan that describes state policies and procedures to assure a free appropriate public education (FAPE) for all children with disabilities residing within the state between the ages of 3 and 21, inclusive, including children with disabilities who have been suspended or expelled from school. The SEA is not required to provide special education and related services to children in the 3- to 5- and 18- to 21-year age groups if the provision of services to those age groups is in conflict with the state law or practice. In addition, states are not required to provide special education and related services to youth ages 18 through 21 who are incarcerated in adult correctional facilities if they were not identified as disabled or did not have an individualized education program (IEP) prior to their incarceration (34 CFR § 300.102).

Under IDEIA—Part B, federal funds are provided to all states that had an acceptable state plan on file with the U.S. DOE prior to the 2004 amendments. The U.S. DOE may require revisions to state plans, but only as necessary to achieve compliance with the 2004 amendments or new interpretations of the law by a federal court or a state's highest court, or following a finding of noncompliance problems (34 CFR § 300.176). To ensure responsiveness to the needs of children with disabilities and their parents, the SEA must provide opportunities for public comment prior to a revision of its plan (34 CFR § 300.165). Each state also must maintain an advisory panel for the purpose of providing policy guidance with respect to special education and related services for children within the state (34 CFR § 300.167).

The Office of Special Education Programs (OSEP) within the U.S. DOE monitors compliance with IDEIA at the level of the state and only indirectly (i.e., through the review of the state plan). States are responsible for monitoring local school districts to ensure compliance with IDEIA regulations and the state's plan (see Reschly & Bersoff, 1999). The OSEP responds to written inquiries regarding interpretation of IDEIA, but it does not attempt to enforce compliance at the level of the individual school district (Zirkel & Kincaid, 1993).

Single-Agency Responsibility

In legislating Pub. L. No. 94-142, Congress sought to ensure that a single state agency was responsible for carrying out the requirements of the law (H. R. Turnbull & Turnbull, 2000). The single-agency responsibility aspect of the law has several implications. First, under IDEIA—Part B, the SEA is the agency responsible for monitoring all educational programs for children with disabilities ages 3 through 21 within the state and ensuring that the programs meet IDEIA standards (34 CFR § 300.101, 300.149). IDEIA—Part B allows the SEA to delegate the responsibility to provide special education and related services to intermediate school districts (or other regional units) and local educational agencies (LEAs). An LEA is usually the board of education of a public school district; the educational administrative unit of a public institution (e.g., school for the deaf or blind); or a charter school that is established as an LEA under state law (34 CFR § 3300.28). The SEA must ensure that policies and programs administered by intermediate and local education agencies are in conformance with IDEIA—Part B requirements. If an LEA is unable or unwilling to provide appropriate services under IDEIA—Part B, the SEA must ensure that special education and related services are available to students with disabilities residing in those areas (H. R. Turnbull & Turnbull, 2000). If a charter school is a part of an LEA, the LEA is required to serve children with disabilities who attend the charter school and to provide funds to charter schools in the same manner as funds are provided to other schools (34 CFR § 300.209).

Second, consistent with the idea of single-agency responsibility, the SEA also must ensure IDEIA—Part B rights and protections to children with disabilities who are enrolled in programs administered by other state agencies. As illustrated by the Joseph McNulty case (see Case 6.1), prior to 1975, many state residential facilities provided custodial care but little training or education for children with disabilities. With the exception of children unilaterally placed in schools or facilities by their parents, the SEA is now responsible for making available an appropriate education for all children with disabilities in the state, including those who are homeless, are residing in mental health facilities or hospitals, and are in homes for individuals with developmental disabilities. IDEIA, however, allows an SEA to delegate its responsibility for providing special education to youth in adult prisons to another agency (e.g., the prison system; 34 CFR § 300.149).

Third, the SEA must ensure that special education and related services are available to children with disabilities enrolled in private schools or facilities. Congress identified two types of private school placements: A child with a disability may be placed in a private school or facility by the SEA or LEA as a means of providing special education and related services, or children may attend private schools or facilities by parental choice.

Private School Placement by the State Educational Agency or Local Educational Agency

Some children with disabilities are placed in a private school or facility as a means of providing the child with appropriate special education and related services. Children placed in a private school or facility by the SEA or LEA must be provided special education and related services in conformance with an IEP developed by an IEP team as described in the law. Publicly placed private school students are entitled to the same benefits and services as those attending public schools. The child must retain all IDEIA rights in the private school setting, and the SEA or LEA must monitor the services provided to ensure compliance with IDEIA requirements (34 CFR § 300.146). When the placement is made by the SEA or LEA, the placement must be at no cost to the parents, including the program, nonmedical care, and room and board if placement is in a residential facility (34 CFR § 300.146, 300.104).

Unilateral Placement by Parents

If an LEA makes available a FAPE for a child with a disability but the parents choose to place their child in a private school, the child does not have an individual right to receive some or all of the special education and related services the child would receive if enrolled in a public school (34 CFR § 300.137). A school system must provide parentally placed private school students Part B programs and services in accordance with a service plan (34 CFR § 300.132). Amounts expended for the provision of services by the LEA must be equal to a proportionate amount of available federal funds, excluding funds expended for child find activities (34 CFR § 300.133, 300.131).

Decisions about the services that will be provided to parentally placed private school children with disabilities are made in consultation with representatives of the private school (34 CFR § 300.134). However, the LEA[4] makes the final decision with respect to the services to be provided to eligible children (34 CFR § 300.137). Based on this consultation and the funding available, the LEA decides which children will receive services; what services will be provided; and how, where, and by whom the services will be provided (34 CFR § 300.134). If a child enrolled in a private school will receive special education or related services from an LEA, the LEA initiates and conducts meetings to develop, review, and revise a service plan for the child and ensures that a representative of the private school attends or otherwise participates (e.g., by telephone) in each meeting (34 CFR § 300.137).

Thus, parentally placed private school students with disabilities may receive a different amount and range of services than children with disabilities in public school (34 CFR § 300.138). School systems are given broad discretion with regard to which private school students with disabilities will receive services and what services will be provided. Parentally placed private school children may receive services on-site at the

---

[4]The regulations read "SEA or LEA" or "the agency." "LEA" is used in this section for simplicity.

child's school, including a religious school, to the extent consistent with law (34 CFR § 300.139). LEAs may not use federal funds to benefit private schools, and LEAs must maintain control over any property, equipment, and supplies that are used to benefit private school students with disabilities (34 CFR § 300.141, 300.144). LEAs may count the cost of transporting children to participate in services as part of their required expenditure on private school students (34 CFR § 300.139).

Parents have, at times, recovered private school tuition costs from the LEA through administrative hearings or lawsuits in which they demonstrated that their school district failed to offer their child an appropriate education program in the public schools, leaving them no option but to place him or her at their own expense (see *Forest Grove School District v. T.A.*, 2009). IDEIA specifically addresses this issue. If the parents of a child with a disability who previously received special education under the authority of an LEA enroll the child in a private school without the consent or referral of the LEA, a court or hearing officer may require the LEA to reimburse the parents for the cost of enrollment if it is found that the LEA failed to make a FAPE available to the child in a timely manner prior to that enrollment (34 CFR § 300.148).

However, IDEIA also states that the cost of reimbursement may be reduced or denied if:

- At the most recent IEP meeting the parents attended prior to removal of the child from the public school, the parents did not inform the IEP team that they were rejecting the placement proposed by the LEA, including stating their concerns and their intent to enroll their child in a private school at public expense.
- The parents did not give the LEA written notice of their concerns and their intent to enroll their child in a private school at public expense at least 10 business days prior to the removal of the child from the public school.
- The LEA notified the parents of its intent to evaluate the child (and the reasons for the evaluation) prior to the parents' removal of the child from the public school, but the parents did not make the child available for such evaluation.
- Or a judicial finding is made that the actions taken by the parents were unreasonable. (34 CFR § 300.148[d])

The cost of reimbursement may not be reduced or denied if the school prevented the parents from providing notice, the parents had not received notice, compliance would likely result in physical or serious emotional harm to the child, or the parents are not literate or cannot write in English (34 CFR § 300.148).

The Zero Reject Principle

The zero reject principle requires states to locate and evaluate students with disabilities and offer them full educational opportunity, regardless of the severity of the disability.

Child Find

Consistent with the court decisions in *P.A.R.C.* and *Mills*, Congress recognized that to assure special education was available to all children with disabilities (i.e., the zero reject principle), it was necessary for the SEA to actively seek to locate every child with a disability within the state. This aspect of the law is called the *child find* requirement. IDEIA requires the SEA to implement policies and procedures to assure that all children with disabilities (including those who are homeless, wards of the state, or attending private schools) are identified, located, and evaluated. The SEA also must identify students who are suspected of being disabled and in need of special education services, even though they are advancing from grade to grade, and highly mobile children, including migrant children (34 CFR § 300.111). Finally, the SEA must ensure that accurate child counts of children receiving services under IDEIA are made to Washington each year (34 CFR § 300.640).

Severity of the Disability

The zero reject principle also encompasses the notion that the SEA must provide full educational opportunity to all children with disabilities, regardless of the severity of their disability. A 1989 court case raised the question of whether some children are so severely impaired that they do not qualify for services under IDEIA. *Timothy W. v. Rochester, New Hampshire School District* (1989) concerned a child who was "profoundly mentally retarded," deaf, blind, a spastic quadriplegic and subject to convulsions (p. 956). The school alleged that Timothy was so impaired he was "not 'capable of benefiting' from an education, and therefore was not entitled to one" (p. 956). In a surprise ruling, the district court agreed with the school. On appeal, however, this decision was reversed. In a lengthy opinion the court stated, "The language of the Act [IDEIA] in its entirety makes clear that a 'zero-reject' policy is at the core of the Act" (p. 960). As the court noted in *Timothy W.*, there is no requirement under IDEIA that a child be able to demonstrate that he or she will benefit from special education in order to be eligible for services.

Exception to the Zero Reject Principle

When Pub. L. No. 94-142 was passed in 1975, its purpose was to assure a free and appropriate education for *all* students with disabilities within a state. If parents failed to consent to the initial special education placement, schools were expected to use due process procedures (e.g., hearings) to override parent refusal of services. Based on a review of case law and special education regulations in the late 1970s, Martin (1979) concluded that "the parent cannot be allowed to block needed services any more than the school can be allowed to offer inadequate services" (p. 103).

In 2004, however, this aspect of special education law was changed. IDEIA *prohibits* schools from using procedural safeguards to overrule a parent's failure to consent to the initial provision of services. Parents now have "the ultimate choice" as to whether their child will receive special education services. IDEIA states that a school is not required to convene an IEP meeting or develop an IEP for a student whose parents do not consent to the initial evaluation or provision of special education. Also, the school will not be considered in violation of the requirement to make available a FAPE to the child if the parent withholds consent to the initial evaluation or placement (34 CFR § 300.300).

What if a child's parents do not agree with each other regarding whether to consent to the provision of special education services? In the opinion of the OSEP, if one parent denies or revokes consent to his or her child's receipt of special education services *in writing*, "no" is the controlling decision. However, both parents must be provided written notice prior to discontinuation of the provision of special education and related services. "The IDEA does not provide a mechanism for parents to resolve disputes with one another; such disputes must be settled privately or through whatever State law processes exist" (Guard, 2009, p. 2).

In summary, Pub. L. No. 94-142 assured a free and appropriate education to all students with disabilities. Federal special education law is now more accurately described as assuring that all states *offer* or *make available* a free and appropriate education to all children with disabilities. IDEIA presumes that parents can and will make educational decisions that are in the best interest of their child.

Children Eligible for Services

The funds available under IDEIA—Part B are earmarked to provide special education and related services only for children with disabilities as defined by the law. Under IDEIA—Part B, a *child with a disability* means a child evaluated in accordance with the procedures in the law as having:

> an intellectual disability,[5] a hearing impairment (including deafness), a speech or language impairment, a visual impairment (including blindness), a serious emotional disturbance (referred to in this part as "emotional disturbance"), an orthopedic impairment, autism, traumatic brain injury, an other health impairment, a specific learning disability, deaf-blindness, or multiple disabilities, and who ... needs special education and related services. (34 CFR § 300.8[a])

It is important to note that eligible children under IDEIA—Part B must have a disability as outlined in one of the 13 disability categories (see Exhibit 4.1), and they must need special education and related services because of that disability. Identification of a student as needing special education is thus "a two-pronged determination: (a) A disability in obtaining an education must be documented, and (b) a need for special education must be established" (Reschly, 2000, p. 87). Also, a child is not eligible for special education and related services if "the determinant factor for that determination is lack of appropriate instruction in reading, including the essential components of reading instruction (as defined in the Elementary and Secondary Education Act of 1965); lack of appropriate instruction in math; or limited English proficiency" (34 CFR § 300.306[b]).

IDEIA—Part B allows states to use a broader definition of disability for children ages 3 through 9 years, or for a subset of that age range (e.g., ages 3 through 5) (34 CFR § 300.111). States may use the term *developmental delay* for a 3- to 9-year-old who is experiencing delays (as defined by the state) in one or more areas of

---

[5]Original text reads "mental retardation."

Exhibit 4.1 Disability Categories Under IDEIA—Part B

Definitions of Disability Terms

The terms used in the definition of disability are defined as follows:

1. (i) *Autism* means a developmental disability significantly affecting verbal and nonverbal communication and social interaction, generally evident before age three, that adversely affects a child's educational performance. Other characteristics often associated with autism are engagement in repetitive activities and stereo-typed movements, resistance to environmental change or change in daily routines, and unusual responses to sensory experiences.
   (ii) Autism does not apply if a child's educational performance is adversely affected primarily because the child has an emotional disturbance, as defined in paragraph (c)(4) of this section.
   (iii) A child who manifests the characteristics of autism after age three could be identified as having autism if the criteria in paragraph (1)(i) of this section are satisfied."

2. *Deaf-blindness* means "concomitant hearing and visual impairments, the combination of which causes such severe communication and other developmental and educational needs that they cannot be accommodated in special education programs solely for children with deafness or children with blindness."

3. *Deafness* means "a hearing impairment that is so severe that the child is impaired in processing linguistic information through hearing, with or without amplification, that adversely affects a child's educational performance."

4. *Emotional disturbance.* See the text under this heading later in this chapter.

5. *Hearing impairment* means "an impairment in hearing, whether permanent or fluctuating, that adversely affects a child's educational performance but that is not included under the definition of deafness in this section."

6. *Intellectual disability* (*mental retardation* in source). See the text under this heading later in this chapter.

7. *Multiple disabilities* means "concomitant impairments (such as intellectual disability—blindness, intellectual disability—orthopedic impairment), the combination of which causes such severe educational needs that they cannot be accommodated in special education programs solely for one of the impairments. Multiple disabilities does not include deaf-blindness."

8. *Orthopedic impairment* means "a severe orthopedic impairment that adversely affects a child's educational performance. The term includes impairments caused by a congenital anomaly, impairments caused by disease (e.g., poliomyelitis, bone tuberculosis), and impairments from other causes (e.g., cerebral palsy, amputations, and fractures or burns that cause contractures)."

9. *Other health impairment.* See the text under this heading later in this chapter.

10. *Specific learning disability.* See the text under this heading later in this chapter.

11. *Speech or language impairment* means "a communication disorder, such as stuttering, impaired articulation, a language impairment, or a voice impairment, that adversely affects a child's educational performance."

12. *Traumatic brain injury* means "an acquired injury to the brain caused by an external physical force, resulting in total or partial functional disability or psychosocial impairment, or both, that adversely affects a child's educational performance. Traumatic brain injury applies to open or closed head injuries resulting in impairments in one or more areas, such as cognition; language; memory; attention; reasoning; abstract thinking; judgment; problem-solving; sensory, perceptual, and motor abilities; psychosocial behavior; physical functions; information processing; and speech. Traumatic brain injury does not apply to brain injuries that are congenital or degenerative, or to brain injuries induced by birth trauma."

13. *Visual impairment including blindness* means "an impairment in vision that, even with correction, adversely affects a child's educational performance. The term includes both partial sight and blindness."

Source: Adapted from 34 CFR § 300.8.

development—physical, cognitive, communication, social or emotional, or adaptive—and who, for that reason, needs special education and related services (34 CFR § 300.8).

What are the appropriate criteria for determining that a child *needs* special education? In *West Chester Area School Dist. v. Bruce C.* (2002), the judge stated: "There is no precise standard for determining whether a student is in need of special education, and well-settled precedent counsels against invoking any bright-line rules for making such a determination" (2002, p. 420). If a child is suspected of being eligible for special education under the definition of *intellectual disability* or *specific learning disability*, it is reasonable to expect that the disability would affect the child's academic achievement. However, academic progress "is not the 'litmus test' for eligibility" (*Corchado v. Board of Education, Rochester City*, 2000, p. 176; also see *G."J" D. v. Wissahickon School District*. 2011). Students with visual, hearing, or physical impairments or emotional or behavior problems may perform well academically but need special education and related services to support their achievement (see Exhibit 4.3).

IDEIA—Part B definitions that concern sensory, motor, and speech or language impairments typically pose few problems. The definitions of *intellectual disability*, *specific learning disability (SLD)*, *emotional disturbance (ED)*, and *other health impairment* frequently have been a source of confusion and disagreement. These definitions are discussed in the text rather than appearing in Exhibit 4.3.

This discussion focuses on the federal definitions of disability categories under IDEIA—Part B. School psychologists also must be knowledgeable of the broader definition of disability under Section 504 of the Rehabilitation Act of 1973 (see Chapter 5) and their state code eligibility requirements. Different states use different names for special education categories (e.g., intellectual disability, cognitive impairment, or developmental cognitive delay), and state classification criteria vary as well (Reschly & Bersoff, 1999). It is important to note that IDEIA does not require states to assign classification "labels" to students with disabilities and some states have adopted a noncategorical system for the delivery of special education services (34 CFR § 300.111). However, states must nevertheless provide data to the U.S. DOE each year regarding the number of children with disabilities by disability category (34 CFR § 300.641).

It is also important to note that a medical diagnosis is not required by *federal* law, nor is it sufficient for determining whether a child is eligible for special education and related services under IDEIA—Part B (Zirkel, 2009a, p. 336). Federal special education law allows schools to use means other than a medical evaluation by a licensed physician to determine whether a child has a disability. States may, however, require a medical evaluation to determine whether a child has a medically related disability. If a medical evaluation is required, it must be done at no cost to the parent. Similarly, a *Diagnostic and Statistical Manual of Mental Disorders (DSM-5)* diagnosis (American Psychiatric Association, 2013) may assist in determining eligibility under IDEIA, but it is neither legally required nor sufficient to determine whether a student is eligible for special education under IDEIA—Part B (Zirkel, 2009a).

Intellectual Disability

The term *intellectual disability*

> means significantly subaverage general intellectual functioning, existing concurrently with deficits in adaptive behavior and manifested during the developmental period, that adversely affects a child's educational performance. (34 CFR § 300.8[c][6])

Prior to the passage of Pub. L. No. 94-142, many children were labeled "mentally retarded" on the basis of a single IQ score (see Case 6.1). The use of an IQ score as the sole criterion for classifying mental retardation in the schools resulted in the overidentification of children as mentally retarded, particularly students from ethnic minority backgrounds and those with limited English proficiency. In the 1950s and 1960s, the American Association of Mental Deficiency argued persuasively for a change in the definition of *mentally retarded*. The group recommended that a diagnosis of mental retardation be based on the finding of deficits in both intellectual functioning and adaptive behavior. This view gained wide acceptance and was incorporated into IDEIA—Part B regulations. In addition, the term *mental retardation* was replaced with *intellectual disability* in 2010. However, this change had not been made in the text of the regulations implementing IDEIA as of April 2015.

Under IDEIA—Part B, eligibility for special education is determined by a team of qualified professionals and the parents of the child. The team generally considers three types of assessment information in determining whether a child has an intellectual disability: general intellectual functioning, adaptive behavior, and school performance. To be eligible for special education under the intellectual disability category, the child must show subaverage performance on a measure of general intellectual functioning. *Subaverage* is usually further defined in state guidelines as performance at least 2 standard deviations below the population mean for the child's age group. Most states recommend the use of IQ tests for this measure. However, this evaluation can be accomplished by testing "or by means other than testing" as long as the procedures are valid and nondiscriminatory (Heumann, 1993, p. 539).

The child also must demonstrate concurrent deficits in adaptive behavior and school performance. Assessment of adaptive behavior focuses on the child's ability to meet age-appropriate standards of personal independence and social responsibility. Such measures typically are based on observations of behavior and competencies provided by an informant, usually a parent or teacher (Sattler & Hoge, 2006). Deficits in school performance typically are documented by individually administered achievement tests.

Specific Learning Disability

The term s*pecific learning disability*

> means a disorder in one or more of the basic psychological processes involved in understanding or in using language, spoken or written, that may manifest itself in an imperfect ability to listen, think, speak, read, write, spell, or to do mathematical calculations, including conditions such as perceptual disabilities, brain injury, minimal brain dysfunction, dyslexia, and developmental aphasia. . . . Specific learning disability does not include learning problems that are primarily the result of visual, hearing, or motor disabilities, of . . . [intellectual disability], of emotional disturbance, or of environmental, cultural, or economic disadvantage. (34 CFR § 300.8[c][10])

Prior to the 2004 amendments, IDEA regulations stated that a team could determine that a child has an SLD only if the child had a severe discrepancy between an area of academic achievement and intellectual ability. Definitions vary, but generally a severe discrepancy occurs when a statistically significant and unusual difference occurs between a child's IQ score (in the normal range) and a below-normal-limits achievement test score in at least one of the IDEIA SLD performance domains. Over the years since the regulations were first introduced in 1977, many experts expressed dissatisfaction with the IQ-achievement discrepancy model for identifying children with SLDs (U.S. DOE OSEP, 2002). Criticisms included inadequate reliability and validity of the model; overidentification of children as having an SLD, particularly ethnic and racial minorities; delayed treatment for young children who do not yet evidence a score discrepancy between ability and achievement; and wide variability in SLD identification practices across schools and states.

Under IDEIA, schools are no longer required to take into consideration whether a child has a severe discrepancy between achievement and intellectual ability. The 2006 regulations allow for the use of any of the following models in identifying learning disabilities: ability–achievement discrepancy, intra-individual differences, clinical judgment, or response to intervention (RTI; Lichtenstein, 2014). An RTI model identifies children who are likely to qualify as having a learning disability through (a) a documented slow rate of learning and (b) large differences from age or grade expectations even after high-quality, scientifically based interventions are put in place for the child (Gresham et al., 2005). Ethical and legal issues associated with using RTI as part of the procedure to determine whether a student is eligible as having a disability under IDEIA are discussed in Burns, Jacob, and Wagner (2008) and Daves and Walker (2012).

In determining whether a student has an SLD, IDEIA regulations specify the group (or team) members who should be involved in eligibility determination. The determination must be made by the child's parents and a team of qualified professionals, which includes the child's general education teacher (or, if the child does not have a general education teacher, a general education teacher qualified to teach a child of his or her age), as well as at least one person qualified to conduct individual diagnostic examinations of children, such as a school psychologist, speech-language pathologist, or remedial reading teacher (34 CFR § 300.308).

The regulations go on to state that a team may determine a child has an SLD if:

(1) The child does not achieve adequately for the child's age or to meet State-approved grade-level standards in one or more of the following areas, when provided with learning experiences and instruction appropriate for the child's age or State-approved grade-level standards:

    (i) Oral expression.

    (ii) Listening comprehension.

    (iii) Written expression.

    (iv) Basic reading skill.

    (v) Reading fluency skills.

    (vi) Reading comprehension.

    (vii) Mathematics calculation.

    (viii) Mathematics problem solving.

(2) (i) The child does not make sufficient progress to meet age or State-approved grade-level standards in one or more of the areas identified in paragraph

(a)(1) of this section when using a process based on the child's response to scientific, research-based intervention; or

(ii) The child exhibits a pattern of strengths and weaknesses in performance, achievement, or both, relative to age, State-approved grade-level standards, or intellectual development, that is determined by the group to be relevant to the identification of a specific learning disability, using appropriate assessments ... ; and

(3) The group determines that its findings under paragraphs (a)(1) and (2) of this section are not primarily the result of—

(i) A visual, hearing, or motor disability;

(ii) ... [Intellectual disability];

(iii) Emotional disturbance;

(iv) Cultural factors;

(v) Environmental or economic disadvantage; or

(vi) Limited English proficiency. (34 CFR § 300.309)

To ensure that the underachievement in a child suspected of having an SLD is not due to lack of appropriate instruction in reading or math, the group must consider whether data demonstrate that prior to (or as a part of) the referral process, the child was provided appropriate instruction in general education settings. The team also must consider, as part of the evaluation, data-based documentation of repeated assessments (at reasonable intervals) of the student's progress during instruction, information that also was provided to the child's parents (34 CFR § 300.309).

Furthermore, the regulations require an observation of the child's academic performance and behavior in the child's learning environment, including the general education classroom, or an age-appropriate setting if not in school (34 CFR § 300.310). The group (team) report and documentation for a child suspected of having an SLD must include statements covering seven items: (1) whether the child has an SLD; (2) the basis for making the determination; (3) the relevant behavior, if any, noted during the observation of the child and the relationship of that behavior to the child's academic functioning; (4) the educationally relevant medical findings, if any; (5) whether the child does not achieve adequately and does not make sufficient progress to meet age or state-approved grade-level standards, or whether the child exhibits a pattern of strengths and weaknesses in performance, achievement, or both, relative to age, state-approved grade-level standards, or intellectual development; (6) the determination of the group concerning the effects of a visual, hearing, or motor disability; intellectual disability; emotional disturbance; cultural factors; environmental or economic disadvantage; or limited English proficiency on the child's achievement level; and (7) the instructional strategies used and the student-centered data collected if a response to a scientific, research-based intervention process was implemented, and documentation showing that the parents were notified regarding this process. Each team member is required to certify in writing whether the report reflects his or her conclusion. If it does not reflect his or her conclusion, the team member must submit a separate statement presenting his or her conclusions (34 CFR § 300.311). (Also see Zirkel, 2013b.)

Emotional Disturbance

Emotional disturbance is defined as follows:

(i) The term means a condition exhibiting one or more of the following characteristics over a long period of time and to a marked degree that adversely affects a child's educational performance:

   (A) An inability to learn that cannot be explained by intellectual, sensory, or health factors.

   (B) An inability to build or maintain satisfactory interpersonal relationships with peers and teachers.

   (C) Inappropriate types of behavior or feelings under normal circumstances.

   (D) A general pervasive mood of unhappiness or depression.

   (E) A tendency to develop physical symptoms or fears associated with personal or school problems.

(ii) Emotional disturbance includes schizophrenia. The term does not apply to children who are socially maladjusted, unless it is determined that they have an emotional disturbance. (34 CFR § 300.8)

The IDEIA—Part B definition of ED has been controversial since it was adopted in 1975. It is a modification of a definition of the "emotionally disturbed schoolchild" first outlined by Bower (1982). Bower's definition grew out of a California study in the late 1950s of children identified by school personnel as emotionally disturbed. This study found that children with emotional disturbance differed from their classmates on a number of characteristics: They were poor learners; they had few, if any, satisfactory interpersonal relationships; they behaved oddly or inappropriately; they were depressed or unhappy; and they developed illnesses or phobias. These characteristics also were found among nondisturbed children; however, the children identified as emotionally disturbed displayed these characteristics of emotional disturbance to *"a marked degree over a long period of time"* (p. 57).

In his definition of emotional disturbance, Bower (1982) did not differentiate between children with emotional disturbance and those with social maladjustment. He believed that emotional disturbance and social maladjustment were not separate and distinct constructs. Federal policy makers, however, feared that a definition of *emotionally disturbed* based on Bower's original description would result in a category of special education eligibility that was too broad and costly for schools. They consequently added a clause excluding children who are socially maladjusted unless they also are emotionally disturbed.

For many years, the IDEIA definition of ED has been criticized as being too vague, subjective, and not empirically supported (Hanchon & Allen, 2013; T. L. Hughes & Bray, 2004; McConaughy & Ritter, 2014). As Hanchon and Allen (2013) observed:

in addition to deciding whether a student's interpersonal relationships are "satisfactory" or his or her feelings are "appropriate" for a given situation, in the absence of a clear definition of ED, the multidisciplinary team's task of determining eligibility is complicated by having to discern a level of severity that sufficiently constitutes a "marked degree," symptom persistence suggesting an "extended period of time," and educational impact qualifying as "adverse." (p. 195)

The portion of the ED definition that excludes children who are socially maladjusted unless they also are emotionally disturbed is also problematic because the federal regulations do not define the term *socially maladjusted*, and, despite advances in differentiation of emotional disturbance and social maladjustment (e.g., Gacono & Hughes, 2004; J. A. Miller, Williams, & McCoy, 2004), distinguishing between the two continues to be challenging. Furthermore, the two categories are not mutually exclusive; some children are emotionally disturbed *and* socially maladjusted (Merrell & Walker, 2004).

Bower (1982), as noted previously, believed that attempts to differentiate between emotional disturbance and social maladjustment are artificial and that such distinctions miss the more important point that both groups of children are in need of special help (also T. L. Hughes & Bray, 2004; Olympia et al., 2004). A number of psychologists and concerned professional associations have called for replacing the term *emotional disturbance* in IDEIA with *emotional or behavior disorders*. Others have called on general education to provide better programs for students who are socially maladjusted but not emotionally disturbed (Merrell & Walker, 2004). At this time, the definition of ED varies across states, with some states eliminating the social maladjustment exclusion from their definition (Olympia et al., 2004).

Thus, aspects of the ED definition are vague, subjective, and controversial. Confusion also arises from the fact that nonschool mental health professionals typically are trained to use a system for classifying childhood disorders that differs from IDEIA. The system of classification that is most frequently used outside the schools is the *DSM-5* (American Psychiatric Association, 2013). As Slenkovich (1988a) observed, psychologists and psychiatrists in nonschool settings often assume (and state in reports to schools) that a child diagnosed with an emotional problem under the *DSM* automatically qualifies for special education and related services as emotionally disturbed. However, to qualify for special education as emotionally disturbed under IDEIA—Part B, a child must be found eligible under the IDEIA—Part B definition (also see Zirkel, 2013a; Zirkel & Rose, 2009).

McConaughy and Ritter (2014) identified best practices in a multimethod assessment of students suspected of qualifying for special education as emotionally disturbed. It is likely that there will be a call for a new definition of ED based on contemporary science the next time that IDEA is amended.

Other Health Impairment

The term *other health impairment*

> means having limited strength, vitality or alertness, including a heightened alertness to environmental stimuli, that results in limited alertness with respect to the educational environment, that—
>
> (i) Is due to chronic or acute health problems such as asthma, attention deficit disorder or attention deficit hyperactivity disorder, diabetes, epilepsy, a heart condition, hemophilia, lead poisoning, leukemia, nephritis, rheumatic fever, sickle cell anemia, Tourette syndrome; and
>
> (ii) Adversely affects a child's educational performance. (34 CFR § 300.8)

Beginning in the 1980s, the courts and the OSEP began to address questions regarding whether students with acquired immune deficiency syndrome (AIDS), alcohol and chemical dependency, and attention-deficit disorder or attention-deficit/hyperactivity disorder (ADD/ADHD) qualify as having a health impairment under Part B. Court rulings have determined that students with conditions such as AIDS qualify under the "other health impairment" classification only if their physical condition is such that it adversely affects educational performance (*Doe v. Belleville Public School District No. 118,* 1987). However, as will be seen in Chapter 5, students with AIDS are protected by Section 504 of the Rehabilitation Act of 1973.

The OSEP also has addressed the question of whether students who are chemically dependent (alcohol or drug addicted) qualify as having a health impairment under IDEIA. According to the OSEP, chemical dependency does not, in and of itself, qualify a child for special education and related services within the "other health impairment" classification (cited in Slenkovich, 1987a). However, students who are receiving treatment for drug or alcohol dependency may be protected by Section 504 (see Chapter 5).

A third question was whether students with ADD/ADHD qualify for special education and related services under the "other health impairment" classification of IDEIA—Part B. Unlike its precursors, IDEA 1997 specifically included ADD/ADHD among the disabling conditions listed under "other health impairment." To be eligible within this category, the child must have limited strength, vitality, or alertness due to the ADD/ADHD, and the condition must adversely impact the child's education performance and result in the need for special education and related services. Thus, some children with ADD/ADHD qualify within the IDEIA definition of *other health impairment*. Other students do not qualify under the "other health impairment" classification but may be eligible for accommodations in general education under Section 504 if the ADD/ADHD *substantially limits* (rather than *adversely affects*) their educational performance (Tobin, Schneider, & Landau, 2014; also see Chapter 5).

Early Intervening Services

In the mid-1980s, some schools began to introduce building-based "child study" teams to assist teachers in planning interventions for children with learning or behavior problems. Such programs provided early assistance to students who were struggling to succeed in the general education classroom, reduced referrals to special education, and were seen as a safeguard against unnecessary referral, testing, and possible misclassification (see Chalfant & Pysh, 1989).

In 2004, the IDEA was amended to allow school districts to use up to 15% of their federal special education funds each year to develop and implement coordinated *early intervening services*. These services are for all students, with a focus on kindergarten through third grade. The services are targeted to those students who "need additional academic and behavior support to succeed in the general education environment" but who have not been identified as needing special education and related services. Funds may be used for professional development to enable staff to deliver "scientifically based academic and behavioral interventions, including scientifically based literacy instruction" and to provide "educational and behavioral evaluations, services, and supports, including scientifically based literacy instruction" services (34 CFR § 300.226). It is hoped that IDEIA's early intervening services result in effective assistance to students before their problems become severe, a reduction of inappropriate referrals for special education, and less misclassification of children as having disabilities for the purpose of providing individualized help. (Also see Chapter 7.)

Evaluation Procedures

This portion of the chapter describes a series of lawsuits concerning the misclassification of racial and ethnic minority students as "mentally retarded," including students whose native language was not English, and the safeguards that Congress subsequently included in special education law to protect against misclassification.

Problem of Misclassification

As noted previously, right-to-education court cases signaled to Congress that federal legislation was needed to ensure educational opportunities for all children with disabilities. A second type of court case was important in shaping the nondiscriminatory testing, classification, and placement procedures required by IDEIA—Part B. These cases concerned the misclassification of ethnic minority group children as "mentally retarded" and their placement in special classes for the educable mentally retarded (EMR). They raised questions regarding school violations of the due process and equal protection guarantees of the 14th Amendment (Bersoff, 1979).

Due Process.   The due process clause of the 14th Amendment protects individuals from arbitrary or unwarranted stigmatization by the state that may interfere with the ability to acquire property. Under the protections of the 14th Amendment, the state (school) may not assign a negative label, such as "mentally retarded," without due process, that is, without some sort of fair and impartial decision-making procedures (Bersoff & Ysseldyke, 1977). In the *P.A.R.C.* ruling, a number of procedural safeguards against misclassification were required. For example, parents were given the right to an impartial hearing if they were dissatisfied with their child's special education classification or placement.

Equal Protection.   With the landmark *Brown v. Board of Education* decision in 1954, the Supreme Court ruled that school segregation by race was a denial of the right to equal protection (equal educational opportunity) under the 14th Amendment. Following this decision, the courts began to scrutinize school practices that suggested within-school segregation, that is, where ethnic minority group children were segregated and treated differently within the schools. A number of suits against the public schools were filed in which minority group children were overrepresented in lower-ability education tracks and special education classes. These lower-ability tracks and special education classes were seen as educationally inferior and a denial of equal education opportunities. The claimants in these cases maintained that many children were misclassified and inappropriately placed based on racially and culturally discriminatory classification and placement procedures (see Exhibit 4.2).

Exhibit 4.2 Cases Concerning Misclassification of Ethnic Minority Children

Hobson v. Hansen (1967, 1969)

The first significant legal challenge to the use of aptitude tests for assigning minority group children to low-ability classes was *Hobson v. Hansen*. In this case, African American children and children from lower socioeconomic backgrounds were disproportionately assigned to the lower-ability tracks in the Washington, DC, public schools on the basis of scores on group-administered aptitude tests. Judge Wright noted that the tracking system was rigid, that it segregated students by race, and that the lower tracks were educationally inferior. He further stated that because the aptitude tests were "standardized primarily on and are relevant to a White middle-class group of students, they produce inaccurate and misleading test scores when given to lower class and Negro students" (*Hobson*, 1967, p. 514). He ruled that the tracking system was a violation of equal protection laws and ordered the system abolished.

Diana v. State Board of Education (1970)

Diana was a class action suit filed in California on behalf of nine Mexican American children placed in classes for the EMR on the basis of Stanford-Binet or Wechsler Intelligence Scale for Children IQ scores. Diana, one of the plaintiffs, came from a Spanish-speaking family and was placed in an EMR classroom based on an IQ score of 30. When she was later retested in Spanish and English by a bilingual psychologist, she scored 49 points higher on the same test and no longer qualified for special class placement (Bersoff & Ysseldyke, 1977). The consent decree in *Diana* required that children be assessed in their primary language or with sections of tests that do not depend on knowledge of English (Reschly, 1979).

Guadalupe Organization, Inc. v. Tempe Elementary School District No. 3 (1972)

Guadalupe was a class action suit filed on behalf of Yaqui Indian and Mexican American students. The consent decree in *Guadalupe* also required assessment in the child's primary language or the use of nonverbal measures if the child's primary language was not English. *Guadalupe*, however, went further than *Diana* in requiring a multifaceted evaluation that included assessment of adaptive behavior and an interview with the parents in the child's home (Reschly, 1979). *Guadalupe* also required due process procedures, including informed consent for evaluation and placement.

Larry P. v. Riles (1984)

Larry P. was a class action suit filed on behalf of African American pupils placed in classes for the EMR in the San Francisco School District. The plaintiffs claimed that many African American children were misclassified as mentally retarded and that IQ tests were the primary basis for classification as EMR. The court asked the schools to demonstrate that their methods of classification (i.e., use of IQ test scores) were "rational" or valid for the purpose of classifying African American children as mentally retarded and in need of special education. The school district was unable to convince the court that IQ tests were valid for the purpose of placing African American children in EMR classes, and in 1972 the court temporarily enjoined the schools from any further placement of African American children in EMR classes on the basis of IQ test results.

In the second phase of *Larry P.*, the trial on the substantive issues, the plaintiffs requested that the court consider their claims under both the 14th Amendment and the new federal statute, Pub. L. No. 94-142. More than 10,000 pages of testimony were presented during this phase. In his lengthy opinion, Judge Peckham characterized the EMR classes as "inferior" and "dead-end." Based on his analysis of the expert testimony, he found IQ tests to be racially and culturally discriminatory. He ruled that the school failed to show that IQ tests were valid for the purpose of selecting African American children for EMR classes, and, in his view, IQ scores weighed so heavily in decision making that they "contaminated" and biased the assessment process. He permanently enjoined the state from using any standardized intelligence tests to identify African American children for EMR classes without prior permission of the court (Bersoff, 1982; Reschly, 1979). In 1986, Judge Peckham banned the use of IQ tests to assign African American children to any special education program except for the state-supported gifted and talented program. In 1988, a group of parents filed a suit claiming that the state's ban on IQ tests discriminated against African American children by denying them an opportunity to take the tests helpful in determining special education needs. In 1992, Judge Peckham issued an order allowing African American children to be given IQ tests with parent consent (*Crawford v. Honig,* 1994). The California State Department of Education continued to prohibit the use of IQ tests with African American children, however. The California Association of School Psychologists made an unsuccessful attempt to challenge the state's ban on IQ testing in 1994 (*California Association of School Psychologists v. Superintendent of Public Instruction,* 1994).

Parents in Action in Special Education (P.A.S.E.) v. Hannon (1980)

This case was filed on behalf of African American children in the Chicago public schools. As Bersoff (1982, p. 81) noted, "the facts, issues, claims and witnesses" were similar to those in *Larry P.*, but the outcome was different. Judge Grady carefully listened to the same expert witnesses who testified in San Francisco. He decided that the issue of racial and cultural bias could best be answered by examining the test questions himself. He proceeded to read aloud every question on the WISC, WISC-R, and Stanford-Binet and every acceptable response. As a result of his analysis, he found only eight items on the WISC or WISC-R to be biased and one item on the Stanford-Binet. He concluded that the use of IQ tests in the context of a multifaceted assessment process as outlined in special education law was not likely to result in racially or culturally discriminatory classification decisions and found in favor of the school system (Bersoff, 1982).

The first three court cases summarized in Exhibit 4.2, along with *P.A.R.C.* and *Mills*, were extremely influential in shaping IDEIA—Part B requirements for nondiscriminatory testing and classification and the procedural or due process safeguards against misclassification. *Larry P. v. Riles* (1984) and *Parents in Action in Special Education (P.A.S.E.) v. Hannon* (1980) addressed the question of whether IQ tests are valid for the purpose of classifying and placing minority group children in special classes. The court in *P.A.S.E.* ruled that the use of IQ tests in the context of the assessment process outlined in IDEIA—Part B was not likely to result in racially or culturally discriminatory placement decisions.

As an additional safeguard against misclassification of ethnic minority children, IDEIA requires each state to gather and examine data to determine whether significant disproportionality based on race and ethnicity is occurring in the state in relation to the identification and/or placement of children with disabilities. If it is determined that a significant disproportionality exists, the state must provide for the review and, if appropriate, revision of policies, procedures, and practices (34 CFR § 300.646). (Also see Chapter 9.)

Conduct of Evaluation

The early court cases concerning the misclassification of students as "mentally retarded" prompted Congress to include a number of standards with regard to both the content and the process of assessment, classification, and special education placement in Pub. L. No. 94-142. IDEIA—Part B requires each SEA or LEA to establish procedures to assure a full and individual evaluation of each child who may qualify as having a disability. These procedures must yield the information necessary to determine if the child has a disability and his or her educational needs. The evaluation must be completed prior to the initial provision of special education and related services and within the time frame identified in state law, or within 60 days of receiving parental consent for the evaluation if no deadline is specified by the state (34 CFR § 300.301). Informed parental consent for an initial assessment and the nondiscriminatory testing and assessment procedures required by IDEIA—Part B are discussed in Chapter 6.

Student Evaluations and Eligibility Determination

In conducting an evaluation, IDEIA—Part B requires the LEA to:

> use a variety of assessment tools and strategies to gather relevant functional, developmental, and academic information about the child, including information provided by the parent that may assist in determining whether the child has a disability ... and the content of the child's IEP, including information related to enabling the child to be involved in and progress in the general curriculum (or, for preschool children, to participate in appropriate activities); not use any single procedure as the sole criterion for determining whether a child has a disability or determining an appropriate educational program for the child; and use technically sound instruments that may assess the relative contribution of cognitive and behavioral factors, in addition to physical or developmental factors. (34 CFR § 300.304[b])

In addition, assessment tools must be validated for the purpose used and be fair, and the child must be assessed in all areas related to the suspected disability (see Chapter 6). The assessment strategies must provide information that directly assists in determining the education needs of the child (34 CFR § 300.304).

After completion of the administration of tests and other evaluation procedures, the determination of whether the child has a disability is made by a team that includes qualified professionals and the parent. The composition of this team will vary depending on the nature of the child's suspected disability. Some or all of the persons who serve on this eligibility determination team may also serve on the IEP team. The parent is given a copy of the evaluation report and documentation of determination of eligibility (34 CFR § 300.306).

Under IDEIA—Part B, parents have the right to obtain an independent educational evaluation (IEE) of their child, and those findings must be considered by the school "in any decision made with respect to the provision of [a FAPE] to the child" (34 CFR § 300.502[a], [c][1]). An IEE is an evaluation conducted by a qualified examiner who is not employed by the district responsible for the education of the child in question. The school is required only to consider, not to adopt, the IEE recommendations (e.g., *James v. Board of Education of Aptakisic-Tripp Community Consolidated School District No. 102*, 2009). The school, on request, must provide parents with information about where an independent educational evaluation may be obtained and the district's criteria for an IEE (34 CFR § 300.502).

Depending on the circumstances, an IEE may be conducted at parent or school expense. If the parent disagrees with the evaluation done by the school, the district is required, with no unnecessary delay, to either ensure that an IEE is conducted at public expense or initiate a due process hearing if it believes its evaluation was appropriate. If the hearing officer determines that the evaluation was appropriate, parents may proceed with an IEE, but at their own expense. The parents are entitled to only one independent educational evaluation at school expense each time the LEA conducts an evaluation with which the parents disagree (34 CFR § 300.502).

When a child is seen for reevaluation, the IEP team and other qualified professionals, as appropriate, review existing evaluation data on the child and, on the basis of that review (along with input from the parents), identify what additional data are needed to determine: (a) whether the child continues to have a disability and the educational needs of the child; (b) the present levels of academic achievement and related developmental needs of the child; (c) whether the child continues to need special education and related services; and (d) whether any additions or modifications to special education and related services are needed to enable the child to meet the measurable annual goals set out in his or her IEP and to participate, as appropriate, in the general education curriculum. For reevaluations, the group may conduct its review without a meeting (34 CFR § 300.305).

If, as part of a reevaluation, it is determined that no additional data are needed to determine whether a child continues to have a disability, the school ensures that the parents are notified of that determination and the reasons for it, along with their right to request an assessment of the child. In this situation, the school is not required to conduct an assessment unless requested by the child's parents. A school is required, however, to evaluate a child before determining that the child no longer qualifies as disabled under Part B. If a student graduates from high school with a regular diploma or exceeds age eligibility for special education under state law, an evaluation is not needed. Schools must provide the graduating student with a summary of his or her academic achievement and functional performance, along with recommendations on how to assist the student in meeting postsecondary goals (34 CFR § 300.305).

Placements

In determining the educational placement of a child with a disability, including preschool children, the LEA is required to ensure that the placement decision is made by a group of persons (including the parents and other persons knowledgeable regarding the child) who consider the evaluation data and the placement options. Placement must be determined at least annually based on the child's IEP, must be in the least restrictive environment (LRE), and must be as close as possible to the child's home. The child must be educated in the school that he or she would attend if not disabled unless the parent agrees otherwise or the child requires some other arrangement because of his or her special education needs. In selecting the LRE, consideration is given to any potential harmful effect on the child or the quality of services that he or she needs, and a child is not removed from education in an age-appropriate general classroom solely because some modifications in the general curriculum are needed (34 CFR § 300.116; also see the section titled "Least Restrictive Environment" later in this chapter).

Individualized Education Program

As previously noted, in the *P.A.R.C.* consent decree, the court required that instructional programs for each child with disabilities be "appropriate for his learning capabilities," and the *Mills* ruling required that each child's education be "suited to his needs." This policy of providing an appropriate education for children with disabilities is achieved in IDEIA—Part B by the IEP. Congress viewed the IEP as a means of preventing functional exclusion of children with disabilities from opportunities to learn, and the yearly review of the IEP was seen as a safeguard against misclassification and as a way to encourage continued parent involvement (H. R. Turnbull & Turnbull, 2000). The students placed in private schools by the SEA or LEA must also receive special education and related services in conformance with an IEP; in contrast, school districts are given broad latitude in developing a service plan that determines which parentally placed private school students with disabilities will receive special education and related services and the types of services to be provided.

The Meeting

The SEA or LEA is responsible for initiating and conducting a meeting for the purpose of developing the child's initial IEP. The initial IEP meeting must be held within 30 calendar days after the determination that the child needs special education and related services. Schools are not required to hold the IEP meeting within 30 days of the *referral* for evaluation; the 30-day countdown to the IEP starts the day that the group making the eligibility determination finds that the child qualifies for and needs special education. Schools must have an IEP for each child with a disability in effect at the beginning of each school year (34 CFR § 300.323).

The Team

The IEP team is composed of: (a) the parents of the child; (b) at least one general education teacher of the child (if the child is, or may be, participating in a general education environment); (c) at least one special education teacher of the child, or, if appropriate, at least one special education provider of the child; (d) a representative of the LEA who is qualified to provide, or supervise the provision of, specially designed instruction to meet the unique needs of children with disabilities, and who is knowledgeable about the general curriculum and the availability of resources of the LEA; (e) an individual who can interpret the instructional implications of evaluation results (who may already be a member of the team in another capacity); (f) at the discretion of the parent or the LEA, other individuals who have knowledge or special expertise regarding the child, including related services personnel as appropriate; and (g) whenever appropriate, the child (34 CFR § 300.321).

If private school placement is under consideration by the IEP team, the LEA must ensure that a representative of the private school attends the meeting or in some way participates in the meeting to develop the initial IEP (e.g., telephone conference call). After a child with a disability enters a private school or facility, any meetings to review and revise the child's IEP may be initiated and conducted by the private school or facility at the discretion of the LEA, as long as the LEA and parents are involved in any decisions about the IEP (34 CFR § 300.325).

If the purpose of the IEP meeting is to consider transition services for the student (services to promote movement from school to postschool activities), the school must invite the student to attend. If the student is not able to attend, the school must take steps to ensure that the student's preferences and interests are considered. With the consent of the parents or the adult student, schools also must invite representatives of agencies responsible for providing or paying for transition services to attend the meeting or in some way participate in the planning of any transition services (34 CFR § 300.321).

Prior to 1975, parents often were not included in special education placement decisions, and school policies of closed records made it difficult for parents to gain access to information about how such decisions were made. Initially clarified in IDEA 1997, the law states that each SEA or LEA must ensure that the parents of a child with a disability are members of any group that makes decisions on the identification, evaluation, and educational placement of their child (34 CFR § 300.501). To ensure parent participation and shared decision making in the development of the IEP, IDEIA—Part B requires the school to provide adequate prior notice of team meetings, and the meetings must be scheduled at a mutually agreed-upon time and place. Notice must include the purpose, time, place, and location of the meetings and who will be in attendance (34 CFR § 300.322). A meeting does not include informal or unscheduled conversations among school personnel or conversations on issues such as teaching methodology, lesson plans, or coordination of services. A meeting also does not include preparatory activities that school personnel engage in to develop a proposal (or a response to a parent proposal) that will be discussed at a later meeting (34 CFR § 300.501).

Schools must make reasonable efforts to ensure that parents understand, and are able to participate in, any group discussions relating to the educational placement of their child, including providing interpreters for parents who are deaf or whose native language is other than English (34 CFR § 300.322). If neither parent can attend, the school must attempt to ensure parent participation using other means, such as telephone conference calls or videoconferencing (34 CFR § 300.501). The IEP meeting may be conducted without parent participation only if the school is unable to convince the parents to attend. The school must document its efforts to arrange a mutually agreed-upon meeting. This documentation might include records of telephone calls and the results of those calls, copies of correspondence to parents and responses, or records of home visits or visits to the parents' place of employment (34 CFR § 300.322; also *Doug C. v. Hawaii Department of Education*, 2013).

The 2004 changes to special education law (IDEIA) introduced greater flexibility with regard to IEP meetings. First, a member of the IEP team is not required to attend the IEP meeting if the parent and the school agree, in writing, that the attendance of that member is not necessary. If the meeting involves discussion related to the excused member's area of expertise, he or she must submit written input to the parent and IEP team prior to the meeting (34 CFR § 300.321). Second, consolidation of the reevaluation and IEP team meetings is encouraged. Third, after the annual IEP meeting for the school year and if the parent and school agree, a child's IEP may be modified in writing without convening additional meetings (34 CFR § 300.324).

Development of the Individualized Educational Program

IDEIA—Part B outlines a number of factors the IEP team is obligated to consider in developing each child's IEP. The team must consider the strengths of the child; the concerns of the parents; the results of the initial evaluation or most recent evaluation of the child; and the academic, developmental, and functional needs of the child. In addition, the team should consider the next five special factors: (1) In the case of a child whose behavior impedes his or her learning or that of others, the team should consider strategies, including positive behavioral interventions and supports, to address that behavior; (2) in the case of a child with limited English proficiency, the team should consider the language needs of the child as those needs relate to his or her IEP; (3) in the case of a child who is blind or visually impaired, the team should consider providing instruction in Braille and the use of Braille, unless the IEP team determines after evaluation of reading and writing skills and needs (including future needs and available media) that use of Braille is not appropriate for the child; (4) in the case of the child who is deaf or hard of hearing, the team should consider the child's full range of needs, including language and communication needs, opportunities for direct communications with peers and professional personnel in the child's language and communication mode, opportunities for direct instruction in the child's language and communication mode, and academic level; and (5) whether the child requires assistive technology devices and services (34 CFR § 300.324).

Content of the Individualized Educational Program

The written IEP must include the following:

- A statement of the child's present levels of academic achievement and functional performance, including how the child's disability affects the child's involvement and progress in the general education curriculum or, for preschool children, as appropriate, how the disability affects the child's participation in appropriate activities.
- For a child who will take regular state and districtwide assessments, a statement of measurable annual goals, including academic and functional goals designed to meet the child's needs that result from his or her disability, to enable the child to be involved in and make progress in the general education curriculum, and to meet each of the child's other educational needs that result from the child's disability. For a child who will take alternate assessments aligned to alternative achievement standards, the IEP includes a description of benchmarks or short-term objectives.
- A description of how the child's progress toward meeting the annual goals will be measured and when periodic reports on the progress the child is making toward meeting the annual goals (such as through the use of quarterly or other periodic reports, concurrent with the issuance of report cards) will be provided.
- A statement of the special education and related services and supplementary aids and services, based on peer-reviewed research to the extent practicable, to be provided to the child or on behalf of the child, and a statement of the program modifications or supports for school personnel that will be provided to enable the child to advance appropriately toward attaining the annual goals, to be involved in and make progress in the general curriculum, to participate in extracurricular and other nonacademic activities, and to be educated and participate with other children with disabilities and nondisabled children.
- An explanation of the extent, if any, to which the child will not participate with nondisabled children in general education and in nonacademic activities.

- A statement of any individual accommodations that are necessary to measure the academic achievement and functional performance of the child on state and districtwide assessments. If the IEP team determines that the child must take an alternate assessment instead of a particular regular state or districtwide assessment of achievement, a statement of why the child cannot participate in the regular assessment and why the particular alternate assessment selected is appropriate for the child.

- The projected date for the beginning of the services and modifications and the anticipated frequency, location, and duration of those services and modifications.

- Beginning not later than the first IEP to be in effect when the child turns 16, or younger if determined appropriate by the IEP team, and updated annually thereafter, the IEP must include appropriate measurable postsecondary goals based on age-appropriate transition assessments related to training, education, employment, and, where appropriate, independent living skills, and the transition services (including courses of study) needed to assist the child in reaching those goals.

- In a state that transfers rights at the age of majority, beginning not later than one year before the child reaches the age of majority under state law, the IEP must include a statement that the child has been informed of his or her rights that will transfer to the child on reaching the age of majority. (Adapted from 34 CFR § 300.320[a])

Parents must be given a copy of the IEP at no cost (34 CFR § 300.322).

Special Education.   The IEP must include a statement of the specific special education and related services to be provided to the child. The term *special education* is defined as "specially designed instruction, at no cost to the parents, to meet the unique needs of a child with a disability, including instruction conducted in the classroom, in the home, in hospitals and institutions, and in other settings" (34 CFR § 300.39[a][1][i]). Special education includes instruction in physical education, vocational education, and travel training (i.e., instruction in the skills necessary to move effectively and safely from place to place), if designed to meet the unique needs of a child with a disability. Speech pathology instruction is included as special education; however, speech pathology also can be a related service (34 CFR § 300.39).

IDEIA—Part B requires schools to provide a statement of needed transition services for students with disabilities beginning at age 16 (or younger if appropriate) as part of the IEP. *Transition services* means a coordinated set of activities for a child with a disability that:

(1) is designed to be within a results-oriented process, that is focused on improving the academic and functional achievement of the child to facilitate the child's movement from school to post-school activities, including postsecondary education, vocational education, integrated employment (including supported employment), continuing and adult education, adult services, independent living or community participation;

(2) is based on the individual child's needs, taking into account the child's strengths, preferences, and interests; and includes instruction; related services; community experiences; the development of employment and other post-school adult living objectives; and, if appropriate, acquisition of daily living skills and provision of a functional vocational evaluation. (34 CFR § 300.43[a][1–2])

Related Services. *Related services* means:

transportation and such developmental, corrective, and other supportive services as are required to assist a child with a disability to benefit from special education, and includes speech-language pathology and audiology services, interpreting services, psychological services, physical and occupational therapy, recreation, including therapeutic recreation, early identification and assessment of disabilities in children, counseling services, including rehabilitation counseling, orientation and mobility services, and medical services for diagnostic or evaluation purposes. Related services also include school health services and school nurse services, social work services in the schools, and parent counseling and training. (34 CFR § 300.34[a])

Under IDEIA—Part B, a related service cannot "stand alone—it must be attached to a special education program, and it must be a necessary service for the child to benefit from special instruction" (Slenkovich, 1988b, p. 168). If the child is not eligible for special education under IDEIA—Part B, there can be no related services, and the child (lacking a disability) is not covered under IDEIA.

Supplementary Aids and Services. *Supplementary aids and services* means "aids, services, and other supports that are provided in general education classes or other education-related settings, and in extracurricular and nonacademic settings, to enable children with disabilities to be educated with nondisabled to the maximum extent appropriate" (34 CFR § 300.42).

Implementation of the Individualized Educational Program

The IEP must be made accessible to each of the child's teachers and service providers, and each must be informed of his or her responsibilities under the IEP and of the specific accommodations, modifications, and supports that must be provided under the IEP (34 CFR § 300.323). The school is accountable for providing the special education instruction and related services outlined in the IEP. The description of services to be provided is an "enforceable promise" (Slenkovich, 1988b, p. 168; *Tyler W. v. Upper Perkiomen School District*, 2013). However, neither the school nor the teacher may be held liable if a student fails to achieve his or her IEP goals. Recommendations for services the school is not required to provide (e.g., for family therapy) should be made separately from the IEP (Slenkovich, 1987b).

Special education and related services are made available as soon as possible following the development of the IEP (34 CFR § 300.323). If the parents and school do not agree on the content of the IEP, either party may request mediation or a due process hearing. Unless parents and the school agree otherwise, the student remains in his or her present placement during any due process proceeding. This is the *stay put* rule (34 CFR § 300.518).

Each child's IEP must be reviewed and revised at least annually, and each child must be seen for reevaluation at least once every three years, or more often if warranted (34 CFR § 300.324, 300.303). However, as noted previously, if the IEP team determines that no additional assessment data are needed as part of a reevaluation, the LEA is not required to conduct additional assessments unless requested by the child's parents or teacher. During the annual review of the IEP, the team must determine whether the annual goals for the child are being achieved and revise the IEP as appropriate to address: (a) any lack of expected progress toward annual goals and progress in the general curriculum, (b) the results of any reevaluations conducted, (c) information about the child provided by the parents, or (d) the child's anticipated needs. The general education teacher is required to participate in the IEP review as appropriate. The LEA also must convene an IEP meeting if an agency fails to provide the transition services described in a child's IEP (34 CFR § 300.324).

Least Restrictive Environment

As noted earlier in the chapter, prior to 1975, children with moderate or severe disabilities often were routinely excluded from school. Children with mild disabilities frequently were segregated in special classes with few opportunities to interact with their nondisabled peers. In some cases, these classes were located in a separate corridor of the school. At times, the less capable teachers were assigned to teach children with disabilities, and typically the classroom facilities and equipment were less adequate than for nondisabled children (H. R. Turnbull & Turnbull, 2000). Few special class children ever returned to the mainstream.

The "least restrictive alternative" doctrine evolved from court decisions starting in the 1960s (e.g., *Wyatt v. Stickney*, 1971). H. R. Turnbull and Turnbull (2000) summarized this constitutionally based doctrine as follows: "Even if the legislative purpose of a government action is appropriate ... the purpose may not be pursued by means that broadly stifle personal liberties if it can be achieved by less oppressive restrictive means" (p. 243). The doctrine of least restrictive alternative was at the foundation of the deinstitutionalization movement in the field of mental health in the late 1960s and early 1970s. The doctrine recognizes that it may be necessary to restrict personal freedoms when treating an individual who is mentally ill, but the state should deprive the patient of his or her liberties only to the extent necessary to provide treatment (H. R. Turnbull & Turnbull, 2000).

This principle also was applied to the education of children with disabilities in special education law with the requirement that special education and related services be provided in a setting that is the LRE appropriate for the child. Congress recognized that integration of children with disabilities into the educational mainstream was not likely to occur without a legal mandate. Many educators and nondisabled students and their parents held negative stereotypes and attitudes toward special education students

(Martin, 1979). Consequently, IDEIA—Part B requires the SEA or LEA to ensure the following:

> To the maximum extent appropriate, children with disabilities, including children in public or private institutions or other care facilities, are educated with children who are nondisabled; and special classes, separate schooling, or other removal of children with disabilities from the regular educational environment occurs only when the nature or severity of the disability is such that education in regular classes with the use of supplementary aids and services cannot be achieved satisfactorily. (34 CFR § 300.114[a][2])

Congress intended that the SEA or LEA make available a continuum of alternative placements to meet the needs of children with disabilities, including instruction in general education classes with supplementary services, special classes, special schools, home instruction, and instruction in hospitals and institutions (34 CFR § 300.115). Congress also intended that decisions about the extent to which students with disabilities can be educated with nondisabled children be made on the basis of the child's individual needs and capabilities.

A number of court decisions have addressed the school's responsibility to ensure that children with disabilities are educated in the least restrictive appropriate environment (e.g., *Daniel R.R. v. Texas Board of Education, El Paso Independent School District*, 1989; *Greer v. Rome City School District*, 1991; *Sacramento City Unified School District, Board of Education v. Rachel H.*, 1994). In *Greer* (1991), the judge noted that "Congress created a statutory preference for educating handicapped children with non-handicapped children" (p. 695). In *Sacramento City Unified School District, Board of Education v. Holland* (1992), the court stated that the IDEA's preference for inclusion of children with disabilities in the general educational environment "rises to the level of a rebuttable presumption" (pp. 877–878). This means that placement decision making must begin with the assumption that the child can be educated in the general education classroom:

> Before the school district may conclude that a handicapped child should be educated outside the regular classroom, it must consider whether supplemental aids and services would permit satisfactory education in the regular classroom. The school district must consider the whole range of supplemental aids and services, including resource rooms and itinerant instruction, for which it is obligated under the Act.... Only when the handicapped child's education may not be achieved satisfactorily, even with one or more of these supplemental aids and services, may the school board consider placing the child outside of the regular classroom. (*Greer*, 1991, p. 696)

In *Holland* (1992) and, on appeal, *Sacramento City Unified School District, Board of Education v. Rachel H.* (1994), the courts established a four-part test for determining compliance with the IDEA's mainstreaming requirement. These rulings concerned Rachel, an elementary school child with moderate mental impairment (IQ 44), whose parents requested full-time placement in a general education classroom with supplemental services. The school district, however, believed that Rachel was "too severely disabled to benefit" from full-time placement in the general education classroom and recommended special education placement for all academic instruction (p. 1403). The Hollands appealed the school's placement decision to a state hearing officer, who ordered the district to place Rachel in a general education classroom with supportive services. The school district appealed this determination to the district court (1992), to the circuit court (1994), and to the Supreme Court (*certiorari denied*, 1994). The courts affirmed the hearing officer's decision that Rachel should be educated in the general education classroom.

In *Holland* (1994, p. 1404), the courts considered these four factors in determining the least restrictive appropriate environment: (1) the educational benefits available in a general education classroom, supplemented with appropriate aids and services, as compared with the educational benefits of a special education classroom; (2) the nonacademic benefits of interaction with children who are not disabled; (3) the effect of the child's presence on the teacher and other children in the classroom; and (4) the cost of educating the child in a general education classroom.

In evaluating the educational benefit of inclusion in the general education classroom, the *Holland* rulings considered the learning opportunities available in alternative settings and the child's likely progress toward IEP goals if placed in the general education classroom. In evaluating nonacademic benefits, the court considered whether the child was likely to interact with and learn from other children in the inclusive placement. As noted in an earlier case, the presumption of inclusion in the general education classroom is not rebutted unless the school shows that the child's disabilities are so severe that he or she will receive little or no educational benefit from inclusion (e.g., *Devries v. Fairfax County School Board*, 1989).

With regard to the effect of the child's presence on the teacher and other children, the court in *Holland* (1994, p. 1401) considered two aspects of disruptive behavior: (1) whether there was detriment because the child was disruptive, distracting, or unruly, and (2) whether the child would take up so much of the teacher's time that the other students would suffer from lack of attention. *Holland* thus suggested that an IEP team may consider the impact of the child's behavior on the setting where services are provided in determining an appropriate placement. However, the education of the other children must be compromised by the inclusion of the child with a disability to justify exclusion on this basis. The child may be excluded from the general education environment only if "after taking all reasonable steps to reduce the burden to the teacher, the other children in the class will still be deprived of their share of the teacher's attention" (*Holland*, 1992, p. 879; see also *B.E.L. v. Hawaii*, 2014; *Daniel R.R. v. Texas Board of Education, El Paso Independent School District*, 1989).

Schools also may consider the cost of providing an inclusive education. However, the cost must be *significantly* more expensive than alternative placements to justify an exclusion from the general education classroom on the basis of cost (*Holland*, 1994).

IDEIA regulations state that "in selecting the [least restrictive environment], consideration is given to any potential harmful effect on the child or on the quality of services that he or she needs; and ... [the] child with a disability is not removed from education in age-appropriate regular classrooms solely because of needed modifications in the general education curriculum" (34 CFR § 300.116[d–e]). However, several court cases suggest that the law does not require general education teachers to "modify the curriculum beyond recognition" (*Daniel R. R. v. Texas Board of Education*, 1989, p. 1048). *Daniel R. R.* and *Brillon v. Klein Independent School District* (2004) suggested that a fifth factor can be considered in making placement decisions, namely, whether the child can benefit from the general education curriculum *without substantial and burdensome curricular modifications*. In *Daniel R. R.* (1989), the court noted: "Mainstreaming would be pointless if we forced instructors to modify the regular education curriculum to the extent that the handicapped child is not required to learn any of the skills normally taught in regular education" (p. 1049). In the *Brillon* (2004) case, the court noted that placement of a second grader with disabilities in general education for social studies and science "required the school district to make unduly burdensome modifications to the regular curriculum" (p. 314). For this reason, the court held that providing social studies and science instruction to the child in the special education setting did not violate the least restrictive environment requirement.

As H. R. Turnbull and Turnbull (2000) noted, the courts have recognized that appropriate sometimes means more, rather than less, separation from the general education classroom. The LRE favors integration but allows separation when separation is needed to achieve a satisfactory educational program for the child. In *A. W. v. Northwest R-1 School District* (1987, p. 163), the judge noted that the mainstreaming requirement is "inapplicable" where it cannot be achieved satisfactorily.

A school placement that allows a child to remain with his or her family is considered to be less restrictive than a residential placement. IDEIA also indicates a preference for a neighborhood school. Part B regulations state that unless "the IEP of a child with a disability requires some other arrangement, the child is educated in the school that he or she would attend if not nondisabled" (34 CFR § 300.116[c]). However, although the law indicates a preference for neighborhood schooling, proximity of the school is only one factor the IEP team must consider in making placement decisions. The court in *Flour Bluff Independent School District v. Katherine M.* (1996) noted, "Distance remains a consideration in determining the least restrictive environment.... The child may have to travel farther, however, to obtain better services" (p. 695).

The SEA or LEA also must ensure that a child with a disability has opportunities to participate with nondisabled children in nonacademic and extracurricular activities (e.g., meals, recess, clubs, and interest groups) to the maximum extent appropriate to the needs of the child (34 CFR § 300.117). However, in several cases (e.g., *Rettig v. Kent City School District*, 1986), the courts ruled that IDEIA—Part B does not require schools to provide nonacademic and extracurricular activities to children with disabilities without regard for their ability to benefit from the experience.

The Meaning of *Appropriate Education*

IDEIA—Part B also requires that children with disabilities be offered a FAPE in the LRE. Since the passage of Pub. L. No. 94-142, a number of court cases have provided further interpretation of *appropriate education*. In their decision making about what is appropriate, the courts have considered several different factors, including whether IDEIA—Part B procedures were followed in developing the IEP and whether the IEP is consistent with the intent of the law (H. R. Turnbull & Turnbull, 2000).

Board of Education of the Hendrick Hudson Central School District v. Rowley (1982) was the first case to reach the Supreme Court in which the Court attempted to define *appropriate education* (see Exhibit 4.3). The Supreme Court's interpretation of appropriate education in *Rowley* has shaped all subsequent court decisions concerning the meaning of *appropriate education* under Part B. *Rowley* suggested that IDEIA ensures only an education program reasonably designed to benefit the student, not the best possible or most perfect education. The *Rowley* decision set forth a two-pronged test of appropriate education, namely, "Were IDEIA procedures followed in developing the IEP?" and "Is the program reasonably designed to benefit the child?"

Since *Rowley*, in a number of court cases, parents have challenged whether their child's special education program was reasonably calculated to enable their child to receive educational benefits. Consistent with the majority opinion in *Rowley*, these decisions suggest that the determination of whether a program is reasonably designed to confer benefit must be made on the basis of the individual child's potential. Furthermore, the program must be likely to provide meaningful benefit, that is, more than de minimis or trivial benefit, in relation to the child's potential (e.g., *Cordrey v. Euckert*, 1990). Also, as foreshadowed in the *Rowley* opinion, schools, not parents,

---

Exhibit 4.3 *Board of Education of the Hendrick Hudson Central School District v. Rowley* (1982)

The case involved Amy, a deaf child with minimal residual hearing, who understood about 50% of spoken language by lip-reading. During her kindergarten year, the school provided an FM hearing aid to amplify speech. Her IEP for first grade included continued use of the hearing aid, instruction from a tutor for the deaf one hour each day, and speech therapy three hours each week.

Amy's parents also requested that the school provide an interpreter for the deaf in the classroom in order for her to make optimal school progress. The school and a hearing officer agreed that an interpreter was too costly and not needed because "'Amy was achieving educationally, academically, and socially' without such assistance" (*Rowley*, p. 185). A district court, however, found in favor of the parents and noted that without the interpreter Amy was not afforded the opportunity to achieve her full potential.

Based on a review of the history of special education law, the Supreme Court concluded that Congress intended only to provide an education program "reasonably calculated to enable the child to receive educational benefits" (p. 207) or a "basic floor of opportunity" (p. 200). It was noted that there is no requirement under the Education for the Handicapped Act (EHA; now IDEIA) that the school provide services that maximize the potential of a child with disabilities; the "furnishing of every special service necessary to maximize each handicapped child's potential is, we think, further than Congress intended to go" (p. 199). The Court found in favor of the school.

have the authority to select specific instructional methodologies as long as the methods chosen are considered to be acceptable evidence-based practice (e.g., *Ridley School District v. M.R.*, 2012).

The courts also have ruled that when two or more appropriate placements are available, IEP team members may consider costs to the school in determining a child's education placement (e.g., *Clevenger v. Oak Ridge School Board*, 1984).

Extended School Year

IDEIA requires extended school year (ESY) services for a child with a disability if they are necessary to ensure an appropriate public education for the child. ESY services are provided beyond the normal school year, in accordance with the child's IEP and at no cost to the child's parents. Such services must be provided only if a child's IEP team determines, on an individual basis, that the services are necessary for the child to receive a free and appropriate public education (34 CFR § 300.106). The following standard for determining whether a child with disabilities is entitled to ESY services has gained acceptance:

> If a child will experience severe or substantial regression during the summer months in the absence of a summer program, the handicapped child may be entitled to year-round services. The issue is whether the benefits accrued to the child during the regular school year will be significantly jeopardized if he is not provided an educational program during the summer months. (*Alamo Heights Independent School District v. State Board of Education*, 1986, p. 1158)

According to *Cordrey* (1990) and *Reusch v. Fountain* (1994), "This standard is satisfied when it is shown that the student will suffer a significant regression of skills or knowledge without a summer program, followed by an insufficient recoupment of the same during the next school year" (*Reusch*, 1994, p. 1434). The courts have ruled that parents do not need empirical data demonstrating regression during summer and slow recoupment to establish that their child is entitled to ESY services (*Cordrey*, 1990; *Johnson v. Independent School District No. 4 of Bixby, Tulsa County, Oklahoma*, 1990). The court in *Cordrey* noted that it is unfair to require that a child demonstrate regression in the absence of summer programming in order to be entitled to such programming in subsequent summers and suggested that decisions about whether a child is entitled to ESY services can be based on predictive factors (i.e., the child is likely to show significant regression and slow recoupment of skills). Furthermore, decisions about whether a child is likely to show regression and slow recoupment may rely on "expert opinion, based on professional individual assessment" when empirical data are not available (*Cordrey*, 1990, p. 1472). Thus, rulings suggest schools may not require definitive empirical evidence of prior regression and slow recoupment in determining whether a child is entitled to ESY services.

Assistive Technology

IDEIA requires schools to ensure that assistive technology devices and services are made available to a child with a disability if the child requires the devices and services to receive an appropriate public education. An *assistive technology device* is "any item, piece of equipment, or product system, whether acquired commercially off the shelf, modified, or customized, that is used to increase, maintain, or improve the functional capabilities of a child with a disability. The term does not include a medical device that is surgically implanted" (e.g., cochlear implants) (34 CFR § 300.5). Schools are not obligated to provide eyeglasses, hearing aids, or braces. However, they must ensure that hearing aids are functioning properly (34 CFR § 300.113). *Assistive technology service* is "any service that directly assists a child with a disability in the selection, acquisition, or use of an assistive technology device" (34 CFR § 300.6). Assistive technology services include evaluation of the needs of a child with a disability; purchasing, leasing, or otherwise providing for the acquisition of an assistive technology device; selecting, designing, fitting, or customizing such devices; coordinating and using devices with other therapies or interventions; and training the child and the professionals involved in the use of the device (34 CFR § 300.6).

Freedom from Harassment

In *Shore Regional High School v. P.S.* (2004) (Exhibit 4.4), a federal court of appeals held that a school district failed to offer a free and appropriate education to a student

---

Exhibit 4.4 *Shore Regional High School v. P.S.* (2004)

P.S. was teased and bullied by other pupils in the early elementary grades, and the physical and verbal harassment intensified in the middle school. He was called names such as "Loser," "Bit Tits," and "Fat Ass"; bullies threw rocks at him; and a student hit him with a padlock in gym class. Bullies warned other students not to interact with him, and when he sat down at a cafeteria table, other students moved away. Despite repeated complaints by P.S.'s parents, the school administration failed to address the bullying.

Because of the severe and relentless harassment by other students, P.S. became depressed in middle school, his grades declined, and he attempted suicide. P.S. was placed in special education, with his school day modified so he could avoid situations where he would likely be harassed. P.S. was scheduled to attend the high school in his district, Shore Regional High School, beginning in ninth grade. Unhappy with the constant and continuing harassment of their son and the school district's failure to address the problem, P.S.'s parents requested a transfer to a public school in a neighboring district. When Shore High refused the transfer, P.S.'s parents unilaterally placed him in an out-of-district school and then took steps to recover out-of-district tuition, related costs, and attorney fees from Shore High. In requesting reimbursement, P.S.'s parents argued that Shore High had not offered P.S. a FAPE in the LRE. The courts ultimately upheld this request for reimbursement, noting that Shore High failed to offer "an education sufficiently free from the threat of harassment to constitute a FAPE" (p. 199).

who was subjected to severe and prolonged harassment by other students (also *T.K. v. New York City Department of Education*, 2011). In response to growing concerns about harassment and bullying of students with disabilities, the OSEP issued a "Dear Colleague Letter" to school districts in 2013 (Musgrove & Yudin, 2013). The letter noted that a student who is bullied may not be receiving an education that confers benefit because of the bullying. Consequently, to fulfill their obligations to students under IDEIA, schools must take steps to prevent and remedy bullying of students with disabilities. The OSEP also advised that, when a student with a disability is the target of bullying, attempting to solve the problem by moving him or her to a more "protected" setting could result in a denial of the student's right to be educated in the least restrictive environment.

Summary

Schools are required to offer a child with a disability an appropriate education reasonably designed to confer benefit. However, consistent with *Rowley*, IDEIA does not require that the school provide a program designed to maximize the potential of a child with disabilities.

Scope of Required Related Services

As noted earlier in the chapter, under IDEIA—Part B, a child must be found eligible for special education before he or she qualifies to receive related services, and the related services must be necessary to assist the child with disabilities to benefit from special education. The related services provision includes school health, school nurse, and counseling services, but medical services are provided only for diagnostic and evaluation purposes to determine a child's medically related disability (34 CFR § 300.34). This is the *medical exclusion*.

Whether certain services fall within the parameters of school health or counseling services (and are thus provided under IDEIA—Part B) has been the focus of a number of court cases. *Irving Independent School District v. Tatro* (1984) (Exhibit 4.5) was a key case in determining the scope of school health services required under IDEIA—Part B. In this case, the Supreme Court ruled that the school must provide clean intermittent catheterization (CIC) for a child with a disability as a related service needed for her to benefit from special education. In the Court's opinion, CIC is not a medical service because it can be performed by a trained layperson and requires only several minutes every three or four hours.

Thus, in accordance with *Tatro*, schools are not responsible for providing school health services that must be performed by a physician rather than a nurse or trained layperson. But what if a child requires *full-time* nursing care? Until 1999, courts ruled that full-time nursing care was beyond the scope of the services that must be provided by the schools (e.g., *Detsel v. Board of Education of the Auburn Enlarged City School District*, 1987). However, in 1999, the Supreme Court decided *Cedar Rapids Community School District v. Garret F. by Charlene F.*, a case concerning a ventilator-dependent student who required continuous, one-on-one nursing services to remain in school. Contrary to previous lower court rulings, the Supreme Court held

---

Exhibit 4.5 *Irving Independent School District v. Tatro* (1984)

Amber Tatro was born with spina bifida and had orthopedic and speech impairments and a neurogenic bladder. Because she was unable to empty her bladder voluntarily, she required CIC every three or four hours. This procedure involves insertion of a catheter into the urethra to drain the bladder and can be performed in a few minutes by a trained layperson.

Amber first received special education services at age 3, and her IEP provided early child development classes, occupational therapy, and physical therapy. There was no provision for CIC as requested by Amber's parents, however. The school held that CIC is a medical service and, under the EHA (now IDEIA), the school is required to provide medical services only for the purpose of diagnosis to determine the child's medically related disability.

Tatro ultimately reached the Supreme Court, and the Court decided in favor of the parents. The Court reasoned that Amber could not attend class (and, therefore, could not benefit from special education) without CIC as a related supportive service and held that CIC is not a medical service because it can be performed by a trained layperson or school nurse (i.e., a physician is not required).

---

that the school must provide full-time nursing services if such services are necessary for a child with a disability to benefit from special education. The Court reiterated *Tatro*, stating that schools are not responsible for services that must be performed by a physician, but made clear that the nursing services a child needs to benefit from special education must be provided without regard to the cost to the school.

Another question that arises under the related services provision of the IDEIA— Part B is: When is the school responsible for the cost of psychotherapy as a related service? Counseling services identified as related services in the regulations include "services provided by qualified social workers, psychologists, guidance counselors, and other qualified personnel" (34 CFR § 300.34[c][2]). Psychological services include "planning and managing a program of psychological services, including psychological counseling for children and parents" (34 CFR § 300.34[c][10][v]). Schools are required to provide these services at no cost to the parents when they are included in the child's IEP.

However, more difficult questions have arisen with regard to psychotherapy provided by a physician (i.e., psychiatric treatment). In *Max M. v. Thompson* (1984, p. 1444), the court held, "The simple fact that a service *could be* or *actually is* rendered by a physician rather than a non-physician does not dictate its removal from the list of required services" under special education law. The court went on to say that the limit to psychiatric services is cost: "A school board can be held liable for no more than the cost of the service as provided by the minimum level health care personnel recognized as competent to perform the related service" (p. 1444). Thus, this ruling (subsequently cited in multiple cases) suggests that in states where a psychologist or social worker is recognized as competent to provide psychotherapy, the school is responsible only for the amount it would cost for a psychologist or social worker to perform the service.

Court decisions have been inconsistent with regard to the school's responsibility when a child is placed in a residential mental health facility. In *Kruelle v. New Castle County School District* (1981, p. 693), the court noted that, in some cases, a child's "social, emotional, medical and educational problems are so intertwined" that a court is not able to determine whether the primary purpose of a residential placement is educational (and therefore the school's financial responsibility under IDEIA) or medical. In *Kruelle*, a student's placement in a residential facility was determined to be the least restrictive appropriate placement for the student and the school was required to assume financial responsibility for the residential placement. However, in a more recent case, the court did not find that the academic and mental health needs of a student were "too intertwined" to determine the primary purpose of the residential placement. In *Munir v. Pottsville Area School District* (2013), the court held that a child who was parentally placed in a mental health facility was so placed because of the child's psychiatric (medical) needs rather than the school's failure to offer a free appropriate education to the child and ruled that the school would not be required to assume financial responsibility for the child's residential mental health placement (see Pedi, 2014).

Coordination of IDEIA, Medicaid, and Private Health Insurance

When a child with a disability has multiple health-related needs, the cost of school health and nursing services can be extraordinarily high. IDEIA, however, typically funds only a small portion of the extra expenses involved in educating a child with a disability. States may set aside up to 10% of their monies for a so-called high-cost fund to be used to reimburse districts when the cost of providing special education and related services to a high-need child with a disability is greater than three times the average pupil expenditure (34 CFR § 300.704).

In 1990, the U.S. Department of Health and Human Services (U.S. HHS) signaled greater willingness to allow Medicaid coverage for health-related services for children receiving special education (see the 1991–1992 "HHS Policy Clarification" prepared by the U.S. HHS in cooperation with the U.S. DOE). In this policy clarification, HHS stated that school districts can bill the Medicaid program for medically necessary health-related services provided at school, at home, or in a residential facility if the child is eligible under the state's Medicaid plan. Medicaid now covers a broad range of medical services (e.g., physician's services, prescription drugs, therapeutic interventions such as occupational therapy, psychological services), and states have considerable flexibility in defining Medicaid eligibility groups. Under IDEIA, the state's governor must ensure interagency agreements regarding Medicaid and other public insurance agencies. Medicaid precedes the financial responsibility of the LEA and SEA, but the SEA remains the payer of last resort (34 CFR § 300.154).

An LEA must obtain parent consent before the school accesses the child's or parent's Medicaid or other insurance for the first time, and it is a one-time consent. The LEA must provide written notification to the child's parents before consent is obtained, and this notice must inform parents of their rights regarding the LEA accessing Medicaid or other insurance. More specifically, parents must be informed that they are not required to sign up for or enroll in public benefits or other insurance programs in order for their child to receive a free and appropriate education under Part B; the school must pay any deductibles or copays; schools also may not use a child's benefits under a public insurance program if that use would decrease the lifetime coverage available, result in the family's paying for care outside of school that would otherwise be covered, or result in increased premiums or discontinuation of insurance. The notice must also inform parents that they have a right to withdraw consent for disclosure of their child's personally identifiable information (PII) to the agency responsible for administering the public benefits or insurance program at any time and that their withdrawal of permission to disclose PII does not relieve the LEA of its responsibility to ensure that all required services are provided at no cost to the parent. Consistent with Family Educational Rights and Privacy Act of 1974 requirements, the written consent form must identify the PII that may be disclosed (e.g., records of the types of services provided to the child), the purpose of the disclosure (e.g., billing for services), and the agency to which the disclosure may be made (e.g., Medicaid or other insurance program). In addition, the consent form must specify that the parent understands and agrees that the LEA may access the child's or parent's public benefits or insurance to pay for services under IDEIA (34 CFR § 300.154).

Procedural Safeguards

A number of Part B procedural safeguards to ensure the rights of children with disabilities and their parents were foreshadowed in the *P.A.R.C.* and *Mills* decisions. Under IDEIA—Part B, the SEA must ensure that each LEA establishes and implements procedures to safeguard the parents' right to confidentiality of records and right to examine records; right to participate in meetings with respect to the identification, evaluation, and placement of their child; right to consent to the initial student evaluation and the initial placement; right to written prior notice before changes are made in identification, evaluation, placement, and special services; right to present findings from an independent evaluation; right to resolution of complaints by mediation; right to resolution of complaints by an impartial hearing officer; and right to bring civil action in court. Notice and consent, transfer of parental rights at age of majority, surrogate parents, and mediation and due process hearings are discussed next.

Consent and Notice

Depending on the proposed school action or refusal to act, IDEIA may require consent or written notice and procedural safeguards notice.

Consent. Under IDEIA—Part B, parental written consent (permission) must be obtained before conducting a preplacement evaluation and before the initial placement of a child in special education. If the parent refuses consent to the initial preplacement evaluation, the LEA may request mediation or a hearing to override a parent's refusal to consent. However, if the parent of a child who is homeschooled or parentally placed in a private school does not provide consent for the initial evaluation or reevaluation, or if the parent fails to respond to a request to provide consent, the LEA may not use the consent override procedures (34 CFR § 300.300).

Parent consent also is required for subsequent reevaluations of a child, unless the school can demonstrate that it has taken reasonable measures to obtain consent and the child's parent failed to respond. It also should be noted that if the parent refuses to consent to the initial *placement* of a child in special education, the school may not use mediation or due process procedures to override parent consent. Thus, consent for initial evaluation should not be misconstrued as consent for placement (34 CFR § 300.300).

Notice. IDEIA divides information sent to parents into two different types of notice: prior written notice and procedural safeguards notice. Prior written notice is required a reasonable time before the proposed school action whenever the SEA or LEA proposes to initiate or change the identification, evaluation, education placement, or program of the child or refuses to change the identification, evaluation, placement, or program. Notice must be provided in a mode of communication understandable to the parent (unless it is clearly not feasible to do so) and must include a description of the proposed action (or refusal to act); an explanation of why the school proposes or refuses to take action; a description of each evaluation procedure, test, record, or report used as the basis for the school's action; a statement that the parents have protection under procedural safeguards and, if the notice is not an initial referral for evaluation, the means by which a copy of a description of the procedural safeguards can be obtained; sources for parents to contact to obtain assistance in understanding these provisions (e.g., nonprofit group that could assist the parents); a description of any other options considered and why those were rejected; and a description of other factors that the IEP team considered and the reasons those options were rejected (34 CFR § 300.503).

A procedural safeguards notice includes information on protections available to the parents of a child with a disability. This information must be provided only one time a school year, except that a copy also must be given to the parents at the time of initial referral or parent request for an evaluation, following registration of a complaint, when a decision is made to make a removal that constitutes a change of placement because of violation of a code of student conduct, and upon parent request (34 CFR § 300.504; also see 34 CFR § 300.530).

The procedural safeguards notice must include a full explanation of the procedural safeguards written in an understandable manner. The content of the notice must include information pertaining to all the procedural safeguards relating to independent educational evaluations, prior written notice, parental consent, access to education records, opportunity to present and resolve complaints, the availability of mediation, the child's placement during the pendency of any due process complaint, procedures for students who are subject to placement in an interim alternative educational setting, requirements for unilateral placements by parents of children in private schools at public expense, hearings on due process complaints, state-level appeals, civil actions, and attorneys' fees (34 CFR § 300.504). Parents of a child with a disability may choose to receive notices by electronic mail, if the school makes that option available (34 CFR § 300.505).

Transfer of Parent Rights at Age of Majority

Under IDEIA, a state may require that when an individual with a disability reaches the age of majority or when a child with a disability is incarcerated in an adult or juvenile correctional facility, all rights accorded to parents transfer to the individual with a disability. The school or other agency must notify the individual and parents of the transfer of rights. For youth who have reached the age of majority and who have not been determined to be incompetent, but who are determined not to have the ability to provide informed consent with respect to their education program, the state will establish procedures for the appointment of the parent of the youth (or other appropriate person if the parent is not available) to represent the educational interest of the youth as long as he or she is eligible for special education under IDEIA (34 CFR § 300.520).

Surrogate Parents

Under IDEIA—Part B, the school must ensure that the rights of a child with disabilities are protected when no parent can be identified; when, after reasonable efforts, the school cannot locate the parents; when the child is a ward of the state under state laws; or when the child is an unaccompanied homeless youth. The school (or a judge overseeing the case of a child who is a ward of the state) must assign a surrogate parent for the child. The surrogate may not be an employee of the school or have interests that conflict with the interests of the child (34 CFR § 300.519).

Complaints, Resolution Meetings, Mediation, and Due Process Hearings

The school and parents may attempt to resolve disputes regarding the identification, evaluation, educational placement, or program of a child through resolution meetings, the mediation process, due process hearings, or civil action. The school and parents may agree to mediation of a disagreement prior to filing a due process complaint or after filing a due process complaint.

Complaints.   A due process complaint must allege that a violation occurred not more than two years before the date the parent or school knew or should have known about the action that forms the basis of the complaint, unless different explicit time limitations are identified in state law (34 CFR § 300.507). IDEIA requires the school to have procedures that require either party (school or parent) to provide the other party a written due process complaint, which must remain confidential. The complaint must include: (a) the name and address of the child and the name of the school he or she is attending; (b) a description of the nature of the problem of the child relating to the proposed or refused initiation or change, including facts relating to the problem; and (c) a proposed resolution of the problem to the extent known and available to the parents at that time. Within five days of receipt of notification, a hearing officer reviews the complaint to determine if it is sufficient or needs amendment. The party receiving the complaint has 10 days to send the other party a response that specifically addresses the issues raised in the due process complaint (34 CFR § 300.508).

Resolution Meetings.   Within 15 days of receiving notice of the parents' due process complaint, and prior to the initiation of a hearing, the school must convene a resolution meeting with the parents and members of the IEP team who have knowledge of the facts identified in the complaint. The purpose of the resolution meeting is to give the school an additional opportunity to attempt to resolve the dispute without a due process hearing. The meeting does not have to be held if the parent and school agree in writing to waive the meeting or if the parent and the school agree to use the mediation process. If a resolution of the dispute is reached at the meeting, the parties sign a legally binding agreement that is enforceable in any state or federal court. If the complaint is not resolved during the resolution meeting, a due process hearing is held within 30 days of the receipt of the due process complaint (34 CFR § 300.510).

Mediation. Any SEA or LEA that receives IDEIA funds must ensure that procedures are established and implemented to allow parties to resolve disputes regarding the identification, evaluation, educational placement, or program of a child through a mediation process. This process must be available to resolve disputes arising prior to the filing of a due process complaint. The procedures must ensure that the mediation process is: (a) voluntary on the part of the parties; (b) not used to deny or delay a parent's right to a due process hearing, or to deny any other parental rights; and (c) conducted by a qualified and impartial mediator who is trained in effective mediation techniques (34 CFR § 300.506).

The SEA or LEA may establish procedures to offer parents and schools that choose not to use the mediation process an opportunity to meet, at a time and location convenient to the parents, with a disinterested party who is under contract with an appropriate alternative dispute resolution agency to explain and discuss the benefits of the mediation process. The SEA is responsible for maintaining a list of qualified mediators and bears the costs of the mediation process. The mediator must be selected on a random, rotational, or other impartial basis. The mediator must not be an employee of the school, and no individual with a personal or professional conflict of interest may serve as mediator. An agreement reached by the parties as a result of mediation is a legally binding document. Discussions that occur during mediation are confidential and may not be used as evidence in any subsequent due process hearing or civil proceeding that arises from the dispute (34 CFR § 300.506).

Due Process Hearings. IDEIA—Part B also grants parents and the school a right to an impartial due process hearing on any matter regarding the identification, evaluation, educational placement, or program of a child. In a 2005 Supreme Court decision, the Court held that the burden of persuasion in an administrative hearing challenging a child's IEP falls on the party seeking relief, whether it is the parent of child with a disability or the school (*Schaffer v. Weast*, 2005). Under the IDEIA—Part B, the due process hearing must be conducted by the SEA or other school agency responsible for the child. Each SEA or LEA must maintain a list of hearing officers and their qualifications. The hearing officer may not be an employee of the school, and no person with a personal or professional interest in the outcome may serve as the hearing officer. The school must inform the parents of any free or low-cost legal and other relevant services available (34 CFR § 300.507) and that they may be able to recover attorney fees if they prevail in a hearing or judicial proceeding (34 CFR § 300.517).

IDEIA—Part B further specifies a number of hearing rights. The hearing must be held at a time and place reasonably convenient to the parents. Each party has a right to be accompanied and advised by legal counsel and other experts and to present evidence and confront, cross-examine, and compel the attendance of witnesses (34 CFR § 300.512). The party requesting the due process hearing may not raise issues at the hearing that were not raised in the due process complaint, unless both parties agree otherwise (34 CFR § 300.511). No evidence may be introduced by any party unless it was disclosed at least five business days before the hearing; each party must disclose to all other parties all evaluations completed by that date and the recommendations based on those evaluations if the findings from such evaluations will be used at the hearing. The parents are afforded the right to have their child present and to have the hearing open to the public (34 CFR § 300.512).

The hearing generally must be held and a final decision reached within 45 days after the expiration of the resolution period (30 days after the receipt of the due process complaint) (34 CFR § 300.515). Each party has a right to a written record of the hearing (or an electronic verbatim recording if the parent so chooses) and to a copy of the written findings of fact and the decision (34 CFR § 300.512). The decision of the hearing officer is final unless a party initiates an appeal or begins a court action. An appeal may be filed by the parent or the school to the SEA for an impartial review of the findings and the decision appealed (34 CFR § 300.514).

Right to Private Action

IDEIA grants the parents and the school the right to civil action if they are not satisfied with the SEA decision. This means that parents may initiate a court action against the school on behalf of a child with a disability if they believe the school has violated the provisions of IDEIA with respect to their child (34 CFR § 300.516). When parents prevail, they typically are awarded tuition reimbursement for private educational services or compensatory education as remedies for a school's failure to offer a free and appropriate education to their child. Except for very unusual circumstances, parents are required to exhaust administrative remedies (e.g., due process hearings) available to them before they pursue a court action. In *Schaffer v. Weast* (2005), the Supreme Court ruled that the burden of proof (the burden of persuasion) in cases challenging the appropriateness of an IEP rests with the challenging party. In *Winkelman v. Parma City School District* (2007), the Supreme Court ruled that parents may pursue a court action under IDEIA without being represented by an attorney.

It is important to note that, in determining whether to award the parent tuition reimbursement or compensatory education, the courts typically focus primarily on the issue of whether the school failed to offer a child with a disability a free and appropriate education reasonably designed to confer benefit. For example, if a child with a disability was assigned an incorrect disability classification (e.g., he or she was identified as qualifying within the Other Health Impairment classification rather than Autism), the court is likely to view this as a harmless error as long as the student's IEP was tailored to meet his or her individual needs (e.g., *Fort Osage R-I School District v. Sims*, 2011; *Weissburg v. Lancaster School District*, 2010). The courts also are likely to disregard minor IDEIA procedural violations by the school if, despite those violations, the school offered a free and appropriate education to the student.

Recovery of Attorney Fees

In 1986, Congress enacted the Handicapped Children's Protection Act (Pub. L. No. 99-372), an amendment to special education law that provides: "In any action or proceeding brought under this subsection, the court, in its discretion, may award reasonable attorneys' fees as part of the costs to the parents or guardian of a handicapped child or youth who is the prevailing party" (20 U.S.C. 1415[a][4][B]). In *Hensley v. Eckerhart* (1983), the Supreme Court found that "plaintiffs may be considered 'prevailing parties' for the purposes of recovery of attorney fees if they succeed on any significant issue in litigation which achieves some of the benefit the parties sought in bringing the suit" (p. 433). IDEIA prohibits recovery of attorney fees for an IEP meeting unless the meeting is convened as a result of an administrative proceeding or a judicial action; for mediation that is conducted prior to filing a complaint; or if the parent declines a written settlement offer and the court later awards the parent a lesser amount. In addition, attorney fees may be reduced if the parent unreasonably protracted the resolution of the dispute, the fees unreasonably exceeded the prevailing rate in the community, the time spent on legal services was excessive in light of the nature of the proceedings, or the attorney representing the parent did not provide the required information to the school district (34 CFR § 300.517).

Abrogation of State Sovereign Immunity

Under IDEIA, states and their departments of education can be sued by private citizens if they violate the law. This provision in IDEIA waives the traditional immunity from private lawsuits that states enjoy under the 11th Amendment to the Constitution.

INFANTS AND TODDLERS WITH DISABILITIES

Pub. L. No. 99-457, the Education for the Handicapped Act Amendments of 1986, provided grants to states to develop and implement a statewide, comprehensive system of early intervention services for infants and toddlers with disabilities and their families. The current IDEIA statute (Pub. L. 108-446), Part C—Infants and Toddlers with Disabilities, identified five reasons for the law:

(1) to enhance the development of infants and toddlers with disabilities and to minimize their potential for developmental delay;

(2) to reduce the education costs to our society, including our Nation's schools, by minimizing the need for special education and related services after infants and toddlers with disabilities reach school age;

(3) to maximize the potential for individuals with disabilities to live independently in society;

(4) to enhance the capacity of families to meet the special needs of their infants and toddlers with disabilities; and

(5) to enhance the capacity of state and local agencies and service providers to identify, evaluate, and meet the needs of all children, particularly minority, low-income, inner-city, and rural children, and infants and toddlers in foster care. (Pub. L. No. 105-17; § 631; 118 Stat. 2644 [2004])

A number of similarities and differences exist between legislation providing a free and appropriate education for children with disabilities in the 3- to 21-year age group (IDEIA—Part B) and the legislation providing grants for early intervention services for infants and toddlers (IDEIA—Part C). Part C is described under the following sections: "Statewide System," "Child Find," "Eligible Children," "Evaluation and Assessment," "Individualized Family Service Plan," "Early Intervention Services," and "Procedural Safeguards."

Statewide System

Prior to 1986, services for infants and toddlers with disabilities typically were provided by a number of different agencies in each state (social services, public health, education), often resulting in service gaps or unnecessary duplication (J. J. Gallagher, 1989). IDEIA—Part C was designed to encourage states to develop and implement a statewide, comprehensive, coordinated, multidisciplinary, interagency program of early intervention services for infants and toddlers with disabilities and their families (34 CFR § 303.1).

The law requires each state to identify a lead agency responsible for administration, supervision, coordination, and monitoring of programs and activities in the state. Different states have chosen different lead agencies, including state departments of health, education, and social welfare (J. J. Gallagher, 1989). To receive funds, each state must have submitted an application to the U.S. DOE that outlines state policies and procedures for the delivery of services consistent with the requirements of Part C. Part C also requires the establishment of a state interagency coordinating council to advise and assist the lead agency; advise and assist regarding the transition of toddlers with disabilities to preschool and other appropriate services; and prepare and submit an annual report to the U.S. DOE on the status of intervention service programs for infants and toddlers with disabilities and their families (34 CFR § 303.604).

Child Find

IDEIA—Part C requires each state to establish a public awareness program and a comprehensive child find system to ensure that eligible infants and toddlers with disabilities are identified, located, and evaluated (34 CFR § 303.301–302). Each state must develop a public central directory that contains information about public and private early intervention services, resources, and experts available in the state and research and demonstration projects being conducted in the state relating to infants and toddlers with disabilities (34 CFR § 303.117).

Eligible Children

IDEIA—Part C defines *infant or toddler with a disability* to mean a child under 3 years of age who needs early intervention services because he or she is experiencing a developmental delay, as measured by appropriate diagnostic assessments, in one or more of these areas—cognitive, physical (including vision and hearing), communication, social or emotional, or adaptive development—or has a diagnosed physical or mental condition that has a high probability of resulting in developmental delay (34 CFR § 303.21). The term also may include, at a state's discretion, at-risk infants and toddlers. The term *at-risk infant or toddler* means a child under 3 years of age who would be at risk of experiencing a substantial developmental delay if early intervention services were not provided. The factors that put the child at risk may be biological or environmental (34 CFR § 303.5).

Evaluation and Assessment

IDEIA—Part C requires a multidisciplinary assessment of the unique strengths and needs of an infant or toddler with a disability and the identification of services appropriate to meet such needs. All evaluations and assessments of the child and family must be conducted by qualified personnel, in a nondiscriminatory manner, and selected and administered so not to be racially or culturally discriminatory. In conducting the evaluation of the child, no single procedure may be used as the sole criterion for determining a child's eligibility and procedures must include administering evaluation instrument(s); taking the child's history (including interviewing the parent); identifying the child's level of functioning in each of the developmental areas; gathering information from other sources, such as family members, other caregivers, medical providers, social workers, and educators, if necessary, to understand the full scope of the child's unique strengths and needs; and reviewing medical, educational, and other records (34 CFR § 303.321).

IDEIA—Part C also requires a family-directed assessment of the resources, priorities, and concerns of the family and the identification of the supports and services necessary to enhance the family's capacity to meet the developmental needs of the infant or toddler. The family-directed assessment must be voluntary on the part of each family member participating in the assessment; be based on information obtained through an assessment tool and also through an interview with those family members who elect to participate in the assessment; and include the family's description of its resources, priorities, and concerns related to enhancing the child's development (34 CFR § 303.321). With the exception of unusual circumstances, the evaluation and initial assessment of each child and family must be completed within 45 days after the lead agency receives the referral (34 CFR § 303.310).

Individualized Family Service Plan

IDEIA—Part C requires a written individualized family service plan (IFSP) rather than an IEP for each infant or toddler. The IFSP is developed at a meeting that includes the parent or parents of the child, and other family members as requested by the parents, if feasible to do so; an advocate or person outside of the family if the parents request that the person participate; the service coordinator designated by the lead agency; a person directly involved in conducting the evaluations and assessment; and, as appropriate, persons who will be providing early intervention services to the child or family. If one of these persons is unable to attend, arrangements must be made for the person's involvement through other means (e.g., telephone call, having a knowledgeable authorized representative attend the meeting, making pertinent records available) (34 CFR § 303.343). The IFSP meetings must be conducted in settings and at times that are convenient for the family and in the native language or other mode of communication used by the family, unless it is clearly not feasible to do so. Written notice of meeting arrangements must be provided to the family and other participants early enough before the meeting date to ensure that they will be able to attend. For the child who has been referred for evaluation for the first time and found eligible, the meeting to develop the IFSP must be conducted within 45 days of the referral (34 CFR § 303.342). With the consent of the parent, services may be provided prior to the completion of the assessment (34 CFR § 303.345).

The IFSP must include: (a) a statement of the infant or toddler with a disability's present levels of physical development (including vision, hearing, and health status), cognitive, communication, social or emotional, and adaptive development based on the information from that child's evaluation and assessments; (b) with the concurrence of the family, a statement of the family's resources, priorities, and concerns relating to enhancing the development of the child; and (c) a statement of the measurable results or outcomes expected to be achieved for the child (including preliteracy and language skills, as developmentally appropriate for the child) and the family, and the criteria, procedures, and timelines used to determine the degree to which progress toward achieving the results and outcomes identified in the IFSP is being made. When appropriate, necessary modifications of the expected outcomes or early intervention services should be identified. Additionally, the IFSP must include: (d) a statement of the specific early intervention services, based on peer-reviewed research (to the extent practical), that are necessary to meet the unique needs of the child and the family to achieve the outcomes, including: the length, duration, frequency, intensity, and method of delivering early intervention services. The IFSP must also include the determination of the appropriate setting for providing early intervention services and a statement that each early intervention service is provided in the natural environment for that child to the maximum extent appropriate, or a justification as to why an early intervention service will not be provided in the natural environment. For each early intervention service, the IFSP must include the location of the services and the payment arrangements, if any. For children who are at least 3 years of age, the IFSP must include an educational component that promotes school readiness and incorporates preliteracy, language, and numeracy skills. (e) To the extent appropriate, the IFSP also must identify medical and other services that the child or family needs or is receiving through other sources but that are neither required nor funded under Part C. If those services are not currently being provided, the IFSP must include a description of the steps the service coordinator or family may take to assist the child and family in securing those services. (f) The IFSP must also include the projected date for the initiation of each early intervention service and the anticipated duration of each service, and (g) the name of the service coordinator responsible for implementing the child's IFSP, including transition services and coordination with other agencies and persons. Last, (h) the IFSP must include the steps and services to be taken to support the smooth transition of the child with a disability to preschool or other appropriate services (34 CFR § 303.344).

The content of the IFSP must be explained fully to the parents, and informed written consent from the parents must be obtained prior to the provision of the early intervention services described in the plan. Each early intervention service must be provided as soon as possible after the parent provides consent for that service. An annual meeting is conducted to evaluate the IFSP, and the family is provided with a review of the plan every six months, or more often if needed (34 CFR § 303.342).

Early Intervention Services

Under Part C, early intervention services include both special instruction and related services; an infant or toddler can receive a related service under Part C without receiving special instruction. (This differs from the requirement under Part B that children with disabilities ages 3 to 21 only receive related services in order to benefit from special education.) The term *early intervention services* means developmental services that are: (a) provided under public supervision; (b) are selected in collaboration with the parents; (c) are provided at no cost except where federal or state law provides a system of payments by families including a schedule of sliding fees; and (d) are designed to meet the developmental needs of an infant or toddler with a disability and the needs of the family to assist appropriately in the infant's or toddler's development in any one or more of the following areas: physical, cognitive, communication, social or emotional, or adaptive development. Types of services include assistive technology device and service; audiology services; family training, counseling, and home visits; health services; medical services; nursing services; nutrition services; occupational therapy; physical therapy; psychological services; service coordination services; sign language and cued language services; social work services; special instruction; speech-language pathology; transportation and related costs; and vision services (34 CFR § 303.13).

Procedural Safeguards

The procedural safeguards under Part C are similar to those under Part B. Parents are afforded the right to confidentiality of PII; the right to examine records; the right to consent to or decline any early intervention service without jeopardizing the right to other services; the right to written prior notice before changes are made in identification, evaluation, placement, or provision of services; the right to use mediation; the right to timely administrative resolution of complaints; and the right to bring civil action in state or federal court (34 CFR § 303.400–449).

CONCLUDING COMMENTS

Pub. L. No. 94-142 was enacted more than 40 years ago. Amendments, court interpretations, changing rules and regulations, and policy statements have further shaped special education law. Education law will continue to change. School psychologists must keep abreast of these changes to ensure that the educational rights of pupils are safeguarded.

STUDY AND DISCUSSION

Questions for Chapter 4

1. Why did Congress require single-agency responsibility for children with disabilities?
2. What is the zero reject principle?
3. What is the purpose of the IEP meeting? Who attends? Briefly describe the content of the IEP.
4. Briefly describe what is meant by *least restrictive appropriate environment* in special education law. Does this aspect of the law mean that all children with disabilities must be integrated into the general education classroom? What are the guiding principles for determining a child's educational placement?
5. How is *appropriate education* defined in *Rowley*?
6. What is the medical exclusion?
7. Under federal law, what is the role of a *DSM-5* diagnosis in determining whether a student is eligible for special education under IDEIA—Part B?
8. What are some of the ways that Part C and Part B differ?

Activities

1. Compare the 13 disability categories under IDEIA—Part B with the categories and eligibility criteria that appear in the special education guidelines of your state.
2. Does your state have model forms for services to students in special education? If yes, review the model forms prepared by your state's department of education. If not, visit the State of Washington Office of the Superintendent of Public Instruction's Web site: http://www.k12.wa.us/SpecialEd/Data/ModelStateForms .aspx and review the model forms provided. Note that these forms were written to ensure compliance with the state's regulations implementing IDEIA and that the model forms are available in several different languages. On the same Web page, access and skim the "IEP Review Form" and the "Evaluation Review Form." These forms were prepared to assist school professionals when reviewing their own evaluations, reevaluations, and IEPs for compliance with state special education rules.

Chapter 5 ———————————————————

SECTION 504 AND THE AMERICANS WITH DISABILITIES ACT

This chapter begins with a summary of those portions of Section 504 of the Rehabilitation Act of 1973 most pertinent to school psychological practice. Special attention is given to similarities and differences between Section 504 and the Individuals with Disabilities Education Improvement Act of 2004 (IDEIA) regarding school responsibilities to students with disabilities. We also provide a brief overview of the Americans with Disabilities Act of 1990 (ADA) and the Americans with Disabilities Amendments Act of 2008 (ADAA).

SECTION 504

Section 504 of the Rehabilitation Act of 1973 is civil rights legislation that prohibits discrimination against students with disabilities in school systems receiving federal financial assistance. Contemporary interpretations suggest that schools must attend to three types of potential discrimination prohibited by law:

1. Section 504 prohibits public schools from excluding students from participating in school programs and activities solely on the basis of a disability.
2. It requires schools to take effective steps to prevent harassment on the basis of disability.
3. It requires schools to make accommodations to ensure that students with disabilities have opportunities to benefit from its programs and activities that are equal to those provided to students without disabilities.

Passed in 1973, Section 504 was initially misunderstood or ignored by the schools. Beginning in the late 1980s, however, Office for Civil Rights (OCR) enforcement activities, court decisions, and parent advocacy efforts heightened awareness of Section 504, and the law subsequently began to impact school practices. School psychologists must be knowledgeable about Section 504 and its role in safeguarding the right to equal educational opportunity for students with a broad range of physical and mental impairments.

Historical Framework

One way Congress attempted to ensure a free and appropriate education for all children with disabilities was through federal grant legislation, such as Pub. L. No. 94-142. A second way the federal government attempted to address the problem of discrimination against students with disabilities was through antidiscrimination laws. One of the first bills that attempted to ensure equal educational opportunity for children with disabilities in the public schools was an amendment to Title VI of the Civil Rights Act of 1964. The bill subsequently became part of the Rehabilitation Act of 1973 (Pub. L. No. 93-112; Martin, 1979). Section 504 of the Rehabilitation Act states, "No otherwise qualified handicapped individual in the United States ... shall, solely by reason of his handicap, be excluded from the participation in, or be denied the benefits of, or be subjected to discrimination under any program or activity receiving Federal financial assistance" (29 U.S.C. § 794).

The intent of Section 504 was to require all states to provide educational opportunities for children with disabilities equal to those provided to children without disabilities. However, the Rehabilitation Act of 1973 is concerned primarily with discrimination in employment settings, and many interpreted Section 504 as a prohibition against employment discrimination in the schools. The 1974 amendments to the Rehabilitation Act (Pub. L. No. 93-516) clarified the intent of the law by specifically prohibiting discrimination against students with physical or mental impairments in schools receiving federal funds (Martin, 1979).

There was still no immediate impact on school policies regarding children with disabilities, however. Advocates for the rights of students with disabilities staged wheelchair sit-ins to encourage the quick development of regulations implementing the law, while school officials quietly protested this legislation as too costly for the public schools (Martin, 1979). The U.S. Department of Health, Education, and Welfare (HEW), caught in the middle, was slow to issue regulations implementing Section 504. As Martin noted, HEW did not require compliance with Section 504 until the 1978–1979 school year, a full five years after the law was passed.

During the same years that HEW was struggling to develop regulations for Section 504, Congress debated and passed several laws providing funds to states to assure educational opportunities for children with disabilities. Following the passage of the Education for All Handicapped Children Act of 1975 (Pub. L. No. 94-142), public school districts typically concentrated on fulfilling their obligation to provide special education and related services to students with disabilities in conformance with its requirements. Many school administrators were unaware that the broad definition of *handicapped* under Section 504 included a number of students who did not qualify as disabled under Pub. L. No. 94-142. They erroneously believed that compliance with special education law meant the school was in full compliance with Section 504 (Martin, 1992).

In the late 1980s, a number of lawsuits and complaints to the OCR were filed on behalf of students in general education programs because schools failed to make accommodations for their Section 504 handicapping conditions (e.g., *Elizabeth S. v. Thomas K. Gilhool*, 1987; Lake Washington [WA] School District No. 414, 1985; Rialto [CA] Unified School District, 1989).[1] Advocacy efforts on behalf of children with attention deficit disorder (ADD) and attention-deficit/hyperactivity disorder (ADHD) also were an important trigger for increased attention to Section 504 requirements.

Passage of the Americans with Disabilities Act of 1990 (Pub. L. No. 101-336) further heightened attention to the requirements of Section 504. As will be seen later in this chapter, the ADA generally requires full compliance with Section 504, but at times it requires more than Section 504 does with regard to the school's obligations to students with physical or mental impairments. In 2008, the ADAA (Pub. L. No. 110-325) was passed, further defining and clarifying the criteria for determining whether a student has a disability under ADAA and is eligible for Section 504 protections and accommodations.[2]

Overview of Section 504

As previously noted, Section 504 of the Rehabilitation Act of 1973 was designed to eliminate discrimination on the basis of disability in any program or activity receiving federal financial assistance. Subpart D applies to preschool, elementary, and secondary education programs and activities. Section 504 is antidiscrimination legislation; it is not a federal grant program. Unlike IDEIA, Section 504 does not provide funds to schools. A state department of education may choose not to pursue monies available under federal grant statutes (e.g., IDEIA—Part C funds for infants and toddlers). However, school districts must comply with antidiscrimination legislation if they receive any federal funds for any purpose.

The OCR, an agency within the U.S. Department of Education (DOE), is charged with investigating Section 504 and ADAA complaints pertaining to U.S. DOE programs or activities. The OCR has the authority to remove federal funds from a district if it is not in compliance with Section 504.

Unlike IDEIA, Section 504 does not require states to develop a written plan to meet the requirements of the law. However, under Section 504, each school district must designate at least one person to coordinate its efforts to comply with the law and adopt grievance procedures that incorporate appropriate due process standards and provide for the prompt and equitable resolution of complaints alleging violations of Section 504 (34 CFR § 104.7).[3] Each school district also must take appropriate and continuing steps to notify students and their parents that it does not discriminate in its programs and activities on the basis of disability (34 CFR § 104.8).

---

[1] References to court cases are italicized; references to OCR opinions and administrative hearings are not.

[2] The ADAA language quoted in this chapter is based on the text of United State Code (U.S.C.) Title 42 Chapter 126 § 12101 et seq., downloaded June 23, 2015, from Legal Information Institute: https://www.law.cornell.edu

[3] Electronic Code of Federal Regulations (e-CFR) current as of June 18, 2015.

Preventing Discrimination in Access to Programs and Services

Section 504 specifically prohibits schools from discriminating on the basis of disability (see Exhibit 5.1 for the Section 504/ADAA definition of disability) in providing any aid, benefit, or service, either directly or through contractual arrangements. Schools must provide accommodations for a student with a Section 504/ADAA disability if the accommodations are necessary to ensure equal educational opportunity for the student. Schools are not required to produce the identical result or level of achievement for students with and without disabilities, but they *must afford students with disabilities equal opportunity* to obtain the same result, to gain the same benefit, or to reach the same level of achievement, in the most integrated setting appropriate to the student's needs. Schools may not provide different or separate aid, benefits, or services to students with disabilities unless such action is necessary to provide them with services that are as effective as those provided to others. When separate programs or activities exist to meet the needs of students with disabilities, a school may not deny a qualified student with a disability the opportunity to participate in programs or activities that are not separate or different (34 CFR § 104.4; also see *Baird v. Rose*, 1999). For example, in recent years, some school districts refused to allow qualified students with disabilities to enroll in advanced placement or other accelerated programs. Such practices are a violation of Section 504 (Monroe, 2007).

Case 5.1 is based on a real-life incident. The school's policy of barring special education classes from the school's computer lab was clearly in violation of Section 504. The policy was changed quickly after it was challenged by the special education teacher and the school psychologist.

Protection From Disability Harassment

Section 504 and Title II of the ADAA protect students from harassment based on disability. The term *harassment* means oral, written, graphic, or physical conduct *relating to an individual's disability* that is sufficiently severe, pervasive, or persistent so as to interfere with or limit the ability of an individual to participate in or benefit from the

---

Case 5.1

Mrs. Drew, a middle school special education teacher, teaches an English class for students with intellectual disabilities who cannot keep pace in the general education English curriculum. After observing that several of Mrs. Drew's students had problems with handwriting, Pearl Meadows offered to take Mrs. Drew and her students to the school's computer lab to show them how to use a simple word processing program for English writing assignments. When Pearl contacted the teacher responsible for scheduling the school's computer lab, she was told that, in accordance with school policy, special education classes were not allowed to use the computer lab because the students were too likely to damage the expensive equipment.

district's programs or activities. Bullying is one type of harassment. Between 2009 and 2014, the OCR received "more than 2,000 complaints regarding bullying of students with disabilities in the nation's elementary and secondary schools" (U.S. DOE Press Office, October 21, 2014).

In a 2014 "Dear Colleague Letter" (Lhamon, 2014), the OCR issued extensive guidance to schools regarding their obligations to address and prevent disability-based harassment and bullying under Section 504 and Title II of the ADAA:

> Bullying of a student on the basis of his or her disability may result in a disability-based harassment violation under Section 504 and Title II.... [W]hen a school knows or should know of bullying conduct based on a student's disability, it must take immediate and appropriate action to investigate or otherwise determine what occurred. If a school's investigation reveals that bullying based on disability created a hostile environment—i.e., the conduct was sufficiently serious to interfere with or limit a student's ability to participate in or benefit from the services, activities, or opportunities offered by a school—the school must take prompt and effective steps reasonably calculated to end the bullying. (footnote numbers omitted, Lhamon, 2014, p. 4)

The 2014 "Dear Colleague Letter" also identified the elements that the OCR would consider to determine whether a disability-based harassment violation occurred under Section 504 and Title II of the ADAA: "(1) a student is bullied based on disability; (2) the bullying is sufficiently serious to create a hostile environment; (3) school officials know or should know about the bullying; and (4) the school does not respond appropriately" (Lhamon, 2014, p. 4).

In addition, some courts have recognized the right of parents to seek monetary damages or another remedy for disability harassment under Section 504 and the ADAA (e.g., *K.M. ex rel. D.G. v. Hyde Park Central School District*, 2005; *Werth v. Board of Directors of the Public Schools of the City of Milwaukee*, 2007). However, as Secunda (2015) observed, such court actions have resulted in "a remarkable lack of success even in the most severe instances of special education student bullying" (p. 175). As will be seen in Chapter 9, the courts use more stringent tests than the OCR to determine whether bullying of a student was a violation of his or her civil rights.

Some students with Section 504/ADAA impairments also qualify as having a disability under IDEIA. As noted in Chapter 4, persistent harassment of a student eligible for special education and related services may be interpreted by the courts to mean that the student's placement does not provide a free and appropriate education in the least restrictive environment (*Shore Regional High School v. P.S.*, 2004).

Section 504/ADAA Definition of *Disability*

To be eligible for special education and related services under IDEIA—Part B, students must be evaluated in accordance with procedures outlined in Part B and found eligible under one of the 13 categories of disability, and they must need special education because of that disability (see Chapter 4). The definition of *disability* under Section 504/ADAA is broader and more open-ended than under IDEIA (Zirkel, 2009a). Under Section 504/ADAA, the term *disability* means a physical or mental impairment that substantially limits one or more of the major life activities of the individual (see Exhibit 5.1). *Major life activities* include, but are not limited to, functions such as caring for oneself, performing manual tasks, seeing, hearing, eating, sleeping, walking, standing, lifting, bending, speaking, breathing, learning, reading, concentrating, thinking, communicating, and working.

Exhibit 5.1 Definition of *Disability* as Amended by the ADAA

Disability means, with respect to an individual, a physical or mental impairment that substantially limits one or more of the major life activities of such individual; a record of such an impairment; or being regarded as having such an impairment.

(1)　(i)　The phrase *physical or mental impairment* means—

　　　(A)　Any physiological disorder or condition, cosmetic disfigurement, or anatomical loss affecting one or more of the following body systems: Neurological, musculoskeletal, special sense organs, respiratory (including speech organs), cardiovascular, reproductive, digestive, genitourinary, hemic and lymphatic, skin, and endocrine;

　　　(B)　Any mental or psychological disorder such as mental retardation, organic brain syndrome, emotional or mental illness, and specific learning disabilities.

　　(ii)　The phrase *physical or mental impairment* includes, but is not limited to, such contagious and noncontagious diseases and conditions as orthopedic, visual, speech and hearing impairments, cerebral palsy, epilepsy, muscular dystrophy, multiple sclerosis, cancer, heart disease, diabetes, mental retardation, emotional illness, specific learning disabilities, HIV disease (whether symptomatic or asymptomatic), tuberculosis, drug addiction, and alcoholism.

　　(iii)　The phrase *physical or mental impairment* does not include homosexuality or bisexuality.

(2)　The phrase *major life activities* means functions such as caring for one's self, performing manual tasks, walking, seeing, hearing, speaking, breathing, learning, and working.

(3)　The phrase *has a record of such an impairment* means has a history of, or has been misclassified as having, a mental or physical impairment that substantially limits one or more major life activities.

(4)　The phrase *is regarded as having an impairment* means—

　　(i)　Has a physical or mental impairment that does not substantially limit major life activities but that is treated by a public entity as constituting such a limitation;

　　(ii)　Has a physical or mental impairment that substantially limits major life activities only as a result of the attitudes of others toward such impairment; or

> (iii) Has none of the impairments defined in paragraph (1) of this definition but is treated by a public entity as having such an impairment.
>
> (5) The term *disability* does not include—
>
>   (i) Transvestism, transsexualism, pedophilia, exhibitionism, voyeurism, gender identity disorders not resulting from physical impairments, or other sexual behavior disorders;
>
>   (ii) Compulsive gambling, kleptomania, or pyromania; or
>
>   (iii) Psychoactive substance use disorders resulting from current illegal use of drugs.
>
>   *Drug* means a controlled substance, as defined in schedules I through V of section 202 of the Controlled Substances Act (21 U.S.C. 812).
>
> ---
>
> Source: 28 CFR § 35.104, Electronic Code of Federal Regulations current as of June 19, 2015.

In 2008, the ADAA clarified that the definition of the term *disability* should be "construed in favor of broad coverage of individuals" (42 United States Code [U.S.C.] § 12102[4][A]). Furthermore, the determination whether a physical or mental impairment substantially limits a major life activity is made without regard to the "ameliorative effects of mitigating measures" such as medication; medical devices (except for ordinary glasses and corrective lens); assistive technology; accommodations, aids, or services; or learned behavioral or adaptive neurological modifications (42 U.S.C. § 12102 [4][E]). Thus, a student with attention-deficit/hyperactivity disorder (ADHD) might qualify as having a disability under Section 504/ADAA even if his or her ADHD is generally well controlled by medication.

Under Section 504/ADAA, the term *disability* also includes persons who can document that they experienced illegal discriminatory actions against them because of the perception of a disability, whether or not they have an actual impairment. For example, if a high school senior was denied admission to college solely on the basis of school education records showing a history of special education placement, Section 504/ADAA safeguards would be triggered. This prong of the definition of Section 504/ADAA disability is most pertinent to discrimination in employment and settings other than elementary and secondary schools.

The ADAA also clarified that the term *substantially limits a major life activity* does not apply to impairments that are transitory, defined as an actual or expected duration of six months or less, and minor (42 U.S.C. § 12102[3][B]). However, an impairment that is "episodic or in remission is a disability if it would substantially limit a major life activity when active" (42 U.S.C. § 2102[4][D]).

The ADAA did not provide any new guidance regarding the appropriate frame of reference to use for determining whether an impairment *substantially limits* a major life activity. Based on a review of relevant case law, Zirkel (2013d) noted that the generally accepted frame of reference is "the average person" (p. 15). Consequently, the performance of children of the same age or in the same grade in the general population should serve as the normative standard for evaluating whether an impairment substantially limits a student's major life activity. As Zirkel observed, parents, school psychologists, and teachers may incorrectly assume that the standard is whether the disability substantially limits the student's ability to reach his or her potential.

Finally, in the portion of the law that addresses discrimination in employment settings, the ADAA states that its protections do not extend to individuals who are disabled by drug addiction if they are "currently engaged in the illegal use of drugs" (42 U.S.C. § 12114[a]). However, the ADAA does protect individuals from discrimination if they have undergone drug rehabilitation successfully and no longer engage in illegal drug use (42 U.S.C. § 12114[b]). Other exclusions from the Section 504/ADAA definition of disability include homosexuality, bisexuality, gender identity disorders, and transgender status. (See Zirkel, 2009c.)

In sum, Section 504 prohibits schools from discriminating on the basis of disability in providing aids, benefits, or services and requires schools to take effective steps to prevent harassment of students with disabilities. Any student who has a disability as defined by Section 504/ADAA and who needs special assistance at school because of his or her impairment may be eligible for individual accommodations under Section 504. All students who are disabled under IDEIA are considered to be disabled under Section 504/ADAA, and are, therefore, afforded the protections of Section 504. Students who are not disabled under IDEIA may nevertheless have a disability under Section 504/ADAA ("504 only" students).

Physical and Mental Health Impairments

A number of schoolchildren have health conditions that substantially impair major life activities, such as caring for oneself, performing manual tasks, walking, seeing, hearing, speaking, breathing, or learning. Students with a wide range of physical health conditions (e.g., diabetes, asthma, severe allergies, impairments from an accident, arthritis, epilepsy) *may* qualify for accommodations under Section 504/ADAA. A student with a temporary Section 504/ADAA impairment also may qualify for accommodations if the impairment has an actual or expected duration of more than six months. (See Zirkel, 2009c.)

The Section 504/ADAA definition of *mental impairment* is also broad and includes any mental impairment that substantially limits a major life activity, including learning, reading, concentrating, thinking, or communicating. For example, a general education student may have a disability within the meaning of Section 504/ADAA because ADHD substantially limits his or her concentration in comparison with other students the same age. However, the student may perform well in general education with classroom accommodations (e.g., shorter homework assignments, more time on tests, behavioral support) and not need special education and related services. Or a general education student may fail to attend school or be otherwise unable to participate in his or her education because of a mental illness such as depression, a sleeping disorder, an anxiety disorder, or oppositional defiant disorder, and therefore require Section 504/ADAA accommodations. (See Zirkel, 2009c.)

Communicable Diseases

State and local school boards have the power and authority to adopt regulations to safeguard the health and safety of students. Schools may deny school access to children who pose a health threat to others (Russo, 2012). The difficulty with serious communicable diseases is in determining whether the health threat posed by the child with a communicable disease is significant enough to outweigh the student's right to schooling in the least restrictive setting.

Section 504/ADAA prohibits schools from discriminating against any "otherwise qualified" student with a communicable disease. This means that schools may not remove a student with a communicable disease from the general education classroom unless a significant risk of transmission of the disease would still exist in spite of reasonable efforts by the school to accommodate the student with a communicable disease (e.g., *Doe v. Belleville Public School District No. 118*, 1987; *School Board of Nassau County, Florida v. Arline*, 1987; *Thomas v. Atascadero Unified School District*, 1987). Court rulings and the Centers for Disease Control have suggested that the decision whether a student with a communicable disease should be excluded from school or school activities (e.g., contact sports in the case of a student with methicillin-resistant *Staphylococcus aureus* [MRSA]) must be made on a case-by-case basis and include consultation with the student's physician (see http://www.cdc.gov/mrsa/community/schools/index.html).

Evaluation of Students to Determine Eligibility for Accommodations

Under Section 504, schools must take steps to "identify and locate" every student with a 504 disability residing in the school's jurisdiction (i.e., a "child find" requirement; 34 CFR § 104.32[a]). An evaluation of a child is required if it is believed that the child may qualify as having a disability under Section 504/ADAA and may need special school services or accommodations. Education experts and court rulings suggest that schools consider whether a student might have a Section 504/ADAA impairment when parents frequently express concern about their child's performance; if the child fails to benefit from research-based instruction; when grade retention, suspension, or expulsion is being considered for the student; when the student exhibits a chronic health condition or is diagnosed with a mental illness; or when a student returns to school after serious injury, illness, or a psychiatric hospitalization (adapted from South Dakota Department of Education, 2010, p. 31).

If a student is evaluated and found not eligible for special education under IDEIA, the school should consider whether the student might be eligible for accommodations under Section 504/ADAA. However, a student should not be "504'd" (found eligible) unless he or she meets the eligibility criteria outlined in Section 504/ADAA (Zirkel, 2013d). School personnel with good intentions may mislabel a student as having a Section 504/ADAA disability so that the student can receive individualized help at school. Unfortunately, such actions result in unnecessary stigmatization of the child and create an unwarranted legal entitlement to special treatment.

Schools are required to advise students with suspected disabilities and their parents of their rights and the school's duties under Section 504/ADAA (34 CFR § 104.32). Although Section 504 is silent on the matter, written parent consent is recommended for the initial evaluation to determine eligibility under Section 504/ADAA and for placement. The OCR has recommended that parents be notified of their procedural safeguard rights under Section 504 at the time the district requests parental permission for an evaluation (e.g., Cobb County [GA] School District, 1992) or when a parent requests an evaluation. When a student is suspected of having a disability under IDEIA, parent rights and school duties under both IDEIA and Section 504 should be clearly identified.

A school must evaluate a student only when the school has reason to believe a child may have a Section 504/ADAA disability (Lim, 1993). Like IDEIA, schools are not required to evaluate children based only on parental suspicion of an impairment. However, when a school does not agree with a parental request for evaluation, it still must inform parents of their right to contest that decision and the procedures for a fair and timely resolution of the evaluation dispute.

When it is suspected that a student may have a Section 504/ADAA disability, Martin (1992) and Zirkel (2013c) interpret the evaluation regulations to require three determinations: (1) Is there a physical or mental impairment within the meaning of Section 504/ADAA?; (2) Does that impairment substantially limit a major life activity?; and (3) What kind of accommodations are required for the student to have an opportunity to benefit from the school's programs that is equal to his or her nondisabled peers? Section 504 does not require a specific categorical label or diagnosis, only the determination that a condition exists that substantially impairs one or more major life activities. (Also see Zirkel, 2009c.)

School psychologists, along with other members of the group of persons involved in making a Section 504/ADAA eligibility determination, should be aware that federal law does not require a medical diagnosis for the purpose of determining whether a child has a disability; the OCR "expressly allows for alternative assessment methods in lieu of medical diagnosis" for determining whether a child has an impairment that substantially limits a major life activity (Zirkel, 2009c, p. 336). The school should, however, consider the findings from a medical evaluation if shared with the school by the parents as part of the eligibility determination process. Furthermore, Section 504, like IDEIA, requires schools to ensure that if the school believes that a medical diagnosis is necessary to determine eligibility, then the diagnosis is made at no cost to the parent. Also, as noted previously, while a *DSM-5* (American Psychiatric Association, 2013) diagnosis may assist in determining eligibility under Section 504/ADAA or IDEIA, it is neither legally required nor sufficient to make an eligibility determination under federal law (Zirkel, 2009c).

The Section 504 regulations regarding evaluation procedures (34 CFR § 104.35) are almost identical to those implementing IDEIA—Part B. Test and evaluation materials must be valid for the purpose used, administered by trained personnel, and fair. The evaluation must be comprehensive enough to assess the nature and extent of the impairment and the needed accommodations and services. In interpreting data and in making placement decisions, schools must "draw upon information from a variety of sources," "establish procedures to ensure that information obtained from all such sources is documented and carefully considered," and ensure that decisions are made by a "group of persons, including persons knowledgeable about the child, the evaluation data, and the placement options" (34 CFR § 104.35). As Zirkel (2009c) noted, "use of a systematic eligibility form facilitates a defensible determination" (p. 340) of whether a child is eligible for accommodations under Section 504/ADAA. The sources of evaluation information and the names and professional roles of the persons who participated in the eligibility determination should be documented (Zirkel, 2013c).

Time lines for the completion of an evaluation and determination of a child's needs are not specified in Section 504 regulations. The OCR has held that although "504 does not specify the time periods permitted at each stage of the process of identification, evaluation, and placement, it is implicit that the various steps in the process will be completed within a reasonable time period" (Cobb County [GA] School District, 1992, p. 29). It also has held that it is reasonable to expect schools to complete evaluations under Section 504 within the same time frame outlined in state guidelines for completion of IDEIA evaluations (East Lansing [MI] Public Schools, 1992).

Section 504 does not require reevaluation of the student every three years, only periodic reevaluation and reevaluation prior to any significant change in placement (34 CFR § 104.35). Courts have ruled that expulsion or long-term suspension (more than 10 days) of a student with a Section 504/ADAA disability is a change of placement requiring reevaluation of the student.

Free Appropriate Public Education

IDEIA and Section 504 both require schools to offer a free appropriate public education (FAPE) to every student with a disability. *Appropriate education* is defined in Section 504 as "the provision of regular or special education and related aids and services (i) that are designed to meet individual educational needs of handicapped persons as adequately as the needs of nonhandicapped persons are met and (ii) [that] are based on adherence to procedures" outlined in the regulations (34 CFR § 104.33). Thus, under Section 504, *appropriate education* is more broadly defined than under IDEIA—Part B, and it can consist of education in general education classes, placement in general education classes with the use of supplementary services, or special education and related services.

Section 504, like IDEIA, also requires schools to "educate, or provide for the education of, each qualified handicapped person in its jurisdiction with persons who are not handicapped to the maximum extent appropriate to the needs of the handicapped person" (34 CFR § 104.34). Students with Section 504 impairments must be placed in the general education environment unless it is determined that the education of the student in the general education classroom with the use of supplementary aids and services cannot be achieved satisfactorily. In providing or arranging for the provision of nonacademic services and extracurricular activities, schools must ensure that students with disabilities participate with nondisabled students to the maximum extent appropriate to their needs (34 CFR § 104.34). They must be provided equal opportunity to participate in, or benefit from, nonacademic services such as "counseling services, physical recreational athletics, transportation, health services, recreational activities, and special interest groups or clubs" (34 CFR 104.37) and school field trips (e.g., Clovis [CA] Unified School District, 2009). In 2013, the OCR reported that students with disabilities were not being afforded equal opportunity to participate in extracurricular athletics. A "Dear Colleague Letter" was issued to provide guidance to schools regarding the legal rights of students with disabilities to participate in extracurricular athletics (see Swenson & Musgrove, 2013).

Section 504 requires the provision of general or special education and related aids and services designed to meet the individual needs of students with impairments. A question raised by parents of children with Section 504/ADAA impairments and school administrators is whether school districts may use IDEIA programs and services in making accommodations for Section 504-only students. The court ruling in *Lyons by Alexander v. Smith* (1993), OCR complaint investigation findings (e.g., Lake Washington [WA] School District No. 414, 1985), and OCR policy statements indicate that children with Section 504/ADAA impairments may have access to all IDEIA programs and services, even if they do not qualify under IDEIA. As the court noted in *Lyons*, a school system may have to provide special education services to a Section 504-only student if such services are necessary to prevent discrimination, that is, to meet the individual educational needs of the student with Section 504 impairments as adequately as those of nondisabled students.

Under Section 504, when a school district places a student with a disability in a program not operated by the school district as a means of providing a free and appropriate education, the district retains responsibility for assuring that Section 504 rights and protections are afforded to the student placed elsewhere (34 CFR § 104.33). When selecting a child's placement, proximity to the child's home must be considered (34 CFR § 104.34). When school districts place students with disabilities in programs not operated by the school itself, the placement must be at no cost to the parent. Schools also must ensure adequate transportation to the placement site at no greater cost to the parent than would be incurred if the student were placed in a program operated by the school (34 CFR § 104.33).

Accommodation Plan

Under Section 504, schools must provide a free and appropriate education designed to meet the individual education needs of children with Section 504/ADAA impairments and that provides education opportunities equal to those of students without disabilities. The law itself does not specifically require a written accommodation plan; however, education law experts recommend that a written plan be developed for students with Section 504/ADAA disabilities (Zirkel, 2009b).

As noted previously, the Section 504/ADAA student accommodation plan must be developed by a group of persons, including persons knowledgeable of the child and the evaluation data. Educators and law experts have recommended that this plan include: (a) a description of the identified impairment(s); (b) a description of how the impairment substantially affects a major life activity; (c) a description of the accommodations that are necessary; (d) the names and roles of each professional responsible for implementing each accommodation; (e) the name and role of the professional responsible for monitoring the implementation of the accommodations; (f) the date the plan will begin; (g) the date when the plan will be reviewed or reassessed; and

(h) the names and titles of the participants at the accommodation plan meeting. The accommodation plan should be reviewed on the predetermined date (South Dakota Department of Education, 2010; Zirkel, 2013c).

Nature of the Required Accommodations

Under Section 504/ADAA, the school is only required to provide the accommodations that are necessary because of a student's identified impairment(s); the school is not required to provide every accommodation that would benefit the child. Furthermore, a school is only required to provide *reasonable* accommodations; it is not required to provide accommodations that pose an "undue hardship" on the school or that would necessitate a "fundamental alteration" of its programs (Zirkel, 2013c, p. 5).

Specific accommodations for a child must always be determined by a group of persons and based on individual student need. However, many years ago, the court settlement in *Elizabeth S. v. Thomas K. Gilhool* (1987) provided early guidance regarding school responsibilities *to students with physical and health impairments* who do not qualify under IDEIA. The court stated that the required school accommodations and services for students with physical or health impairments might include, but are not limited to, development of a plan to address any medical emergencies, school health services including assistance in monitoring of blood sugar levels and arrangements for a child to take injections or medications, assistance with toileting, adjustment of class schedules, home instruction, use of an elevator or other accommodations to make school facilities accessible, adaptive transportation, and adaptive physical education and/or occupational therapy.

Some schools have been reluctant to allow staff to administer medications and to allow students to self-medicate (e.g., use a nebulizer or inhaler during an asthma attack) because of concerns about district legal liability. While medical diagnosis is not necessary or controlling in determining eligibility under Section 504/ADAA, schools may require a physician's diagnosis and instructions for certain health services at school, such as providing medication. However, based on a review of OCR opinions, Gelfman and Schwab (2005a) concluded that under Section 504, schools "no longer have a choice of whether to agree to administer medication when the student has a condition that interferes with a major life function and administration of medication during school hours is necessary" (p. 361). The OCR also has held that schools may not require parents to attend a school program to provide health services to their child (e.g., diabetes monitoring) because this imposes an obligation on the parents of a child with a health impairment that is not imposed on other parents (e.g., Clovis [CA] Unified School District, 2009). (For additional discussion of services for students with 504 health impairments, see Gelfman & Schwab, 2005a.)

Several administrative hearings and OCR investigations have addressed *accommodations for students with mental health impairments*. These cases concerned students who did not qualify under IDEIA—Part B as having an emotional disturbance but who were deemed to have a mental impairment that substantially limited a major life activity. Accommodations and services for a student with a mental health impairment under Section 504 also must be based on individual need. However, schools must, at a minimum, provide assistance to ensure equal educational opportunity. For example, as a result of a hearing involving Howard County, Maryland, Public Schools ("Failure to Provide," 2005), parents of a high school student diagnosed with depression were awarded funds to cover all expenses they incurred from unilaterally placing their son in a private facility (tuition, room and board, psychological services) after it was determined that the school failed to offer any services to address the student's depression and inability to participate in his education. (See Zirkel, 2009c, for additional examples.)

Procedural Safeguards Under Section 504

Procedural safeguards in Section 504 regulations are stated in more general terms than those in IDEIA—Part B. Under 504, schools are required "to make available a system of procedural safeguards that permit parents to challenge actions regarding the identification, evaluation, or educational placement of their handicapped child whom they believe needs special education or related services" (DOE, 1991; also 34 CFR § 104.36). The system of procedural safeguards must include "notice, an opportunity for the parents or guardian to examine relevant records, an impartial hearing with opportunity for participation by the person's parents or guardian and representation by counsel, and a review procedure" (34 CFR § 104.36). School districts may not require parents to exhaust their internal complaint resolution procedures such as mediation before requesting a due process hearing under Section 504 (e.g., Talbot County [MD] Public Schools, 2008).

As noted previously, the OCR is charged with investigating Section 504 complaints pertaining to DOE programs or activities. The OCR investigates individual complaints, and a parent may trigger an investigation of school district compliance with Section 504 by filing a complaint with the OCR (Zirkel & Kincaid, 1993).

In addition, parents have the right to initiate a court action against the school on behalf of a child with Section 504/ADAA impairments if they believe the school has violated the provisions of Section 504 with respect to their child. In accordance with the Handicapped Children's Protection Act of 1986 (Pub. L. No. 99-372), if a Section 504 claim can be remedied under IDEIA, parents must first attempt to remedy the problem under IDEIA before filing a civil action on a Section 504 claim. The courts may award reasonable attorney fees as part of the costs to parents when they are the prevailing party in a Section 504 suit.

AMERICANS WITH DISABILITIES ACT

Congress passed more than 20 laws prohibiting discrimination against individuals with disabilities between 1973 and 1990 (Burgdorf, 1991). The Americans with Disabilities Act of 1990 (ADA) (Pub. L. No. 101-336) is considered to be the most significant federal law ensuring the civil rights of all individuals with disabilities.

The ADA was first introduced as a bill in Congress in 1988. In its statement of findings, Congress reported widespread discrimination against individuals with disabilities in all spheres of life, including employment, housing, public accommodations, education, transportation, communication, recreation, health services, and access to public services (Pub. L. No. 101-336 § 2[a][1]). Additionally, testimony to Congress documented a strong link between disability and poverty, joblessness, lack of education, and failure to participate in social and recreational opportunities (Burgdorf, 1991). The ADA was signed into law in 1990.

The ADA differed from earlier laws because it extended to programs and activities outside the federal sphere and it included a detailed set of standards prohibiting discrimination (Burgdorf, 1991). The law guaranteed equal opportunity to individuals with disabilities in employment, public services, transportation, state and local government services, and telecommunications. It specifically prohibited discrimination on the basis of disability in public and private schools that are not controlled by a religious entity, regardless of whether the private school receives federal funds (Zirkel, 2009a). The protections of ADA extended only to those persons who have a disability as defined by the law. However, the ADA's definition of *disability* was broad. Between 1999 and 2002, several Supreme Court decisions narrowed the interpretation of disability under the ADA, particularly in employment settings (e.g., *Sutton v. United Air Lines, Inc.*, 1999; *Toyota Motor Manufacturing, Kentucky, Inc. v. Williams*, 2002). The Americans with Disabilities Amendments Act (ADAA) was passed in 2008 to restore the original, broad scope of the definition of *disability* as intended by Congress in 1990 and to explicitly reject the narrower Supreme Court interpretations of *disability*. The ADAA definition of *disability* also applies to Section 504 of the Rehabilitation Act of 1973.

The ADAA regulations state that, unless otherwise noted, the ADAA "shall not be construed to apply a lesser standard" than Section 504 (28 CFR § 35.103). ADAA generally requires full compliance with Section 504, but at times it requires more than Section 504 in school obligations to students with disabilities, such as the removal of architectural barriers.

The OCR within the U.S. Department of Education was designated as the agency responsible for enforcing the ADAA with regard to public schools. Complaints regarding ADAA violations may be filed with the OCR. The remedies of Section 504 are the remedies of Title II of ADAA.

Whistle-Blower Protection

School psychologists also should be familiar with the ADAA's protection against retaliation or coercion for whistle-blowers:

(a) No private or public entity shall discriminate against any individual because that individual has opposed any act or practice made unlawful by this part or because that individual made a charge, testified, assisted, or participated in any manner in an investigation, proceeding or hearing under the Act or this part.

(b) No private or public entity shall coerce, intimidate, threaten, or interfere with any individual in the exercise or enjoyment of, or on account of his having exercised or enjoyed, or on account of his or her having aided or encouraged any other individual in the exercise of enjoyment of, any right granted or protected by the Act or this part. (28 CFR § 35.134)

This portion of the law was designed in part to protect individuals who advocate for the rights of persons with disabilities from retaliation by the agency involved. Thus, if a school district failed to meet its obligations to students with disabilities under the ADAA and a school employee assisted those students in obtaining their rights under the Act, the school district would be prohibited from retaliating against the employee. If the school did retaliate by firing or in some way demoting the employee, the employee would have the right to file a lawsuit against the school district under the ADAA's protection against retaliation. For example, in 2001, a federal jury awarded almost $1 million to a former special education teacher who was fired after persistently complaining that students with disabilities received less adequate time, equipment, and facilities for physical education than their nondisabled peers (Chestnut, 2001; *Settlegoode v. Portland Public Schools*, 2004).

CONCLUDING COMMENTS

Contemporary interpretations of Section 504 suggest that schools must attend to three types of potential discrimination prohibited by the law. First, Section 504 prohibits public schools from excluding students from participating in school programs and activities solely on the basis of a disability. Second, it requires schools to take steps to prevent harassment on the basis of disability. Third, it requires schools to make accommodations to ensure that students with disabilities have equal opportunity to benefit from its programs and activities.

STUDY AND DISCUSSION

Questions for Chapter 5

1. What type of legislation is Section 504 of the Rehabilitation Act of 1973? How does it differ from IDEIA in purpose, scope, and funding?
2. How is student eligibility determined under Section 504/ADAA?
3. Must a child have a permanent mental or physical impairment to be eligible for accommodations under Section 504/ADAA?
4. What is the meaning of *free appropriate public education* within Section 504/ADAA?
5. Describe the content of an accommodation plan under Section 504/ADAA, and describe how one is developed.

Activities

Visit the Department of Education's Office for Civil Rights "Reading Room" Web site (http://www2.ed.gov/about/offices/list/ocr/frontpage/faq/readingroom.html). Click on "Case Resolutions" and then "By statute" and "Disability." Skim the outcome of an OCR compliance investigation in the public schools. This is a good way to understand how OCR conducts compliance investigations and the application of policy, regulations, and law to actual cases.

Vignette

D.G.'s school records indicated that he was often sad or "down" as early as fourth grade and that he focused on things that he didn't like about himself. In grade 6, signs of depression were evident, and D.G. made threats of suicide while at school. The principal informed D.G.'s parents that they were required to have D.G. evaluated privately and at their own expense; otherwise, D.G. would be removed from school if his suicidal statements persisted. In grades 7 and 8, D.G. engaged in defiant and aggressive actions. School personnel never referred D.G. for any type of school psychological evaluation. In high school. D.G. was hospitalized for depression, and, contrary to a request from his parents, the school only provided them with his textbooks, but no syllabi or list of homework assignments, during the time he was hospitalized.

D.G.'s parents repeatedly asked the school to evaluate their child for possible special education placement, but these requests were denied (orally but not in writing) with the special education director explaining that a school evaluation was not required because D.G. "can do the work." D.G.'s parents were never informed of their right to dispute this decision or provided with information about their rights under IDEIA or Section 504.

D.G. frequently failed to attend classes his last year of high school because of his depression. He was not permitted to graduate with his classmates because he missed too many classes. He also was not permitted to walk in the school's graduation ceremony or attend the senior class breakfast. (Vignette adapted from *D.G. v. Somerset Hills School District*, 2008.)

In your opinion, did the school violate Section 504/ADAA in this scenario? If yes, in what ways—and at what points in D.G.'s education—did the school violate its obligations under Section 504/ADAA? If you believe D.G. was eligible for accommodations under Section 504, what accommodations would you have recommended? D.G. and his parents subsequently filed a court action against the school district, asserting, among other claims, violation of Section 504/ADAA. If you were the judge in this case, would you rule in favor of D.G. and his parents or the school? Why?

Chapter 6

ETHICAL AND LEGAL ISSUES IN PSYCHOEDUCATIONAL ASSESSMENT

> Psychological testing and assessment techniques, in common with most tools, can be used for a diversity of purposes, some destructive and some constructive, and their use cannot be separated from the training, competence, and ethical values of the clinical-user (Matarazzo, 1986, p. 18).

This chapter focuses on ethical and legal issues associated with the assessment of individual students within the context of an established school psychologist–client relationship.

TESTING VERSUS ASSESSMENT

In their work with teachers, parents, and children (and in their own thinking), it is important for school psychologists to distinguish between *testing* and *assessment*. Testing and assessment are not synonymous, interchangeable terms (Matarazzo, 1986). A test is a tool that may be used to gather information as part of the assessment process. Assessment is a broader term. Mowder (1983) defined the assessment process as "the planning, collection, and evaluation of information pertinent to a psychoeducational concern" (p. 145). A psychoeducational assessment of a student referred for individual evaluation is conducted by a psychologist trained to gather a variety of different types of information (e.g., school and health history; cultural, language, and experiential background; observations; test results) from a number of different sources (e.g., student, teacher, parents) and to interpret or give meaning to that information in light of the unique characteristics of the student and his or her situation.

Practitioners also need to be familiar with the distinction between the medical and ecological models of school psychological assessment. In past years, practitioners often were trained to accept a medical model that views learning and behavior problems as a result of within-child disorders or disabilities. In contrast, the ecological model encourages an assessment approach that takes into account the multiple factors that affect learning and behavior, including classroom variables, teacher and instructional variables, characteristics of the referred student, and support available from the home for school achievement. The ecological perspective has gained acceptance because it is viewed as potentially more beneficial to the child. To reverse a student's pattern of poor progress, systematic assessment of factors in the child's learning environment is needed (Ysseldyke & Christenson, 1988). Messick (1984) suggested that, ethically, a child should not be exposed to the risk of misdiagnosis unless deficiencies in instruction first have been ruled out (also NASP-PPE II.3.1).

The psychologist has certain preassessment responsibilities to the parent and student. After discussing these responsibilities, we address ethical-legal concerns associated with assessment planning; the selection and evaluation of tests and testing practices; data collection and interpretation; report writing, and sharing findings. Nondiscriminatory assessment and projective personality assessment then are discussed. The final portions of the chapter focus on the professional issues of competence and autonomy in conducting psychoeducational evaluations and ethical-legal issues associated with computer-assisted assessment, including the use of Web-based digital assessment platforms.

Codes of ethics, professional testing standards, and law provide guidelines for psychological assessment in schools. The National Association of School Psychologists (NASP) "Principles for Professional Ethics" (2010b) and the American Psychological Association's (APA's) "Ethical Principles of Psychologists and Code of Conduct" (2010) each include ethical principles for psychological assessment. The *Standards for Educational and Psychological Testing*, or *Standards* (American Educational Research Association, APA, & National Council on Measurement in Education, 2014)[1], provides criteria for psychologists and educators to use in the evaluation of assessment practices. The *Standards* has no official legal status. However, the *Standards* has been referred to in federal regulations concerning acceptable testing practices, and it has have been cited in Supreme Court cases as an authoritative source on issues concerning the technical adequacy of testing practices (Adler, 1993).

The Individuals with Disabilities Education Improvement Act of 2004 (IDEIA) and Section 504 of the Rehabilitation Act of 1973 each outline legal requirements for evaluation procedures used in the identification of children with disabilities. The regulations for IDEIA—Part B pertaining to tests and evaluation procedures are shown in Exhibit 6.1.

PREASSESSMENT RESPONSIBILITIES

Consistent with the ethical obligation "to respect the right of persons to participate in decisions affecting their own welfare" (NASP-PPE I.1), school psychologists "encourage and promote parent participation in school decisions affecting their children" (NASP-PPE I.1.1). However, as will be discussed here and in Chapter 7, not all of their assessment services require informed parent consent.

Parental Involvement and Consent

Practitioners are ethically obligated to seek informed consent to establish a psychologist–client relationship for the purpose of conducting a school psychological evaluation of a student (NASP-PPE I.1.2), and consent, oral or written, should

---

[1]The *Standards for Educational and Psychological Testing* (American Educational Research Association, American Psychological Association, & National Council on Measurement in Education, 2014) includes explanatory text (cited by page number) and numbered standards (cited by standard number, e.g. "3.13").

Exhibit 6.1   Excerpts from IDEIA Regulations on Evaluation Procedures

Sec. 300.304 Evaluation procedures.

(a) Notice. The public agency must provide notice to the parents of a child with a disability, in accordance with Sec. 300.503, that describes any evaluation procedures the agency proposes to conduct.

(b) Conduct of evaluation. In conducting the evaluation, the public agency must—

   (1) Use a variety of assessment tools and strategies to gather relevant functional, developmental, and academic information about the child, including information provided by the parent, that may assist in determining—

      (i) Whether the child is a child with a disability under Sec. 300.8; and

      (ii) The content of the child's IEP [individual education program], including information related to enabling the child to be involved in and progress in the general education curriculum (or for a preschool child, to participate in appropriate activities);

   (2) Not use any single procedure as the sole criterion for determining whether a child is a child with a disability and for determining an appropriate educational program for the child; and

   (3) Use technically sound instruments that may assess the relative contribution of cognitive and behavioral factors, in addition to physical or developmental factors.

(c) Other evaluation procedures. Each public agency must ensure that—

   (1) Assessments and other evaluation materials used to assess a child under this part—

      (i) Are selected and administered so as not to be discriminatory on a racial or cultural basis;

      (ii) Are provided and administered in the child's native language or other mode of communication and in the form most likely to yield accurate information on what the child knows and can do academically, developmentally, and functionally, unless it is clearly not feasible to so provide or administer;

      (iii) Are used for the purposes for which the assessments or measures are valid and reliable;

      (iv) Are administered by trained and knowledgeable personnel; and

      (v) Are administered in accordance with any instructions provided by the producer of the assessments.

(2) Assessments and other evaluation materials include those tailored to assess specific areas of educational need and not merely those that are designed to provide a single general intelligence quotient.

(3) Assessments are selected and administered so as best to ensure that if an assessment is administered to a child with impaired sensory, manual, or speaking skills, the assessment results accurately reflect the child's aptitude or achievement level or whatever other factors the test purports to measure, rather than reflecting the child's impaired sensory, manual, or speaking skills (unless those skills are the factors that the test purports to measure).

(4) The child is assessed in all areas related to the suspected disability, including, if appropriate, health, vision, hearing, social and emotional status, general intelligence, academic performance, communicative status, and motor abilities;

(5) Assessments of children with disabilities who transfer from one public agency to another public agency in the same academic year are coordinated with those children's prior and subsequent schools, as necessary and as expeditiously as possible, consistent with Sec. 300.301(d)(2) and (e), to ensure prompt completion of full evaluations.

(6) In evaluating each child with a disability under Sec. Sec. 300.304 through 300.306, the evaluation is sufficiently comprehensive to identify all of the child's special education and related services needs, whether or not commonly linked to the disability category in which the child has been classified.

(7) Assessment tools and strategies that provide relevant information that directly assists persons in determining the educational needs of the child are provided.

Authority: 20 U.S.C. 1414[b][1–3], 1412[a][6][B]

be appropriately documented (APA-EP 3.10d, 9.03; NASP-PPE I.1.3; *Standards* 8.4). Consent is given by the parent of a minor child or another adult acting in the place of a parent. A student who has reached the age of majority or who is an emancipated minor typically may consent on his or her own behalf (see Chapter 3).[2] Under IDEIA, written consent (34 CFR § 300.9) of the parent is needed to conduct an initial evaluation of a child to determine if the child has a disability as defined in the law. However, it is important to understand that parent consent for an initial evaluation "must not be

[2]The term *parent* is used here to refer to an individual who has the legal authority to provide consent and make decisions.

construed as consent for the initial provision of special education and related services" (34 CFR § 300.300[a][1][ii]); that is, parents have a legal right to consent to an evaluation but may later refuse special education and related services even if their child is found to be a child with a disability under IDEIA. IDEIA also requires parent consent for subsequent reevaluations, unless the school can demonstrate that it has taken reasonable measures to obtain consent and the child's parent failed to respond (34 CFR § 300.300[c]).

Parent consent is not required for a review of existing student data as part of an evaluation or reevaluation (34 CFR § 300.300[d][1][i]). In addition, "the screening of a student by a teacher or specialist to determine appropriate instructional strategies for curriculum implementation is not considered to be an evaluation requiring parental consent under IDEA" (34 CFR § 300.302). *Screening* is "typically a relatively simple and quick process" to "identify strategies a teacher may use to more effectively teach children" (U.S. DOE, 2006, p. 46639). The question of who is considered a "specialist" is left to the discretion of the school district. Consequently, school psychologists may participate in the screening of students without parent consent if the purpose of the screening is to inform the teacher about appropriate instructional strategies for children (U.S. DOE, 2006, p. 46639). (Also see Chapter 7.)

Professional standards and IDEIA are highly similar with regard to the necessary components of the informed consent agreement for psychoeducational assessment. According to the *Standards* (8.4) and consistent with IDEIA (34 CFR § 300.9), the parent granting permission for the psychoeducational evaluation should be made aware of the reasons for the assessment, the types of tests and evaluation procedures to be used, what the assessment results will be used for, the types of records (paper and digital) that will be created, and who will have access to those records. This information must be presented to the parent in his or her native language or other mode of communication (also see NASP-PPE I.1.3). Parents must be informed that their consent is voluntary and they may revoke it at any time (34 CFR § 300.9; also NASP-PPE I.1). School psychologists also are ethically obligated to "respect the wishes of parents who object to school psychological services and attempt to guide parents to alternative resources" (NASP-PPE I.1.5).

In recent years, tension sometimes has arisen between school psychology practitioners and parents (or their advocates) regarding the tests and other assessment materials to be used in evaluating a child suspected of having a disability. For example, in *G.J. v. Muscogee County School District* (2012), the parents of a child with a disability added an addendum to the school's proposed assessment plan with seven conditions the school had to agree to before the parents would consent to having their child reevaluated under IDEIA. The parents would not consent to an IDEIA reevaluation unless all of the specific instruments to be used were pre-identified in the assessment plan and the psychological evaluation was conducted by a named licensed psychologist. The school declined to agree to the addendum conditions. The parents subsequently filed a lawsuit against the school. The court held that the school has the right to develop the assessment plan and the parent has the right to accept or decline the proposed plan. The parent has no legal right to negotiate the assessment plan. Thus, while it is "best practice" to listen and respond respectfully to the parents' input about the proposed assessment plan for their child, the school, not the parent, has the right to determine who will conduct an assessment of a child with a suspected IDEIA disability and the assessment instruments to be used.

Many states and school districts have developed materials for parents describing evaluation procedures and the assessment instruments used by multidisciplinary team members. Many districts also have developed forms for parents to sign to consent to a school psychological evaluation of their child. However, school-based practitioners are cautioned to ensure that they have a shared understanding with the individual providing consent regarding the nature and scope of the proposed psychological evaluation. For example, are parents providing informed consent for an evaluation of whether their child has a disability as defined by IDEIA and/or a disability as defined by Section 504 of the Rehabilitation Act of 1973? Are they providing consent for psychological diagnosis (e.g., *Diagnostic and Statistical Manual of Mental Disorders [DSM-5]*, American Psychiatric Association, 2013)? Although *DSM-5 criteria* may be used in identifying children with disabilities under IDEIA or Section 504 (e.g., autism or attention deficits), parents and eligible students should be given an explicit choice regarding whether they consent to a *DSM-5 diagnosis* as part of a school district's psychoeducational evaluation.

Most parents cooperate with school attempts to secure approval for psychoeducational assessment. However, under IDEIA, if the parent fails to provide consent for an initial evaluation of a child with a suspected disability, the school *may* use mediation and other due process procedures (e.g., a hearing by an impartial hearing officer) in an effort to overrule parent failure to consent. However, schools are *not required* to pursue an initial evaluation of a child with a suspected disability if the parent fails to provide consent to do so (34 CFR § 300.300[a][3][i]). Furthermore, if the parent of a child who is homeschooled or parentally placed in a private school does not provide consent for an initial evaluation or reevaluation under IDEIA, or fails to respond to a request for consent, the school may not use IDEIA consent override procedures, and it is not required to consider the child as eligible for services (34 CFR § 300.300[d][4]).

Consistent with our ethical standards for consent, school psychologists should be aware that, under IDEIA, the parents or an adult student may withdraw consent for assessment or special education placement or services at any time, and this withdrawal of consent must be honored (34 CFR 300.9[c][1]). If a parent revokes consent for assessment, it is "not retroactive," that is, "it does not negate an action that has occurred after the consent was given and before the consent was revoked" (34 CFR 300.9[c][2]). School psychologists should not destroy records of a partially completed evaluation without first notifying the parent.

Responsibilities to the Student

In addition to prior parental consent to initiate a psychoeducational evaluation of an individual student, school psychologists also have a number of obligations to the student. As noted in Chapter 3, children are not seen as *legally* competent to make autonomous decisions about whether to participate in a psychological assessment; minors have no *legal* right "to consent, assent, or object to proposed psychoeducational evaluations" (Bersoff, 1983, p. 153). In our opinion, it is ethically permissible to assess a minor child without his or her explicit assent if the assessment promises to benefit his or her welfare (e.g., the planning of an individualized instructional program to enhance student learning). We concur with Corrao and Melton (1988) that it is disrespectful to solicit the assent of the child if refusal will not be honored (NASP-PPE I.1.4). Consistent with good testing practices, practitioners need to make full use of their professional skills to gain the active cooperation of the student.

Every student has the right to be fully informed about the scope and nature of the assessment process, whether or not the student is given a choice to assent to or refuse services. Practitioners are obligated ethically to explain the assessment process to the student in a manner that is understood by the student (NASP-PPE I.1.4). This explanation includes how the assessment results will be used, who will receive information, and possible implications of results. Even preschoolers and children with development disabilities should receive an explanation in a language they can understand as to why they are being seen by the school psychologist (*Standards* 8.4).

ASSESSMENT PLANNING

Each phase of the assessment process—assessment planning, information gathering, and interpretation of findings—requires data-based decision making and professional judgment (Ysseldyke et al., 2006). School psychologists are obligated to make decisions that promote the welfare of the student in each phase of the assessment process and to accept responsibility for decisions made (NASP-PPE I, II.2, II.3). Case 6.1 illustrates how psychological test results can have a powerful impact on the lives of children.

Case 6.1

Joseph McNulty was the unwanted child of a woman who was raped. He was placed in Willowbrook State Hospital in 1966 at the age of 4, after being diagnosed as "an imbecile" on the basis of an IQ score of 32. Subsequent reevaluations suggested that Joseph had some hearing problems, but those findings were "initially ignored or simply not seen." Joseph grew up among children and adults diagnosed with severe mental retardation, and during his stay at Willowbrook, he was given high doses of drugs, including Valium, Thorazine, and Haldol. In 1976, when Joseph was 14, an audiologist observed that Joseph showed a greater interest in learning than other youth with severe intellectual disabilities and confirmed that Joseph was hearing-impaired. After years of intensive therapy, Joseph's IQ tested in the normal range in 1980. In his late 20s, Joseph was not yet able to live independently, and he continued to need therapy and training. In 1988, he won a $1.5 million damage suit against the state of New York for medical malpractice.

Source: Adapted from Bauder, 1989, p. B-1.

Five Ethical-Legal Concerns

Psychologists have long recognized that the use of an IQ score in isolation is not sound practice in the identification of individuals with intellectual disabilities. However, prior to the passage of Pub. L. No. 94-142 in 1975, IQ test scores were frequently the sole basis for labeling children as "mentally retarded" (Matarazzo, 1986). The 1960s and 1970s were years of increasing court and federal government involvement in the regulation of school psychological testing as a result of this type of misuse of tests.

Five broad ethical-legal concerns emerge from an analysis of our codes of ethics, professional standards, and federal laws that address psychological assessment: Psychologists must strive to ensure that psychoeducational evaluations are *multifaceted*, *comprehensive*, *fair*, *valid*, and *useful*. We address each of these concerns briefly in the following pages and then discuss the selection and evaluation of tests and testing procedures.

Multifaceted

Psychoeducational assessment of a child with learning or behavior problems must be based on information "gathered from multiple measures and multiple informants" (D. N. Miller & Nickerson, 2007, p. 48). Under IDEIA and consistent with codes of ethics, evaluation procedures must include findings from a variety of assessment tools and strategies "to gather relevant functional, developmental, and academic information, including information provided by the parent" (34 CFR § 304[b][1], also [c][2]; NASP-PPE II.3.3). School psychologists base their opinions on "information and techniques sufficient to substantiate their findings" (APA-EP 9.01). No important decisions (e.g., special education eligibility) should be made on the basis of findings from a single test score or assessment procedure (34 CFR § 300.304[b][2]; NASP-PPE II.3.3; *Standards* 12.10).

Comprehensive

Children with suspected disabilities must be assessed "in all areas related to the suspected disability, including, if appropriate, health, vision, hearing, social and emotional status, general intelligence, academic performance, communicative status, and motor abilities" (34 CFR § 300.304[c][4]; also NASP-PPE II.3.4). As was apparent in Case 6.1, failure to have a child evaluated for possible sensory impairments can result in misdiagnosis with tragic consequences for the child. Furthermore, the term *comprehensive* should be interpreted broadly to include assessing the child in all areas that likely impact his or her learning even if the assessments are not required to determine eligibility for a specific disability classification. For example, in *G. "J" D. v. Wissahickon School District* (2011), the court held that the school psychological evaluation of the child was inadequate and that the school failed its child find obligations under IDEIA. The student had a known history of attentional and behavior problems that impeded learning. However, the psychoeducational evaluation focused solely on cognitive potential and academic progress. The judge opined that the school psychologist had an obligation to assess and address the child's attentional and behavior problems in a systematic way (e.g., functional behavior assessment and behavior management plan) and that failure to do so resulted in a denial of a free and appropriate education under IDEIA.

Fair

School psychologists strive to conduct fair and valid assessments. "They actively pursue knowledge of the student's disabilities, and developmental, cultural, linguistic, and experiential background and then select, administer, and interpret assessment instruments and procedures in light of those characteristics" (NASP-PPE II.3.5; also APA-EP 9.02). IDEIA outlines requirements for the assessment of English language learners; children with disabilities; and children from diverse cultural, ethnic, and racial backgrounds.

English Language Learners.   Under IDEIA, tests and other assessment tools used in the evaluation of children with suspected disabilities are "provided and administered in the child's native language or other mode of communication and in the form most likely to yield accurate information on what the child knows and can do academically, developmentally, and functionally, unless it is not feasible to so provide or administer" (34 CFR § 300.304[c][1][ii]; also APA-EP 9.02; NASP-PPE II.3.5; *Standards* 3.13). Furthermore, materials and procedures used to assess English language learners are selected and administered to ensure that they measure the extent to which the child has a disability and needs special education rather than measuring the child's English language skills (34 CFR § 300.304[c][3]). *Native language* is defined as "the language normally used by the child in the home or learning environment" (34 CFR § 300.29[a][2]).

According to Carvalho, Dennison, and Estrella (2014), Dana (2000), Ortiz (2008), and Paredes Scribner (2002), among others, competent assessment of children from culturally and linguistically diverse backgrounds requires the practitioner to gather information about the student's and family's degree of acculturation from the student, family, and cultural agents and to assess the child's language proficiency *prior* to selecting assessment tools.

Cummins (1999) observed that immigrant children often learn basic interpersonal conversational skills before they acquire the English language proficiency necessary to support academic learning. A child's fluency in conversational English can cause teachers and school psychologists to overestimate the child's cognitive-academic English language proficiency. Consequently, the practitioner must assess the child's language proficiency in the languages to which the child has been exposed prior to selecting assessment tools (Carvalho et al., 2014). This assessment should include evaluation of spoken and written language skills in each language, using both formal and informal measures, to obtain a full picture of functional language usage (Lopez, 1997). Language proficiency information is needed to guide selection and interpretation of measures of aptitude, achievement, and adaptive behavior and in planning instruction and interventions (see Paredes Scribner, 2002). Even if a child from a linguistically diverse background demonstrates some proficiency in spoken or written English, it is important to remember that commonly used tests (e.g., Wechsler Intelligence Test for Children V; Wechsler, 2014) tap the language, symbols, and knowledge children encounter in the dominant U.S. culture and schools.

Carvalho et al. (2014) have provided a detailed sequence of steps to follow to conduct a valid assessment of a student who is an English language learner.

The NASP maintains a directory of bilingual school psychologists who may be available to assist in the assessment of a child who is an English language learner. When a bilingual psychologist is not available and the services of an interpreter are used during psychological assessment, the psychologist is obligated ethically to obtain consent for the use of the interpreter, ensure that the interpreter is adequately trained to assist in the assessment (including following standardized test procedures and maintaining confidentiality and test security), and describe any limitations regarding the validity of the results obtained (APA-EP 9.03; NASP-PPE II.3.6; also *Standards* 3.14). In addition, the practitioner is obligated to ensure that he or she has the necessary skills to work effectively with an interpreter (Lopez, 2008). Practitioners are advised not to translate (or have an interpreter translate) items from a test developed for English-speaking examinees into the child's native language because translation of an item is likely to change item difficulty (Rogers et al., 1999). An on-the-spot translation of a test or subtest thus results in scores of unknown validity.

If a student is an English language learner and it is not feasible to conduct an assessment in the language in which the child is most proficient, the examiner should exercise caution in interpreting test results, especially if the results will be used to make an important decision, such as special education eligibility. English-only assessments of cognitive ability, adaptive behavior, or achievement may result in scores that reflect construct-irrelevant factors (limited English, lack of familiarity with the culture) rather than measuring the intended construct (Carvalho et al., 2014). See Carvalho et al. (2014) and Rhodes, Ochoa, and Ortiz (2005) for additional information on assessing linguistically diverse children.

Children With Disabilities.   IDEIA—Part B also mandates careful selection of assessment procedures for children with sensory, motor, or speech impairments. Children with deafness or blindness or no written language must be evaluated using the mode of communication that he or she uses, such as sign language, Braille, or oral communication (34 CFR § 300.29). Furthermore, assessments are "selected and administered so as best to ensure that if an assessment is administered to a child with impaired sensory, manual, or speaking skills, the assessment results accurately reflect that child's aptitude or achievement level or whatever other factors the test purports to measure, rather than reflecting the child's impaired sensory, manual, or speaking skills (unless those are the factors which the test purports to measure)" (34 CFR § 300.304[c][3].

Children From Diverse Cultural, Ethnic, and Racial Backgrounds.   Codes of ethics, professional standards, and special education law also mandate *nondiscriminatory* assessment of children from diverse cultural, ethnic, and racial backgrounds. As the issue of nondiscriminatory assessment is complex, it is discussed separately later in the chapter.

Valid

"School psychologists use assessment techniques and practices that the profession considers to be responsible, research-based practice" (NASP-PPE II.3.2). They "select assessment instruments and strategies that are reliable and valid for the child and the purpose of the assessment" (NASP-PPE II.3.2; also 34 CFR § 300.304[c][1][iii]; APA-EP 9.02; *Standards*, 2014, pp. 11–22). To ensure reliable and valid findings, IDEIA also requires that assessment and evaluation materials be administered by trained and knowledgeable personnel, in accordance with any instructions provided by the producer of such assessments (34 CFR § 300.304[c][1][iv, v]; also NASP-PPE II.3.2, II.5.2).

Useful

School psychologists use their expertise in assessment for the purpose of improving the quality of life for the child (NASP-PPE Introduction). Evaluation procedures are selected to provide a profile of the child's strengths and difficulties that will assist parents, educators, and other helping professionals to make informed decisions about the child's needs and aid in instructional planning. IDEIA requires that assessment tools and strategies "provide relevant information that directly assists persons in determining the educational needs of the child" (34 CFR § 300.304[c][7]).

Evaluating Tests and Testing Practices

School psychology practitioners select assessment techniques that are consistent with the highest standard for responsible professional practices (APA-EP 9.02; NASP-PPE II.3). The *Standards* was developed to "promote sound testing practices and to provide a basis for evaluating the quality of those practices. The *Standards* "is intended for professionals who specify, develop or select tests and for those who interpret, or evaluate the technical quality of tests" (2014, p. 1). Evaluating the adequacy of assessment practices ultimately rests with the test user and involves professional judgment; the *Standards* provides a frame of reference for ensuring relevant issues are addressed.

When assessment results play an important role in decision making for the individual student, the school psychologist is obligated to choose the best available assessment procedures. Considerable agreement exists in the school psychology literature that a variety of different types of information are appropriate within the framework of a *successive-levels model* of psychoeducational assessment. Consistent with this model, primary emphasis is given to scores and information from the most reliable and valid sources (composite scores on technically adequate measures) in interpretation and decision making. However, findings from less reliable and valid sources (scores on various subtest groups, individual subtest scores, performance on individual items, observations, and impressions) also may play a role in generating hypotheses about the student's profile of abilities, skills, and needs. These hypotheses then may be confirmed or abandoned by collecting additional information that verifies (cross-validates) or disconfirms the hypothesis (Kaufman, 1994).

According to the *Standards*, it is the responsibility of the test user to determine whether there is evidence for "(a) the validity of the interpretation for intended uses of the scores, (b) the reliability/precision of the scores, (c) the applicability of the normative data available in the test manual, and (d) the potential positive and negative consequences of use" (2014, p. 139).

Reliability

Reliability, or precision, refers to the consistency of test scores across testing procedures (e.g., tasks, contexts, raters) (*Standards*, 2014). Generally, reliability is evaluated through the use of reliability coefficients. Two types of reliability information should be reported in the manuals for tests to be used in psychoeducational decision making: test stability and internal consistency reliability. *Test stability* or *test-retest reliability* studies provide information about the consistency of scores from one testing session to another. This information typically is obtained by administering the same test to the same group of examinees on two occasions and correlating the resultant test scores (Salvia, Ysseldyke, & Bolt, 2013). *Internal consistency coefficients* are based on scores obtained during one administration of the test. The reliability coefficient obtained in this manner provides information about the extent to which items on the test are intercorrelated. According to the *Standards* (2.6), coefficients of internal consistency should not be substituted for estimates of stability unless evidence supports that interpretation in a particular context.

How reliable must a test be? There is no simple answer to this question. Shorter, less time-consuming, and less reliable measures may be adequate when tests are selected to provide information about groups rather than individuals (as in program evaluation and research) or when the results are used for decisions that are tentative and reversible (as when teacher-made tests are used to group children for reading instruction). A review of the literature suggests that some consensus exists in the field of school psychology about desirable levels of reliability for tests used in the schools. Test retest reliability coefficients of .60 to .65 are seen as adequate for measures of group performance; coefficients of .80 to .85 are acceptable for screening instruments; and correlations of .90 or above are desirable for instruments that play a key role in making educational decisions about individual students (Hammill, Brown, & Bryant, 1989).

Test publishers have primary responsibility to report reliability information for each of the intended subgroups of the test (*Standards* 2.11). Unlike some types of validity information (e.g., predictive validity) that require a longitudinal design, reliability data can be gathered during test development and standardization and should be included in the supporting manuals when the test is marketed. The *Standards* (2.3) recommends that reliability estimates be provided for each total score, subscore, or combination of scores that the test reports. Reliability coefficients should be reported for each age or grade level and population for which the test is intended (*Standards* 2.11, 2.12). The test user is responsible for evaluating this information to ensure that the test selected is reliable for its intended use (NASP-PPE II.3.2).

Validity

Validity is the single most important consideration in evaluating tests and assessment procedures (*Standards*, 2014, p. 11). Validity refers to "the degree to which evidence and theory support the interpretations of test scores for proposed uses of tests" (*Standards*, 2014, p. 11). However, "no test is valid for all purposes or valid in the abstract"; tests are valid (or not valid) for a specific purpose (Sattler, 2008, p. 117). IDEIA requires that assessment materials used in the identification of children with suspected disabilities "are used for purposes for which the assessments or measures are valid and reliable" (34 CFR § 300.304[c][iii]).

Test producers gather validity evidence from a variety of sources, including evidence based on: (a) test content, (b) response processes, (c), internal structure, (d) relations to other variables, and (e) validity and consequences of testing (*Standards*, 2014, pp. 13–21). In terms of test content, the evidence needs to be evaluated on the degree to which the sample of items, tasks, or questions (as well as the procedures for administration and scoring of those items) on a test is representative of the domain that the test is supposed to measure (Salvia et al., 2013). Test authors are obligated to specify adequately the universe of content that a test is intended to represent and provide evidence that the test content agrees with specifications of what the test should measure (*Standards* 1.11). Likewise, if there are assumptions about the cognitive processes followed by test takers (e.g., test takers are using mathematical reasoning when completing a task purported to measure mathematical reasoning), theoretical or empirical evidence should be provided that those items measure the intended processes (*Standards* 1.12).

When a test allows interpretations based on intratest score differences or score profiles, evidence regarding the internal structure of the test should be provided to support such interpretations (*Standards* 1.13). More specifically, "the distinctiveness and reliability of the separate scores should be demonstrated, and the interrelationships of those scores should be shown to be consistent with the construct(s) being assessed" (*Standards,* 2014, p. 27).

Tests used in psychoeducational assessment often cite criterion-related studies as evidence of validity. Test-criterion relationships typically are reported as a correlation between scores on the test and scores on some type of outcome of interest called the "criterion" measure. Traditionally, test-criterion relationships have been evaluated using concurrent and predictive studies (Salvia et al., 2013). Concurrent validity studies involve obtaining information from the predictor and criterion measures at the same point in time. Predictive validity studies involve administering the criterion measure after a specified time interval to evaluate how well a test correlates with future performance.

What levels of criterion-related validity are acceptable for tests used in psychoeducational assessment? Again, no simple answer exists. Estimates of criterion-related validity are affected by a number of factors, including the extent to which the predictor and criterion tests measure the same traits and abilities, the reliability of the predictor and criterion measures, the heterogeneity or spread of scores on either measure, and the time interval between the administration of the two measures (see Gregory, 2007). Criterion-related validity studies should be described by the test producer in enough detail to enable test users to evaluate the adequacy of the research design and findings. This description should include the types of test takers; research procedures, including the time interval between tests; and statistical analysis, including any correction for attenuation of range of scores. The psychometric characteristics of the criterion measure also should be described in detail (*Standards*, 2014, pp. 28–29).

If a test is purported to be a measure of a construct (psychological characteristic or trait) such as intelligence, scholastic ability, anxiety, or sociability, evidence regarding the relationships of the test's scores with conceptually related constructs should be provided (*Standards* 1.16). As Messick (1965) noted, no single study can establish the construct validity of a test or other measure; an accumulation of evidence based on a multitrait, multimethod construct validation paradigm is needed. This model of construct validation suggests that evidence should be provided showing that the test correlates well with other measures of the same construct (convergent evidence) but does not correlate highly with measures of theoretically unrelated constructs (discriminate evidence) (Campbell & Fiske, 1959).

Last, evidence based on the consequences of tests needs to be evaluated. It is the responsibility of the test user to evaluate the unintended consequences of using a particular test. Further, when unintended consequences arise, the user should attempt to understand whether those consequences resulted from the test's sensitivity to factors other than the desired construct of interest or from the test's inability to fully measure the construct of interest (*Standards* 1.25).

It is also important to note that, in accordance with the *Standards*, when a test is translated and adapted from one language to another, the test producer is obligated to describe the methods used in establishing the adequacy of the adaptation and provide evidence of validity of test score interpretations for its intended use (*Standard* 3.12). Since many dialects and differences in word usage exist among groups with the same official language (e.g., Spanish), the test producer should identify the intended target linguistic groups for the test (e.g., Cubans, Puerto Ricans, or Mexicans) and provide evidence of score validity for each linguistic group (*Standards* 3.12).

How do you decide whether validity evidence is sufficient? Both the quality and quantity of the supporting evidence are important (*Standards*, 2014, pp. 21–22). Although the test manual and supportive materials are starting points for test review, practitioners are obligated ethically to keep abreast of the research related to the validity of tests used in psychoeducational assessment (NASP-PPE II.3.2).

Adequacy of Test Norms

Tests that provide norm-referenced scores allow us to interpret a child's test performance in comparison with a reference group of children of the same age, in the same grade, or perhaps with the same type of disability. In selecting tests with norm-referenced scores, the school psychologist has a responsibility to evaluate the adequacy and appropriateness of the test norms for the intended use of the test. Test norms must be: (a) based on a sample representative of the intended target population for the test, (b) recent, and (c) appropriate for the child being evaluated.

Test producers have a responsibility to identify the intended target population for a test and to describe fully the extent to which the norm group is characteristic of that specific population. Norming studies should be described in the test manual or supportive materials in sufficient detail for the user to evaluate their adequacy and appropriateness for intended test use (*Standards* 5.9). Test users have a responsibility to evaluate the extent to which the children they test are represented in the published norms (NASP-PPE II.3.2).

INFORMATION GATHERING

Ethical-legal concerns that arise during information gathering include ensuring that assessment procedures are administered by qualified examiners under appropriate conditions and that family and student privacy are respected.

Invasion of Privacy

The school psychologist seeks to gather the information needed to develop a picture of the student that is comprehensive enough to be useful in decision making and in planning appropriate interventions. However, in responsible psychological assessment, the practitioner also remains sensitive to student and family privacy (Matarazzo, 1986). School psychologists are obligated ethically to respect the privacy of others (APA-EP Principle E; NASP-PPE I.2). They do not seek or store personal information about the student, parents, or others that is not needed in the provision of services (APA-EP 4.04; NASP-PPE I.2.2).

Assessment Conditions

School psychologists must ensure that the assessment conditions are in the best interests of the student being evaluated. The testing environment should be of "reasonable comfort and with minimal distractions" (*Standards* 6.4); otherwise, findings may not be accurate or valid. Testing done by computers should be monitored to ensure that results are not adversely affected by a lack of computer test-taking skills or by problems with the equipment (NASP-PPE II.3.2, *Standards* 10.9).

In accordance with professional standards and law, tests and other assessment procedures must be "administered by trained and knowledgeable personnel ... in accordance with any instructions provided by the producer of the assessments" (34 CFR § 300.304[c][1][iv, v]). Practitioners are obligated to "follow carefully the standardized procedures for administration and scoring specified by the test developer and any instructions from the test user" (*Standards* 6.1). Modifications are based on carefully considered professional judgment. Furthermore, if an assessment is not conducted under standard conditions, a description of the extent to which it varied from standard conditions should be included in the evaluation report (APA-EP 9.06; NASP-PPE II.3.2; *Standards* 6.3).

Psychological and educational tests should be administered only by individuals qualified to do so (APA-EP 9.07). "School psychologists do not promote or condone the use of restricted psychological and educational tests or other assessment tools or procedures by individuals who are not qualified to use them" (NASP-PPE II.5.2).

Test Security

The development of valid assessment instruments requires extensive research and considerable expense. Inappropriate release of information about the underlying principles or specific content of a test is likely to decrease its validity for future examinees.

The APA's ethics code states that psychologists are obligated to "make reasonable efforts to maintain the integrity and security of test materials and other assessment techniques consistent with law, contractual obligations, and in a manner that permits adherence to this Ethics Code" (APA-EP 9.11; also NASP-PPE II.5, II.5.1–3; *Standards* 9.21–9.23). (Also see Chapter 3, "Parent Access to Test Protocols.")

ASSESSMENT INTERPRETATION

"School psychologists adequately interpret findings and present results in clear, understandable terms so that the recipient can make informed choices" (NASP-PPE II.3.8). As noted previously, in reporting assessment results, psychologists indicate any reservations that exist concerning validity due to assessment circumstances or norm appropriateness (APA-EP 9.06; NASP-PPE II.3.2). Psychologists also are obligated to ensure that assessment results are useful in planning interventions (34 CFR § 300.304[c][7]). Data from student progress monitoring are likely to provide an empirically sound basis for planning interventions (see Chapter 7).

School psychologists may be asked to make recommendations for a student based on findings from a psychoeducational evaluation conducted by another psychologist. This might happen, for example, when a child moves from one locale to another. According to the NASP's code of ethics, "It is permissible for school psychologists to make recommendations based solely on a review of existing records. However, they should utilize a representative sample of records, and explain the basis for, and the limitations of, their recommendations" (NASP-PPE II.3.7; also APA-EP 9.01b, 9.01c).

Classification

Depending on his or her work setting and prior training, a school psychologist might use one or more of several different diagnostic or classification systems. In school-based practice, practitioners most typically are involved in determination of whether a student is eligible for special education under IDEIA and/or whether the student has an impairment and is eligible for accommodations in accordance with Section 504 of the Rehabilitation Act of 1973. Some school psychologists also have been trained to use the *DSM-5* (American Psychiatric Association, 2013) to diagnose mental disorders. As noted previously, *decisions regarding eligibility under IDEIA or Section 504 must be based on the disability criteria outlined in those laws.*

When included in a report written by or for a physician or mental health care provider, a *DSM-5* diagnosis may be helpful in assisting a student to acquire appropriate services. However, school-based practitioners should not render a *DSM-5* diagnosis without the prior consent of the parent (or adult student). Dr. Kim (Case 6.2), like other school psychologists, needs to think carefully about the privacy rights of students and their families and the meaning of the need-to-know principle when making decisions about what information to disclose to others within the school setting. For this reason, school-based practitioners, in collaboration with parents, should decide whether it is in the child's best interests to include a *DSM-5* diagnosis

=== **Case 6.2** ===

After completing his Ph.D., David Kim became a licensed psychologist as well as a certified school psychologist and has continued to work as a school-based practitioner. He received a referral to evaluate Ana, a 12-year-old student in sixth grade, to determine whether she might be eligible for special education services as a student with a learning disability in mathematics calculation and reasoning under IDEIA. Ana's school records indicated that she is a shy and anxious student who has struggled in math since first grade. Her mathematics achievement test scores are below the 4th percentile, even after multiple individualized interventions were attempted in the fourth and fifth grades. Ana's father has consented to a school psychological evaluation in the hope that his daughter will receive additional individualized help in mathematics.

As a result of his interview with Ana, her father, and her teachers, Dr. Kim learns that Ana's mother died from uterine cancer when Ana was in third grade. Since that time, Ana's school records show many absences due to illness and that she frequently goes home early from school because of complaints of an upset stomach. Ana's father reports that their family doctor has found no medical cause for her recurring stomachaches and that, despite reassurances from adults, Ana worries excessively that she is dying from "cancer in the tummy."

Based on his observations, assessment results, and interview findings, Dr. Kim determines that, in addition to possible eligibility under IDEIA as having a learning disability in mathematics, Ana meets the diagnostic criteria for somatic symptom disorder, a diagnosis based on the *DSM-5* (American Psychiatric Association, 2013). Dr. Kim recognizes that he has a number of ethical decisions to make regarding what information to include and what to exclude from his section of the multidisciplinary report that is being prepared for the individualized education program (IEP) team.

in a multidisciplinary report for use by the group of persons determining eligibility under IDEIA or Section 504. Dr. Kim and Ana's father together decide to not include the *DSM-5* diagnosis of somatic symptom disorder in Ana's multidisciplinary report because nonpsychologists sometimes confuse the disorder with malingering. However, Dr. Kim will collaborate with Ana's physician, the school nurse, and Ana's teacher to ensure that appropriate strategies are implemented to help Ana cope with her stomachaches at school. Ana's father has also requested a referral to a child therapist. Dr. Kim will provide him with a list of qualified mental health providers who are skilled in working with children and a letter summarizing the *DSM-5* diagnostic findings.

Last, it is important to note that, legally and ethically, practitioners are obligated to ensure that when classification labels are assigned, they are based on valid assessment procedures and sound professional judgment. Furthermore, when labels are used, "care should be taken to avoid labels with unnecessary stigmatizing implications" (*Standards*, 2014, p. 136).

Report Writing and Sharing Findings

School psychologists typically share their assessment findings in written reports and orally in meetings with the individuals involved.

Report Writing

The written psychological report documents the assessment process and outcomes and outlines recommendations to assist the child. A school psychological evaluation report may be used in making special education decisions and identifying instructional needs. It may serve as a history of performance for subsequent evaluations of student progress or deterioration. It also may be used as a communication tool in referrals to professionals outside the school setting and as documentation in legal proceeding such as hearings and court procedures (Sattler, 2008).

In preparing school psychological evaluation reports, practitioners must consider their obligation to ensure that their findings are understandable and useful to the intended recipient (NASP-PPE II.3.8) as well as their obligation to safeguard the confidentiality of sensitive private information about the student and family (NASP-PPE I.2). Although parents (and eligible students) have access to all school psychological assessment findings, school-based practitioners, in collaboration with parents, need to make careful choices about what information to include in psychological reports prepared for different purposes (e.g., Case 6.2). It may be ethically appropriate (and legally advisable) to exclude sensitive family and student information from a report written for the purpose of making special education decisions or identifying instructional needs. However, *with parent permission*, this information could be shared with others in the school setting or included in a report prepared for a professional outside the school. Walrath, Willis, and Dumont (2014) recommended that, in sensitive situations, psychologists report only the information necessary to allow teachers and staff to implement the recommendations. They also suggested that psychologists consider whether potentially sensitive information could prejudice school staff toward the child and/or family or embarrass the child if inappropriately disclosed.

School psychologists accept responsibility for their professional work (NASP-PPE II.2). They "review all of their written documents for accuracy, signing them only when correct. They may add an addendum, dated and signed, to a previously submitted report if information is found to be inaccurate or incomplete" (NASP-PPE II.2.1). School psychologists who supervise practicum students and interns are responsible for the professional practices of their supervisees (NASP-PPE II.2.4, IV.4.2). Reports prepared by school psychology trainees should be cosigned by the supervising school psychologist. IDEIA requires that parents be given a copy of their child's evaluation report (34 CFR § 300.306[a][2]).

Sharing Findings With the Parent and Student

School psychologists secure continuing parental involvement by honest and forthright reporting of their findings within the promised time frame (APA-EP 9.10; NASP-PPE III; *Standards* 10.11), and they "encourage and promote parental participation in designing interventions for their children" (NASP-PPE II.3.10). Practitioners "discuss with parents the recommendations and plans for assisting their children. This discussion takes into account the ethnic/cultural values of the family and includes alternatives that may be available" (NASP-PPE II.3.10). (Also see Chapter 8.)

School psychologists also discuss the outcomes of the psychoeducational evaluation with the child. Recommendations for program changes or additional services are discussed with the student, along with any alternatives that may be available (NASP-PPE II.3.11). Consistent with ethical principles, students should be afforded opportunities to participate in decisions that affect them.

NONDISCRIMINATORY ASSESSMENT

In Chapter 1, we suggested that psychologists have an ethical obligation to help ensure that the science of psychology is used to promote human welfare in the schools, neighborhoods, and communities in which they work and in the larger society (also NASP-PPE IV). Unfortunately, American history is replete with examples of the ways the supposed science of psychology has been used to oppress culturally and linguistically diverse students in the United States and to justify discriminatory practices in society and in our schools. For example, following the introduction of the Stanford-Binet Intelligence Scales in 1916 and the development of group ability tests, IQ tests were used to characterize Black persons as members of a genetically inferior race and justify discriminatory treatment in society, to characterize non-Anglo immigrants as intellectually inferior and therefore undesirable, and to support laws allowing sterilization of women of below-normal IQ without their consent (Gould, 1996). In schools, IQ and other cognitive assessments have been used: to segregate culturally and linguistically diverse students in inferior, dead-end classes; to deny them access to the college preparatory curriculum; to misclassify them as having intellectual disabilities; and to justify their placement in poorly equipped special education classes taught by inadequately trained staff (see Exhibit 4.2). School psychology practitioners need to be knowledgeable about the history of the misuse of tests in the United States so that they can understand the roots of contemporary controversies regarding the use of IQ tests with children from diverse backgrounds as well as the concerns of parents of culturally and linguistically diverse students referred for psychological testing (also see Ortiz, 2008).

Today, nondiscriminatory assessment is both an ethical and a legal mandate. IDEIA requires that assessment and other evaluation materials must be "selected and administered so as not to be discriminatory on a racial or cultural basis" (34 CFR § 300.304[c][1][i]). Our codes of ethics and professional standards include multiple statements regarding valid and fair assessment of students from culturally diverse backgrounds. The APA's code of ethics addresses these issues in General Principles D (Justice) and E (Respect for People's Rights and Dignity), and in its "Ethical Standards" sections 2.01 (Competence), 2.05 (Delegation of Work to Others), 3.01 (Unfair Discrimination), 9.02 (Use of Assessments), and 9.06 (Interpreting Assessment Results). The NASP's code also includes multiple statements with regard to valid and fair assessment of diverse students (NASP-PPE I.3, II.3.2, II.3.5, II.3.6).

Although the ethical, professional, and legal mandate for nondiscriminatory assessment is clear, it is not easy to translate the nondiscrimination principle into practice. As Reschly and Bersoff (1999) noted, "widely varying" (p. 1085) interpretations of the meaning of nondiscriminatory assessment have appeared in the professional literature and court interpretations. Ortiz (2014) described nondiscriminatory assessment as:

> fair and equitable assessment, irrespective of the individual being evaluated, which adopts a process that dutifully considers all factors that may influence the meaning assigned to any collected data. The only difference between what might be called "typical" assessment practices and those that constitute "nondiscriminatory" assessment practices is that in some cases there are simply more relevant variables at play that thereby merit increased and deliberate attention on the part of the evaluator as compared to what might be needed in cases where few such variables are present. (p. 61)

Culture and Acculturation

There appears to be growing agreement in the professional literature that competent assessment of children from culturally diverse backgrounds requires the practitioner to seek knowledge of the child's culture and how that background may influence development, behavior, and school learning and to gather information about the student's degree of acculturation (Dana, 2000; Ortiz, 2014; Rogers et al., 1999; *Standards*, 2014, p. 56).

With regard to the student's degree of acculturation, Dana (2000) viewed *cultural orientation* on a continuum ranging from traditional (retention of original culture) to nontraditional (assimilation into the majority Anglo-American culture). Information about cultural orientation can be gathered through interviews with the student and his or her family. Information about acculturation should inform test selection, examiner interactional style, assessment interpretation, and intervention planning. The closer a student's cultural orientation falls toward the traditional end of the continuum, the greater the need for caution in use and interpretation of IQ measures that draw on knowledge of language, symbols, and information specific to the dominant U.S. culture. Furthermore, if an intellectual disability is suspected and adaptive behavior at home and in school is assessed, careful attention should be given to how cultural experiences may have affected the child's behavior (Carvalho et al., 2014). Finally, *acculturation stress*, the "stress of adapting to two or more cultures," should be considered in mental health evaluations of a student (p. 78).

Test Bias

For the purposes of the following discussion, bias in assessment is discussed in terms of *test bias, bias in clinical application*, and *fairness of consequences*.

Test bias here refers to the psychometric adequacy of the instrument, that is, evidence that a test or procedure is not equally valid when used with children from differing ethnic or racial backgrounds (Messick, 1965, 1980; Reynolds, Lowe, & Saenz, 1999). In selecting tests for use with culturally diverse students, the practitioner needs to ask: "Is this test a valid measure of what it purports to measure for examinees from this particular group?"

Test bias may be defined and evaluated in terms of the content validity, criterion-related validity, and construct validity. "An item or subscale of a test is considered to be biased in content when it is demonstrated to be relatively more difficult for members of one group than another when the general ability level of the groups being compared is held constant and no reasonable theoretical rationale exists to explain group differences on the item (or subscale) in question" (Reynolds et al., 1999, p. 564).

The question of content bias is resolved by research that shows equal (or unequal) item difficulties for various groups (Flaugher, 1978). Biased items usually can be identified and eliminated during the test development phase. Reynolds et al. (1999) reviewed available studies and found little evidence of any consistent content bias in well-prepared, standardized tests when such tests are used with English-speaking examinees. When content bias was found, it accounted for a relatively small proportion of the variance (2%–5%) in the group score differences associated with minority group membership.

Test bias also may be defined in terms of differential concurrent or predictive (criterion-related) validity. "A test is considered biased with respect to predictive validity if the inference drawn from the test score is not made with the smallest feasible random error or if there is constant error in an inference or prediction as a function of membership in a particular group" (Reynolds et al., 1999, p. 577). A test may be shown to be nonbiased in criterion-related validity if it predicts the criterion measure performance equally well for children from different ethnic backgrounds. Based on a review of the school psychology literature, R. T. Brown, Reynolds, and Whitaker (1999) concluded that "empirical evidence overwhelmingly supports the conclusion that well-developed, currently-used mental tests are of equivalent predictive validity for American-born, English-speaking individuals regardless of their subgroup membership" (p. 231). Less is known about bias in adaptive behavior and personality assessment instruments.

Test bias also may be defined in terms of construct validity. "Bias exists in regard to construct validity when a test is shown to measure different hypothetical traits (psychological constructs) for different groups; that is, differing interpretations of a common performance are shown to be appropriate as a function of ethnicity, gender, or another variable of interest" (Reynolds et al., 1999, p. 573). Studies that show a test has the same factor structure for children from different ethnic backgrounds provide evidence that the test is measuring the same construct for different groups—that it is nonbiased with respect to construct validity. Reynolds et al. reported that "no consistent evidence of bias in construct validity" was found with any of the well-constructed and well-standardized tests they investigated (p. 577).

The *Standards* (3.8) recommends that test developers research and report results for relevant subgroups for whom there may be differential prediction of future test performance. The practitioner is obligated to evaluate the research on test bias when selecting instruments for culturally, ethnically, and racially diverse students and to choose the fairest and most appropriate instruments available.

Bias in Clinical Application

Bias in clinical application refers to fairness in administration, interpretation, and decision making. The use of biased tests may lead to unfair decisions. However, poor decisions can be made on the basis of fair tests because of atmosphere bias and bias in interpretation or decision making. *Atmosphere bias* refers to factors in the testing situation that may inhibit performance of children from ethnic minority backgrounds (Flaugher, 1978). As noted previously, practitioners are obligated to seek knowledge of the child's background so that they can build and maintain rapport during testing in a culturally sensitive manner. Atmosphere bias may occur because of limited test-taking skills (e.g., lack of responsiveness to speed pressures); wariness of the examiner (e.g., race of the examiner effects, reluctance to verbalize); and differences in cognitive style and test achievement motivation that hinder optimal performance. Sattler (2008) suggested that atmosphere bias can be minimized by a competent, well-trained examiner who is sensitive to the child's personal, linguistic, and cultural background. (See Frisby, 1999a, 1999b, for a comprehensive review of the empirical literature on culture/ethnicity of the examinee, test session behaviors, and test performance.)

As Ortiz (2014) observed, "Although psychometric data in particular are often viewed as representing objective measurement, data have no inherent meaning and derive significance only from interpretation with the broader, ecological context of the examinee" (p. 63). To minimize bias in data collection and interpretation, he suggested that psychologists adhere to the null hypothesis that "an individual's learning problems are related to extrinsic or situational, not intrinsic, variables" until the collected data suggest otherwise.

Fairness of Consequences

A third area of concern is *fairness of consequences* of test use. This involves an appraisal of the outcomes or consequences of test use for a particular group (Messick, 1980). If testing and assessment practices result in children from a particular ethnic group being placed in inferior educational programs, the outcomes or consequences of testing are biased and unfair (Reschly, 1997; also *Standards*, 2014, p. 56).

Closing Comments on Nondiscriminatory Assessment

In these closing comments on nondiscriminatory assessment, we refer the reader back to Messick's (1984) statement that, consistent with responsible, ethical practice, no child should be seen for psychological evaluation unless deficiencies in instruction have first been ruled out. A service delivery model that emphasizes early intervening services may help safeguard ethnically, racially, and linguistically diverse children from unnecessary testing and the risk of misdiagnosis or misclassification. By working with teachers and parents to pinpoint learning and behavior problems before they become severe and by intervening early, many problems can be remedied without formal psychological assessment.

If, however, such efforts to remediate problems are unsuccessful and a psychological assessment is needed, practitioners can minimize assessment bias by adhering to seven "best practice" recommendations:

1. Be knowledgeable of the child's culture and able to establish and maintain rapport in a culturally sensitive manner.
2. Consider the influence of English language proficiency, culture, and the degree of acculturation in selecting assessment methods.
3. Gather developmental, health, family, and school history information.
4. Observe the child in the classroom and other settings as appropriate to the problem.
5. Consider teacher characteristics, instructional variables, classroom factors, and support available from the home in understanding the child's difficulties and possible interventions.
6. Use a variety of formal and less formal assessment strategies, including interviews, behavioral assessments, evaluation of classroom work samples, curriculum-based assessment, testing the limits, and response to intervention.
7. Interpret findings in light of the child's background to ensure a valid and useful picture of the child's abilities and educational needs.

Ortiz (2014) outlined a systematic, step-by-step procedure to guide school psychologists in conducting nondiscriminatory assessments. Practitioners also assume responsibility for monitoring the outcomes of assessment for culturally and linguistically diverse students in their schools to ensure that the consequences of testing are fair and in the best interests of the children.

PERSONALITY ASSESSMENT

Three ethical-legal concerns associated with the use of personality tests in the schools, in particular projective techniques, have been identified in the literature. First, there has been a long-standing concern among psychologists that the use of personality tests may result in unwarranted invasion of privacy. Personality tests have been a special focus of concern because, unlike achievement or ability tests, questions on personality tests are often indirect, and the test taker may unknowingly reveal aspects of the self, including emotional problems, that he or she is not prepared to unveil (Messick, 1965). Two strategies to safeguard privacy in the use of personality tests have been suggested. First, consistent with ethical codes and legal requirements (e.g., IDEIA), explicit informed consent should be obtained before administering such tests. Second, the school psychologist must consider carefully whether the use of such tests is justified in assisting the student; that is, the psychologist must weigh the risk of intrusion on student and family privacy against the likelihood that such techniques will result in information helpful in promoting student welfare.

A second ethical-legal issue specific to the use of projective personality tests in the schools focuses on whether such tests meet professional and legal standards for demonstrated test validity. A number of writers have argued that evidence for the technical adequacy of many projective techniques is lacking or does not support their use with children and that projective test results appear to lack educational relevance (Batsche & Peterson, 1983). D. N. Miller and Nickerson (2007) questioned the use of projective techniques in school-based practice because of their lack of *incremental validity*, namely "the extent to which an assessment method contributes to the understanding of an individual beyond that which is already known, as well as the degree to which it can provide information that cannot be gained in some other, easier way" (pp. 50–51). More specifically, are there other assessment procedures (such as direct observations and rating scales) that have better evidence of diagnostic validity and clearer implications for school-based interventions?

An additional concern about the use of personality tests, including projectives, is that school psychologists may not be adequately trained in their use. Consistent with the broad ethical principle of responsible caring, school psychologists must evaluate their own competence to use particular assessment strategies. Practitioners who use personality tests need to have skills in the administration and interpretation of the particular assessment tool and competent judgment about when to use the test or strategy. Projective tests should be used only by psychologists with verifiable training in their use.

PROFESSIONAL COMPETENCE AND AUTONOMY

To ensure valid results, psychologists must offer assessment services only within the boundaries of their competence, and they must insist on professional autonomy in the selection of assessment methods.

Competence

Practitioners are ethically obligated to ensure that they have the competence to conduct a valid psychoeducational assessment of the students whom they typically serve in their work setting (see APA-EP 2.01; also NASP-PPE II, II.1, II.1.1, II.1.2; *Standards* 9.1). Psychologists who step beyond their competence in assessing children place students at risk for misdiagnosis, misclassification, miseducation, and possible psychological harm. Practitioners are well advised to develop a directory of colleagues with expertise in evaluating children from special backgrounds or with low-incidence disabilities. Seeking assistance through supervision, consultation, and referral are appropriate strategies for psychologists faced with a difficult or unusual case (NASP-PPE II.1.1). However, practitioners who plan to shift or expand their services to a new age group or special student population are obligated to seek formal training or professional supervision before offering such services.

Professional Autonomy

IDEIA—Part B requires the consideration of certain types of information in the evaluation of children with suspected disabilities. For example, intellectual ability, achievement, adaptive behavior, and developmental history all must be considered in the evaluation of children who may be eligible within the IDEIA classification of intellectual disability. State education laws and local district policy may specify additional *types* of information to be considered in evaluation of children with suspected disabilities. School psychologists need to be knowledgeable of these requirements. In some school districts, administrators have attempted to dictate the specific tests that psychologists must use to determine special education eligibility. To serve the best interests of students, however, school psychologists must insist on professional autonomy in the selection of specific assessment instruments. *District-mandated test batteries* are inconsistent with professional standards, may result in unsound assessment choices for the student being evaluated, and violate the intent of special education law that requires tests be selected in light of the unique characteristics of the individual child (APA-EP 9.02; NASP-PPE II.3.2, II.3.5).

COMPUTER-ASSISTED PSYCHOEDUCATIONAL ASSESSMENT

A number of psychological and educational tests can now be computer administered, scored, and interpreted via the Internet or computer software programs (L. D. Armistead, 2014b). A special challenge of this technology is to interpret codes of ethics, professional standards, and special education laws as they relate to computer-assisted assessment (APA, 1986; L. D. Armistead, 2014b; Harvey & Carlson, 2003; Naglieri et al., 2004; Pfohl & Jarmuz-Smith, 2014).

As Harvey and Carlson (2003) suggested, school practitioners have an ethical responsibility to consider the ways computers can improve assessment practices. Computer-administered tests and interviews can result in quick and accurate scores and facilitate fair assessment of students with disabilities as well as those from diverse linguistic backgrounds. For example, features such as variable text and image size and digitalized voice may improve testing of students with visual impairments; response devices such as joysticks, the mouse, and touch-sensitive screens and pads can facilitate assessment of students with physical and communicative disabilities. A digitalized voice or video clips providing instructions or asking questions in the child's native language and dialect may assist in assessment of children from linguistically and culturally diverse backgrounds and permit parents who do not speak English to provide child history information in their native language (Black & Ponirakis, 2000). In addition, computer-administered tests allow easy and efficient use of adaptive testing formats (where the computer is programmed to select and administer test questions based on the examinee's pattern of correct answers) to assess academic skills or cognitive abilities. Furthermore, research suggests that some examinees are more candid when answering sensitive questions administered via computer (e.g., drug use, suicidal thoughts) when compared to in-person interviews, resulting in more valid results (Black & Ponirakis, 2000). Finally, another benefit is the convenience to parents and teachers when they can complete an online version of a behavioral/social-emotional questionnaire or rating scale. Some practitioners report better compliance with requests to complete online forms than when paper forms are sent home (L. D. Armistead, personal communication, July 12, 2015).

Computer-assisted scoring likely reduces scoring errors, such as failure to correctly calculate a child's chronological age and mistakes in raw-to-scaled-score conversions.

Computer-assisted score analysis also can provide interpretive guidance to the practitioner. Computer-generated interpretations, based on research findings and the knowledge of the expert clinicians who developed the underlying algorithms, can encourage the practitioner to consider appropriate alternative diagnostic hypotheses (Harvey & Carlson, 2003).

Web-based testing may allow test developers to offer less expensive products and revisions and translations more quickly (Naglieri et al., 2004). When a Web-based assessment platform is used for test scoring, the test publisher can monitor item statistics (e.g., index of difficulty, index of discrimination) and identify language or other content that is outdated. Test publishers also can identify items that are not measuring what was anticipated when the test was originally developed. Web-based testing also makes it possible for publishers to update test norms tables with less cost and in a timely manner. Finally, online scoring allows the use of sophisticated algorithms that differentially weigh items or subtests in determining scores.

In addition to the possible benefits of computer-assisted assessment, practitioners must be sensitive to the ethical-legal questions associated with the use of this technology (L. D. Armistead, 2014b; Harvey & Carlson, 2003; Pfohl & Jarmuz-Smith, 2014; Reidenberg et al., 2013). First, and perhaps most important, it is the psychologist's responsibility to ensure that all assessment procedures, including those that are computer-assisted, yield valid results prior to using the results in decision making (APA, 1986, p. 8; NASP-PPE II.3.2). Selection of computer-administered tests and scoring and interpretation programs should be limited to those programs that have been reviewed by experts in the field and found to meet high standards for professional practice (Harvey & Carlson, 2003; NASP-PPE II.3.2; Schulenberg & Yutrzenka, 2004). In addition, when the practitioner considers using a computer-administered instrument that was originally developed for a traditional pencil-and-paper administrative format, he or she is obligated to review the technical information provided on the equivalency of scores when the instrument is computer-administered as compared to the traditional administrative format. Also, as noted previously, when a child is required to respond to test items presented on a tablet or other device, the examiner must ensure that results are not adversely affected by a lack of familiarity with the device or by problems with the equipment (NASP-PPE II.3.2, *Standards* 10.9). Finally, computer-generated test interpretations should be considered to be a tool that is to be used in conjunction with the clinical judgment of a well-trained professional (NASP-PPE II.3.2; Schulenberg & Yutrzenka, 2004, *Standards* 9.10).

Several major test publishers have created online digital assessment platforms. Examples include Pearson's Q-global®, Multi-Health Systems' Online Assessment Center, PAR's PARiConnect, and Riverside's Woodcock Johnson® IV online scoring and reporting system. These Web-based platforms typically allow the presentation of test questions and the recording of the examinee's answers on a computer screen and online scoring and results reporting. Some allow integration of the results of multiple tests and assessments administered to an examinee. In addition, Pearson offers Q-interactive®, an assessment system that uses two iPads® linked by encrypted Bluetooth technology. One iPad, for the examiner, has the test instructions, and is used to record and score responses and control presentation of items on the student's iPad. The student uses the second iPad to view and respond to test stimuli. Tests available in the Q-interactive battery include the Wechsler Intelligence Scales and achievement, speech and language, memory, and neuropsychological tests.

Use of a Web-based digital assessment platform as part of a psychoeducational evaluation of an individual student raises new ethical-legal concerns. In the paragraphs that follow, we attempted to answer some of the questions raised by NASP members in posts to the NASP's online member exchange or in email queries to the first author of this book. These answers are based on a review of contemporary resources, ethics codes, and relevant law. Readers are cautioned that there is a diversity of ethical opinions on these issues and that relevant law is evolving; the information provided here should not be viewed as legal advice.

Is parent consent legally required for a school psychology practitioner to transmit personally identifiable student psychological test answers and scores to a third-party Web-based digital assessment platform provider? Probably not. As discussed in Chapter 3, under the Family Educational Rights and Privacy Act of 1974 (FERPA), parent consent is not required for the school to release personally identifiable information (PII) to parties to whom a school has outsourced schools services or functions if certain conditions are met (34 CFR § 99.31). The agreement is between *the school* and the assessment platform provider; consequently, individual practitioners should ensure that the district approves the use of the Web-based assessment provider for school psychological assessment.[3]

Ethically, is parent consent required to use a Web-based platform in the assessment of a child? Both the APA and the NASP require practitioners to *notify* clients of the electronic storage and transmission of personally identifiable student information and any known risks to privacy (APA-EP 4.02c; NASP-PPE II.4.1). However, we recommend that parents be asked whether they consent to the use of a Web-based platform for individual psychological assessment of their child.[4] We make this recommendation for two reasons. First, unlike Web-administered districtwide achievement tests, some measures that might be individually administered by a school psychologist using a Web-based platform (e.g., depression scales) yield sensitive information about a child that could cause harm in the unlikely event of a breach of Web site security. Second, some parents are strongly opposed to the "uploading" of personal information to the Internet. In such situations, the practitioner might suggest that the child's assessment information be entered using an identifier other than the child's real name. If that is not acceptable to parents, practitioners are encouraged to respect the parents' wishes and offer traditional assessment alternatives (Lustgarten, 2015).

Is parent consent required for a test company to use test scores and other data collected from examinees during Web-based assessments for product assessment and development? Probably not. The use of existing data for research and product development does not require parent consent under FERPA or human research subjects protection guidelines (see Chapter 10) as long as the data are de-identified before being used for research and product development purposes.

---

[3]Although it is likely not relevant to the school psychologist's use of a Web-based assessment platform, practitioners also should be familiar with the Children's Online Privacy Protection Act of 1998 (COPPA, Pub. L. No. 106-277). COPPA regulates the online or Web-based *collection of personal information directly from children* age 12 or under.

[4]Note that parent consent is not required when schools use Web-based tests to conduct school- or districtwide achievement testing.

Does the Web-based assessment platform adequately protect the privacy and security of personally identifiable student assessment information during transmission to and from the Web site and when stored by the Web-based assessment platform provider? Although school-based psychologists typically are required to comply with FERPA and not the Health Insurance Portability and Accountability Act of 1996 (HIPAA), practitioners should ensure that the Web-based assessment platform provider is in compliance with HIPAA "best practices" standards for data security during transmission and storage. Access to student data should require a password. All data should be encrypted when stored (Pfohl & Jarmuz-Smith, 2014) and online connections should be secure (e.g., use of a Secure Sockets Layer [SSL] that authenticates the identity of the Web site and user and encrypts information sent across the Internet between the Web site and user; "https" signifies use of an SSL). Practitioners also need to ensure that a password is required to log onto tablets used for test administration and that all testing administration files are password protected and encrypted.

Finally, school psychologists should ensure that the agreement between the school and the Web-based assessment platform provider guarantees the deletion of personally identifiable examinee answers, scores, and other information when it is no longer needed by the practitioner. Also, consistent with ethically and legally sound record-keeping practices (Chapter 3), the practitioner should ensure that he or she can obtain a record of the student's responses when tests are administered via a digital assessment platform.

Advances in computer-assisted assessment have moved forward rapidly in recent years. School psychologists interested in using Web-based digital assessments must gain competence in evaluation and selection of these products and competence in their use (Pfohl & Jarmuz-Smith, 2014). Practitioners should be prepared to discuss the benefits and risks associated with new psychoeducational assessment products with their school administrators and with parents.

CONCLUDING COMMENTS

In recent years, many school psychologists have modified their job role so they can devote more time to consultation and intervention activities and less time to student assessment to determine eligibility for special education services. Although current job roles may now place more emphasis on consultation and intervention, school psychologists continue to be among the members of a school's staff who are most knowledgeable about assessment. Consequently, school psychologists must continue to accept responsibility for ensuring that tests and assessment procedures are used only in ways that protect the rights and promote the well-being of students.

STUDY AND DISCUSSION

Questions for Chapter 6

1. What is the difference between *testing* and *assessment?*
2. Identify the school psychologist's ethical-legal obligations to the parent prior to beginning an assessment and during interpretation of findings.

3. Describe five ethical-legal concerns a psychologist should consider in planning and conducting psychoeducational assessments.
4. What are test bias, bias in clinical application, and fairness of consequences?
5. Identify the ethical concerns associated with the use of projective personality tests with schoolchildren.
6. Identify the ethical-legal issues associated with the selection and use of Web-based and computer-assisted test administration, scoring, and interpretation programs.

Discussion

Pearl Meadows supervises school psychology specialist-level graduate students who are completing their training at the university in the town where Pearl is employed. A professor in the school psychology training program received a grant to purchase Apple iPads and capacitive-enabled styluses so that school psychology students could learn to administer assessments using Pearson's Q-interactive digital assessment system. The grant includes funding to provide iPads and styluses to several internship supervisors, including Pearl.

Make a list of the ethical-legal questions and issues Pearl should consider/address prior to using Q-interactive at her school. Then visit http://www.helloq.com. Watch the Q-global and Q-interactive videos. Click on the "Privacy Policy" at the bottom of the page. Is de-identified test data used for research purposes? Is it possible to delete personally identifiable student information from the system? Go to http://www.helloq .com/research.html. Why is this Web site important to Pearl's decision making? Visit http://www.pearsonclinical.com. Search for the "Legal" information tab. Click on "HIPAA." Does the Q-interactive system meet HIPAA guidelines for protecting the security of personally identifiable information?

Vignettes

1. Carrie Johnson's caseload includes a school located on an island in the Great Lakes. Ferry service is available only between April and November; in winter months, Carrie must use the charter air carrier to provide services at the island school. She has been following the literature on remote psychological assessment via telemental health technologies and found that it has been used effectively for some types of assessments of adults (Luxton, Pruitt, & Osenbach, 2014). However, Carrie has not located any research on telemental health assessments of children.

   Carrie loves technology and has thought about conducting remote psychoeducational assessments of children at the island school. She knows it would be easy to use her home computer's webcam to send a live feed of herself to a computer screen in the testing room at the island school. Two Dropcams® positioned in the testing room could be used to capture images of a child's face and hands, with one also capturing sound. A speech and language professional who lives on the island has expressed a willingness to be trained to assist in the administration of the Wechsler Intelligence Scales for Children–V and several achievement tests.

The speech teacher would manipulate the testing materials (e.g., Block Design presentation) and help maintain rapport with the child while Carrie, via computer, would ask the child questions, query answers as needed, read instructions to the child, and score the protocol.

If Carrie goes forward with her plan to conduct remote psychoeducational assessments, what ethical-legal issues are involved?

2. During his internship in a suburban school district, David Kim receives a disproportionately high number of referrals for special education evaluation of children who live in federally funded low-income housing in his district. Most of these children are African American or Hispanic but attending predominately White elementary schools. David is concerned about potential overidentification of African American and Hispanic children for special education in his district. What are some strategies he might use to prevent this problem?

3. Each May, the elementary schools in Carrie Johnson's district invite children who will enter kindergarten in the fall and their parents to a kindergarten roundup. During the roundup, hearing, vision, and speech screenings are conducted, and Carrie administers the Vocabulary and Picture Completion subtests from the Wechsler Preschool and Primary Scale of Intelligence–IV (Wechsler, 2012) to identify children who might need further evaluation of their learning needs. A new resort-hotel complex is being built near one of her schools, and the hotel management has recruited several families from Dominica for job openings. Carrie is delighted when a Dominican child comes to her screening table. Relying on the French she learned in college, Carrie speaks to the child in French and attempts an on-the-spot translation of the WPPSI–IV subtests from English to French. What are the ethical issues in this situation?

4. Wanda Rose receives a note from the principal of an elementary school where she provides school psychological services. The note says: "Wanda, please give a WISC–V to Timmy O'Brien, in second grade, and let me know his IQ. His teacher and I think he's just 'slow' like his brothers. We don't want to bother with parent consent and all the IDEIA paperwork so let's just consider this a 'screening.' His parents will probably never even know he was tested." What are the ethical and legal issues in this situation? How should Wanda respond to the principal's request?

Activities

A 7-year-old child has been referred for psychoeducational assessment because of her slow academic progress. Her teacher suspects that she may be eligible for special education as a child with an intellectual disability. Role-play your initial meeting with the child's parents during which you seek informed consent for assessment. Role-play your meeting with the child during which you describe the scope and nature of the assessment process.

Chapter 7 ———————————————

ETHICAL AND LEGAL ISSUES IN SCHOOL-BASED INTERVENTIONS

As noted in Chapter 1, school-based practitioners often provide consultative services that are not within the scope of an established psychologist–client relationship to school districts, to student assistance teams, or within classrooms. In this chapter, we first explore the ethical-legal issues associated with delivering services within a multitiered system of academic and behavioral support. Then we explore the ethical-legal issues associated with providing counseling and other therapeutic interventions within the context of a school psychologist–client relationship.

MULTITIERED SYSTEMS OF ACADEMIC AND BEHAVIORAL SUPPORT

In 2006, a task force composed of experts in the field of school psychology completed the document titled *School Psychology: A Blueprint for Training and Practice III* (Ysseldyke et al. 2006), in which the authors suggested that the goals of improving educational and mental health outcomes for all students, and the capacity of systems to meet the needs of all students, can best be achieved by a three-tier model of service delivery (p. 13), now referred to as a *multitiered system of support* (MTSS). *Tier I* or *universal services* are systems-level programs and services designed to meet the academic and social-behavior needs of the majority of students. Examples include "use of evidence-based approaches to reading and math instruction or the implementation of a positive school-wide discipline program to reduce problems with behavior management" (Ysseldyke et al., 2006, p. 13; also Stoiber, 2014). At Tier I, school psychology practitioners might assist in developing a universal (districtwide) screening process to identify students at risk of not making adequate progress in the general education curriculum. *Tier II* or *targeted interventions* are for students who do not succeed in response to Tier I services and address "specific academic or social-emotional skill or performance deficits" (Ysseldyke et al., 2006, p. 13). At Tier II, school psychologists might provide consultation to student assistance teams or in classrooms with the goal of implementing evidence-based interventions and monitoring their effectiveness. *Tier III* or *intensive interventions* are tailored to the needs of the individual student (Stoiber, 2014). Tier III interventions might include special education and related services, therapeutic interventions in the context of a school psychologist–client relationship, and/or assistance provided through interagency collaborations.

Classroom Interventions

Beginning in the mid-1980s, some school districts introduced building-based prereferral child study teams to assist teachers in planning academic and behavioral interventions for students in general education classes. Researchers found that such efforts were a safeguard against inappropriate referral for special education eligibility evaluation, unnecessary testing, and misclassification (e.g., Chalfant & Pysh, 1989; Graden, Casey, & Bonstrom, 1985). A statewide system of prereferral intervention also was found to be one means of reducing the overrepresentation of African American students in special education (e.g., *Lee v. Lee County Bd. of Education*, 2007). In the 1990s, federal policy makers encouraged schools to implement prereferral child study teams as a component of a district's child find procedures under the Individuals with Disabilities Education Act and Section 504 (Shrag, 1991). The 2004 amendments to special education law, the Individuals with Disabilities Improvement Act (IDEIA), allow school districts to use up to 15% of their federal special education funds each year to develop and implement coordinated *early intervening services*. These services are for students in all grades who require additional academic and behavior support to be successful in general education, but who have not been identified as needing special education and related services (34 CFR § 300.226).

A distinction is made in the contemporary school psychology literature between the terms *response to intervention* (RTI) and *positive behavior supports* (PBS), with *RTI* described as the systematic, data-driven use of evidence-based interventions to assist students who are struggling academically and *PBS* referring to systematic, data-driven evidence-based interventions to assist students with challenging behaviors (see Stoiber, 2014). However, consistent with the language used by the U.S. Department of Education (DOE) Office of Special Education Services (e.g., Musgrove, 2011) and for the purposes of this chapter, *response to intervention* will serve as an umbrella term that includes strategies to address the behavioral functioning of students as well as their academic performance. The RTI process generally involves providing effective instruction for students within general education, monitoring student progress, providing more individualized assistance for students who do not demonstrate adequate progress, and monitoring progress again. Students who still do not respond satisfactorily might be referred for a special education or Section 504 eligibility evaluation (Burns, Jacob, & Wagner, 2008; Walker & Daves, 2010).

The next portion of the chapter focuses on ethical-legal issues associated with academic and behavioral interventions in the classroom including: (1) parent involvement, consent, and child find obligations within a multitiered model; (2) selecting classroom interventions; (3) documenting interventions and monitoring progress; and (4) special considerations associated with the use of behavioral interventions.

Parent Involvement, Consent, and Child Find Obligations Within a Multitiered Model

As discussed in Chapters 1 and 3, school psychologists are ethically obligated to promote parental participation in school decisions affecting children (NASP-PPE, I.1.2, II.3.10). However, consistent with IDEIA, in cases where school psychologists are members of the school's instructional support staff, not all of their services require informed parent consent. It is ethically and legally permissible "to provide school-based consultation services regarding a child or adolescent to a student assistance team or teacher without informed parent consent as long as the resulting interventions are *under the authority of the teacher* and within the scope of typical classroom interventions" (NASP-PPE I.1.1, emphasis added).

Furthermore, consistent with IDEIA:

> Parent consent is not ethically required for a school-based school psychologist to review a student's education records, conduct classroom observations, assist in within-classroom interventions and progress monitoring, or to participate in educational screenings conducted as part of a regular program of instruction. Parent consent is required if the consultation about a particular child or adolescent is likely to be extensive and ongoing and/or if school actions may result in a significant intrusion on student or family privacy beyond what might be expected in the course of ordinary school activities. (NASP-PPE I.1.1)

The NASP's code of ethics goes on to recommend that a school district's parent handbook inform families that school psychologists routinely assist teachers in planning classroom instruction and monitoring its effectiveness and that district policy does not require parent notice or consent for such involvement in student support (NASP-PPE, footnote to I.1.2).

The U.S. DOE's Office of Special Education Programs and the courts have generally supported the use of "less drastic alternatives" such as RTI prior to evaluation of a student for eligibility under IDEIA or Section 504 as long as the student's progress is monitored and a referral for evaluation is made as soon as a disability is suspected (e.g., *A. P. v. Woodstock Board of Education*, 2008; *El Paso Independent School District v. Richard R.*, 2008; also Musgrove, 2011). Under IDEIA, parents must be *notified* if RTI is being implemented *as part of the process to determine whether their child is suspected of having a disability*. More specifically, the parents must be notified about state policies dictating the amount and nature of student performance data to be collected and the general education services that will be provided, strategies that will be implemented for increasing the child's rate of learning, and the parents' right to request an evaluation of their child for IDEIA eligibility at any time (34 CFR § 300.311[a][7]).

If, at any point during the process of providing early intervening services, a student is suspected of having a disability, the school is required to seek parent consent to conduct an individual evaluation in accordance with IDEIA or Section 504 procedures and time lines (Musgrove, 2011). Because RTI is a widely accepted evidence-based general education instructional method and because schools, not parents, have the authority to select specific instructional methodologies (e.g., *Board of Education of the Hendrick Hudson Central School District v. Rowley*, 1982; *Ridley School District v. M.R.,* 2012), the school (not the parent) determines which students receive RTI services, the instructional strategies implemented for each child, and how student progress is monitored. In short, parent notice is required if RTI will be used as part of a process of determining whether a student is suspected of a having a disability; parent consent is required before conducting a comprehensive individual evaluation of a child to determine if he or she has a disability, but parent consent is not required for the initial or continuing provision of RTI services.

Furthermore, if parents request a special education or Section 504 eligibility evaluation *during* the RTI process and the school decides not to evaluate the student, the school must provide parents with written notice of its refusal to evaluate along with information describing parent rights to challenge that decision (Musgrove, 2011). School districts may not require that RTI be implemented for a predetermined number of weeks before responding to a parent request for an evaluation under IDEIA or Section 504 (Musgrove, 2011). For example, an Office for Civil Rights investigation was triggered by a parent's complaint that the school did not respond to her request for evaluation of her child under Section 504 or provide notice of parent rights under the law. The investigation found that the school required an eight-week RTI intervention period before a student could be considered for a Section 504 evaluation, at which time parents would be provided notice of their rights. The complaint resolution stated that "the use of RTI does not offend Section 504," but RTI may not, without violating Section 504, be implemented in such a manner that denies parents notice of their rights under Secton 504 at the time they request an evaluation of their child, including their right to "persist in their request for an evaluation or to seek procedural safeguards" (Acalanes [CA] Union High School District Office for Civil Rights, Western Division, San Francisco [California], 2009, p. 8).

In sum, the implementation of prereferral recommendations by student assistance teams or the use of RTI is not likely to be seen as an unreasonable delay of the child find requirements of IDEIA and Section 504/Americans with Disabilities Act Amendments as long as student progress is documented and a referral for evaluation is made as soon as a disability is suspected. If parents request a special education or Section 504 eligibility evaluation during the RTI process and the school decides not to evaluate the child, the school must provide parents with written notice of the refusal to evaluate along with information describing parent rights to challenge that decision.

Selecting Classroom Interventions

Both the No Child Left Behind Act of 2001 (Pub. L. No. 89-10) and IDEIA called on school psychologists and other educational specialists to use scientifically based academic and behavioral interventions. In the Every Student Succeeds Act of 2015 (ESSA, Pub. L. No. 114-95), the term *scientifically based* was with replaced with *evidence-based* interventions (EBI). The term *evidence-based* generally means a state or school activity that:

(i) demonstrates a statistically significant effect on improving student outcomes or other relevant outcomes based on—

    (I) strong evidence from at least 1 well-designed and well-implemented experimental study;

    (II) moderate evidence from at least 1 well-designed and well-implemented quasi-experimental study; or

    (III) promising evidence from at least 1 well-designed and well-implemented correlational study with statistical controls for selection bias; or

(ii) (I) demonstrates a rationale based on high quality research findings or positive evaluation that such activity, strategy, or intervention is likely to improve student outcomes or other relevant outcomes; and

 (II) includes ongoing efforts to examine the effects of such activity, strategy, or intervention. (S.1177 Sec. 8002 [21][A]i–ii])

A reliance on applied learning sciences in making intervention choices also is consistent with codes of ethics. Standard II.3.9 of the NASP's code requires school psychologists to "use a problem-solving process to develop interventions appropriate to the presenting problems and that are consistent with data collected" and to give preference "to interventions described in the peer-reviewed professional research literature and found to be efficacious" (also APA-EP 2.04). However, while practitioners give preference to interventions reported to be effective, they also must adapt those interventions to the setting and the individual needs of the child. In other words, practitioners must strive for fidelity to the treatment program as it is described in the research literature while at the same time adapting the intervention to the unique characteristics of the setting and student (Bailey & Burch, 2011). Similarly, the ESSA acknowledges the importance of evidence-based interventions that are also *place-based*, that is, the interventions are selected and modified by local educators to take into account the setting and the characteristics and needs (culture, language, ethnic identity) of targeted student groups (U.S. DOE, 2016, p. 1; also ESSA, Sec. 6004 [a][4]).

Documenting Interventions and Monitoring Progress

School psychologists are ethically obligated to use a data-based problem-solving process to plan and monitor the effectiveness of interventions. The NASP's code of ethics specifically requires practitioners to:

> actively monitor the impact of their recommendations and intervention plans. They revise a recommendation, or modify or terminate an intervention plan, when data indicate the desired outcomes are not being attained. (NASP-PPE II.2.2)

Furthermore, documenting the interventions attempted, collecting progress monitoring data, and modifying interventions when they do not achieve the desired result are essential components of legally defensible RTI practices. RTI data must be available for review by the parents when used by the school in answering any of these questions: (1) Is the student a child with a suspected disability? (2) Is the student eligible for special education and related services under IDEIA? and (3) Based on RTI data, what are the appropriate components of an individualized instructional program be designed to benefit the student?

In *M.M. v. Lafayette School District* (2014), for example, the school district cited a student's RTI data as one basis for its determination of a free appropriate public education (FAPE) for a child with a disability. The RTI data were not used for eligibility determination; however, the data were identified by the school as one source of information for planning an appropriate instructional program. The school did not make the child's RTI data available to the parents. The court opined that, whether or not the RTI data were the primary basis for developing a FAPE, the school had violated IDEIA's requirement that parents be provided access to the documentation that provided the basis for determining special education services (34 CFR § 300.306[a][2]).

In a due process hearing under IDEIA, a parent sought compensatory education for her child because the school failed to evaluate her child for special education services during the academic year, even though her child exhibited extensive and continuing behavioral problems from the first day of school. The school also failed to provide her with notice of parent rights under IDEIA. In its defense, the school argued in part that the child had not been referred for evaluation of IDEIA eligibility because RTI methods were being implemented prior to initiating an evaluation. However, the school had no written documentation of an RTI plan and no evidence of progress monitoring or that the RTI interventions were modified based on student progress. The hearing officer found in favor of the parent, awarding considerable compensatory education for the child at school district expense (Delaware College Preparatory Academy and the Red Clay Consolidated School District Delaware State Educational Agency, 2009).[1]

Special Considerations Associated With the Use of Behavioral Interventions

For many years, school psychologists have provided consultation to teachers on the use of behavioral techniques (applied behavior analysis) to reduce problematic student behaviors. For the purpose of this discussion, *behavioral intervention* means the planned and systematic use of learning principles, particularly operant techniques and modeling theory, to change the behavior of students. This portion of the chapter provides a brief overview of the ethical-legal issues associated with the use of behavioral interventions in school-based practice. Readers are encouraged to also consult the "Guidelines for Responsible Conduct for Behavior Analysts" adopted by the Behavior Analysis Certification Board (Behavior Analyst Certification Board, 2012) and Bailey and Burch (2011).

Selection of Goals. An ethical concern that arises in the use of behavioral interventions is whether the goals of the intervention are in the best interests of the student. Classroom behavior modification programs introduced in the late 1960s often focused on teaching children to "be still, be quiet, and be docile" (Winett & Winkler, 1972, p. 499), what Conoley and Conoley (1982) later referred to as "dead man behaviors." Such goals may assist the teacher in maintaining a quiet, orderly classroom, but they are not likely to improve learning or foster the healthy personal-social development of children (Winett & Winkler, 1972). The school psychologist is obligated ethically to ensure that behaviors selected to replace undesired behaviors "enhance the long-term well-being of the child" (A. Harris & Kapche, 1978, p. 27; also Bailey & Burch, 2011) and are consistent with the long-range goal of self-management. Goals must be selected to ensure that the student will develop appropriate adaptive behaviors and not just suppress inappropriate ones (Van Houten et al., 1988).

---

[1]Court cases are italicized; Office for Civil Rights and state due process hearing officer decisions are not italicized.

Selection of Interventions.   Considerable research support exists for the practice of selecting behavioral interventions based on a systematic evaluation of the function a problem behavior serves for the child (Bailey & Burch, 2011; Steege & Scheib, 2014). Two assessment methodologies have been developed to assist in identifying the functions served by a behavior. *Functional assessment* is based on naturalistic observations and involves direct observation and the use of informants (e.g., teacher interviews and rating scales) to gather information. *Functional analysis* involves controlled observation; that is, the factors that are believed to maintain the behavior are experimentally manipulated (Martens, Witt, Daly, & Vollmer, 1999). Both assessment strategies allow evaluation of the child and the environmental factors associated with the problem behavior, including examination of the setting events, antecedents, and consequences of behavior (also see Steege & Scheib, 2014).

School psychologists are obligated ethically to select (or assist in the selection of) change procedures that have demonstrated effectiveness (NASP-PPE II.3.9). Consistent with the least restrictive alternative doctrine that evolved from court decisions (e.g., *Wyatt v. Stickney*, 1971) and the broad ethical principle of nonmaleficence, practitioners are obligated to select the least drastic procedures and those that minimize the risk of adverse side effects and that are also likely to be effective. The literature reflects some consensus about the acceptability of various behavior-change procedures. First-choice strategies are *positive behavioral interventions* typically based on differential reinforcement (reinforcing appropriate behaviors incompatible with problem behaviors). Second-choice strategies are based on extinction (withdrawing of reinforcement for undesired behavior). Third-choice strategies include removal of desirable stimuli (e.g., time-out procedures). The least acceptable strategies are those that involve presentation of aversive stimuli (Alberto & Troutman, 2013).

Under IDEIA, if a child's behavior impedes his or her learning or that of others, the individualized education plan (IEP) team is required to consider "the use of positive behavioral interventions and support, and other strategies to address that behavior" in developing the IEP (34 CFR § 300.324[a][2][i]). It is important for school psychologists to ensure that a functional behavioral assessment is conducted and to assist in the development of a behavior intervention plan when such strategies are essential to the provision of quality early intervening services or to the development of a student's IEP or Section 504 plan (e.g., *Denita Harris v. District of Columbia*, 2008). In addition, functional behavioral assessment and intervention services are required following a disciplinary infraction that was determined to be a manifestation of the student's disability (34 CFR § 300.530[d][ii]).

In the 1970s, a number of behavioral control or change procedures came under the scrutiny of the courts. These early cases concerned youth in juvenile correction facilities (e.g., *Morales v. Turman*, 1974; *Pena v. New York State Division for Youth*, 1976) or residential mental health facilities (e.g., *New York State Association for Retarded Children v. Carey*, 1975) and provided some insight into the minimal standards that must be adhered to in the use of behavioral methods so as not to violate the constitutional rights of the children involved. More specifically, these rulings suggested that behavioral control methods must not deprive students of their basic rights to food, water, shelter (including adequate heat and ventilation), sleep, and exercise periods (also see APA-EP 1.03).

In the 1980s, the courts addressed the use of behavioral methods in the public schools. As noted previously, the systematic use of differential reinforcement is considered to be a first-choice strategy. Access to privileges (e.g., use of a computer to play games), special luxuries (e.g., colorful stickers), and social reinforcers (e.g., smiles and praise) are types of reinforcers that typically present no special concerns. However, court rulings have been interpreted to suggest that not all types of reinforcers are acceptable. Some teachers use token economies to manage behavior. In token economies, tokens or points may be earned for appropriate behavior, and the tokens subsequently are exchanged for rewards. The use of token economies should not result in denial of basic rights (e.g., access to food at lunchtime), and students should not be denied educational opportunities that are part of the child's expected program, such as gym or art (Hindman, 1986).

Time-out is a behavioral intervention based on removal of desirable stimuli. K. R. Harris (1985) identified three different types of time-out: (1) nonexclusion, which involves removing the child from the reinforcing situation but still allowing the child to observe the ongoing activity; (2) exclusion, which involves removing the child from the reinforcing situation but not from the room; and (3) isolation, which involves the removal of the child from the reinforcing situation and placing him or her in a different area or room. It is important to note the difference between the terms *isolation time-out* and *seclusion*. The U.S. DOE defines the term *seclusion* as:

> The involuntary confinement of a student alone in a room or area *from which the student is physically prevented from leaving*. It does not include a timeout, which is a behavior management technique that is part of an approved program, involves the monitored separation of the student in a *non-locked setting*, and is implemented for the purpose of calming the student. (U.S. DOE, 2012, p. 10, emphasis added)

Discussion here focuses primarily on the use of exclusion and isolation time-out procedures. Seclusion and restraint are discussed in the chapter section titled "Behavior Intervention in Crisis Situations: Use of Physical Restraint and Seclusion."

Legal challenges to the use of time-out in the public schools found it to be an acceptable procedure to safeguard other students from disruptive behavior (*Dickens by Dickens v. Johnson County Board of Education*, 1987; *Hayes v. Unified School District No. 377*, 1987; see also *Honig v. Doe*, 1988).[2] In *Dickens,* the court noted that "judicious use of behavioral modification techniques such as 'time-out' should be favored over expulsion in disciplining disruptive students, particularly the handicapped" (p. 158). However, the use of time-out must meet reasonable standards safeguarding the rights and welfare of students. In finding the use of time-out permissible, the judge in *Dickens* also noted, "This is not to say that educators may arbitrarily cage students in a corner of the classroom for an indeterminate length of time" (p. 158). The court considerations in *Dickens*, *Hayes*, and earlier cases suggest some general parameters for the use of time-out: School personnel must monitor a secluded student to ensure his or her well-being; the room must have adequate ventilation (*Morales*, 1974); the time-out

---

[2] In *Dickens,* time-out procedures involved having the child sit at a desk placed inside a three-sided refrigerator carton in the corner of the classroom, where the child could not see classmates but could hear the teacher and sometimes see the teacher and chalkboard. *Hayes* involved removing the child to a different room.

room itself must not present a fire or safety hazard (*Hayes*, 1987); students must be permitted to leave time-out for appropriate reasons (*Dickens*, 1987); and the door to the time-out room must remain unlocked (*New York State Association for Retarded Children*, 1975).

Students should be given prior notice about the types of behaviors that will result in being placed in time-out (*Hayes*, 1987), and school personnel must ensure that time-out, when used as punishment, is "not unduly harsh or grossly disproportionate" to the offense (*Dickens*, 1987, p. 158). Placement in time-out should not result in "a total exclusion from the educational process for more than a trivial period" (*Goss v. Lopez*, 1975, p. 575). Use of time-out combined with instruction in the time-out room, or requiring the child to do schoolwork while segregated, is recommended (*Dickens*, 1987). (See Turner & Watson, 1999, for a review of research-based best practices in the use of time-out.)

A highly controversial area in behavioral intervention is the use of *aversive conditioning*, in which a discomforting stimulus is presented contingent on the student's undesirable behavior. Some psychologists and educators believe that aversive conditioning must never be used; others believe its use may be justified in the treatment of extremely self-injurious or dangerously aggressive behaviors. It is beyond the scope of this book to explore the controversy fully; interested readers are referred to Jacob-Timm (1996), National Institutes of Health (1991), and Repp and Singh (1990).

Evaluation of Intervention Integrity and Effectiveness.   Consistent with codes of ethics, school psychologists ensure that intervention integrity is monitored and modify or terminate the intervention plan when data indicate it is not achieving the desired goals (NASP-PPE II.2.2, II.2.3; Bailey & Burch, 2011). The monitoring of intervention integrity and effectiveness is particularly important when students evidence challenging behaviors. Change agents, including teachers and parents, may resort to more punitive behavior control practices if they are frustrated by a lack of success using positive behavioral interventions or the intervention plan is too difficult to implement.

Behavior Intervention in Crisis Situations: Use of Physical Restraint and Seclusion. School personnel, particularly those who work with students with behavior disorders, must be trained and prepared to respond immediately and appropriately when a crisis occurs involving potential student self-injury or dangerously aggressive behaviors. Restraint and seclusion historically have been used in psychiatric hospitals, where their use is highly regulated under federal law protecting the safety of patients (Yankouski & Massarelli, 2014). In recent years, public attention has been drawn to the use of restraint and seclusion in public schools, with allegations of abuse. In 2009, the U.S. Government Accountability Office (GAO) conducted an investigation and found no federal laws restricting the use of seclusion and restraints in public and private schools, and inconsistent laws at the state level. Further, no entity collects data about the use of seclusion and restraints in schools. The GAO reviewed 10 closed cases from the prior two decades where the use of seclusion or restraints resulted in a criminal conviction, finding of civil or administrative liability, or a large financial settlement. Themes from the case review indicated that: (a) the majority of the incidents were against students with disabilities; (b) children who died from the use of restraints were held in facedown restraints or restraints that blocked the child's airway; (c) and staff members were not trained in the use of physical restraints (Kutz, 2009). Several bills (e.g., Keeping All Kids Safe Act) have been introduced in the U.S. House of Representatives and Senate regarding the use of restraints and seclusion in schools, but, as of fall 2015, no bill had passed in both the House and Senate. However, the ESSA requires states to identify how they will support local school districts in efforts to reduce "the use of aversive behavioral interventions that compromise student health and safety" (Sec. 1111 [g][1][C][iii]).

A review of cases conducted by the U.S. Senate Health, Education, Labor, and Pensions (HELP) committee (2014) found that families of children who have been injured or traumatized, or even those whose children have died, as a result of restraint and seclusion practices, have very little legal recourse. This review indicated that families are not informed that these procedures are being used with their children, and when families do seek information about their usage, they are unable to determine the frequency, intensity, or duration of use. Moreover, in many cases, families were required to exhaust all of their due process options under IDEIA before a case could be brought to court, even in situations of obvious abuse. Families were also under the burden to prove psychological harm and had to overcome the assumptions that schools are safe and that school personnel acted appropriately.

The HELP committee (2014) put forth a number of recommendations to increase preventive strategies and reduce the risk of death or injury due to inappropriate practices, including the use of school- and districtwide positive behavior supports and training all school personnel on techniques that do not require the use of restraints or seclusion when confronted with challenging behavior. Additionally, they recommended that restraints and seclusion be used only as a last resort when there is serious imminent threat of harm to a student or others and that schools inform parents when they are used. If seclusion or restraint is used, the child must be continuously and visually observed and monitored (U.S. DOE, 2012). School psychologists can assist school personnel in implementing positive behavioral supports to reduce the occurrence of challenging behavior and also can assist in the use of least restrictive behavioral interventions in times of crisis (Yankouski & Massarelli, 2014). Ethically, "any behavior intervention must be consistent with the child's right to be treated with dignity and to be free from abuse" (U.S. DOE, 2012, p. iii; also NASP-PPE Principle I.1).

THERAPEUTIC INTERVENTIONS WITHIN THE CONTEXT OF A SCHOOL PSYCHOLOGIST–CLIENT RELATIONSHIP

We first address ethical and legal issues associated with providing counseling in the schools and then explore challenging special situations, such as suspected child abuse and working with students who are potentially dangerous to others or a threat to themselves. The chapter concludes with a brief discussion of psychopharmacologic interventions.

Counseling: Ethical and Legal Issues

Tharinger and Stafford (1995) described counseling in the schools as a process of ongoing, planned interactions between a student and a mental health professional. The school psychologist works to alleviate the student's distress by improving the child's psychological functioning and/or facilitating change in his or her environment, in particular the school and family systems. More specifically, the goals of counseling may include:

> alleviating the child's emotional and cognitive distress, changing the child's behavior, assisting with self-understanding, helping the child meet current developmental tasks successfully, supporting needed environmental changes, and promoting a more positive fit between the child and the systems in which she or he resides (e.g., school and family). (p. 896)

School psychologists have a number of ethical and legal obligations to students and their parents prior to providing ongoing counseling services. The NASP's code of ethics states:

> Except for urgent situations or self-referrals by a minor student, school psychologists seek parent consent (or the consent of an adult student) prior to establishing a school-psychologist client relationship... to provide ongoing individual or group counseling or other non-classroom therapeutic intervention. (NASP-PPE I.1.2)

In the school setting, informed consent to establish a school psychologist–client relationship usually rests with the parents of a minor. However, the practitioner is ethically obligated to respect the dignity, autonomy, and self-determination of the student. The decision to allow a student the opportunity to choose or refuse psychological intervention may involve consideration of a number of factors, including law, ethical issues (self-determination versus welfare of the student), the child's competence to make choices, and the likely consequences of affording choices (e.g., enhanced functioning versus choice to refuse treatment). We concur with Weithorn's (1983) suggestion that practitioners permit and encourage student involvement in decision making to the maximum extent appropriate to the child and the situation. Practitioners have an ethical obligation to inform students of the scope and nature of the proposed intervention, whether or not they are given a choice about participating (see NASP-PPE I.1.4).

Self-Referrals for Counseling

Young children are unlikely to seek help or initiate a counseling relationship on their own. However, at the high school level, referrals for counseling may be self-referrals. Students may wish to see a school psychologist on the condition that their parents are not notified. This raises the question of whether students who are minors can ever be seen by the school psychologist for counseling without parental permission. We are not aware of any case law decisions that specifically address this question. The NASP's code of ethics states:

> When a student who is a minor self-refers for assistance, it is ethically permissible to provide psychological assistance without parent notice or consent for one or several meetings to establish the nature and degree of the need for services and assure the child is safe and not in danger. It is ethically permissible to provide services to mature minors without parent consent where allowed by state law and school district policy. However, if the student is *not* old enough to receive school psychological assistance independent of parent consent, the school psychologist obtains parent consent to provide continuing assistance to the student beyond the preliminary meetings or refers the student to alternative sources of assistance that do not require parent notice or consent. (NASP-PPE I.1.2)

The preliminary meetings can serve to ensure that the child is not in danger (C. Osip, quoted in Canter, 1989). During these meetings, the school psychologist also can discuss the need for parental consent for further counseling sessions, offer to contact the parent on behalf of the student, or offer to meet jointly with the student and parents to discuss consent and ensure ongoing parent support. Unless there is a conflict with state law, we believe school districts should adopt written policies stating that students may be seen by the school psychologist or other mental health professional for one or several meetings without parent notice or consent to ensure that the student is not in danger (e.g., child abuse, suicidal) or if it is suspected the student may be a danger to others (see footnote at NASP-PPE I.1.2).

Some states allow minors to consent to outpatient mental health services independent of parent notice or consent, with the minor's treatment records considered to be under his or her own control. Because of the Family Educational Rights and Privacy Act of 1974, it may be problematic for school-based practitioners to keep records about individual students that are not accessible by the parent (see Chapter 3). For this reason, school-based practitioners at times may choose to refer students who desire assistance without parent involvement to community-based providers. Such referrals are ethically permissible (NASP-PPE I.1.2).

Planning Counseling and Other Therapeutic Interventions.   School psychologists are obligated to use counseling or other therapeutic intervention techniques that the profession considers to be "responsible, research-based practice" (NASP-PPE II.3.9; also APA-EP 2.04). Practitioners "encourage and promote parental participation in designing interventions for their children" (NASP-PPE II.3.10) and, to "the maximum extent appropriate, students are invited to participate in selecting and planning interventions" (II.3.11). The proposed options should consider all resources (school and community) available to assist the student and family, the support and assistance that can be made available to the teacher, and the values and skills of the parents (NASP-PPE II.3.10). School practitioners "respect the wishes of parents who object to school psychological services and attempt to guide parents to alternative resources" (NASP-PPE I.1.5).

Interventions with Culturally Diverse Clientele.   School psychologists have five special obligations when working with students and families whose background characteristics are different from their own (NASP-PPE I.3.2).

1. Psychologists need to be aware of how their own cultural heritage, gender, class, ethnic-racial identity, sexual orientation, and age cohort shape personal values and beliefs, including assumptions and biases related to those who are different (N. D. Hansen, Pepitone-Arreola-Rockwell, & Greene, 2000; Rogers et al., 1999).

2. Practitioners need to learn about the student's background, values, beliefs, and worldview and how those cultural and experiential factors may influence development and behavior.

3. To provide sensitive and effective services, practitioners must be able to demonstrate an understanding and respect for cultural and experiential differences in interacting with the student.

4. Practitioners are obligated to seek knowledge of best practices in selecting, designing, and implementing intervention plans for diverse clientele with learning or behavior problems (N. D. Hansen et al., 2000; Lynch & Hanson, 2011; Rogers et al., 1999).

5. When working with diverse students, practitioners should assist the students and their parents to better understand the culture of the school and community so that they can make informed choices relevant to schooling and mental health services (Hays, 2001; Rogers et al., 1999).

Practitioners also are obligated to self-assess their multicultural competence (N. D. Hansen et al., 2000; Nagy, 2012). More specifically, they need to consider when circumstances (personal biases; lack of requisite knowledge, skills, or language fluency) may negatively influence the effectiveness of professional services and adapt accordingly, that is, by obtaining needed information, consultation, or supervision, or referring the student to a better qualified professional (NASP-PPE II.1.2; N. D. Hansen et al., 2000).

DUTY TO PROTECT

As noted in Chapter 2, school-based practitioners have a legal as well as an ethical obligation to take reasonable steps to protect all students from reasonably foreseeable harm.

Child Abuse

The Child Abuse Prevention and Treatment Act (CAPTA), as amended by the CAPTA Reauthorization Act of 2010, defined *child abuse and neglect* as:

> Any act or failure to act on the part of a parent or caretaker which results in death, serious physical or emotional harm, sexual abuse or exploitation; or an act or failure to act, which presents an imminent risk of serious harm. (U.S. Department of Health and Human Services, 2015a, p. viii)

Variations exist with regard to the exact language states use to define *child abuse and neglect*. All 50 states have enacted legislation requiring school professionals to report suspected cases of child abuse to child welfare or protection agencies.

In 2013 (federal fiscal year), there were about 3.5 million reports to child protective service agencies of possible abuse and neglect, with an estimated 679,000 substantiated cases of child maltreatment that year (U.S. Department of Health and Human Services, 2015a). Researchers estimate that reported cases of child abuse constitute only about 40% of all cases (Kalichman, 1999). School psychologists are legally required to report all cases of suspected child abuse. As mandated reporters, their role is to ensure a report is made to child protective services each time an incident of child abuse is suspected. In *Pesce v. J. Sterling Morton High School* (1987), the court held that the duty to protect schoolchildren by reporting suspected child abuse outweighs any right to confidentiality of the school psychologist–client relationship.

In their survey of NASP school psychology practitioners, Dailor and Jacob (2011) found that, of eight types of ethical dilemmas experienced in the previous year, the dilemma reported by the largest percentage of respondents was whether there was a reasonable suspicion of child abuse that would warrant contacting child protective services. Kalichman (1999) reviewed studies of reporting decisions and found that physical signs of abuse were most influential in the decision to report, followed by child verbal reports of physical or sexual abuse. Parent or other adult reports that a child was abused also were likely to trigger a report.

In many situations, however, the determination of whether a reasonable suspicion of child abuse exists is complicated. In general, teachers and other school staff who work closely with children should be encouraged to respond to ambiguous child disclosures with open-ended questions and in a warm, calm, nonjudgmental manner. For example, a child's statement that "Mommy hurt me" might be followed by "Oh, I'm sorry to hear that. What happened?" (See Horton & Cruise, 2001, pp. 39–52.) Schools are well advised to ensure that each building has a physical or mental health professional with expertise in child abuse and a positive working relationship with child protective services. This individual can seek guidance from child protective services when difficult questions arise and also assist in making reports when abuse is suspected.

It is critically important for school staff to recognize that it is the responsibility of the child protection agency, not school personnel, to confirm or disconfirm the existence of suspected abuse or neglect. The courts have held that it is not necessary for school personnel to be certain that the abuse took place, only that there is reason to suspect abuse (e.g., *State v. Grover*, 1989). In a news story described as a "wake-up" call for educators, a school principal asked the school psychologist and several teachers to interview a 9-year-old to confirm a parent's report of suspected abuse prior to contacting child protective services. Six educators, including the school psychologist, were subsequently investigated by the school district for failing to promptly report suspected child abuse. Although the school psychologist and teachers were cleared of any wrongdoing, the principal was dismissed (Saunders, 2007).

School attorneys advise school psychologists to report suspected abuse promptly and to document that the call was made rather than to attempt to confirm abuse suspicions on their own (Saunders, 2007). Experts in law and developmental psychology have crafted research-based protocols for interviewing children if abuse is suspected. These interview protocols are based on a *forensic* (rather than a clinical) perspective.

To meet forensic standards, interviews with suspected victims of abuse should be conducted by individuals specifically trained to gather, evaluate, and interpret evidence of child abuse using accepted interview techniques (e.g., Poole, in press).

All states provide immunity from civil or criminal action for filing a child abuse report to the appropriate authorities. This means that a school psychologist who files a report of suspected abuse cannot be sued for damages that might arise from making such a report (e.g., defamation), as long as the report is made in good faith and the procedures for filing a report under state law are followed (Small, Lyons, & Guy, 2002). Penalties for not reporting may include civil or criminal liability and loss of certification or license. Fines for failure to report range from $25 to $5,000; possible jail sentences range from 10 days to one year (Small et al., 2002).

One concern about making a report about suspected child abuse by a family member is the potential loss of rapport with the student and his or her family as a result of making a report. However, based on a review of the available studies, Kalichman (1999) concluded that "little evidence exists to support the popular perceptions that reporting abuse has detrimental effects on the quality and efficacy of professional services. In fact, studies specifically addressing these issues in clinical settings find that reporting sometimes benefits the treatment process" (p. 61).

Threat to Self

Suicide is the third leading cause of death among adolescents. It is estimated that 4,600 youth between the ages of 10 and 24 take their own lives each year (Centers for Disease Control and Prevention [CDC], 2015a). The *Kelson v. The City of Springfield* (1985) and *Eisel v. Board of Education of Montgomery County* court decisions (Cases 7.1. and 7.2), among others (e.g., *Wyke v. Polk County School Board*, 1997), have been interpreted to suggest that schools should develop clear suicide prevention policies and procedures that include notifying parents and should ensure adequate staff orientation to district policy and procedures.

In *Kelson* (1985; Case 7.1), Brian's parents filed a negligence suit against the school and city in state court and a Section 1983 lawsuit against the school and city in federal

---

Case 7.1

Brian, a 14-year-old, confronted his teacher during class with a .38-caliber revolver. The teacher persuaded Brian to talk with the vice principal alone in an empty classroom. Brian showed the vice principal a suicide note he had written and asked to speak with his favorite teacher; he was not allowed to do so. When Brian and the vice principal left the classroom, Brian was met by a police officer who told him he was "in trouble with the law." Brian (still armed with the gun) entered the boy's restroom, where he shot himself. He died later that morning.

Source: Adapted from *Kelson v. The City of Springfield*, 1985.

Case 7.2

"Nina," a 13-year-old middle school student, became involved in Satanism and developed an obsessive interest in death. She told several friends that she intended to kill herself. Nina's friends reported her suicidal intentions to their school counselor (at a different school), who conveyed the information to Nina's school counselor. Both counselors met with Nina and questioned her about her statements concerning suicide, but she denied making them. Neither counselor informed Nina's parents about her suicidal statements. One week after telling her friends about her suicidal intentions, Nina and another 13-year-old girl consummated a murder-suicide pact in a public park some distance from the middle school she attended.

Source: Adapted from *Eisel v. Board of Education of Montgomery County*, 1991.

court, alleging that the state interfered with their constitutionally protected liberty interest in the companionship of their son. When the Section 1983 lawsuit reached the U.S. Court of Appeals, the judge advised Brian's parents to file an amended claim against the school district after ruling on several legal questions raised by the case. In so doing, the judge raised the question of a possible relationship between school policy (namely, inadequate suicide training for its staff) and Brian's death.

In *Eisel* (1991; Case 7.2), Nina's father filed a negligence suit against the two school counselors based on their failure to communicate information to him concerning Nina's contemplated suicide. Nina's father believed he could have prevented his daughter's death had he been told about her statements. The court held that a school has a duty to protect a student from foreseeable harm and that "school counselors have a duty to use reasonable means to attempt to prevent a suicide when they are on notice of a child or adolescent's suicidal intent" (p. 456). The school counselors were viewed as having little discretion regarding whether to contact parents once information suggested a potential suicide.[3]

When it is suspected that a student is suicidal, the situation should be reported to a designated professional who has training in assessment of suicide risk and suicide prevention. The school psychologist might serve as one of the designated staff members. The student should be assessed for the lethality of suicidal ideation because the degree of lethality determines the appropriate course of action. A suicide risk assessment interview involves seeking a variety of different types of information, including how the student currently feels; past and present feelings of sadness and hopelessness; past and current suicidal ideation; perceptions of being a burden to others and not belonging; current stressors at home and school; history of drug use; previous suicide attempts; presence or absence of a suicide plan and ability (physical, cognitive) to carry

---

[3]This decision did not determine the school's liability; the decision only allowed action in another court to rule on the school's liability. The school counselors ultimately were not held liable for the $1 million in damages the father sought.

it out; access to lethal means; current support systems; and reasons to live (Boccio, 2015; D. N. Miller, 2011, p. 89). Readers are referred to Boccio (2015) for information about conducting suicide risk assessments.

Although research has shown that psychologists cannot predict suicide attempts with a high degree of accuracy, they are expected to apply "skill and care in assessing suicidal potential and ... a reasonable degree of care and skill in preventing the suicide" (Knapp, 1980, p. 609). Some psychologists recommend asking suicidal clients to sign a "no-suicide contract." Although do-no-harm contracts may be clinically useful, it is important to recognize that such contracts do not substitute for a careful risk assessment and appropriate intervention based on the assessed risk (Simon, 1999).

Parents must be contacted in all cases, whether the risk is determined to be low or high. As Poland (1989) noted, the question is not whether to tell the parents but how to elicit a supportive reaction from them. Parents of medium- or high-risk students should be contacted as soon as possible. The high-risk student should not be left alone, and his or her parents should be required to come to school for a conference and to pick up their child (Poland, 1989). Poland recommended that two staff members conduct the parent notification conference and noted that some districts have parents sign a form acknowledging that they have been notified that their child is suicidal. The psychologist needs to ensure that parents understand the seriousness of the situation, and parents should be advised to increase supervision at home and remove access to weapons and other means of self-harm, such as medications. The practitioner should be prepared to refer the family to a community mental health professional who has expertise in working with suicidal youth. Poland also provided a number of recommendations for eliciting a supportive response from the parents.

School psychologists are well advised to develop consultative relationships with clinicians who have expertise in suicide assessment and management whom they can contact for assistance in evaluating and managing a potential suicide situation (Jobes & Berman, 1993). Practitioners also are advised to document their actions regarding risk assessment and management of students who may be suicidal. School-based practitioners should become familiar with community resources for referral, including the procedures for hospitalization of suicidal minors and adult students. Furthermore, school psychologists also need to consider the long-range needs of the suicidal student with regard to follow-up educational and mental health services. Unfortunately, as D. N. Miller and Eckert (2009) noted, many youths do not receive any form of treatment following a suicide attempt. Additionally, many questions remain regarding the most effective treatment for suicidal youth.

The courts generally have not held schools liable for failure to prevent a student suicide. One notable exception is when school actions are so reckless as to "shock the conscience" by placing the student at substantial increased risk of immediate self-harm. In *Armijo v. Wagon Mound Public Schools* (1998), a 13-year-old boy shot and killed himself after he was driven home by the school counselor and left alone even though both the school principal and the counselor knew that the boy was upset about a disciplinary infraction, had a history of suicide attempts, and had access to firearms at his house.

In a national survey of school psychology practitioners, Debski, Spadafore, Jacob, Poole, and Hixson (2007) found that most respondents had participated in a suicide-risk assessment in the previous two years. It has become increasingly important for school practitioners to obtain professional competence in assessment and management of suicidal students. Additionally, psychologists who acquire special expertise in suicide prevention can play an important role in the development of their school district's planned response to suicidal students. Recent publications have addressed best practices in school-based suicide prevention programs (e.g., D. N. Miller, 2011).

Threat to Others

School violence that results in the death of a student is rare (CDC, 2015b). Nevertheless, violence in our schools is a concern of educators and parents. In 2012, approximately 750,000 nonfatal violent victimizations occurred at school. Based on a nationally representative sample of students in grades 9 to 12, 8% reported being in a physical fight at school in the year prior to the survey, 7% reported not going to school one or more days because of feeling unsafe in the 30 days prior to the survey, 5% reported carrying a weapon to school on one or more days in the 30 days prior to the survey, 7% reported that they were threatened or injured with a weapon at school during the previous 12 months, and 20% reported being bullied on school property during the previous year, with 15% being bullied electronically (CDC, 2015b). Our focus here is on assessment of whether an individual student poses a danger to others.

The assessment of whether a student poses a danger to others is not an easy task. School personnel may become concerned about a student because of his or her aggressive, antisocial behavior (fighting, explosive temper). For such students, the task is to determine the risk for future violent acts and how to reduce the likelihood of future violence. Borum (2000) provided guidelines regarding how to conduct a systematic assessment of violence potential in such situations. His approach takes into account the student's past violent acts, the precipitants to those acts, and the protective factors—that is, factors that would help the student avoid situations likely to trigger violent actions. A student also may come to the attention of the school psychologist because the student made direct or indirect threats to injure others. The term *targeted violence* is used to refer to situations in which both the potential perpetrator and the target(s) are identifiable prior to a violent attack (Vossekuil, Reddy, Fein, Borum, & Modzeleski, 2000). As Borum noted, a different assessment approach is recommended in situations involving targeted violence.

When students make threats to injure others, such threats should be taken seriously (*D.J.M. v. Hannibal Public School District #60*, 2011; *Mirand v. Board of Education of the City of New York*, 1994; M. Reddy et al., 2001). A report sponsored by the Federal Bureau of Investigation (FBI) recommended a multidisciplinary team approach to threat assessment (FBI Academy, 2000). This team might include mental health professionals, school administrators, and law enforcement professionals. In *Milligan et al. v. City of Slidell* (2000), a federal court ruled that it is permissible for school officials and police to detain and question a student thought to be planning an act of violence at school because the school's interest in deterring school violence outweighs a student's limited Fourth Amendment privacy rights in such situations.

The risk factors for targeted violence do not appear to be the same as the risk factors associated with general aggression and violence recidivism among youth (M. Reddy et al., 2001). M. Reddy et al. outlined a model for evaluating whether a student is on a path to targeted violence. Their model is based on three principles: (1) Targeted violence is a result of an interaction among the student, situation, target, and setting; there is no single type of student prone to such acts; (2) evaluators must make a distinction between a student who makes threats versus one who actually poses a threat; and (3) targeted violence is often the product of an understandable pattern of thinking and behavior. The model involves evaluating the student's behavior and pattern of conduct using information from multiple sources. Information gathering might involve interviewing the student and his or her family, teachers, and friends and reviewing student records. Key questions that guide the threat assessment evaluation include the following: Does the student have ideas about or plans for targeted violence? Has the student shown an interest in violence, acts of violence by others, or weapons? Has the student engaged in any attack-related behavior, including menacing, harassing, or stalking? Is the student cognitively and physically capable of carrying out a plan of violence? Has the student experienced a recent loss or loss of status, and has this led to feelings of desperation and despair? What factors in the student's life and/or environment might increase or decrease the likelihood of the student becoming violent? Cornell (2014) provided guidelines for responding to student threats of violence.

In making a decision regarding whether a student is potentially dangerous, the psychologist is well advised to consult with other professionals. In court decisions, therapists have not been held liable for failure to warn "when the propensity toward violence is unknown or would be unknown by other psychotherapists using ordinary skill" (Knapp & VandeCreek, 1982, p. 515). Similarly, the courts generally have not held a school district liable for student-on-student violence if the actions of the perpetrator were not foreseeable (e.g., *Kok v. Tacoma School District No. 10*, 2013).

Consistent with the guidelines for other situations involving danger, schools need to develop written procedures regarding when and how to notify school officials and legal authorities (police, the student's probation officer) if school staff become aware of a potentially assaultive student. These procedures should ensure that the intended victim is warned. If a student poses a threat to another student, the parents of the threatened child should be notified. Parents of a potentially assaultive student also must be informed of the situation. The potentially violent student should be supervised in the school setting and at home, with steps taken to ensure that there is no access to weapons. School psychology practitioners should know and follow school policies regarding dangerous students and document their actions in the management of a student who may become violent. In addition, they should be prepared to refer the family to a community mental health agency and, again, be knowledgeable of procedures for the involuntary commitment of minors and adult students (Pitcher & Poland, 1992).

Practitioners also must consider the long-range needs of students at risk for violence with regard to follow-up educational and mental health services. They need to ensure that the student receives well-coordinated assistance from the family, school, and community mental health professionals. Furthermore, as is true of many mental health concerns in the school setting, efforts aimed at preventing student violence on a systemwide basis are preferable to the dilemmas of managing the assault-prone student. Readers are referred to Brock and Jimerson's (2012) *Best Practices in School Crisis Prevention and Intervention*.

Substance Abuse

Alcohol is the substance most commonly used by minors. In 2014, 9% of students in grade 8, 24% of students in grade 10, and 37% of students in grade 12 reported having consumed alcohol within the year. In the same year, 27% of students for all grades combined reported using illicit drugs (National Institute on Drug Abuse, 2014). School psychologists—particularly those who work with middle and senior high students—need to be knowledgeable about drugs commonly used by adolescents and the symptoms of alcohol and drug abuse.

Forman, Bry, and Urga (2006) defined *substance abuse* as "the use of alcohol or other drugs in ways that negatively affect life functions" (p. 1011) and went on to note that most youth "who use alcohol and drugs do not use them in ways that are considered abuse." At times, however, the frequency, duration, or type of substance used (e.g., amphetamines, inhalants) may pose a threat to the student's physical or mental health.

Unfortunately, the laws regarding disclosure of a student's substance abuse to his or her parents are complicated. If a minor student discloses risky substance abuse to a school-based psychologist within the context of a professional relationship, the school psychologist may disclose this information to the child's parent and work with the parent in locating treatment. However, with the exception of a medical emergency, federal law provides confidentiality protection to students, *including minors*, who specifically seek drug and alcohol evaluation and treatment (part of the Public Health Service Act codified at 42 U.S.C. § 290dd; 42 CFR Part 2). For this reason, if a student requests drug or alcohol treatment or a referral for treatment and he or she does not want his or her parents to be notified, the request is absolutely confidential, and the school psychologist should identify treatment options for the student that do not require parental notice or consent (Cohn, Gelfman, & Schwab, 2005; also see English, Bass, Boyle, & Eshragh, 2010).

If a school psychologist gains knowledge of substance abuse that involves other students in the school setting, the practitioner may need to discuss the situation with appropriate school authorities (without disclosing the identity of the student-client) to ensure the safety of others. Practitioners must be cautious to avoid involvement in searches of students for illegal drugs, particularly if such activities are not part of their formal job responsibilities (see Chapter 2).

School-based practitioners are encouraged to assume a leadership role in the development of educational programs for the school and for parents regarding student substance abuse prevention. They also can support the development of evidence-based school or community-based programs for students who are struggling with drug or alcohol use (Forman et al., 2006).

Students Who Disclose Criminal Acts

If, within the context of a psychologist–client relationship, a student or other client discloses that he or she committed a crime and was never arrested, does the psychologist have a legal obligation to report the crime to the police or the building principal? In 1790, the U.S. Congress passed *misprision of felony* laws, making it a criminal offense "to conceal and ... not as soon as possible make known" a felony committed by another person (U.S.C., Title 18, § 4). Subsequent court decisions have held that misprision of felony occurs only if an individual takes affirmative steps to conceal a felony committed by another person (e.g., suppressing evidence, providing false statements to authorities, hiding stolen property); *simple failure to report a felony is not a crime* (*U.S. v. Farrar*, 1930). Although state laws vary with regard to misprision of felony statutes, Appelbaum and Meisel (1986) concluded that "American law at the federal and state levels rejects the imposition of criminal liability for mere failure to report a crime and requires overt assistance rendered to a felon for there to be a criminal offense" (p. 227). Thus, school psychologists generally do not have a legal duty to report a crime committed by student-clients or their parents, unless it involves suspected child abuse or other state-mandated reporting.

If there is no legal duty to report a crime committed by a client, is it permissible for the school psychologist to do so without client consent? As noted in Chapter 3 under "Nondisclosure Laws and Privileged Communication," if a psychologist discloses privileged client information to others without first obtaining client consent (consent of an adult student or the parents of a minor child), the practitioner has violated the trust of the psychologist–client relationship and may put him- or herself at risk for a malpractice suit. In *McDuff v. Tamborlane* (1999; Case 3.4), the mother of a student-client told the school psychologist that her child had committed larceny. The mother subsequently filed a malpractice suit against the school psychologist after the school psychologist disclosed information about the student's past crime to school authorities without parent consent to do so and the student was arrested. The mother assumed that the information she provided to the school psychologist was confidential, and the judge supported her contention, noting that a parent would naturally assume that communications to a school psychologist were confidential. The judge also noted that there was no imminent danger to the student or others that justified the breach of confidentiality.

The federal courts have recognized that individuals who receive mental health services generally expect their disclosures to a psychologist to be held in strict confidence unless they are told otherwise (see Beam & Whinery, 2001). As discussed in Chapter 3, school practitioners are ethically obligated to inform student-clients and their parents that they have a duty to share confidential information with others if the disclosure is necessary to ensure the safety of the student-client or others or if there is a mandatory duty to report (child abuse, elder abuse) under state law. In light of laws governing privilege, it also may be appropriate for a practitioner to forewarn student-clients and their parents that, if it is disclosed that the student committed a serious criminal act, the psychologist cannot promise to keep the disclosure confidential (see *People v. Vincent Moreno*, 2005; Case 3.5).

As happened in *People v. Vincent Moreno* (2005), student-clients may confess to criminal acts even if they are forewarned about the limits of confidentiality. If a school-based psychologist believes the past crimes of a minor student should be reported to legal authorities, the issue should first be discussed with the student and parents, if feasible. The student's parents *should be encouraged to report the crime but to obtain legal representation for their child before they contact legal authorities* (Applebaum & Meisel, 1986). If the parents cannot be persuaded to report the crime themselves and the psychologist believes the situation is so serious that it must be reported, the practitioner should consult the school's attorney regarding how to proceed.

Pregnancy, Birth Control, and Sexually Transmitted Disease

In the following paragraphs, we provide a brief overview of the legal issues associated with student pregnancy, birth control counseling, and sexually transmitted disease (STD).

Pregnancy

In 2010, there were an estimated 625,000 pregnancies in the 15- to 19-year-old age group, and 11,000 pregnancies for girls age 14 and younger (Kost & Henshaw, 2014). A student may tell a school psychologist that she is pregnant. Except for situations in which disclosure to the parent might mean more harm than nondisclosure, the student should be encouraged to disclose her pregnancy to a parent. If involvement of a parent or other adult family member is not an acceptable option, it is permissible under current *federal* law (Case 7.3) for school personnel to refer the student to a family planning clinic without notifying a parent. The practitioner should, ideally, refer the student to a family planning clinic or an area physician known to provide pregnant teens sensitive and supportive care. Family planning clinic staff are knowledgeable of state laws regarding the right of minors to consent to various reproductive health care services and trained to identify and manage circumstances requiring parent involvement.

In *Arnold v. Board of Education of Escambia* (1990; Case 7.3), the court opined that federal law does not require school personnel to notify the parents of a student who

---

Case 7.3

In *Arnold v. Board of Education of Escambia* (1990), a 15-year-old female student ("Jane Doe") was referred to a school counselor because a physical education coach suspected Jane might be pregnant. After the pregnancy was confirmed, the counselor encouraged Jane to inform her mother, or her aunt, with whom she lived. The student refused to do so because she had already been thrown out of her mother's home, where there also was a history of physical abuse, and she feared her aunt would ask her to leave if she was pregnant. The counselor and a social worker explored options with the student, including adoption. The student made her own decision to choose an abortion. A grandparent of the unborn child later filed suit against the school, claiming that the school counselor and social workers coerced Jane to have an abortion and refrained from notifying parents about the pregnancy and that their actions interfered with parental guidance. The court decided for the school, noting that Jane was of age to consent to an abortion under state law and that there was no requirement for a school to notify the parents of the pregnancy of a minor student under federal or state law.

is pregnant. However, practitioners must be familiar with state law and school district policy regarding parental notification when an unemancipated minor is pregnant. In some circumstances, it may be necessary for school personnel to inform parents about their daughter's pregnancy to safeguard the student's health and well-being.

If a school psychologist continues to work with a pregnant student after she has been seen by a health care provider, all alternatives to pregnancy management should be discussed and explored (*Arnold*, 1990; Case 7.3). The Guttmacher Institute provides state-by-state information regarding a minors' right to consent to confidential prenatal care, the right of minors to place their children for adoption, and state laws regarding access to abortion for minors (see http://www.guttmacher.org).

Birth Control Information

The issue of school involvement in the provision of family planning information is highly controversial and involves deep-rooted family and community values. School policies run the gamut, from those that forbid discussion of birth control with individual students to programs that allow easy student access to family planning information and contraceptives (e.g., health clinics on or adjacent to school grounds).

Although minors should be encouraged to discuss sexual activity and sexual health issues with a parent, many adolescents are not willing to do so. D. M. Reddy, Fleming, and Swain (2002) found that about one-half of girls under age 18 would forgo visiting a sexual health care clinic if accessing their services involved mandatory parental notification; however, of those girls, 99% would continue having sexual intercourse. Twenty-six states and the District of Columbia allow minors to consent to contraceptive services without parent notice or consent; in four states, the decision to provide contraception to a minor rests with the physician. Other states allow only certain groups of minors to consent to contraceptive services (e.g., already pregnant or a parent) (see Guttmacher Institute, 2015, for a state-by-state summary of policies). Unless school policy dictates otherwise, it is likely legally permissible for a school psychologist to refer a minor to a family planning clinic for contraceptive advice in those states that allow minors access to contraceptives without parent notification. Practitioners are encouraged to consult their school nurse or local family planning clinic for advice.

Sexually Transmitted Disease

In the United States, an estimated 20 million new cases of STD occur each year, and almost half of them are among teenagers and young adults 15 to 24 years of age (CDC, 2014). The spread of chlamydia, gonorrhea, syphilis, human papillomavirus, and human immunodeficiency (HIV) among adolescents is a cause of national concern. If a school psychologist believes that a student-client may have or is at risk of contracting an STD, the student should be encouraged to talk with a parent. However, practitioners also should recognize that some teens will not do so and may avoid screening and treatment if they believe their parents will be notified. All states allow minors to consent to confidential testing and treatment of STDs. Eighteen states allow a physician to inform a minor's parents that their child is seeking or receiving STD services if the physician believes it is in the best interests of the minor

(Guttmacher Institute, 2015). It is likely legally permissible to refer a student for STD screening and treatment without notifying the parent unless school policy bars such referrals. Practitioners, again, may wish to consult a school nurse or a public health clinic regarding the best course of action.

What if a student-client has tested positive for HIV and engages in unprotected sex with partners who are uninformed of his or her HIV status? First-step strategies for the school psychologist include encouraging the student to discontinue sexual activity unless sexual partners are informed about his or her HIV status and to practice safe sex. The student should be reminded that, under most state laws, knowingly transmitting an STD could result in legal action against him or her.

Little consistency exists in the laws of various states regarding a psychologist's duty to protect a client's sexual partner from exposure to HIV, and ethical opinions on the matter are contradictory (see Huprich, Fuller, & Schneider, 2003). If the student-client fails to take responsibility to protect others from exposure to possible infection, the psychologist may have a duty to protect the student-client's sexual partners from risk of HIV. As noted in Chapter 3, a minor has no *legal* right to confidentiality independent of the parent. If the student-client with HIV is a minor, talking with his or her parents about the situation may be appropriate. If the parents are uncooperative or not likely to be of assistance or if the student is an adult, practitioners are advised to seek guidance regarding how to handle the situation from their state public health agency. Penalties likely exist under state law if school personnel disclose to third parties that a student-client is infected with an STD. However, these same state laws typically allow school personnel to contact public health agencies for assistance without penalty (also NASP-PPE I.2.7). Public health clinics have the authority to notify partners of individuals diagnosed with an STD of their exposure to an STD.

It is important to remember that young adolescents often think they are invincible and may deny any risk for an STD. School psychologists can play an important role in encouraging the development of programs to prevent teen pregnancies and reduce the incidence of STDs among teenagers.

Summary

Within the protection of a confidential relationship, students may report any number of behaviors that, although not immediately dangerous, have that potential. Such actions as failure to take prescribed medications, eating disorders, criminal activity, engaging in unprotected sex, and sexual promiscuity might fall into this category. Anticipating all possible circumstances in counseling that may prove to be a problem is not possible. The five keys to dealing with most cases successfully are:

1. a candid discussion of confidentiality and its limits at the outset of offering services;
2. a good working relationship with the student;
3. knowledge of state laws and regulations as well as school policies;
4. familiarity with resources in the community and how to access them; and
5. dealing openly and honestly with the student about your concerns and possible course of action.

COMPETENCE AND RESPONSIBILITY

Consistent with the principle of responsible caring, school psychologists are obligated to "recognize the strengths and limitations of their training and experience, engaging only in practices for which they are qualified" (NASP-PPE II.1.1; also APA-EP 2.01).

Competence

A problem for psychologists is to determine what constitutes an acceptable and recognized level of competency to provide specific services. Seeking assistance through supervision, consultation, and referral is an appropriate strategy for handling a difficult case (NASP-PPE II.1.1). However, practitioners who plan to introduce new counseling techniques or expand the scope of their services must complete appropriate and verifiable training before offering such services (APA-EP 2.01).

Practitioners also must evaluate their competence to provide services to students whose background characteristics are outside the scope of their supervised experience. Is Carrie Johnson competent to provide psychological counseling to Tamika (Case 7.5)? Ignoring or minimizing the importance of client characteristics such as race, ethnicity, sexual orientation, or socioeconomic background may result in approaches that are ineffective (NASP-PPE II.1.2; N. D. Hansen et al., 2000; Rogers et al., 1999).

Is Maria (Case 7.4) competent to provide group counseling to teens with eating disorders? The question of her competence relates to both the adequacy of the workshop she attended and her background. If she has had extensive training in group counseling, including prior supervised experience, she is able to claim more competence to attempt this new technique than if this workshop was her first exposure to the group counseling process. Group counseling techniques require a high degree of skill and prior supervised experience (Fischer & Sorenson, 1996).

An issue related to the question of competence is whether the school psychologist is the most competent professional available to provide the counseling service. School psychologists recognize the competence of other professionals and encourage the use of all resources to best meet the needs of students (NASP-PPE III.3.1). Carrie Johnson (Case 7.5) may have some expertise in helping children cope with loss. However, she should consider whether Tamika might benefit more from counseling provided by a professional who has experience working with African American children and their families.

Case 7.4

Maria Delgado, school psychologist, has developed expertise in eating disorders and has successfully counseled a number of students on a one-to-one basis. She became interested in providing a counseling group for students with eating disorders and attended a one-day workshop on using group counseling methods with anorexic and bulimic teens. She is now using this group counseling technique with students in her schools.

Case 7.5

Tamika, a new student in Mr. March's fifth-grade class, recently transferred from an inner-city school located in a poverty-ridden neighborhood. She came to live with her grandparents after her mother's death. She is one of only a few African American students in her new school, which, along with her use of African American Vernacular English, sets her apart from her classmates. Tamika's records from her previous school indicate that she was an average student, and there is no mention of disciplinary problems. According to Mr. March, Tamika appears to be scared and angry. She refuses to talk in class, has made no friends, and does not complete assignments. Her classmates complain that she is "mean," and that she shoves or punches when no teachers are in sight. When Carrie Johnson, the school psychologist, phoned Tamika's grandparents to discuss her school adjustment and invite them in for a conference, Tamika's grandmother responded, "The Lord brought Tamika to us, and He will show us the way." She declined to come in for a conference but agreed to allow Carrie to work with Tamika to identify possible interventions. Carrie has received training in helping children cope with grief and loss, but she has little experience working with African American students or their families, particularly students from low-income, inner-city homes who may be mistrusting of White school professionals.

School psychologists also are ethically obligated to refrain from any activity in which their personal problems or conflicts may interfere with professional effectiveness. "When personal beliefs, conflicts of interest, or multiple relationships threaten to diminish professional effectiveness ... school psychologists ask their supervisor for a reassignment of responsibilities, or they direct the client to alternative services" (NASP-PPE III.4.2).

Responsibility

The APA code of ethics states: "Psychologists terminate therapy when it becomes reasonably clear that the client/patient ... is not likely to benefit, or is being harmed by continued service" (APA-EP 10.10). If the practitioner determines that he or she is not able to be of professional assistance to the client, the psychologist should "suggest alternative service providers as appropriate" (APA-EP 10.10; also NASP-PPE II.2.2).

PSYCHOPHARMACOLOGIC INTERVENTIONS

This portion of the chapter alerts the practitioner to ethical and legal issues associated with the use of medications to treat children with school learning or behavior problems. The number of children treated with psychotropic medication has increased dramatically in recent decades. School psychologists should be aware that, because drug trials with children raise ethical concerns, some drugs commonly prescribed to youth have not yet been adequately tested for safety and effectiveness in children (Hale, Semrud-Clikeman, & Kubas, 2014). Discussion here is limited to the use of Ritalin (methylphenidate hydrochloride), a drug that has been approved by the Food and Drug Administration (FDA) for the treatment of attention-deficit/hyperactivity disorder (ADHD) in children aged 6 years and older (U.S. FDA, 2013). Ritalin is widely prescribed for schoolchildren in the United States, and it provides an excellent example of both the promise and potential pitfalls of drug therapy.

Substantial research has shown that stimulant medication can be effective in the treatment of ADHD (Hale et al., 2014). However, the use of Ritalin or other drugs to treat difficulties such as ADHD places the child at risk for physical or psychological harm because of the problems of potential misdiagnosis and drug side effects. A number of different types of hyperactivity exist, and stimulant medication is not appropriate for all types. Furthermore, Ritalin is generally considered safe, but harm can result from its side effects. Common side effects include nervousness, headache, stomachache, trouble sleeping, nausea, and decreased appetite. Serious side effects include growth suppression, seizures, eyesight changes or blurred vision, and painful and prolonged erections. Other reported side effects (U.S. FDA, 2013) include: sudden death in persons who have heart problems; increased blood pressure and heart rate; psychotic symptoms; aggressive behavior or hostility; agitation; and the development of tics or Tourette's syndrome, especially among individuals with a family history of tics or Tourette's syndrome.

A number of lawsuits have been filed against public schools and physicians by parents of children prescribed Ritalin. In many of these suits, children suffered physical (e.g., Tourette's syndrome) or psychological harm (e.g., suicidal behavior) as a result of drug treatment recommended to them by school personnel (see Case 7.6). In some instances, parents report that they were pressured by school officials to seek drug treatment for their son or daughter with threats of exclusion from school if they failed to comply (*Valerie J. v. Derry Coop. School District*, 1991).

To receive IDEIA funds, states must prohibit school personnel from requiring parents to obtain a prescription for a controlled substance as a condition of attending school. The law does not, however, prohibit school personnel from "consulting or sharing classroom-based observations with parents or guardians regarding a student's academic and functional performance" (34 CFR § 300.174). Thus, decisions to prescribe drugs must be made by a physician (a point that should be clearly communicated to parents), and parents must be free to choose or refuse the use of such medication without pressure from the school.

The court settlement in *Benskin* (1980) provides some guidance to schools regarding psychopharmacological interventions with students. Drug treatment requires careful physician-school-parent collaboration. The school psychologist should ensure that parents have been provided information regarding the potential benefits of drug treatment (e.g., improved working memory, reduced disruptive behavior) and any known risks (drug side effects and adverse reactions). Through cooperative efforts with the physician, school psychologists can assist in the monitoring of the effectiveness of drug treatments and thereby provide important feedback to the physician and parents (see Carlson & Shahidullah, 2014; Hale et al., 2014).

Case 7.6

In 1980, a California court approved the settlement of a lawsuit filed by 18 students and their parents against the school district. In the suit, the parents made claims against the school district and staff (including the school psychologist) stemming from the district's intrusion into the decision whether a child should take Ritalin to control what the schools alleged was hyperactive behavior. The parents contended that they had been subjected to extremely strong pressure to agree to the administration of the drug. One parent reported being called in before an array of school district staff and told that she would be a "foolish parent" if she refused to give the drug to her son. Others were told that their children could not possibly succeed in school without the drug or that they would not be able to remain in general education classes unless they took it. Nothing was mentioned about the potentially dangerous side effects of the drug, and when parents asked about this, they were told that the drug was as harmless as aspirin. Only the most superficial of medical examinations of the children were done prior to prescribing or recommending the drug, and no follow-up monitoring was done. No efforts were made to alter any environmental factors (such as poor teaching) that might have contributed to the children's difficult behavior.

The suit was filed after two of the children experienced their first grand mal epileptic seizures while taking the drug. Other children complained of aches and pains, insomnia, loss of appetite, apathy, moodiness, nosebleeds, and other problems associated with the drug Ritalin. Expert witnesses for the parents testified that many of the children were perfectly normal and should never have been candidates for drug therapy and that the school's procedures for diagnosis and prescription were woefully inadequate.

The settlement agreement ordered by the court included a lump sum of $210,000, which the court allocated among the plaintiffs according to the severity of harm each child suffered. In addition, the settlement agreement set forth a number of policy clarifications that precluded the school district from diagnosing hyperactivity or recommending in any way that a child take behavior-modification drugs.

Source: Adapted from *Benskin v. Taft City School District*, 1980.

CONCLUDING COMMENTS

Teenaged parents. Academic failure. Substance abuse. Youth suicide. Divorce. AIDS. Childhood depression. Juvenile delinquency. Sexual abuse. The list of problems facing students in our schools today continues to grow and seemingly is endless. Yet, our time and resources remain limited. (Zins & Forman, 1988, p. 539)

Today we must add fear of terrorism and school shootings and the problem of student-on-student harassment and victimization, including cyberbullying. Partly in response to court decisions and high-profile crisis events, many schools are beginning to recognize the importance of a planned response to crisis situations and many are beginning to place a greater emphasis on the prevention of student academic and mental health problems.

STUDY AND DISCUSSION

Questions for Chapter 7

1. When a school psychologist becomes aware of a potentially assaultive student, what actions are appropriate?
2. When a school psychologist becomes aware of a potentially suicidal student, what actions are appropriate?
3. When a school psychologist suspects child abuse or child neglect, what actions are appropriate?
4. Develop a list of guidelines for teachers on how to safeguard the ethical and legal rights of students when behavioral interventions are planned and implemented.
5. May a school require a child to take medication as a precondition for school attendance? Identify the ethical-legal issues associated with the use of medications to treat schoolchildren with learning and behavior problems.

Discussion

In *D.J.M. v. Hannibal Public School District #60* (2011), a student used instant messaging from a location outside of his school to make threats of "deadly acts" (p. 765) that would take place inside his school.

Use Google Scholar to retrieve the case. You may Google by the names of the parties in the case or its legal citation: 647 F.3d 754. Do you agree with the court outcome on the question of whether the student's First Amendment free speech rights were violated? Do you feel the actions of the adults in this situation were appropriate and reasonable in light of the content of the instant messages and other facts of the situation? What steps would you have taken if you were the first adult contacted by C.M.?

Vignettes

1. Leslie is a 14-year-old girl who has a history of suicide attempts and psychiatric hospitalization. Maria Delgado, school psychologist, provides individual counseling to Leslie once a week as part of a Section 504 plan to monitor Leslie's emotional well-being and assist her in self-understanding and developing healthy social relationships. During the first four weeks of counseling sessions, Leslie talked incessantly about her romantic interest in a boy named "Ethan," who is in one of her classes. She repeatedly attempted to interact with him in socially appropriate ways, but he has shown little interest in developing a friendship with her. In their fifth counseling session, Leslie discloses that, after

getting his cell phone number from a classmate, she sexted Ethan several nude pictures of herself because the pictures "will get him interested in me." Using her cell phone, Leslie shows Maria one of the pictures she sexted to Ethan. Maria is aware that Leslie and Ethan are now at risk for being criminally prosecuted under a state law that prohibits distribution and possession of child pornography. She is also aware that her school district's policy states that school personnel who discover images of nude minors on a student's electronic device should promptly and directly contact law enforcement (see Goodno, 2011). However, Maria is employed in a state that explicitly recognizes communications in a school psychologist–client relationship as privileged. Maria did not forewarn Leslie or her parents that disclosure of a criminal act might result in a breach of confidentiality. How should Maria handle this situation? Consider all parties involved, including Ethan. Why do you think attorneys recommend that school personnel contact law enforcement directly if they discover sexting by minors rather than confiscating the pictures and forwarding them to school administrators?

2. An English teacher at the middle school stopped in to see James Lewis, school psychologist, to discuss concerns about one of her eighth-grade students, Melinda. The teacher reported that Melinda's grades have declined over the past six weeks and that she appears to be sad and tired in class. Because the district's policy allows a student to be seen by any mental health professional without parent notice to ensure the student is safe and not in danger, the teacher hopes that James has time to meet with Melinda to make sure that she is all right. The teacher believes that Melinda spends quite a lot of time online and mentioned that there is growing concern about cyberbullying among the girls at the middle school. The teacher goes on to suggest that James also gather information about Melinda's well-being by visiting her Facebook page. James is unsure whether this would be appropriate. Use a problem-solving model to consider the ethical-legal issues raised by this situation. (This vignette was adapted from Dailor and Jacob, 2010, p. 161. Also see Kaslow, Patterson, & Gottlieb, 2011; Lehavot, Barnett, & Powers, 2010.)

3. David Kim, school psychologist, developed good rapport with Frank Green, a 10th grader, when he counseled Frank about some problems in adjusting to a new stepfather. Later in the year, Frank makes an appointment to see David and reports that things seem to be going better at home. He confides that he stopped by to talk to David because he is worried about a girl in his woodshop class named Heidi. Heidi is a friendly 16-year-old who has an intellectual disability. Recently, three boys in the woodshop class began to show a special interest in her. Frank saw the boys take Heidi into a storeroom near the woodshop on two occasions after class, and he thinks the boys are doing something bad to Heidi. How should David handle this situation?

4. Cindy, a troubled 14-year-old whom Maria Delgado has seen previously for counseling, comes to her without an appointment. She is upset because two of her best friends, Tara and Trisha, have made plans to "ambush and beat up"

another girl after school because of an argument about a boy. She knows that Tara and Trisha have been in trouble at school before for fighting, and she is worried they will be kicked out of school if they follow through on their plans, and that they may really hurt their intended victim. How should Maria respond to this situation? What are the ethical-legal issues involved?

5. Nora, a 16-year-old, makes an appointment to see Carrie Johnson, the school psychologist. Nora confides that she is worried that her friend Jason may be planning to kill himself. She reports that Jason's father recently lost his job, and Jason has been upset since he overheard his parents arguing about how they will pay for Jason's costly psychiatrist visits and antidepressant medication. Jason feels he has become a burden to his family. How should Carrie handle this situation?

6. John Salvage, school psychologist, started a counseling group for middle school boys who have a history of disciplinary problems. Because he hoped to establish and maintain a positive rapport with them, John communicated with them using his social media accounts in addition to their meetings at school. In one posting, he teased a student about the student's girlfriend, and the student responded, "don't be jealous cause you can't get any lol :)" John replied, "What makes you think I want any? I'm not jealous. I just like to have fun and goof on you guys. If you don't like it, KISS MY BRASS! LMAO." Do you think this is a violation of professional boundaries between a school psychologist and student-clients? (See Lehavot et al., 2010.) Do you think John could face sanctions from the school district for behavior unbecoming a professional? (Situation adapted from *Spanierman v. Hughes*, 2008.)

Activities

According to the NASP's code of ethics, it is permissible to delay the discussion of the boundaries of confidentiality if a student is in immediate need of assistance (NASP-PPE I.2.3). Except for such situations, school psychologists "inform students and other clients of the boundaries of confidentiality at the outset of establishing a professional relationship" (NASP-PPE I.2.3). You, the school psychologist, are responsible for defining the boundaries of confidentiality and explaining them in a language that is understood by the client(s). Role-play the following situations:

1. A teenager (age 14) has made an appointment for a counseling session with you, the school psychologist. Role-play the initial meeting during which the psychologist defines the parameters of confidentiality and discusses parent consent issues.

2. A parent, Mrs. Fox, has made an appointment with you to discuss her concerns about Bill, her 15-year-old son. She reports that Bill has become moody and difficult and that his grades recently have declined markedly. She would like you to meet with Bill to see whether you can discover what the problems are and report your findings back to her. Role-play the initial meeting with Mrs. Fox, including a discussion of consent, assent, and confidentiality issues.

3. During a precounseling screening session, Joan Bellows, a 16-year-old, confides in you that she might be pregnant. Role-play how you might handle this situation.

4. A 13-year-old boy has been referred to you for counseling. The student has a history of truancy, running away from home, and being involved in physical fights at school, and he is suspected of stealing from other students. Role-play the initial meeting with the student's parents during which you seek consent to provide counseling and discuss confidentiality issues. Role-play your meeting with the student during which you seek assent and discuss confidentiality and its limits.

Chapter 8

INDIRECT SERVICES I: ETHICAL-LEGAL ISSUES IN WORKING WITH TEACHERS AND PARENTS

Chapter 8 first addresses ethical-legal issues associated with professional-to-professional consultation, focusing on teachers as consultees. As will be seen, the adoption of multitiered systems of support and response to intervention (MTSS/RTI) has prompted school psychologists to rethink some of our traditional ideas about school psychologist–teacher consultation. Ethical issues in working with parents are also addressed. Systems-level consultation is addressed in Chapter 9.

CONSULTATION WITH TEACHERS

The term *consultation* is used here to refer to "a process for providing psychological and educational services in which a specialist (consultant) works cooperatively with a staff member (consultee) to improve the learning and adjustment of a student (client) or group of students" (Erchul & Martens, 2010, p. 12). Consultative relationships typically are *voluntary*, meaning that the consultant makes an informed choice to enter into the consultative relationship. However, in schools that have adopted MTSS/RTI, some consultative services may not be voluntary on the part of the teacher (Erchul & Young, 2014). Unlike supervision, consultation is nonhierarchical; the consultant and consultee share coordinate status (Sandoval, 2014). The consultee remains an autonomous professional and generally retains the right to accept or reject suggestions made by the consultant (Gutkin & Curtis, 1999). Again, however, when MTSS/RTI is adopted at the systems level, the teacher may have limited autonomy in selecting instructional and behavioral strategies because interventions must be evidence-based, and he or she also may have little choice in how interventions are to be implemented due to the requirements for treatment integrity (Erchul & Young, 2014). Although the consultee retains responsibility for decisions, the consultant encourages alternative solutions until the goals of the consultative relationship are achieved (Sandoval, 2014). Like supervision, the goals of consultation in the schools should be work-related (Gutkin & Curtis, 1999).

Integrity in Consultative Relationships With Teachers

Consistent with the broad ethical principle of integrity in professional relationships, the psychologist/consultant strives to be honest and straightforward in interactions with the consultee. Consultants "explain their professional competencies, roles, assignments, and working relationships to recipients of services and others in their work setting in a forthright and understandable manner" (NASP-PPE III.2.1, III.2.4; also Codding, Sanetti, & Reed, 2014).

Gutkin and Curtis (1999) suggested that the consultation role be clearly defined to the school community prior to offering consultative services (APA-EP 3.11; NASP-PPE III.2). Discussions of consultative services should include role definition, the process of goal setting during consultation, the responsibilities of the consultant and consultee, and the parameters of confidentiality. Although initially this may occur at the level of the school, the same entry-stage issues are discussed subsequently with individual teachers at the beginning of establishing a consultative relationship.

A means of ensuring a mutual understanding of the parameters of a consultative relationship is through contracting. "A contract is a verbal or written agreement between the consultant and the consultee that specifies the parameters of the relationship" (Conoley & Conoley, 1982, p. 115; also Erchul & Young, 2014). The contract might include these five elements: (1) general goals of consultation and how specific goals will be selected; (2) tentative time frame; (3) consultant responsibilities (services to be provided, methods to be used, time commitment, and how the success of the consultation will be evaluated); (4) the nature of consultee responsibilities; and (5) confidentiality rules (adapted from Gallessich, 1982, pp. 272–273; also Rosenfield, 2014).

Respect for the Dignity of Persons (Welfare of Consultee and Student)

When providing consultation to teachers, the broad principle of respect for the dignity of persons encompasses the obligation to safeguard the autonomy and self-determination of the consultee and student(s); to make known and respect boundaries of confidentiality; and to promote understanding among consultants, consultees, and students from culturally and linguistically diverse backgrounds.

Autonomy and Self-Determination

Although in consultation the teacher is the recipient of services, student welfare "must be of primary importance to a school-based consultant" (Davis & Sandoval, 1982, p. 549; also Erchul & Young, 2014; T. L. Hughes, Kolbert, & Crothers, 2014; NASP-PPE III.2.3).

Students. School psychologists consider the rights and welfare of students to be their primary responsibility. The school psychologist is obligated to work with the teacher to ensure that consultation goals and intervention strategies are selected that are likely to be ultimately beneficial to the student (NASP-PPE II.3, III.2.3). A number of strategies can be used for safeguarding student welfare, autonomy, and self-determination when providing consultative services. These include involving the student as much as is feasible in the selection of goals and intervention strategies and selecting goals to promote student self-management (Newman, 1993).

Teacher/Consultee. In providing consultation services to the teacher, the teacher/consultee remains an autonomous professional and generally retains the right to accept or reject suggestions made by the consultant. The psychologist discourages teacher dependence on the consultant (Fanibanda, 1976) and also is careful to avoid stepping into the role of counselor/therapist to the consultee (Sandoval, 2014). Because the psychologist and teacher have differing fields of specialization, they may have differing perspectives on how to address a student's difficulties (T. L. Hughes et al., 2014). It is important that, as consultants, we "sufficiently understand the values of the community, institution, consultee, and clients with whom we work so that we will not merely impose our values on them" (Davis & Sandoval, 1982, p. 545; also NASP-PPE I.3.2, IV.1.1). As Fanibanda (1976) pointed out, our obligation to the welfare of the student may require us to advocate for certain decisions even if they conflict with the apparent value orientation of the consultee. Candid discussion of values and goals throughout consultation is a safeguard for teacher autonomy (D. Brown, Pryzwansky, & Schulte, 2011).

Consultants also must address possible barriers to an effective school psychologist–teacher consultative relationship. Barriers might include a teacher's limited skills in implementing certain evidence-based strategies with integrity; teacher uncertainty regarding a school psychologist's expertise and credibility as a consultant; or negative attitudes toward the consultative process (e.g., teacher perception that it is too time-consuming, a threat to professional autonomy, and/or an evaluation of teacher competence) (Burns, Jacob, & Wagner, 2008; Codding et al., 2014; Kratochwill, Altschaefl, & Bice-Urbach, 2014; Rosenfield, 2014; Sandoval, 2014). Consistent with our ethical codes, school psychologists address these barriers by working in full cooperation with teachers in a relationship based on *mutual respect* (NASP-PPE III, III.2.3). It is important to remember that teachers are our most important resource in helping children in the school setting.

Informed Consent

In consultative services to the teacher, the use of a verbal or written contract helps to ensure his or her informed consent for services. As discussed in Chapter 7, informed consent of the parent is needed if an intervention is planned for a student that diverges from ordinary, expected schooling.

Confidentiality

The parameters of confidentiality must be discussed at the outset of the delivery of consultative services, and, at a minimum, teachers should clearly understand what and how information will be used, by whom, and for what purposes (APA-EP 4.02; NASP-PPE I.2.3; also Erchul & Young, 2014; Sandoval, 2014). The confidentiality agreement is likely to vary depending on the nature of the consultative services being provided. When a consultative relationship is established between an individual school psychologist and a teacher, the parameters of confidentiality are likely to be similar to those of a traditional psychologist–client relationship (see Chapter 3; also Fanibanda, 1976; Sandoval, 2014). Today, however, school psychologists often are members of a team that provides instructional and behavioral consultation to teachers. As Erchul and Young noted (2014), "with the increasing adoption of RTI [response to intervention]/multitiered systems of support models, confidentiality may well vanish as a core characteristic of school consultation because considerable information is now shared freely among [team] participants" (p. 452). RTI goals for a child, intervention methods, and progress monitoring data are likely to be shared with parents as well. In such situations, the school psychologist must clarify that the school psychologist–teacher consultative relationship is not confidential. Regardless of the nature of the consultative services, the school psychologist is responsible for communicating the boundaries of confidentiality to the consultee. Violation of the confidentiality agreement in consultation with teachers is likely to result in a loss of trust in the school psychologist and may impair his or her ability to work with the consultee and others.

When school psychology consultation services are provided within the context of an individual school psychologist–client relationship, what are the appropriate limits to confidentiality? The school psychologist has an ethical obligation to safeguard the welfare of students. Consequently, the school psychologist should inform the consultee that third parties (e.g., the building principal) may be notified if the consultee "chronically and stubbornly" persists in activities that put students at risk for foreseeable harm (Conoley & Conoley, 1982, p. 216; also J. N. Hughes, 1986; Newman, 1993). However, "before breaching confidentiality, the consultant must have expended all resources at influencing the consultee to take collaborative action" (J. N. Hughes, 1986, p. 491). Such a breach of confidentiality would be appropriate only in unusual circumstances, namely when the consultee's actions are harmful or potentially harmful to students: "The consultee's approach toward the client [student] actually must be detrimental to the child rather than a less than optimal approach." The consultant is obligated to discuss the anticipated breach of confidentiality with the consultee prior to disclosure of information to third parties.

Fairness and Nondiscrimination

The broad ethical principle of respect for the dignity of persons also encompasses the values of fairness and nondiscrimination. School psychologists deal justly and impartially with each consultee regardless of his or her personal, political, cultural, racial, linguistic, or religious characteristics. As noted in Chapter 1, practitioners have an ethical obligation to become knowledgeable of the values, beliefs, and worldview of the consultee so as to be able to provide consultative services in a culturally sensitive manner (NASP-PPE I.3, II.1.2).

Providing consultation across culturally diverse consultant-consultee-student groups can pose special challenges. To provide consultation services that foster school success for all students, James Lewis (Case 8.1) needs to ensure that Mrs. Dolan and other teachers understand the backgrounds, cultures, prior school experiences, and interests of the African American and Latino students who now attend Littlefield Elementary and how to select materials and modify instruction as needed to meet their needs. He also can help families new to Littlefield better understand the culture and expectations of the school and work to assist them in supporting their children's achievement. Conceptual frameworks for cross-cultural consultation and best

---

Case 8.1

James Lewis provides school psychological services to Littlefield Elementary. Over the past 10 years, a change occurred in the ethnic-racial composition of Littlefield Elementary, from 60% White students to almost 90% African American and Latino students. Littlefield Elementary now has a dynamic African American principal and a staff composed of many new teachers of diverse racial and ethnic backgrounds as well as older White teachers. James is concerned because a White second-grade teacher, Mrs. Dolan, recommends five or six of her students for grade retention each year, all African American boys.

Source: Adapted from Rogers et al., 1999.

---

practices in providing services across culturally diverse consultant-consultee-client groups have been addressed in the literature (see Ingraham, 2000, 2014).

Responsible Caring

Psychologists are obligated ethically to provide consultation only within the boundaries of their competence, to evaluate the impact of consultative services on consultees and students, and to modify consultative plans as needed to ensure effectiveness.

Professional Responsibility in Teacher Consultation

Although multiple models of consultation exist, many emphasize the use of a systematic problem-solving process within the relationship of consultant, consultee, and client (Kratochwill et al., 2014). Models of consultation often include four stages: an entry phase, problem identification/clarification, intervention/problem solution, and evaluation. The fourth stage of the consultation process, evaluation, encourages professional responsibility on the part of both the school psychologist and the consultee. During this final stage, consistent with ethical obligations (NASP-PPE II.2.2), the consultant and the consultee assess whether the intervention was successful in meeting the agreed-on goals, and if not, the consultant and the consultee recycle back to the stages of problem identification/clarification or intervention/solution.

However, in the course of the consultative process, it may become apparent to the psychologist that he or she is unable to assist the consultee. If so, the psychologist is obligated ethically to refer the consultee to another professional (NASP-PPE II.2.2). This situation could occur when the consultee has emotional difficulties that interfere with effective functioning. As noted earlier, the practitioner generally must avoid the dual roles of consultant and counselor/therapist to the teacher. It also may become apparent during the consultative process that another professional is better able to assist the consultee (e.g., another psychologist with different skills or perhaps a well-respected teacher with special expertise in the problem area).

Special problems with regard to professional responsibility sometimes occur when the practitioner steps into the role of *consultant/trainer* and provides an in-service education workshop to teachers in the district. Although at first it might seem that the use of informational methods such as in-service training raises no special ethical concerns, problems may arise when there is no planned follow-up on the way the information provided is understood and used by teachers or other staff. For example, a number of writers noted that brief workshop methods of teaching applied behavior analysis techniques to teachers are inadequate and may result in unintended harmful consequences for students. As Conoley and Conoley (1982) suggested, consultant/trainers are well advised to view in-service training as "a *means*, not an *end*" (p. 134). A number of options exist for follow-up consultation to ensure that new ideas and techniques introduced during in-service training are used appropriately in the classroom (see Crothers, Kolbert, & Hughes, 2014, for suggestions).

Competence

Effective competencies needed by the consultant include: positive interpersonal communication skills; self-awareness of values, attitudes, and beliefs, particularly those relating to culture, ethnicity, socioeconomic status, religion, and gender differences; knowledge about evidenced-based interventions and treatment integrity; and an understanding of how schools function at an organizational level (Erchul & Young, 2014; Sheridan, Clarke, & Christenson, 2014). In addition, to provide services effectively, practitioners must be knowledgeable about the organization, philosophy, goals, and methodology of the schools where they provide services (NASP-PPE, IV.1.1), and they must be familiar with the areas of competence of other professionals in their setting.

SPECIAL ISSUES IN WORKING WITH PARENTS

Family–school partnerships have been linked to improved student achievement and higher academic aspirations, higher rates of academic engagement and attendance, and a reduction of suspensions and early school withdrawals (Esler, Godber, & Christenson, 2008; Sheridan et al., 2014).

Respect for the Dignity of Persons

We again utilize the framework provided by the code of ethics of the National Association of School Psychologists (NASP, 2010b) to discuss the issues involved in working with families.

Autonomy and Self-Determination

Historically, prior to the 1970s, parents were expected simply to be passive recipients of decisions made by school professionals. Parents often were considered to be the source of their children's problems and treated poorly. Today, in contrast, parents are viewed as collaborative partners in family–school relationships (Fish, 2002;

Sheridan et al., 2014; A. P. Turnbull & Turnbull, 2001). However, if parents are to assume the role of "equal and full partners with educators and school systems" (A. P. Turnbull & Turnbull, 2001, p. 13), schools must actively encourage and enable parents to do so.

As a result of advocacy efforts by parents and court rulings, the presumption that parents should be viewed as collaborators in educational decision making for their children has been incorporated into our codes of ethics and education law (Fish, 2002). The Individuals with Disabilities Education Act of 1997 placed greater emphasis on parent involvement in special education decision making than previous versions of the law. Establishing an effective working relationship with parents became even more essential with the 2004 changes in special education law. Under the 2004 Individuals with Disabilities Education Improvement Act (IDEIA), parents may withdraw consent for assessment or special education placement or services at any time, and this withdrawal of consent must be honored (34 CFR 300.9[c][1]). Because addressing the needs of the student is the top priority of school psychologists, practitioners must ensure genuine and ongoing communication with parents, listening carefully to family concerns and questions and emphasizing the shared goal of making decisions that are in the best interests of the child (Blue-Banning, Summers, Frankland, Nelson, & Beegle, 2004; McIntyre & Garbacz, 2014; Sheridan et al., 2014).

In addition, according to the NASP's code of ethics, when a student experiences school difficulties, school psychologists encourage parent involvement in all phases of the problem identification and remediation process (NASP-PPE I.1.1, II.3.10). They clearly explain their services so that they are understood by parents (NASP-PPE I.1.3, III.2.1) and "respect the wishes of parents who object to school psychological services," guiding them to alternative resources (NASP-PPE I.1.5). Findings and recommendations are communicated to parents in language they can understand, and when interpreters are used, school psychologists adhere to ethical guidelines and best practices regarding their use (APA-EP 2.05; NASP-PPE II.3.6). Furthermore, practitioners propose alternative recommendations to parents, ensuring that options take into account the values and cultural background of the family and the types of support for school achievement the family is able to provide the child (NASP-PPE II.3.10).

It is important to recognize that not all educators are willing to grant parents a partnership role. Furthermore, because of individual and cultural differences, not all parents may wish to assume a coequal role, and some are not capable of doing so (Webb, 2001). In such situations, because the school psychologist's "greatest responsibility is to those persons in the most vulnerable position," practitioners have a special obligation to speak up for the rights and wishes of the parent and student (Canadian Psychological Association, 2000, Principle I).

Managing the Conflicting Interests of Parent, Child, and School

How do school psychologists provide guidance, advice, and intervention while respecting parent autonomy and encouraging parent empowerment? What if the wishes of the parent do not coincide with the school psychologist's view of what is best for the child? How do school-based practitioners balance the needs of the particular family with the larger needs of the school (Friedman, Helm, & Marrone, 1999)? The problem of conflicting interests of multiple parties (parent, student, school) can arise in a variety of contexts (Dailor & Jacob, 2011). We provide two examples that focus on special education decision making.

In Case 8.2, consistent with the principle of respect for autonomy, Pearl should encourage the parents to exercise their right to make their wishes known and understood. One way to foster parents' autonomy and safeguard their legal rights in special education decision making is to ensure that parents understand the assessment findings, alternative recommendations, the process of decision making (including factors the team is legally required to consider), and their role in that process. For example, at the beginning of the individualized education program (IEP) team meeting to determine Jane's placement, Pearl might remind all team members that, as educators and parents, they share the goal of developing the best possible program the district can offer Jane—a program that, at a minimum, meets the legal standard of "reasonably designed to confer meaningful educational benefit." Pearl also might summarize issues that must be considered by the team under IDEIA in making the placement decision: The presumption is placement in general education with supplementary supports and services; placement in a more restrictive setting must be justified on the basis of greater academic or social benefit, or the presence of behavior that interferes with the learning of others in the general education classroom (see Chapter 4). The goal of providing such information is to put parents on an equal footing with other team members in the decision-making process. In addition, Pearl must ensure that Jane's parents understand the benefits and shortcomings of the alternative decisions. However, she must take care not to usurp their right to an independent opinion and voice about desired services for their child (see Hartshorne, 2002; but also Friedman et al., 1999). Lasser and Klose (2007, p. 497) identified social psychological phenomena that can influence decision making by parents and other members of an IEP team and encouraged school psychologists to learn strategies "to promote meaningful involvement of all team members."

How do school psychologists balance the needs of the particular family with the larger needs of the school? The NASP's code of ethics recognizes that school-based practitioners provide services to multiple parties, including children, parents, and systems, and states that school psychologists should support conclusions that are in the best interests of the child (NASP-PPE Introduction, III.2.3; also see "Advocacy" in

---

Case 8.2

Pearl Meadows is asked to conduct a reevaluation of a girl, Jane, who has a developmental disability and who will be entering junior high next fall. Consistent with parental wishes, Jane has been in an inclusive setting since kindergarten. Following her assessment, Pearl feels very strongly that Jane will receive much greater academic benefit from an outstanding self-contained program in the junior high. However, the parents have made it clear that they wish to continue with an inclusive program for their daughter.

========================== Case 8.3 ==========================

The parents of a 5-year-old boy with developmental disabilities have requested that their child be fully included in the kindergarten at his neighborhood school. Because of the child's unique needs, David Kim, the school psychologist, and the boy's parents believe he should be in a full-day program. Consequently, the parents have requested that their son be in both sections of kindergarten, morning and afternoon. Prior to the boy's IEP meeting, the school district's assistant superintendent contacts David. She has heard about the possible request for a full-day kindergarten placement and is concerned because, by teacher contract, a child with special needs counts as two children in a classroom. This boy would take the space of four children in kindergarten. Because this is a desirable school in the district, this means that three children will be turned away by the school and assigned to other elementary schools in the district.

Definition of Terms). David Kim in Case 8.3, like Pearl Meadows in Case 8.2, may want to remind IEP team members of the legal parameters of the placement decision at the IEP team meeting. A full-day program must be provided if that is what is necessary to confer meaningful educational benefit. Then David should advocate for the full-day kindergarten program he believes meets the intent of IDEIA and is in the best interests of the child, even if it puts him in conflict with district wishes.

Privacy and Confidentiality

School psychologists respect family privacy and do not seek information that is not needed in the provision of services (NASP-PPE I.2.2). Practitioners must be sensitive to cultural differences regarding the concept of privacy and recognize that, in some cultures, discussing personal problems with individuals outside of the family is "taboo" (Webb, 2001, p. 343). In such situations, it is critically important that practitioners follow culturally appropriate protocols to build a relationship with family members before initiating discussion of the student's difficulties (see Case 1.2). Practitioners also should discuss confidentiality and its limits with family members before seeking information from them, carefully identifying the types of information that might be shared with other school personnel or outside agencies, for what purpose, and under what circumstances (NASP-PPE I.2.3). The concept of confidentiality may not be familiar to parents from some cultures, whereas parents from other backgrounds may be very concerned that information will not be held in confidence (Webb, 2001).

Professional Competence and Responsibility

Consistent with the principle of beneficence (responsible caring), school psychologists must consider whether they are competent to provide services in light of family characteristics (e.g., language, cultural background) and the nature of the concern, and whether the family might benefit more from services provided by another professional (see Case 1.2 and Case 7.5; NASP-PPE II.1.2). Webb (2001) reviewed the available research on cultural matching of psychologist and client and reported that, for some groups, racial matching between practitioner and client results in more positive outcomes (also see Behring, Cabello, Kushida, & Murguia, 2000). Webb goes on to note, however, that for most clients who participated in these studies, *"the practitioner's personal qualities of sensitivity and competence were more important than was similarity of ethnicity and race"* (p. 344).

Integrity in Relationships With Parents

Practitioner–family partnerships are ideally based on honesty, trust, shared responsibility, and mutual support (Sheridan et al., 2014). Practitioners must avoid conflicts of interest; that is, they refrain from taking on a professional role when their own interests (personal, professional, financial) could reasonably be expected to impair their objectivity, competence, or effectiveness or expose clients to harm or exploitation (APA-EP Principle B, 3.06; NASP-PPE III.4, III.4.2–4.4). In situations where there is a potential conflict of interest, practitioners ask their supervisor to assign a different school psychologist. If that is not feasible or acceptable, the practitioner should attempt to guide the parents to alternative resources (NASP-PPE III.4.2).

School psychologists also must consider potential problems associated with multiple relationships. In working with parents, multiple relationships occur when the school psychologist is in a professional role in relation to a student's parents and at the same time has another relationship with the parents or a person closely associated with the parents. For example, a school psychologist might be asked to provide services to a student whose parents are his or her close personal friends, or the parent with whom the school psychologist is consulting might be the teacher of the psychologist's own child.

Psychologists refrain from entering into multiple relationships if the relationship reasonably could be expected to impair the psychologist's performance (APA-EP 3.05; NASP-PPE III.4.2). Again, in such situations, the parents should be offered the services of another school psychologist in the district; if that is not feasible, the practitioners should attempt to guide them to alternative resources. However, multiple relationships "that would not reasonably be expected to cause impairment or risk exploitation or harm are not unethical" (APA-EP 3.05). If, due to unforeseen circumstances, a potentially harmful multiple relationship arises, the school psychologist attempts to resolve it with due regard for the best interests of the client and others involved (APA-EP 3.05; NASP-PPE III.4.2).

For many years, psychotherapists were cautioned to avoid social or other nonprofessional contacts with their patients because a blurring of professional boundaries could impair the therapist's objectivity or effectiveness. More recently, however, codes of ethics have been modified to recognize that not all social contacts between psychologists and their clients pose a risk of harm. Social contacts with families may, in fact, improve family–school relationships. For example, Latino families may expect relationships with the school psychologist to involve *personalismo*, namely a warm, friendly relationship in which the psychologist demonstrates an interest and concern

============================ **Case 8.4** ============================

Maria Delgado is trying to establish a working partnership with a Puerto Rican couple whose 15-year-old daughter is pregnant. The family has appreciated Maria's openness with them and recently invited her to the girl's baby shower. Should Maria attend?

Source: Situation suggested by Congress, 2001.

about the individual student and his or her family. Making a personal connection with the family may be the only way to establish a partnership (Congress, 2001). Maria Delgado (Case 8.4) should consider both the potential benefits and disadvantages of social interaction with her student-client and family in deciding whether to attend the baby shower.

Diversity Issues

School psychologists are obligated ethically to provide services to students and their families that are respectful of diverse backgrounds and circumstances (APA-EP 2.01; NASP-PPE I.3, I.3.2). Furthermore, to build and maintain positive school–parent partnerships, school psychologists must help teachers and others in the school setting recognize "the inherent strengths in all families … in contrast to attitudes that consider family members as having deficits that need to be treated, trained or altered" (Sheridan et al., 2014, p. 441).

Webb (2001) identified several common sources of misunderstanding that can arise when the mental health practitioner works with a family whose background is different from his or her own. Confusion can arise because of "the practitioner's lack of understanding about the … stresses of the client's situation in the context of the client's specific cultural and family environment" (p. 339). School psychologists must strive to understand family circumstances; they cannot assume that the parents' reality is the same as theirs (Ortiz, Flanagan, & Dynda, 2008).

When James Lewis is able to contact Adam's mother (Case 8.5), he learns that she is a widow who works the second shift as a press operator in a stamping plant. Adam and his sisters go to a neighbor's house after school, where she picks them up after midnight. She noticed that Adam has had some congestion but did not want to take him out of school to see the doctor and cannot afford to miss work. Now that she knows he is having problems at school, she promises to take him to the doctor and contact the teacher. In a tactful and respectful manner, James will work to help Mrs. Barbos appreciate the strengths of this family and that the mother's failure to participate in school events is not due to a lack of caring about the well-being and school success of her children.

A second area of potential misunderstanding involves "engaging, communicating, and agreeing about the problem" and determining whether, in fact, a problem exits (Webb, 2001, p. 339; also Lopez & Bursztyn, 2013). Practitioners must be able to

---

Case 8.5

James Lewis received a referral for an African American boy, Adam, who is experiencing difficulty learning to read. James arranges to meet with Adam's teacher, Mrs. Barbos, who reports that Adam does not seem to be able to distinguish different phonemes. Adam has a "nonstop" runny nose and congestion, and Mrs. Barbos wonders if he is experiencing ear infections and possible hearing difficulties. Mrs. Barbos goes on to explain that Adam's parents did not show up for school open house or fall conferences. She has tried to contact them by phone many times after school and at night, but no one answers. Exasperated, she comments, "How can we be expected to help these kids when their parents don't care?"

---

establish rapport with parents and communicate the school's concerns in culturally sensitive ways, and they should seek to understand the parents' perceptions of their child's development, learning, and behavior. Parents often can provide important insights into the meaning of their child's behaviors at school. Gathering this information is essential when working with children from diverse cultures and backgrounds. For example, a teacher might refer a child for evaluation because the child avoids eye contact with adults. In the absence of information from the parents, the school psychology practitioner may not know that children in some cultures are taught that it is disrespectful to look an adult in the eyes.

A third area of potential misunderstanding concerns "different ideas about seeking help and dealing with the problem situation" (Webb, 2001, p. 339). It is likely that culturally sensitive modifications in the psychologist's approach will be needed to work effectively with families from different backgrounds. For some families, attempts to establish a collaborative partnership may not be culturally appropriate (Behring et al., 2000; Lynch & Hanson, 2011). For example, some families with Asian roots place great importance on expert opinion and prefer a directive rather than a collaborative approach (Behring et al., 2000).

It is also important to recognize that many families prefer to seek and receive help from other family members, friends, or religious leaders rather than schools or social service agencies. Some mistrust school personnel (Webb, 2001). Practitioners are obligated ethically to identify alternative sources of assistance available in the community (NASP-PPE, I.1.5) and should work to support, rather than supplant, existing community-based helping relationships. At the same time, school psychologists should consider whether systems-level changes are needed to promote parent trust and partnerships (Sheridan et al., 2014).

Finally, misunderstandings can occur because of the "different values and worldviews of the practitioner and the client" (Webb, 2001, p. 339). School psychologists need to recognize that the way in which some parents prioritize their child's needs (e.g., socialization with general education students versus academic benefits of individualized special education classroom instruction) may differ considerably from the way in which the school psychologist might prioritize a student's needs (Case 8.2; also NASP-PPE I.3.2).

Lopez and Rogers (2001) identified a comprehensive list of cross-cultural competencies for school psychologists. Four apply to working with parents, including having knowledge about "differences in family structures across cultures," "differences in authority, hierarchies, communication patterns, belief systems, values, and gender roles," "attitudes of culturally diverse parents towards different forms of interventions," and "attitudes that culturally diverse parents have towards educational institutions and teachers." School psychologists should also be skilled in "implementing home-school collaboration programs and interventions" (p. 130).

In addition to cultural, racial, socioeconomic, and language diversity, school psychologists also must be knowledgeable of best practices for establishing school–parent partnerships when families are headed by same-sex parents. A greater number of gay and lesbian parents are identifying themselves to school personnel than in past years, and this trend is likely to continue as more same-sex couples marry. In research studies, gay- and lesbian-headed families identified multiple risks associated with disclosing their family constellation to school personnel. Some choose not to disclose that they are parents with same-sex partners because they fear discrimination in housing or employment or social rejection or harassment of their children by classmates, or that they would not be welcome at school. Some worry that their children will not be treated well by teachers (Herbstrith, Tobin, Hesson-McInnis, & Schneider, 2013; Kosciw, Greytak, Diaz, & Bartkiewicz, 2010; Ryan & Martin, 2000).

Available research findings suggest that many school systems are not prepared to work with families headed by lesbian, gay, bisexual, or transgender (LGBT) parents. "Attitudes towards homosexuality remain negative, teachers report little to no training on sexual orientation issues, and LGBT parents and their children report bullying and harassment that goes unreported or unpunished and exclusion from school activities and curricula" (Herbstrith, 2014, p. 214) Using a multitiered framework, Herbstrith (2014) identified best practices for fostering positive school–parent partnerships with LGBT parents.

In Case 8.6, a school secretary engages in discrimination against a gay parent that is illegal under Title IX of the Education Amendments of 1972 (see Chapter 9). This case illustrates that school district training on LGBT issues must be targeted to *all* of the members of the school staff.

Responsibility to Families, Community, and Society

As noted in Chapter 1, school psychologists have an ethical obligation to use psychological knowledge to benefit students and the larger school community. Family–school partnerships have been found to enhance the success of students. Practitioners can assist in developing a school environment that is welcoming to all families and provide consultation on best practices in promoting positive school–parent partnerships (see Sheridan et al., 2014).

Case 8.6

Carrie Johnson's two friends, Jason and George, were married after the Supreme Court decision in *Obergell v. Hodges* (2015) reversed the ban on same-sex marriage in their state. Jason and George have been partners for 15 years, and they have three children who attend an elementary school where Carrie is the school psychologist. At a social gathering, George remarks to Carrie that he completed an application to become a parent volunteer at the elementary school. He now has health insurance coverage as Jason's spouse which allows him to be a stay-at-home dad, and he would love to volunteer at the school. George goes on to say that he received an e-mail from the school district's Human Resource Office stating that his criminal background check had been completed and that he was approved to volunteer. However, that was in September, and now, six months later, he's disappointed because he has never been contacted by the school principal to participate in the parent volunteer program. The following Monday, Carrie stops by the principal's office to ask whether there has been a paperwork "mix-up" concerning George's interest in being a parent volunteer at the school. The school secretary shuts the door and then tells Carrie in hushed tones that George's approved application is in a file in her office, but she didn't provide his volunteer form or contact information to the principal because "I wouldn't want someone like that working with my children and the other parents wouldn't either."

CONCLUDING COMMENTS

Effective problem solving and intervention for students who are experiencing difficulties in social or emotional development, school learning, or behavior depend on using the combined skills and resources of teachers, other professionals, and the family. School psychologists can play an important role in drawing together these resources to bring about positive change for individual students, classrooms, and schools.

Practitioners undoubtedly will encounter difficult teachers and parents in the course of their careers. Regardless of their personal feelings and frustrations, school psychologists ethically are obligated to engage in conduct that is respectful of all persons (NASP-PPE I). Research with physicians has demonstrated the importance of sensitive and tactful communication with clients and consultees (Knapp & VandeCreek, 2012). For example, Levinson, Roter, Mullooly, Dull, and Frankel (1997) audiotaped two groups of physicians interacting with patients during routine office visits. One group of physicians had a history of one or more malpractice claims against them; the second group had no history of malpractice claims. Results indicated significant differences in the communication behaviors of no-claims physicians in comparison with the claims physicians. No-claims physicians spent more time educating their patients regarding what to expect, laughed and used humor more, and showed better listening skills (asked patients their opinions, checked understanding, encouraged patients to talk). This and subsequent research suggests that physical and mental health care providers who are courteous, tactful, and good listeners are more likely to achieve excellence in their profession and are less likely to be the targets of complaints.

STUDY AND DISCUSSION

Questions for Chapter 8

1. What information should be provided in describing the consultant's role to the school, community, and individual consultees?

2. What parameters of confidentiality are appropriate when a school psychologist is a member of an instructional assistance team providing instructional or behavioral consultation to a teacher? What parameters of confidentiality are generally appropriate when an individual school psychologist provides consultation within the context of a consultant–consultee professional relationship? Under what circumstances, if any, might it be appropriate for the psychologist/consultant to breach the confidentiality of a consultative relationship with a teacher?

3. Although the idea that parents should be viewed as collaborators in educational decision making has been incorporated into education law and our codes of ethics, it is not always realized in practice. Identify two barriers to parents assuming the role of "equal and full partners with educators and school systems." (Also see Lasser & Klose, 2007.)

4. Throughout the text, the authors have stressed the idea that the school psychologist's responsibility goes beyond being impartial and unprejudiced in the delivery of services. Identify some of the practitioner's special obligations in working with families from backgrounds different from his or her own.

Vignettes

1. Mrs. French, a middle school English teacher, stops by to see the school psychologist, Maria Delgado. Mrs. French is upset about a love note she intercepted between two students in one of her classes. The note was written by a 14-year-old boy named Derek to another boy in the class. Derek knows that Mrs. French has read and kept the note, but she has not spoken with him about the matter. Mrs. French wants Maria to confront Derek with the note and talk with Derek's parents so that he will "get help to cure him of this sick stuff before it's too late." How should Maria respond to this situation? (Adapted from Eversole, 1993; also see *Sterling v. Borough of Minersville*, 2000, in Chapter 2.)

2. Victor and Margaret Lee attend school in Pearl Meadows's district. Their father, who speaks almost no English, is the cook at their family-owned Chinese restaurant, while their mother, who is fluent in English, manages the restaurant and is very actively involved in her children's education. One Monday morning, Pearl is saddened to hear of Mrs. Lee's unexpected death over the weekend. While Margaret, in eighth grade, slowly adjusts to her loss, Victor, a fifth grader, continues to

struggle with his grief many months after his mother's death, and he has begun to show signs of serious depression. Pearl would like to meet with Mr. Lee to discuss Victor's depression. The principal suggests that Margaret serve as the interpreter during the conference. What are the ethical issues regarding choice and use of interpreters? (See APA-EP 2.05; NASP-PPE II.3.6; Lopez, 2008.) Evaluate the appropriateness of the principal's suggestion in light of the hierarchical family structure of many Asian families (see Webb, 2001, p. 342) and the psychologist's ethical obligations to Victor.

3. Reread Case 8.6. How should Carrie respond to the school secretary's disclosure that she did not give George's approved application to be a school volunteer to the principal?

Chapter 9

INDIRECT SERVICES II: SPECIAL TOPICS IN SYSTEMS-LEVEL CONSULTATION

As used in this chapter, the term *systems-level consultation* refers to cooperative problem solving between the school psychologist (consultant) and consultee(s) (principal, district-level administrators) with a goal of improving school policies, practices, and programs so as to better serve the mental health and educational needs of all students. In 1991, Prilleltensky foreshadowed contemporary thinking when he suggested that "school psychologists have a moral responsibility to promote not only the well-being of their clients but also of the environments where their clients function and develop" (p. 2000). The code of ethics of the National Association of School Psychologists (NASP, 2010b) states:

> School psychologists use their professional expertise to promote changes in schools and community service systems that will benefit children and other clients. They advocate for school policies and practices that are in the best interests of children and that respect and protect the legal rights of students and parents. (NASP-PPE IV.1.2)

To be competent to provide systems-level consultation, school psychologists need expertise in understanding human behavior from a social systems perspective, well-developed skills in collaborative planning and problem-solving procedures, and knowledge of principles for organizational change (Castillo & Curtis, 2014; also NASP-PPE IV.1.1).

The first portion of the chapter summarizes the ethical and legal issues associated with three special topics in school consultation: large-scale assessment programs, including high-stakes achievement testing, minimum competency testing, and screening to identify students at risk of harm to self or others. Next, legal issues associated with the following instructional practices are addressed: grade retention, student ability grouping and disproportionality, and programs for English language learners (ELL) and gifted and talented students. Then an overview of law and ethical issues pertinent to school discipline is provided, including discussions of corporal punishment, suspension and expulsion, and school-wide positive behavior support systems. Finally, recent court decisions and Office for Civil Rights (OCR) policies pertinent to discrimination against, and harassment of, students protected by civil rights law are addressed, ending with a brief summary of law, ethics, and bullying. These topics were chosen because they are issues of long-standing or contemporary concern.

LARGE-SCALE ASSESSMENT PROGRAMS

Thus far, the portions of this book that addressed assessment generally focused on psychoeducational evaluation of individual students, not districtwide assessments. It is important to recognize, however, that in many school districts, the school psychologist is the professional with the greatest expertise in measurement. Consequently, practitioners can assume valuable consultative roles related to large-scale assessment programs. To be prepared for such roles, practitioners need to be knowledgeable of the *Standards for Educational and Psychological Testing* (hereafter *Standards*; American Educational Research Association, American Psychological Association, & National Council on Measurement in Education, 2014). Practitioners also need to be familiar with the legal issues associated with large-scale assessment programs.

State- and Districtwide Academic Achievement Testing

A heightened emphasis on school accountability gave impetus to the development of statewide student performance assessment programs. The No Child Left Behind Act of 2001 (NCLB) required each state to develop challenging academic content standards for mathematics, reading or language arts, and science and measurable achievement standards for those content areas (Pub. L. No. 107-110 § 1111[a][1]). Each state also was required to implement a set of high-quality, yearly student academic standardized assessments to serve as the primary means of determining the performance of the state, school district, and school. States identified target starting goals (e.g., 80% of all students will demonstrate proficiency on the reading and mathematics tests) and were required to then increase the target percentage of students who test as proficient each year until 100% were proficient in 2013–2014. Sanctions were imposed on schools based on the number of years the school failed to meet adequate yearly progress expectations. Unfortunately, the NCLB "overidentified schools as 'failing' even when they demonstrated growth, hindering school reform and innovation" and demoralizing educators, parents, and students (U.S. Department of Education [DOE], n.d.[a], p. 1).

After years of dissatisfaction with NCLB, the Every Student Succeeds Act (ESSA) was signed into law December 10, 2015. This law was a result of bi-partisan efforts to remedy the problems caused by NCLB including its sole reliance on statewide achievement test scores to evaluate school quality and its sanctions for low performing schools. The lawmakers who crafted ESSA sought to preserve NCLB's emphasis on high expectations for school performance and to strengthen support for students who are struggling academically. Like its precursor, the ESSA requires states to establish a statewide accountability system that includes challenging academic standards and high-quality assessments in mathematics, reading or language arts, and science (Sec. 1111 [b][1][C]; Sec. 1111 [b][2][A−C]). However, states now have greater discretion to select their own goals and academic achievement standards and select assessments aligned to those standards, as long as the measures are technically adequate and valid for the pur-posed used (Sec. 1111[b][1] [G][ii]; Sec. 1111[b][2][B][iii]). Under ESSA, mathematics and reading or language arts assessment must be administered in grades 3 through 8 and at least once in grades 9 through 12; science tests are administered at least once in grades 3 through 5, 6 through 9, and 10 through 12 (Sec. 1111 [b][2][A−C]).

The state's accountability system must disaggregate and report separately the academic assessment scores of students who are economically disadvantaged, members of major racial and ethnic groups, children with disabilities, and those who are English learners (Sec. 1111 [b][2][B][xi]; also see English Language Learners, this chapter). Furthermore, for the first time, state accountability measures must include an assessment of school quality *other than* academic achievement test scores. This quality indicator must be an assessment of school attributes or student success such as a measure of student engagement, educator engagement, student completion of advanced coursework, postsecondary readiness, or school climate and safety (Sec. 1111 [c][4][B][v][I–VIII]; also Klein, 2016).

Under ESSA and consistent with IDEIA, students with disabilities are also required to participate in statewide student proficiency assessment programs (Sec. 1111 [b][2][D]). They may take their statewide assessment with or without individualized testing accommodations and/or with modified proficiency standards, or they may take an alternative assessment specifically designed to document progress in relation to the student's individualized education program (IEP) objectives (see Braden & Joyce, 2008; Braden & Tayrose, 2008). Alternative assessments are intended for students with "the most significant cognitive disabilities" who cannot meaningfully participate in the state assessments taken by other students. The ESSA allows 1 percent of all students (about 10 percent of students with disabilities) to take alternative statewide assessments (Sec. 1111 [b][2][D]; also Klein, 2016).

High-stakes testing is a term that refers to situations in which test outcomes have a direct impact on the lives of stakeholders (Braden & Tayrose, 2008; *Standards*, 2014). Results of statewide proficiency assessments have been used to evaluate the performance of individual teachers and schools. Low-scoring schools may suffer negative publicity and increased external scrutiny and control, while high-scoring schools receive public praise, increased autonomy, and, in some states, financial rewards. In some districts, teachers are awarded bonuses based on the test performance of their students. Unfortunately, high-stakes testing programs can encourage school practices that are not in the best interests of students. Unintended consequences of high-stakes testing can include narrowing the district's curriculum to match test content (e.g., eliminating music and art) and teacher and student demoralization due to repeated low performance (Braden & Tayrose, 2008; also see Decker & Bolt, 2008).

High-stakes testing programs also have fostered dishonest school practices in test administration and scoring. The 2015 conviction of Atlanta, Georgia, educators for racketeering marked the close of the largest test cheating scandal in the nation (see Case 9.1) The district has since ended teacher bonuses related to students' test scores (Binder, 2015).

High-stakes testing programs have also been linked to lax supervision of examinees with concomitant student cheating and breaches of test security. For example, three Colorado teachers were reprimanded in 2015 for failure to properly supervise students taking a statewide assessment test that was developed in collaboration with Pearson Education. The teachers were instructed to ensure that students did not have access to their cellphones or other electronic devices during the administration of the test. However, students under their supervision took pictures of test items and posted them on social media sites. These test security breaches were discovered by Pearson as a result

---

Case 9.1

Based on an analysis of test scores on the statewide academic achievement test, a 2009 newspaper article reported "statistically unlikely" scores, including "extraordinary gains," in 19 Georgia public schools. Twelve of the schools were located in Atlanta (Perry & Vogell, 2009). A subsequent investigation by the Georgia Bureau of Investigation found "'widespread'" conspiracy among teachers and administrators in the Atlanta Public Schools to change answers on student answer sheets, threaten whistle-blowers, and hide the cheating, with 178 teachers and principals named in the scandal (Jonsson, 2011). In April 2015, ten Atlanta Public School teachers and administrators were convicted of racketeering. Eight were sentenced to prison, and two defendants chose to negotiate a lighter sentence in exchange for admission of guilt and an apology (E. Brown, 2015).

---

of its routine monitoring of social media for test security violations (Cavanagh, 2015; Gerwitz, 2015). Similar problems were reported in California (Associated Press, 2013). School personnel have an obligation to ensure that assessments are administered in accordance with the instructions provided by the producer and to supervise examinees with vigilance sufficient to prevent cheating and protect test security (*Standards* 6.1, 6.6, 6.7, 9.21, 9.22, 9.23). Cheating may result in sanctions for those involved.

School psychologists can assume important consultative roles related to districtwide testing programs, such as assisting administrators in making informed decisions regarding whether a particular testing or screening program is needed; assisting in the selection of tests and assessment tools that are technically adequate and valid for the intended purpose; assisting in the alignment of the curriculum with what is measured by the statewide achievement testing program tests; providing consultation on best practices in reporting data to parents and the community; and assisting in the identification of reasonable test accommodations for students with disabilities (Braden & Joyce, 2008; Braden & Tayrose, 2008; Niebling & Kurz, 2014). In addition, when high-stakes testing is required, practitioners might assist in the development of school guidelines for appropriate test proctoring practices to ensure that proctors understand their roles and responsibilities, including the obligation to establish appropriate testing conditions and supervise in ways that discourage cheating and violations of test security. Practitioners also can take part in efforts to improve student test-taking skills and raise awareness among students of the seriousness and potential consequences of cheating and disclosure of confidential test content (*Standards* 8.9). Finally, practitioners can work to foster a school climate that values truthfulness and honesty among those who administer tests and the students who take them.

Minimum Competency Testing

Minimum competency testing is the practice of requiring a student to achieve a certain score on a standardized test in order to be promoted or to receive a high school diploma (Medway & Rose, 1986). There have been a number of legal challenges to the policy of requiring students to pass an examination before they are awarded a high school diploma. *Debra P. v. Turlington* (1984) is probably the most important decision in this area.

In 1978, Florida passed legislation requiring high school seniors to pass a state-mandated competency test to receive a high school diploma. Students unable to pass the test were awarded a certificate of high school completion but not a diploma. *Debra P.* was a class action suit filed on behalf of African American students in the state of Florida. The plaintiffs argued that they had a property interest in receiving a diploma because students who do not receive one may not be accepted into college or trade school or the military, or be competitive for a well-paying job. Further, they claimed that use of the competency exam was a denial of the equal protection clause of the 14th Amendment because the test was discriminatory against African Americans.

The court ultimately upheld the right of the state to require students to pass a competency test to receive a diploma. The court identified several issues that must be addressed in evaluating whether such tests are legally permissible. The first is whether *adequate notice* exists, that is, an adequate phase-in period before the test is used to determine the award of a diploma. Other issues are whether the test has adequate curricular validity and whether the school can document acceptable instructional validity. *Curricular validity* addresses the question of whether the curriculum of the school matches what is measured by the test. *Instructional validity* is whether the students are, in fact, taught what is outlined in the curriculum, that is, whether the curriculum is implemented (Fischer & Sorenson, 1996; also *Debra P.*, 1984, p. 1408).

Legally, students with disabilities also may be required to pass a competency test to receive a high school diploma. The school must ensure that tests used with students who have disabilities are a valid measure of school achievement and that no student is penalized due to his or her disability (Fischer & Sorenson, 1996). Medway and Rose (1986) suggested that special education students who might be able to pass a high school competency test have appropriate instructional goals outlined in their IEPs and that teachers be able to document that adequate instruction was provided.

Screening to Identify Students "at Risk" for Harm to Self or Others

The use of districtwide screening programs to identify students at risk for harm to self or others raises several legal and ethical concerns. First, as systems-level consultants, school psychologists should ensure that the school district's protocol for such screenings meets ethical-legal requirements for consent and assent.[1] The Protection of Pupil Rights Amendment (2001, Pub. L. No. 107-110) requires schools that receive any federal funds to notify parents prior to administering a questionnaire or other measure to students that seeks information about mental or psychological problems potentially embarrassing to the student or his or her family (see Chapter 2). Parents must be given an opportunity to inspect the measure prior to its distribution and to remove their child from participation if they so desire. School psychologists also are ethically required to ensure that students are informed about the purpose of

---

[1]Portions of this text appeared in Jacob (2009).

the screening and who, in addition to their parents, will have access to the results. Note that if a teacher is conducting a behavior screening and reporting on "public" or visible student behavior, then neither parent notice nor consent would be required under federal law as long as the screening is not part of an assessment to determine that the student is suspected of having a disability under the Individuals with Disabilities Education Improvement Act of 2004 (IDEIA; see Chapter 7). However, prior parent notice of behavior screenings would be consistent with the goal of building open and positive parent–school communications.

Second, consistent with codes of ethics, school psychologists must consider whether screening results are valid, fair, and useful for identification of students at risk for harm to self or others and whether the potential benefits of such screenings outweigh possible harm. Although the emotional impact of student-on-student violence or student suicide is enormous, screening results are not highly predictive of suicide or targeted violence (e.g., Hanson, 2009; D. N. Miller & Eckert, 2009). Also, it is important for school psychologists to remember that students have a constitutional right to be free from unjustified stigmatization by the school. Consequently, the risk-benefit analysis of large-scale screenings must take into account the possibility that such screenings will result in harm to those students who are false positives (i.e., inaccurately identified as being at risk for violence), including the stigma and embarrassment of being subjected to an unnecessary follow-up mental health evaluation.

Third, school personnel have at times misunderstood the purpose and significance of mental health screening test results. Screening test scores alone do not have technical adequacy for decision making about individual students and should be used only to identify those students in need of further evaluation or for schoolwide needs-assessment purposes. School psychologists must help ensure that no student is "labeled" or treated differently from other students by teachers or school officials solely on the basis of screening test results.

Fourth, school personnel should be encouraged to consider the *incremental validity* of a mental health screening instrument—that is, "the extent to which an assessment method contributes to the understanding of an individual beyond that which is already known, as well as the degree to which it can provide information that cannot be gained in some other, easier way" (D. N. Miller & Nickerson, 2007, pp. 50–51). For example, in the Miami-Dade County Public Schools, a student intervention profile is developed for each student. This profile is based on a review of existing information about each student by school professionals in seven areas of concern, such as academic performance, effort, conduct, attendance, and involvement with school police (Zenere & Lazarus, 2009). Students identified as demonstrating difficulty in three or more areas are seen by a school counselor who assesses student needs and works in collaboration with a student support team to plan individualized interventions (e.g., counseling or more intensive mental health services) with the goal of reducing risk for suicidal behavior or violence toward others.

Finally, school psychologists must consider whether the school has access to the resources necessary to provide individualized evaluations of the students who are identified as at risk by large-scale screenings (Gutierrez & Osman, 2009). It is unethical to screen for risk of harm to self or others but then fail to provide individualized follow-up evaluation and intervention.

INSTRUCTIONAL PROGRAMS, POLICIES, AND PRACTICES

In this section, we explore legal issues associated with grade retention and delayed school entry, instructional grouping and disproportionality with regard to student race and ethnicity, and programs for ELLs and gifted and talented students.

Grade Retention

Grade retention, or nonpromotion, is the practice of requiring a student to repeat a grade due to poor academic achievement. A number of studies have found no lasting beneficial effect of grade retention (see Jimerson et al., 2006, for a review). Some research suggests that grade retention actually may be detrimental, especially in the areas of student self-concept and personal and social adjustment.

In general, the courts have preferred not to interfere with school promotion or retention decisions. However, the court considerations in *Sandlin v. Johnson* (1981) suggested that a decision to retain a child cannot be arbitrary; that is, the method for assignment to a particular grade must be reasonably related to the purpose of providing appropriate instruction and furthering education. Furthermore, any method of determining retention that results in a disproportionate representation by race or ethnicity among retained students may be scrutinized more closely as a possible denial of equal educational opportunities. School psychologists can assist in providing effective early intervention for students who are experiencing school difficulties and help ensure that retention is not used inappropriately. Alternatives to retention are discussed in Rafoth and Parker (2014).

Delayed School Entry

Public schools may not require that parents postpone kindergarten entry for a child that the school perceives to be "not ready" for kindergarten. After a child reaches the age of school eligibility, the child has a property interest (created by the state or local school board) in receiving a public school education. The legal reasoning of *Pennsylvania Association for Retarded Children (P.A.R.C.) v. Commonwealth of Pennsylvania* (1972) consent decree can be seen to apply in all school districts (Kirp, 1973); that is, public school districts must offer an education program to all children who are age-eligible for school entry in their district under the equal protection clause of the 14th Amendment. The education program must be offered at district expense, and no child can be turned away (see *P.A.R.C.*, 1972, p. 1262).

Instructional Grouping and Racial and Ethnic Disproportionality

With the landmark *Brown v. Board of Education* decision in 1954, the courts ruled that school segregation by race was a denial of the right to equal educational opportunity under the 14th Amendment. Following this decision, the courts began to scrutinize school practices that suggested within-school segregation—that is, where certain racial and ethnic groups were segregated and treated differently within the schools.

Instructional Grouping

A number of court cases were filed against the public schools in which African American children were overrepresented in the lower educational tracks and special education classes. *Hobson v. Hansen* (1967, 1969) was the first significant challenge to the disproportionate assignment of African American children to lower-ability tracks.[2] The judge in this case noted that the tracking system was rigid, the lower tracks offered inferior educational opportunities, and children were grouped on the basis of racially biased group ability tests. He ruled that the tracking system was a violation of the equal protection clause of the 14th Amendment and ordered the system abolished. He did not find that ability grouping was per se unconstitutional.

Consistent with the *Hobson v. Hansen* (1967, 1969) decision, court rulings in the 1990s found that grouping students by ability is not per se unconstitutional (*Georgia State Conference of Branches of NAACP v. State of Georgia*, 1985; *Simmons v. Hooks*, 1994). In these cases, the courts held that ability grouping that results in within-school racial segregation may be permissible if the school district can demonstrate that its grouping practices will remedy the results of past segregation by providing better educational opportunities for children. *Georgia* was a class action suit filed on behalf of African American students because of their disproportionate assignment to the lower-achievement groups, resulting in intraschool racial segregation. In this case, information about grouping practices showed that students typically were assigned to achievement rather than ability groups on the basis of a combination of factors, including assessment of skill level in a basal series, achievement test results, and teacher recommendations. In defending their grouping practices, the schools noted that the achievement groupings were flexible (students could move easily from one group to another) and likely to benefit students as instruction was matched to skill level. They also presented achievement data to show that students in the lower tracks did, in fact, benefit from the instructional grouping. The schools consequently were able to show that their grouping practices resulted in enhanced educational opportunities for African American students. The court found in favor of the schools.

Simmons (1994) involved a school district in which students were placed in whole-class ability tracks in kindergarten through third grade, with a disproportionate number of African American students placed in the low-ability classes. In grades 4 through 6, students were placed in heterogeneous classes, with within-class instructional grouping for reading, math, and language arts. The district was not able to show that whole-class ability grouping resulted in better educational opportunities for students in grades kindergarten through grade 3, and the court found this practice unconstitutionally segregative. The court did not find heterogeneous class assignment with within-class grouping for reading, math, and language arts unconstitutionally segregative.

In summary, the grouping practice that has raised the most concern is ability-grouped class assignment, in which students are assigned to self-contained classes based on ability. Research suggests that assignment to self-contained classes based

---

[2] Tracking involves assigning students to classes or a curriculum based on a measure of the student's academic potential, such his or her score on a group-administered IQ test score. Students are placed in classes with others of similar ability. Tracking was a more common practice in the 1950s and 1960s than it is today.

on ability level does not improve school achievement and may result in lowered self-esteem and educational aspirations for students placed in the lower tracks. School psychologists should be knowledgeable of the various types of instructional grouping and encourage the use of grouping methods that are in the best interests of all children (see R. P. Ross & Harrison, 2006).

Disproportionality in Special Education

The disproportionate representation of African American, Latino, Native American, and ELLs in special education has been documented as a persistent problem since the late 1960s (Hosp & Reschly, 2003; A. L. Sullivan, 2011). Overrepresentation can occur when the percentage of students in special education from a particular group is higher than one would expect based on that group's prevalence in a broader population, or it can occur when the rate of identification of a particular group of students is higher than the rate of identification for other groups of students (Skiba et al., 2008).

Disproportionality in special education is a complex problem with multiple factors contributing to its persistence (see Losen & Orfield, 2002, and Skiba et al., 2008, for reviews). The IDEIA requires states to take steps to prevent and reduce its occurrence. In particular, states must have policies and procedures in place to prevent the inappropriate overidentification or disproportionate representation by race or ethnicity of students with disabilities (34 CFR § 300.173). Each state that receives IDEIA—Part B funds must collect and examine special education data to determine if significant disproportionality is occurring at the state or local levels with respect to disability, placement in particular settings, or disciplinary actions (e.g., suspensions, expulsions) (34 CFR § 300.346[a]). If significant disproportionality is found, states must review and, if appropriate, revise the policies, practices, and procedures used in the identification and placement of students with disabilities. Local agencies that are found to have significant disproportionality must devote the maximum amount of funds (15% of IDEIA—Part B) to providing comprehensive coordinated early intervening services directed particularly (but not exclusively) toward children from groups found to be disproportionately represented (34 CFR § 300.646[b]).

Instructional Programs for English Language Learners

In 1974, the Supreme Court decided a landmark case, *Lau v. Nichols*, concerning the education of children who were ELLs. This case was based on a class action suit filed on behalf of non-English-speaking Chinese students in the San Francisco Unified School District. At that time, more than half of the Chinese students were ELLs but they were taught solely in English and no instruction was provided to help them learn the English language. Furthermore, proficiency in English was a requirement for high school graduation. The plaintiffs in this case claimed that the school's practice was a denial of equal opportunity under the 14th Amendment.

The case was decided on statutory grounds (Civil Rights Act of 1964) rather than the equal protection clause of the 14th Amendment. The 1964 Civil Rights Act prohibits discrimination in programs receiving federal assistance. In his decision in favor of the plaintiffs, Justice William O. Douglas wrote, "There is no equality of treatment merely by providing students with the same facilities, textbooks, teachers, and curriculum; for students who do not understand English are effectively foreclosed from meaningful education" (*Lau*, 1974, p. 566). *Lau* has been interpreted to mean that schools must provide assistance or "take affirmative steps" to ensure that students who are ELLs have access to a meaningful education. It is not interpreted as requiring bilingual instruction for each child who is an ELL.

Thus, no federal mandate requires bilingual education for a student who is an ELL. However, in 1968, the Bilingual Education Act was added as an amendment to the Elementary and Secondary Education Act of 1965 (ESEA) (Pub. L. No. 100-297), providing funds for bilingual education. The previous re-authorization of ESEA, namely NCLB, addressed the needs of ELL solely under Title III, a part of the law that authorizes funds to states for English language instruction. Although the Every Student Succeeds Act continues to fund English language acquisition programs under Title III, the law shifted *accountability* for students who are ELL to Title I. This means that states and schools will be held accountable for the English language acquisition and school performance of students who are English learners. Each state must adopt English language proficiency standards in speaking, listening, reading, and writing, and school districts must annually assess the English proficiency of all of their students who are English learners. In accordance with Title I accountability requirements, although some exceptions are allowed, English learners generally must take the same academic assessments (in English) used to measure the achievement of all students and state academic assessment results must be disaggregated by English proficiency status. States are not required to include the academic assessment scores of English-learning students who have arrived from other countries until those students have attended school in the U.S. for three or more consecutive years (excluding Puerto Rico) (Sec. 1111 [b]). Each state has the flexibility to implement the evidence- and place-based English language acquisition programs it believes to be most effective to ensure that "all English learners, including immigrant children and youth, attain English proficiency and develop high levels of academic achievement in English" (Sec. 3102 [1]) and to assist ELL to meet "the same challenging State academic standards that all children are expected to meet" (Sec. 3102 [2]). School psychologists who serve ELLs need to maintain up-to-date knowledge of best practices in assessment and instruction of ELLs.

Instructional Programs for Gifted and Talented Students

No federal legislation requires schools to provide specialized education to gifted and talented students. In 1988, the Jacob K. Javits Gifted and Talented Students Education Act was passed (part of ESEA). This legislation provided funds for programs designed to meet the special instructional needs of gifted and talented students. The Jacob K. Javits Gifted and Talented Students Education Act of 2001 (Pub. L. No. 107-110 §§ 5461–5466) reaffirmed the purposes of the 1988 Act. However, Congress did not approve funds for the Javits gifted and talented student programs in 2011 to 2013; $10 million was approved for 2015 (U.S. DOE, 2015). The ESSA again re-affirmed and authorized funds for the Jacob. K. Javits Gifted and Talented Students Education Program (see Sec. 4644).

Many disagreements exist regarding how to identify gifted and talented children and how to provide them with effective educational programs (see R. M. Gallagher, Caterino, & Bisa-Kendrick, 2014; Worrell & Erwin, 2011). School psychologists involved in the identification of gifted and talented students and the development of instructional programs are obligated to keep abreast of literature in this area.

SCHOOL DISCIPLINE

Under the general mandate to operate the public school, school officials have been given "a wide latitude of discretion" to fulfill their duty to maintain order, ensure student safety, and educate children (*Burnside v. Byars*, 1966, p. 748). Historically, school administrators and teachers were allowed to function quite autonomously in maintaining school and classroom discipline. In recent years, however, the courts have been called on to consider the constitutionality of school rules and disciplinary methods.

In considering the constitutionality of school rules, the courts generally have held that school rules and regulations must be a reasonable exercise of the power and discretion of the school's authority, related to the purpose of maintaining order and discipline (*Burnside*, 1966), and enforced in a nondiscriminatory manner. The courts also generally have held that school rules should be clearly stated and that the consequences for conduct code violations should be reasonably explicit. Students should be informed of expectations for appropriate conduct through written statements or instruction (Russo, 2012). The methods of school discipline that frequently have been the focus of judicial scrutiny include corporal punishment, suspension, and expulsion.

School discipline is the job responsibility of the building principal, not the school psychologist. However, because of their role as consultant to principals and teachers regarding mental health principles and students with behavior problems, practitioners need a sound working knowledge of the ethical-legal aspects of disciplinary practices.

Corporal Punishment

Why is it that school children remain the last Americans that can be legally beaten? (Messina, 1988, p. 108)

Corporal punishment by the teacher or other school official generally is defined as the infliction of pain on the body as a penalty for conduct disapproved of by the punisher. Forms of corporal punishment include spanking, beating, whipping, gagging, punching, shoving, knuckle rapping, arm twisting, shaking, and ear and hair pulling (Gershoff, Holas, & Purtell, 2015; Hyman, 1990). Social science evidence suggests that corporal punishment in the schools can be psychologically harmful to children and that alternative approaches to maintaining school discipline are preferable and more effective. Furthermore, children throughout the country have suffered severe and sometimes permanent physical injuries as a result of corporal punishment administered in the schools, including injuries to the head, neck, spine, kidneys, and genitals; perforated eardrums and hearing loss; facial and body scars; and chipped teeth (Hyman, 1990). Unfortunately, the use of corporal punishment is a disciplinary practice that has a long history in American schools and, even today, many southern states continue to permit its use with schoolchildren (Gershoff et al., 2015).

The following subsections summarize case law and statutory law regarding corporal punishment and then discuss the role of the school psychologist in promoting alternatives to corporal punishment.

Case Law

Historically, English common law viewed teachers as having the authority to use corporal punishment under the doctrine of in loco parentis. According to this doctrine, a child's father delegated part of his parental authority to the tutor or schoolmaster. The tutor or schoolmaster then "stood in the place of the parent" and was permitted to use "restraint and correction" as needed to teach the child (Gersoff et al., 2015). In the United States, the notion that educators have the authority to use corporal punishment under the common law doctrine of in loco parentis dates back to colonial times, but it has been replaced gradually with the view that the state (school) has the right to administer corporal punishment because of the school's legitimate interest in maintaining order for the purpose of education.

Baker v. Owen (1975) raised the question of whether the parent can "undelegate," or take away, the school's authority to use corporal punishment. In this case, Mrs. Baker told the school principal she did not want her son, Russell, corporally punished because he was a fragile child. Following a minor school infraction, his teacher took a drawer divider and spanked him with it twice, causing some bruises. Mrs. Baker filed a complaint in federal court alleging that her fundamental right to the care, control, and custody of her child had been violated when the school used corporal punishment despite her prohibition. The court in *Baker* held that the school's interest in maintaining order by the use of reasonable corporal punishment outweighs parents' rights to determine the care and control of their child, including how a student shall be disciplined. Under this ruling, schools were free to use reasonable corporal punishment for disciplinary purposes, despite parental objections to the practice.

In *Ingraham v. Wright*, a 1977 Supreme Court ruling, the parents of two schoolchildren contended that corporal punishment was a violation of a child's basic constitutional rights. The Court in *Ingraham* agreed to consider whether corporal punishment in the schools is "cruel and unusual punishment" under the Eighth Amendment, the extent to which paddling is constitutionally permissible, and whether paddling requires due process protection under the 14th Amendment.

The Court found that corporal punishment to maintain discipline in the schools does not fall under the "cruel and unusual punishment" prohibition of the Eighth Amendment because the amendment was designed to protect those accused of crimes. The Court noted that "the schoolchild has little need for the protection of the Eighth Amendment" because the openness of the schools and supervision by the community afford significant safeguards from the abuse of corporal punishment by teachers (*Ingraham*, 1977, p. 669).

Justice Powell, who wrote the majority opinion, acknowledged that the 14th Amendment protects the right to be free from unjustified intrusions on personal security and that liberty interests are "implicated" if punishment is unreasonable.

However, he went on to state that "there can be no deprivation of substantive rights as long as disciplinary corporal punishment is within the limits of common law privilege" (*Ingraham*, 1977, p. 675) and held that due process safeguards do not apply. Thus, the Supreme Court in *Ingraham* found that corporal punishment of schoolchildren is not unconstitutional per se. However, the opinion left unanswered the question of whether corporal punishment *is ever* unconstitutional.

Subsequent decisions at the level of the U.S. Circuit Court of Appeals suggest that excessive corporal punishment is likely to be viewed as unconstitutional in most, but not all, federal circuit courts. For example, in *Hall v. Tawney* (1980) and *Garcia by Garcia v. Miera* (1987), the parents of schoolchildren filed Section 1983 civil rights lawsuits against school officials after their children were severely beaten as part of disciplinary actions. The actions of the school personnel in these cases were seen as a violation of the substantive rights of the child to be free of state intrusions into realms of personal privacy and bodily security through means the court viewed as so "brutal and demeaning" as to "shock the conscience of the court." In *Neal v. Fulton County Board of Education* (2000), a high school student was struck in the head with a metal weight lock by a football coach as punishment for misconduct. The blow knocked the student's eye out of its socket and permanently blinded him in that eye. Consistent with the *Hall* and *Garcia* cases, the federal circuit court in *Neal* held that the school's actions were a violation of the student's substantive due process right to be free from excessive corporal punishment.

Case 9.2 provides an example of a different outcome. Do you think the case was decided 20 or 30 years ago, or do you think this is a contemporary case? Look in the Appendix C: Table of Cases for the answer.

Statutory Law

As of 2015, 31 states had adopted legislation or issued regulations banning the use of corporal punishment in public schools (Gunderson National Child Protection Agency, 2015). Most state laws that prohibit corporal punishment allow teachers and others in the school setting to use reasonable physical restraint as necessary to protect people from immediate physical danger or to protect property. Michigan's law, for example, allows an individual to use reasonable physical force for self-defense and in defense of others, to prevent self-injury, to obtain a weapon, and to restrain or remove a disruptive student who refuses to refrain from further disruptive behaviors when told to do so (Public Act 521 as amended by Act No. 6 of the Public Acts of 1992).

School psychology practitioners can work to abolish corporal punishment by promoting alternatives to its use through in-service training and consultation (see the section titled "Schoolwide Positive Behavior Support Systems," this chapter). They also may serve an important role by sensitizing school staff to the potential legal sanctions for the use of corporal punishment. The use of corporal punishment can be costly to the principal or teacher in terms of time and legal defense fees, even if he or she is ultimately found innocent of any wrongdoing. In districts that have banned the use of corporal punishment, its use is likely to result in disciplinary action by the local school board, possibly including suspension or loss of employment. Even in states that allow the use of corporal punishment in the schools, parents who are upset by its use with

---

Case 9.2

"Tom" (not his real name) Clayton, a student in eighth grade, found another student sitting in his assigned seat when he arrived for English class. As a result, he chose a different seat. His English teacher subsequently sent him to the school library to discipline him for not sitting in his assigned seat. In the library, the assistant principal, Mr. Martin, reprimanded Tom for his noncompliant behavior. Mr. Martin, who appeared to be "angry and agitated," told Tom to follow him to his office, where Mr. Martin struck Tom "three times on the buttocks with a paddle" with "excessive and great force." The paddling "left visible bruising and welts on Clayton's buttocks, which were visible days thereafter." Immediately after being paddled, Tom fainted and fell face-first onto the concrete floor. "When Clayton regained consciousness he was bleeding, five of his teeth were shattered, and, it was later determined, his jaw was broken" (*Clayton v. Tate County School District*, ****, p. 295). Tom's mother filed a Section 1983 lawsuit against the school and Mr. Martin in federal court, claiming, among other claims, that Mr. Martin's actions violated Tom's constitutional right to be free from excessive corporal punishment by the school. Citing *Ingraham v. Wright* (1977) and case precedent in the Fifth Circuit, the federal court judge dismissed all of Tom's claims.

Source: Adapted from *Clayton v. Tate County School District*, ****; an unpublished decision.

---

their child may pursue several courses of legal action. The majority of corporal punishment cases are filed in state courts under charges of battery, assault and battery, or negligent battery. Parents also may file a complaint under state child abuse laws. In addition, a number of parents have filed actions in federal court under Section 1983 (Henderson, 1986).

Suspension and Expulsion

Schools have been given the authority to suspend or expel students to maintain order and carry out the purpose of education. *Short-term suspension* typically is defined as an exclusion of 10 days or less from school or from participation in classes and activities (in-school suspension). In most districts, school principals are given the authority to suspend students. *Expulsion* means exclusion of the student for a period longer than 10 consecutive school days or the equivalent, with "equivalent" determined by factors such as the number and proximity of excluded days (Hindman, 1986). Student expulsion usually requires action by the school board.

The specific grounds for disciplinary suspensions and expulsions vary from state to state. School codes are likely to allow suspension or expulsion of students guilty of persistent noncompliance with school rules and directives, weapon- and drug-related offenses, repeated use of obscene language, stealing or vandalizing property on school grounds, and using violence or encouraging the use of violence (Hindman, 1986;

Russo, 2012). The NCLB gun-free schools requirement is re-designated as Sec. 8561 in ESSA. This legislation requires each state receiving federal funds under the Act to have in effect a state law requiring schools to expel for a period of not less than one year a student who brings a firearm to school. However, the law must allow the chief school administrator to modify the expulsion requirement on a case-by-case basis, and states may allow students expelled from their regular schools to receive educational services in an alternative setting.

In 1975, *Goss v. Lopez* was decided by the Supreme Court. This case was filed on behalf of several high school students suspended without any sort of formal or informal due process hearing. The Court ruled that because education is a state-created property right, a school may not suspend or expel students without some sort of due process procedures to protect students from arbitrary or wrongful infringement of their interests in schooling. In writing the majority opinion, Justice White outlined the minimal due process procedures required for suspensions of 10 days or less:

> Students facing temporary suspension have interest qualifying for protection of the Due Process Clause, and due process requires, in connection with a suspension of 10 days or less, that the student be given oral or written notice of the charges against him and, if he denies them, an explanation of the evidence the authorities have and an opportunity to present his side of the story. The Clause requires at least these rudimentary precautions against unfair or mistaken findings of misconduct and arbitrary exclusion from school. (p. 581)

Justice White further noted that "longer suspensions or expulsions for the remainder of the school term, or permanently, may require more formal procedures" (p. 584). He also noted that, generally, the notice and hearing should precede the removal of the student from the school. However, students "whose presence poses a continuing danger to persons or property or an ongoing threat of disrupting the academic process may be immediately removed from school. In such cases, the necessary notice and rudimentary hearing should follow as soon as practicable" (pp. 582–583).

When immediate removal of a student is under consideration, it is important to remember that suspension may serve as a trigger for suicide attempts or violence against others. Consequently, parents should be notified if it is necessary to remove their child from school, and students who are suspended during the school day should not be sent home to an empty house (see *Armijo v. Wagon Mound Public Schools*, 1998).

It is also important to note that, because of concerns about school district reliance on suspension and expulsion to discipline students, the ESSA requires states to identify how they will support local school districts in efforts to reduce "the overuse of discipline practices that remove students from the classroom" (Sec. 1111 [g][1][C][ii]; Sec. 1112 [b][11]). Furthermore, research indicates that African American and Latino students are disproportionately affected by punitive school discipline practices. Skiba et al. (2011) found that these students were more likely to receive an expulsion or out-of-school suspension than their White counterparts for the same or similar behavior. School psychologists can advocate for evidence-based alternatives to suspension that have been effective in reducing problem behaviors and teaching students appropriate behaviors (Chin, Dowdy, Jimerson, & Rime, 2012; "Schoolwide Positive Behavior Support Systems," this chapter).

Suspension and Expulsion of Students With Disabilities

When Congress passed Pub. L. No. 94-142 in 1975, it was recognized that schools might rely on suspension and expulsion policies to exclude children with disabilities from public schools, particularly students with emotional and behavioral difficulties. Consequently, IDEIA includes special protections with regard to disciplinary removals of children with disabilities.

Disciplinary Removals. The IDEIA—Part B regulations regarding disciplinary removals of students with disabilities are complex; only a brief overview of the federal regulations is provided here.[3]

Disciplinary Removals for 10 Days or Less. The IDEIA allows school officials to remove a child with a disability who violates a student conduct code from his or her current placement to an appropriate interim alternative educational setting, another setting, or suspension for not more than 10 consecutive school days to the extent that those alternatives are applied to children without disabilities (34 CFR § 300.530[b][1]). A school is not required to provide services to a child with a disability who has been removed from his or her current placement for 10 school days or less in the school year, if services are not provided to children without disabilities who have been similarly removed (34 CFR § 300.530[d][3]).

Additional Removals. It is helpful for practitioners to be familiar with the term *change of placement because of disciplinary removals* before reading the text that follows. A change of placement occurs if:

(1) The removal is for more than 10 consecutive school days; or
(2) The child has been subjected to a series of removals that constitute a pattern—
   (i) Because the series of removals total more than 10 school days in a school year;
   (ii) Because the child's behavior is substantially similar to the child's behavior in previous incidents that resulted in the series of removals; and
   (iii) Because of such additional factors as the length of each removal, the total amount of time the child has been removed, and the proximity of the removals to one another. (34 CFR § 300.536[a][b])

The IDEIA provides schools with the flexibility to consider any unique circumstances on a case-by-case basis when determining whether a change in placement is appropriate for a child with a disability following a disciplinary infraction (34 CFR § 300.530[a]). More specifically, the law permits additional removals of not more than 10 consecutive school days in the same school year for separate incidents of misconduct as long as the child has not been subject to a series of removals that constitute a pattern indicative of a change of placement (34 CFR § 300.530[b][1]). However, after a child

---

[3]Readers may wish to locate their state's flow chart on discipline of special education students or download the one available from Massachusetts: www.doe.mass.edu/sped/IDEA2004/spr_meetings/disc_chart.pdf

with a disability has been removed from his or her current placement for more than 10 school days in the same school year, during any subsequent days of removal, the school must provide education services so as to enable the child to continue to participate in the general curriculum, although in another setting, and to progress toward meeting his or her IEP goals and receive, as appropriate, a functional behavioral assessment and behavioral intervention services to address the behavior violation so that it does not recur (34 CFR § 300.530[b][2], [d]).

If the current removal is not a change of placement, school personnel, in consultation with at least one of the child's teachers, determine the extent to which services are needed to enable the child to continue to participate in the general education curriculum, although in another setting, and to progress toward meeting the goals set out in the child's IEP (34 CFR § 300.530[d][4]). If the removal is determined to be a change of placement, the child's IEP team decides what services are appropriate.

Manifest Determination Review.   If a disciplinary action is contemplated as a result of weapons, drugs, or potential injury to self or others, or if a disciplinary action involving a change of placement is contemplated for a child with a disability who engaged in behavior that violated any school rule or code, a manifest determination review must be conducted. This review is conducted by the IEP team, including the parents, within 10 days of the decision to change the placement of a child with a disability because of a violation of a code of student conduct. For the purpose of a manifest determination, the IEP team reviews all relevant information in the student's file, including the child's IEP, teacher observations, and information provided by the parents, to determine if the conduct in question was caused by, or had a direct and substantial relationship to, the child's disability, or if the conduct in question was the direct result of the district's failure to implement the IEP (34 CFR § 300.530[e]). School psychologists should not share information at the manifest determination review that was disclosed within the context of a school psychologist–client relationship with the expectation it would be held in confidence by the psychologist unless the parent grants permission to do so (see Chapter 3). Readers are referred to Kubick and Lavik (2014) for additional information on manifestation determination reviews.

When Misconduct Is a Manifestation of a Disability.   If the IEP team determines that the disciplinary infraction was caused by the child's disability or failure to implement the IEP, the conduct is considered to be a manifestation of the child's disability. Furthermore, if the disciplinary infraction is determined to be a manifestation of the child's disability, the IEP team is required to conduct a functional behavioral assessment and implement a behavior intervention plan for the child (34 CFR § 300.530[f][1][i]).

If the child had a behavior plan prior to the disciplinary action, the IEP team is required to review the plan and modify it as necessary to address the problem behavior. The child is returned to the placement from which he or she was removed, unless the parent and school agree to a change of placement as part of the modification of the behavioral intervention plan, or special circumstances exist (34 CFR § 300.530[f][1–2]).

When Misconduct Is Not a Manifestation of a Disability. If, as a result of the manifestation review, it is determined that behavior of the child with a disability was not a manifestation of the child's disability, the relevant disciplinary procedures applicable to children without disabilities may be applied to the child in the same manner that they would be applied to other children (e.g., long-term suspension), except that children with disabilities under IDEIA must continue to receive a free appropriate public education (34 CFR § 300.530[c–d]). Educational services must be provided to enable the child to continue to participate in the general education curriculum, although in another setting, and to continue to progress toward meeting the goals set out in the child's IEP and receive, as appropriate, a functional behavioral assessment and interventions designed to address the behavior violation so that it does not recur. Services are determined by the IEP team. Schools may discontinue educational services to students who qualify as having a disability under Section 504 but who are not also eligible for special education under IDEIA, as long as nondisabled students receive identical treatment ("Discipline under Section 504," 1996).

Special Circumstances. School officials may order placement of a child with a disability into an appropriate interim alternative educational setting (IAES) for not more than 45 days if the child: carried a weapon to school or to a school function; inflicted serious bodily injury on another person while at school, on school premises, or at a school function; or knowingly possessed or used illegal drugs or sold or solicited the sale of a controlled substance while at school or a school function. Placement in an IAES for these reasons can be made without regard to whether the behavior is determined to be a manifestation of the child's disability (34 CFR § 300.530[g]). Parents must be notified on the date that the decision is made to make a removal that constitutes a change of placement of a child with a disability because of a violation of a code of student conduct and must be provided with the procedural safeguards notice (34 CFR § 300.530[h]). The interim alternative setting is determined by the IEP team (34 CFR § 300.531).

Appeals. The parent of a child with a disability who disagrees with any decision regarding placement or the manifest determination, or a school that believes that maintaining a child's current placement is likely to result in injury to the child or others, may request a hearing (34 CFR § 300.532[a]). A hearing officer makes a determination regarding the appeal. The officer may return a child with a disability to the placement from which the child was removed or order a change in placement to an appropriate interim alternative setting for not more than 45 school days if he or she determines that maintaining the current placement is substantially likely to result in injury to the child or others (34 CFR § 300.532[a][2]).

The school is responsible for arranging an expedited due process hearing, which must occur within 20 school days of the date the complaint requesting the hearing is filed. The hearing officer must make a determination within 10 school days after the hearing (34 CFR § 300.532[c][2]). During an appeal, the child remains in the interim alternative setting pending the decision of the hearing officer or until the expiration of the 45-day time limit, whichever comes first, unless the parent and school agree otherwise (34 CFR § 300.533).

Changes to the manifest determination criteria in the IDEIA 2004 regulations have resulted in less protection for students with disabilities. In a review of all the published hearing and review officer and court decisions that applied the manifest determination provisions of IDEIA, Zirkel (2010, 2015) found that case law tended to rule that the child's behavior was not a manifestation of his or her disability. School psychologists can assist students who exhibit challenging behaviors by implementing evidence-based practices to reduce the likelihood of disciplinary infractions and by educating others on the disadvantages of removing students with disabilities from school settings (see "Schoolwide Positive Behavior Support Systems," this chapter, and Kubick & Lavik, 2014).

Protections for Children Not Yet Eligible for Special Education. A child who has not been determined to be eligible for special education and who engaged in behavior that violated any school rule or code may seek IDEIA protections by asserting that the school knew the child had a disability before the behavior leading to disciplinary action occurred. The school is "deemed to have knowledge" that a child has a disability if: (a) the parents had expressed concern in writing that their child is in need of special education, (b) the parents requested an evaluation of the child, or (c) the teacher or other school personnel expressed concern about the child to the special education director or by making a referral (34 CFR § 300.534[b]). If a request is made for evaluation of a child during the time the child is subjected to disciplinary measures, the evaluation will be conducted in an expedited manner, and if found eligible, the child will receive special education and related services (34 CFR § 300.534[d][2]).

Monitoring of Suspension and Expulsion Rates. Under IDEIA, states are required to collect and examine data to determine if significant discrepancies are occurring in the rate of long-term suspensions and expulsions of children with disabilities among school districts or compared to the rates for children without disabilities. If discrepancies are occurring, the state educational agency must review and, if appropriate, revise policies, procedures, and practices related to the development and implementation of IEPs, the use of behavioral interventions, and procedural safeguards (34 CFR § 300.170).

Schoolwide Positive Behavior Support Systems

School discipline strategies that emphasize punishment for misconduct, including corporal punishment and suspension and expulsion, "may stop a problem temporarily, but are rarely effective in producing long-lasting [positive] behavior changes and do not teach students to engage in desired behaviors." The schoolwide positive behavior interventions and support system (SWPBIS) is an alternative to traditional punitive school discipline approaches. SWPBIS is an evidence-based set of strategies that focus on creating "school environments that promote and support [the] appropriate behavior of all students" and in all situations (McKevitt & Fynaardt, 2014, p. 165; also see Bear, 2008). SWPBIS strategies generally are considered to be ethically and legally sound, and their use is supported by the U.S. Department of Education (DOE) as a means of preventing the school exclusion of students with challenging behaviors (OSEP Technical Assistance Center, 2015). However, one question that has been raised is whether parent consent is required for schoolwide implementation of SWPBIS and the monitoring of students' behaviors. In response to a letter of inquiry, the Office of

Special Education Programs indicated that parent consent would not be required when SWPBIS is used to improve behavior in the entire school unless the school decides to require consent from all parents (Musgrove, 2013). Schoolwide notice is advisable in the interest of "transparency" and fostering positive school–parent relationships.

DISCRIMINATION, HARASSMENT, AND BULLYING

School psychologists "assume a proactive role in identifying social injustices that affect children and schools and strive to reform systems-level patterns of injustice" (NASP-PPE IV). In this section, we address discrimination against, and harassment of, students who are members of classes legally protected by interpretations of the U.S. Constitution and federal antidiscrimination law. Because of continuing concerns, our focus is on discrimination and harassment based on sexual orientation, gender identity, and gender expression; race; and religion. Discrimination and harassment based on disability was discussed in Chapter 5. This section closes with a brief discussion of law pertinent to the protection of all students from bullying.

Discrimination and Harassment: LGBT Students

Schools can be cruel and dangerous places for students who are lesbian, gay, biattractional, or transgender or who simply do not conform to gender-role stereotypes (hereafter "LGBT") (Kosciw, Greytak, Diaz, & Bartkiewicz, 2010). LGBT students are more likely than their non-LGBT peers to report being threatened or injured with a weapon at school, to have their property damaged at school, and to stay home from school or drop out because of feeling unsafe (Massachusetts Department of Education, 2006). Despite media attention to incidents of physical assault on LGBT youth and suicides triggered by student-on-student harassment, many school districts have not taken steps to reduce the bullying of youth who do not conform to gender-role expectations.[4]

Lawsuits Based on the 14th Amendment

Federal statutory law does not explicitly prohibit discrimination in the public schools based on sexual orientation, gender identity, or gender expression. Consequently, early efforts to address the problem of discrimination against LGBT students were based on the equal protection clause of the 14th Amendment of the Constitution. For example, in *Massey v. Banning* (2003), Ashley, a 14-year-old student, was permanently barred from the girl's locker room and from participating in gym class after the gym teacher overheard Ashley identify herself as a lesbian. Ashley's parents filed a lawsuit against the school alleging that the school's actions violated Ashley's constitutional right to equal educational opportunity under the 14th Amendment. A federal court ruled the case would not be dismissed, noting "school officials who engage in such sexual orientation-based *discrimination*" (emphasis added) could be held liable under Section 1983 (p. 15).

---

[4]Portions of this section appeared in Jacob (2013).

Similarly, early lawsuits concerning harassment of LGBT students were based on the claim that a school's failure to protect an LGBT youth from harassment to the same extent that the school protected other students from harassment was an unconstitutional violation of the 14th Amendment's equal protection clause. Case 9.3 summarizes one of the best-known lawsuits based on the claim that a school's failure to stop the repeated victimization of a gay student was a violation of his constitutional right to equal protection.

Case 9.3

In 1996, the U.S. Court of Appeals for the Seventh Circuit issued its ruling in *Nabozny v. Podlesny*. The case concerned Jamie, a boy who was harassed continually and physically abused by his fellow students throughout his middle school and high school years because he was homosexual. Classmates referred to him as "faggot" and "queer." In seventh grade, two students performed a mock rape on him in science class in front of 20 other students who looked on and laughed. When Jamie reported the incident, the principal told him that "boys will be boys" and that he should expect such treatment from his fellow students if he was going to be openly gay. No action was taken against the students involved. In eighth and ninth grades, Jamie suffered assaults in the school bathroom, including an incident in which he was pushed into a urinal and urinated on by his attackers. In 10th grade, he was pelted with steel nuts and bolts. That same year, he was beaten in school by eight boys while other students looked on and laughed. When Jamie reported the incident, the school official in charge of discipline laughed and told him that he deserved such treatment because he was gay. Jamie later collapsed from internal bleeding that resulted from the beating. Although a school counselor encouraged administrators to take steps to protect Jamie and discipline the perpetrators, nothing was done. For more than four years, Jamie and his parents repeatedly asked school officials to protect him and to punish his assailants. Despite the fact that the school had a policy of investigating and punishing student-on-student sexual harassment, the administrators turned a deaf ear to Jamie's requests. Jamie eventually filed suit against several school officials and the district under Section 1983, alleging, among other claims, that his 14th Amendment rights to equal protection had been violated by school officials because they denied him the protection extended to other students. The court concluded that it would allow a lawsuit for damages against school officials because, if the facts presented were true, school officials had violated Jamie's 14th Amendment right to equal protection by failing to protect him from harassment to the same extent as other students because he was gay. The court also concluded that the law establishing the defendant's liability was sufficiently clear for the defendants to know that their conduct was unconstitutional. Jamie Nabozny was ultimately awarded nearly $1 million.

Federal Antidiscrimination Law

Title IX of the Educational Amendments of 1972 allows schools to receive federal funds on the condition the school protects its students from discriminatory practices based on gender. It is administered by the U.S. DOE OCR. Sexual harassment is a form of discrimination prohibited by Title IX when such harassment interferes with a student's right to equal educational opportunity. After receiving notice of a violation, the OCR may order a school district to engage in remedial actions to correct the discrimination. If voluntary compliance cannot be achieved through informal actions, the OCR may take steps to suspend federal funding to the school.

In *Gebser v. Lago Vista Independent School District* (1998), the Supreme Court considered the remedies that should be available under Title IX to a student who was sexually harassed by a school employee and concluded Title IX does not allow recovery of monetary damages solely because of a school's failure to comply with the DOE's Title IX administrative requirements. However, Title IX confers a right of private action; that is, students who are victims of sexual harassment may seek to hold school officials or the district liable for monetary damages through lawsuits under Section 1983 or state law. In *Gebser*, the Court noted that federal agencies, such as the DOE, have the power to "promulgate and enforce requirements that effectuate [Title IX's] nondiscrimination mandate" (*Gebser,* p. 292) that extend beyond events and circumstances that would give rise to a claim for money damages (OCR, 2001, p. ii; *Gebser,* p. 292). *The OCR thus has the authority to craft detailed regulations for compliance with Title IX and reduce the flow of federal funds to schools that refuse to comply. The courts, however, determine the legal tests that must be met before a school official or district school can be held liable for monetary damages in a Title IX lawsuit filed by a victim of sexual harassment under Section 1983 or state law. Gebser* also held that, before a school district and/or administrators can be held responsible for sexual harassment, the district must have actual knowledge of the harassment. This replaced previous "knew or should have known" language.

In 1999, the U.S. Supreme Court decided *Davis v. Monroe County Board of Education*, a Title IX lawsuit filed against school officials under Section 1983. The case was brought by the mother of a girl who, as a fifth grader, was subjected to a prolonged pattern of sexual harassment by one of her male classmates. The unwanted sexual advances included attempts to touch the girl's breasts and genital areas. The teacher and school administrators did not respond to complaints from the girl or her mother, and the school did not take steps to stop the harassment by disciplining the boy or separating the two (e.g., changing the girl's seat in class so she did not have to sit next to him).

In *Davis*, the Supreme Court ruled that Title IX applies to student-on-student sexual harassment, and the Court ruled in favor of the victim. The opinion stated that "damages are not available for simple acts of teasing and name-calling among school children" but rather for behavior "so severe, pervasive, and objectively offensive" (p. 652) that it denies its victims the equal access to education as guaranteed under Title IX.

OCR Interprets Title IX to Include LGBT Students

In 2001, the U.S. DOE's OCR published an updated *Sexual Harassment Guidance* document that extended its interpretation of Title IX to include LGBT students. The legal underpinnings for doing so included the Supreme Court decisions in *Davis* (1999) (i.e., student-on-student harassment can result in a denial of equal educational opportunities) and its interpretations of the meaning of *sexual harassment* in cases from employment settings. For example, in *Oncale v. Sundowner Offshore Services* (1998), the Supreme Court held that *same-sex sexual harassment* in the workplace is in violation of federal laws that prohibit discrimination on the basis of sex. In *Price Waterhouse v. Hopkins* (1989), the Court held that *harassment based on gender stereotyping is harassment based on sex*. Finally, in *Harris v. Forklift Systems* (1993), the Court held that a work *environment that is hostile* to an employee because of his or her gender violates antidiscrimination law.

In a 2010 "Dear Colleague Letter" (DCL), the OCR clarified that, as part of national efforts to reduce bullying in schools and to ensure equal educational opportunity for all students, the OCR now explicitly interprets Title IX as protecting *all* students from gender-based harassment. Title IX thus makes schools that receive any federal funds responsible for taking reasonable steps to remedy student-on-student harassment based on gender when it is sufficiently severe, pervasive, *or* persistent so as to interfere with or limit the ability of an individual to participate in or benefit from the district's programs or activities. The DCL stated the OCR interprets Title IX to prohibit gender-based harassment "of both male and female students regardless of the sex of the harasser—i.e., even if the harasser and target are of the same sex" (Ali, 2010, p. 7). The DCL also stated that Title IX is interpreted as protecting students from harassment based on nonconformity to gender-role stereotypes. Furthermore, if harassment based on gender or nonconformity to gender-role stereotypes results in *a hostile learning environment* for a student, schools "have an obligation to take immediate and effective action to eliminate the hostile environment" (p. 8). Public school administrators, school psychologists, and teachers should be aware that, in recent years, the OCR has aggressively pursued complaints regarding discrimination against, and harassment of, LGBT students in the schools. These investigations result in public documents that detail the actions—or inaction—by various named school professionals.

Consistent with OCR guidance, school districts are advised to have written policies to ensure that all students are free from discrimination, harassment, and bullying. However, in developing and applying policies to prevent discrimination and harassment, schools must take care to avoid violating student First Amendment rights to free speech and expression. (See U.S. DOE & Bias Crimes Task Force of the National Association of Attorneys General, 1999, for guidance in developing appropriate policies.) For example, in *Glowacki v. Howell Public School District* (2013, 2014, an unpublished case), a high school teacher recognized "Anti-Bullying Day" by beginning his classes with a video about a youth who committed suicide after being bullied because he was gay and a class discussion about bullying. In one of his classes, a student stated multiple times that he did not accept gays because he is Catholic. The teacher ultimately told the boy to leave the class and go to the office. The parents of the student who made the religious-based antigay comments subsequently filed a section 1983 lawsuit against the school district. Citing *Tinker v. Des Moines Independent County School District* (1969), the court ruled that the student's First Amendment right to freedom of speech had been violated and awarded the parents $1.00 in nominal damages.

Discrimination and Harassment: Race and Religion

Discrimination against, and harassment of, students due to race and religion continues to be a problem in the public schools.

Case 9.4 particularly is important because it put school districts "on notice" that simply disciplining the perpetrators following incidents of harassment is not likely to be viewed by the courts as an adequate response to repeated harassment of a student protected by civil rights law.

Lawsuits claiming discrimination and harassment due to a student's religion appear to be somewhat less common than claims of racial harassment. Citing *Nabozny v. Podlesny* (1996), the courts have held that school district indifference to persistent harassment and bullying of a student due to his or her religion is a violation of the 14th Amendment's equal protection clause (e.g., *Shively v. Green Local School District*, 2014). In addition, the OCR also specifically extended its protections to include harassment and discrimination based on a student's religion (Ali, 2010).

Bullying

Federal antidiscrimination law only explicitly protects students from harassment and bullying based on race, color, or national origin, sex, or disability. The OCR's interpretations of antidiscrimination law have extended protection to include harassment and bullying based on LGBT status and religion. However, "students can be bullied for many reasons that do not fall into the conventional categories of civil rights protection" (Cornell & Limber, 2015, p. 341). As of 2015, all 50 states had adopted antibullying laws and/or policies (U. S. Department of Health and Human Services, 2015b), but it is not clear whether these initiatives have impacted local school practices. The ESSA requires states to identify how they will support local school districts in efforts "to improve school conditions for student learning by reducing incidences of bullying and harassment" (Sec. 1111 [g][1][C][i]; Sec. 1112 [b][11]). This provision will likely provide further impetus for states and schools to take steps to prevent and address bullying of any student regardless of the reason.

School psychologists have an ethical responsibility to help ensure that *all* youth have equal opportunities to attend school, learn, and develop their personal identities in an environment free from discrimination, harassment, violence, and abuse (NASP-PPE I.3.4, IV.1; Felix, Green, & Sharkey, 2014). Recent years have witnessed substantial growth in the literature on bullying prevention (e.g., Bradshaw, 2015; Felix et al., 2014; S. W. Ross & Horner, 2014; Rossen & Cowan, 2012; Swearer & Hymel, 2015), including

========== **Case 9.4** ==========

Soon after Anthony Zeno enrolled in the ninth grade at Stissing Mountain High School, he became a target of racial harassment. Anthony, a dark-skinned boy who is half White and half Latino, was one of a small number of non-White students at the school. The harassment began when "a student—a stranger to Anthony—charged toward him screaming that he would 'rip [Anthony's] face off and … kick [Anthony's] ass,' and that 'we don't want your kind here.' Other students held the aggressor back, while unidentified students call Anthony a 'nigger' and told him to go back to where he came from." When Anthony's mother expressed her concerns to the principal, his response was "this is a small town and … you don't want to start burning your bridges." For the remainder of the year, Anthony was subject to continuing verbal racial epithets, threats of violence, and vandalism of his property (*Zeno v. Pine Plains Central School District*, 2012, p. 659). The harassment escalated during Anthony's second year at the school. Incidents included graffiti in the boy's bathroom warning "Zeno is dead," a homemade CD circulated among students using racial insults, threats that Anthony would be lynched, attempted physical assaults, and repeated vandalism of his locker. These incidents were reported to school officials, who responded by disciplining the students involved with a warning or short-term suspension. However, the harassment continued for more than three years. The school principal never took any proactive steps to end the harassment, and school officials made no meaningful attempts to improve the school environment for Anthony. Although Anthony was making progress toward a high school diploma, his family made the difficult choice for him to accept a special education diploma so that he could graduate with fewer credits "rather than endure further harassment." As noted in the court opinion, students with a special education diploma "can attend certain community colleges, but employers, the military, four-year colleges, apprenticeship programs, and business or trade schools generally do not accept them" (p. 663).

Anthony filed a Section 1983 lawsuit against the school district claiming that the district violated Title VI of the Civil Rights Act of 1964 by allowing other students to racially harass him for more than three years. The district court found the harassment to be severe and pervasive but opined that the school district was not deliberately indifferent to the harassment because it disciplined individual harassers. However, the court found the school district's response to the racial harassment to be inadequate and ineffective, resulting in a racially hostile school environment and denial of equal educational opportunity (*Zeno v. Pine Plains Central School District*, 2009). At the level of the circuit court, the school district was again criticized for its slow response and failure to take systems-level action to stop the harassment. Anthony was awarded $1 million in damages (*Zeno v. Pine Plains Central School District*, 2012).

cyberbullying (Goodno, 2011; Thomas, Connor, & Scott, 2015). As systems-level consultants, school psychologists can help to develop and implement school policies, procedures, and programs to protect students from discrimination, harassment, and bullying. Through advocacy and education of staff and students, we can work to foster a school climate that promotes not only understanding and acceptance of, but also respect for and valuing of, individual differences.

CONCLUDING COMMENTS

As Dawson (1987) observed some time ago, "School psychologists are often in a position to influence educational policy and administrative practices" (p. 349). Maintaining up-to-date knowledge of school policies and practices that have an impact on the welfare of children and sharing that expertise in consultation with school principals and other decision makers "may enable school psychologists to effect organizational change that can have a positive impact on large numbers of children" (p. 348).

STUDY AND DISCUSSION

Questions for Chapter 9

1. What are some of the consultative roles school psychologists can assume related to districtwide testing programs? What does the term *high-stakes testing* mean?
2. Under IDEIA, must special education students participate in statewide assessment programs? May schools require special education students to pass a minimum competency test prior to the award of a high school diploma?
3. Identify the ethical-legal issues associated with schoolwide screening for students who may be at risk of harm to self and others.
4. Are public schools required to provide bilingual instruction under federal law? Are public schools required to provide specialized instruction for gifted and talented students under federal law?
5. Is the use of paddling (spanking) for disciplinary purposes in the schools constitutionally permissible?
6. What strategies does a school have under IDEIA for handling a special education student who violates school rules? What is a manifest determination review?

Discussion

Discuss the OCR's 2010 "Dear Colleague Letter" on harassment and bullying (Ali, 2010). In what ways did this letter mark a turning point with regard to school district responsibilities to address discrimination and harassment? In what ways did the letter extend the OCR's protections beyond the classes of individuals explicitly identified in federal civil rights law? (The letter may be found by simply Googling "Dear Colleague Letter on Harassment and Bullying").

Vignettes

1. Susan Doe was designated male at birth but began to express a female gender identity by age 2. In kindergarten through third grade, she wore gender-neutral clothes. In third grade, she was referred to as "she," and by grade 4 she dressed exclusively as a girl. In 2007, when Susan was in fourth grade, a Section 504 plan was developed for her. The Americans with Disabilities Amendments Act of 2008/Section 504 excludes gender identity disorder and transgender status from its definition of a disability. However, Susan was diagnosed with a gender identity disorder and concomitant emotional and social stresses that impaired her ability to join in and benefit from school life. As a result, school professionals, along with Susan's parents, felt that accommodations were necessary at school to support Susan's mental health and address the impact of gender identity issues on her school experiences. The Section 504 plan included encouraging students and staff to refer to Susan by her female name and allowing Susan to use the communal girl's bathroom. The plan was initially implemented smoothly and without complications until a boy, encouraged by his grandfather, entered the girl's bathroom, claiming that he too had a right to be there. This incident triggered media coverage and controversy. As a result, school administrators decided that Susan would not be permitted to use the girl's bathroom. She was instructed to use the staff unisex bathroom and was the only student permitted and required to do so. Susan's parents filed a complaint in state court asserting unlawful discrimination based on the state's human rights law that prohibits discrimination against transgender persons in public facilities. In the court opinion, Judge Silver wrote "Susan is a girl" and must be given the same access to the girl's bathroom as other girls (*John Doe v. Regional School Unit 26*, 2014, p. 16), The court held that "[w]here it had been clearly established that a student's psychological well-being and educational success depended on being permitted to use the communal bathroom consistent with her gender identity, denying access to the appropriate bathroom" was discriminatory under state law (p. 1). (Adapted from *John Doe v. Regional School Unit 26*, 2014.) Discuss the ethical issues associated with this situation, taking care to consider all parties who are affected. Do you agree with the court's decision allowing a male-to-female transgender student to use the girl's bathroom? Do you think that requiring Susan to be the only student to use the staff unisex bathroom would have been a better way to resolve the situation? Why or why not? The principal of Susan's school testified that it wasn't "safe" for Susan to use the boy's bathroom. Do you agree, and why or why not? As a systems-level consultant, what steps would you recommend to foster a school climate that is safe and welcoming for transgender students? (Also see *G.G. Grimm v. Gloucester School Board*, 2015, for a different court opinion.)

2. In Pearl Meadows's school district, many of the students are the sons and daughters of university faculty who have high expectations for the academic performance of their children and who are quick to be critical of teachers and the quality of instruction when their children do not achieve high scores on standardized achievement tests. Pearl is in the high school to do paperwork on a day that statewide student achievement testing is done. It is a warm day, and many teachers have left their classroom doors open. As she passes by classrooms, she notices that some teachers are sitting at their desks, preoccupied with their cellphones and not monitoring the students who are taking tests. She also notices students who appear to be using their cellphones during the test. Discuss the ethical-legal issues involved with this situation. What steps, if any, should Pearl take as a result of her observations?

3. Goodno (2011) raised some thought-provoking questions about cyberbullying. Consider the next situation, adapted from Goodno (2011, pp. 642–643).

> Jane and Joe are students at the same middle school. Joe punches Jane in the school cafeteria at lunch. The school has the authority to suspend Joe. Joe punches Jane on a Saturday in the public park. The school does not have the authority to discipline Joe. On his own computer at home, Joe creates an animated video game showing himself and other students punching Jane. He then posts the game on the Internet, and it is quickly shared and accessed by more than 100 students. Many students join in the virtual punching of Jane online, some using electronic devices to play the game at school and others at home. Jane is afraid to go to school. Do school officials have the authority to punish Joe or any other students? Is Joe's game free speech protected by the First Amendment? How should school officials respond to this situation, if at all? How do school officials protect targeted students from cyberbullying without violating the constitutional rights of other students (e.g., free speech)?

Goodno (2011) noted, "Neither the legislatures nor the courts have been able to give public schools clear and consistent guidelines on how to answer these questions" (pp. 642–643). What strategies would you recommend to a school district to prevent and respond to cyberbullying?

Use Google Scholar to access Goodno's model cyberbullying policy for public schools. The citation is: Goodno, N. H. (2011). How public schools can constitutionally halt cyberbullying: A model cyberbullying policy that considers First Amendment, due process, and Fourth Amendment challenges. *Wake Forest Law Review, 46*, 641–700. The rationale for the model policy appears in section III of the law review article; the model policy itself is in Appendix B of the law review article. Do you agree with Goodno's recommendations? Why or why not?

4. An 8-year-old girl, Celia, complained to her teacher that another student (a 13-year-old boy) was "playing games" with her. As it was apparent that the games involved inappropriate sexual contact, the teacher informed the school psychologist. The school psychologist counseled Celia without notifying her mother of the problem. The school principal was informed of the incidents and told the boy involved not to "bother" Celia any more. The principal also failed to notify Celia's mother about the incidents. Meanwhile, the assaults on Celia

continued over a three-month period, both on school premises and en route to school. Celia became increasingly despondent and withdrawn. The sexual assaults ultimately led to rape. The victim's mother, after learning what had happened, filed a lawsuit against the school psychologist, teacher, and principal. (Adapted from *Phillis P. v. Claremont Unified School District*, 1986.) What are the ethical-legal issues involved in this situation?

Activities

Visit the U.S. Department of Education's Web site on bullying (http://www.ed.gov/category/keyword/bullying). Skim the guidance documents on bullying prepared for school districts and teachers.

Chapter 10

RESEARCH IN THE SCHOOLS: ETHICAL AND LEGAL ISSUES

In this chapter, we explore the ethical and legal aspects of research in the schools. There are a number of sources of guidance in the conduct of research with human participants. The codes of ethics of both the American Psychological Association (APA, 2010) and the National Association of School Psychologists (NASP, 2010b) include standards for research. In recognition of some of the special problems posed by research with children, the Society for Research in Child Development (SRCD) also developed ethical standards specifically for research with children (SRCD, 2007).[1]

The National Research Act of 1974 (Pub. L. No. 93-348) outlined federal policies for research with human participants. It is interesting to note that the basic elements of our federal policies for research with human participants can be traced back to the Nuremberg Code, a judicial summary made at the war trials of Nazi physicians who conducted medical experiments on war prisoners and were indicted for crimes against humanity (Keith-Spiegel, 1983). The National Research Act mandated the formation of the National Commission for the Protection of Human Subjects of Biomedical and Behavioral Research (National Commission). One of the charges to the commission was to identify the fundamental ethical principles that should underlie the conduct of research involving human subjects; a second charge was to develop guidelines to ensure that research involving human participants is conducted in accordance with those principles.

In 1979, the National Commission published *The Belmont Report: Ethical Principles and Guidelines for the Protection of Human Subjects of Biomedical and Behavioral Research*. The report identified three broad ethical principles relevant to research with human subjects:

1. *Respect for persons*—the obligation to respect the autonomy of individuals and protect individuals with diminished autonomy.
2. *Beneficence*—the obligation to do no harm, to maximize possible benefits and minimize possible harm.
3. *Justice*—the obligation to ensure that all persons share equally in the burdens and benefits of research.

---

[1] The SRCD's (2007) "Ethical Standards for Research with Children" has 16 principles that will be referred to by number in this chapter.

Federal regulations for the protection of human research participants are issued by the U. S. Department of Health and Human Services (HHS) and published at 45 CFR Subtitle A, Part 46. Institutions that receive federal *research* support are required to establish an *institutional review board* (IRB) that reviews studies proposed by researchers affiliated with the institution to ensure that HHS standards for the protection of human subjects are met. Researchers who are affiliated with a university that receives federal research support, including graduate students, must obtain IRB approval prior to initiating a study that involves human subjects or the personally identifiable records (e.g., medical, educational) of human subjects.

Most preschool, elementary, and secondary schools do not receive federal research funds. For this reason, studies conducted by schools typically are not subject to HHS regulations. Nevertheless, school psychologists should be knowledgeable of federal human subject research protections because the regulations provide well-established and accepted guidance on the ethical conduct of needs-assessment studies, program evaluation, or more basic human subjects research.

COMPETENCE, RESPONSIBILITY, AND WELFARE OF PARTICIPANTS

The broad ethical principles of respect for the dignity and welfare of persons and professional competence and responsibility provide the foundation for ethical decision making in the conduct of research in the schools.

Professional Competence and Responsibility

In all types of data-gathering activities, whether it is decision-oriented action research or more basic research, school psychologists are ethically obligated to take responsibility for protecting the rights and welfare of research participants and to conduct research that is scientifically sound (APA-EP Ethical Standards 2, 8; C. B. Fisher & Vacanti-Shova, 2012; NASP-PPE II.1.1).

> The formidable task of ensuring ethical competence in psychological research depends on sensitive and informed planning by scientists who possess the ethical commitment, awareness, and competence to ensure that research meets the highest principles of scientific design and human participant protections. (C. B. Fisher & Vacanti-Shova, 2012, p. 335)

As Koocher and Keith-Spiegel (2008) noted, poorly designed research is likely to result in invalid and perhaps misleading findings. Misleading findings may result in the introduction or continuation of ineffective practices and a potential disservice to students, teachers, parents, and others. Poorly designed studies also are unfair to research participants who volunteer in hopes of contributing to the knowledge base of psychology and education. For these reasons, school psychologists with limited expertise in research design should consult with experienced researchers to ensure that a planned study is methodologically sound.

Welfare of the Participant

In planning research and data collection, priority always must be given to the welfare of the participant. The researcher is obligated ethically to identify any potential risks for the research participants and collect data in ways that will avoid or minimize such risks (APA, 1982, p. 17; National Commission, 1979, Principle 2; C. B. Fisher & Vacanti-Shova, 2012; SRCD Principle 1; 45 CFR § 46.111). The six major types of risk are physical, psychological, social, economic, legal, and dignitary (National Research Council, 2003, pp. 27–28). Potential risks of research participation may include pain or physical injury, exposure to stressful procedures and possible emotional discomfort or harm, invasion of privacy, loss of community standing, exposure to criminal prosecution, loss of employment or potential monetary gain, denial of potentially beneficial treatment, and violations of confidentiality.

Ethical and legal standards for research are consistent in recommending that the researcher ask the advice of others regarding the acceptability of proposed research procedures (NASP-PPE IV.5.2). The greater the potential risks, the greater the obligation to seek advice and observe stringent safeguards. Consistent with the regulations implementing the National Research Act, colleges and universities typically have IRBs that evaluate the ethical acceptability of research proposed by their faculty and students. The NASP's code of ethics requires school psychologists and graduate students affiliated with a university or an agency subject to HHS regulation of human subjects research to first obtain IRB approval prior to initiating a study (NASP-PPE IV.5.2). In addition, research in the schools that is *funded* by the U.S. Department of Education also is required to comply with HHS protections of human subjects.

The NASP's code of ethics recommends peer review of any and all research involving children (NASP-PPE IV.5.2), even if a school-based practitioner is not required to obtain IRB approval. Policies and procedures for review and approval of research activities in the public schools vary; some school districts have their own research review boards. School practitioners should consult with principals, teachers, parents, and others about the acceptability of planned research studies and obtain formal school district administrative approval for proposed research (NASP-PPE IV.5.2).

The remaining portions of this chapter explore informed consent for research; the risks of invasion of privacy, exposure to stress or harm, and denial of beneficial treatment; post-data-collection responsibilities; concealment and deception; confidentiality of data; research with culturally and linguistically diverse populations; and scientific misconduct.

INFORMED CONSENT AND PRIVACY

Case 10.1 summarizes the circumstances that prompted Sylvia Merriken, the mother of an eighth grader named Michael, to file a complaint against the school system that was subsequently decided in a federal district court in Pennsylvania in 1973. Although this incident occurred more than 40 years ago, it is not hard to imagine the occurrence of similar events today as school districts continue to struggle with the problem of substance abuse.

Case 10.1

School administrators, teachers, and members of the school board were alarmed by reports of high levels of drug abuse by students in the school district. They decided to hire a private consultant in hopes of developing an effective drug abuse prevention program for junior high students. The initial phase of the program involved research to identify eighth graders at risk for drug abuse. As part of the research phase, questionnaires were administered to eighth graders and their teachers. Students were asked to rate themselves on a number of personality variables, such as level of self-confidence, and they were asked about their relationship to their parents (e.g., Did one or both of your parents hug and kiss you good night when you were small? Do they make you feel unloved?). Teachers were asked to identify students with antisocial behavior patterns, and students were asked to identify classmates with problem behavior patterns. The private consultant planned to collect and analyze the data and prepare a list of "potential drug abusers" for the school superintendent that could be used to identify students in need of drug abuse prevention therapy. The therapy program would use peer-pressure techniques to combat potential drug abuse, and teachers would serve as the therapists. A letter was sent to parents informing them of the diagnostic testing and prevention program and assuring confidentiality of the results. Parents' silence in response to the letter was construed as consent for their child to participate.

Source: Adapted from *Merriken v. Cressman*, 1973; Bersoff, 1983.

Sylvia Merriken's complaint alleged that the school's drug abuse prevention program, particularly the research phase, violated her constitutional rights and those of her son, including the right to privacy. A central issue in this case was the school's failure to seek informed consent for the collection of personal, private information about Michael and his family. As mentioned in Chapter 3, case law, government regulations, and our codes of ethics concur that waiver of an individual's right to privacy must be based on informed consent. The key elements of informed consent are that it must be knowing, competent, and voluntary. The court held that the school's program violated Sylvia Merriken's right to privacy, and an injunction was issued.

Consent Must Be Knowingly Given

Informed consent in research is an agreement between the researcher and the research participant that identifies the obligations and responsibilities of each party. The investigator informs the participant of all aspects of the research that may be expected to influence willingness to participate and answers all questions about the nature of the research procedures (APA-EP 8.02; NASP-PPE IV.5.2; SRCD Principles 2, 3; 45 CFR § 46.116). The researcher may incur special obligations to study participants if the principle of fully informed consent must be comprised because of the nature and purpose of the study (see the section titled "Concealment and Deception" later in this chapter).

Who Gives Consent?

The individual giving consent to volunteer for research must be legally competent to do so (Bersoff, 1983). In the HHS protections for children involved as research subjects, a distinction is made between *consent*, what a person may do autonomously, and *permission*, what a person may do on behalf of another, as when a parent or guardian grants permission for a child to participate in research (46 CFR § 46.402). When research involves children (minors) as study participants, legal standards and codes of ethics (SRCD Principles 2, 3) suggest that the researcher should seek informed consent or permission of the parent or legal guardian for the child to participate and the child's assent to participate. *Assent* is defined as "a child's affirmative agreement to participate in research" (46 CFR § 46.402[b]). This means that the child "shows some form of agreement to participate without necessarily comprehending the full significance of the research necessary to give informed consent" (SRCD Principle 2). HHS regulations note that a child's ability to make informed decisions about participation in research depends on his or her age and maturity (46 CFR § 46.408[a]).

Ferguson (1978) observed that individual level of cognitive development and the complexity of the research situation must be taken into account in determining a child's capacity to make choices regarding research participation. She suggested that informed parental permission is both necessary and sufficient for research with infants and toddlers. The preschool-age child, however, is able to understand explanations stated in here-and-now concrete terms, with a straightforward description of what participation means for the child. Consequently the researcher is obligated to seek both parental permission and affirmative assent for the child of preschool age or older. Ferguson provided some helpful guidelines for explaining research to children of various ages (pp. 118–120). (See V. A. Miller, Drotar, & Kodish, 2004, for a review of the empirical literature on children's competence to assent to research participation; also see Masty & Fisher, 2008.)

The SRCD suggested that the informed consent of any person whose interaction with the child is the subject of the study also be obtained (SRCD Principle 4). For example, a study of the association between children's positive or negative feelings about their classroom teacher and academic achievement would require parental permission, the child's assent to participate, and the teacher's informed consent.

Freedom From Coercion

The third characteristic of informed consent is that it must be voluntary. HHS regulations specify that research participants (the parent or legal representative in the case of a minor child) should be given "sufficient opportunity" to decide whether to choose to participate in the research and should be informed that they may refuse to participate without incurring any penalty (46 CFR § 46.116[a][8]). The investigator also must respect the individual's freedom to discontinue participation at any time

(APA-EP 8.02; SRCD Principles 2, 3, 4; 45 CFR § 46.116[a][8]). Consistent with the values of respect for self-determination and autonomy, researchers must attract consent and assent without coercion, duress, pressure, or undue enticement or influence (Koocher & Keith-Spiegel, 2008; also APA-EP 8.06; SRCD Principle 5).

In the school setting, it is important to allow potential volunteers (students, teachers) the opportunity to decline to participate without embarrassment (SRCD Principles 2, 3, 4). In the *Merriken* decision (1973, p. 915), Judge Davis noted that the school did not afford the students an opportunity to decline to participate without being marked for "scapegoating" and unpleasant treatment by peers.

It also is important to remember that researchers may not promise benefits from research participation unless they are able to ensure the promised outcomes. For example, a researcher may not guarantee that participation in an experimental counseling group for overweight teens will result in weight loss for each participant, although weight loss might be identified as a *possible* benefit from participation.

Minimal Risk Research

Informed consent is not always required for research in the schools. As C. B. Fisher and Vacanti-Shova (2012) explained:

> Ethical justification for waiving the informed consent requirement for special types of research conducted in educational settings is predicated on the right and responsibility of education institutions to evaluate their own programs, practices, and policies to improve services as long as the research procedures do not create distress or harm. (p. 350)

Researchers whose studies are subject to IRB review should be aware that, under HHS regulations, minimal risk research in school settings may not require informed consent if the information is recorded and reported in a way that individuals cannot be identified. *Minimal risk research* generally means that the study poses little likelihood of invasion of privacy, exposure to stress, or psychological or physical harm as a result of participation in the study. HHS regulations at A—Basic HHS Policy for Protection of Human Research Subjects specifically exempt these types of research from its informed consent requirements: "research conducted in established or commonly accepted educational settings, involving normal educational practices" and research involving "the use of educational tests (cognitive, diagnostic, aptitude, achievement)" if information taken from these sources is recorded in such a manner that subjects cannot be identified (45 CFR § 46.101[b][1]). Research involving the study of existing school records also would be viewed as minimal risk research under HHS regulations as long as information is recorded in such a manner that subjects cannot be identified directly or through identifiers linked to the subjects (45 CFR § 46.101[b][4]).

However, as mentioned previously, few preschool, elementary, or secondary schools receive federal research funds. Consequently, research conducted by, or on behalf of, schools typically is not subject to HHS human subjects protections. School-based research and program evaluation should, nevertheless, meet accepted standards for the ethical treatment of human subjects and be in compliance with relevant federal education law. The Family Educational Rights and Privacy Act of 1974 (FERPA) and the Protection of Pupil Rights Act (PPRA) were passed to protect privacy of student and family information in schools that receive any type of federal funds; they are not research acts. However, both have implications for research in schools.

FERPA was amended in 2008 to clarify, among other issues, the conditions under which consent is *not* required to disclose personally identifiable student information for educational research studies. More specifically, a school may disclose information protected by FERPA without parent consent if the disclosure is to organizations conducting studies for, or on behalf of, educational agencies or institutions to develop, validate, or administer predictive tests, or improve instruction, and if the following conditions are met:

(A) The study is conducted in a manner that does not permit personal identification of parents and students by individuals other than representatives of the organization that have legitimate interests in the information;

(B) The information is destroyed when no longer needed for the purposes for which the study was conducted; and

(C) The educational agency or institution ... enters into a written agreement with the organization that—

    (1) Specifies the purpose, scope, and duration of the study or studies and the information to be disclosed;

    (2) Requires the organization to use personally identifiable information from education records only to meet the purpose or purposes of the study as stated in the written agreement;

    (3) Requires the organization to conduct the study in a manner that does not permit personal identification of parents and students ... by anyone other than representatives of the organization with legitimate interests; and

    (4) Requires the organization to destroy or return to the educational agency or institution all personally identifiable information when the information is no longer needed for the purposes for which the study was conducted and specifies the time period in which the information must be returned or destroyed. ...
(34 CFR § 99.31[a][6][iii])[2]

As noted in Chapter 3, there has been growing public concern about the release of students' personally identifiable information (PII) to third-party service providers contracted to provide *data analytic functions* for school districts or state departments of education. *Data analytic services* are designed to: aggregate and analyze student data; report on performance trends; pinpoint areas for district-wide performance improvement; and identify schools, teachers, and students "in need of assistance" (Reidenberg et al., 2013, p. 17). Public concern has focused on multiple issues including the security of PII released for data analytic functions, whether third parties would use PII in unauthorized ways, whether schools were releasing PII that was not needed for data analytic functions, and whether data were destroyed when no longer needed. School psychology practitioners should be aware that guidelines are available assist school personnel in making sound decisions about the outsourcing of data analytic services (see Reidenberg et al., 2013).

---

[2]From *Electronic Code of Federal Regulations*, current as of August 21, 2015.

Chapter 3 also addressed PPRA. PPRA requires local school districts that receive any federal funds to develop policies, in consultation with parents, to notify parents when the school intends to request one or more of these eight types of information from students:

1. Political affiliations or beliefs of the student or the student's parent
2. Mental and psychological problems potentially embarrassing to the student or his or her family
3. Sex behavior and attitudes
4. Illegal, antisocial, self-incriminating, and demeaning behavior
5. Critical appraisals of other individuals with whom respondents have close family relationships
6. Legally recognized privileged and analogous relationships
7. Religious practices, affiliations, or beliefs of the student or student's parent
8. Income, other than required by law to determine eligibility for participation in a program or for receiving financial assistance under a program.

The parent of a student must be given the opportunity to inspect the survey, on request, prior to its distribution. Parents also must be given the opportunity to have their student opt out of the information-gathering activity or physical examination.

Components of the Informed Consent Agreement

The HHS outlined a number of requirements for informed consent for research (46 CFR § 46.116). The consent agreement is a written agreement, but it may be presented orally to the individual giving consent. Oral presentation should be witnessed by a third party. The informed consent information must be presented in a language understandable to the participant or guardian granting permission for the child to participate, and the researcher may not include language that implies a release from ethical and legal responsibility to the subjects of the study.

There are eight basic components of the informed consent agreement:

1. A description of the nature and purpose of the research and the procedures and expected duration of participation
2. A description of "any reasonably foreseeable risks or discomforts" for the participant or to others
3. A description of any potential benefits to the participant that can reasonably be expected
4. A description of available alternative treatments that might be advantageous
5. A description of the extent to which confidentiality of information will be maintained
6. Instructions concerning who may be contacted to answer questions about the research

7. A statement that participation is voluntary and that the participant may discontinue the study at any time without penalty

8. For studies that involve more than minimal risk, a description of any compensation and medical treatment available if injury occurs as a result of participation (46 CFR § 46.116[a])

The SRCD also suggested that the professional and institutional affiliation of the researcher be identified (SRCD Principle 3). The consent form should be signed by the parent or guardian of a minor child or by the research participant if he or she is an adult. HHS has procedures for requesting a waiver of the parent consent requirement if requesting parent consent might jeopardize subject welfare (e.g., research with abused children) (45 CFR § 46.408). Grunder (1978) recommended using reading-level determination formulas to evaluate the readability of the consent form to ensure that it is understandable.

EXPOSURE TO STRESS OR HARM AND DENIAL OF BENEFICIAL TREATMENT

Consistent with the principle of responsible caring, researchers take steps to protect study participants from physical and emotional discomfort, harm, and danger (APA, 1982, p. 51; C. B. Fisher & Vacanti-Shova, 2012; SRCD Principle 1). We can think of no ethically permissible studies by school psychologists that involve exposing a study participant to harm and danger. Research on the use of medications in the treatment of behavior or learning problems (e.g., the use of Ritalin in the treatment of hyperactivity) exposes the child to potentially dangerous medical side effects (see Chapter 7). Although data regarding the effects of medications might be gathered in the school setting, any research involving the administration of drugs must be conducted under the supervision of a physician knowledgeable of the necessary medical and legal safeguards (see APA, 1982, pp. 57–58).

Prior to beginning a study, the researcher is obligated to determine whether proposed research procedures are stressful and to explore ways to avoid or minimize stress by modifying the research methodology (SRCD Principle 1). Psychological discomfort is likely to result: from failure experiences; from temptations to lie, cheat, or steal; or if the investigator asks the research participant to reveal personal information that is embarrassing or to perform disturbing tasks, such as rating parents (APA, 1982, pp. 58–59). The survey questions for students in the *Merriken* case, for example, were likely to be quite stressful for some eighth graders.

In evaluating the acceptability of a study that places the participants at risk for discomfort, the researcher is obligated to seek the advice of others and carefully consider whether the potential benefits of the study outweigh the risks, often called a risk-benefit analysis (SRCD Principle 1). The researcher must obtain fully informed consent for any study that exposes the subjects to potential discomfort or harm (APA, 1982, p. 53). HHS regulations recommend that informed consent be sought for any research that exposes volunteers to risks greater than "those ordinarily encountered in daily life" (46 CFR § 46.102[h]–[i]). The HHS Secretary's Advisory Committee on Human Research Protection further suggested that the evaluation of minimal risk for children "be indexed to risks in daily life and routine medical or psychological examinations experienced by children the same age and developmental status as the subject population" (Prentice, 2005).

Assessing the potential risks of research participation for children can be a difficult and complex task. The researcher is obligated to consider developmental factors, prior experiences, and individual characteristics of the study participants in evaluating children's vulnerability to research risk. The likelihood of distress, embarrassment, and diminished self-esteem should be evaluated within a developmental context. For example, after age 7 or 8, children have greater self-awareness and capacity to make inferences about the meaning of others' behavior, and consequently they become increasingly more sensitive to both explicit and implied judgments of their performance in research situations. There also are developmental changes with regard to embarrassment from intrusions on privacy. The privacy concerns of young children center on their bodies and possessions. As children mature, privacy concerns extend to include informational privacy, namely, a desire to keep private information about their peer group, activities, and interests. Adolescents are highly sensitive to privacy intrusions and may view requests for personal information as intrusive and threatening (Thompson, 1990; also Masty & Fisher, 2008).

The researcher also must be alert to the fact that the data-collection procedures may result in unanticipated discomfort or harm. It is important to monitor the research procedures, particularly when research involves children. Children are likely to be highly sensitive to failure, and "seemingly innocuous" questions may be stressful for some (APA, 1982, p. 59). If a research participant appears to show a stressful reaction to the procedures, the researcher is obligated "to correct these consequences" and should consider altering the data-collection procedures (SRCD Principle 10).

In planning research investigations of the effectiveness of new treatments or interventions, school psychologists are obligated to select an alternative treatment known to be beneficial (a contrast group) rather than using a no-treatment control group, if at all feasible. If the new or experimental intervention is found to be effective, contrast or control group participants should be given access to the new treatment (APA, 1982, p. 68; also see APA-EP 8.02).

POST-DATA-COLLECTION RESPONSIBILITIES

The investigator is obligated to end the data-collection session with "a positive and appropriate debriefing" (APA, 1982, p. 67). After the data are collected, the investigator provides participants with information about the nature of the study and attempts to remove any misconceptions participants may have (APA-EP 8.08). The investigator also is obligated to remove or correct any undesirable consequences that result from research participation (APA, 1982, p. 66; SRCD Principles 10, 12). As Holmes (1976) observed, stress is likely to occur when participants acquire an awareness of their own inadequacies and weaknesses as a result of participation in research. Researchers are obligated to introduce procedures to desensitize participants when this occurs; that is, the investigator must eliminate any distress that results from self-knowledge acquired as a result of research.

As the APA (1982) noted, investigators have special postexperimental responsibilities in research with children. The investigator must "ensure that the child leaves the research situation with no undesirable after-effects of participation." This may mean "that certain misconceptions should not be removed or even that some new misconceptions should be induced. If children erroneously believe that they have done well on a research task, there may be more harm than good in trying to correct this misconception than in permitting it to remain." When children feel that they have done poorly, corrective efforts are needed. Such efforts might include introducing a special experimental procedure "to guarantee the child a final success experience" (p. 66).

Investigators also are obligated to consider any long-range aftereffects from participation in research. Research that introduces the possibility of irreversible aftereffects should not be conducted (APA, 1982, p. 59). In *Merriken* (1973), Judge Davis admonished the school for its failure to acknowledge the risks of harm introduced by its drug prevention program. He noted that on the basis of responses to an unvalidated survey, a student could be erroneously labeled as a "potential drug abuser," possibly resulting in stigma, peer rejection, or a self-fulfilling prophesy and be subjected to group therapy sessions conducted by untrained and inexperienced therapists (the teachers) (p. 920).

CONCEALMENT AND DECEPTION

Case 10.2 provides an illustration of deception and concealment in research.

Concealment

The nature and purpose of a study may require a compromise of the principle of fully informed consent (APA, 1982, p. 36; Kimmel, 2012; SRCD Principle 6). The term *concealment* is used to refer to studies in which the investigator gathers information about individuals without their knowledge or consent; that is, the study subject may not know he or she has participated in a research study (APA, 1982, p. 36). These studies often involve covert (hidden) or unobtrusive observation. The National Research Act regulations and the APA's code of ethics (APA-EP 8.5) suggest that covert observation or unobtrusive observational studies can be considered minimal risk research and exempt from informed consent requirements as long as: data are recorded so that subjects cannot be identified directly or indirectly; the behaviors observed are public; the research does not deal with sensitive or illegal behaviors (sexual behaviors, drug abuse); the experience of the person is not affected by the research (i.e., the research procedures are nonreactive); and the person is not put at risk in the event of a breach of confidentiality (criminal or civil liability, financial damage, or loss of employment) (45 CFR § 46.101[b][2]; APA, 1982, pp. 36–39). The research described in Case 10.2 appears to present minimal risk for the students observed in the study.

========================= **Case 10.2** =========================

Carrie Johnson, school psychologist, decided to conduct a study of differences in teacher behaviors toward general education and special education students to fulfill the research requirements for her Ed.D. degree. She plans to observe time samples of reading instruction in five second-grade classrooms in a district near her university and code the number of positive and negative comments the teachers make to general education students and their special education classmates. She is concerned that knowledge of the purpose of the study might alter teacher behavior, so she misinforms the teachers that the purpose of the research is to study the peer interaction patterns of special education students. The findings from her study show that all teachers observed gave special education students more negative and fewer positive comments during reading instruction compared with their general education classmates. Carrie places a form letter in the faculty mailbox of each teacher/participant and the building principal, thanking them for their help and briefly summarizing her findings. Two of the teacher/participants are angry about the deception and demand that their observation data be destroyed. A third teacher is dismayed and embarrassed by her biased treatment of students with disabilities and considers abandoning her career in teaching.

Deception

The term *deception* typically is used to refer to studies in which participants are misinformed about the purpose of the study or the meaning of their behavior (APA, 1982, p. 40). Carrie Johnson's study (Case 10.2) illustrates the use of deception with the teacher/participants; she deliberately misinformed them of the purpose of the study so as to avoid altering their typical teaching behaviors.

Studies that involve deception are controversial. The investigator has a responsibility to seek peer review and carefully evaluate whether the use of deception is justified by the value of the study and to consider alternative procedures (APA, 1982, p. 41; APA-EP 8.07; Kimmel, 2012; SRCD Principle 6). C. B. Fisher and Fryberg (1994) suggested that researchers ask nonparticipants from the same subject pool about the acceptability of the deception before proceeding with the study. Another alternative is forewarning subjects—that is, gaining the informed consent of participants to use deception as part of the research procedure. Some researchers maintain that the intentional use of deception with children is never justified as "children may be left with the distinct impression that lying is an *appropriate* way for adults to achieve their goals" (Keith-Spiegel, 1983, p. 201).

If, after consultation with others, it is determined that the use of deception is necessary and justified by the value of the study, the researcher incurs additional obligations to the study participants. After the completion of the data collection, the researcher must fully inform each participant of the nature of the deception, detect and correct any stressful aftereffects, and provide an opportunity for the participant to withdraw from the study after the deception is revealed (APA, 1982, p. 41; also APA-EP 8.08; Kimmel, 2012; SRCD Principle 6).

In Case 10.2, Carrie did not fulfill her postexperimental obligations to the teacher/participants. An individual or small-group meeting was needed to explain the nature of the deception, introduce appropriate desensitization procedures, and assure the confidentiality of the data gathered. It would have been beneficial for the teacher/participants to know that their differential treatment of low-achieving students is normal teacher behavior and most likely an unconscious response to student behavior; that is, student behavior may condition teacher behavior (Brophy & Good, 1974). Offering to work with the teachers to help modify these behaviors would have been appropriate and in the best interests of everyone involved.

Confidentiality of Data

Codes of ethics, case law, and legal regulations are consistent in requiring a clear prior agreement between the investigator and the research participant about who will have access to information gathered during research and what types of information, if any, will be shared with others.

> Information obtained about the research participant during the course of an investigation is confidential unless otherwise agreed on in advance. When the possibility exists that others may obtain access to such information, this possibility, together with the plans for protecting confidentiality, is explained to the participants as part of the procedure for obtaining informed consent. (APA, 1982, p. 70; also SRCD Principle 11)

In his *Merriken* (1973) decision, Judge Davis noted that the school made a blanket promise to parents that survey results would be confidential. However, documents describing the program indicated that, to the contrary, it was anticipated that a "massive data bank" would be developed, and information would be shared with guidance counselors, athletic coaches, Parent-Teacher Association officers, and school board members, among others (p. 916). The judge also noted that the list of "potential drug abusers" could be subpoenaed by law enforcement authorities. Investigators are obligated to forewarn research participants of any such risks of violation of confidentiality.[3]

The APA (1982, p. 82) recommends removing identifying information from research protocols immediately. If a coding key that links the individual to his or her data is necessary because of the nature of the research, it should be kept in a secure location or password-protected file. The use of any permanent recordings during data collection (e.g., videotapes) increases the risk of loss of anonymity. The researcher should seek informed consent to create and maintain such records (APA, 1982, p. 37; also APA-EP 8.03; C. B. Fisher & Vacanti-Shova, 2012).

---

[3]Investigators planning research on sensitive topics, such as drug abuse, may apply to HHS's Office for Human Research Protections for a confidentiality certificate to protect subject identity from disclosure in legal proceedings.

Codes of ethics and research regulations do not prohibit the sharing of research information if informed consent to do so is obtained. Information obtained in the course of research (e.g., test scores) may be helpful in educational planning for an individual child. However, it is of critical importance that researchers in the schools have a clear prior understanding with all parties involved, including students, parents, teachers, and administrators, regarding what research information will be shared and with whom, and what information will not be disclosed (APA, 1982, pp. 70–71). School administrators may believe they have a legitimate right to information gathered about individual teachers, and parents are likely to believe they have a right to information about their child's performance in a research situation unless they are advised ahead of time that the research information gathered is for research purposes only.

Student researchers are advised against offering to share information from psychological tests with parents or teachers. The interpretation of psychological tests by students outside the supervised internship setting raises legal questions regarding the practice of psychology without certification or licensure (see also SRCD Principle 13).

In unusual circumstances, a researcher may choose to disclose confidential information deliberately for the protection of the research participant or the protection of others. "The protection afforded research participants by the maintenance of confidentiality may be compromised when the investigator discovers information that serious harm threatens the research participant or others" (APA, 1982, p. 69). The researcher may uncover information about the participant that has important implications for his or her well-being, such as emotional or physical problems. Such situations are most likely rare in school settings. If deliberate disclosure is warranted, however, the research volunteer (parent or guardian of a minor child) should be counseled about the problem identified by someone qualified to interpret and discuss the information gathered and handle any resultant distress. If disclosure of information to a third party is anticipated, this also should be discussed with the research participant (or parent or guardian) (APA, 1982, p. 72; C. B. Fisher & Vacanti-Shova, 2012; SRCD Principle 9).

School psychologists must be sensitive to potential loss of confidentiality as a result of presentation or publication of research findings. As the APA (1982) has noted, there are rarely problems with loss of confidentiality when data on groups are published. However, school psychology practitioners may be interested in presenting or publishing case studies. Often the data from case studies were obtained as part of an intervention plan and follow-up, and informed consent to use the data for research was not obtained. If a psychologist plans to present or publish case information, this should be discussed with the individuals involved (students, parents, teachers), and informed consent should be obtained. The researcher also should make a sincere effort to disguise the identity of the research participants (APA-EP 4.07; NASP-PPE IV.5.3; SRCD Principle 11).

It is usually appropriate to offer research participants a brief summary of the findings from the study based on the data from all study participants. This summary should preserve the anonymity of the participants and the confidentiality of the data gathered from individual participants (SRCD Principle 12).

RESEARCH WITH CULTURALLY AND LINGUISTICALLY DIVERSE POPULATIONS

In conducting research that involves culturally and linguistically diverse groups, researchers must give special consideration to the selection and recruitment of research participants, research methodology, evaluation of potential risks and benefits, and reporting of results. In the 1960s, a number of research investigations came to the attention of the U.S. Congress in which vulnerable groups carried the burden of research but often were denied its benefits. Perhaps the best known of these was the Tuskegee Study, conducted by the U.S. Public Health Service, in which 400 African American men with syphilis were observed until autopsy to determine the natural course of the disease. The study lasted from 1932 to 1972. The men were left untreated even when penicillin became available.

According to White (2000), the facts of the Tuskegee Study were more complex than presented in the public forum (e.g., penicillin treatment at that time typically was limited to early syphilis, and many study participants had late-latent syphilis). However, growing concern about this and other research studies gave impetus to the formation of the National Commission for the Protection of Human Subjects of Biomedical and Behavioral Research (discussed earlier) and heightened awareness of the importance of the ethical principle of justice, namely, the obligation to ensure that all persons share equally in the burdens and benefits of research. In accordance with this principle, researchers must select and recruit participants in an equitable manner, or for reasons directly related to the research question, instead of selecting subjects because of their easy availability or tractability (Frankel & Siang, 1999).

Researchers also have special obligations when planning research studies of culturally and linguistically diverse groups. Researchers must be sensitive to the ways their own background and biases may impact how they conceptualize and design research studies (Rogers et al., 1999). In addition, it is critically important for researchers to have or to acquire knowledge of the culture and history of the group under study, including an understanding of how to convey respect for that culture in the conduct of research. Researchers are advised to seek input from members of the group being studied in planning the research project. Doing this can help to ensure that the research targets the needs of the study population, that research questions and methods are culturally appropriate, and that risks and benefits are evaluated in light of the special circumstances of the group participating in the study (C. B. Fisher & Vacanti-Shova, 2012; Gil & Bob, 1999).

In addition, researchers must be cautious in interpretation of findings. As Atkinson (1993) has stated, "We each have our own way of interpreting data based on the cultural lenses through which we view the world" (p. 220). Again, seeking to understand the experiences and worldview of the study group and seeking input from members of that group regarding the possible meaning of data may help the researcher avoid inaccurate and biased interpretation (Gil & Bob, 1999). Also, in the dissemination of research, researchers should consider how their findings might be misrepresented and how to minimize the likelihood that their findings will result in unintended harm (Sieber, 2000).

SCIENTIFIC MISCONDUCT

The term *scientific misconduct* here refers to reporting research findings in a biased or misleading way, fabricating or falsifying data, plagiarism, or taking credit for work that is not one's own. Consistent with APA and NASP codes of ethics, school psychologists strive to collect and report research information so as to make an honest contribution to knowledge and minimize the likelihood of misinterpretation and misunderstanding. In publishing reports of their research, they acknowledge the limitations of their study and the existence of disconfirming data and identify alternate explanations of their findings (APA-EP Principle C; NASP-PPE IV.5.1, IV.5.6).

The publication of scientific misinformation based on false or fabricated data is a serious form of misconduct that potentially can result in harm to others. In 1988, Dr. Stephen Breuning, a psychopharmacologist, pleaded guilty to charges of fabricating research data. The charges followed an investigation of his research that reported improved functioning for children with intellectual disabilities who were treated with Ritalin or Dexedrine, research that "helped shape drug treatment policy for mentally retarded" individuals in several states (Hostetler, 1988, p. 5). This was the nation's first federal conviction for falsifying scientific data. Breuning was ordered to pay over $11,000 in restitution and was sentenced to 60 days in jail and five years of probation (Coughlin, 1988). Breuning's case triggered much discussion of the need to protect the public from misinformation. Psychologists and others involved in investigating the case hoped that it would serve as a warning to others about the seriousness of falsifying data in scientific research (Hostetler, 1988). Although they are infrequent, incidents of falsifying research data unfortunately have continued (Jha, 2012).

Another type of scientific misconduct is plagiarism. Plagiarism "occurs when the words, ideas, or contributions of others are appropriated in writing or speech without proper citation or acknowledgment" (McGue, 2000, p. 83). Psychologists are ethically and legally obligated to acknowledge the source of their ideas when publishing or making a professional presentation (NASP-PPE IV.5.8; also APA-EP 8.11; Barnett & Campbell, 2012). Both published and unpublished material that influenced the development of the manuscript or presentation materials must be acknowledged.

Finally, psychologists take credit "only for work they have actually performed or to which they have contributed" (APA-EP 8.12). "Principal authorship and other publication credits accurately reflect the relative scientific or professional contributions of the individuals involved.... Minor contributions to the research or to the writing for publications are acknowledged appropriately, such as in footnotes or in an introductory statement" (APA-EP 8.12; also NASP-PPE IV.5.9.) (See Barnett & Campbell, 2012.)

CONCLUDING COMMENTS

As in other areas of service delivery, school psychologists most likely can avoid ethical-legal dilemmas in research by maintaining up-to-date knowledge of relevant guidelines, by careful planning of proposed research activities, and by seeking consultation and advice from others when questions arise. School psychologists conducting research need to be knowledgeable of the organization and methodology of the school and to work within the organizational framework, taking care to build and maintain good public relations within and outside of the school community during all phases of a research project.

STUDY AND DISCUSSION

Questions for Chapter 10

1. Identify the key codes of ethics and legal documents that provide guidelines for research.
2. What is the single most important ethical consideration in conducting research?
3. Identify six types of potential risks for research participants.
4. What are the key elements of informed consent for research?
5. What is the difference between consent and assent for research participation?
6. We do not always seek children's assent for the provision of psychological services. Why should we seek their assent to participate in psychological research?
7. Do we always need informed parent consent for research in the schools? What is minimal risk research?

Discussion

In 2001, third and fifth graders in a California school participated in a study conducted by a school therapist as part of her graduate degree requirements. The consent form sent home to parents said nothing about the survey's content. Angry parents contacted the school after learning that the survey asked children questions such as whether they were "thinking about having sex," "touching my private parts too much," and "thinking about touching other people's private parts" (Bowman, 2002).

What are the ethical and legal issues associated with this research situation? What risks for children are associated with participation in this study? What mechanisms to protect schoolchildren in human subjects research apparently failed in this situation? What are some ways researchers can evaluate whether their research designs and data-gathering instruments are developmentally appropriate and appropriate in light of special characteristics (e.g., students with learning difficulties) that may heighten vulnerability to research risks? (See Thompson, 1990.)

Vignettes

1. Christa Jones, a second-year student in a school psychology program, administered IQ tests to children in area nursery schools as part of her thesis research. Two months after she completed the data collection, the director of one of the nursery schools requests IQ test information for a preschooler she feels is delayed developmentally as a first step toward requesting a full evaluation of the child's

developmental status. How should Christa respond? What are the ethical-legal issues involved?

2. After seeing a newspaper article on how Internet chat rooms reduced feelings of isolation for some lesbian, gay, and bisexual (LGB) youth, Brad Gilman, a school psychology student, decided to conduct his master's thesis research on the life stories of gay teens. To gather his data, he pretended to be a gay teen, entered several chat rooms popular among LGB youth, asked questions to prompt chat room participants to share information about their lives, and then recorded their conversations verbatim. In his thesis write-up, he identified the chat rooms he visited and included many direct quotes, attributing the quotes to the speakers' undisguised online pseudonyms. What are the ethical issues involved in this research project? (See Frankel & Siang, 1999; also Hoerger & Currell, 2012).

3. Marrisa Garcia, a school psychologist, is concerned about the failure of her district to successfully involve Latino families in home-school collaboration efforts. After receiving approval from her district and a small research grant from a private corporation, she began an interview study with Latino families to identify the barriers to their participation in school meetings, parent conferences, and school outreach activities. Perhaps because she is of Latino descent and fluent in Spanish, Marrisa was able to establish rapport with families, gain their trust, and solicit their informed consent for research participation. During the interviews, Marrisa has been surprised to learn that several of the families have avoided involvement with the schools because one or more family members entered the country illegally and they fear detection. What are the ethical and legal issues associated with this research situation? (See Henning-Stout, 1996.)

4. To complete the requirements for her specialist degree, Shantelle Brown decided to conduct a study of the effectiveness of a drug education program in reducing substance abuse at the middle school level. She plans to individually interview middle school students to ask about their patterns of drug use before and after their participation in the new drug education program. What are the ethical and legal issues associated with a study of this type?

Activities

If you are required to complete a research project as part of your program of graduate studies and the project will involve human subjects, complete the research ethics training program (usually online) required by your university's institutional review board.

Chapter 11

ETHICAL AND LEGAL ISSUES IN SUPERVISION

Supervision can occur in a variety of settings (school, hospital, mental health clinic) and for a variety of different purposes. School psychologists may serve as supervisors of interns or of practitioners seeking full certification or licensure; and, in larger school districts with more than one psychologist, they may assume a supervisory role as lead psychologist or director of school psychological services (Harvey, Struzziero, & Desai, 2014). The goal of this chapter is to provide an introduction to some of the ethical and legal issues associated with field-based supervision of interns and beginning practitioners in a school setting.

Goodyear and Rodolfa (2012) defined *clinical supervision* as

> an intervention that is provided by a more senior member of a profession to a more junior member of the profession, is evaluative, extends over time, and has the simultaneous purposes of helping the supervisee develop professionally in addition to protecting the vulnerable public. (p. 261)

In clinical supervision, unlike consultation, the supervisor has ultimate responsibility for client welfare (Knapp & VandeCreek, 1997). "When supervising graduate students' field experiences or internships, school psychologists are responsible for the work of their supervisees" (NASP-PPE II.2.4). The supervisor is ethically obligated to take steps to ensure that supervisees "perform services responsibly, competently, and ethically" (Knapp & VandeCreek, 1997, p. 591; also APA-EP 2.05; NASP-PPE II.2.4, IV.4.2). Some differences exist, however, in the supervisor's role and duties depending on the level of training of the supervisee. The supervisor assumes greater control, and is obligated to provide more intensive supervision, to interns and other trainees who do not hold a credential to practice when compared to supervisees with a preliminary credential who are pursuing full certification or licensure (Knapp & VandeCreek, 1997).

A supervisor's role may include clinical supervision (working with supervisees to promote skill development) and/or administrative functions (providing effective leadership and management of school psychological services, hiring, delegating work assignments, evaluation of job performance for contract renewal) (Harvey et al., 2014). Some psychologists routinely assume both roles, particularly those who serve as lead psychologist or director of psychological services. Numerous legal issues are associated with hiring employees, employee performance evaluation, and contract renewal or nonrenewal that are beyond the scope of this book. Interested readers are referred to Harvey and Struzziero (2008) and Russo (2012).

PROFESSIONAL STANDARDS FOR SUPERVISION

Both the American Psychological Association (APA) and the National Association of School Psychologists (NASP) include guidelines pertinent to supervision in their codes of ethics (APA-EP 7.06; NASP-PPE IV.4). The NASP's code of ethics states. "As part of their obligation to students, schools, society, and their profession, school psychologists mentor less experienced practitioners and graduate students to assure high quality services, and they serve as role models for sound ethical and professional practices and decision making" (IV.4).

In addition, the NASP (2010a) identified recommended professional standards for supervision in school psychology in its *Model of Comprehensive and Integrated Services by School Psychologists*. Organizational Principle 5 addresses supervision and mentoring and outlines these criteria for being a supervisor of school psychological services: Supervisors must be state certified and have three years of experience as a practicing school psychologist. The NASP *Model* Organizational Principle 6 goes on to state that professional development and supervision should be ongoing, not simply restricted to students in training.

The NASP (2010d) *Standards for Graduate Preparation of School Psychologists* specifies standards for field experiences and internships that must be met by school psychology training programs to receive NASP training program approval. Similarly, the APA's Office of Program Consultation and Accreditation (2013) publishes standards for internships and postdoctoral residencies that must be met to be eligible for accreditation. In addition, the NASP's (2010c) *Standards for the Credentialing of School Psychologists* outlines recommended predegree and postdegree supervision requirements for states to consider when developing their standards for the credentialing of school psychologists and describes the required supervised field experiences to become a Nationally Certified School Psychologist (NCSP).

School psychology internship standards are undergoing change as a result of the shift towards competency-based preparation of psychologists. This movement requires training programs to identify observable and measurable professional competencies that school psychology interns must demonstrate before they graduate, with the capstone internship experience serving as "the gatekeeper" for entry into the profession. The Council of Directors of School Psychology Programs formed a task force in 2009 to seek consensus on measurable internship outcome competencies appropriate for school psychology specialist- and doctoral-level interns (Caterino et al., 2010; Phelps & Swerdlik, 2011).

PROFESSIONAL DISCLOSURE STATEMENT AND INDIVIDUALIZED LEARNING PLAN

Consistent with the ethical principles of integrity in professional relationships and respect for the supervisee's right to make informed choices, Cobia and Boes (2000) recommended that the parameters of the supervisory relationship be outlined in a *professional disclosure statement.* This written agreement is similar to an informed consent agreement between a school psychologist and a client or a consultative contract between a psychologist and a teacher/consultee.

The professional disclosure statement is a means of ensuring a mutual understanding between the supervisor and the supervisee regarding the rights and responsibilities of all parties and helps to ensure that the supervisee is able to make an informed choice about entering the supervisor–supervisee relationship. The professional disclosure statement might include these nine components:

1. Description of the supervision site, clientele, and types of services typically provided
2. Credentials of the supervisor
3. General goals of supervision and how specific objectives will be selected
4. Time frame, frequency, and length of supervision contacts, and type of supervision provided (individual versus group supervision)
5. Rights and responsibilities of supervisor and supervisee
6. Potential risks and benefits of supervision
7. Parameters of confidentiality
8. Record keeping
9. Methods of evaluation (Cobia & Boes, 2000; also NASP-PPE III, IV.4.4)

Lamb, Cochran, and Jackson (1991) and J. R. Sullivan et al. (2014), among others, suggested that supervised practicum and internship experiences should promote supervisee growth and learning in four broad areas of professional functioning: (1) competency; (2) ethical sensitivity, knowledge, decision making, and behavior; (3) understanding of and respect for individual and cultural differences; and (4) emotional awareness and ability to self-reflect on professional competence and performance. In addition to these broad goals, it is recommended that the supervisee, in cooperation with his or her supervisor, develop a written *individualized learning plan* outlining: the supervisee's specific learning objectives; activities for the achievement of those objectives (supervised experiences, reading, attending workshops); and how progress toward mastery of objectives will be evaluated. This individualized learning plan provides further clarification of the expectations and responsibilities of both the supervisor and the supervisee and sets the stage for the establishment of a collaborative supervisory relationship (Cobia & Boes, 2000; Harvey et al., 2014). The plan should be reviewed and modified periodically and serve as the basis for ongoing feedback to the supervisee.

Although the professional disclosure statement and individualized learning plan clarify rights and responsibilities of supervisors and supervisees, a written university–internship site affiliation agreement is also advisable. This agreement outlines the duties of the university as well as the internship site with regard to an intern's field experience (also see the NASP's *Standards for Graduate Preparation of School Psychologists,* 2010d).

ETHICAL PRINCIPLES AND SUPERVISION

Ethical principles and standards pertinent to supervision in school psychology are discussed in this section. The chapter closes with a brief discussion of liability issues.

Respect for the Dignity of Persons (Welfare of the Client and Supervisee)

In providing supervision, the supervisor must consider the rights and welfare of multiple parties: the student who is the recipient of services, parents, teachers, other students, and the supervisee. However, consistent with the NASP's code of ethics, protecting the welfare of the schoolchildren is of primary importance (NASP-PPE Introduction). In Case 11.1, Wanda and Morgan have mutually agreed on a plan that ensures infants and their parents will receive school psychological services that meet high professional standards while Morgan is gaining competence in infant assessment and working with parents.

A number of issues should receive attention early in supervision to help safeguard the well-being of schoolchildren. Supervisees should receive explicit instructions regarding how and under what circumstances to contact their supervisor immediately (Knapp & VandeCreek, 1997). School-based supervisees also should receive verifiable training in the school district's crisis prevention and response procedures, including written instructions regarding what to do in situations in which it is suspected a student might be a danger to self, a danger to others, or in danger (e.g., child abuse). Additionally, it is important to remind school psychology trainees not to leave schoolchildren unsupervised after they remove them from their classrooms for assessment or intervention services.

Although the welfare of schoolchildren is of primary importance, the supervisor also is obligated to consider the welfare of the supervisee. Supervisors are in a position of greater power than supervisees and are expected to advocate for the welfare of the supervisee (Barnett, Erickson Cornish, Goodyear, & Lichtenberg, 2007;

Case 11.1

Wanda Rose has agreed to supervise a school psychologist intern, Morgan LaLone, who is interested in infant assessment and intervention. Morgan administered the Bayley Scales a number of times as part of her university practicum experience but feels she is not yet ready to conduct an infant assessment on her own. Consequently, in preparing Morgan's individualized learning plan, Wanda and Morgan agree that they will conduct a number of infant assessments together before Morgan undertakes such evaluations independently. This will afford Morgan the opportunity to observe Wanda interact with babies and their parents as well as practice administration of infant scales before she begins conducting infant assessments on her own.

===== **Case 11.2** =====

When Carrie Johnson's cooperative special services unit hired a new school psychologist, Ben Pennington, Carrie agreed to serve as supervisor for his first year. A year of supervision by a certified school psychologist is required for Ben to be eligible for full rather than preliminary certification under state law. Carrie also recognizes the importance of providing professional support for her new colleague. During one of their weekly meetings, she learns that the special education coordinator in one of Ben's three schools has assigned Ben the responsibility of scheduling all individualized education program (IEP) team meetings in the building. Carrie is indignant, because IEP scheduling is part of the job description of the special education coordinator, not the school psychologist. It appears that the special education coordinator is attempting to take advantage of a new employee.

Knapp & VandeCreek, 1997). In Case 11.2, Carrie needs to work with Ben to choose a course of action that will relieve Ben of the inappropriately assigned duties but still make it possible for him to have a positive working relationship with the special education director involved. Practitioners new to a school district may feel overwhelmed by requests for assistance from teachers and others, particularly when faced with a backlog of referrals. Consequently, it is advisable for supervisors to introduce beginning practitioners and interns at a school staff meeting and to clarify their role and how work assignments will be delegated and prioritized (NASP-PPE IV.4.2; also III.2; also J. R. Sullivan, Svenkerud, & Conoley, 2014).

Autonomy and Self-Determination

As described previously, the use of a professional disclosure statement is a means of ensuring that the supervisee makes an informed choice when entering a supervisor-supervisee relationship. Consistent with the principle of respect for autonomy and self-determination, the supervisor and supervisee should work together to identify specific objectives and experiences to include in the supervisee's individualized learning plan, taking into account the supervisee's current and desired competencies. The supervisor is obligated to encourage increasingly autonomous professional functioning on the part of the supervisee (see the section titled "Responsible Caring" later in this chapter).

Psychologists also have an obligation to ensure that parents (or other persons providing consent to services) have an opportunity to make an informed choice about whether to accept services provided by a graduate student or an uncertified intern under supervision. "Any service provision by interns, practicum students, or other trainees is explained and agreed to in advance, and the identity and responsibilities of the supervising school psychologist are explained prior to the provision of services" (NASP-PPE I.1.3). Parents should be given information about how to contact the supervisor in the event they are not satisfied with the services provided (Knapp & VandeCreek, 1997). In addition, written consent of the parents and child assent should be obtained prior to audio- or videotaping students as part of the supervision process, and, unless parents agree otherwise, such tapes should be destroyed as soon as they are no longer needed for supervision purposes (APA-EP 4.03; Harvey & Struzziero, 2008).

Privacy and Confidentiality

In general, the guarantees of client confidentiality apply to the supervisor–supervisee relationship. However, supervision often involves evaluations of supervisee performance that must be shared with others (e.g., the university intern supervisor). Consequently, the professional disclosure statement should identify the circumstances under which information regarding the performance of the supervisee will be disclosed to others and the nature and types of information that may be disclosed. Furthermore, supervisees should be informed that supervisors have a duty to breach confidentiality if such action is necessary to safeguard the welfare of clients.

Supervisors are well advised to review ethical and legal principles with supervisees regarding respect for privacy and maintaining client confidentiality and to discuss district policies regarding privacy of student education records. In a study of ethical transgressions by school psychology graduate students, Tryon (2000) found that failure to maintain the privacy and confidentiality of others was an area of difficulty for graduate students.

Fairness, Nondiscrimination, and Diversity Issues

Psychologists are ethically obligated to be respectful of cultural, racial, linguistic, and other differences in providing supervision to interns and other supervisees (APA-EP Principle E; also NASP-PPE I.3). Like consultation across culturally diverse groups, supervision across culturally diverse supervisor–supervisee–client groups can be challenging, particularly with regard to building understanding and trust (Elkund, Aros-O'Malley, & Murrieta, 2014; Harvey et al., 2014).

Although Donita (Case 11.3) has been able to open channels of communication with African American parents, she has inadvertently alienated some teachers and administrators. Case 11.3 raises issues that are often uncomfortable to talk about, namely race, social class, and linguistic prejudice, and there are no simple answers to the issues raised. James will share the feedback from the principals and teachers with Donita and suggest that they use a problem-solving model together to consider the issues raised. James's willingness to openly discuss difficult issues and his use of a problem-solving model with Donita is likely to reinforce her trust in him and foster a safe supervision environment in which she feels comfortable initiating discussions of difficult issues (see J. R. Sullivan et al., 2014).

Responsible Caring in Supervision

Supervisors have an ethical responsibility to ensure that they are competent to provide effective supervision (APA-EP Standard 2; NASP-PPE II.I). Harvey et al. (2014, p. 570) and Goodyear and Rodolfa (2012) identified professional skills necessary

=========== Case 11.3 ===========

James Lewis was pleased when asked to provide field-based supervision for an African American intern. His district has had difficulty recruiting African American school psychologists, and he is hopeful that his new intern, Donita Mason, might be interested in future employment with his district. Donita came to the internship with strong assessment and intervention skills for an entry-level practitioner. She grew up in the inner city in a low-income family and she is bi-dialectal, that is, she is able to switch easily between "standard" English and African American Vernacular English (AAVE). Donita has been able to establish a warm, positive rapport with a number of African American parents who previously were uninvolved with the school. James received several negative evaluations of Donita, however, from principals and teachers because they overheard her using AAVE when conversing with parents before and after meetings. The teachers and principals feel that the use of AAVE is inappropriate for a school professional.

for supervisory competence. Unfortunately, few school psychology supervisors have received formal training in supervision (Harvey & Pearrow, 2010; Phelps & Swerdlik, 2011). School psychologists who wish to provide supervision should assess their competence to do so and pursue continuing education in effective supervisory methods. In addition, supervisors are advised to periodically self-assess their performance as a supervisor and to seek feedback from former supervisees and others regarding the effectiveness of their supervision methods (Harvey et al., 2014; J. R. Sullivan et al., 2014).

To foster the supervisee's professional development and safeguard the well-being of clients, supervisors should offer and provide supervision only within the areas of their own competence (Cobia & Boes, 2000). The supervisor is obligated to be forthcoming and accurate in describing to potential supervisees the areas in which he or she is qualified to provide supervision and may wish to include this information in the professional disclosure statement. As illustrated by Case 11.4, supervision by another professional

=========== Case 11.4 ===========

Pearl Meadows's district accepted a school psychology intern, Roberto Otero, for the upcoming academic year. Roberto is Latino and bilingual. He would like to gain supervised experience working with students and families whose native language is Spanish and consulting with teachers in the district's English as a second language (ESL) classrooms. Because Pearl is not competent to provide psychological services to bilingual students, she has arranged for Roberto to receive supervision from the district's Spanish-bilingual psychologist for the second half of his internship year.

with appropriate credentials, training, and skills should be arranged if the supervisee would like to gain experience in areas outside of the competence of the supervisor; otherwise, such experiences should not be offered.

The supervisor also is obligated to ensure that client welfare is not compromised because of the supervisee's lack of competence. In her study of school psychology graduate students, Tryon (2000) found that, in addition to respecting privacy and confidentiality, working within the boundaries of competence was also an area of difficulty for school psychology graduate students. Supervisors must "delegate responsibilities carefully and deliberately to their supervisees" (Knapp & VandeCreek, 1997, p. 591). The supervisor has a duty to carefully assess the skill level of the supervisee by review of past training and experiences, face-to-face discussion, evaluation of work samples, use of audio- and videotape and direct observation, and inviting feedback from recipients of the supervisee's services (Falender & Shafranske, 2007; J. R. Sullivan et al., 2014). As in Wanda's supervision of her intern Morgan (Case 11.1), it may be appropriate and necessary for the supervisor to work very closely with the supervisee in certain practice areas before allowing the supervisee to function more autonomously in providing services.

Furthermore, consistent with ethical obligations and the legal requirements of most states, supervisors review and cosign psychological reports prepared by interns and supervisees who do not yet hold a credential to practice in the state (NASP-PPE IV.4.2).

Bosk (1979) observed that there are dilemmas inherent in the supervisor's role of selecting and assigning responsibilities to the beginning practitioner. To master new skills and situations, beginners must be given the opportunity to try new experiences and learn from their successes and mistakes. At the same time, the supervisor must protect the client from the supervisee's errors and make sure the supervisee is not overly discouraged by his or her mistakes. *Technical errors* occur when trainees are performing their role conscientiously but their skills fall short of what the task requires. Similarly, *judgmental errors* occur when trainees are performing conscientiously but select an incorrect strategy or intervention. Supervisors should assure trainees that technical errors and errors in professional judgment are "inevitable and forgivable" during training and should seek to create an atmosphere in which supervisees can openly admit and discuss such mistakes without fear. Open discussion of errors encourages trainees to learn from their mistakes and take responsibility for them (Bosk, 1979; also Barnett, Erickson Cornish, et al., 2007; Elkund et al., 2014; J. R. Sullivan et al., 2014).

In contrast, *normative errors* constitute a more serious failure, possibly resulting in the need for reprimand, probation, or dismissal (Bosk, 1979). Normative errors occur when a supervisee fails to discharge his or her role responsibilities conscientiously or violates fundamental expectations for proper conduct in the profession, such as covering up mistakes. Normative errors are a breach of psychologist–client and supervisor–supervisee trust.

Consistent with the principle of responsible caring, supervision must be provided "on a scheduled basis with additional supervision available as needed," and supervisees should be provided timely and straightforward evaluations of their progress (Knapp & VandeCreek, 1997, p. 593). Supervisors are ethically obligated to use accurate and fair methods for evaluating their supervisees (NASP-PPE IV.4.3, 4.4; also APA-EP

7.06; Barnett, Erickson Cornish, et al., 2007; Falender & Shafranske, 2007; Goodyear & Rodolfa, 2012; Harvey & Struzziero, 2008). As recommended by Cobia and Boes (2000), the professional disclosure statement should outline the methods and timetable for evaluation. Evaluations should occur early and often enough in supervision to make and implement modifications in the individualized learning plan if the supervisee is not making the desired progress toward goals and objectives. As Knapp and VandeCreek (1997) suggested, the final evaluation of supervisee performance should "never come as a surprise to a supervisee" (p. 594).

Records of supervisee performance should be maintained on an ongoing basis and with sufficient detail to provide support for summative appraisals and any final recommendations (e.g., for or against approval for state certification). Supervisors should maintain a record of supervisory contacts to document that supervision was provided as promised in the professional disclosure statement and consistent with professional standards. In unusual circumstances, it may be necessary to terminate a supervisory relationship before the end of the agreed-on supervision period. In such situations, supervisors "should summarize the progress made by the supervisee, discuss the supervisee's additional need for supervision and training, draw generalizations from the supervision, resolve interpersonal issues, review the written evaluation with the supervisee in a personal interview, and bring supervision to a closure" (Harvey & Struzziero, 2008, pp. 59–60; also Goodyear & Rodolfa, 2012).

Integrity in Supervisor–Supervisee Professional Relationships

Supervisory relationships ideally are based on honesty, objectivity, and mutual respect. Supervisors "must be continually careful not to abuse the inherent power in the supervisor–supervisee relationship" (Vasquez, 1992, p. 200). Practitioners refrain from taking on a supervisory role when their own interests (personal, professional, financial) could reasonably be expected to impair their objectivity, competence, or effectiveness in providing supervision or place the supervisee at risk of exploitation or harm (APA-EP Principles A, B; NASP-PPE III.4.2–4.4; Gottlieb, Robinson, & Younggren, 2007). Supervisors are cautioned not to step into the dual role of therapist and supervisor to the supervisee (Goodyear & Rodolfa, 2012). When a supervisee displays signs of serious personal problems, the "appropriate role of the supervisor is to listen carefully, provide support, and refer the supervisee for additional counseling as appropriate" (Harvey & Struzziero, 2008, p. 46).

Psychologists also must consider potential problems associated with multiple relationships. In working with supervisees, multiple relationships occur when the psychologist is in a supervisory role and at the same time has another role with the same person, or a relationship with a person closely associated with or related to the supervisee (APA-EP 3.05; NASP-PPE III.4.2, III.4.4; Gottlieb et al., 2007). For example, a practitioner might be asked to accept the daughter or son of a close personal friend as a supervisee. The school psychologist is obligated to refrain from entering into a multiple relationship if the relationship could reasonably be expected to impair his or her performance as a supervising psychologist or might otherwise risk exploitation or harm to the supervisee (APA-EP 3.05).

University-based internship supervisors are obligated to comply with Title IX of the Education Amendments of 1972, a federal law that prohibits sexual harassment of students by university faculty. Under Title IX, sexual harassment in education can take two forms: quid pro quo and hostile environment.

> Quid pro quo harassment occurs when a school employee causes a student to believe that he or she must submit to unwelcome sexual conduct in order to participate in a school program or activity. It can also occur when an employee causes a student to believe that the employee will make an educational decision based on whether or not the student submits to unwelcome sexual conduct. For example, when a teacher threatens to fail a student unless the student agrees to date the teacher, it is quid pro quo harassment.
>
> Hostile environment harassment occurs when unwelcome conduct of a sexual nature is sufficiently serious that it affects a student's ability to participate in or benefit from an education program or activity, or creates an intimidating, threatening, or abusive educational environment. (Office for Civil Rights, 2014, p. 1)

Field-based supervisors of school psychology trainees also must take steps to ensure a training environment that is free of sexual harassment (NASP-PPE III.4.3). Sexual harassment in the workplace is a violation of Title VII of the Civil Rights Act of 1964. The U.S. Equal Employment Opportunity Commission (n.d.) defines sexual harassment as "unwelcome sexual advances, requests for sexual favors, and other verbal or physical conduct of a sexual nature ... when this conduct explicitly or implicitly affects an individual's employment, unreasonably interferes with an individual's work performance, or creates an intimidating, hostile, or offensive work environment" (p. 1).

It is not illegal for a supervisor to engage in a consensual sexual relationship with an adult supervisee or for a university faculty member to engage in a consensual sexual relationship with a graduate student. However, our ethical codes recognize the inherent imbalance of power between supervisors and supervisees and between professors and their students (C. B. Fisher, 2012). *Ethically,* school psychologists are prohibited from "engaging in sexual relationships with individuals over whom they have evaluation authority, including college students in their classes or program, or any other trainees, or supervisees" (NASP-PPE III.4.3; also APA-EP 3.02, 3.08, 7.07).

As Cobia and Boes (2000) and others (e.g., Harvey & Struzziero, 2008; Johnson et al., 2008) observed, the role of supervisor in psychology often involves the dual roles of evaluator and growth facilitator of the supervisee, and balancing these two roles may cause "ethical tugs" for the supervisor. As part of the supervision process, supervisors encourage supervisees to be open and self-disclosing, particularly regarding strengths and difficulties in professional functioning. However, as in Case 11.5, it is possible that the supervisee, as a result of the supervisor's encouragement, may disclose material that leads to the conclusion that the supervisee has serious skill deficits or personal problems and is perhaps not suited for the professional role of school psychologist (Cobia & Boes, 2000). Pearl (Case 11.5) may feel she has betrayed Jack's trust because, after encouraging his self-disclosure, she must now terminate his internship on the basis of the information disclosed.

=============================== **Case 11.5** ===============================

Jack Western was a capable and conscientious intern during his first semester as Pearl Meadows's supervisee. After winter vacation, however, Jack was often late to school, was sporadically absent due to illness, and appeared disorganized and unprepared for meetings. When Pearl expressed concern about this change in his performance, Jack apologized, attributed his tardiness and disorganization to the stress of completing his master's thesis, and promised to do better. The following week, however, when reviewing a student assessment he had completed, Pearl noticed that Jack had failed to record any of the child's verbatim responses on the Vocabulary and Comprehension WISC–V subtests and that his report was poorly written, with little attention to integration and interpretation of findings. Then, after lunch that day, Pearl thought she smelled alcohol on his breath. When Pearl queries Jack about the incomplete WISC–V protocol and hastily written report during their supervision meeting, Jack discloses that his wife left him over the winter holidays and that he is devastated by their separation. He never administered all the WISC–V subtests and simply fabricated the scores. When asked whether alcohol is a problem, he confides that he has been drinking heavily.

However, in supervision, ethical priority always must be given to the welfare of current and future clients. A distinction is made in the literature between supervisee *distress* and *professional competence problems* (previously termed *professional impairment*[1]). *Distress* occurs when the supervisee is experiencing stress or discomfort but still is able to provide services adequately and, with the support and guidance of the supervisor, make progress toward internship goals (Knapp & VandeCreek, 1997). In more serious situations, the supervisee may exhibit *professional competence problems*. This means that the supervisee is unable to perform his or her professional responsibilities competently, placing the client at risk for misdiagnosis, inappropriate and inadequate treatment, and possible harm. Distress and professional competence problems may "occur on a continuum with all practitioners having some degree of distress which, in turn, may lead (or has already led to) some degree" of compromised professional competence (Mahoney & Morris, 2012, p. 342). When a supervisee exhibits persistent substandard performance despite corrective efforts or engages in serious normative errors, it is ethically appropriate and necessary for the supervisor to recommend a failing internship grade, suspend or terminate the internship, or deny endorsement for state credentialing. These risks, along with the potential benefits of supervision, should be outlined in the professional disclosure statement (Johnson et al., 2008; Sherry, 1991).

---

[1] Historically, the term *professional impairment* was used in the literature. As Collins, Falender, and Shafranske (2011) noted, however, this term created confusion because *impairment* connotes a disability as defined by the Americans with Disabilities Act.

LIABILITY ISSUES

It is well established in common law that psychologists in private practice or health care settings may be held liable for their own actions or the actions of supervisees that result in harm to clients (Knapp & VandeCreek, 1997). The legal principle of *respondent superior* ("let the master answer" for the wrongful acts of his servant) provides the foundation for liability suits against a supervisor when the actions of a supervisee result in harm to a client (H. C. Black, 1983). As discussed in Chapter 2, however, states generally hold individual school employees immune from liability under state law during the performance of duties within the scope of their employment. The provision of supervision to school psychology trainees or employees should be included in the job description of practitioners who provide such services.

Inappropriate actions by a supervisee that result in harm to a schoolchild could trigger a negligence suit against the school under state law and possibly result in reprimand of the supervisor if it is determined that the supervisor failed to provide proper supervision to the supervisee. Supervisees should be reminded that they have a legal duty to take steps to protect students from reasonably foreseeable risk of harm, and, as noted previously, supervisees should receive verifiable training regarding how to respond to situations that suggest a potential danger to students or others. In addition, if a supervisee violates a student's constitutional rights or other rights under federal law, parents could file suit against the supervisor and supervisee under Section 1983 of the Civil Rights Act of 1871.

Also, parents who are not satisfied with the identification, evaluation, or placement of their child with a disability under special education law may request mediation, initiate a due process hearing, and pursue court action when administrative remedies are exhausted (see Chapters 4 and 5). Supervisors are advised to select their cases for interns and beginning practitioners carefully, avoiding those that might be expected to trigger difficult school–parent disagreements.

Although the likelihood of an intern being involved in a lawsuit in the school setting is probably small, we encourage supervisors and interns to consider purchasing professional liability insurance. Interns may not be covered by the school district's liability insurance if they are not also employees of the district (see Chapter 2).

CONCLUDING COMMENTS

Quality supervision helps to ensure that practitioners are trained and prepared to provide school psychological services that meet high professional standards (Harvey & Pearrow, 2010). School psychologists should consider ways they can contribute to the field by providing quality supervision to interns and beginning practitioners and ways they might contribute to our knowledge of effective supervision practices by conducting or participating in research on supervision.

STUDY AND DISCUSSION

Questions for Chapter 11

1. Compare *clinical supervision* to *consultation* in terms of ultimate responsibility for client welfare.
2. What is a *professional disclosure statement*? What purpose does it serve? What is an *individualized learning plan*? What purpose does it serve?
3. What are *technical errors, judgmental errors*, and *normative errors*?
4. What is *quid pro quo* sexual harassment?
5. Why is a consensual sexual relationship between a university professor and his or her adult graduate student considered to be unethical?
6. What is the difference between *supervisee distress* and *professional competence problems*?
7. Can supervisors be held responsible for the inappropriate actions of their supervisees?

Discussion

1. In Case 11.3, both the supervisor, James Lewis, and the supervisee, Donita Mason, are African American, and a situation arises that requires them to discuss race, dialect, and social class as part of the supervision process. Do you think that the situation described in Case 11.3 would be more difficult for a supervisor to handle if the supervisor was White? Why? What are a supervisor's ethical obligations with regard to working with a supervisee from a different cultural, racial, or experiential background? Read the "best practice considerations in multicultural supervision" in Elkund, Aros-O'Malley, and Murrieta (2014). We suspect that it is unlikely that a supervisor would initiate a conversation with the supervisee by saying "Donita, let's talk about the use of African American Vernacular English." So, how would you talk about the issue of dialect usage and linguistic prejudice in a culturally sensitive manner?
2. Reread Case 11.5 about Pearl Meadows and her supervisee, Jack Western. What information do you think Pearl should share with Jack's university supervisor, and why? What information should Pearl disclose to the school district regarding the termination of Jack's internship, and why? Do you believe Pearl should recommend to the university that Jack be permanently dismissed from his graduate training program? Or do you believe Jack should be allowed to complete an internship after he has received treatment for alcohol abuse and personal problems? What are the ethical reasons for or against each course of action? See Lamb et al. (1991) for a discussion of suggested procedures for identifying and responding to a supervisee's problematic behaviors or professional competence problems.

Epilogue: Ethics, Law, and Advocacy ———

The code of ethics of the National Association of School Psychologists (NASP, 2010a) states: "School psychologists consider the interests and rights of children and youth to be their highest priority in decision making and act as advocates for all students" (NASP-PPE Introduction). In addition, consistent with the general ethical principle of responsible caring and our commitment to building the capacity of systems, practitioners promote scientifically sound school policies to enhance the welfare of all students. They also are encouraged to work as advocates for change at the state and national level to better address the needs of children (NASP-PPE IV.1, IV.1.2; also Duncan & Fodness, 2008; Nastasi, 2008).

Many different definitions of *advocacy* exist. The NASP's "Principles for Professional Ethics" describes advocacy in this way:

> School psychologists have a special obligation to speak up for the rights and welfare of students and families, and to provide a voice to clients who cannot or do not wish to speak for themselves. Advocacy also occurs when school psychologists use their expertise in psychology and education to promote changes in schools, systems, and laws that will benefit school children, other students, and families. Nothing in this code of ethics, however, should be construed as requiring school psychologists to engage in insubordination (willful disregard of an employer's lawful instructions) or to file a complaint about school district practices with a federal or state regulatory agency as part of their advocacy efforts. (NASP-PPE Definition of Terms)

In 1974, a special issue of NASP's *School Psychology Digest* (now *School Psychology Review*) addressed emerging ethical and legal issues in school psychology (Kaplan, Crisci, & Farling, 1974). One concern expressed by multiple authors was the challenge of managing conflicts inherent in the dual roles of child advocate and school employee. Not surprisingly, in several subsequent research studies, school-based psychologists reported pressure from their supervisors to put the administrative needs of the district (e.g., to contain costs, to maintain discipline) ahead of the rights and needs of students (Dailor & Jacob, 2011; Helton, Ray, & Biderman, 2000; Jacob-Timm, 1999). Although school administrators also are committed to promoting the welfare of all students, they face pressures to base decisions on "the good of the whole" rather than the needs of individual students and to carefully manage limited resources (Denig & Quinn, 2001). As is evident from the F. L. Miller's (2009) experiences detailed in Exhibit E.1, advocating for the best interests of the student and upholding ethical standards, while at the same time facing pressure from administrators to simply defer to their judgments, continues to be a challenge for school-based psychological practitioners.

Exhibit E.1 Excerpt from "Advocacy: The Risks and Rewards"
by Frank L. Miller

School psychologists are very different from other public school employees—teachers, counselors, and paraprofessionals. We are *required* by our ethical guidelines to speak up. While most employees defer to the administrator, we cannot, and as such we often stand out as the fly in the ointment. We must always be ready to offer reasonable alternatives to administrators frustrated in their attempts to maintain a safe and orderly building. We must, in a quiet and yet determined fashion, also help administrators to understand that in protecting the disabled student, we are also protecting the school district, and we are protecting them. The fine line between advocacy and insubordination is just that, a fine line, but as long as we understand our role, and communicate it loudly and clearly to our superiors, they can choose to respect what we have to say, or they can simply remove us from the case. They do this, however, at their own peril. And never give up; there's a reason school psychologists are part of this process: We know the law, we understand the psychological dynamics of behavior, and we understand our role as a powerful and sometimes lonesome advocate for students.

Source: F. L. Miller, 2009, pp. 17–18.

Throughout this book, we have focused on the ways in which our codes of ethics protect the rights and interests of children and their parents in the school setting. In this epilogue, we discuss the complex legal landscape for school-based practitioners who wish to advocate for students when they encounter unjust or ineffective school practices and offer suggestions for speaking up effectively without facing disciplinary action or dismissal by employers. We then identify several general guidelines for developing an ethical practice.

ADVOCACY AND A COMPLEX LEGAL LANDSCAPE

As noted in Chapter 2, tension exists between the school psychologist's obligation to speak up as an advocate for schoolchildren and the limits of his or her free speech rights as a public school employee. The most important U.S. Supreme Court decision specifically addressing the right of a school employee to comment publicly on school practices is *Pickering v. Board of Education of Township High School District 205, Will County* (1968). *Pickering* concerned a public school teacher, Marvin L. Pickering, who wrote a letter to the editor of a local newspaper criticizing the way in which the board of education handled proposals to increase revenue for the schools. He subsequently was dismissed on the grounds that the letter was detrimental to the operation of the school.

In *Pickering*, the appellant claimed that his dismissal for writing the letter was a violation of his First Amendment right to freedom of speech.

Supreme Court Justice Marshall delivered the opinion of the Court. He wrote that it is necessary "to arrive at a balance between the interests of the teacher, as a citizen, in commenting on matters of public concern and the interest of the State, as an employer, in promoting the efficiency of the public services it performs through its employees" (*Pickering*, p. 568). He opined that the statements in Pickering's letter were "in no way directed towards any person with whom appellant [Pickering] would normally be in contact in the course of his daily work as a teacher" (pp. 569–570). No evidence was found that the letter interfered with the operation of the school (p. 567) or Pickering's performance of his duties as a teacher (p. 572). The letter also did not diminish the authority of supervisors or harmony among coworkers or violate expectations of confidentiality within the school (p. 570). Justice Marshall concluded that, "in the absence of proof of false statements knowingly or recklessly made by the teacher, his right to speak on issues of public importance could not furnish the basis for his dismissal, and that under the circumstances ... his dismissal violated his constitutional right to free speech" (p. 563).

Pickering thus suggested that when school psychologists speak as private citizens *on matters of public concern,* their speech is protected, and it typically cannot be the basis for disciplinary action. However, they should take care to ensure that their facts and statements are accurate and in good faith. Furthermore, open criticism of specific school administrators (by name or position) is not likely to be protected speech because it likely would be viewed as undermining their authority. Subsequent court decisions addressed the meaning of the phrase *matters of public concern.* In *Connick v. Myers* (1983), the Supreme Court noted that whether an employee's speech "is a matter of public concern is determined by the content, form, and context of a given statement, as revealed by the whole record" (pp. 147–148). More recently, the Supreme Court opined that speech involves matters of public concern "when it can be 'fairly considered as relating to any matter of political, social, or other concern to the community,' or when it 'is a subject of legitimate news interest; that is, a subject of general interest and value and concern to the public'" (*Snyder v. Phelps,* 2011, p. 453).

A 2006 U.S. Supreme Court decision seemed to place new emphasis on the right of government employers to restrict the speech of their employees. In *Garcetti v. Ceballos* (2006), the Court opined that "when public employees make statements pursuant to their official duties, they are not speaking as citizens for First Amendment purposes, and the Constitution does not insulate their communications from employer discipline." The opinion went on to state: "Without a significant degree of control over its employees' words and actions, a government employer would have little chance to provide public services efficiently.... Thus, a government entity has *broad discretion to restrict speech when it acts in its employer role*, but the restrictions it imposes must be directed at speech that has some potential to affect its operations" (p. 419, emphasis added). It is important to note that the opinion did acknowledge the significance of federal and state whistle-blower protections of employees who expose unlawful actions by their employers (see *Settlegoode v. Portland Public Schools*, 2004; Chapter 5). In addition, speech related to teaching and scholarship was explicitly excluded from the decision.

In his *Garcetti* (2006) opinion, Justice Kennedy made observations particularly relevant to the advocacy role of school psychologists. He noted: "A public employer that wishes to encourage its employees to voice concerns privately retains the option of instituting internal policies and procedures that are receptive to employee criticism. Giving employees an internal forum for their speech will discourage them from concluding that the safest avenue of expression is to state their views in public" (p. 424). Consistent with this observation, school psychologists are well advised to ask administrators to identify and agree on communication channels and forums that are appropriate within-district venues for staff to voice concerns about ineffective school policies and practices without fear of disciplinary sanctions for speaking out. Furthermore, school-based practitioners are wise to emphasize the potential positive effects of implementing new policies and practices in their advocacy efforts rather than simply criticizing existing practices.

As noted, Justice Kennedy stated that the *Garcetti* (2006) decision was not applicable to "speech related to scholarship or teaching" (p. 425). However, *Garcetti* subsequently was cited as a basis for lower court decisions concerning public K–12 and college employees. In the 2014 *Lane v. Franks* ruling, the Supreme Court provided some additional clarification of the meaning of *Garcetti* for public school employees. *Lane v. Franks* concerned an employee (Lane) of a community college who testified in a federal criminal case against an employee whom he had fired and who was now on trial for mail fraud and theft of monies from a program receiving federal funds. Lane subsequently was terminated from the college. He filed suit against the community college president because he believed his termination was in retaliation for testifying against the employee whom he had terminated. When the case reached the 11th Circuit Court, the court, citing *Garcetti*, held that, as a public employee, Lane's speech was not protected by the First Amendment when he testified against a former employee.

Lane appealed to the U.S. Supreme Court. Like the 11th Circuit Court, the Supreme Court also deliberated about whether Lane's testimony was speech as a private citizen on matters of public concern and protected by the First Amendment or speech pursuant to his official job duties and therefore not protected by the First Amendment. Justice Sotomayer wrote the majority opinion:

> [T]he mere fact that a citizen's speech concerns information acquired by virtue of his public employment does not transform that speech into employee—rather than citizen—speech. The critical question under *Garcetti* is whether the speech at issue is itself ordinarily within the scope of an employee's duties, not whether it merely concerns those duties. (*Lane v. Franks*, 2014, p. 2379)

After establishing that his testimony at the trial of a former employee was outside the scope of Lane's ordinary job duties, Justice Sotomayer went on to hold that his speech was on a matter of public concern (corruption in a public program) and therefore protected by the First Amendment. Justice Sotomayer also noted that the employer (the community college) had no legitimate interest in silencing Lane's speech and that Lane did not inappropriately disclose sensitive, confidential, or privileged information. The Supreme Court reversed the ruling of the 11th Circuit Court.

The Supreme Court decision in *Lane* thus clarified that the Court distinguishes between speech within the scope of an employee's duties (not protected by First

Amendment) and "citizen" speech that involves information acquired in his or her employment setting (possibly protected by the First Amendment if the speech does not interfere with the functioning of the school, impair within-school relationships, or breach confidentiality expectations).

In sum, the speech of school-employed school psychologists made pursuant to their official job duties is not protected by the First Amendment. Under *Pickering* and *Lane*, citizen speech (speech that is not pursuit to job duties) on matters of public concern *may* be protected by the First Amendment even if it involves information the employee acquired in his or her employment setting. Under *Pickering* and *Garcetti*, school psychologists can be disciplined for what they say or write—whether employee or citizen speech, on or off school grounds—if their speech: threatens to undermine the authority of school administrators; potentially disrupts relationships in the school, especially those based on trust and confidentiality; would likely impair the employee's performance of his or her duties; or could disrupt the learning atmosphere of the school. School-based practitioners should never assume that electronic communications are confidential (at home or at work).

Case law to date provides limited insight into how the courts might respond if a school psychologist was dismissed for speaking out in an appropriate, factual manner about a legitimate concern related to the welfare of students and he or she subsequently challenged the dismissal in court. For example, if a school psychologist spoke out publicly against the use of corporal punishment in his or her school district and was dismissed, would the courts consider his or her speech a matter of public concern protected by the First Amendment? Would the courts use a balancing test that weighs the interest of the school in maintaining order, the school psychologist's ethical duty to promote student welfare, *and the interests of the students* in a safe and orderly learning environment, one that is free from the potential harms known to be associated with corporal punishment (Harvard Law Review Association, 2011)?

Regardless of the answers to these questions, school psychologists, as noted previously, are wise to emphasize the potential positive effects of implementing new policies and practices in their advocacy efforts rather than simply criticizing existing practices. They are also well advised to advocate for evidence-based effective practices using factual and verifiable statements. Using corporal punishment as an example, school psychologists could, through appropriate channels, advocate for the introduction of a schoolwide positive behavior interventions and support system as an alternative to punitive and ineffective school discipline approaches (Chapter 9). Although it often is persuasive to share anecdotal incidents to illustrate why change is needed, practitioners must avoid disclosing confidential information about students and families, school staff, or others as part of their advocacy efforts. Furthermore, regardless of personal feelings and frustrations, practitioners are ethically obligated to engage in conduct that is respectful of all persons at all times. In addition, "to best meet the needs of children, school psychologists cooperate with other professionals in relationships based on mutual respect" (NASP-PPE Principle III.3). School change requires collaborative partnerships and open channels of communication among many stakeholders.

As noted, school-based practitioners are not ethically required to engage in insubordination (willful disregard of an employer's lawful instructions) as part of their efforts to advocate for children (NASP-PPE Definition of Terms). Although widely varying definitions of the term *insubordination* exist across states, dismissal of school employees for insubordination has been upheld in many court cases (McCarthy, Cambron-McCabe, & Thomas, 2004). If a school psychologist believes it is necessary to engage in insubordination to safeguard fundamental human rights, the practitioner should seek legal advice (American Psychological Association Committee on Professional Practice and Standards, 2003).

PROACTIVE SURVIVAL STRATEGIES FOR ADVOCATES

In this section, we offer some considerations and strategies to assist practitioners in balancing the roles of employee and advocate.

- If at all feasible, negotiate a job description that encompasses advocacy for evidence-based practices and the freedom to adhere to the NASP and American Psychological Association codes of ethics.
- Some districts have privatized their school psychology services. If feasible, only accept a job position as a school district employee, either full-time or part-time or by contracting directly with the school. Be extremely cautious of jobs offered by health care companies that hire school psychologists to provide services to one or multiple districts. Such companies may advertise attractive salaries and benefits. However, private sector employees likely have no union protection again arbitrary and unfair dismissal. Also, an employee of a private sector health care provider, unlike an employee of a school system, may not receive supervision to foster professional growth or yearly performance evaluations documenting good work. Furthermore, health care companies may provide no professional liability protection. If, nevertheless, you are interested in employment at such an agency, read the contract offered to you very carefully. What is the job description? Are you a "fire at will" employee? If yes, how might that impact your ability to advocate respectfully for a child's best interests if those interests conflict with school pressures to make certain decisions?
- If you are a school employee, join and support your teachers' union. Union membership can help ensure that you are treated fairly if your advocacy efforts result in tensions with school administrators and the district threatens disciplinary action against you.
- Join and support your state school psychology association. Even if you cannot be active in association leadership, your membership dues may help support a lobbyist who can advocate for legislation that supports a comprehensive model of school psychological services. Your state association also can alert you to upcoming state legislative issues that affect K–12 schools, children, and school psychologists, allowing you to make an informed choice about whether to voice your concerns to a legislator.
- Learn about the views of candidates for local (e.g., school board), state, and federal elected positions in the areas of school policies and funding, curricular issues, children's needs, and teachers' unions. Exercise your right to vote.

- Interpersonal or social power is the potential for one individual to affect the attitudes, perceptions, and/or behavior of another (French & Raven, 1959). Two forms of social power available to a school psychologist are *expert power* and *referent power*. With expert power, the principal, teacher, or parent perceives that the school psychologist has the skills and knowledge to help him or her accomplish goals. Referent power, in contrast, is attributed to the school psychologist when the principal, teacher, or parent perceives the psychologist as trustworthy and as having values similar to his or her own, especially with regard to caring about the welfare of children. Practitioners are advised to build social power patiently and thoughtfully prior to attempting a leadership role in systems-level change. This means creating a record of exemplary service and actively pursuing collaborative partnerships with district and building administrators; with teachers, particularly those who are the school's opinion leaders; with health professionals in the school and in the community (nurses, social workers, counselors); with community leaders, including religious leaders; and with influential parents and parent groups. By first developing social power, the school psychologist increases the likelihood that he or she will be able to influence stakeholders in advocacy efforts and garner their support for change.
- If a school district seeks to discipline or dismiss an employee because of his or her advocacy efforts, it is likely that the district will claim the employee performed his or her job poorly or that he or she engaged in insubordination. For this reason, it is wise to document your advocacy actions carefully and retain records of your performance appraisals in the unlikely event that your employer disciplines you for speaking up for change in school policies and practices.

DEVELOPING AN ETHICAL PRACTICE

The next guidelines for developing an ethical school psychology practice were first suggested in Jacob (2008, pp. 1930–1931) and are reprinted here with some modifications. By developing an ethical practice, we enhance our credibility and ability to effectively advocate for children on the individual and systems levels.

- Keep up-to-date regarding developments in ethics and law by reading professional publications and newsletters and attending conferences and workshops. Lifelong learning is necessary to achieve and maintain expertise in applied professional ethics (Armistead, 2014a; Ysseldyke et al., 2006).
- Be sensitive to the ethical and legal components of service delivery and adopt a proactive stance; that is, work to anticipate and avoid ethical and legal problems. When difficult situations arise, use a decision-making model to choose the best course of action.
- Develop a positive approach to ethics; that is, strive for excellence rather than meeting minimal obligations outlined in codes of ethics and law (Knapp & VandeCreek, 2012). Be candid about commitments and priorities, and foster a reputation for being a psychologist who is dedicated to high standards of service delivery and whose primary concern is to promote the best interests of children.

- Take care to discuss confidentiality and its limits with each student, his or her parents, and other clients at the outset of establishing a school psychologist–client relationship, and maintain confidentiality as promised.
- Consistent with the broad ethical principles of beneficence, responsible caring, and responsibility to community and society, work to build the capacity of systems to better address the academic, wellness, and mental health needs of children (Ysseldyke et al., 2006).
- As noted in Chapter 8, school psychologists encounter difficult teachers, administrators, colleagues, staff, parents, and students in the course of their careers. Regardless of personal feelings and frustrations, engage in conduct that is respectful of all persons at all times (NASP-PPE I). Practitioners who are courteous, tactful, sensitive, and good listeners are more likely to foster positive working relationships with their clientele, build and maintain trust, avoid client complaints, and achieve excellence in their profession.

CONCLUDING COMMENTS

In attempting to write as current a book as we could, we have been impressed by the speed with which law and ethics change. You, the school psychologist, must take it from here. This means maintaining your currency regarding new developments in ethics and law and also working proactively for school policies and law to better serve the interests and rights of children.

Appendix A

National Association of School Psychologists

Principles for Professional Ethics

2010

TABLE OF CONTENTS

I. RESPECTING THE DIGNITY AND RIGHTS OF ALL PERSONS

School psychologists engage only in professional practices that maintain the dignity of all individuals. In their words and actions, school psychologists demonstrate respect for the autonomy of persons and their right to self-determination, respect for privacy, and a commitment to just and fair treatment of all persons.

II. PROFESSIONAL COMPETENCE AND RESPONSIBILITY

Beneficence, or responsible caring, means that the school psychologist acts to benefit others. To do this, school psychologists must practice within the boundaries of their competence, use scientific knowledge from psychology and education to help clients and others make informed choices, and accept responsibility for their work.

III. HONESTY AND INTEGRITY IN PROFESSIONAL RELATIONSHIPS

To foster and maintain trust, school psychologists must be faithful to the truth and adhere to their professional promises. They are forthright about their qualifications, competencies, and roles; work in full cooperation with other professional disciplines to meet the needs of students and families; and avoid multiple relationships that diminish their professional effectiveness.

IV. RESPONSIBILITY TO SCHOOLS, FAMILIES, COMMUNITIES, THE PROFESSION, AND SOCIETY

School psychologists promote healthy school, family, and community environments. They assume a proactive role in identifying social injustices that affect children and schools and strive to reform systems-level patterns of injustice. They maintain the public trust in school psychologists by respecting law and encouraging ethical conduct. School psychologists advance professional excellence by mentoring less experienced practitioners and contributing to the school psychology knowledge base.

National Association of School Psychologists

Principles for Professional Ethics
2010

INTRODUCTION

The mission of the National Association of School Psychologists (NASP) is to represent school psychology and support school psychologists to enhance the learning and mental health of all children and youth. NASP's mission is accomplished through identification of appropriate evidence-based education and mental health services for all children; implementation of professional practices that are empirically supported, data driven, and culturally competent; promotion of professional competence of school psychologists; recognition of the essential components of high-quality graduate education and professional development in school psychology; preparation of school psychologists to deliver a continuum of services for children, youth, families, and schools; and advocacy for the value of school psychological services, among other important initiatives.

School psychologists provide effective services to help children and youth succeed academically, socially, behaviorally, and emotionally. School psychologists provide direct educational and mental health services for children and youth, as well as work with parents, educators, and other professionals to create supportive learning and social environments for all children. School psychologists apply their knowledge of both psychology and education during consultation and collaboration with others. They conduct effective decision making using a foundation of assessment and data collection. School psychologists engage in specific services for students, such as direct and indirect interventions that focus on academic skills, learning, socialization, and mental health. School psychologists provide services to schools and families that enhance the competence and well-being of children, including promotion of effective and safe learning environments, prevention of academic and behavior problems, response to crises, and improvement of family-school collaboration. The key foundations for all services by school psychologists are understanding of diversity in development and learning; research and program evaluation; and legal, ethical, and professional practice. All of these components and their relationships are depicted in Appendix A [Figure A.1], a graphic representation of a national model for comprehensive and integrated services by school psychologists. School psychologists are credentialed by state education agencies or other similar state entities that have the statutory authority to regulate and establish credentialing requirements for professional practice within a state. School psychologists typically work in public or private schools or other educational contexts.

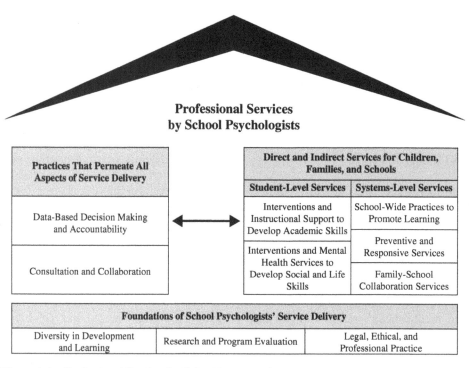

**Professional Services
by School Psychologists**

Practices That Permeate All Aspects of Service Delivery		Direct and Indirect Services for Children, Families, and Schools	
		Student-Level Services	Systems-Level Services
Data-Based Decision Making and Accountability	◄──►	Interventions and Instructional Support to Develop Academic Skills	School-Wide Practices to Promote Learning
Consultation and Collaboration		Interventions and Mental Health Services to Develop Social and Life Skills	Preventive and Responsive Services
			Family-School Collaboration Services

Foundations of School Psychologists' Service Delivery		
Diversity in Development and Learning	Research and Program Evaluation	Legal, Ethical, and Professional Practice

Figure A.1   Professional Services by School Psychologists

The NASP *Principles for Professional Ethics* is designed to be used in conjunction with the NASP *Standards for Graduate Preparation of School Psychologists*, *Standards for the Credentialing of School Psychologists*, and *Model for Comprehensive and Integrated School Psychological Services* to provide a unified set of national principles that guide graduate education, credentialing, professional practices, and ethical behavior of effective school psychologists. These NASP policy documents are intended to define contemporary school psychology; promote school psychologists' services for children, families, and schools; and provide a foundation for the future of school psychology. These NASP policy documents are used to communicate NASP's positions and advocate for qualifications and practices of school psychologists with stakeholders, policy makers, and other professional groups at the national, state, and local levels.

The formal principles that elucidate the proper conduct of a professional school psychologist are known as *ethics*. In 1974, the National Association of School Psychologists (NASP) adopted its first code of ethics, the *Principles for Professional Ethics* (*Principles*), and revisions were made in 1984, 1992, 1997, and 2000. The purpose of the *Principles* is to protect the public and those who receive school psychological services by sensitizing school psychologists to the ethical aspects of their work, educating them about appropriate conduct, helping them monitor their own behavior, and providing standards to be used in the resolution of complaints of unethical conduct.[1] NASP members and school psychologists who are certified by the National School Psychologist Certification System (NCSP) are bound to abide by NASP's code of ethics.[2]

The NASP *Principles for Professional Ethics* were developed to address the unique circumstances associated with providing school psychological services. The duty to educate children and the legal authority to do so rests with state governments. When school psychologists employed by a school board make decisions in their official roles, such acts are seen as actions by state government. As state actors, school-based practitioners have special obligations to all students. They must know and respect the rights of students under the U.S. Constitution and federal and state statutory law. They must balance the authority of parents to make decisions about their children with the needs and rights of those children, and the purposes and authority of schools. Furthermore, as school employees, school psychologists have a legal as well as an ethical obligation to take steps to protect all students from reasonably foreseeable risk of harm. Finally, school-based practitioners work in a context that emphasizes multidisciplinary problem solving and intervention.[3] For these reasons, psychologists employed by the schools may have less control over aspects of service delivery than practitioners in private practice. However, within this framework, it is expected that school psychologists will make careful, reasoned, and principled ethical choices[4] based on knowledge of this code, recognizing that responsibility for ethical conduct rests with the individual practitioner.

School psychologists are committed to the application of their professional expertise for the purpose of promoting improvement in the quality of life for students, families, and school communities. This objective is pursued in ways that protect the dignity and rights of those involved. School psychologists consider the interests and rights of children and youth to be their highest priority in decision making, and act as advocates for all students. These assumptions necessitate that school psychologists "speak up" for the needs and rights of students even when it may be difficult to do so.

The *Principles for Professional Ethics*, like all codes of ethics, provide only limited guidance in making ethical choices. Individual judgment is necessary to apply the code to situations that arise in professional practice. Ethical dilemmas may be created by situations involving competing ethical principles, conflicts between ethics and law, the conflicting interests of multiple parties, the dual roles of employee and pupil advocate, or because it is difficult to decide how statements in the ethics code apply to a particular situation.[5] Such situations are often complicated and may require a nuanced application of these *Principles* to effect a resolution that results in the greatest benefit for the student and concerned others. When difficult situations arise, school psychologists are advised to use a systematic problem-solving process to identify the best course of action. This process should include identifying the ethical issues involved, consulting these *Principles*, consulting colleagues with greater expertise, evaluating the rights and welfare of all affected parties, considering alternative solutions and their consequences; and accepting responsibility for the decisions made.[7]

The NASP *Principles for Professional Ethics* may require a more stringent standard of conduct than law, and in those situations in which both apply, school psychologists are expected to adhere to the *Principles*. When conflicts between ethics and law occur, school psychologists are expected to take steps to resolve conflicts by problem solving with others and through positive, respected, and legal channels. If not able to resolve the conflict in this manner, they may abide by the law, as long as the resulting actions do not violate basic human rights.[8]

In addition to providing services to public and private schools, school psychologists may be employed in a variety of other settings, including juvenile justice institutions, colleges and universities, mental health clinics, hospitals, and private practice. The principles in this code should be considered by school psychologists in their ethical decision making regardless of employment setting. However, this revision of the code, like its precursors, focuses on the special challenges associated with providing school psychological services in schools and to students. School psychologists who provide services directly to children, parents, and other clients as private practitioners, and those who work in health and mental health settings, are encouraged to be knowledgeable of federal and state law regulating mental health providers, and to consult the American Psychological Association's (2002) *Ethical Principles of Psychologists and Code of Conduct* for guidance on issues not directly addressed in this code.

Four broad ethical themes[9] provide the organizational framework for the 2010 *Principles for Professional Ethics*. The four broad ethical themes subsume 17 ethical principles. Each principle is then further articulated by multiple specific standards of conduct. The broad themes, corollary principles, and ethical standards are to be considered in decision making. NASP will seek to enforce the 17 ethical principles and corollary standards that appear in the *Principles for Professional Ethics* with its members and school psychologists who hold the NCSP credential in accordance with NASP's *Ethical and Professional Practices Committee Procedures* (2008). Regardless of role, clientele, or setting, school psychologists should reflect on the theme and intent of each ethical principle and standard to determine its application to his or her individual situation.

The decisions made by school psychologists affect the welfare of children and families and can enhance their schools and communities. For this reason, school psychologists are encouraged to strive for excellence rather than simply meeting the minimum obligations outlined in the NASP *Principles for Professional Ethics*[10], and to engage in the lifelong learning that is necessary to achieve and maintain expertise in applied professional ethics.

DEFINITION OF TERMS AS USED IN THE *PRINCIPLES FOR PROFESSIONAL ETHICS*

Client: The *client* is the person or persons with whom the school psychologist establishes a professional relationship for the purpose of providing school psychological services. A school psychologist–client professional relationship is established by an informed agreement with client(s) about the school psychologist's ethical and other duties to each party.[11] While not *clients* per se, classrooms, schools, and school systems also may be recipients of school psychological services and often are parties with an interest in the actions of school psychologists.

Child: A *child*, as defined in law, generally refers to a minor, a person younger than the age of majority. Although this term may be regarded as demeaning when applied to teenagers, it is used in this document when necessary to denote minor status. The term *student* is used when a less precise term is adequate.

Informed Consent: Informed consent means that the person giving consent has the legal authority to make a consent decision, a clear understanding of what it is he or she is consenting to, and that his or her consent is freely given and may be withdrawn without prejudice.[12]

Assent: The term *assent* refers to a minor's affirmative agreement to participate in psychological services or research.

Parent: The term *parent* may be defined in law or district policy, and can include the birth or adoptive parent, an individual acting in the place of a natural or adoptive parent (a grandparent or other relative, stepparent, or domestic partner), and/or an individual who is legally responsible for the child's welfare.

Advocacy: School psychologists have a special obligation to speak up for the rights and welfare of students and families, and to provide a voice to clients who cannot or do not wish to speak for themselves. *Advocacy* also occurs when school psychologists use their expertise in psychology and education to promote changes in schools, systems, and laws that will benefit school children, other students, and families.[13] Nothing in this code of ethics, however, should be construed as requiring school psychologists to engage in insubordination (willful disregard of an employer's lawful instructions) or to file a complaint about school district practices with a federal or state regulatory agency as part of their advocacy efforts.

School-based versus Private Practice: School-based practice refers to the provision of school psychological services under the authority of a state, regional, or local educational agency. School-based practice occurs if the school psychologist is an employee of the schools or contracted by the schools on a per case or consultative basis. *Private practice* occurs when a school psychologist enters into an agreement with a client(s) rather than an educational agency to provide school psychological services and the school psychologists' fee for services is the responsibility of the client or his or her representative.

I. Respecting the Dignity and Rights of All Persons

School psychologists engage only in professional practices that maintain the dignity of all with whom they work. In their words and actions, school psychologists demonstrate respect for the autonomy of persons and their right to self-determination, respect for privacy, and a commitment to just and fair treatment of all persons.

Principle I.1 Autonomy and Self-Determination (Consent and Assent)
School psychologists respect the right of persons to participate in decisions affecting their own welfare.

Standard I.1.1 School psychologists encourage and promote parental participation in school decisions affecting their children (see Standard II.3.10). However, where school psychologists are members of the school's educational support staff, not all of their services require informed parent consent. It is ethically permissible to provide school-based consultation services regarding a child or adolescent to a student assistance team or teacher without informed parent consent as long as the resulting interventions are under the authority of the teacher and within the scope of typical classroom interventions.[14] Parent consent is not ethically required for a school-based school psychologist to review a student's educational records, conduct classroom observations, assist in within-classroom interventions and progress monitoring, or to participate in educational screenings conducted as part of a regular program of instruction. Parent consent is required if the consultation about a particular child or adolescent is likely to be extensive and on-going and/or if school actions may result in a significant intrusion on student or family privacy beyond what might be expected in the course of ordinary school activities.[15] Parents must be notified prior to the administration of school- or classroom-wide screenings for mental health problems and given the opportunity to remove their child or adolescent from participation in such screenings.

Standard I.1.2 Except for urgent situations or self-referrals by a minor student, school psychologists seek parent consent (or the consent of an adult student) prior to establishing a school psychologist–client relationship for the purpose of psychological diagnosis, assessment of eligibility for special education or disability accommodations, or to provide ongoing individual or group counseling or other non-classroom therapeutic intervention.*

- It is ethically permissible to provide psychological assistance without parent notice or consent in emergency situations or if there is reason to believe a student may pose a danger to others; is at risk for self-harm; or is in danger of injury, exploitation, or maltreatment.

- When a student who is a minor self-refers for assistance, it is ethically permissible to provide psychological assistance without parent notice or consent for one or several meetings to establish the nature and degree of the need for services and assure the child is safe and not in danger. It is ethically permissible to provide services to mature minors without parent consent where allowed by state law and school district policy. However, if the student is *not* old enough to receive school psychological assistance independent of parent consent, the school psychologist obtains parent consent to provide continuing assistance to the student beyond the preliminary meetings or refers the student to alternative sources of assistance that do not require parent notice or consent.

Standard I.1.3 School psychologists ensure that an individual providing consent for school psychological services is fully informed about the nature and scope of services offered, assessment/intervention goals and procedures, any foreseeable risks, the cost of services to the parent or student (if any), and the benefits that reasonably can be expected.

*It is recommended that school district parent handbooks and web sites advise parents that a minor student may be seen by school health or mental health professionals (e.g., school nurse, counselor, social worker, school psychologist) without parent notice or consent to ensure that the student is safe or is not a danger to others. Parents should also be advised that district school psychologists routinely assist teachers in planning classroom instruction and monitoring its effectiveness and do not need to notify parents of, or seek consent for, such involvement in student support.

The explanation includes discussion of the limits of confidentiality, who will receive information about assessment or intervention outcomes, and the possible consequences of the assessment/intervention services being offered. Available alternative services are identified, if appropriate. This explanation takes into account language and cultural differences, cognitive capabilities, developmental level, age, and other relevant factors so that it may be understood by the individual providing consent. School psychologists appropriately document written or oral consent. Any service provision by interns, practicum students, or other trainees is explained and agreed to in advance, and the identity and responsibilities of the supervising school psychologist are explained prior to the provision of services.[16]

Standard I.1.4 School psychologists encourage a minor student's voluntary participation in decision making about school psychological services as much as feasible. Ordinarily, school psychologists seek the student's assent to services; however, it is ethically permissible to by-pass student assent to services if the service is considered to be of direct benefit to the student and/or is required by law.[17]

- If a student's assent for services is not solicited, school psychologists nevertheless honor the student's right to be informed about the services provided.

- When a student is given a choice regarding whether to accept or refuse services, the school psychologist ensures the student understands what is being offered, honors the student's stated choice, and guards against overwhelming the student with choices he or she does not wish or is not able to make.[18]

Standard I.1.5 School psychologists respect the wishes of parents who object to school psychological services and attempt to guide parents to alternative resources.

Principle I.2 Privacy and Confidentiality
School psychologists respect the right of persons to choose for themselves whether to disclose their private thoughts, feelings, beliefs, and behaviors.

Standard I.2.1 School psychologists respect the right of persons to self-determine whether to disclose private information.

Standard I.2.2 School psychologists minimize intrusions on privacy. They do not seek or store private information about clients that is not needed in the provision of services. School psychologists recognize that client-school psychologist communications are privileged in most jurisdictions and do not disclose information that would put the student or family at legal, social, or other risk if shared with third parties, except as permitted by the mental health provider-client privilege laws in their state.[19]

Standard I.2.3 School psychologists inform students and other clients of the boundaries of confidentiality at the outset of establishing a professional relationship. They seek a shared understanding with clients regarding the types of information that will and will not be shared with third parties. However, if a child or adolescent is in immediate need of assistance, it is permissible to delay the discussion of confidentiality until the immediate crisis is resolved. School psychologists recognize that it may be necessary to discuss confidentiality at multiple points in a professional relationship to ensure client understanding and agreement regarding how sensitive disclosures will be handled.

Standard I.2.4 School psychologists respect the confidentiality of information obtained during their professional work. Information is not revealed to third parties without the agreement of a minor child's parent or legal guardian (or an adult student), except in those situations in which failure to release information would result in danger to the student or others, or where otherwise required by law. Whenever feasible, student assent is obtained prior to disclosure of his or her confidences to third parties, including disclosures to the student's parents.

Standard I.2.5 School psychologists discuss and/or release confidential information only for professional purposes and only with persons who have a legitimate need to know. They do so within the strict boundaries of relevant privacy statutes.

Standard I.2.6 School psychologists respect the right of privacy of students, parents, and colleagues with regard to sexual orientation, gender identity, or transgender status. They do not share information about the sexual orientation, gender identity, or transgender status of a student (including minors), parent, or school employee with anyone without that individual's permission.[20]

Standard I.2.7 School psychologists respect the right of privacy of students, their parents and other family members, and colleagues with regard to sensitive health information (e.g., presence of a communicable disease). They do not share sensitive health information about a student, parent, or school employee with others without that individual's permission (or the permission of a parent or guardian in the case of a minor). School psychologists consult their state laws and department of public health for guidance if they believe a client poses a health risk to others.[21]

Principle I.3 Fairness and Justice

In their words and actions, school psychologists promote fairness and justice. They use their expertise to cultivate school climates that are safe and welcoming to all persons regardless of actual or perceived characteristics, including race, ethnicity, color, religion, ancestry, national origin, immigration status, socioeconomic status, primary language, gender, sexual orientation, gender identity, gender expression, disability, or any other distinguishing characteristics.

Standard I.3.1 School psychologists do not engage in or condone actions or policies that discriminate against persons, including students and their families, other recipients of service, supervisees, and colleagues based on actual or perceived characteristics including race; ethnicity; color; religion; ancestry; national origin; immigration status; socioeconomic status; primary language; gender; sexual orientation, gender identity, or gender expression; mental, physical, or sensory disability; or any other distinguishing characteristics.

Standard I.3.2 School psychologists pursue awareness and knowledge of how diversity factors may influence child development, behavior, and school learning. In conducting psychological, educational, or behavioral evaluations or in providing interventions, therapy, counseling, or consultation services, the school psychologist takes into account individual characteristics as enumerated in Standard I.3.1 so as to provide effective services.[22]

Standard I.3.3 School psychologists work to correct school practices that are unjustly discriminatory or that deny students, parents, or others their legal rights. They take steps to foster a school climate that is safe, accepting, and respectful of all persons.

Standard I.3.4 School psychologists strive to ensure that all children have equal opportunity to participate in and benefit from school programs and that all students and families have access to and can benefit from school psychological services.[23]

II. Professional Competence and Responsibility

Beneficence, or responsible caring, means that the school psychologist acts to benefit others. To do this, school psychologists must practice within the boundaries of their competence, use scientific knowledge from psychology and education to help clients and others make informed choices, and accept responsibility for their work.[24]

Principle II.1 Competence
To benefit clients, school psychologists engage only in practices for which they are qualified and competent.

Standard II.1.1 School psychologists recognize the strengths and limitations of their training and experience, engaging only in practices for which they are qualified. They enlist the assistance of other specialists in supervisory, consultative, or referral roles as appropriate in providing effective services.

Standard II.1.2 Practitioners are obligated to pursue knowledge and understanding of the diverse cultural, linguistic, and experiential backgrounds of students, families, and other clients. When knowledge and understanding of diversity characteristics are essential to ensure competent assessment, intervention, or consultation, school psychologists have or obtain the training or supervision necessary to provide effective services, or they make appropriate referrals.

Standard II.1.3 School psychologists refrain from any activity in which their personal problems may interfere with professional effectiveness. They seek assistance when personal problems threaten to compromise their professional effectiveness (also see III.4.2).

Standard II.1.4 School psychologists engage in continuing professional development. They remain current regarding developments in research, training, and professional practices that benefit children, families, and schools. They also understand that professional skill development beyond that of the novice practitioner requires well-planned continuing professional development and professional supervision.

Principle II.2 Accepting Responsibility for Actions
School psychologists accept responsibility for their professional work, monitor the effectiveness of their services, and work to correct ineffective recommendations.

Standard II.2.1 School psychologists review all of their written documents for accuracy, signing them only when correct. They may add an addendum, dated and signed, to a previously submitted report if information is found to be inaccurate or incomplete.

Standard II.2.2 School psychologists actively monitor the impact of their recommendations and intervention plans. They revise a recommendation, or modify or terminate an intervention plan, when data indicate the desired outcomes are not being attained. School psychologists seek the assistance of others in supervisory, consultative, or referral roles when progress monitoring indicates that their recommendations and interventions are not effective in assisting a client.

Standard II.2.3 School psychologists accept responsibility for the appropriateness of their professional practices, decisions, and recommendations. They correct misunderstandings resulting from their recommendations, advice, or information and take affirmative steps to offset any harmful consequences of ineffective or inappropriate recommendations.

Standard II.2.4 When supervising graduate students' field experiences or internships, school psychologists are responsible for the work of their supervisees.

Principle II.3 Responsible Assessment and Intervention Practices

School psychologists maintain the highest standard for responsible professional practices in educational and psychological assessment and direct and indirect interventions.

Standard II.3.1 Prior to the consideration of a disability label or category, the effects of current behavior management and/or instructional practices on the student's school performance are considered.

Standard II.3.2 School psychologists use assessment techniques and practices that the profession considers to be responsible, research-based practice.

- School psychologists select assessment instruments and strategies that are reliable and valid for the child and the purpose of the assessment. When using standardized measures, school psychologists adhere to the procedures for administration of the instrument that are provided by the author or publisher or the instrument. If modifications are made in the administration procedures for standardized tests or other instruments, such modifications are identified and discussed in the interpretation of the results.
- If using norm-referenced measures, school psychologists choose instruments with up-to-date normative data.
- When using computer-administered assessments, computer-assisted scoring, and/or interpretation programs, school psychologists choose programs that meet professional standards for accuracy and validity. School psychologists use professional judgment in evaluating the accuracy of computer-assisted assessment findings for the examinee.

Standard II.3.3 A psychological or psychoeducational assessment is based on a variety of different types of information from different sources.

Standard II.3.4 Consistent with education law and sound professional practice, children with suspected disabilities are assessed in all areas related to the suspected disability.

Standard II.3.5 School psychologists conduct valid and fair assessments. They actively pursue knowledge of the student's disabilities and developmental, cultural, linguistic, and experiential background and then select, administer, and interpret assessment instruments and procedures in light of those characteristics (see Standards I.3.1 and I.3.2).

Standard II.3.6 When interpreters are used to facilitate the provision of assessment and intervention services, school psychologists take steps to ensure that the interpreters are appropriately trained and are acceptable to clients.[25]

Standard II.3.7 It is permissible for school psychologists to make recommendations based solely on a review of existing records. However, they should utilize a representative sample of records and explain the basis for, and the limitations of, their recommendations.[26]

Standard II.3.8 School psychologists adequately interpret findings and present results in clear, understandable terms so that the recipient can make informed choices.

Standard II.3.9 School psychologists use intervention, counseling and therapy procedures, consultation techniques, and other direct and indirect service methods that the profession considers to be responsible, research-based practice:

- School psychologists use a problem-solving process to develop interventions appropriate to the presenting problems and that are consistent with data collected.
- Preference is given to interventions described in the peer-reviewed professional research literature and found to be efficacious.

Standard II.3.10 School psychologists encourage and promote parental participation in designing interventions for

their children. When appropriate, this includes linking interventions between the school and the home, tailoring parental involvement to the skills of the family, and helping parents gain the skills needed to help their children.

- School psychologists discuss with parents the recommendations and plans for assisting their children. This discussion takes into account the ethnic/cultural values of the family and includes alternatives that may be available. Subsequent recommendations for program changes or additional services are discussed with parents, including any alternatives that may be available.
- Parents are informed of sources of support available at school and in the community.

Standard II.3.11 School psychologists discuss with students the recommendations and plans for assisting them. To the maximum extent appropriate, students are invited to participate in selecting and planning interventions.[27]

Principle II.4 Responsible School-Based Record Keeping

School psychologists safeguard the privacy of school psychological records and ensure parent access to the records of their own children.

Standard II.4.1 School psychologists discuss with parents and adult students their rights regarding creation, modification, storage, and disposal of psychological and educational records that result from the provision of services. Parents and adult students are notified of the electronic storage and transmission of personally identifiable school psychological records and the associated risks to privacy.[28]

Standard II.4.2 School psychologists maintain school-based psychological and educational records with sufficient detail to be useful in decision making by another professional and with sufficient detail to withstand scrutiny if challenged in a due process or other legal procedure.[29]

Standard II.4.3 School psychologists include only documented and relevant information from reliable sources in school psychological records.

Standard II.4.4 School psychologists ensure that parents have appropriate access to the psychological and educational records of their child.
- Parents have a right to access any and all information that is used to make educational decisions about their child.
- School psychologists respect the right of parents to inspect, but not necessarily to copy, their child's answers to school psychological test questions even if those answers are recorded on a test protocol (also see II.5.1).[30]

Standard II.4.5 School psychologists take steps to ensure that information in school psychological records is not released to persons or agencies outside of the school without the consent of the parent except as required and permitted by law.

Standard II.4.6 To the extent that school psychological records are under their control, school psychologists ensure that only those school personnel who have a legitimate educational interest in a student are given access to the student's school psychological records without prior parent permission or the permission of an adult student.

Standard II.4.7 To the extent that school psychological records are under their control, school psychologists protect electronic files from unauthorized release or modification (e.g., by using passwords and encryption), and they take reasonable steps to ensure that school psychological records are not lost due to equipment failure.

Standard II.4.8 It is ethically permissible for school psychologists to keep private notes to use as a memory aid that are not made accessible to others. However, as noted in Standard II.4.4, any and all information that is used to make educational decisions about a student must be accessible to parents and adult students.

Standard II.4.9 School psychologists, in collaboration with administrators and other school staff, work to establish district policies regarding the storage and disposal of school psychological records that are consistent with law and sound professional practice. They advocate for school district policies and practices that:
- safeguard the security of school psychological records while facilitating appropriate parent access to those records;
- identify time lines for the periodic review and disposal of outdated school psychological records that are consistent with law and sound professional practice;
- seek parent or other appropriate permission prior to the destruction of obsolete school psychological records of current students;
- ensure that obsolete school psychology records are destroyed in a way that the information cannot be recovered.

Principle II.5 Responsible Use of Materials

School psychologists respect the intellectual property rights of those who produce tests, intervention materials, scholarly works, and other materials.

Standard II.5.1 School psychologists maintain test security, preventing the release of underlying principles and specific content that would undermine or invalidate the use of the instrument. Unless otherwise required by law or district policy, school psychologists provide parents with the opportunity to inspect and review their child's test answers rather than providing them with copies of their child's test protocols. However, on parent request, it is permissible to provide copies of a child's test protocols to a professional who is qualified to interpret them.

Standard II.5.2 School psychologists do not promote or condone the use of restricted psychological and educational tests or other assessment tools or procedures by individuals who are not qualified to use them.

Standard II.5.3 School psychologists recognize the effort and expense involved in the development and publication of psychological and educational tests, intervention materials, and scholarly works. They respect the intellectual property rights and copyright interests of the producers of such materials, whether the materials are published in print or digital formats. They do not duplicate copyright-protected test manuals, testing materials, or unused test protocols without the permission of the producer. However, school psychologists understand that, at times, parents' rights to examine their child's

test answers may supersede the interests of test publishers.[31, 32]

III. Honesty and Integrity in Professional Relationships

To foster and maintain trust, school psychologists must be faithful to the truth and adhere to their professional promises. They are forthright about their qualifications, competencies, and roles; work in full cooperation with other professional disciplines to meet the needs of students and families; and avoid multiple relationships that diminish their professional effectiveness.

Principle III.1 Accurate Presentation of Professional Qualifications

School psychologists accurately identify their professional qualifications to others.

Standard III.1.1 Competency levels, education, training, experience, and certification and licensing credentials are accurately represented to clients, recipients of services, and others. School psychologists correct any misperceptions of their qualifications. School psychologists do not represent themselves as specialists in a particular domain without verifiable training and supervised experience in the specialty.

Standard III.1.2 School psychologists do not use affiliations with persons, associations, or institutions to imply a level of professional competence that exceeds that which has actually been achieved.

Principle III.2 Forthright Explanation of Professional Services, Roles, and Priorities

School psychologists are candid about the nature and scope of their services.

Standard III.2.1 School psychologists explain their professional competencies, roles, assignments, and working relationships to recipients of services and others in their work setting in a forthright and understandable manner. School psychologists explain all professional services to clients in a clear, understandable manner (see I.1.2).

Standard III.2.2 School psychologists make reasonable efforts to become integral members of the client service systems to which they are assigned. They establish clear roles for themselves within those systems while respecting the various roles of colleagues in other professions.

Standard III.2.3 The school psychologist's commitment to protecting the rights and welfare of children is communicated to the school administration, staff, and others as the highest priority in determining services.

Standard III.2.4 School psychologists who provide services to several different groups (e.g., families, teachers, classrooms) may encounter situations in which loyalties are conflicted. As much as possible, school psychologists make known their priorities and commitments in advance to all parties to prevent misunderstandings.

Standard III.2.5 School psychologists ensure that announcements and advertisements of the availability of their publications, products, and services for sale are factual and professional. They do not misrepresent their degree of responsibility for the development and distribution of publications, products, and services.

Principle III.3 Respecting Other Professionals

To best meet the needs of children, school psychologists cooperate with other professionals in relationships based on mutual respect.

Standard III.3.1 To meet the needs of children and other clients most effectively, school psychologists cooperate with other psychologists and professionals from other disciplines in relationships based on mutual respect. They encourage and support the use of all resources to serve the interests of students. If a child or other client is receiving similar services from another professional, school psychologists promote coordination of services.

Standard III.3.2 If a child or other client is referred to another professional for services, school psychologists ensure that all relevant and appropriate individuals, including the client, are notified of the change and reasons for the change. When referring clients to other professionals, school psychologists provide clients with lists of suitable practitioners from whom the client may seek services.

Standard III.3.3 Except when supervising graduate students, school psychologists do not alter a report completed by another professional without his or her permission to do so.

Principle III.4 Multiple Relationships and Conflicts of Interest

School psychologists avoid multiple relationships and conflicts of interest that diminish their professional effectiveness.

Standard III.4.1 The *Principles for Professional Ethics* provide standards for professional conduct. School psychologists, in their private lives, are free to pursue their personal interests, except to the degree that those interests compromise professional effectiveness.

Standard III.4.2 School psychologists refrain from any activity in which conflicts of interest or multiple relationships with a client or a client's family may interfere with professional effectiveness. School psychologists attempt to resolve such situations in a manner that provides greatest benefit to the client. School psychologists whose personal or religious beliefs or commitments may influence the nature of their professional services or their willingness to provide certain services inform clients and responsible parties of this fact. When personal beliefs, conflicts of interests, or multiple relationships threaten to diminish professional effectiveness or would be viewed by the public as inappropriate, school psychologists ask their supervisor for reassignment of responsibilities, or they direct the client to alternative services.[33]

Standard III.4.3 School psychologists do not exploit clients, supervisees, or graduate students through professional relationships or condone these actions by their colleagues. They do not participate in or condone sexual harassment of children, parents, other clients, colleagues, employees, trainees, supervisees, or research participants. School psychologists do not engage in sexual relationships with individuals over whom they have evaluation authority, including college students in their classes or program, or any other trainees, or supervisees. School psychologists do not engage in sexual relationships with

their current or former pupil-clients; the parents, siblings, or other close family members of current pupil-clients; or current consultees.

Standard III.4.4 School psychologists are cautious about business and other relationships with clients that could interfere with professional judgment and effectiveness or potentially result in exploitation of a client.

Standard III.4.5 NASP requires that any action taken by its officers, members of the Executive Council or Delegate Assembly, or other committee members be free from the appearance of impropriety and free from any conflict of interest. NASP leaders recuse themselves from decisions regarding proposed NASP initiatives if they may gain an economic benefit from the proposed venture.

Standard III.4.6 A school psychologist's financial interests in a product (e.g., tests, computer software, professional materials) or service can influence his or her objectivity or the perception of his or her objectivity regarding that product or service. For this reason, school psychologists are obligated to disclose any significant financial interest in the products or services they discuss in their presentations or writings if that interest is not obvious in the authorship/ownership citations provided.

Standard III.4.7 School psychologists neither give nor receive any remuneration for referring children and other clients for professional services.

Standard III.4.8 School psychologists do not accept any remuneration in exchange for data from their client data base without the permission of their employer and a determination of whether the data release ethically requires informed client consent.

Standard III.4.9 School psychologists who provide school-based services and also engage in the provision of private practice services (dual setting practitioners) recognize the potential for conflict of interests between their two roles and take steps to avoid such conflicts. Dual setting practitioners:

- are obligated to inform parents or other potential clients of any psychological and educational services available at no cost from the schools prior to offering such services for remuneration;
- may not offer or provide private practice services to a student of a school or special school program where the practitioner is currently assigned;
- may not offer or provide private practice services to the parents or family members of a student eligible to attend a school or special school program where the practitioner is currently assigned;
- may not offer or provide an independent evaluation as defined in special education law for a student who attends a local or cooperative school district where the practitioner is employed;
- do not use tests, materials, equipment, facilities, secretarial assistance, or other services belonging to the public sector employer unless approved in advance by the employer;
- conduct all private practice outside of the hours of contracted public employment; and
- hold appropriate credentials for practice in both the public and private sectors.

IV. Responsibility to Schools, Families, Communities, the Profession, and Society

School psychologists promote healthy school, family, and community environments. They assume a proactive role in identifying social injustices that affect children and schools and strive to reform systems-level patterns of injustice. They maintain the public trust in school psychologists by respecting law and encouraging ethical conduct. School psychologists advance professional excellence by mentoring less experienced practitioners and contributing to the school psychology knowledge base.

Principle IV.1 Promoting Healthy School, Family, and Community Environments
School psychologists use their expertise in psychology and education to promote school, family, and community environments that are safe and healthy for children.

Standard IV.1.1 To provide effective services and systems consultation, school psychologists are knowledgeable about the organization, philosophy, goals, objectives, culture, and methodologies of the settings in which they provide services. In addition, school psychologists develop partnerships and networks with community service providers and agencies to provide seamless services to children and families.

Standard IV.1.2 School psychologists use their professional expertise to promote changes in schools and community service systems that will benefit children and other clients. They advocate for school policies and practices that are in the best interests of children and that respect and protect the legal rights of students and parents.[34]

Principle IV.2 Respect for Law and the Relationship of Law and Ethics

School psychologists are knowledgeable of and respect laws pertinent to the practice of school psychology. In choosing an appropriate course of action, they consider the relationship between law and the *Principles for Professional Ethics*.

Standard IV.2.1 School psychologists recognize that an understanding of the goals, procedures, and legal requirements of their particular workplace is essential for effective functioning within that setting.

Standard IV.2.2 School psychologists respect the law and the civil and legal rights of students and other clients. The *Principles for Professional Ethics* may require a more stringent standard of conduct than law, and in those situations school psychologists are expected to adhere to the *Principles*.

Standard IV.2.3 When conflicts between ethics and law occur, school psychologists take steps to resolve the conflict through positive, respected, and legal channels. If not able to resolve the conflict in this manner, they may abide by the law, as long as the resulting actions do not violate basic human rights.[35]

Standard IV.2.4 School psychologists may act as individual citizens to bring about change in a lawful manner. They identify when they are speaking as private citizens rather than as employees. They also identify when they speak as individual professionals rather than as representatives of a professional association.

Principle IV.3 Maintaining Public Trust by Self-Monitoring and Peer Monitoring

School psychologists accept responsibility to monitor their own conduct and the conduct of other school psychologists to ensure it conforms to ethical standards.

Standard IV.3.1 School psychologists know the *Principles for Professional Ethics* and thoughtfully apply them to situations within their employment context. In difficult situations, school psychologists consult experienced school psychologists or state associations or NASP.

Standard IV.3.2 When a school psychologist suspects that another school psychologist or another professional has engaged in unethical practices, he or she attempts to resolve the suspected problem through a collegial problem-solving process, if feasible.

Standard IV.3.3 If a collegial problem-solving process is not possible or productive, school psychologists take further action appropriate to the situation, including discussing the situation with a supervisor in the employment setting, consulting state association ethics committees, and, if necessary, filing a formal ethical violation complaint with state associations, state credentialing bodies, or the NASP Ethical and Professional Practices Committee in accordance with their procedures.

Standard IV.3.4 When school psychologists are concerned about unethical practices by professionals who are not NASP members or do not hold the NCSP, informal contact is made to discuss the concern if feasible. If the situation cannot be resolved in this manner, discussing the situation with the professional's supervisor should be considered. If necessary, an appropriate professional organization or state credentialing agency could be contacted to determine the procedures established by that professional association or agency for examining the practices in question.

Principle IV.4 Contributing to the Profession by Mentoring, Teaching, and Supervision

As part of their obligation to students, schools, society, and their profession, school psychologists mentor less experienced practitioners and graduate students to assure high quality services, and they serve as role models for sound ethical and professional practices and decision making.

Standard IV.4.1 School psychologists who serve as directors of graduate education programs provide current and prospective graduate students with accurate information regarding program accreditation, goals and objectives, graduate program policies and requirements, and likely outcomes and benefits.

Standard IV.4.2 School psychologists who supervise practicum students and interns are responsible for all professional practices of the supervisees. They ensure that practicum students and interns are adequately supervised as outlined in the NASP *Graduate Preparation Standards for School Psychologists*. Interns and graduate students are identified as such, and their work is co-signed by the supervising school psychologist.

Standard IV.4.3 School psychologists who employ, supervise, or train professionals provide appropriate working conditions, fair and timely evaluation, constructive supervision, and continuing professional development opportunities.

Standard IV.4.4 School psychologists who are faculty members at universities or who supervise graduate education field experiences apply these ethical principles in all work with school psychology graduate students. In addition, they promote the ethical practice of graduate students by providing specific and comprehensive instruction, feedback, and mentoring.

Principle IV.5 Contributing to the School Psychology Knowledge Base

To improve services to children, families, and schools, and to promote the welfare of children, school psychologists are encouraged to contribute to the school psychology knowledge base by participating in, assisting in, or conducting and disseminating research.

Standard IV.5.1 When designing and conducting research in schools, school psychologists choose topics and employ research methodology, research participant selection procedures, data-gathering methods, and analysis and reporting techniques that are grounded in sound research practice. School psychologists identify their level of training and graduate degree to potential research participants.

Standard IV.5.2 School psychologists respect the rights, and protect the well-being, of research participants. School psychologists obtain appropriate review and approval of proposed research prior to beginning their data collection.

- Prior to initiating research, school psychologists and graduate students affiliated with a university, hospital, or other agency subject to the U.S. Department of Health and Human Services (DHHS) regulation of research first obtain approval for their research from their institutional review board (IRB) for research involving human subjects as well as the school or other agency in which the research will be conducted. Research proposals that have not been subject to IRB approval should be reviewed by individuals knowledgeable about research methodology and ethics and approved by the school administration or other appropriate authority.

• In planning research, school psychologists are ethically obligated to consider carefully whether the informed consent of research participants is needed for their study, recognizing that research involving more than minimum risk requires informed consent, and that research with students involving activities that are not part of ordinary, typical schooling requires informed consent. Consent and assent protocols provide the information necessary for potential research participants to make an informed and voluntary choice about participation. School psychologists evaluate the potential risks (including risks of physical or psychological harm, intrusions on privacy, breach of confidentiality) and benefits of their research and only conduct studies in which the risks to participants are minimized and acceptable.

Standard IV.5.3 School psychologists who use their assessment, intervention, or consultation cases in lectures, presentations, or publications obtain written prior client consent or they remove and disguise identifying client information.

Standard IV.5.4 School psychologists do not publish or present fabricated or falsified data or results in their publications and presentations.

Standard IV.5.5 School psychologists make available their data or other information that provided the basis for findings and conclusions reported in publications and presentations, if such data are needed to address a legitimate concern or need and under the condition that the confidentiality and other rights of research participants are protected.

Standard IV.5.6 If errors are discovered after the publication or presentation of research or other information, school psychologists make efforts to correct errors by publishing errata, retractions, or corrections.

Standard IV.5.7 School psychologists only publish data or other information that make original contributions to the professional literature. They do not report the same study in a second publication without acknowledging previous publication of the same data. They do not duplicate significant portions of their own or others' previous publications without permission of copyright holders.

Standard IV.5.8 When publishing or presenting research or other work, school psychologists do not plagiarize the works or ideas of others. They appropriately cite and reference all sources, print or digital, and assign credit to those whose ideas are reflected. In inservice or conference presentations, school psychologists give credit to others whose ideas have been used or adapted.

Standard IV.5.9 School psychologists accurately reflect the contributions of authors and other individuals who contributed to presentations and publications. Authorship credit is given only to individuals who have made a substantial professional contribution to the research, publication, or presentation. Authors discuss and resolve issues related to publication credit as early as feasible in the research and publication process.

Standard IV.5.10 School psychologists who participate in reviews of manuscripts, proposals, and other materials respect the confidentiality and proprietary rights of the authors. They limit their use of the materials to the activities relevant to the purposes of the professional review. School psychologists who review professional materials do not communicate the identity of the author, quote from the materials, or duplicate or circulate copies of the materials without the author's permission.

NOTES

[1] Jacob, S., Decker, D. M., & Hartshorne, T. S. (in press). *Ethics and law for school psychologists* (6th ed.). Hoboken, NJ: John Wiley & Sons.

[2] National Association of School Psychologists. (2008). *Ethical and Professional Practices Committee Procedures.* Available: http://www.nasponline.org.

[3] Russo, C. J. (2006). *Reutter's the law of public education* (6th ed.). New York: Foundation Press.

[4] Haas, L. J., & Malouf, J. L. (2005). *Keeping up the good work: A practitioner's guide to mental health ethics* (4th ed.). Sarasota, FL: Professional Resource Press.

[5] Jacob-Timm, S. (1999). Ethical dilemmas encountered by members of the National Association of School Psychologists. *Psychology in the Schools, 36,* 205–217.

[6] McNamara, K. (2008). Best practices in the application of professional ethics. In A. Thomas & J. Grimes (Eds.), *Best practices in school psychology V* (pp. 1933–1941).

Bethesda, MD: National Association of School Psychologists.

[7] Williams, B., Armistead, L., & Jacob, S. (2008). *Professional ethics for school psychologists: A problem-solving model casebook.* Bethesda, MD: National Association of School Psychologists.

[8] American Psychological Association. (2002). Ethical principles of psychologists and code of conduct. *American Psychologist, 57,* 1060–1073.

[9] Adapted from the Canadian Psychological Association. (2000). *Canadian code of ethics for psychologists* (3rd ed.). Available: http://www.cpa.ca.

[10] Knapp. S., & VandeCreek, L. (2006). *Practical ethics for psychologists: A positive approach.* Washington, DC: American Psychological Association.

[11] Fisher, M. A. (2009). Replacing "who is the client" with a different ethical question. *Professional Psychology: Research and Practice, 40,* 1–7.

[12] Dekraai, M., Sales, B., & Hall, S. (1998). Informed consent, confidentiality, and duty to report laws in the conduct of child therapy. In T. R. Kratochwill & R. J. Morris (Eds.), *The practice of child therapy* (3rd ed., pp. 540–559). Boston: Allyn & Bacon.

[13] Masner, C. M. (2007). *The ethic of advocacy.* Doctoral dissertation, University of Denver. Available: http://www.dissertation.com.

[14] Burns, M. K., Jacob, S., & Wagner, A. (2008). Ethical and legal issues associated with using response-to-intervention to assess learning disabilities. *Journal of School Psychology, 46,* 263–279.

[15] Corrao, J., & Melton, G. B. (1988). Legal issues in school-based therapy. In J. C. Witt, S. N. Elliot, & F. M. Gresham (Eds.), *Handbook of behavior therapy in education* (pp. 377–399). New York: Plenum Press.

[16] Weithorn, L. A. (1983). Involving children in decisions affecting their own welfare: Guidelines for professionals. In G. B. Melton, G. P.

Koocher, & M. J. Saks (Eds.), *Children's competence to consent* (pp. 235–260). New York: Plenum Press.

[17] Weithorn, L. A. (1983). Involving children in decisions affecting their own welfare: Guidelines for professionals. In G. B. Melton, G. P. Koocher, & M. J. Saks (Eds.), *Children's competence to consent* (pp. 235–260). New York: Plenum Press.

[18] Weithorn, L. A. (1983). Involving children in decisions affecting their own welfare: Guidelines for professionals. In G. B. Melton, G. P. Koocher, & M. J. Saks (Eds.), *Children's competence to consent* (pp. 235–260). New York: Plenum Press.

[19] Jacob, S., & Powers, K. E. (2009). Privileged communication in the school psychologist–client relationship. *Psychology in the Schools, 46*, 307–318.

[20] Sterling v. Borough of Minersville, 232 F.3d 190, 2000 U.S. App. LEXIS 27855 (3rd Cir. 2000)

[21] Jacob, S., Decker, D. M., & Hartshorne, T. S. (in press). *Ethics and law for school psychologists* (6th ed.). Hoboken, NJ: John Wiley & Sons.

[22] Flanagan, R., Miller, J. A., & Jacob, S. (2005). The 2002 revision of APA's ethics code: Implications for school psychologists. *Psychology in the Schools, 42*, 433–444.

[23] Flanagan, R., Miller, J. A., & Jacob, S. (2005). The 2002 revision of APA's ethics code: Implications for school psychologists. *Psychology in the Schools, 42*, 433–445.

[24] Jacob, S., Decker, D. M., & Hartshorne, T. S. (in press). *Ethics and law for school psychologists* (6th ed.). Hoboken, NJ: John Wiley & Sons.

[25] American Psychological Association. (2002). Ethical principles of psychologists and code of conduct. *American Psychologist, 57*, 1060–1073.

[26] American Psychological Association. (2002). Ethical principles of psychologists and code of conduct. *American Psychologist, 57*, 1060–1073.

[27] Weithorn, L. A. (1983). Involving children in decisions affecting their own welfare: Guidelines for professionals. In G. B. Melton, G. P. Koocher, & M. J. Saks (Eds.), *Children's competence to consent* (pp. 235–260). New York: Plenum Press.

[28] American Psychological Association. (2002). Ethical principles of psychologists and code of conduct. *American Psychologist, 57*, 1060–1073.

[29] Nagy, T. F. (2000). *Ethics in plain English*. Washington, DC: American Psychological Association.

[30] Reschly, D. J., & Bersoff, D. N. (1999). Law and school psychology. In C. R. Reynolds & T. B. Gutkin (Eds.), *Handbook of school psychology* (3rd ed., pp. 1077–1112). New York: John Wiley & Sons. Note: this chapter summarizes Department of Education policy letters on the matter of parent inspection of test protocols.

[31] Reschly, D. J., & Bersoff, D. N. (1999). Law and school psychology. In C. R. Reynolds & T. B. Gutkin (Eds.), *Handbook of school psychology* (3rd ed., pp. 1077–1112). New York: John Wiley & Sons. Note: this chapter summarizes Department of Education policy letters on the matter of parent inspection of test protocols.

[32] Newport-Mesa Unified School District v. State of California Department of Education, 371 F. Supp. 2d 1170; 2005 U.S. Dist. LEXIS 10290 (C.D. Cal. 2005).

[33] American Psychological Association. (2002). Ethical principles of psychologists and code of conduct. *American Psychologist, 57*, 1060–1073.

[34] Prilleltensky, I. (1991). The social ethics of school psychology: A priority for the 1990s. *School Psychology Quarterly, 6*, 200–222.

[35] American Psychological Association. (2002). Ethical principles of psychologists and code of conduct. *American Psychologist, 57*, 1060–1073.

Appendix B

American Psychological Association

Ethical Principles of Psychologists and Code of Conduct

With the 2010 Amendments

INTRODUCTION AND APPLICABILITY

The American Psychological Association's (APA's) Ethical Principles of Psychologists and Code of Conduct (hereinafter referred to as the Ethics Code) consists of an Introduction, a Preamble, five General Principles (A–E), and specific Ethical Standards. The Introduction discusses the intent, organization, procedural considerations, and scope of application of the Ethics Code. The Preamble and General Principles are aspirational goals to guide psychologists toward the highest ideals of psychology. Although the Preamble and General Principles are not themselves enforceable rules, they should be considered by psychologists in arriving at an ethical course of action. The Ethical Standards set forth enforceable rules for conduct as psychologists. Most of the Ethical Standards are written broadly, in order to apply to psychologists in varied roles,

although the application of an Ethical Standard may vary depending on the context. The Ethical Standards are not exhaustive. The fact that a given conduct is not specifically addressed by an Ethical Standard does not mean that it is necessarily either ethical or unethical.

This Ethics Code applies only to psychologists' activities that are part of their scientific, educational, or professional roles as psychologists. Areas covered include but are not limited to the clinical, counseling, and school practice of psychology; research; teaching; supervision of trainees; public service; policy development; social intervention; development of assessment instruments; conducting assessments; educational counseling; organizational consulting; forensic activities; program design and evaluation; and administration. This Ethics Code applies to these activities across a variety of contexts, such as in person, postal, telephone, Internet, and other electronic transmissions. These activities shall be distinguished from the purely private conduct of psychologists, which is not within the purview of the Ethics Code.

Membership in the APA commits members and student affiliates to comply with the standards of the APA Ethics Code and to the rules and procedures used to enforce them. Lack of awareness or misunderstanding of an Ethical Standard is not itself a defense to a charge of unethical conduct.

The procedures for filing, investigating, and resolving complaints of unethical conduct are described in the current Rules and Procedures of the APA Ethics Committee. APA may impose sanctions on its members for violations of the standards of the Ethics Code, including termination of APA membership, and may notify other bodies and individuals of its actions. Actions that violate the standards of the Ethics Code may also lead to the imposition of sanctions on the psychologists or students whether or not they are APA members by bodies other than APA, including state psychological associations, other professional groups, psychology boards, other state or federal agencies, and payors for health services. In addition, APA may take action against a member after his or her conviction of a felony, expulsion or suspension from an affiliated state psychological association, or suspension or loss of licensure. When the sanction to be imposed by APA is less than expulsion, the 2001 Rules and Procedures do not guarantee an opportunity for an in-person hearing, but generally provide that complaints will be resolved only on the basis of a submitted record.

The Ethics Code is intended to provide guidance for psychologists and standards of professional conduct that can be applied by the APA and by other bodies that choose to adopt them. The Ethics Code is not intended to be a basis of civil liability. Whether a psychologist has violated the Ethics Code does not by itself determine whether the psychologist is legally liable in a court action, whether a contract is enforceable, or whether other legal consequences occur.

The modifiers used in some of the standards of this Ethics Code (e.g., *reasonably, appropriate, potentially*) are included in the standards when they would (1) allow professional judgment on the part of psychologists, (2) eliminate injustice or inequality that would occur without the modifier, (3) ensure applicability across the broad range of activities conducted by psychologists, or (4) guard against a set of rigid rules that might be quickly outdated. As used in this Ethics Code, the term *reasonable* means the prevailing professional judgment of psychologists engaged in similar activities in similar circumstances, given the knowledge the psychologist had or should have had at the time.

In the process of making decisions regarding their professional behavior, psychologists must consider this Ethics Code in addition to applicable laws and psychology board regulations. In applying the Ethics Code to their professional work, psychologists may consider other materials and guidelines that have been adopted or endorsed by scientific and professional psychological organizations and the dictates of their own conscience, as well as consult with others within the field. If this Ethics Code establishes a higher standard of conduct than is required by law, psychologists must meet the higher ethical standard. If psychologists' ethical responsibilities conflict with law, regulations, or other governing legal authority, psychologists make known their commitment to this Ethics Code and take steps to resolve the conflict in a responsible manner in keeping with basic principles of human rights.

PREAMBLE

Psychologists are committed to increasing scientific and professional knowledge of behavior and people's understanding of themselves and others and to the use of such knowledge to improve the condition of individuals, organizations, and society. Psychologists respect and protect civil and human rights and the central importance of freedom of inquiry and expression in research, teaching, and publication. They strive to help the public in developing informed judgments and choices concerning human behavior. In doing so, they perform many roles, such as researcher, educator, diagnostician, therapist, supervisor, consultant, administrator, social interventionist, and expert witness. This Ethics Code provides a common set of principles and standards upon which psychologists build their professional and scientific work.

This Ethics Code is intended to provide specific standards to cover most situations encountered by psychologists. It has as its goals the welfare and protection of the individuals and groups with whom psychologists work and the education of members, students, and the public regarding ethical standards of the discipline.

The development of a dynamic set of ethical standards for psychologists' work-related conduct requires a personal commitment and lifelong effort to act ethically; to encourage ethical behavior by students, supervisees, employees, and colleagues; and to consult with others concerning ethical problems.

GENERAL PRINCIPLES

This section consists of General Principles. General Principles, as opposed to Ethical Standards, are aspirational in nature. Their intent is to guide and inspire psychologists toward the very highest ethical ideals of the profession. General Principles, in contrast to Ethical Standards, do not represent obligations and should not form the basis for imposing sanctions. Relying upon General Principles for either of these reasons distorts both their meaning and purpose.

Principle A: Beneficence and Non-Maleficence

Psychologists strive to benefit those with whom they work and take care to do no harm. In their professional actions, psychologists seek to safeguard the welfare and rights of those with whom they interact professionally and other affected persons, and the welfare of animal subjects of research. When conflicts occur among psychologists' obligations or concerns, they attempt to resolve these conflicts in a responsible fashion that avoids or minimizes harm. Because psychologists' scientific and professional judgments and actions may affect the lives of others, they are alert to and guard against personal, financial, social, organizational, or political factors that might lead to misuse of their influence. Psychologists strive to be aware of the possible effect of their own physical and mental health on their ability to help those with whom they work.

Principle B: Fidelity and Responsibility

Psychologists establish relationships of trust with those with whom they work. They are aware of their professional and scientific responsibilities to society and to the specific communities in which they work. Psychologists uphold professional standards of conduct, clarify their professional roles and obligations, accept appropriate responsibility for their behavior, and seek to manage conflicts of interest that could lead to exploitation or harm. Psychologists consult with, refer to, or cooperate with other professionals and institutions to the extent needed to serve the best interests of those with whom they work. They are concerned about the ethical compliance of their colleagues' scientific and professional conduct. Psychologists strive to contribute a portion of their professional time for little or no compensation or personal advantage.

Principle C: Integrity

Psychologists seek to promote accuracy, honesty, and truthfulness in the science, teaching, and practice of psychology. In these activities psychologists do not steal, cheat, or engage in fraud, subterfuge, or intentional misrepresentation of fact. Psychologists strive to keep their promises and to avoid unwise or unclear commitments. In situations in which deception may be ethically justifiable to maximize benefits and minimize harm, psychologists have a serious obligation to consider the need for, the possible consequences of, and their responsibility to correct any resulting mistrust or other harmful effects that arise from the use of such techniques.

Principle D: Justice

Psychologists recognize that fairness and justice entitle all persons to access to and benefit from the contributions of psychology and equal quality in the processes, procedures, and services being conducted by psychologists. Psychologists exercise reasonable judgment and take precautions to ensure that their potential biases, the boundaries of their competence, and the limitations of their expertise do not lead to or condone unjust practices.

Principle E: Respect for People's Rights and Dignity

Psychologists respect the dignity and worth of all people, and the rights of individuals to privacy, confidentiality, and self-determination. Psychologists are aware that special safeguards may be necessary to protect the rights and welfare of persons or communities whose vulnerabilities impair autonomous decision making. Psychologists are aware of and respect cultural, individual, and role differences, including those based on age, gender, gender identity, race, ethnicity, culture, national origin, religion, sexual orientation, disability, language, and socioeconomic status and consider these factors when working with members of such groups. Psychologists try to eliminate the effect on their work of biases based on those factors, and they do not knowingly participate in or condone activities of others based upon such prejudices.

ETHICAL STANDARDS

1.   Resolving Ethical Issues

1.01   Misuse of Psychologists' Work

If psychologists learn of misuse or misrepresentation of their work, they take reasonable steps to correct or minimize the misuse or misrepresentation.

1.02 Conflicts Between Ethics and Law, Regulations, or Other Governing Legal Authority

If psychologists' ethical responsibilities conflict with law, regulations, or other governing legal authority, psychologists clarify the nature of the conflict, make known their commitment to the Ethics Code, and take reasonable steps to resolve the conflict consistent with the General Principles and Ethical Standards of the Ethics Code. Under no circumstances may this standard be used to justify or defend violating human rights.

1.03 Conflicts Between Ethics and Organizational Demands

If the demands of an organization with which psychologists are affiliated or for whom they are working are in conflict with this Ethics Code, psychologists clarify the nature of the conflict, make known their commitment to the Ethics Code, and take reasonable steps to resolve the conflict consistent with the General Principles and Ethical Standards of the Ethics Code. Under no circumstances may this standard be used to justify or defend violating human rights.

1.04 Informal Resolution of Ethical Violations

When psychologists believe that there may have been an ethical violation by another psychologist, they attempt to resolve the issue by bringing it to the attention of that individual, if an informal resolution appears appropriate and the intervention does not violate any confidentiality rights that may be involved. (See also Standards 1.02, Conflicts Between Ethics and Law, Regulations, or Other Governing Legal Authority, and 1.03, Conflicts Between Ethics and Organizational Demands.)

1.05 Reporting Ethical Violations

If an apparent ethical violation has substantially harmed or is likely to substantially harm a person or organization and is not appropriate for informal resolution under Standard 1.04, Informal Resolution of Ethical Violations, or is not resolved properly in that fashion, psychologists take further action appropriate to the situation. Such action might include referral to state or national committees on professional ethics, to state licensing boards, or to the appropriate institutional authorities. This standard does not apply when an intervention would violate confidentiality rights or when psychologists have been retained to review the work of another psychologist whose professional conduct is in question. (See also Standard 1.02, Conflicts Between Ethics and Law, Regulations, or Other Governing Legal Authority.)

1.06 Cooperating With Ethics Committees

Psychologists cooperate in ethics investigations, proceedings, and resulting requirements of the APA or any affiliated state psychological association to which they belong. In doing so, they address any confidentiality issues. Failure to cooperate is itself an ethics violation. However, making a request for deferment of adjudication of an ethics complaint pending the outcome of litigation does not alone constitute noncooperation.

1.07 Improper Complaints

Psychologists do not file or encourage the filing of ethics complaints that are made with reckless disregard for or willful ignorance of facts that would disprove the allegation.

1.08 Unfair Discrimination Against Complainants and Respondents

Psychologists do not deny persons employment, advancement, admissions to academic or other programs, tenure, or promotion, based solely upon their having made or their being the subject of an ethics complaint. This does not preclude taking action based upon the outcome of such proceedings or considering other appropriate information.

2. Competence

2.01 Boundaries of Competence

(a) Psychologists provide services, teach, and conduct research with populations and in areas only within the boundaries of their competence, based on their education, training, supervised experience, consultation, study, or professional experience.

(b) Where scientific or professional knowledge in the discipline of psychology establishes that an understanding of factors associated with age, gender, gender identity, race, ethnicity, culture, national origin, religion, sexual orientation, disability, language, or socioeconomic status is essential for effective implementation of their services or research, psychologists have or obtain the training, experience, consultation, or supervision necessary to ensure the competence of their services, or they make appropriate referrals, except as provided in Standard 2.02, Providing Services in Emergencies.

(c) Psychologists planning to provide services, teach, or conduct research involving populations, areas, techniques, or technologies new to them undertake relevant education, training, supervised experience, consultation, or study.

(d) When psychologists are asked to provide services to individuals for whom appropriate mental health services are not available and for which psychologists have not obtained the competence necessary, psychologists with closely related prior training or experience may provide such services in order to ensure that services are not denied if they make a reasonable effort to obtain the competence required by using relevant research, training, consultation, or study.

(e) In those emerging areas in which generally recognized standards for preparatory training do not yet exist, psychologists nevertheless take reasonable steps to ensure the competence of their work and to protect clients/patients, students, supervisees, research participants, organizational clients, and others from harm.

(f) When assuming forensic roles, psychologists are or become reasonably familiar with the judicial or administrative rules governing their roles.

2.02 Providing Services in Emergencies

In emergencies, when psychologists provide services to individuals for whom other mental health services are not available and for which psychologists have not obtained the necessary training, psychologists may provide such services in order to ensure that services are not denied. The services are discontinued as soon as the emergency has ended or appropriate services are available.

2.03 Maintaining Competence

Psychologists undertake ongoing efforts to develop and maintain their competence.

2.04 Bases for Scientific and Professional Judgments

Psychologists' work is based upon established scientific and professional knowledge of the discipline. (See also Standards 2.01e, Boundaries of Competence, and 10.01b, Informed Consent to Therapy.)

2.05 Delegation of Work to Others

Psychologists who delegate work to employees, supervisees, or research or teaching assistants or who use the services of others, such as interpreters, take reasonable steps to (1) avoid delegating such work to persons who have a multiple relationship with those being served that would likely lead to exploitation or loss of objectivity; (2) authorize only those responsibilities that such persons can be expected to perform competently on the basis of their education, training, or experience, either independently or with the level of supervision being provided; and (3) see that such persons perform these services competently. (See also Standards 2.02, Providing Services in Emergencies; 3.05, Multiple Relationships; 4.01, Maintaining Confidentiality; 9.01, Bases for Assessments; 9.02, Use of Assessments; 9.03, Informed Consent in Assessments; and 9.07, Assessment by Unqualified Persons.)

2.06 Personal Problems and Conflicts

(a) Psychologists refrain from initiating an activity when they know or should know that there is a substantial likelihood that their personal problems will prevent them from performing their work-related activities in a competent manner.

(b) When psychologists become aware of personal problems that may interfere with their performing work-related duties adequately, they take appropriate measures, such as obtaining professional consultation or assistance, and determine whether they should limit, suspend, or terminate their work-related duties. (See also Standard 10.10, Terminating Therapy.)

3. Human Relations
3.01 Unfair Discrimination

In their work-related activities, psychologists do not engage in unfair discrimination based on age, gender, gender identity, race, ethnicity, culture, national origin, religion, sexual orientation, disability, socioeconomic status, or any basis proscribed by law.

3.02 Sexual Harassment

Psychologists do not engage in sexual harassment. Sexual harassment is sexual solicitation, physical advances, or verbal or nonverbal conduct that is sexual in nature, that occurs in connection with the psychologist's activities or roles as a psychologist, and that either (1) is unwelcome, is offensive, or creates a hostile workplace or educational environment, and the psychologist knows or is told this or (2) is sufficiently severe or intense to be abusive to a reasonable person in the context. Sexual harassment can consist of a single intense or severe act or of multiple persistent or pervasive acts. (See also Standard 1.08, Unfair Discrimination Against Complainants and Respondents.)

3.03 Other Harassment

Psychologists do not knowingly engage in behavior that is harassing or demeaning to persons with whom they interact in their work based on factors such as those persons' age, gender, gender identity, race, ethnicity, culture, national origin, religion, sexual orientation, disability, language, or socioeconomic status.

3.04 Avoiding Harm

Psychologists take reasonable steps to avoid harming their clients/patients, students, supervisees, research participants, organizational clients, and others with whom they work, and to minimize harm where it is foreseeable and unavoidable.

3.05 Multiple Relationships

(a) A multiple relationship occurs when a psychologist is in a professional role with a person and (1) at the same time is in another role with the same person, (2) at the same time is in a relationship with a person closely associated with or related to the person with whom the psychologist has the professional relationship, or (3) promises to enter into another relationship in the future with the person or a person closely associated with or related to the person.

A psychologist refrains from entering into a multiple relationship if the multiple relationship could reasonably be expected to impair the psychologist's objectivity, competence, or effectiveness in performing his or her functions as a psychologist, or otherwise risks exploitation or harm to the person with whom the professional relationship exists.

Multiple relationships that would not reasonably be expected to cause impairment or risk exploitation or harm are not unethical.

(b) If a psychologist finds that, due to unforeseen factors, a potentially harmful multiple relationship has arisen, the psychologist takes reasonable steps to resolve it with due regard for the best interests of the affected person and maximal compliance with the Ethics Code.

(c) When psychologists are required by law, institutional policy, or extraordinary circumstances to serve in more than one role in judicial or administrative proceedings, at the outset they clarify role expectations and the extent of confidentiality and thereafter as changes occur. (See also Standards 3.04, Avoiding Harm, and 3.07, Third-Party Requests for Services.)

3.06 Conflict of Interest

Psychologists refrain from taking on a professional role when personal, scientific, professional, legal, financial, or other interests or relationships could reasonably be expected to (1) impair their objectivity, competence, or effectiveness in performing their functions as psychologists or (2) expose the person or organization with whom the professional relationship exists to harm or exploitation.

3.07 Third-Party Requests for Services

When psychologists agree to provide services to a person or entity at the request of a third party, psychologists attempt to clarify at the outset of the service the nature of the relationship with all individuals or organizations involved. This clarification includes the role of the psychologist (e.g., therapist, consultant, diagnostician, or expert witness), an identification of who is the client, the probable uses of the services provided or the information obtained, and the fact that there may be limits to confidentiality. (See also Standards 3.05, Multiple Relationships, and 4.02, Discussing the Limits of Confidentiality.)

3.08 Exploitative Relationships

Psychologists do not exploit persons over whom they have supervisory, evaluative, or other authority such as clients/patients, students, supervisees, research participants, and employees. (See also Standards 3.05, Multiple Relationships; 6.04, Fees and Financial Arrangements; 6.05, Barter With Clients/Patients; 7.07, Sexual Relationships With Students and Supervisees; 10.05, Sexual Intimacies With Current Therapy Clients/Patients; 10.06, Sexual Intimacies With Relatives or Significant Others of Current Therapy Clients/Patients; 10.07, Therapy With Former Sexual Partners; and 10.08, Sexual Intimacies With Former Therapy Clients/Patients.)

3.09 Cooperation With Other Professionals

When indicated and professionally appropriate, psychologists cooperate with other professionals in order to serve their clients/patients effectively and appropriately. (See also Standard 4.05, Disclosures.)

3.10 Informed Consent

(a) When psychologists conduct research or provide assessment, therapy, counseling, or consulting services in person or via electronic transmission or other forms of communication, they obtain the informed consent of the individual or individuals using language that is reasonably understandable to that person or persons except when conducting such activities without consent is mandated by law or governmental regulation or as otherwise provided in this Ethics Code. (See also Standards 8.02, Informed Consent to Research; 9.03, Informed Consent in Assessments; and 10.01, Informed Consent to Therapy.)

(b) For persons who are legally incapable of giving informed consent, psychologists nevertheless (1) provide an appropriate explanation, (2) seek the individual's assent, (3) consider such persons' preferences and best interests, and (4) obtain appropriate permission from a legally authorized person, if such substitute consent is permitted or required by law. When consent by a legally authorized person is not permitted or required by law, psychologists take reasonable steps to protect the individual's rights and welfare.

(c) When psychological services are court ordered or otherwise mandated, psychologists inform the individual of the nature of the anticipated services, including whether the services are court ordered or mandated and any limits of confidentiality, before proceeding.

(d) Psychologists appropriately document written or oral consent, permission, and assent. (See also Standards 8.02, Informed Consent to Research; 9.03, Informed Consent in Assessments; and 10.01, Informed Consent to Therapy.)

3.11 Psychological Services Delivered To or Through Organizations

(a) Psychologists delivering services to or through organizations provide information beforehand to clients and when appropriate those directly affected by the services about (1) the nature and objectives of the services, (2) the intended recipients, (3) which of the individuals are clients, (4) the relationship the psychologist will have with each person and the organization, (5) the probable uses of services provided and information obtained, (6) who will have access to the information, and (7) limits of confidentiality. As soon as feasible, they provide information about the results and conclusions of such services to appropriate persons.

(b) If psychologists will be precluded by law or by organizational roles from providing such information to particular individuals or groups, they so inform those individuals or groups at the outset of the service.

3.12 Interruption of Psychological Services

Unless otherwise covered by contract, psychologists make reasonable efforts to plan for facilitating services in the event that psychological services are interrupted by factors such as the psychologist's illness, death, unavailability, relocation, or retirement or by the client's/patient's relocation or financial limitations. (See also Standard 6.02c, Maintenance, Dissemination, and Disposal of Confidential Records of Professional and Scientific Work.)

4. Privacy and Confidentiality

4.01 Maintaining Confidentiality

Psychologists have a primary obligation and take reasonable precautions to protect confidential information obtained through or stored in any medium, recognizing that the extent and limits of confidentiality may be regulated by law or established by institutional rules or professional or scientific

relationship. (See also Standard 2.05, Delegation of Work to Others.)

4.02 Discussing the Limits of Confidentiality

(a) Psychologists discuss with persons (including, to the extent feasible, persons who are legally incapable of giving informed consent and their legal representatives) and organizations with whom they establish a scientific or professional relationship (1) the relevant limits of confidentiality and (2) the foreseeable uses of the information generated through their psychological activities. (See also Standard 3.10, Informed Consent.)

(b) Unless it is not feasible or is contraindicated, the discussion of confidentiality occurs at the outset of the relationship and thereafter as new circumstances may warrant.

(c) Psychologists who offer services, products, or information via electronic transmission inform clients/patients of the risks to privacy and limits of confidentiality.

4.03 Recording

Before recording the voices or images of individuals to whom they provide services, psychologists obtain permission from all such persons or their legal representatives. (See also Standards 8.03, Informed Consent for Recording Voices and Images in Research; 8.05, Dispensing With Informed Consent for Research; and 8.07, Deception in Research.)

4.04 Minimizing Intrusions on Privacy

(a) Psychologists include in written and oral reports and consultations, only information germane to the purpose for which the communication is made.

(b) Psychologists discuss confidential information obtained in their work only for appropriate scientific or professional purposes and only with persons clearly concerned with such matters.

4.05 Disclosures

(a) Psychologists may disclose confidential information with the appropriate consent of the organizational client, the individual client/patient, or another legally authorized person on behalf of the client/patient unless prohibited by law.

(b) Psychologists disclose confidential information without the consent of the individual only as mandated by law, or where permitted by law for a valid purpose such as to (1) provide needed professional services; (2) obtain appropriate professional consultations; (3) protect the client/patient, psychologist, or others from harm; or (4) obtain payment for services from a client/patient, in which instance disclosure is limited to the minimum that is necessary to achieve the purpose. (See also Standard 6.04e, Fees and Financial Arrangements.)

4.06 Consultations

When consulting with colleagues, (1) psychologists do not disclose confidential information that reasonably could lead to the identification of a client/patient, research participant, or other person or organization with whom they have a confidential relationship unless they have obtained the prior consent of the person or organization or the disclosure cannot be avoided, and (2) they disclose information only to the

extent necessary to achieve the purposes of the consultation. (See also Standard 4.01, Maintaining Confidentiality.)

4.07 Use of Confidential Information for Didactic or Other Purposes

Psychologists do not disclose in their writings, lectures, or other public media, confidential, personally identifiable information concerning their clients/patients, students, research participants, organizational clients, or other recipients of their services that they obtained during the course of their work, unless (1) they take reasonable steps to disguise the person or organization, (2) the person or organization has consented in writing, or (3) there is legal authorization for doing so.

5. Advertising and Other Public Statements

5.01 Avoidance of False or Deceptive Statements

(a) Public statements include but are not limited to paid or unpaid advertising, product endorsements, grant applications, licensing applications, other credentialing applications, brochures, printed matter, directory listings, personal resumes or curricula vitae, or comments for use in media such as print or electronic transmission, statements in legal proceedings, lectures and public oral presentations, and published materials. Psychologists do not knowingly make public statements that are false, deceptive, or fraudulent concerning their research, practice, or other work activities or those of persons or organizations with which they are affiliated.

(b) Psychologists do not make false, deceptive, or fraudulent statements concerning (1) their training, experience, or competence; (2) their academic degrees; (3) their credentials; (4) their institutional or association affiliations; (5) their services; (6) the scientific or clinical basis for, or results or degree of success of, their services; (7) their fees; or (8) their publications or research findings.

(c) Psychologists claim degrees as credentials for their health services only if those degrees (1) were earned from a regionally accredited educational institution or (2) were the basis for psychology licensure by the state in which they practice.

5.02   Statements by Others

(a) Psychologists who engage others to create or place public statements that promote their professional practice, products, or activities retain professional responsibility for such statements.

(b) Psychologists do not compensate employees of press, radio, television, or other communication media in return for publicity in a news item. (See also Standard 1.01, Misuse of Psychologists' Work.)

(c) A paid advertisement relating to psychologists' activities must be identified or clearly recognizable as such.

5.03   Descriptions of Workshops and Non-Degree- Granting Educational Programs

To the degree to which they exercise control, psychologists responsible for announcements, catalogs, brochures, or advertisements describing workshops, seminars, or other non-degree-granting educational programs ensure that they accurately describe the audience for which the program is intended, the educational objectives, the presenters, and the fees involved.

5.04   Media Presentations

When psychologists provide public advice or comment via print, Internet, or other electronic transmission, they take precautions to ensure that statements (1) are based on their professional knowledge, training, or experience in accord with appropriate psychological literature and practice; (2) are otherwise consistent with this Ethics Code; and (3) do not indicate that a professional relationship has been established with the recipient. (See also Standard 2.04, Bases for Scientific and Professional Judgments.)

5.05   Testimonials

Psychologists do not solicit testimonials from current therapy clients/patients or other persons who because of their particular circumstances are vulnerable to undue influence.

5.06   In-Person Solicitation

Psychologists do not engage, directly or through agents, in uninvited in-person solicitation of business from actual or potential therapy clients/patients or other persons who because of their particular circumstances are vulnerable to undue influence. However, this prohibition does not preclude (1) attempting to implement appropriate collateral contacts for the purpose of benefiting an already engaged therapy client/patient or (2) providing disaster or community outreach services.

6. Record Keeping and Fees

6.01 Documentation of Professional and Scientific Work and Maintenance of Records

Psychologists create, and, to the extent the records are under their control, maintain, disseminate, store, retain, and dispose of records and data relating to their professional and scientific work in order to (1) facilitate provision of services later by them or by other professionals, (2) allow for replication of research design and analyses, (3) meet institutional requirements, (4) ensure accuracy of billing and payments, and (5) ensure compliance with law. (See also Standard 4.01, Maintaining Confidentiality.)

6.02 Maintenance, Dissemination, and Disposal of Confidential Records of Professional and Scientific Work

(a) Psychologists maintain confidentiality in creating, storing, accessing, transferring, and disposing of records under their control, whether these are written, automated, or in any other medium. (See also Standards 4.01, Maintaining Confidentiality, and 6.01, Documentation of Professional and Scientific Work and Maintenance of Records.)

(b) If confidential information concerning recipients of psychological services is entered into databases or systems of records available to persons whose access has not been consented to by the recipient, psychologists use

coding or other techniques to avoid the inclusion of personal identifiers.

(c) Psychologists make plans in advance to facilitate the appropriate transfer and to protect the confidentiality of records and data in the event of psychologists' withdrawal from positions or practice. (See also Standards 3.12, Interruption of Psychological Services, and 10.09, Interruption of Therapy.)

6.03 Withholding Records for Nonpayment

Psychologists may not withhold records under their control that are requested and needed for a client's/patient's emergency treatment solely because payment has not been received.

6.04 Fees and Financial Arrangements

(a) As early as is feasible in a professional or scientific relationship, psychologists and recipients of psychological services reach an agreement specifying compensation and billing arrangements.

(b) Psychologists' fee practices are consistent with law.

(c) Psychologists do not misrepresent their fees.

(d) If limitations to services can be anticipated because of limitations in financing, this is discussed with the recipient of services as early as is feasible. (See also Standards 10.09, Interruption of Therapy, and 10.10, Terminating Therapy.)

(e) If the recipient of services does not pay for services as agreed, and if psychologists intend to use collection agencies or legal measures to collect the fees, psychologists first inform the person that such measures will be taken and provide that person an opportunity to make prompt payment. (See also Standards 4.05, Disclosures; 6.03, Withholding Records for Nonpayment; and 10.01, Informed Consent to Therapy.)

6.05   Barter With Clients/Patients

Barter is the acceptance of goods, services, or other nonmonetary remuneration from clients/patients in return for psychological services. Psychologists may barter only if (1) it is not clinically contraindicated, and (2) the resulting arrangement is not exploitative. (See also Standards 3.05, Multiple Relationships, and 6.04, Fees and Financial Arrangements.)

6.06   Accuracy in Reports to Payors and Funding Sources

In their reports to payors for services or sources of research funding, psychologists take reasonable steps to ensure the accurate reporting of the nature of the service provided or research conducted, the fees, charges, or payments, and where applicable, the identity of the provider, the findings, and the diagnosis. (See also Standards 4.01, Maintaining Confidentiality; 4.04, Minimizing Intrusions on Privacy; and 4.05, Disclosures.)

6.07   Referrals and Fees

When psychologists pay, receive payment from, or divide fees with another professional, other than in an employer-employee relationship, the payment to each is based on the services provided (clinical, consultative, administrative, or other) and is not based on the referral itself. (See also Standard 3.09, Cooperation With Other Professionals.)

7.   Education and Training

7.01   Design of Education and Training Programs

Psychologists responsible for education and training programs take reasonable steps to ensure that the programs are designed to provide the appropriate knowledge and proper experiences, and to meet the requirements for licensure, certification, or other goals for which claims are made by the program. (See also Standard 5.03, Descriptions of Workshops and Non-Degree-Granting Educational Programs.)

7.02   Descriptions of Education and Training Programs

Psychologists responsible for education and training programs take reasonable steps to ensure that there is a current and accurate description of the program content (including participation in required course- or program-related counseling, psychotherapy, experiential groups, consulting projects, or community service), training goals and objectives, stipends and benefits, and requirements that must be met for satisfactory completion of the program. This information must be made readily available to all interested parties.

7.03   Accuracy in Teaching

(a) Psychologists take reasonable steps to ensure that course syllabi are accurate regarding the subject matter to be covered, bases for evaluating progress, and the nature of course experiences. This standard does not preclude an instructor from modifying course content or requirements when the instructor considers it pedagogically necessary or desirable, so long as students are made aware of these modifications in a manner that enables them to fulfill course requirements. (See also Standard 5.01, Avoidance of False or Deceptive Statements.)

(b) When engaged in teaching or training, psychologists present psychological information accurately. (See also Standard 2.03, Maintaining Competence.)

7.04 Student Disclosure of Personal Information

Psychologists do not require students or supervisees to disclose personal information in course- or program-related activities, either orally or in writing, regarding sexual history, history of abuse and neglect, psychological treatment, and relationships with parents, peers, and spouses or significant others except if (1) the program or training facility has clearly identified this requirement in its admissions and program materials or (2) the information is necessary to evaluate or obtain assistance for students whose personal problems could reasonably be judged to be preventing them from performing their training- or professionally related activities in a competent manner or posing a threat to the students or others.

7.05 Mandatory Individual or Group Therapy

(a) When individual or group therapy is a program or course requirement, psychologists responsible for that program allow students in undergraduate and graduate programs the option of selecting such therapy from practitioners unaffiliated with the program. (See also Standard 7.02, Descriptions of Education and Training Programs.)

(b) Faculty who are or are likely to be responsible for evaluating students' academic performance do not themselves provide that therapy. (See also Standard 3.05, Multiple Relationships.)

7.06 Assessing Student and Supervisee Performance

(a) In academic and supervisory relationships, psychologists establish a timely and specific process for providing feedback to students and supervisees. Information regarding the process is provided to the student at the beginning of supervision.

(b) Psychologists evaluate students and supervisees on the basis of their actual performance on relevant and established program requirements.

7.07 Sexual Relationships With Students and Supervisees

Psychologists do not engage in sexual relationships with students or supervisees who are in their department, agency, or training center or over whom psychologists have or are likely to have evaluative authority. (See also Standard 3.05, Multiple Relationships.)

8. Research and Publication

8.01 Institutional Approval

When institutional approval is required, psychologists provide accurate information about their research proposals and obtain approval prior to conducting the research. They conduct the research in accordance with the approved research protocol.

8.02 Informed Consent to Research

(a) When obtaining informed consent as required in Standard 3.10,

Informed Consent, psychologists inform participants about (1) the purpose of the research, expected duration, and procedures; (2) their right to decline to participate and to withdraw from the research once participation has begun; (3) the foreseeable consequences of declining or withdrawing; (4) reasonably foreseeable factors that may be expected to influence their willingness to participate such as potential risks, discomfort, or adverse effects; (5) any prospective research benefits; (6) limits of confidentiality; (7) incentives for participation; and (8) whom to contact for questions about the research and research participants' rights. They provide opportunity for the prospective participants to ask questions and receive answers. (See also Standards 8.03, Informed Consent for Recording Voices and Images in Research; 8.05, Dispensing With Informed Consent for Research; and 8.07, Deception in Research.)

(b) Psychologists conducting intervention research involving the use of experimental treatments clarify to participants at the outset of the research (1) the experimental nature of the treatment; (2) the services that will or will not be available to the control group(s) if appropriate; (3) the means by which assignment to treatment and control groups will be made; (4) available treatment alternatives if an individual does not wish to participate in the research or wishes to withdraw once a study has begun; and (5) compensation for or monetary costs of participating including, if appropriate, whether reimbursement from the participant or a third-party payor will be sought. (See also Standard 8.02a, Informed Consent to Research.)

8.03 Informed Consent for Recording Voices and Images in Research

Psychologists obtain informed consent from research participants prior to recording their voices or images for data collection unless (1) the research consists solely of naturalistic observations in public places, and it is not anticipated that the recording will be used in a manner that could cause personal identification or harm, or (2) the research design includes deception, and consent for the use of the recording is obtained during debriefing. (See also Standard 8.07, Deception in Research.)

8.04 Client/Patient, Student, and Subordinate Research Participants

(a) When psychologists conduct research with clients/patients, students, or subordinates as participants, psychologists take steps to protect the prospective participants from adverse consequences of declining or withdrawing from participation.

(b) When research participation is a course requirement or opportunity for extra credit, the prospective participant is given the choice of equitable alternative activities.

8.05 Dispensing With Informed Consent for Research

Psychologists may dispense with informed consent only (1) where research would not reasonably be assumed to create distress or harm and involves (a) the study of normal educational practices, curricula, or classroom management methods conducted in educational settings; (b) only anonymous questionnaires, naturalistic observations, or archival research for which disclosure of responses would not place participants at risk of criminal or civil liability or damage their financial standing, employ-ability, or reputation, and confidentiality is protected; or (c) the study of factors related to job or organization effective-ness conducted in organizational settings for which there is no risk to participants' employability and confidentiality is protected or (2) where otherwise per-mitted by law or federal or institutional regulations.

8.06 Offering Inducements for Research Participation

(a) Psychologists make reason-able efforts to avoid offering excessive or inappropriate financial or other induce-ments for research participation when such inducements are likely to coerce participation.

(b) When offering professional services as an inducement for research participation, psychologists clarify the nature of the services, as well as the risks, obligations, and limitations. (See also Standard 6.05, Barter With Clients/Patients.)

8.07 Deception in Research

(a) Psychologists do not conduct a study involving deception unless they have determined that the use of decep-tive techniques is justified by the study's significant prospective scientific, educa-tional, or applied value and that effective nondeceptive alternative procedures are not feasible.

(b) Psychologists do not deceive prospective participants about research

that is reasonably expected to cause phys-ical pain or severe emotional distress.

(c) Psychologists explain any deception that is an integral feature of the design and conduct of an exper-iment to participants as early as is feasible, preferably at the conclusion of their participation, but no later than at the conclusion of the data collection, and permit participants to withdraw their data. (See also Standard 8.08, Debriefing.)

8.08 Debriefing

(a) Psychologists provide a prompt opportunity for participants to obtain appropriate information about the nature, results, and conclusions of the research, and they take reasonable steps to correct any misconceptions that participants may have of which the psychologists are aware.

(b) If scientific or humane values justify delaying or withholding this infor-mation, psychologists take reasonable measures to reduce the risk of harm.

(c) When psychologists become aware that research procedures have harmed a participant, they take reason-able steps to minimize the harm.

8.09 Humane Care and Use of Animals in Research

(a) Psychologists acquire, care for, use, and dispose of animals in com-pliance with current federal, state, and local laws and regulations, and with professional standards.

(b) Psychologists trained in research methods and experienced in the care of laboratory animals supervise all procedures involving animals and are responsible for ensuring appropriate consideration of their comfort, health, and humane treatment.

(c) Psychologists ensure that all individuals under their supervision who are using animals have received instruction in research methods and in the care, maintenance, and handling of the species being used, to the extent appropriate to their role. (See also Standard 2.05, Delegation of Work to Others.)

(d) Psychologists make reasonable efforts to minimize the discomfort, infection, illness, and pain of animal subjects.

(e) Psychologists use a procedure subjecting animals to pain, stress, or privation only when an alternative procedure is unavailable and the goal is justified by its prospective scientific, educational, or applied value.

(f) Psychologists perform surgical procedures under appropriate anesthesia and follow techniques to avoid infection and minimize pain during and after surgery.

(g) When it is appropriate that an animal's life be terminated, psychologists proceed rapidly, with an effort to minimize pain and in accordance with accepted procedures.

8.10 Reporting Research Results

(a) Psychologists do not fabricate data. (See also Standard 5.01a, Avoidance of False or Deceptive Statements.)

(b) If psychologists discover significant errors in their published data, they take reasonable steps to correct such errors in a correction, retraction, erratum, or other appropriate publication means.

8.11 Plagiarism

Psychologists do not present portions of another's work or data as their own, even if the other work or data source is cited occasionally.

8.12 Publication Credit

(a) Psychologists take responsibility and credit, including authorship credit, only for work they have actually performed or to which they have substantially contributed. (See also Standard 8.12b, Publication Credit.)

(b) Principal authorship and other publication credits accurately reflect the relative scientific or professional contributions of the individuals involved, regardless of their relative status. Mere possession of an institutional position, such as department chair, does not justify authorship credit. Minor contributions to the research or to the writing for publications are acknowledged appropriately, such as in footnotes or in an introductory statement.

(c) Except under exceptional circumstances, a student is listed as principal author on any multiple-authored article that is substantially based on the student's doctoral dissertation. Faculty advisors discuss publication credit with students as early as feasible and throughout the research and publication process as appropriate. (See also Standard 8.12b, Publication Credit.)

8.13 Duplicate Publication of Data

Psychologists do not publish, as original data, data that have been previously published. This does not preclude republishing data when they are accompanied by proper acknowledgment.

8.14 Sharing Research Data for Verification

(a) After research results are published, psychologists do not withhold the data on which their conclusions are based from other competent professionals who seek to verify the substantive claims through reanalysis and who intend to use such data only for that purpose, provided that the confidentiality of the participants can be protected and unless legal rights concerning proprietary data preclude their release. This does not preclude psychologists from requiring that such individuals or groups be responsible for costs associated with the provision of such information.

(b) Psychologists who request data from other psychologists to verify the substantive claims through reanalysis may use shared data only for the declared purpose. Requesting psychologists obtain prior written agreement for all other uses of the data.

8.15 Reviewers

Psychologists who review material submitted for presentation, publication, grant, or research proposal review respect the confidentiality of and the proprietary rights in such information of those who submitted it.

9. Assessment

9.01 Bases for Assessments

(a) Psychologists base the opinions contained in their recommendations, reports, and diagnostic or evaluative statements, including forensic testimony, on information and techniques sufficient to substantiate their findings. (See also Standard 2.04, Bases for Scientific and Professional Judgments.)

(b) Except as noted in 9.01c, psychologists provide opinions of the psychological characteristics of individuals only after they have conducted an examination of the individuals adequate to support their statements or conclusions. When, despite reasonable efforts, such an examination is not practical, psychologists document the efforts they made and the result of those efforts, clarify the probable impact of their limited information on the reliability and validity of their opinions, and appropriately limit the nature and extent of their conclusions or recommendations. (See also Standards 2.01, Boundaries of Competence, and 9.06, Interpreting Assessment Results.)

(c) When psychologists conduct a record review or provide consultation or supervision and an individual examination is not warranted or necessary for the opinion, psychologists explain this and the sources of information on which they based their conclusions and recommendations.

9.02 Use of Assessments

(a) Psychologists administer, adapt, score, interpret, or use assessment techniques, interviews, tests, or instruments in a manner and for purposes that are appropriate in light of the research on or evidence of the usefulness and proper application of the techniques.

(b) Psychologists use assessment instruments whose validity and reliability have been established for use with members of the population tested. When such validity or reliability has not been established, psychologists describe the strengths and limitations of test results and interpretation.

(c) Psychologists use assessment methods that are appropriate to an individual's language preference and competence, unless the use of an alternative language is relevant to the assessment issues.

9.03   Informed Consent
in Assessments

(a) Psychologists obtain informed consent for assessments, evaluations, or diagnostic services, as described in Standard 3.10, Informed Consent, except when (1) testing is mandated by law or governmental regulations; (2) informed consent is implied because testing is conducted as a routine educational, institutional, or organizational activity (e.g., when participants voluntarily agree to assessment when applying for a job); or (3) one purpose of the testing is to evaluate decisional capacity. Informed consent includes an explanation of the nature and purpose of the assessment, fees, involvement of third parties, and limits of confidentiality and sufficient opportunity for the client/patient to ask questions and receive answers.

(b) Psychologists inform persons with questionable capacity to consent or for whom testing is mandated by law or governmental regulations about the nature and purpose of the proposed assessment services, using language that is reasonably understandable to the person being assessed.

(c) Psychologists using the services of an interpreter obtain informed consent from the client/patient to use that interpreter, ensure that confidentiality of test results and test security are maintained, and include in their recommendations, reports, and diagnostic or evaluative statements, including

forensic testimony, discussion of any limitations on the data obtained. (See also Standards 2.05, Delegation of Work to Others; 4.01, Maintaining Confidentiality; 9.01, Bases for Assessments; 9.06, Interpreting Assessment Results; and 9.07, Assessment by Unqualified Persons.)

9.04   Release of Test Data

(a) The term *test data* refers to raw and scaled scores, client/patient responses to test questions or stimuli, and psychologists' notes and recordings concerning client/patient statements and behavior during an examination. Those portions of test materials that include client/patient responses are included in the definition of *test data*. Pursuant to a client/patient release, psychologists provide test data to the client/patient or other persons identified in the release. Psychologists may refrain from releasing test data to protect a client/patient or others from substantial harm or misuse or misrepresentation of the data or the test, recognizing that in many instances release of confidential information under these circumstances is regulated by law. (See also Standard 9.11, Maintaining Test Security.)

(b) In the absence of a client/patient release, psychologists provide test data only as required by law or court order.

9.05   Test Construction

Psychologists who develop tests and other assessment techniques use appropriate psychometric procedures and current scientific or professional knowledge for test design, standardization, validation, reduction or elimination of bias, and recommendations for use.

9.06 Interpreting Assessment Results

When interpreting assessment results, including automated interpretations, psychologists take into account the purpose of the assessment as well as the various test factors, test-taking abilities, and other characteristics of the person being assessed, such as situational, personal, linguistic, and cultural differences, that might affect psychologists' judgments or reduce the accuracy of their interpretations. They indicate any significant limitations of their interpretations. (See also Standards 2.01b and c, Boundaries of Competence, and 3.01, Unfair Discrimination.)

9.07 Assessment by Unqualified Persons

Psychologists do not promote the use of psychological assessment techniques by unqualified persons, except when such use is conducted for training purposes with appropriate supervision. (See also Standard 2.05, Delegation of Work to Others.)

9.08 Obsolete Tests and Outdated Test Results

(a) Psychologists do not base their assessment or intervention decisions or recommendations on data or test results that are outdated for the current purpose.

(b) Psychologists do not base such decisions or recommendations on tests and measures that are obsolete and not useful for the current purpose.

9.09 Test Scoring and Interpretation Services

(a) Psychologists who offer assessment or scoring services to other professionals accurately describe the purpose, norms, validity, reliability, and applications of the procedures and any special qualifications applicable to their use.

(b) Psychologists select scoring and interpretation services (including automated services) on the basis of evidence of the validity of the program and procedures as well as on other appropriate considerations. (See also Standard 2.01b and c, Boundaries of Competence.)

(c) Psychologists retain responsibility for the appropriate application, interpretation, and use of assessment instruments, whether they score and interpret such tests themselves or use automated or other services.

9.10 Explaining Assessment Results

Regardless of whether the scoring and interpretation are done by psychologists, by employees or assistants, or by automated or other outside services, psychologists take reasonable steps to ensure that explanations of results are given to the individual or designated representative unless the nature of the relationship precludes provision of an explanation of results (such as in some organizational consulting, preemployment or security screenings, and forensic evaluations), and this fact has been clearly explained to the person being assessed in advance.

9.11 Maintaining Test Security

The term test *materials* refers to manuals, instruments, protocols, and test questions or stimuli and does not include *test data* as defined in Standard 9.04, Release of Test Data. Psychologists make reasonable efforts to maintain the integrity and security of test materials and other assessment techniques consistent with law and contractual obligations, and in a manner that permits adherence to this Ethics Code.

10. Therapy

10.01 Informed Consent to Therapy

(a) When obtaining informed consent to therapy as required in Standard 3.10, Informed Consent, psychologists inform clients/patients as early as is feasible in the therapeutic relationship about the nature and anticipated course of therapy, fees, involvement of third parties, and limits of confidentiality and provide sufficient opportunity for the client/patient to ask questions and receive answers. (See also Standards 4.02, Discussing the Limits of Confidentiality, and 6.04, Fees and Financial Arrangements.)

(b) When obtaining informed consent for treatment for which generally recognized techniques and procedures have not been established, psychologists inform their clients/patients of the developing nature of the treatment, the potential risks involved, alternative treatments that may be available, and the voluntary nature of their participation. (See also Standards 2.01e, Boundaries of Competence, and 3.10, Informed Consent.)

(c) When the therapist is a trainee and the legal responsibility for the treatment provided resides with the supervisor, the client/patient, as part of the informed consent procedure, is informed that the therapist is in training and is being supervised and is given the name of the supervisor.

10.02 Therapy Involving Couples or Families

(a) When psychologists agree to provide services to several persons who have a relationship (such as spouses, significant others, or parents and children), they take reasonable steps to clarify at the outset (1) which of the individuals are clients/patients and (2) the relationship the psychologist will have with each person. This clarification includes the psychologist's role and the probable uses of the services provided or the information obtained. (See also Standard 4.02, Discussing the Limits of Confidentiality.)

(b) If it becomes apparent that psychologists may be called on to perform potentially conflicting roles (such as family therapist and then witness for one party in divorce proceedings), psychologists take reasonable steps to clarify and modify, or withdraw from, roles appropriately. (See also Standard 3.05c, Multiple Relationships.)

10.03 Group Therapy

When psychologists provide services to several persons in a group setting, they describe at the outset the roles and responsibilities of all parties and the limits of confidentiality.

10.04 Providing Therapy to Those Served by Others

In deciding whether to offer or provide services to those already receiving mental health services elsewhere, psychologists carefully consider the treatment issues and the potential client's/patient's welfare. Psychologists discuss these issues with the client/patient or another legally authorized person on behalf of the client/patient in order to minimize the risk of confusion and conflict, consult with the other service providers when appropriate, and proceed with caution and sensitivity to the therapeutic issues.

10.05 Sexual Intimacies With Current Therapy Clients/ Patients

Psychologists do not engage in sexual intimacies with current therapy clients/patients.

10.06 Sexual Intimacies With Relatives or Significant Others of Current Therapy Clients/Patients

Psychologists do not engage in sexual intimacies with individuals they know to be close relatives, guardians, or significant others of current clients/patients. Psychologists do not terminate therapy to circumvent this standard.

10.07 Therapy With Former Sexual Partners

Psychologists do not accept as therapy clients/patients persons with whom they have engaged in sexual intimacies.

10.08 Sexual Intimacies With Former Therapy Clients/ Patients

(a) Psychologists do not engage in sexual intimacies with former clients/patients for at least two years after cessation or termination of therapy.

(b) Psychologists do not engage in sexual intimacies with former clients/patients even after a two-year interval except in the most unusual circumstances. Psychologists who engage in such activity after the two years following cessation or termination of therapy and of having no sexual contact with the former client/patient bear the burden of demonstrating that there has been no exploitation, in light of all relevant factors, including (1) the amount of time that has passed since therapy terminated; (2) the nature, duration, and intensity of the therapy; (3) the circumstances of termination; (4) the client's/patient's personal history; (5) the client's/patient's current mental status; (6) the likelihood of adverse impact on the client/patient; and (7) any statements or actions made by the therapist during the course of therapy suggesting or inviting the possibility of a post-termination sexual or romantic relationship with the client/patient. (See also Standard 3.05, Multiple Relationships.)

10.09 Interruption of Therapy

When entering into employment or contractual relationships, psychologists make reasonable efforts to provide for orderly and appropriate resolution of responsibility for client/patient care in the event that the employment or contractual relationship ends, with paramount consideration given to the welfare of the client/patient. (See also Standard 3.12, Interruption of Psychological Services.)

10.10 Terminating Therapy

(a) Psychologists terminate therapy when it becomes reasonably clear that the client/patient no longer needs the service, is not likely to benefit, or is being harmed by continued service.

(b) Psychologists may terminate therapy when threatened or otherwise endangered by the client/patient or another person with whom the client/patient has a relationship.

(c) Except where precluded by the actions of clients/patients or third-party payors, prior to termination psychologists provide pretermination counseling and suggest alternative service providers as appropriate.

HISTORY AND EFFECTIVE DATE

The American Psychological Association's Council of Representatives adopted this version of the APA Ethics Code during its meeting on August 21, 2002. The Code became effective on June 1, 2003. The Council of Representatives amended this version of the Ethics Code on February 20, 2010. The amendments became effective on June 1, 2010. Inquiries concerning the substance or interpretation of the APA Ethics Code should be addressed to the Director, Office of Ethics, American Psychological Association, 750 First Street, NE, Washington, DC 20002-4242. The standards in this Ethics Code will be used to adjudicate complaints brought concerning alleged conduct occurring on or after the effective date. Complaints will be adjudicated on the basis of the version of the Ethics Code that was in effect at the time the conduct occurred.

The APA has previously published its Ethics Code as follows:

American Psychological Association. (1953). *Ethical standards of psychologists*. Washington, DC: Author.

American Psychological Association. (1959). Ethical standards of psychologists. *American Psychologist, 14,* 279–282.

American Psychological Association. (1963). Ethical standards of psychologists. *American Psychologist, 18,* 56–60.

American Psychological Association. (1968). Ethical standards of psychologists. *American Psychologist, 23,* 357–361.

American Psychological Association. (1977, March). Ethical standards of psychologists. *APA Monitor*, 22–23.

American Psychological Association. (1979). *Ethical standards of psychologists*. Washington, DC: Author.

American Psychological Association. (1981). Ethical principles of psychologists. *American Psychologist, 36,* 633–638.

American Psychological Association. (1990). Ethical principles of psychologists (Amended June 2, 1989). *American Psychologist, 45,* 390–395.

American Psychological Association. (1992). Ethical principles of psychologists and code of conduct. *American Psychologist, 47,* 1597–1611.

American Psychological Association. (2002). Ethical principles of psychologists and code of conduct. *American Psychologist, 57,* 1060–1073.

Request copies of the APA's Ethical Principles of Psychologists and Code of Conduct from the APA Order Department, 750 First Street, NE, Washington, DC 20002–4242, or phone (202) 336–5510.

Appendix C

TABLE OF CASES

Agostini v. Felton, 522 U.S. 803 (1997).

Alamo Heights Independent School District v. State Board of Education, 790 F.2d 1153 (5th Cir. 1986).

Altman v. Bedford Central School District, 45 F. Supp. 2d 368 (S.D.N.Y. 1999).

Ambach v. Norwick, 441 U.S. 68 (1979).

A.P. v. Woodstock Board of Education, 572 F. Supp. 2d 221 (D. Conn. 2008).

Armijo v. Wagon Mound Public Schools, 159 F.3d 1253 (10th Cir. 1998).

Arnold v. Board of Education of Escambia, 754 F. Supp. 853 (S.D. Ala. 1990).

A.W. v. Northwest R-1 School District, 813 F.2d 158 (8th Cir. 1987), *cert. den.*, 108 S. Ct. 144 (1987).

Baird v. Rose, 192 F.3d 462 (4th Cir. 1999).

Baker v. Owen, 395 F. Supp. 294 (M.D. N.C., 1975), *aff'd*, 423 U.S. 908 (1975).

B.E.L. v. Hawaii, 63 F. Supp. 3d 1215 (D. Haw. 2014).

Benskin v. Taft City School District, 14 Clearinghouse Review 529 (1980).

Bethel School District No. 403 v. Fraser, 478 U.S. 675 (1986).

Board of Education of the Hendrick Hudson Central School District v. Rowley, 458 U.S. 176 (1982).

Brillon v. Klein Independent School District, 100 Fed. Appx. 309 (5th Cir. 2004).

Brown v. Board of Education, 347 U.S. 483 (1954).

Burnside v. Byars, 363 F.2d 744 (5th Cir. 1966).

California Association of School Psychologists v. Superintendent of Public Instruction, 21 IDELR 130 (N.D. Cal. 1994).

Cedar Rapids Community School District v. Garret F. by Charlene F., 526 U.S. 66 (1999).

Clayton v. Tate County School District, 560 Fed.Appx. 293 (5th Cir. 2014).

Clevenger v. Oak Ridge School Board, 774 F.2d 514 (6th Cir. 1984).

Connick v. Myers, 461 U.S. 138 (1983).

Corchado v. Board of Educ., Rochester City, 86 F.Supp.2d 168 (W.D.N.Y. 2000).

Cordrey v. Euckert, 917 F.2d 1460 (6th Cir. 1990).

Crawford v. Honig, 37 F.3d 485 (9th Cir. 1994).

Daniel R.R. v. Texas Board of Education, El Paso Independent School District, 874 F.2d 1036 (5th Cir. 1989).

Davis v. Monroe County Board of Education, 526 U.S. (1999).

Debra P. v. Turlington, 730 F.2d 1405 (11th Cir. 1984).

Denita Harris v. District of Columbia, 561 F. Supp. 2d 63 (D.D.C. 2008).

Detsel v. Board of Education of the Auburn Enlarged City School District, 637 F. Supp. 1022 (N.D.N.Y. 1986), *aff'd*, 820 F.2d 587 (2nd Cir. 1987), *cert. den.*, 108 S. Ct. 495 (1987).

Devries v. Fairfax County School Board, 882 F.2d 876 (4th Cir. 1989).

D.G. v. Somerset Hills School District, 559 F. Supp. 2d 484 (D. N.J. 2008).

Diana v. State Board of Education, Civ. Act. No. C-70-37 (N.D. Cal., 1970, *further order*, 1973).

Dickens by Dickens v. Johnson County Board of Education, 661 F. Supp. 155 (E.D. Tenn. 1987).

D.J.M. v. Hannibal Public School District #60, 647 F.3d 754 (8th Cir. 2011).

Doe v. Belleville Public School District No. 118, 672 F. Supp. 342 (S.D. Ill. 1987).

Donohue v. Copiague Union Free School District, 391 N.E.2d 1352 (N.Y. 1979).

Doug C. v. Hawaii Department of Education, 720 F.3d 1038 (9th Cir. 2013).

Eastwood v. Depart. of Corrections of State of Okl., 846 F.2d 627 (10th Cir. 1988).

Eisel v. Board of Education of Montgomery County, 597 A.2d 447 (Md. 1991).

Elizabeth S. v. Thomas K. Gilhool, 558 Educ. of the Handicapped L. Rep. 461 (M.D. Pa. 1987).

El Paso Independent School District v. Richard R., 567 F.Supp.2d 918 (W.D. Tex. 2008).

Epperson v. State of Arkansas, 393 U.S. 97 (1968).

Fay v. South Colonie Central School District, 802 F.2d 21 (2nd Cir. 1986).

Flour Bluff Independent School District v. Katherine M., 91 F.3d 689 (5th Cir. 1996).

Forest Grove School District v. T.A., 129 S. Ct. 2484 (2009).

Fort Osage R-1 School District v. Sims, 641 F.3d 996 (8th Cir. 2011).

Gallimore v. Henrico County School District, 38 F. Supp. 3d 721 (E.D. Va. 2014).

Garcetti v. Ceballos, 547 U.S. 410 (2006).

Garcia by Garcia v. Miera, 817 F.2d 650 (10th Cir. 1987).

Gebser v. Lago Vista Independent School District, 524 U.S. 274 (1998).

Georgia State Conference of Branches of NAACP v. State of Georgia, 775 F.2d 1403 (11th Cir. 1985).

G.G. Grimm v. Gloucester County School Board, ___ F. Supp.3d ___, 2015 WL 5560190 (E.D. Va. 2015).

G.J. v. Muscogee County School District, 668 F.3d 1258 (11th Cir. 2012).

G. "J" D. v. Wissahickon School District, 832 F.Supp. 2d 455 (E.D. Pa. 2011).

Glowacki v. Howell Public School District, No. 11-15481 (E.D. Mich. 2013), *aff'd*, No. 13-2231 (6th Cir. 2014).

Gonzaga University v. John Doe, 122 S. Ct. 2268 (2002).

Goss v. Lopez, 419 U.S. 565 (1975).

Greer v. Rome City School District, 950 F.2d 688 (11th Cir. 1991).

Guadalupe Organization, Inc. v. Tempe Elementary School District No. 3, 587 G.2d 1022 Civ. No. 71-435 (D. Ariz. 1972).

Hall v. Tawney, 621 F.2d 607 (4th Cir. 1980).

Harlow v. Fitzgerald, 457 U.S. 800 (1982).

Harris v. Forklift Systems Inc., 510 U.S. 14, 22 (1993).

Hayes v. Unified School District No. 377, 669 F. Supp. 1519 (D. Kan. 1987).

Hensley v. Eckerhart, 461 U.S. 424 (1983).

Hobson v. Hansen, 269 F. Supp. 401, 514 (D.D.C. 1967), *aff'd sub nom Smuck v. Hobson*, 408 F.2d 175 (D.C. Cir. 1969).

Honig v. Doe, 108 S. Ct. 592 (1988).

Ingraham v. Wright, 430 U.S. 651 (1977).

Irving Independent School District v. Tatro, 468 U.S. 883 (1984).

Jaffee v. Redmond, 518 U.S. 1 (1996).

James v. Board of Education of Aptakisic-Tripp Community Consolidated School District No. 102, 642 F. Supp. 2d 804 (N.D. Ill. 2009).

J.N. v. Bellingham School District No. 501, 74 Wn. App. 49, 871 P.2d 1106 (Wash. App. 1994).

John Doe v. Regional School Unit 26, 2014 ME 11, 86 A.3d 600 (Me. 2014).

John K. and Mary K. v. Board of Education for School District #65, Cook County, 504 N.E.2d 797 (Ill. App. 1987).

Johnson v. Independent School District No. 4 of Bixby, Tulsa County, Oklahoma, 921 F.2d 1022 (10th Cir. 1990).

Kelson v. The City of Springfield, 767 F.2d 651 (9th Cir. 1985).

K.M. ex rel. D.G. v. Hyde Park Central School District, 381 F. Supp. 2d 343 (S.D.N.Y. 2005).

Kok v. Tacoma School District No. 10, 179 Wn. App. 10, 317 P.3d 481 (Wash. App. 2013).

Kruelle v. New Castle County School District, 642 F.2d 687 (3rd Cir. 1981).

Lane v. Franks, 134 S. Ct. 2369 (2014).

Landstrom v. Illinois Department of Children and Family Services, 892 F.2d 670 (7th Cir. 1990).

Larry P. v. Riles, 343 F. Supp. 1306 (D.C. N.D. Cal., 1972), *aff'd*, 502 F.2d 963 (9th Cir. 1974), *further proceedings*, 495 F. Supp. 926 (D.C. N.D. Cal., 1979), *aff'd*, 502 F.2d 693 (9th Cir. 1984).

Lau v. Nichols, 414 U.S. 563 (1974).

Lee v. Lee County Bd. of Education, 476 F. Supp. 2d 1356 (M.D. Ala. 2007).

Lyons by Alexander v. Smith, 829 F. Supp. 414 (D.D.C. 1993).

Marshall v. American Psychological Association, No. 87-1316 (D.D.C. 1987).

Massey v. Banning, 256 F.Supp. 2d 1090 (C.D. Cal. 2003).

Max M. v. Thompson, 592 F. Supp. 1437, 1450 (N.D. Ill. 1984).

McDuff v. Tamborlane, 1999 Conn. Super. LEXIS 1771 (Conn. Super. 1999).

Merriken v. Cressman, 364 F. Supp. 913 (E.D. Pa. 1973).

Milligan et al. v. City of Slidell, No. 98-31335, 2000 WL 1285260 (5th Cir. 2000).

Mills v. Board of Education of District of Columbia, 348 F. Supp. 866 (1972); *contempt proceedings*, 551 Educ. of the Handicapped L. Rep. 643 (D.D.C. 1980).

Mirand v. Board of Education of the City of New York, 84 N.Y.2d 44, 637 N.E.2d 263, 614 N.Y.S.2d 372 (N.Y. 1994).

M.M. v. Lafayette School District, 767 F.3d 842 (9th Cir. 2014).

Morales v. Turman, 383 F. Supp. 53 (E.D. Tex. 1974).

Morse v. Frederick, 127 S.Ct. 2618 (2007).

Munir v. Pottsville Area School District, 723 F.3d 423 (3rd Cir. 2013).

Nabozny v. Podlesny, 92 F.3d 446 (7th Cir. 1996).

Neal v. Fulton County Board of Education, 229 F.3d 1069 (11th Cir. 2000).

New Jersey v. T.L.O., 469 U.S. 325 (1985).

Newport-Mesa Unified School District v. State of California Department of Education, 371 F. Supp. 2d 1170 (C.D. Cal. 2005).

New York State Association for Retarded Children v. Carey, 393 F. Supp. 715 (E.D.N.Y. 1975).

Obergell v. Hodges, 135 S. Ct. 1039 (2015).

Oncale v. Sundowner Offshore Services, Inc., 523 U.S. 75 (1998).

Owasso Independent School District No. I-011 v. Falvo, 534 U.S. 426 (2002).

Parents Against Abuse in Schools v. Williamsport Area School District, 594 A.2d 796 (Pa. Commw. 1991).

Parents in Action in Special Education (P.A.S.E.) v. Hannon, 506 F. Supp. 831 (N.D. Ill. 1980).

Parham v. J.R., 422 U.S. 584 (1979).

Pena v. New York State Division for Youth, 419 F. Supp. 203 (S.D.N.Y. 1976).

Pennsylvania Association for Retarded Children (P.A.R.C.) v. Commonwealth of Pennsylvania, 334 F. Supp. 1257 (D.C. E.D. Pa. 1971), 343 F. Supp. 279 (E.D. Pa. 1972).

People v. Vincent Moreno, 2005 N.Y. App. Div. LEXIS 2363 (N.Y. 2005).

Pesce v. J. Sterling Morton High School, 830 F.2d 789 (7th Cir. 1987).

Peter W. v. San Francisco Unified School District, 60 Cal. App. 3d 814 (1976).

Phillis P. v. Claremont Unified School District, 183 Cal. App. 3d 1193 (Cal. App. 1986).

Pickering v. Board of Education of Township High School District 205, Will County, 391 U.S. 563 (1968).

Price Waterhouse v. Hopkins, 490 U.S. 228, 251 (1989).

Rettig v. Kent City School District, 788 F.2d 328 (6th Cir. 1986).

Reusch v. Fountain, 872 F. Supp. 1421 (D. Md. 1994).

Richerson v. Beckon, 2008 U.S. Dist. LEXIS 29346 (W.D. Wash. 2008), *aff'd sub nom. Richerson v. Beckon*, 2009 U.S. App. LEXIS 12870 (9th Cir. Wash. 2009).

Ridley School District v. M.R., 680 F.3d 260 (3rd Cir. 2012).

S.A. v. Tulare County Office of Education, 2009 U.S. Dist. LEXIS 93170 (E.D. Cal. 2009).

Sacramento City Unified School District, Board of Education v. Holland, 786 F. Supp. 874 (E.D. Cal. 1992), *aff'd sub nom. Sacramento City Unified School District, Board of Education v. Rachel H.*, 14 F.3d 1398 (9th Cir. 1994), *cert. denied sub nom. Sacramento City Unified School District, Board of Education v. Holland*, 114 S. Ct. 2697 (1994).

Safford Unified School District No. 1 v. Redding, 129 S. Ct. 2633 (2009).

San Antonio Independent School District v. Rodriguez, 411 U.S. 1 (1973).

Sandlin v. Johnson, 643 F.2d 1027 (4th Cir. 1981).

Schaffer v. Weast, 546 U.S. 49 (2005).

School Board of Nassau County, Florida v. Arline, 107 S. Ct. 1123 (1987).

Settlegoode v. Portland Public Schools, 371 F.3d 503 (9th Cir. 2004).

Shively v. Green Local School District Board of Education, 579 Fed.Appx. 348 (6th Cir. 2014).

Shore Regional High School v. P.S., 381 F.3d 194 (3rd Cir. 2004).

Simmons v. Hooks, 843 F. Supp. 1296 (E.D. Ark. 1994).

Snyder v. Millersville University, 2008 U.S. Dist. LEXIS 97943 (E.D. Pa. 2008).

Snyder v. Phelps, 562 U.S. 443 (2011).

Spanierman v. Hughes, 576 F.Supp. 2d 292 (D. Conn. 2008).

State v. Grover, 437 N.W.2d 60 (Minn. 1989).

Sterling v. Borough of Minersville, 232 F.3d 190 (3rd Cir. 2000).

Sutton v. United Air Lines, Inc., 527 U.S. 471 (1999).

Tarasoff v. Regents of California, 118 Cal. Rptr. 129, 529 P.2d 553 (Cal. 1974). (Tarasoff I).
   Tarasoff v. Regents of California, 131 Cal. Rptr. 14, 551 P.2d 334 (Cal. 1976). (Tarasoff II).

Thomas v. Atascadero Unified School District, 662 F. Supp. 376 (C.D. Cal. 1987).

Timothy W. v. Rochester, New Hampshire School District, 875 F.2d 954 (1st Cir. 1989).

Tinker v. Des Moines Independent Community School District, 393 U.S. 503 (1969).

T.K. v. New York City Department of Education, 779 F.Supp.2d 289 (E.D.N.Y., 2011).

Toyota Motor Manufacturing, Kentucky, Inc. v. Williams, 534 U.S. 181 (2002).

Tyler W. v. Upper Perkiomen School District, 963 F. Supp.2d 427 (E.D. Pa. 2013).

U.S. v. Farrar, 38 F.2d 515 (D. Mass. 1930).

Valerie J. v. Derry Coop. School District, 771 F. Supp. 492 (D.N.H. 1991).

Whalen v. Roe, 429 U.S. 589 (1977).

Weissburg v. Lancaster School District, 591 F.3d 1255 (9th Cir. 2010).

Werth v. Board of Directors of the Public Schools of the City of Milwaukee, 472 F. Supp.2d 113 (E.D. Wis. 2007).

West Chester Area School Dist. v. Bruce C., 194 F.Supp.2d 417 (E.D. Pa. 2002).

Winkelman v. Parma City School District, 550 U.S. 516 (2007).

Wisconsin v. Constantineau, 400 U.S. 433 (1971).

Wolman v. Walter, 433 U.S. 229 (1977).

Woods v. Northport Public School, 487 Fed. Appx. 968 (6th Cir. 2012).

Wyatt v. Stickney, 325 F. Supp. 781 (M.D. Ala. N.D. 1971).

Wyke v. Polk County School Board, 129 F.3d 560 (11th Cir. 1997).

Zelman v. Simmons-Harris, 536 U.S. 639 (2002).

Zeno v. Pine Plains Central School District, 2009 U.S. Dist. LEXIS 42848 (S.D.N.Y. 2009), *aff'd*, 702 F.3d 655 (2nd Cir. 2012).

Appendix D ————————————————————

TABLE OF FEDERAL LEGISLATION

Americans with Disabilities Act of 1990 or "ADA" (Pub. L. No. 101-336) is codified at 42 U.S.C. §§ 12101 et seq.

Americans with Disabilities Act Amendments of 2008 or "ADAA". ADAA language quoted in this volume is based on the text of United State Code Title 42 Chapter 126 § 12101 et seq., downloaded June 23, 2015, from Legal Information Institute: https://www.law.cornell.edu

Bilingual Education Act of 1968 was added as an amendment to the Elementary and Secondary Education Act of 1965. Most recently amended by the Every Student Succeeds Act of 2015 (Pub. L. No. 114-95).

Civil Rights Act of 1871 or "Section 1983," 42 U.S.C. § 1983.

Civil Rights Act of 1964 (Pub. L. No. 88-352), 42 U.S.C. § 2000d.

Education Amendments of 1972 (Pub. L. No. 92-318), 20 U.S.C. § 1681.

Education for All Handicapped Children Act of 1975 or "EHA" (Pub. L. No. 94-142, 20 U.S.C. Chapter 33.

Education for the Handicapped Act Amendments of 1986 (Pub. L. No. 99-457); now Part C of the Individuals with Disabilities Education Improvement Act.

Elementary and Secondary Education Act of 1965 or "ESEA" (Pub. L. No. 89-750).

Every Student Succeeds Act of 2015 or "ESSA" (Pub. L. No. 114-95, 129 Stat. 1802). The ESSA includes the most recent amendments to the Elementary and Secondary Education Act of 1965. Citations to ESSA in this text are to (Senate Bill) S. 117, available at https://www.gpo .gov/fdsys/pkg/BILLS-114s1177enr/pdf/BILLS-114s1177enr.pdf

Family Educational Rights and Privacy Act of 1974 or "FERPA" (a part of Pub. L. No. 93-380), 20 U.S.C. § 1232g. Regulations implementing FERPA appear at 34 CFR § Part 99.

Handicapped Children's Protection Act of 1986 (Pub. L. No. 99-372), now part of the Individuals with Disabilities Education Improvement Act.

Health Insurance Portability and Accountability Act of 1996 or "HIPPA" (Pub. L. No. 104191), 26 U.S.C. § 294, 42 U.S.C. §§ 201, 1395b-5. Regulations implementing the "Privacy Rule" can be found at 45 CFR Part 160 and Part 164.

Federal statutes are compiled and published in the *United States Code* (U.S.C.). Rules and regulations implementing a law first appear in a daily publication called the *Federal Register* (Fed. Reg.) and subsequently are published in the *Code of Federal Regulations* (CFR). The *Code of Federal Regulations* has 50 titles, and each volume is updated once each calendar year. These government publications can be found at https://www.gpo .gov and in state and university libraries. In addition, the Electronic Code of Federal Regulations (e-CFR) can be accessed on the Internet at www.ecfr.gov. The e-CFR is updated daily but it is not considered to be the "official" legal edition of federal regulations. The U.S. Department of Education Web site also has links to statutes and regulations pertinent to education (http://www.ed.gov).

Individuals with Disabilities Education Act of 1990 or "IDEA" (Pub. L. No. 101-476), 20 U.S.C. Chapter 33. Amended by Pub. L. No. 105-117 in June 1997. Amended by the Individuals with Disabilities Education Improvement Act of 2004.

Individuals with Disabilities Education Improvement Act of 2004, commonly referred to as "IDEIA" or simply "IDEA" (Pub. L. No. 108-446), 20 U.S.C. §§ 1400 *et seq.* Regulations appear at 34 CFR Part 300.

Jacob K. Javits Gifted and Talented Students Education Act of 1988 (Pub. L. No. 100-297). Amended by the Every Student Succeeds Act of 2015 (Pub. L. No 114-95).

National Research Act of 1974 (Pub. L. No. 93-348), 42 U.S.C. § 289. Regulations appear at 45 CFR Part 46.

Protection of Pupil Rights Act or "PPRA." A 1978 amendment to ESEA. Amended in 1994 by Pub. L. No. 103-227 and in 2001 by Pub. L. No. 107-110.

Rehabilitation Act of 1973, commonly called "Section 504"(Pub. L. No. 93-112), 29 U.S.C. § 794. Regulations implementing Section 504 appear at 34 CFR Part 104.

Appendix E

FREQUENTLY USED ACRONYMS

The following is a list of acronyms that are frequently used in this volume.

ADA	Americans with Disabilities Act of 1990
ADAA	Americans with Disabilities Amendments Act of 2008
APA	American Psychological Association
APA-EP	American Psychological Association's "Ethical Principles of Psychologists and Code of Conduct" (2010)
CPA	Canadian Psychological Association
CFR	Code of Federal Regulations
DCL	"Dear Colleague Letter"
DOE	U.S. Department of Education
DSM-5	*Diagnostic and Statistical Manual of Mental Disorders* (5th ed.; American Psychiatric Association, 2013)
EBI	evidence-based intervention
ED	emotional disturbance
ELL	English language learner (or simply English learner)
ESEA	Elementary and Secondary Education Act of 1965
ESSA	Every Student Succeeds Act of 2015
FAPE	free appropriate public education
FERPA	Family Educational Rights and Privacy Act of 1974
HHS	U.S. Department of Health and Human Services
HIPAA	Health Insurance Portability and Accountability Act of 1996
IDEA	Individuals with Disabilities Education Act of 1997
IDEIA	Individuals with Disabilities Education Improvement Act of 2004
IEE	independent educational evaluation
IEP	individualized education program
IRB	institutional review board for the protection of human subjects in research
LEA	local educational agency
LGBT	lesbian, gay, biattractional, transgender
LRE	least restrictive environment
MTSS	multitiered system of support

NASP	National Association of School Psychologists
NASP-PPE	National Association of School Psychologists' "Principles for Professional Ethics" (2010b)
NCSP	Nationally Certified School Psychologist
OCR	U.S. Department of Education Office for Civil Rights
OSEP	U.S. Department of Education Office of Special Education Programs
PBS	positive behavior supports
PHI	protected health information
PII	personally identifiable information
PPRA	Protection of Pupil Rights Act of 1978
RTI	response to intervention
SDE	state department of education
Section 504	Section 504 of the Rehabilitation Act of 1973
Section 1983	Section 1983 of the Civil Rights Act of 1871
SLD	specific learning disability
SRCD	Society for Research on Child Development; see "Ethical Standards for Research with Children" (2007)
Standards	*Standards for Educational and Psychological Testing* (American Educational Research Association, American Psychological Association, & National Council on Measurement in Education, 2014)
SWPBIS	schoolwide positive behavior interventions and support system
U.S.C.	United States Code

For a more complete list of acronyms commonly used in the schools, visit the Center for Parent Information and Resources: http://www.parentcenterhub.org/repository/acronyms/

References

Abramovitch, R., Freedman, J. L., Henry, K., & Van Brunschot, M. (1995). Children's capacity to agree to psychological research: Knowledge of risks and benefits and voluntariness. *Ethics and Behavior, 5*, 25–48. doi:10.1207/s15327019eb0501_3

Acalanes (CA) Union High School District Office for Civil Rights, Western Division, San Francisco (California). (2009). 109 LRP 32284. Retrieved from Special Education Connection, http://www.specialedconnection.com

Adler, T. (1993, September). APA, two other groups to revise test standards. *APA Monitor*, pp. 24–25.

Alberto, P. A., & Troutman, A. C. (2013). *Applied behavior analysis for teachers* (9th ed.). Upper Saddle River, NJ: Pearson.

Ali, R. (2010, October 26). *Dear colleague letter*. U.S. Department of Education Office for Civil Rights. Retrieved from http://www2.ed.gov/about/offices/list/ocr/letters/colleague-201010.html

American Educational Research Association, American Psychological Association, & National Council on Measurement in Education. (2014). *Standards for educational and psychological testing*. Washington, DC: American Educational Research Association.

American Psychiatric Association. (2013). *Diagnostic and statistical manual of mental disorders* (5th ed.). Washington, DC: Author.

American Psychological Association. (1981). Ethical principles of psychologists. *American Psychologist, 36*, 633–638.

American Psychological Association. (1982). *Ethical principles in the conduct of research with human participants*. Washington, DC: Author.

American Psychological Association. (1986). *Guidelines for computer-based tests and interpretations*. Washington, DC: Author.

American Psychological Association. (2002). Ethical principles of psychologists and code of conduct. *American Psychologist, 57*, 1060–1073. doi:10.1037/0003-066X.57.12.1060

American Psychological Association. (2007a). *APA ethics committee rules and procedures*. Retrieved from http://www.apa.org/ethics/code/committee.aspx

American Psychological Association. (2007b). Record keeping guidelines. *American Psychologist, 62*, 993–1004.

American Psychological Association. (2010). *Ethical principles of psychologists and code of conduct with the 2010 amendments*. Retrieved from http://www.apa.org/ethics/code

American Psychological Association. (2015). Report of the ethics committee, 2014. *American Psychologist, 70*, 444–453. http://dx.doi.org/10.1037/a0039370

American Psychological Association Committee on Legal Issues. (1996). Strategies for private practitioners coping with subpoenas or compelled testimony for client records or test data.

Professional Psychology: Research and Practice, 27, 245–251. http://dx.doi.org/10.1037/0735-7028.27.3.245

American Psychological Association Committee on Professional Practice and Standards. (2003). Legal issues in the professional practice of psychology. *Professional Psychology: Research and Practice, 34*, 595–600.

American Psychological Association Office of Program Consultation and Accreditation. (2013). *Guidelines and principles for accreditation of programs in professional psychology.* Retrieved from http://www.apa.org/ed/accreditation/about/policies/guiding-principles.pdf

Appelbaum, P. S., & Meisel, A. (1986). Therapists' obligations to report their patients' criminal acts. *Bulletin of the American Academy of Psychiatry and the Law, 14*, 221–230.

Armistead, L. D. (2014a). Best practices in continuing professional development for school psychologists. In P. L. Harrison & A. Thomas (Eds.), *Best practices in school psychology: Foundations* (pp. 611–626). Bethesda, MD: National Association of School Psychologists.

Armistead, L. D. (2014b). Ethical and professional best practices in the digital age. In P. L. Harrison & A. Thomas (Eds.), *Best practices in school psychology: Foundations* (pp. 459–474). Bethesda, MD: National Association of School Psychologists.

Armistead, L. D., Williams, B. B., & Jacob, S. (2011). *Professional ethics for school psychologists: A problem-solving model casebook* (2nd ed.). Bethesda, MD: National Association of School Psychologists.

Armistead, R. J., & Smallwood, D. L. (2014). The National Association of School Psychologists model for comprehensive and integrated school psychological services. In P. L. Harrison & A. Thomas (Eds.), *Best practices in school psychology: Data-based and collaborative services* (pp. 9–23). Bethesda, MD: National Association of School Psychologists.

Aronson, R. H. (2001). Symposium: The Uniform Rules of Evidence (1999): The mental health provider privilege in the wake of *Jaffee v. Redmond. Oklahoma Law Review, 54*, 591–612.

Associated Press. (2013, August 21). Calif. students share photos of state test answers. *Education Week*, p. 4. http://www.edweek.org/ew/articles/2013/08/21/01brief-b1.h33.html

Atkinson, D. R. (1993). Who speaks for cross-cultural counseling research? *Counseling Psychologist, 21*, 218–224. http://dx.doi.org/10.1177/0011000093212003

Austin, W., Rankel, M., Kagan, L., Bergum, V., & Lemermeyer, G. (2005). To stay or to go, to speak or stay silent, to act or not to act: Moral distress as experienced by psychologists. *Ethics & Behavior, 15*, 197–212. doi:10.1207/s15327019eb1503_1

Bailey, J., & Burch, M. (2011). *Ethics for behavior analysts* (2nd ed.). New York, NY: Routledge. http://dx.doi.org/10.4324/9780203831250

Bailey, J. A. (1980, March). School counselors: Test your ethics. *School Counselor*, 285–293.

Baldick, T. L. (1980). Ethical discrimination ability of intern psychologists: A function of training in ethics. *Professional Psychology, 11*, 276–282. http://dx.doi.org/10.1037/0735-7028.11.2.276

Ballantine, H. T. (1979). The crisis in ethics, anno domini 1979. *New England Journal of Medicine, 301*, 634–638. http://dx.doi.org/10.1056/nejm197909203011204

Barnett, J. E., & Campbell, L. F. (2012). Ethics issues in scholarship. In S. J. Knapp, M. C. Gottlieb, M. M. Handelsman, & L. D. VandeCreek (Eds.), *APA handbook of ethics in psychology* (Vol. 2, pp. 309–332). Washington, DC: American Psychological Association. http://dx.doi.org/10.1037/13272-015

Barnett, J. E., Erickson Cornish, J. A., Goodyear, R. K., & Lichtenberg, J. W. (2007). Commentaries on the ethical and effective practice of clinical supervision. *Professional Psychology: Research and Practice, 38*, 268–275. http://dx.doi.org/10.1037/0735-7028.38.3.268

Barnett, J. E., Wise, E. H., Johnson-Greene, D., & Bucky, S. (2007). Informed consent: Too much of a good thing or not enough? *Professional Psychology: Research and Practice, 38,* 179–186. http://dx.doi.org/10.1037/0735-7028.38.2.179

Bartow, C., Jacob, S., Malta, R., Schmittel, M., & Zielinski, J. (2014, February). *State laws regarding access to mental health services by minors.* Poster presented at the National Association of School Psychologists Convention, Washington, DC.

Bashe, A., Anderson, S. K., Handelsman, M. M., & Klevansky, R. (2007). An acculturation model for ethics training: The ethics autobiography and beyond. *Professional Psychology: Research and Practice, 38,* 60–67. http://dx.doi.org/10.1037/0735-7028.38.1.60

Batsche, G. M., & Peterson, D. W. (1983). School psychology and projective assessment: A growing incompatibility. *School Psychology Review, 12,* 440–445.

Bauder, D. (1989, February 6). Misdiagnosed as mentally retarded, deaf man spent years in institutions. *Midland Daily News,* p. B–1.

Beam, A. C., & Whinery, L. H. (2001). Uniform Rules of Evidence. *Oklahoma Law Review, 54,* 449–511.

Bear, G. G. (2008). Best practices in classroom discipline. In A. Thomas & J. Grimes (Eds.), *Best practices in school psychology V* (pp. 1403–1420). Bethesda, MD: National Association of School Psychologists.

Beauchamp, T. L., & Childress, J. F. (2013). *Principles of biomedical ethics* (7th ed.). New York, NY: Oxford University Press.

Behavior Analyst Certification Board. (2012). *Guidelines for responsible conduct for behavior analysts.* Retrieved from http://www.bacb.com

Behnke, S. H., & Jones, S. E. (2012). Ethics and ethics codes for psychologists. In S. J. Knapp, M. C. Gottlieb, M. M. Handelsman, & L. D. VandeCreek (Eds.), *APA handbook of ethics in psychology* (Vol. 1, pp. 43–74). Washington, DC: American Psychological Association. http://dx.doi.org/10.1037/13271-002

Behring, S. T., Cabello, B., Kushida, D., & Murguia, A. (2000). Cultural modifications to current school-based consultation approaches reported by culturally diverse beginning consultants. *School Psychology Review, 29,* 354–367.

Benjamin, G. A. H., Kent, L., & Sirikantraporn, S. (2009). Duty to protect statutes. In J. L. Werth, E. R. Welfel, & G. A. H. Benjamin (Eds.), *The duty to protect: Ethical, legal, and professional responsibilities of mental health professionals* (pp. 9–28). Washington, DC: American Psychological Association. http://dx.doi.org/10.1037/11866-011

Bennett, B. E., Bricklin, P. M., Harris, E., Knapp, S., VandeCreek, L., & Younggren, J. N. (2006). Assessing and managing risk in psychological practice: An individualized approach. Rockville, MD: The Trust. http://dx.doi.org/10.1037/14293-000

Bernard, J., & Jara, C. (1986). The failure of clinical psychology graduate students to apply understood ethical principles. *Professional Psychology: Research and Practice, 17,* 313–315. http://dx.doi.org/10.1037//0735-7028.17.4.313

Bernstein, B. E., & Hartsell, T. L. (1998). *The portable lawyer for mental health professionals.* New York, NY: Wiley.

Bersoff, D. N. (1979). Regarding psychologists testily: The legal regulation of psychological assessment in the public schools. *Maryland Law Review, 39,* 27–120. http://dx.doi.org/10.1037/10085-002

Bersoff, D. N. (1982). Larry P. and PASE: Judicial report cards on the validity of individual intelligence tests. In T. Kratochwill (Ed.), *Advances in school psychology* (Vol. 2, pp. 61–95). Hillsdale, NJ: Erlbaum.

Bersoff, D. N. (1983). Children as participants in psychoeducational assessment. In G. B. Melton, G. P. Koocher, & M. J. Saks (Eds.), *Children's competence to consent* (pp. 149–177). New York, NY: Plenum Press. doi:10.1007/978-1-4684-4289-2_9

Bersoff, D. N. (1994). Explicit ambiguity: The 1992 ethics code as an oxymoron. *Professional Psychology: Research and Practice, 25*, 382–387. http://dx.doi.org/10.1037/0735-7028.25.4.382

Bersoff, D. N., & Hofer, P. T. (1990). The legal regulation of school psychology. In C. R. Reynolds & T. B. Gutkin (Eds.), *The handbook of school psychology* (2nd ed., pp. 937–961). New York, NY: Wiley.

Bersoff, D. N., & Koeppl, P. M. (1993). The relation between ethical codes and moral principles. *Ethics and Behavior, 3*, 345–357. doi:10.1080/10508422.1993.9652112

Bersoff, D. N., & Prasse, D. (1978). Applied psychology and judicial decision making: Corporal punishment as a case in point. *Professional Psychology, 9*, 400–411. http://dx.doi.org/10.1037/0735-7028.9.3.400

Bersoff, D. N., & Ysseldyke, J. E. (1977). Non-discriminatory assessment: The law, litigation, and implications for the assessment of learning disabled children. In S. Jacob (Ed.), *The law: Assessment and placement of special education students* (pp. 65–92). Lansing, MI: Michigan Department of Education.

Binder, A. (2015, April 1). Atlanta educators convicted in school cheating scandal. *New York Times*. Retrieved from http://www.nytimes.com/2015/04/02/us/verdict-reached-in-atlanta-school-testing-trial.html?_r=2

Black, H. C. (1983). *Black's law dictionary* (5th ed., abridged). St. Paul, MN: West Group.

Black, M. M., & Ponirakis, A. (2000). Computer-administered interviews with children about maltreatment. *Journal of Interpersonal Violence, 15*, 682–695. http://dx.doi.org/10.1177/088626000015007002

Blue-Banning, M., Summers, J. A., Frankland, H. C., Nelson, L. L., & Beegle, G. (2004). Dimensions of family and professional partnerships: Constructive guidelines for collaboration. *Exceptional Children, 70*, 167–184. doi:10.1177/001440290407000203

Boccio, D. E. (2015). A school-based suicide risk assessment protocol. *Journal of Applied School Psychology, 31*, 31–62. doi:10.1080/15377903.2014.963272

Borum, R. (2000). Assessing violence risk among youth. *Journal of Clinical Psychology, 56*, 1263–1288. doi:10.1002/1097-4679(200010)56:10<1263::AID-JCLP3>3.0.CO;2-D

Bosk, C. L. (1979). *Forgive and remember: Managing medical failure*. Chicago, IL: University of Chicago Press. http://dx.doi.org/10.7208/chicago/9780226924687.001.0001

Bower, E. M. (1982). Defining emotional disturbance: Public policy and research. *Psychology in the Schools, 19*, 55–60. doi:10.1002/1520-6807(19820108)19:1<55::AID-PITS2310190112>3.0.CO;2-2

Bowman, D. H. (2002, February 6). Survey's sexuality questions anger elementary parents. *Education Week*, p. 10. http://www.edweek.org/ew/articles/2002/01/09/16privacy.h21.html

Braden, J. P., & Joyce, L. B. (2008). Best practices in making assessment accommodations. In A. Thomas & J. Grimes (Eds.), *Best practices in school psychology V* (pp. 589–603). Bethesda, MD: National Association of School Psychologists.

Braden, J. P., & Tayrose, M. P. (2008). Best practices in educational accountability: High-stakes testing and educational reform. In A. Thomas & J. Grimes (Eds.), *Best practices in school psychology V* (pp. 575–588). Bethesda, MD: National Association of School Psychologists.

Bradshaw, C. P. (2015). Translating research to practice in bullying prevention. *American Psychologist, 70*, 322–332. http://dx.doi.org/10.1037/a0039114

Brock, S. E., & Jimerson, S. R. (Eds.). (2012). *Best practices in school crisis prevention and response* (2nd ed.). Bethesda, MD: National Association of School Psychologists.

Brophy, J. E., & Good, T. L. (1974). *Teacher-student relationships*. New York, NY: Holt, Rinehart & Winston.

Brown, D., Pryzwansky, W. B., & Schulte, A. C. (2011). *Psychological consultation and collaboration: Introduction to theory and practice* (7th ed.). Boston, MA: Pearson.

Brown, D. T. (1979). Issues in accreditation certification, and licensure. In G. D. Phye & D. J. Reschly (Eds.), *School psychology: Perspectives and issues* (pp. 49–82). New York, NY: Academic Press.

Brown, E. (2015, April 14). Nine Atlanta educators in test-cheating case are sentenced to prison. *Washington Post*. Retrieved from https://www.washingtonpost.com/local/education/eight-atlanta-educators-in-test-cheating-case-sentenced-to-prison/2015/04/14/08a9d26e-e2bc-11e4-b510-962fcfabc310_story.html

Brown, R. T., Reynolds, C. R., & Whitaker, J. S. (1999). Bias in mental testing since *Bias in Mental Testing*. *School Psychology Quarterly, 14*, 208–238. http://dx.doi.org/10.1037/h0089007

Burgdorf, R. L. (1991). The Americans with Disabilities Act: Analysis and implications of a second-generation civil rights statute. *Harvard Civil Rights–Civil Liberties Law Review, 26*, 413–522.

Burns, M. K., Jacob, S., & Wagner, A. (2008). Ethical and legal issues associated with using responsiveness-to-intervention to assess learning disabilities. *Journal of School Psychology, 46*, 263–279. doi:10.1016/j.jsp.2007.06.001

Campbell, D. T., & Fiske, D. W. (1959). Convergent and discriminate validation by the multitrait-multimethod matrix. *Psychological Bulletin, 56*, 81–105. http://dx.doi.org/10.1037/h0046016

Canadian Psychological Association. (2000). *Canadian code of ethics for psychologists* (3rd ed.). Retrieved from http://www.cpa.ca

Canter, A. (1989, November). Is parent permission always necessary? *Communiqué*, p. 9.

Canter, A. (2001a, May). Test protocols: Pt. 1. Right to review and copy. *Communiqué*, pp. 30, 32.

Canter, A. (2001b, September). Test protocols: Pt. 2. Storage and disposal. *Communiqué*, pp. 16–19.

Carlson, J. S., & Shahidullah, J. D. (2014). Best practices in assessing the effects of psychotropic medication on student performance. In P. L. Harrison & A. Thomas (Eds.), *Best practices in school psychology: Systems-level services* (pp. 361–373). Bethesda, MD: National Association of School Psychologists.

Carvalho, C., Dennison, A., & Estrella, I. (2014). Best practices in the assessment of English language learners. In P. L. Harrison & A. Thomas (Eds.), *Best practices in school psychology: Foundations* (pp. 75–87). Bethesda, MD: National Association of School Psychologists.

Castillo, J. M., & Curtis, M. J. (2014). Best practices in systems-level change. In P. L. Harrison & A. Thomas (Eds.), *Best practices in school psychology: Systems-level services* (pp. 11–28). Bethesda, MD: National Association of School Psychologists.

Caterino, L., Chieh, L., Hansen, A., Forman, S., Harris, A., & Miller, G. (2010). *Practicum competencies outline: A reference for school psychology doctoral programs*. Council of Directors of School Psychology Programs 2010 mid-winter meeting report. https://docs.google.com/viewer?a=v&pid=sites&srcid=ZGVmYXVsdGRvbWFpbnxjZHNwcGhvbWV8Z3g6 MWVmODQ1ZGUwMjQzZWIxZg

Cavanagh, S. (2015, March 25). Pearson, PARCC knocked for monitoring students' social media. *Education Week*, p. 4. www.edweek.org/ew/articles/2015/03/25/pearson-parcc-knocked-for-monitoring-students-social.html

Centers for Disease Control and Prevention. (2014, December). *Reported STDs in the United States: 2013 national data for chlamydia, gonorrhea, and syphilis.* Retrieved from http://stacks.cdc.gov/view/cdc/26427

Centers for Disease Control and Prevention. (2015a, March 15). *Suicide prevention, youth suicide.* Retrieved from http://www.cdc.gov/violenceprevention/suicide/youth_suicide.html

Centers for Disease Control and Prevention. (2015b). *Understanding school violence: Fact sheet.* Retrieved from http://www.cdc.gov/violenceprevention/pdf/School_Violence_Fact_Sheet-a.pdf

Chalfant, J., & Pysh, M. (1989). Teacher assistance teams: Five descriptive studies on 96 teams. *Remedial and Special Education, 10*(6), 49–58. doi:10.1177/074193258901000608

Chalk, R., Frankel, M. S., & Chafer, S. B. (1980). *AAAS professional ethics project.* Washington, DC: American Association for the Advancement of Science.

Chestnut, C. R. (2001, September 17). Jury awards $1 million to fired special ed teacher. *Oregonian.* Retrieved from http://www.kafourymcdougal.com/headline-victories/employment-law/el-hv-2/

Chin, J. K., Dowdy, E., Jimerson, S. R., & Rime, W. J. (2012). Alternative to suspensions: Rationale and recommendations. *Journal of School Violence, 11*, 156–173. doi:10.1080/15388220.2012.652912

Clovis (CA) Unified School District, Office for Civil Rights, Western Division, San Francisco (CA). (2009, April 23). *Individuals with Disabilities Education Law Report, 52*, 167. SpecialEdConnection. Horsham, PA: LRP Publications. Retrieved from http://www.specialedconnection.com

Cobb County (GA) School District. (1992). OCR complaint investigation letter of findings. *Individuals with Disabilities Education Law Report, 19*, 29–32.

Cobia, D. C., & Boes, S. R. (2000). Professional disclosure statements and formal plans for supervision: Two strategies for minimizing the risk of ethical conflicts in post-master's supervision. *Journal of Counseling and Development, 78*, 293–296. doi:10.1002/j.1556-6676.2000.tb01910.x

Codding, R. S., Sanetti, L. M. H., & Reed, F. D. D. (2014). Best practices in facilitating consultation and collaboration with teachers and administrators. In P. L. Harrison & A. Thomas (Eds.), *Best practices in school psychology: Data-based and collaborative decision making* (pp. 525–539). Bethesda, MD: National Association of School Psychologists.

Cohn, S. D., Gelfman, M. H. B., & Schwab, N. C. (2005). Adolescent issues and rights of minors. In N. C. Schwab & M. H. B. Gelfman (Eds.), *Legal issues in school health services: A resource for school administrators, school attorneys, school nurses* (pp. 231–250). New York, NY: Authors Choice Press.

Collins, C., Falender, C. A., & Shafranske, E. P. (2011). Commentary on Rebecca Schwartz-Mette's 2009 article, "Challenges in addressing graduate student impairment in academic professional psychology programs." *Ethics & Behavior, 21*, 428–430. doi:10.1080/10508422.2011.604547

Congress, E. P. (2001). Ethical issues in work with culturally diverse children and their families. In N. B. Webb (Ed.), *Culturally diverse parent–child and family relationships* (pp. 29–53). New York, NY: Columbia University Press.

Conoley, J. C., & Conoley, C. W. (1982). *School consultation: A guide to practice and training.* New York, NY: Pergamon Press.

Conoley, J. C., & Sullivan, J. R. (2002). Best practices in the supervision of interns. In A. Thomas & J. Grimes (Eds.), *Best practices in school psychology IV* (pp. 131–144). Bethesda, MD: National Association of School Psychologists.

Cooper, S. (1984). Minors' participation in therapy decisions: A written therapist–child agreement. *Journal of Child Adolescent Psychotherapy, 1*, 93–96.

Cornell, D. (2014). Best practices in threat assessment in the schools. In P. L. Harrison & A. Thomas (Eds.), *Best practices in school psychology: Systems-level services* (pp. 259–272). Bethesda, MD: National Association of School Psychologists.

Cornell, D., & Limber, S. P. (2015). Law and policy on the concept of bullying at school. *American Psychologist, 70*, 333–343. http://dx.doi.org/10.1037/a0038558

Corrao, J., & Melton, G. B. (1988). Legal issues in school-based behavior therapy. In J. C. Witt, S. N. Elliot, & F. M. Gresham (Eds.), *Handbook of behavior therapy in education* (pp. 377–399). New York, NY: Plenum Press.

Cottone, R. R. (2012). Ethical decision making in mental health contexts: Representative models and an organizational framework. In S. J. Knapp, M. C. Gottlieb, M. M. Handelsman, & L. D. VandeCreek (Eds.), *APA handbook of ethics in psychology* (Vol. 1, pp. 99–122). Washington, DC: American Psychological Association. http://dx.doi.org/10.1037/13271-004

Coughlin, E. K. (1988, November 30). Psychologist sentenced for giving false data to federal government. *Chronicle of Higher Education*, p. A5.

Crothers, L. M., Kolbert, J. B., & Hughes, T. L. (2014). Best practices in providing inservices for teachers and principals. In P. L. Harrison & A. Thomas (Eds.), *Best practices in school psychology: Data-based and collaborative services* (pp. 583–593). Bethesda, MD: National Association of School Psychologists.

Cummins, J. (1999). BICs and CALP: Clarifying the distinction. Retrieved from ERIC database. (ED438 551) http://files.eric.ed.gov/fulltext/ED438551.pdf

Curtis, M. J., Castillo, J. M., & Gelley, C. (2012). School psychology 2010: Demographics, employment, and the context for professional practice. *Communiqué, 40*(7), pp. 28–30.

Dailor, A. N., & Jacob, S. (2010). Ethical and legal challenges: Negotiating change. In J. Kaufman, T. L. Hughes, & C. A. Riccio (Eds.), *Handbook of education, training, and supervision of school psychologists in school and community* (Vol. 2, pp. 153–168). New York, NY: Routledge, Taylor & Francis.

Dailor, A. M., & Jacob, S. (2011). Ethically challenging situations reported by school psychologists: Implications for training. *Psychology in the Schools, 48*, 619–631. doi:10.1002/pits.20574

Dana, R. H. (2000). Psychological assessment in the diagnosis and treatment of ethnic group members. In J. F. Aponte & J. Wohl (Eds.), *Psychological intervention and cultural diversity* (2nd ed., pp. 59–74). Boston, MA: Allyn & Bacon.

Daves, D. P., & Walker, D. W. (2012). RTI: Court and case law—confusion by design. *Learning Disability Quarterly, 35*, 68–71. doi:10.1177/0731948711433091

Davis, J. M., & Sandoval, J. (1982). Applied ethics for school-based consultants. *Professional Psychology, 13*, 543–551. http://dx.doi.org/10.1037/0735-7028.13.4.543

Dawson, M. M. (1987). Beyond ability grouping: A review of the effectiveness of ability grouping and its alternatives. *School Psychology Review, 16*, 348–369.

Debski, J., Spadafore, C. D., Jacob, S., Poole, D. A., & Hixson, M. D. (2007). Suicide intervention: Training, roles, and knowledge of school psychologists. *Psychology in the Schools, 44*, 157–170. doi:10.1002/pits.20213

Decker, D. M., & Bolt, S. E. (2008). Challenges and opportunities for promoting student achievement through large-scale assessment results. *Assessment for Effective Intervention, 34*, 43–51. doi:10.1177/1534508408314173

Dekraai, M., Sales, B., & Hall, S. (1998). Informed consent, confidentiality, and duty to report laws in the conduct of child therapy. In T. R. Kratochwill & R. J. Morris (Eds.), *The practice of child therapy* (3rd ed., pp. 540–559). Boston, MA: Allyn & Bacon.

de las Fuentes, C., & Willmuth, M. E. (2005). Competency training in ethics education and practice. *Professional Psychology: Research and Practice, 36*, 362–366. http://dx.doi.org/10.1037/0735-7028.36.4.362

Delaware College Preparatory Academy and the Red Clay Consolidated School District Delaware State Educational Agency. (2009). 109 LRP 59893. Retrieved from Special Education Connection, http://www.specialedconnection.com

DeMers, S. T., & Schaffer, J. B. (2012). The regulation of professional psychology. In S. J. Knapp, M. C. Gottlieb, M. M. Handelsman, & L. D. VandeCreek (Eds.), *APA handbook of ethics in psychology* (Vol. 1, pp. 453–482). Washington, DC: American Psychological Association. http://dx.doi.org/10.1037/13271-018

Denig, S. J., & Quinn, T. (2001). Ethical dilemmas for school administrators. *High School Journal, 84*(4), 43–49. doi:10.1353/hsj.2001.0009

Devereaux, R. L., & Gottlieb, M. C. (2012). Recording keeping in the cloud: Ethical considerations. *Professional Psychology: Research and Practice, 43*, 627–632. doi:10.1037/a0028268

Discipline under Section 504. (1996, November 22). *Special Educator, 12*(1), 6–8.

Doll, B., Strein, W., Jacob, S., & Prasse, D. P. (2011). Youth privacy when educational records include psychological records. *Professional Psychology: Research and Practice, 42*, 259–268. doi:10.1037/a0023685

Dreyfus, H. L. (1997). Intuitive, deliberative, and calculative models of expert performance. In C. E. Zsambok & G. Klein (Eds.), *Naturalistic decision making* (pp. 17–28). Mahwah, NJ: Erlbaum.

Duncan, B., & Fodness, R. (2008). Best practices in engaging in legislative activity to promote student academic achievement and mental health. In A. Thomas & J. Grimes (Eds.), *Best practices in school psychology V* (pp. 2013–2028). Bethesda, MD: National Association of School Psychologists.

Eades, R. W. (1986). The school counselor or psychologist and problems of defamation. *Journal of School Law, 15*, 117–120.

East Lansing (MI) Public Schools. (1992). OCR complaint investigation letter of findings. *Individuals with Disabilities Education Law Report, 19*, 40–43.

Eberlein, L. (1987). Introducing ethics to beginning psychologists: A problem-solving approach. *Professional Psychology: Research and Practice, 18*, 353–359. http://dx.doi.org/10.1037/0735-7028.18.4.353

Elias, C. L. (1999). The school psychologist as expert witness: Strategies and issues in the courtroom. *School Psychology Review, 28*, 44–59.

Elkund, K., Aros-O'Malley, M., & Murrieta, I. (2014). Multicultural supervision: What difference does it make? *Contemporary School Psychology, 28*, 295–204. doi:10.1007/s40688-014-0024-8

English, A., Bass, L., Boyle, A. D., & Eshragh, F. (2010). *State minor consent laws: A summary* (3rd ed.). Chapel Hill, NC: Center for Adolescent Health & the Law.

Erchul, W. P., & Martens, B. K. (2010). *School consultation: Conceptual and empirical bases of practice* (3rd ed.). New York, NY: NY: Springer.

Erchul, W. P., & Young, H. L. (2014). Best practices in school consultation. In P. L. Harrison & A. Thomas (Eds.), *Best practices in school psychology: Data-based and collaborative services* (pp. 449–460). Bethesda, MD: National Association of School Psychologists.

Ericsson, K. A., & Williams, A. M. (2007). Capturing naturally occurring superior performance in the laboratory: Translational research on expert performance. *Journal of Experimental Psychology: Applied, 13*, 115–123. http://dx.doi.org/10.1037/1076-898X.13.3.115

Esler, A. N., Godber, Y., & Christenson, S. L. (2008). Best practices in supporting school–family relationships. In A. Thomas & J. Grimes (Eds.), *Best practices in school psychology V* (pp. 917–936). Bethesda, MD: National Association of School Psychologists.

Esseks, J. D. (April 12, 2012). *Dear school administrator letter*. American Civil Liberties Union, Legal Department, Lesbian, Gay, Bisexual, Transgender & AIDS Project. https://www.aclu.org/files/assets/model_letter_-_schools_privacy_letter_4_6_2012.pdf

Evans, W. J. (1997). Torts. In C. J. Russo (Ed.), *The yearbook of school law 1997* (pp. 183–212). Dayton, OH: Education Law Association.

Eversole, T. (1993, September). Lesbian, gay and bisexual youth in school. *Communiqué*, pp. 9–10.

Fagan, T. K. (2014). Trends in the history of school psychology in the United States. In P. L. Harrison & A. Thomas (Eds.), *Best practices in school psychology: Foundations* (pp. 383–399). Bethesda, MD: National Association of School Psychologists.

Fagan, T. K., & Wise, P. S. (2007). *School psychology: Past, present, and future* (3rd ed.). Bethesda, MD: National Association of School Psychologists.

Failure to provide Section 504 to depressed teen was misjudgment. (2005, February 18). *Special Educator, 20*(4). Horsham, PA: LRP Publications.

Falender, C. A., & Shafranske, E. P. (2007). Competence in competency-based supervision practice: Construct and application. *Professional Psychology: Research and Practice, 38*, 232–240. http://dx.doi.org/10.1037/0735-7028.38.3.232

Fanibanda, D. K. (1976). Ethical issues of mental health consultation. *Professional Psychology, 7*, 547–552. http://dx.doi.org/10.1037/0735-7028.7.4.547

FBI Academy. (2000). *The school shooter: A threat assessment perspective*. Retrieved from https://www.fbi.gov/stats-services/publications/school-shooter

Felix, E. D., Green, J. G., & Sharkey, J. D. (2014). Best practices in bullying prevention. In P. Harrison, & A. Thomas (Eds.), *Best practices in school psychology: Systems-level practices* (pp. 245–258). Bethesda, MD: National Association of School Psychologists.

Ferguson, L. R. (1978). The competence and freedom of children to make choices regarding participation in research: A statement. *Journal of Social Issues, 34*, 114–121. doi:10.1111/j.1540-4560.1978.tb01033.x

Fine, M. A., & Ulrich, L. P. (1988). Integrating psychology and philosophy in teaching a graduate course in ethics. *Professional Psychology: Research and Practice, 19*, 542–546. http://dx.doi.org/10.1037/0735-7028.19.5.542

Fischer, L., & Sorenson, G. P. (1996). *School law for counselors, psychologists, and social workers* (3rd ed.). White Plains, NY: Longman.

Fish, M. C. (2002). Best practices in collaborating with parents of children with disabilities. In A. Thomas & J. Grimes (Eds.), *Best practices in school psychology IV* (pp. 363–376). Bethesda, MD: National Association of School Psychologists.

Fisher, C. B. (2012). *Decoding the ethics code* (3rd ed.). Thousand Oaks, CA: Sage.

Fisher, C. B., & Fryberg, D. (1994). Participant partners: College students weigh the costs and benefits of deceptive research. *American Psychologist, 49*, 417–427. http://dx.doi.org/10.1037/0003-066X.49.5.417

Fisher, C. B., & Vacanti-Shova, K. (2012). The responsible conduct of psychological research: An overview of ethical principles, APA ethics code standards, and federal regulations.

In S. J. Knapp, M. C. Gottlieb, M. M. Handelsman, & L. D. VandeCreek (Eds.), *APA handbook of ethics in psychology* (Vol. 2, pp. 335–369). Washington, DC: American Psychological Association. http://dx.doi.org/10.1037/13272-016

Fisher, M. A. (2013). *The ethics of conditional confidentiality*. New York, NY: Oxford University Press.

Flanagan, R., Miller, J. A., & Jacob, S. (2005). The 2002 revision of APA's ethics code: Implications for school psychologists. *Psychology in the Schools, 42*, 433–445. doi:10.1002/pits.20097

Flaugher, R. L. (1978). The many definitions of test bias. *American Psychologist, 33*, 671–679. http://dx.doi.org/10.1037/0003-066X.33.7.671

Fleming, E. R., & Fleming, D. C. (1987). Involvement of minors in special educational decision-making. *Journal of Law and Education, 16*, 389–402. http://eric.ed.gov/?id=EJ367372

Forman, S. G., Bry, B. H., & Urga, P. (2006). Substance abuse. In G. G. Baer & K. M. Minke (Eds.), *Children's needs III: Development, prevention, and intervention* (pp. 1011–1023). Bethesda, MD: National Association of School Psychologists.

Frankel, M. S., & Siang, S. (1999). *Ethical and legal aspects of human subjects research on the Internet*. Retrieved from http://www.aaas.org/sites/default/files/migrate/uploads/report2.pdf

French, J. R. P., & Raven, B. H. (1959). The bases of social power. In D. Cartright (Ed.), *Studies in social power* (pp. 150–167). Ann Arbor, MI: University of Michigan Institute for Social Research.

Friedman, S. L., Helm, D. T., & Marrone, J. (1999). Caring, control, and clinicians' influence: Ethical dilemmas in developmental disabilities. *Ethics and Behavior, 9*, 349–364. doi:10.1207/s15327019eb0904_5

Frisby, C. L. (1999a). Culture and test session behavior: Pt. 1. *School Psychology Quarterly, 14*, 263–280.

Frisby, C. L. (1999b). Culture and test session behavior: Pt. 2. *School Psychology Quarterly, 14*, 281–303.

Gacono, C. B., & Hughes, T. L. (2004). Differentiating emotional disturbance from social maladjustment: Assessing psychopathy in aggressive youth. *Psychology in the Schools, 41*, 849–860. doi:10.1002/pits.20041

Gallagher, J. J. (1989). A new policy initiative: Infants and toddlers with handicapping conditions. *American Psychologist, 44*, 387–391. http://dx.doi.org/10.1037/0003-066X.44.2.387

Gallagher, R. M., Caterino, L. C., & Bisa-Kendrick, T. (2014). Best practices in services for gifted students. In P. L. Harrison & A. Thomas (Eds.), *Best practices in school psychology: Student-level services* (pp. 157–171). Bethesda, MD: National Association of School Psychologists.

Gallessich, J. (1982). *The profession and practice of consultation*. San Francisco, CA: Jossey-Bass.

Gelfman, M. H. B., & Schwab, N. C. (2005a). Discrimination in school: § 504, ADA, and Title IX. In N. C. Schwab & M. H. B. Gelfman (Eds.), *Legal issues in school health services* (pp. 335–371). New York, NY: Authors Choice Press.

Gelfman, M. H. B., & Schwab, N. C. (2005b). School health records and documentation. In N. C. Schwab & M. H. B. Gelfman (Eds.), *Legal issues in school health services* (pp. 297–316). New York, NY: Authors Choice Press.

Gershoff, E. T., Holas, I., & Purtell, K. M. (2015). Corporal punishment in U.S. public schools: Legal precedents, current practices, and future policy. New York, NY: Springer. doi:10.1007/978-3-319-14818-2

Gerwitz, C. (2015, May 16). Students snap pictures of PARCC test, teachers disciplined. *Education Week*, p. 8. http://blogs.edweek.org/edweek/curriculum/2015/05/Students_snap_pictures_of_parcc_test_teachers_disciplined.html

Gil, E. F., & Bob, S. (1999). Culturally competent research: An ethical perspective. *Clinical Psychology Review, 19*, 45–55. doi:10.1016/S0272-7358(98)00019-1

Glosoff, H. L., Herlihy, B., & Spence, E. B. (2000). Privileged communication in the counselor–client relationship. *Journal of Counseling & Development, 78*, 454–462. doi:10.1002/j.1556-6676.2000.tb01929.x

Goodno, N. H. (2011). How public schools can constitutionally halt cyberbullying: A model cyberbullying policy that considers First Amendment, due process, and Fourth Amendment challenges. *Wake Forest Law Review, 46*, 641–700.

Goodyear, R. K., & Rodolfa, E. (2012). Negotiating the complex ethical terrain of clinical supervision. In S. J. Knapp, M. C. Gottlieb, M. M. Handelsman, & L. D. VandeCreek (Eds.), *APA handbook of ethics in psychology* (Vol. 2, pp. 261–275). Washington, DC: American Psychological Association. http://dx.doi.org/10.1037/13272-013

Gottlieb, M. C. (2006). A template for peer ethics consultation. *Ethics & Behavior, 16*, 151–162. doi:10.1207/s15327019eb1602_5

Gottlieb, M. C., Robinson, K., & Younggren, J. N. (2007). Multiple relations in supervision: Guidance for administrators, supervisors, and students. *Professional Psychology: Research and Practice, 38*, 241–247. http://dx.doi.org/10.1037/0735-7028.38.3.241

Gould, S. J. (1996). *The mismeasure of man*. New York, NY: Norton.

Graden, J. L., Casey, A., & Bonstrom, O. (1985). Implementing a prereferral intervention system: Pt. 2. The data. *Exceptional Children, 51*, 487–496. doi:10.1177/001440298505100605

Gregory, R. J. (2007). *Psychological testing: History, principles, and applications* (5th ed.). Boston, MA: Pearson.

Gresham, F. M., Reschly, D. J., Tilly, W. D. Fletcher, J., Burns, M.K., Christ, T. ... & Shinn, M. (2005). Comprehensive evaluation of learning disabilities: A response to intervention perspective. *School Psychologist, 59*(1), 26–30. http://www.apadivisions.org/division-16/publications/newsletters/school-psychologist/2005/01-issue.pdf

Grisso, T., & Vierling, L. (1978). Minors' consent to treatment: A developmental perspective. *Professional Psychology, 9*, 412–427. http://dx.doi.org/10.1037/0735-7028.9.3.412

Grunder, T. M. (1978). Two formulas for determining the readability of subject consent forms. *American Psychologist, 33*, 773–774. http://dx.doi.org/10.1037/0003-066X.33.8.773

Guard, P. J. (2007, August 7). *Letter to Honorable Bill Shuster*. Retrieved from http://www2.ed.gov/policy/speced/guid/idea/memosdcltrs/all2007.html

Guard, P. J. (2009, August 21). *Letter to H. Douglas Cox*. Retrieved from http://www2.ed.gov/policy/speced/guid/idea/memosdcltrs/all2009.html

Gunderson National Child Protection Agency. (2015). *Discipline and the law: State laws*. Retrieved from http://www.gundersenhealth.org/ncptc/center-for-effective-discipline/discipline-and-the-law/state-laws

Gutierrez, P. M., & Osman, A. (2009). Getting the best return on your screening investment: Maximizing sensitivity and specificity of the Suicide Ideation Questionnaire and the Reynolds Adolescent Depression Scale. *School Psychology Review, 38*, 200–217.

Gutkin, T. B., & Curtis, M. J. (1999). School-based consultation theory and practice: The art and science of indirect service delivery. In C. R. Reynolds & T. B. Gutkin (Eds.), *Handbook of school psychology* (3rd ed., pp. 598–637). New York, NY: Wiley.

Guttmacher Institute. (2015, August 1). *State policies in brief: An overview of minors' consent law*. Retrieved from http:www.guttmacher.org/statecenter/spibs/spib_OMCL.pdf

Haas, L. J., & Malouf, J. L. (2005). *Keeping up the good work: A practitioner's guide to mental health ethics* (4th ed.). Sarasota, FL: Professional Resources Press.

Haas, L. J., Malouf, J. L., & Mayerson, N. H. (1986). Ethical dilemmas in psychological practice: Results of a national survey. *Professional Psychology: Research and Practice, 17*, 316–321. http://dx.doi.org/10.1037/0735-7028.17.4.316

Hale, J. B., Semrud-Clikeman, M., & Kubas, H. A. (2014). Best practices in medication treatment for children with emotional and behavioral disorders: A primer for school psychologists. In P. L. Harrison & A. Thomas (Eds.), *Best practices in school psychology: Systems-level Services* (pp. 347–360). Bethesda, MD: National Association of School Psychologists.

Hammill, D. D., Brown, L., & Bryant, B. R. (1989). *A consumer's guide to tests in print*. Austin, TX: Pro-Ed.

Hanchon, T. A., & Allen, R. A. (2013). Identifying students with emotional disturbance: School psychologists' practices and perceptions. *Psychology in the Schools, 50*, 193–208. doi:10.1002/pits.21668

Handelsman, M. M. (1986). Problems with ethics training by "osmosis." *Professional Psychology: Research and Practice, 17*, 371–372. http://dx.doi.org/10.1037/0735-7028.17.4.371

Handelsman, M. M., Gottlieb, M. C., & Knapp, S. (2005). Training ethical psychologists: An acculturation model. *Professional Psychology: Research and Practice, 36*, 59–65. http://dx.doi.org/10.1037/0735-7028.36.1.59

Hansen, J. C., Himes, B. S., & Meier, S. (1990). *Consultation: Concepts and practices*. Englewood Cliffs, NJ: Prentice-Hall.

Hansen, N. D., & Goldberg, S. G. (1999). Navigating the nuances: A matrix of considerations for ethical-legal dilemmas. *Professional Psychology: Research and Practice, 30*, 495–503. http://dx.doi.org/10.1037/0735-7028.30.5.495

Hansen, N. D., Pepitone-Arreola-Rockwell, F., & Greene, A. F. (2000). Multicultural competence: Criteria and case examples. *Professional Psychology: Research and Practice, 31*, 652–660. http://dx.doi.org/10.1037/0735-7028.31.6.652

Hanson, R. K. (2009). The psychological assessment of risk for crime and violence. *Canadian Psychology, 50*, 172–182. http://dx.doi.org/10.1037/a0015726

Hare, R. (1981). The philosophical basis of psychiatric ethics. In S. Bloch & P. Chodoff (Eds.), *Psychiatric ethics* (pp. 31–45). Oxford, UK: Oxford University Press.

Harris, A., & Kapche, R. (1978). Behavior modification in schools: Ethical issues and suggested guidelines. *Journal of School Psychology, 16*, 25–33. doi:10.1016/0022-4405(78)90019-5

Harris, K. R. (1985). Definitional, parametric, and procedural considerations in timeout interventions and research. *Exceptional Children, 51*, 279–288.

Harrison, P. L., & Thomas, A. (Eds.) (2014). *Diversity in development and learning*. In *Best practices in school psychology: Foundations* (Section 1, pp. 1–254). Bethesda, MD: National Association of School Psychologists.

Hartshorne, T. S. (2002). Mistaking courage for denial: Family resilience after the birth of a child with severe disabilities. *Journal of Individual Psychology, 58*, 263–278.

Harvard Law Review Association. (2011). Constitutional law—First Amendment—Sixth circuit holds that primary and secondary school teachers' curricular decisions are not entitled to free speech protection.—*Evans-Marshall v. Board of Education. Harvard Law Review, 124*, 2107–2114.

Harvey, V. S., & Carlson, J. F. (2003). Ethical and professional issues with computer-related technology. *School Psychology Review, 32*, 92–107.

Harvey, V. S., & Pearrow, M. (2010). Identifying challenges in supervising school psychologists. *Psychology in the Schools, 47*, 567–581. doi:10.1002/pits.20491

Harvey, V. S., & Struzziero, J. A. (2008). *Professional development and supervision of school psychologists: From intern to expert* (2nd ed.). Thousand Oaks, CA: Joint Publication of National Association of School Psychologists and Corwin Press.

Harvey, V. S., Struzziero, J. A., & Desai, S. (2014). Best practices in supervision and mentoring of school psychologists. In P. L. Harrison & A. Thomas (Eds.), *Best practices in school psychology: Foundations* (pp. 567–580). Bethesda, MD: National Association of School Psychologists.

Hays, P. A. (2001). *Addressing cultural complexities in practice.* Washington, DC: American Psychological Association. http://dx.doi.org/10.1037/10411-000

Hehir, T. (1993, October 25). Response to letter of inquiry from McDonald. *Individuals with Disabilities Education Law Report, 20*, 1159–1160.

Helton, G. B., Ray, B. A., & Biderman, M. D. (2000). Responses of school psychologists and teachers to administrative pressures to practice unethically: A national survey. *Special Services in the Schools, 16*, 111–134. doi:10.1300/J008v16n01_08

Henderson, D. H. (1986). Constitutional implications involving the use of corporal punishment in the public schools. *Journal of Law and Education, 15*, 255–269.

Henning-Stout, M. (1996). ¿Que podemos hacer? Roles for school psychologists with Mexican and Latino migrant children and families. *School Psychology Review, 25*, 152–164.

Herbstrith, J. C. (2014). Best practices in working with LGBT parents and their families. In P. L. Harrison & A. Thomas (Eds.). *Best practices in school psychology V: Foundations* (pp. 205–215). Bethesda, MD: National Association of School Psychologists.

Herbstrith, J. C., Tobin, R. M., Hesson-McInnis, M. S., & Schneider, W. J. (2013). Preservice teacher attitudes toward gay and lesbian parents. *School Psychology Quarterly, 28*, 183–194. doi:10.1037/spq0000022

Heumann, J. E. (1993). Response to letter of inquiry from G. *Warrington. Individuals with Disabilities Education Law Report, 20*, 539–540.

Hindman, S. E. (1986). The law, the courts, and the education of behaviorally disordered students. *Behavior Disorders, 11*, 280–289.

Hoerger, M., & Currell, C. (2012). Ethical issues in Internet research. In S. J. Knapp, M. C. Gottlieb, M. M. Handelsman, & L. D. VandeCreek (Eds.), *APA handbook of ethics in psychology* (Vol. 2, pp. 385–400). Washington, DC: American Psychological Association. http://dx.doi.org/10.1037/13272-018

Holmes, D. S. (1976). Debriefing after psychological experiments: Pt. 2. Effectiveness of post-experimental desensitizing. *American Psychologist, 31*, 868–875. http://dx.doi.org/10.1037/0003-066X.31.12.858

Holmes, D. S., & Urie, R. C. (1975). Effects of preparing children for psychotherapy. *Journal of Consulting and Clinical Psychology, 43*, 311–318. http://dx.doi.org/10.1037/h0076735

Hopkins, B. R., & Anderson, B. S. (1985). *The counselor and the law* (2nd ed.). Alexandria, VA: American Association for Counseling and Development.

Horton, C. B., & Cruise, T. K. (2001). *Child abuse and neglect: The school's response.* New York, NY: Guilford Press.

Hosp, J. L., & Reschly, D. J. (2003). Referral rates for intervention and assessment: A meta-analysis of racial differences. *Journal of Special Education, 37*, 67–81. doi:10.1177/00224669030370020201

Hostetler, A. J. (1988, June). Indictment: Congress sends message on fraud. *APA Monitor*, p. 5.

Hubsch, A. W. (1989). Education and self-government: The right to education under state constitutional law. *Journal of Law and Education, 18*, 93–133.

Hughes, J. N. (1986). Ethical issues in school consultation. *School Psychology Review, 15*, 489–499.

Hughes, T. L., & Bray, M. A. (2004). Differentiation of emotional disturbance and social maladjustment: Introduction to the special issue. *Psychology in the Schools, 41*, 819–821. doi:10.1002/pits.20038

Hughes, T. L., Kolbert, J. B., & Crothers, L. M. (2014). Best practices in behavioral/ecological consultation. In P. L. Harrison & A. Thomas (Eds.). *Best practices in school psychology V: Data-based and collaborative decision making* (pp. 483–492). Bethesda, MD: National Association of School Psychologists.

Hummel, D. L., Talbutt, L. C., & Alexander, M. D. (1985). *Law and ethics in counseling.* New York, NY: Van Nostrand–Reinhold.

Huprich, S. K., Fuller, K. M., & Schneider, R. B. (2003). Divergent ethical perspectives on the duty-to-warn principle with HIV patients. *Ethics and Behavior, 13*, 263–278. doi:10.1207/S15327019EB1303_05

Hyman, I. A. (1990). *Reading, writing, and the hickory stick.* Lexington, MA: Lexington Books.

Ingraham, C. L. (2000). Consultation through a multicultural lens: Multicultural and cross-cultural consultation in schools. *School Psychology Review, 29*, 320–343.

Ingraham, C. L. (2014). Studying multicultural aspects of consultation. In W. P. Erchul & S. M. Sheridan (Eds.), *Handbook of research in school consultation* (2nd ed., pp. 323–348). New York, NY: Routledge.

Jacob, S. (2008). Best practices in developing ethical school psychological practice. In A. Thomas & J. Grimes (Eds.), *Best practices in school psychology V* (pp. 1921–1932). Bethesda, MD: National Association of School Psychologists.

Jacob, S. (2009). Putting it all together: Implications for school psychology. *School Psychology Review, 38*, 239–243.

Jacob, S. (2013). Creating safe and welcoming schools for LGBT students: ethical and legal issues. *Journal of School Violence, 12*, 98–115. http://dx.doi.org/10.1080/15388220.2012.724356

Jacob, S., Drevon, D. D., Abbuhl, C. M., & Taton, J. (2010). Preparing school psychologists to address the needs of gay, lesbian, biattractional, transgender, and questioning youth. In J. Kaufman, T. L. Hughes, & C. A. Riccio (Eds.), *Handbook of education, training and supervision of school psychologists in school and community* (Vol. 2, pp. 205–225). New York, NY: Routledge, Taylor & Francis.

Jacob, S., & Powers, K. E. (2009). Privileged communication in the school psychologist–client relationship. *Psychology in the Schools, 46*, 307–318. doi:10.1002/pits.20377

Jacob-Timm, S. (1996). Ethical and legal issues associated with the use of aversives in the public schools: The SIBIS controversy. *School Psychology Review, 2*, 184–198.

Jacob-Timm, S. (1999). Ethical dilemmas encountered by members of the National Association of School Psychologists. *Psychology in the Schools, 36*, 205–217.

Jha, A. (2012, September 13). False positives: fraud and misconduct are threatening scientific research. *The Guardian.* Retrieved from https://www.theguardian.com/science/2012/sep/13/scientific-research-fraud-bad-practice

Jimerson, S. R., Graydon, K., Pletcher, S. M., Schnurr, B., Kundert, D., & Nickerson, A. (2006). Grade retention and promotion. In G. G. Baer & K. M. Minke (Eds.), *Children's needs III: Development, prevention, and intervention* (pp. 601–613). Bethesda, MD: National Association of School Psychologists.

Jobes, D. A., & Berman, A. L. (1993). Suicide and malpractice liability: Assessing and revising policies, procedures, and practice in outpatient settings. *Professional Psychology: Research and Practice, 24*, 91–99. http://dx.doi.org/10.1037/0735-7028.24.1.91

Johnson, W. B., Barnett, J. E., Elman, N. S., Forrest, L., & Kaslow, N. J. (2012). The competent community: Towards a vital reformulation of professional ethics. *American Psychologist, 67*, 557–569. doi:10.1037/a0027206

Johnson, W. B., Elman, N. S., Forrest, L., Robiner, W. N., Rodolfa, E., & Schaffer, J. B. (2008). Addressing professional competence problems in trainees: Some ethical considerations. *Professional Psychology: Research and Practice, 39*, 589–599. http://dx.doi.org/10.1037/a0014264

Jonsson, P. (2011, July 5). America's biggest teacher and principal cheating scandal unfolds in Atlanta. *Christian Science Monitor.* Retrieved from http:www.csmonitor.com/USA/Education/2011/0705/America-s-biggest-teacher-and-principal-cheating-scandal-unfolds-in-Atlanta

Kalichman, S. C. (1999). *Mandated reporting of suspected child abuse: Ethics, law, and policy* (2nd ed.). Washington, DC: American Psychological Association.

Kaplan, M. S., Crisci, P. E., & Farling, W. (1974). Editorial comment [Special issue on ethical and legal issues]. *School Psychology Digest, 3*(1).

Kaser-Boyd, N., Adelman, H. S., & Taylor, L. (1985). Minors' ability to identify risks and benefits of therapy. *Professional Psychology: Research and Practice, 16*, 411–417. http://dx.doi.org/10.1037/0735-7028.16.3.411

Kaslow, F. W., Patterson, T., & Gottlieb, M. (2011). Ethical dilemmas in psychologists accessing Internet data: Is it justified? *Professional Psychology: Research and Practice, 42*, 105–112. http://dx.doi.org/10.1037/a0022002

Kaufman, A. S. (1994). *Intelligent testing with the WISC-III.* New York, NY: Wiley.

Keith-Spiegel, P. (1983). Children and consent to participate in research. In G. B. Melton, G. P. Koocher, & M. J. Saks (Eds.), *Children's competence to consent* (pp. 179–211). New York, NY: Plenum Press. doi:10.1007/978-1-4684-4289-2_10

Kimmel, A. J. (2012). Deception in research. In S. J. Knapp, M. C. Gottlieb, M. M. Handelsman, & L. D. VandeCreek (Eds.), *APA handbook of ethics in psychology* (Vol. 2, pp. 401–421). Washington, DC: American Psychological Association. http://dx.doi.org/10.1037/13272-019

Kirp, D. (1973). Schools as sorters. *University of Pennsylvania Law Review, 121*, 705–797.

Kitchener, K. S. (1986). Teaching applied ethics in counselor education: An integration of psychological processes and philosophical analysis. *Journal of Counseling and Development, 64*, 306–310. doi:10.1002/j.1556-6676.1986.tb01117.x

Kitchener, K. S. (2000). *Foundations of ethical practice, research, and teaching.* Mahwah, NJ: Erlbaum.

Klein, A. (January 6, 2016). New law, fresh challenges. *Education Week*, p. 10–12. http://www.edweek.org/ew/articles/2016/01/06/under-essa-states-districts-to-share-more.html

Klose, L. M., & Lasser, J. (2014). Best practices in the application of professional ethics. In P. L. Harrison & A. Thomas (Eds.), *Best practices in school psychology: Foundations* (pp. 449–458). Bethesda, MD: National Association of School Psychologists.

Knapp, S. (1980). A primer on malpractice for psychologists. *Professional Psychology, 11*, 606–612. http://dx.doi.org/10.1037/0735-7028.11.4.606

Knapp, S. J., Bennett, B., & VandeCreek, L. (2012). Risk management for psychologists. In S. J. Knapp, M. C. Gottlieb, M. M. Handelsman, & L. D. VandeCreek (Eds.), *APA handbook of ethics in psychology* (Vol. 1, pp. 483–518). Washington, DC: American Psychological Association. http://dx.doi.org/10.1037/13271-019

Knapp, S., Gottlieb, M., Berman, J., & Handelsman, M. M. (2007). When laws and ethics collide: What should psychologists do? *Professional Psychology: Research and Practice, 38*, 54–59. http://dx.doi.org/10.1037/0735-7028.38.1.54

Knapp, S. J., Gottlieb, M. C., Handelsman, M. M., & VandeCreek, L. D. (Eds.). (2012). *APA handbook of ethics in psychology* (Vol. 1 & Vol. 2). Washington, DC: American Psychological Association. doi: 10.1037/13271-000

Knapp, S., & VandeCreek, L. (1982). Tarasoff: Five years later. *Professional Psychology, 13*, 511–516. http://dx.doi.org/10.1037/0735-7028.13.4.511

Knapp, S., & VandeCreek, L. (1985). Psychotherapy and privileged communications in child custody cases. *Professional Psychology: Research and Practice, 16*, 398–407. http://dx.doi.org/10.1037/0735-7028.16.3.398

Knapp, S., & VandeCreek, L. (1997). Ethical and legal aspects of clinical supervision. In C. E. Watkins (Ed.), *Handbook of psychotherapy supervision* (pp. 589–599). New York, NY: Wiley.

Knapp, S. J., & VandeCreek, L. D. (2012). *Practical ethics for psychologists: A positive approach* (2nd ed.). Washington, DC: American Psychological Association. http://dx.doi.org/10.1037/11331-000

Knauss, L. K. (2001). Ethical issues in psychological assessment in school settings. *Journal of Personality Assessment, 77*, 231–241. doi:10.1207/S15327752JPA7702_06

Koocher, G. P., & Keith-Spiegel, P. (2008). *Ethics in psychology and the mental health professions: Standards and cases.* New York, NY: Oxford University Press.

Kosciw, J. G., Greytak, E. A., Diaz, E. M., & Bartkiewicz, M. J. (2010). *The 2009 National School Climate Survey: The experiences of lesbian, gay, bisexual and transgender youth in our nation's schools.* New York, NY: GLSEN. https://www.glsen.org/download/file/NDIyMw==

Kost, K., & Henshaw, S. (2014, May). *U.S. Teenage pregnancies, births and abortions, 2010: National and state trends by age, race and ethnicity.* Guttmacher Institute. Retrieved from http://www.guttmacher.org/pubs/USTPtrends10.pdf

Kratochwill, T. R., Altschaefl, M. R., & Bice-Urbach, B. B. (2014). Best practices in school-based problem-solving consultation: Applications in prevention and intervention services. In P. L. Harrison & A. Thomas (Eds.). *Best practices in school psychology V: Data-based and collaborative decision making* (pp. 461–482). Bethesda, MD: National Association of School Psychologists.

Kubick, R. J., & Lavik, K. B. (2014). Best practices in making manifest determinations. In P. Harrison, & A. Thomas (Eds.), *Best practices in school psychology: Student-level services* (pp. 399–413). Bethesda, MD: National Association of School Psychologists.

Kutz, G. D. (2009). *Seclusions and restraints: Selected cases of death and abuse at public and private schools and treatment centers.* GAO-09-7191T. Washington, DC: United States Government Accountability Office. Retrieved from http://www.gao.gov/new.items/d09719t.pdf

Lake Washington (WA) School District No. 414. (1985, June 28). OCR complaint investigation letter of findings. *Individuals with Disabilities Education Law Report, 257* (Suppl. 150), 611–615.

Lamb, D. H., Cochran, D. J., & Jackson, V. R. (1991). Training and organizational issues associated with identifying and responding to intern impairment. *Professional Psychology: Research and Practice, 22*, 291–296.

Lasser, J., & Klose, L. M. (2007). School psychologists' ethical decision making: Implications from selected social psychological phenomena. *School Psychology Review, 36*, 484–500.

Legal Information Institute. (n.d.[a]). *Evidence: An overview.* Retrieved from https://www.law .cornell.edu/wex/evidence

Legal Information Institute. (n.d.[b]). *What are uniform laws?* Retrieved from http://www.law .cornell.edu/uniform/uniform.html

Lehavot, K., Barnett, J. E., & Powers, D. (2010). Psychotherapy, professional relationships, and ethical considerations in the MySpace generation. *Professional Psychology: Research and Practice, 41*, 160–166. http://dx.doi.org/10.1037/a0018709

Levinson, W., Roter, D. L., Mullooly, J. O., Dull, V. T., & Frankel, R. M. (1997). Physician–patient communication: The relationship with malpractice claims among primary care physicians and surgeons. *Journal of the American Medical Association, 277*, 553–559. doi:10.1001/jama.1997.03540310051034

Lhamon, C. E. (2014, October 21). *Dear colleague letter.* Retrieved from http://www2.ed.gov/ about/offices/list/ocr/letters/colleague-bullying-201410.pdf

Lichtenstein, R. (2014). Best practices in the identification of learning disabilities. In P. L. Harrison & A. Thomas (Eds.), *Best practices in school psychology: Data-based and collaborative services* (pp. 331–354). Bethesda, MD: National Association of School Psychologists.

Lim, J. (1993, May 19). OCR policy letter to regional offices. *Special Education Report*, p. 5.

Lopez, E. C. (1997). The cognitive assessment of limited-English-proficient and bilingual children. In D. P. Flanagan, J. L. Genshaft, & P. L. Harrison (Eds.), *Contemporary intellectual assessment* (pp. 503–516). New York, NY: Guilford Press. http://dx.doi.org/10.1037/ 1099-9809.3.2.117

Lopez, E. C. (2008). Best practices in working with school interpreters. In A. Thomas & J. Grimes (Eds.), *Best practices in school psychology V* (pp. 1751–1769). Bethesda, MD: National Association of School Psychologists.

Lopez, E. C. (2014). Best practices in conducting assessments via school interpreters. In P. L. Harrison & A. Thomas (Eds.), *Best practices in school psychology: Foundations* (pp. 113–128). Bethesda, MD: National Association of School Psychologists.

Lopez, E. C., & Bursztyn, A. M. (2013). Future challenges and opportunities: Toward culturally responsive training in school psychology. *Psychology in the Schools, 50*, 212–228. doi:10.1002/pits.21674

Lopez, E. C., & Rogers, M. R. (2001). Conceptualizing cross-cultural school psychology competencies. *School Psychology Quarterly, 16*, 270–302. http://dx.doi.org/10.1521/scpq.16.3.270 .19889

Losen, D. J., & Orfield, G. E. (Eds.). (2002). *Racial inequity in special education.* Cambridge, MA: Harvard Educational Publishing Group.

Lustgarten, S. D. (2015). Emerging ethical threats to client privacy in cloud communication and data storage. *Professional Psychology: Research and Practice, 46*, 154–160. http:// dx.doi.org/10.1037/pro0000018

Luxton, D. D., Pruitt, L. D., & Osenbach, J. E. (2014). Best practices for remote psychological assessment via telehealth technologies. *Professional Psychology: Research and Practice, 45*, 27–35. doi:10.1037/a0034547

Lynch, E. W., & Hanson, M. J. (2011). *Developing cross-cultural competence* (4th ed.). Baltimore, MD: Paul H. Brookes.

Mahoney, E. B., & Morris, R. J. (2012). Practicing school psychology while impaired: Ethical, professional, and legal issues. *Journal of Applied School Psychology, 28*, 338–353. doi:10.1080/15377903.2012.722180

Martens, B. K., Witt, J. C., Daly, E. J., & Vollmer, T. R. (1999). Behavior analysis: Theory and practice in educational settings. In C. R. Reynolds & T. B. Gutkin (Eds.), *Handbook of school psychology* (3rd ed., pp. 350–382). New York, NY: Wiley.

Martin, R. (1979). *Educating handicapped children: The legal mandate.* Champaign, IL: Research Press.

Martin, R. (1992). *Continuing challenges in special education law* [looseleaf]. Urbana, IL: Carle Media.

Massachusetts Department of Education. (2006). *2005 youth risk behavior survey results: Executive summary.* Retrieved from http://www.doe.mass.edu/cnp/hprograms/yrbs/05/default.html

Masty, J., & Fisher, C. (2008). A goodness-of-fit approach to informed consent for pediatric intervention research. *Ethics & Behavior, 18*, 139–160. doi:10.1080/10508420802063897

Matarazzo, J. D. (1986). Computerized clinical psychological test interpretations: Unvalidated plus all mean and no sigma. *American Psychologist, 41*, 14–24.

McCarthy, M. M., Cambron-McCabe, N. H., & Thomas, S. B. (2004). *Legal rights of teachers and students.* Boston, MA: Pearson Education.

McConaughy, S. H., & Ritter, D. R. (2014). Best practices in multimethod assessment of emotional and behavioral disorders. In P. L. Harrison & A. Thomas (Eds.), *Best practices in school psychology: Data-based and collaborative services* (pp. 367–389). Bethesda, MD: National Association of School Psychologists.

McGue, M. (2000). Authorship and intellectual property. In B. D. Sales & S. Folkman (Eds.), *Ethics in research with human participants* (pp. 75–95). Washington, DC: American Psychological Association.

McIntyre, L. L., & Garbacz, S. A. (2014). Best practices in systems-level organization and support for family-school partnerships. In P. L. Harrison & A. Thomas (Eds.), *Best practices in school psychology: Systems-level services* (pp. 455–465). Bethesda, MD: National Association of School Psychologists.

McKevitt, B. C., & Fynaardt, A. B. (2014). Best practices in developing a positive behavior support system at the school level. In P. L. Harrison & A. Thomas (Eds.), *Best practices in school psychology: Systems-level services* (pp. 165–179). Bethesda, MD: National Association of School Psychologists.

McKinney Independent School District Texas State Educational Agency. (2010). *Individuals with Disabilities Education Law Report, 54*, p. 303.

Medway, F. J., & Rose, J. S. (1986). Grade retention. In T. R. Kratochwill (Ed.), *Advances in school psychology* (Vol. 5, pp. 141–175). Hillsdale, NJ: Erlbaum.

Melton, G. B., Koocher, G. P., & Saks, M. J. (Eds.). (1983). *Children's competence to consent.* New York, NY: Plenum Press. doi:10.1007/978-1-4684-4289-2_1

Merrell, K. W., & Walker, H. M. (2004). Deconstructing a definition: Social maladjustment versus emotional disturbance and moving the EBD field forward. *Psychology in the Schools, 41*, 899–910. doi:10.1002/pits.20046

Messick, S. (1965). Personality measurement and the ethics of assessment. *American Psychologist, 20*, 136–142. http://dx.doi.org/10.1037/h0021712

Messick, S. (1980). Test validity and the ethics of assessment. *American Psychologist, 35*, 1012–1027. http://dx.doi.org/10.1037/0003-066X.35.11.1012

Messick, S. (1984). Assessment in context: Appraising student performance in relation to instructional quality. *Educational Researcher, 13*, 3–8. doi:10.1002/j.2330-8516.1983 .tb00024.x

Messina, D. J. (1988). Corporal punishment versus classroom discipline: A case of mistaken identity. *Loyola Law Review, 34*, 35–110.

Miller, D. N. (2011). *Child and adolescent suicidal behavior*. New York, NY: Guilford Press.

Miller, D. N., & Eckert, T. L. (2009). School-based suicide prevention: Research advances and practice implications [Special series]. *School Psychology Review, 38*, 153–248.

Miller, D. N., & Nickerson, A. (2007). Projective techniques and the school-based assessment of childhood internalizing disorders: A critical analysis. *Journal of Projective Psychology & Mental Health, 14*, 48–58.

Miller, F. L. (2009). Advocacy: The risks and rewards. *Communiqué, 38*(1), 17–18.

Miller, J. A., Williams, S. J., & McCoy, E. L. B. (2004). Using multimodal functional behavioral assessment to inform treatment selection for children with either emotional disturbance or social maladjustment. *Psychology in the Schools, 41*, 867–877. doi:10.1002/pits.20043

Miller, V. A., Drotar, D., & Kodish, E. (2004). Children's competence for assent and consent: A review of empirical findings. *Ethics and Behavior, 14*, 255–295. doi:10.1207/s15327019 eb1403_3

Miranda, A. H. (2014). Best practices in increasing cross-cultural competency. In P. L. Harrison & A. Thomas (Eds.), *Best practices in school psychology: Foundations* (pp. 9–19). Bethesda, MD: National Association of School Psychologists.

Monroe, S. J. (2007, December 26). *OCR response to "Dear Colleague" letter*. Retrieved from http://www.specialedconnection.com

Mowder, B. (1983). Assessment and intervention in school psychological services. In G. W. Hynd (Ed.), *The school psychologist* (pp. 145–167). Syracuse, NY: Syracuse University Press.

Muehleman, T., Pickens, B. K., & Robinson, F. (1985). Informing clients about the limits to confidentiality, risks, and their rights: Is self-disclosure inhibited? *Professional Psychology: Research and Practice, 16*, 385–397. http://dx.doi.org/10.1037/0735-7028.16.3.385

Musgrove, M. (2011, January 21). *Memorandum to: State Directors of Special Educa-tion*. Retrieved from http://www2.ed.gov/policy/speced/guid/idea/memosdcltrs/osep11-07rtimemo.pdf

Musgrove, M. (2013, April 2). *Letter to Gallo*. Retrieved from http://www2.ed.gov/policy/speced/guid/idea/memosdcltrs/acc-12-017845r-ut-gallo-fba-4-2-13.pdf

Musgrove, M., & Yudin, M. K. (2013, August 20). *Dear colleague letter*. Retrieved from http://www2.ed.gov/policy/speced/guid/idea/letters/2013-3/bullyingdcl082013bullying3q2013 .pdf

Naglieri, J. A., Drasgow, F., Schmit, M., Handler, I., Prifitera, A., Margolis, A., & Velasquez, R. (2004). Psychological testing on the Internet. *American Psychologist, 59*, 150–162. http://dx.doi.org/10.1037/0003-066x.59.3.150

Nagy, T. F. (2012). Competence. In S. J. Knapp, M. C. Gottlieb, M. M. Handelsman, & L. D. VandeCreek (Eds.), *APA handbook of ethics in psychology* (Vol. 1, pp. 147–174). Washington, DC: American Psychological Association. doi:10.1037/13271-006

Nastasi, B. K. (2008). Social justice and school psychology. *School Psychology Review, 37*, 487–492.

National Association of School Psychologists. (2010a). *Model for comprehensive and integrated school psychological services.* Retrieved from https://www.nasponline.org/assets/Documents/Standards%20and%20Certification/Standards/2_PracticeModel.pdf

National Association of School Psychologists. (2010b). *Principles for professional ethics.* Retrieved from https://www.nasponline.org/Documents/Standards%20and%20Certification/Standards/1_%20Ethical%20Principles.pdf

National Association of School Psychologists. (2010c). *Standards for credentialing of school psychologists.* Retrieved from http://www.nasponline.org/assets/Documents/Standards%20and%20Certification/Standards/2_Credentialing_Standards.pdf

National Association of School Psychologists. (2010d). *Standards for graduate preparation of school psychologists.* Retrieved from http://www.nasponline.org/Documents/Standards%20and%20Certification/Standards/1_Graduate_Preparation.pdf

National Association of School Psychologists Ethical and Professional Practices Committee. (2014a, December). *Committee and board report.* Unpublished report. Available from jacob1s@cmich.edu

National Association of School Psychologists Ethical and Professional Practices Committee. (2014b). *Ethical and Professional Practices Committee procedures.* Retrieved from https://www.nasponline.org/assets/Documents/EPPC%20Procedures--2014%20Revision.pdf

National Association of School Psychologists Ethical and Professional Practices Committee. (2015, June). *Committee and board report.* Unpublished report. Available from jacob1s@cmich.edu

National Commission for the Protection of Human Subjects of Research. (1979). *The Belmont Report: Ethical principles and guidelines for the protection of human subjects of biomedical and behavioral research.* Washington, DC: U.S. Government Printing Office. Retrieved from http://www.hhs.gov/ohrp/humansubjects/guidance/belmont.html

National Institutes of Health. (1991). National Institutes of Health consensus development conference statement. In *NIH consensus development conference on the treatment of destructive behaviors in persons with developmental disabilities.* NIH Publication No. 91-2410, pp. 1–29. Washington, DC: U.S. Government Printing Office.

National Institute on Drug Abuse. (2014, December). *DrugFacts: High school and youth trends.* Retrieved from http://www.drugabuse.gov/publications/drugfacts/high-school-youth-trends

National Research Council. (2003). *Protecting participants and facilitating social and behavioral sciences research.* C. F. Citro, D. R. Ilgen, & C. B. Marrett (Eds.). Washington, DC: National Academies Press.

National Task Force on Confidential Student Health Information. (2000). *Guidelines for protecting confidential student health information.* Kent, OH: American School Health Association. Summary available at http://smhp.psych.ucla.edu/qf/confid_qt/guidelinesforprotecting.pdf

New America Foundation. (2015, June 5). Individuals with Disabilities Education Act Funding Distribution. Retrieved from http://atlas.newamerica.org/individuals-disabilities-education-act-funding-distribution

Newman, J. L. (1993). Ethical issues in consultation. *Journal of Counseling and Development, 72,* 148–156.

Niebling, B. C., & Kurz, A. (2014). Best practices in curriculum alignment. In P. L. Harrison & A. Thomas (Eds.), *Best practices in school psychology: Systems-level services* (pp. 57–70). Bethesda, MD: National Association of School Psychologists.

Olympia, D., Farley, M., Christiansen, E., Pettersson, H., Jenson, W., & Clark, E. (2004). Social maladjustment and students with behavioral and emotional disorders. *Psychology in the Schools*, *41*, 835–847. doi:10.1002/pits.20040

Ortiz, S. O. (2008). Best practices in nondiscriminatory assessment. In A. Thomas & J. Grimes (Eds.), *Best practices in school psychology V* (pp. 661–678). Bethesda, MD: National Association of School Psychologists.

Ortiz, S. O. (2014). Best practices in nondiscriminatory assessment. In P. L. Harrison & A. Thomas (Eds.), *Best practices in school psychology: Foundations* (pp. 61–74). Bethesda, MD: National Association of School Psychologists.

Ortiz, S. O., Flanagan, D. P., & Dynda, A. M. (2008). Best practices in working with culturally diverse children and families. In A. Thomas & J. Grimes (Eds.), *Best practices in school psychology V* (pp. 1721–1738). Bethesda, MD: National Association of School Psychologists.

OSEP Technical Assistance Center. (2015). *PBIS and the law*. Retrieved from http://www.pbis .org/school/pbis-and-the-law

Page, E. B. (1980). Tests and decisions for the handicapped: A guide to evaluation under the new laws. *Journal of Special Education*, *14*, 423–483. http://dx.doi.org/10.1177/00224669 8001400404

Paredes Scribner, A. (2002). Best assessment and intervention practices with second language learners. In A. Thomas & J. Grimes (Eds.), *Best practices in school psychology IV* (pp. 337–351). Bethesda, MD: National Association of School Psychologists.

Pedi, N. (2014). Third Circuit review: Bright "IDEA" or missing the mark? The Third Circuit restricts reimbursement for residential placement under the Individuals with Disabilities Education Act. *Villanova Law Review*, *59*, 847–876.

Perry, J., & Vogell, H. (2009, October, reprinted online July 5, 2011). Are drastic swings in CRCT scores valid? *Atlanta Journal-Constitution*. Retrieved from http://www.ajc.com/news/news/ local/are-drastic-swings-in-crct-scores-valid/nQYQm/

Pfohl, W., & Jarmuz-Smith, S. (2014). Best practices in using technology. In P. L. Harrison & A. Thomas (Eds.), *Best practices in school psychology: Foundations* (pp. 475–487). Bethesda, MD: National Association of School Psychologists.

Pham, A. V. (2014). Navigating social networking and social media in school psychology: Ethical and professional considerations in training programs. *Psychology in the Schools*, *5*, 767–778. doi:10.1002/pits.21774

Phelps, L., & Swerdlik, M. E. (2011). Evolving internship issues in school psychology preparation. *Psychology in the Schools*, *49*, 911–921. doi:10.1002/pits.20602

Phillips, B. N. (1983). Law-related training in school psychology: A national survey of doctoral programs. *Journal of School Psychology*, *21*, 253–259. doi:10.1016/0022-4405(83)90020-1

Pinard, M. (2003). From the classroom to the courtroom: Reassessing Fourth Amendment standards in public school searches involving law enforcement authorities. *Arizona Law Review*, *45*, 1067–1125.

Pipes, R. B., Holstein, J. E., & Aguirre, M. G. (2005). Examining the personal–professional distinction. *American Psychologist*, *60*, 325–334. http://dx.doi.org/10.1037/0003-066X.60.4.325

Pitcher, G., & Poland, S. (1992). *Crisis intervention in the schools*. New York, NY: Guilford Press.

Poland, S. (1989). *Suicide intervention in the schools*. New York, NY: Guilford Press.

Poole, D. A. (in press). *Interviewing children: The science of conversation in forensic contexts*. Washington, D.C.: American Psychological Association.

Pope, K. S., Tabachnick, B. G., & Keith-Spiegel, P. (1987). Ethics of practice: The beliefs and behaviors of psychologists as therapists. *American Psychologist, 42,* 993–1006. http://dx.doi.org/10.1037/0003-066X.42.11.993

Prentice, E. D. (2005, July 28). *SACHRP chair letter to HHS secretary regarding recommendations.* Retrieved from http://www.hhs.gov/ohrp/sachrp/sachrpltrtohhssec.html#

Prilleltensky, I. (1991). The social ethics of school psychology: A priority for the 1990s. *School Psychology Quarterly, 6,* 200–222. http://dx.doi.org/10.1037/h0088814

Prilleltensky, I. (1997). Values, assumptions, and practices: Assessing the moral implications of psychological discourse and action. *American Psychologist, 52,* 517–535. http://dx.doi.org/10.1037/0003-066X.52.5.517

Psychologist-patient privilege did not exist when student admitted homicide to school psychologist. (2002). *DOI Summaries, New York Law Journal, 222,* 17.

Rafoth, M. A., & Parker, S. W. (2014). Preventing academic failure and promoting alternatives to retention. In P. Harrison, & A. Thomas (Eds.), *Best practices in school psychology: Student-level services* (pp. 143–155). Bethesda, MD: National Association of School Psychologists.

Reddy, D. M., Fleming, R., & Swain, C. (2002). Effect of mandatory parental notification on adolescent girls' use of sexual health care services. *Journal of American Medical Association, 288,* 710–714. doi:10.1001/jama.288.6.710

Reddy, M., Borum, R., Berglund, J., Vossekuil, B., Fein, R., & Modzeleski, W. (2001). Evaluating risk for targeted violence in schools: Comparing risk assessment, threat assessment, and other approaches. *Psychology in the Schools, 38,* 157–172. doi:10.1002/pits.1007

Reidenberg, J., Russell, N. C., Kovnot, J., Norton, T. B., Cloutier, R., & Alvarado, D. (2013). Privacy and cloud computing in public schools (Book 2). Center on Law and Information Policy at Fordham University School of Law. Retrieved from http://ir.lawnet.fordham.edu/clip/2

Repp, A. C., & Singh, N. N. (Eds.). (1990). *Perspectives on the use of nonaversive and aversive interventions with persons with developmental disabilities.* Pacific Grove, CA: Brooks/Cole.

Reschly, D. J. (1979). Nonbiased assessment. In G. D. Phye & D. J. Reschly (Eds.), *School psychology: Perspectives and issues* (pp. 215–253). New York, NY: Academic Press.

Reschly, D. J. (1997). Diagnostic and treatment utility of intelligence tests. In D. P. Flanagan, J. L. Genshaft, & P. L. Harrison (Eds.), *Contemporary intellectual assessment* (pp. 437–456). New York, NY: Guilford Press.

Reschly, D. J. (2000). Assessment and eligibility determination in the Individuals with Disabilities Education Act of 1997. In C. F. Telzrow & M. Tankersley (Eds.), *IDEA amendments of 1997* (pp. 65–104). Bethesda, MD: National Association of School Psychologists.

Reschly, D. J., & Bersoff, D. N. (1999). Law and school psychology. In C. R. Reynolds & T. B. Gutkin (Eds.), *Handbook of school psychology* (3rd ed., pp. 1077–1112). New York, NY: Wiley.

Reynolds, C. R., Lowe, P. A., & Saenz, A. L. (1999). The problem of bias in psychological assessment. In C. R. Reynolds & T. B. Gutkin (Eds.), *Handbook of school psychology* (2nd ed., pp. 549–595). New York, NY: Wiley.

Rhodes, R. L., Ochoa, S. H., & Ortiz, S. O. (2005). *Assessing culturally and linguistically diverse students: A practical guide.* New York, NY: Guilford Press.

Rialto (CA) Unified School District. (1989). OCR complaint investigation letter of findings. *Education for the Handicapped Law Report, 353* (Suppl. 241), 201–204.

Rogers, M. R., Ingraham, C. L., Bursztyn, A., Cajigas-Segredo, N., Esquivel, G., Hess, R., … Lopez, E. C. (1999). Providing psychological services to racially, ethnically, culturally, and linguistically diverse individuals in the schools: Recommendations for practice. *School Psychology International, 20,* 243–264. doi:10.1177/0143034399203001

Rogers, M. R., & Lopez, E. C. (2002). Identifying critical cross-cultural school psychology competencies. *Journal of School Psychology, 40,* 115–141. doi:10.1016/S0022-4405(02)00093-6

Rooker, L. S. (2005, September 13). *Letter to Mr. Gary S. Mathews.* Retrieved from http: http://www2.ed.gov/policy/speced/guid/idea/letters/revpolicy/tpconfedr.html

Rooker, L. S. (2008, June 30). *Response to "Letter to Anonymous," Family Policy Compliance Office.* 12 FAB 27; 109 LRP 7789. SpecialEdConnection Case Report. Horsham, PA: LRP Publications. Retrieved from http://www.specialedconnection.com

Rosenfeld, S. J. (2010). Must school districts provide test protocols to parents? *Communiqué, 38* (8), 22–26.

Rosenfield, S. (2014). Best practices in instructional consultation and instructional consultation teams. In P. L. Harrison & A. Thomas (Eds.). *Best practices in school psychology V: Data-based and collaborative decision making* (pp. 509–524). Bethesda, MD: National Association of School Psychologists.

Ross, R. P., & Harrison, P. L. (2006). Ability grouping. In G. G. Baer & K. M. Minke (Eds.), *Children's needs III: Development, prevention, and intervention* (pp. 579–588). Bethesda, MD: National Association of School Psychologists.

Ross, S. W., & Horner, R. (2014). Bully prevention in positive behavior support: Preliminary evaluation of third-, fourth-, and fifth-grade attitudes toward bullying. *Journal of Emotional and Behavioral Disorders, 22,* 225–236. doi:10.1177/1063426613491429

Ross, W. D. (1930). *The right and the good.* Oxford, UK: Clarendon Press.

Rossen, E. (2014). Best practices in national certification and credentialing in school psychology. In P. L. Harrison & A. Thomas (Eds.), *Best practices in school psychology: Foundations* (pp. 541–552). Bethesda, MD: National Association of School Psychologists.

Rossen, E., & Cowan, K. C. (2012). *A framework for school-wide bullying prevention and safety* [Brief]. Bethesda, MD: National Association of School Psychologists.

Rossen, E., & Williams, B. B. (2013). The life and times of the National School Psychology Certification System. *Communiqué, 41*(7), 1, 28–30.

Russell Sage Foundation. (1970). *Guidelines for the collection, maintenance, and dissemination of pupil records.* Hartford, CT: Connecticut Printers.

Russo, C. J. (2012). *Reutter's The law of public education* (8th ed.). New York, NY: Foundation Press.

Ryan, D., & Martin, A. (2000). Lesbian, gay, bisexual, and transgender parents in the school systems. *School Psychology Review, 29,* 207–216.

Sales, B. D., Miller, M. O., & Hall, S. R. (2005). *Laws affecting clinical practice.* Washington, DC: American Psychological Association. http://dx.doi.org/10.1037/11218-000

Salvia, J., Ysseldyke, J., & Bolt, S. (2013). *Assessment: In special and inclusive education* (12th ed.) Belmont, CA: Wadsworth.

Sandoval, J. (2014). Best practices in school-based mental health/consultee-centered consultation by school psychologists. In P. L. Harrison & A. Thomas (Eds.), *Best practices in school psychology: Data-based and collaborative services* (pp. 493–507). Bethesda, MD: National Association of School Psychologists.

Sattler, J. M. (2008). *Assessment of children: Cognitive foundations* (5th ed.). San Diego, CA: Sattler.

Sattler, J. M., & Hoge, R. D. (2006). *Assessment of children: Behavioral, social, and clinical foundations* (5th ed.). San Diego, CA: Sattler.

Saunders, S. (2007, June 1). What you need to know about child abuse: A cautionary tale from Bedford Hills. *New York Teacher*. Article available from jacob1s@cmich.edu.

Schill, K. (1993, Fall). Violence among students: Schools' liability under Section 1983. *School Law Bulletin*, 1–11.

Schimmel, D., & Fischer, L. (1977). *The rights of parents in the education of their children*. Columbia, MD: National Committee for Citizens in Education.

Schulenberg, S. E., & Yutrzenka, B. A. (2004). Ethical issues in the use of computerized assessment. *Computers in Human Behavior, 20*, 477–490. https://numerons.files.wordpress.com/2012/04/ethical-issues-in-cba-ii.pdf

Schwab, N. C., & Gelfman, M. H. B. (2005a). Confidentiality: Principles and practice issues. In N. C. Schwab & M. H. B. Gelfman (Eds.), *Legal issues in school health services: A resource for school administrators, school attorneys, school nurses* (pp. 261–295). New York, NY: Authors Choice Press.

Schwab, N. C., & Gelfman, M. H. B. (Eds.). (2005b). *Legal issues in school health services: A resource for school administrators, school attorneys, school nurses*. New York, NY: Authors Choice Press.

Schwab, N. C., Rubin, M., Maire, J. A., Gelfman, M. H. B., Bergren, M. D., Mazyck, D. . . . Hine, B. (2005). *Protecting and disclosing student health information: How to develop school district policies and procedures*. Kent, OH: American School Health Association.

Secunda, P. M. (2015). Overcoming deliberate indifference: Reconsidering effective legal protections for bullied special education students. *University of Illinois Law Review*, p. 175–215.

Sheridan, S. M., Clarke, B. L., & Christenson, S. L. (2014). Best practices in promoting family engagement in education. In P. L. Harrison & A. Thomas (Eds.), *Best practices in school psychology: Systems-level services* (pp. 439–453). Bethesda, MD: National Association of School Psychologists.

Sherry, P. (1991). Ethical issues in the conduct of supervision. *Counseling Psychologist, 19*, 566–584. doi:10.1177/0011000091194006

Shrag, J. A. (1991). Response to letter of inquiry from J. V. Osowaski. *Individuals with Disabilities Education Law Report, 18*, 532–543.

Shriberg, D., & Moy, G. (2014). Best practices in school psychologists acting as agents of social change. In P. L. Harrison & A. Thomas (Eds.), *Best practices in school psychology: Foundations* (pp. 21–32). Bethesda, MD: National Association of School Psychologists.

Shriberg, D., Bonner, M., Sarr, B. J., Walker, A. M., Hyland, M., & Chester, C. (2008). Social justice through a school psychology lens: Definition and applications. *School Psychology Review, 37*, 453–468.

Sieber, J. E. (2000). Planning research: Basic ethical decision-making. In B. D. Sales & S. Folkman (Eds.), *Ethics in research with human participants* (pp. 13–26). Washington, DC: American Psychological Association.

Siegel, M. (1979). Privacy, ethics, and confidentiality. *Professional Psychology, 10*, 249–258. http://dx.doi.org/10.1037/0735-7028.10.2.249

Simon, R. I. (1999). The suicide prevention contract: Clinical, legal, and risk management issues. *Journal of the American Academy of Psychiatry and the Law, 27*, 445–450. http://www.jaapl.org/content/27/3.toc

Sinclair, C. (1998). Nine unique features of the *Canadian Code of Ethics for Psychologists*. *Canadian Psychology, 39*, 167–176. http://dx.doi.org/10.1037/h0086805

Skiba, R. J., Horner, R. H., Chung, C. G., Rausch, M. K., May, S. L., & Tobin, T. (2011). Race is not neutral: A national investigation of African American and Latino disproportionality in school discipline. *School Psychology Review, 40*, 85–107.

Skiba, R. J., Simmons, A. B., Ritter, S., Gibb, A. C., Rausch, M. K., Cuadrado, J., & Chung, C.-G. (2008). Achieving equity in special education: History, status, and current challenges. *Exceptional Children, 74*, 264–288. doi:10.1177/001440290807400301

Slenkovich, J. E. (1987a, June). Chemical dependency doesn't fit within "other health impaired." *Schools' Advocate*, p. 132.

Slenkovich, J. E. (1987b, December). Counseling not same as psychological services. *Schools' Advocate*, p. 143.

Slenkovich, J. E. (1988a, February). The seriously emotionally disturbed definition. *Schools' Advocate*, pp. 153–164.

Slenkovich, J. E. (1988b, March). When is a service a related service? *Schools' Advocate*, p. 168.

Small, M. A., Lyons, P. M., & Guy, L. S. (2002). Liability issues in child abuse and neglect reporting statutes. *Professional Psychology: Research and Practice, 33*, 13–18. http://dx.doi.org/10.1037/0735-7028.33.1.13

Smith, T. S., McGuire, J. M., Abbott, D. W., & Blau, B. I. (1991). Clinical ethical decision making: An investigation of the rationales used to justify doing less than one believes one should. *Professional Psychology: Research and Practice, 22*, 235–239. http://dx.doi.org/10.1037/0735-7028.22.3.235

Society for Research in Child Development. (2007). *SRCD ethical standards for research with children*. http://www.srcd.org/about-us/ethical-standards-research

Solomon, R. S. (1984). *Ethics: A brief introduction*. New York, NY: McGraw-Hill.

South Dakota Department of Education. (2010). *Guidelines for educators and administrators for implementing Section 504 of the Rehabilitation Act of 1973—Subpart D*. Retrieved from https://www.doe.sd.gov/oess/documents/sped_section504_Guidelines.pdf

Steege, M. W., & Scheib, M. A. (2014). Best practices in conducting functional behavioral assessments. In P. L. Harrison & A. Thomas (Eds.), *Best practices in school psychology: Data-based and collaborative services* (pp. 272–286). Bethesda, MD: National Association of School Psychologists.

Stefkovich, J. A. (2006). *Best interests of the student: Applying ethical constructs to legal cases in education*. Mahwah, NJ: Erlbaum.

Steinberg, L., Cauffman, E., Woolard, J., Graham, S., & Banich, M. (2009). Are adolescents less mature than adults? *American Psychologist, 64*, 583–594. http://dx.doi.org/10.1037/a0014763

Stoiber, K. C. (2014). A comprehensive framework for multitiered systems of support in school psychology. In P. L. Harrison & A. Thomas (Eds.), *Best practices in school psychology: Data-based and collaborative services* (pp. 41–70). Bethesda, MD: National Association of School Psychologists.

Sullivan, A. L. (2011). Disproportionality in special education identification and placement of English language learners. *Exceptional Children, 77*, 317–334. doi:10.1177/001440291107700304

Sullivan, J. R., Svenkerud, N., & Conoley, J. C. (2014). Best practices in the supervision of interns. In P. L. Harrison & A. Thomas (Eds.), *Best practices in school psychology: Foundations* (pp. 527–540). Bethesda, MD: National Association of School Psychologists.

Swearer, S. M., & Hymel, S. (2015). Understanding the psychology of bullying: Moving toward a social-ecological diathesis-stress model. *American Psychologist, 70*, 344–353. http://dx.doi.org/10.1037/a0038929

Swenson, S., & Musgrove, M. (2013, January 25). *Dear colleague letter. U.S. Department of Education Office for Civil Rights.* Retrieved from http://www2.ed.gov/about/offices/list/ocr/letters/colleague-201301-504.html

Taft, R. (1965). Comments of Senator Robert Taft. *U.S. Code Congressional and Administrative News*, p. 1450.

Talbot County (MD) Public Schools. (2008). *Individuals with Disabilities Education Law Report, 51*, 205 (OCR 2008). Retrieved from http://www.specialedconnection.com

Taylor, L., & Adelman, H. S. (1989). Reframing the confidentiality dilemma to work in children's best interests. *Professional Psychology: Research and Practice, 20*, 79–83. http://dx.doi.org/10.1037/0735-7028.20.2.79

Taylor, L., Adelman, H. S., & Kaser-Boyd, N. (1985). Minors' attitude and competence toward participation in psychoeducational decisions. *Professional Psychology: Research and Practice, 16*, 226–235. http://dx.doi.org/10.1037/0735-7028.16.2.226

Tharinger, D., & Stafford, M. (1995). Best practices in individual counseling of elementary age students. In A. Thomas & J. Grimes (Eds.), *Best practices in school psychology III* (pp. 893–907). Washington, DC: National Association of School Psychologists.

Thomas, H. J., Connor, J. P., & Scott, J. G., (2015). Integrating traditional and cyberbullying: Challenges of definition and measurement in adolescents—a review. *Educational Psychology Review, 27*, 135–152. doi:10.1007/s10648-014-9261-7

Thompson, R. A. (1990). Vulnerability in research: A developmental perspective on research risk. *Child Development, 61*, 1–16. doi:10.1111/j.1467-8624.1990.tb02756.x

Tobin, R. M., Schneider, W. J., & Landau, S. (2014). Best practices in the assessment of youth with attention deficit hyperactivity disorder within a multitiered services framework. In P. L. Harrison & A. Thomas (Eds.), *Best practices in school psychology: Data-based and collaborative services* (pp. 391–404). Bethesda, MD: National Association of School Psychologists.

Tryon, G. S. (2000). Ethical transgressions of school psychology graduate students: A critical incidents survey. *Ethics and Behavior, 10*, 271–279. doi:10.1207/S15327019EB1003_5

Tryon, G. S. (2001). School psychology students' beliefs about their preparation and concern with ethical issues. *Ethics and Behavior, 11*, 375–394. doi:10.1207/S15327019EB1104_02

Turnbull, A. P., & Turnbull, H. R. (2001). *Families, professionals, and exceptionality: A special partnership collaborating for empowerment* (4th ed.). Upper Saddle River, NJ: Merrill.

Turnbull, H. R., & Turnbull, A. P. (2000). *Free appropriate public education* (6th ed.). Denver, CO: Love.

Turner, H. S., & Watson, T. S. (1999). Consultant's guide for the use of time-out in the preschool and elementary classroom. *Psychology in the Schools, 36*, 135–148. doi:10.1002/(SICI)1520-6807(199903)36:2<135::AID-PITS6>3.0.CO;2-3

Tymchuk, A. J. (1981). Ethical decision-making and psychological treatment. *Journal of Psychiatric Treatment and Evaluation, 3*, 507–513.

Tymchuk, A. J. (1985). Ethical decision-making and psychology students' attitudes toward training in ethics. *Professional Practice of Psychology, 6*, 219–232.

Tymchuk, A. J. (1986). Guidelines for ethical decision making. *Canadian Psychology, 27*, 36–43. http://dx.doi.org/10.1037/h0079866

U.S. Copyright Office. (2012). *Works made for hire.* Washington, DC: Author. Retrieved from doi:10.1007/BF02763793 http://copyright.gov/circs/circ09.pdf

U.S. Department of Education. (n.d.[a]). *The opportunity of ESEA flexibility.* [Brochure.] Retrieved from https://www2.ed.gov/policy/elsec/guid/esea-flexibility/resources/esea-flex-brochure.pdf

U.S. Department of Education. (n.d.[b]). *ESEA flexibility*. [Web page.] Retrieved from http://www2.ed.gov/policy/elsec/guid/esea-flexibility/index.html

U.S. Department of Education. (1999, March 12). Assistance to states for the education of children with disabilities and the early intervention program for infants and toddlers with disabilities, final regulations, attachment 1—analysis of comments and changes. *Federal Register*, *64*(48), 12641. https://www.gpo.gov/fdsys/pkg/FR-1999-03-12/pdf/99-5754.pdf

U.S. Department of Education. (2000, July 6). Family Educational Rights and Privacy Act final rule, appendix B, analysis of comments and changes. *Federal Register*, *65*(130), 41856. https://www.gpo.gov/fdsys/pkg/FR-2000-07-06/pdf/FR-2000-07-06.pdf

U.S. Department of Education. (2006, August 14). Assistance to states for the education of children with disabilities and preschool grants for children with disabilities, final regulations, analysis of comments and changes. *Federal Register*, *71*, 46639. https://www.gpo.gov/fdsys/pkg/FR-2006-08-14/pdf/06-6656.pdf

U.S. Department of Education. (2008, December 9). Family Educational Rights and Privacy Act final rule, analysis of comments and changes, outsourcing (Sec. 99.31(a)(1)(i)(B)). *Federal Register*, *73*(237), 74813–74818. https://www2.ed.gov/legislation/FedRegister/finrule/2008-4/120908a.html

U.S. Department of Education. (2011a, December 2). Family Educational Rights and Privacy Act final regulations, general comments, cloud computing. *Federal Register*, *76*(232), 75612. http://familypolicy.ed.gov/sites/fpco.ed.gov/files/2011-30683.pdf

U.S. Department of Education. (2011b December 2). Appendix B: Model notification of rights under FERPA for elementary and secondary schools. *Federal Register*, *76*(232), 75654. http://familypolicy.ed.gov/sites/fpco.ed.gov/files/2011-30683.pdf

U.S. Department of Education. (2012, May). *Restraint and seclusion: Resource document*. Retrieved from http://www2.ed.gov/policy/seclusion/index.html

U.S. Department of Education. (2015, February 12). *Jacob K. Javits Gifted and Talented Students Education Program, Funding status*. Retrieved from http://www2.ed.gov/programs/javits/funding.html

U.S. Department of Education. (2016). Every Student Succeeds Act (ESSA). [Webpage]. http://www.ed.gov/essa

U.S. Department of Education & Bias Crimes Task Force of the National Association of Attorneys General. (1999). *Protecting students from harassment and hate crime*. Available as an archived document from http://www2.ed.gov/offices/OCR/archives/Harassment/harassment.pdf

U.S. Department of Education Office for Civil Rights. (2001, January). *Revised sexual harassment guidance: Harassment of students by school employees, other students, or third parties. Title IX*. Retrieved from http://www2.ed.gov/about/offices/list/ocr/docs/shguide.html

U.S. Department of Education Office for Civil Rights. (2014, April 28). *Frequently asked questions about sexual harassment, including sexual violence*. http://www2.ed.gov/about/offices/list/ocr/faqs.html, click on sex discrimination

U.S. Department of Education, Office of Special Education Programs. (2002). *Specific learning disabilities: Finding common ground*. A report developed by 10 organizations participating in the Learning Disabilities Roundtable. http://www.ldonline.org/article/5720/

U.S. Department of Education Press Office. (2014, October 21). Bullying of students with disabilities addressed in guidance to America's schools. http://www.ed.gov/news/press-releases/bullying-students-disabilities-addressed-guidance-america%E2%80%99s-schools

U.S. Department of Health and Human Services. (1991–1992). HHS policy clarification. *Individuals with Disabilities Education Law Report, 18*, 558–565.

U.S. Department of Health and Human Services. (2006, December 12). *HIPAA security guidance.* Retrieved from http://www.hhs.gov/sites/default/files/ocr/privacy/hipaa/administrative/securityrule/remoteuse.pdf

U.S. Department of Health and Human Services (2015a, January 15). *Child maltreatment 2013.* Retrieved from http://www.acf.hhs.gov/programs/cb/resource/child-maltreatment-2013

U.S. Department of Health and Human Services. (2015b). *Policies & laws.* Retrieved from http://www.stopbullying.gov/laws/index.html

U.S. Department of Health and Human Services & U.S. Department of Education. (2008, November). *Joint guidance on the application of the Family Educational Rights and Privacy Act (FERPA) and the Health Insurance Portability and Accountability Act of 1996 (HIPAA) to student health records.* Retrieved from http://www.ed.gov/policy/gen/guid/fpco/doc/ferpa-hippa-guidance.pdf

U.S. Equal Employment Opportunity Commission. (n.d.). *Facts about sexual harassment.* Retrieved from http://www.eeoc.gov/eeoc/publications/fs-sex.cfm

U.S. Food and Drug Administration. (2013). *Medication guide: Ritalin.* http://www.fda.gov/downloads/Drugs/DrugSafety/ucm089090.pdf

U.S. Senate Health, Education, Labor, and Pensions Committee. (2014). *Dangerous use of seclusion and restraints in schools remains widespread and difficult to remedy: A review of ten cases.* Retrieved from http://www.help.senate.gov/imo/media/doc/Seclusion%20and%20Restraints%20Final%20Report.pdf

Van Houten, R., Axelrod, S., Bailey, J. S., Favell, J. E., Foxx, R. N., Iwata, B. A., &Lovaas, O. I. (1988). The right to effective behavioral treatment. *Behavior Analyst, 11*, 111–114. doi:10.1901/jaba.1988.21-381

Vasquez, M. T. (1992). Psychologist as clinical supervisor: Promoting ethical practice. *Professional Psychology: Research and Practice, 23*, 196–202. http://dx.doi.org/10.1037/0735-7028.23.3.196

Vossekuil, B., Reddy, M., Fein, R., Borum, R., & Modzeleski, W. (2000). *U.S.S.S. safe school initiative: An interim report on the prevention of targeted violence in the schools.* Washington, DC: U.S. Secret Service, National Threat Assessment Center. Retrieved from http://cecp.air.org/download/ntac_ssi_report.pdf

Waldman, E. G. (2015). Show and tell? Students' personal lives, schools, and parents. *Connecticut Law Review, 47*, 699–740. http://connecticutlawreview.org/articles/show-and-tell-students-personal-lives-schools-and-parents/

Walker, D. W., & Daves, D. (2010). Response to intervention and the courts: Litigation-based guidance. *Journal of Disability Policy Studies, 21*, 40–46. http://dps.sagepub.com/content/21/1/40

Walrath, R., Willis, J. O., & Dumont, R. (2014). Best practices in writing assessment reports. In P. L. Harrison & A. Thomas (Eds.), *Best practices in school psychology: Data-based and collaborative services* (pp. 433–445). Bethesda, MD: National Association of School Psychologists.

Webb, N. B. (2001). Strains and challenges of culturally diverse practice. In N. B. Webb (Ed.), *Culturally diverse parent–child and family relationships* (pp. 337–350). New York, NY: Columbia University Press.

Wechsler, D. (2003). Wechsler Intelligence Scale for Children IV. San Antonio, TX : Harcourt Assessment.

Wechsler, D. (2012). *Wechsler Preschool and Primary Scale of Intelligence IV*. San Antonio, TX: Pearson Clinical Assessment.

Wechsler, D. (2014). *Wechsler Intelligence Scale for Children V*. San Antonio, TX: Pearson Clinical Assessment.

Weinstein, B. S. (2005). Note: A right with no remedy: Forced disclosure of sexual orientation and public "outing" under 42 U.S.C. 1983. *Cornell Law Review, 90*, 811–838. http://cornelllawreview.org/articles/a-right-with-no-remedy-forced-disclosure-of-sexual-orientation-and-public-outing-under-42-u-s-c-%C2%A7-1983/

Weithorn, L. A. (1983). Involving children in decisions affecting their own welfare: Guidelines for professionals. In G. B. Melton, G. P. Koocher, & M. J. Saks (Eds.), *Children's competence to consent* (pp. 235–260). New York, NY: Plenum Press. doi:10.1007/978-1-4684-4289-2_12

Welfel, W. R. (2012). Teaching ethics: Models, methods, and challenges. In S. J. Knapp, M. C. Gottlieb, M. M. Handelsman, & L. D. VandeCreek (Eds.), *APA handbook of ethics in psychology*, (Vol. 2, pp. 277–305). Washington, DC: American Psychological Association.

Welfel, E. R., & Kitchener, K. S. (1992). Introduction to the special section: Ethics education—An agenda for the '90s. *Professional Psychology: Research and Practice, 23*, 179–181.

Welfel, E. R., & Lipsitz, N. E. (1984). Ethical behavior of professional psychologists: A critical analysis of the research. *Counseling Psychologist, 12*, 31–41. doi: 10.1177/0011000084123004

Wells, M. L. (2004). Symposium: Association of American Law Schools: Private parties as defendants in civil rights litigation: Identifying state actors in constitutional litigation: Reviving the role of substantive context. *Cardozo Law Review, 26*, 99–125.

White, R. M. (2000). Unraveling the Tuskegee study of untreated syphilis. *Archives of Internal Medicine, 160*, 585–598. doi:10.1001/archinte.160.5.585

Williams, B. B., Sinko, A., & Epifanio, F. J. (2010). Teaching ethical and legal issues. In J. Kaufman, T. L. Hughes, & C. A. Riccio (Eds.), *Handbook of education, training, and supervision of school psychologists in school and community* (Vol. 1, pp. 109–127). New York, NY: Routledge, Taylor & Francis.

Winett, R. A., & Winkler, R. C. (1972). Current behavior modification in the classroom: Be still, be quiet, be docile. *Journal of Applied Behavior Analysis, 5*, 499–504. doi:10.1901/jaba.1972.5-499

Wonderly, D. (1989, April). Introductory comments. *Ethical behavior: Is there adequate training and support?* Symposia presented at the National Association of School Psychologists Convention, Boston.

Wood, R. C., & Chestnutt, M. D. (1995). Violence in U.S. schools: The problems and some responses. *West's Education Law Quarterly, 4*, 413–428.

Woody, R. H. (1988). *Protecting your mental health practice*. San Francisco, CA: Jossey-Bass.

Worrell, F. C., & Erwin, J. O., (2011). Best practices in identifying students for gifted and talented programs. *Journal of Applied School Psychology, 27*, 319–340. doi:10.1080/15377903.2011.615817

Yankouski, B. M., & Massarelli, T. (2014). Best practices in promoting appropriate use of restraint and seclusion in schools. In P. L. Harrison & A. Thomas (Eds.), *Best practices in school psychology: Student-level services* (pp. 381–397). Bethesda, MD: National Association of School Psychologists.

Ysseldyke, J., Burns, M., Dawson, P., Kelley, B., Morrison, D., Ortiz, S., … Telzrow, C. (2006). *School psychology: A blueprint for training and practice III*. Reprinted in A. Thomas & J. Grimes (Eds.), (2008), *Best practices in school psychology V* (pp. 37–69). Bethesda, MD: National Association of School Psychologists.

Ysseldyke, J. E., & Christenson, S. L. (1988). Linking assessment to intervention. In J. L. Graden, J. E. Zins, & M. J. Curtis (Eds.), *Alternative educational delivery systems* (pp. 91–109). Washington, DC: National Association of School Psychologists.

Zenere, F. J., & Lazarus, P. J. (2009). Research brief: The sustained reduction of youth suicidal behavior in an urban multicultural school district. *School Psychology Review, 38*, 189–199.

Zingaro, J. C. (1983). Confidentiality: To tell or not to tell. *Elementary School Guidance and Counseling, 17*, 261–267.

Zins, J. E., & Forman, S. G. (1988). Primary prevention in the schools: What are we waiting for? *School Psychology Review, 17*, 539–541.

Zirkel, P. (2009a). The ADAA and its effect on Section 504 students. *Journal of Special Education Leadership, 22*, 3–8.

Zirkel, P. A. (2009b). Section 504: Student eligibility update. *The Clearing House, 82*, 209–211.

Zirkel, P. (2009c). A step-by-step process for § 504/ADA eligibility determinations: An update. *West's Education Law Reporter, 239*, 333–343.

Zirkel, P. A. (2010). Manifestation determinations under the new Individuals with Disabilities Education Act: An update. *Remedial and Special Education, 31*, 378–384. doi:10.1177/0741932509355993

Zirkel, P. A. (2012). Lore v. law: Prevailing beliefs and objective knowledge. *Principal Leadership, 13*, 50–54.

Zirkel, P. (2013a). Checklist for identifying students eligible under the IDEA classification of emotional disturbance: An update. *West's Education Law Reporter, 286*, 7–11.

Zirkel, P. (2013b). The legal meaning of specific learning disability for IDEA eligibility: The latest case law. *Communiqué, 41*(5), 10–14.

Zirkel, P. (2013c). Section 504/ADA and K–12 students: Supplemental materials. Retrieved from https://www.alsde.edu/sec/ses/Presentations/504 ADA supplement for MEGA 2010 by Perry Zirkel.pdf

Zirkel, P. (2013d). Top five Section 504 errors redux. *ELA Notes, 48*, p. 14–15.

Zirkel, P. A. (2015). Manifest determinations under the IDEA: The latest cases. *Communiqué, 43*(5), 8–10.

Zirkel, P. A., & Kincaid, J. M. (1993). *Section 504, the ADA, and the schools* [Looseleaf]. Horsham, PA: LRP Publications.

Zirkel, P., & Rose, T. (2009). Special education law update X. *West's Education Law Reporter, 240*, 503–523.

Author Index

Subject Index